# Performance of Financial Institutions
## *Efficiency, Innovation, Regulation*

The efficient operation of financial intermediaries – banks, insurance and pension fund firms, government agencies, and so on – is instrumental for the efficient functioning of the financial system and the fueling of the economies of the 21st century. But what drives the performance of these institutions in today's global environment? This volume brings an interdisciplinary and international perspective to developing a deep understanding of the drivers of performance of financial institutions. World-renowned scholars from economics, finance, operations management, and marketing, and leading industry professionals, bring their expertise to bear on the issues. Primary among these issues are the definition and measurement of efficiency of a financial institution, benchmarks of efficiency, identification of the drivers of performance and measurement of their effects on efficiency, the impact of financial innovation and information technologies on performance, the effects of process design, human resource management policies, and regulations on efficiency, and interrelationships between risk management and operational efficiency.

*Patrick T. Harker* is Professor of Operations and Information Management and Senior Fellow in the Financial Institutions Center at the Wharton School, University of Pennsylvania. He is currently the Dean of the Wharton School. He previously directed Wharton's Fishman-Davidson Center for the Study of the Service Sector from 1989 to 1994 and chaired the Systems Engineering department in the university's School of Engineering and Applied Science. Professor Harker has published five books and more than 80 professional articles and serves as editor-in-chief of *Operations Research*, the leading journal in the field. He is currently co-principal investigator of a multi-million dollar project funded by the Sloan Foundation to study productivity and technological impacts in financial services.

*Stavros A. Zenios* is Professor of Management Science at the University of Cyprus, where he also served as the first Dean of the School of Economics and Management, and Senior Fellow in the Financial Institutions Center at the Wharton School, University of Pennsylvania. He has published six books, including *Financial Optimization* (Cambridge University Press, 1996), and more than 130 professional articles. Professor Zenios is currently principal investigator with the HERMES Laboratory for Financial Modeling and Simulations, and is internationally known for his work in computational finance and operations research. He has taught at Wharton and held visiting appointments at the Massachusetts Institute of Technology and the Universities of Vienna, Haifa, Bergamo, Milan, and Urbino.

Advance Praise for *Performance of Financial Institutions*

"Research on bank efficiency and financial sector innovation has advanced rapidly in recent years. This book provides a thorough review of the state of the art. It is a group of up-to-date papers that present the methodologies for analyzing the issues and summarize the results in the literature. *Performance of Financial Institutions* will give the reader a thorough understanding of the factors that are changing the structure of the banking industry. Banking in the United States and elsewhere is undergoing a fundamental change and this book tells you why."

– Paul Wachtel, *New York University*

"I found the papers in this book both interesting to read and a very valuable source of summaries and critical reviews of research. I know of no comparable volume nor any more efficient way for one to understand what has been learned about the performance of financial institutions."

– George Benston, *Emory University*

# Performance of Financial Institutions
## Efficiency, Innovation, Regulation

Edited by

PATRICK T. HARKER
*University of Pennsylvania*

and

STAVROS A. ZENIOS
*University of Cyprus*

CAMBRIDGE
UNIVERSITY PRESS

PUBLISHED BY THE PRESS SYNDICATE OF THE UNIVERSITY OF CAMBRIDGE
The Pitt Building, Trumpington Street, Cambridge, United Kingdom

CAMBRIDGE UNIVERSITY PRESS
The Edinburgh Building, Cambridge CB2 2RU, UK
http: //www.cup.cam.ac.uk
40 West 20th Street, New York, NY 10011-4211, USA
http: //www.cup.org
10 Stamford Road, Oakleigh, Melbourne 3166, Australia
Ruiz de Alarcón 13, 28014 Madrid, Spain

© Patrick T. Harker, Stavros A. Zenios   2000

First published 2000

Printed in the United States of America

*Typeface* Times New Roman 10/12 pt.   *System* QuarkXPress [BTS]

*A catalog record for this book is available from the British Library.*

*Library of Congress Cataloging in Publication data*
Performance of financial institutions: efficiency, innovation,
    regulation / edited by Patrick T. Harker, Stavros A. Zenios.
        p.   cm.
    ISBN 0-521-77154-4 (hb)
    1. Performance of financial institutions.   I. Harker,
Patrick T., 1958–   .   II. Zenios, Stavros Andrea.
HG173.F5124   2000
332.1 – dc21                                        99-28371
                                                        CIP


ISBN   0 521 77154 4   hardback
ISBN   0 521 77767 4   paperback

# CONTENTS

# FOREWORD

The Wharton Financial Institutions Center (WFIC) has been studying the dynamic changes in the financial sector for the past seven years through a generous grant from the Alfred P. Sloan Foundation. With a group of more than two dozen faculty and an equal number of professional staff and graduate students, the Center has engaged in basic, yet relevant research on this important sector of the economy.

Its work has been divided into three parts. The first and most advanced area of its portfolio is the efficiency and performance issues facing the sector. The second analyzes financial risk management systems employed in the industry, while the third looks at the regulatory and competitive issues. In each case, under the direction of Wharton faculty and affiliated scholars, the Center studies the key drivers of change within the sector and seeks to add new understanding of its revolutionary transformation.

The issues surrounding efficiency and productivity were some of the first studied, because of both their importance and the industry's awareness of their impact on performance. Led by Professor Patrick Harker, the team investigated the key drivers of performance from both the macro level of the industry and the micro level of firm-specific processes and structures. The results of this work can be found in a number of research papers and the message has been spread by many of the involved scholars.

To further the academic work on efficiency and to link it to performance of the firm, a major international conference took place at Wharton in May 1997. The results of this event are the subject of this volume, edited by Patrick Harker and Stavros Zenios, two of the key investigators on the project. The research that it contains is cutting edge in technique and in the quality of the contributions. However, it is also relevant and vital to the future viability of firms operating within the financial sector. It pushes the field of knowledge to new lengths and offers insights to practitioners in a way unique to the WFIC project design. The papers ask vital questions and offer answers that are "actionable" and relevant to management within the sector.

I trust you will enjoy reading the results of our efforts. For sure, the volume will be a benchmark in financial institution research and "must reading" for scholars in the field. Moreover, it will prove pivotal in the research agenda as it brings researchers to the question of performance from diverse fields and with many different kinds of expertise. In the end, the message should be clear that performance is the result of many different factors all properly aligned to enhance product quality, delivery, and value. Understanding performance goes beyond one discipline, e.g., finance, and encompasses a knowledge of the diverse drivers of performance from operations, technology, human resource practices, as well as finance. Regulation and government policy also play a role.

For all of us who toil in these fields, I wish to thank the researchers who have added to our understanding through their contribution to this volume and to the organizers for their efforts to bring them all together.

Anthony M. Santomero
Richard K. Mellon Professor of Finance
Director, Financial Institutions Center
The Wharton School
University of Pennsylvania, PA

# PREFACE

While the efficiency of *financial markets* is widely and extensively studied, little has been done to develop our understanding of what drives the performance of the *institutions* that operate in these markets. Unavoidably, however, the efficient operation of financial intermediaries – banks, insurance and pension fund firms, government agencies, and so on – is instrumental for the efficient functioning of the financial system.

This volume brings an interdisciplinary and international perspective in developing a deep understanding of the drivers of performance of financial institutions. Scholars from economics, finance, operations management, and marketing bring their expertise to bear on the following issues: definition and measurement of efficiency of a financial institution, benchmarks of efficiency, identification of the drivers of performance and measurement of their effects on efficiency, the impact of financial innovation and information technologies on performance, the effects of process design, human resource management policies, and regulations on efficiency, interrelationships between risk management and operational efficiency, and so on.

The contents of this volume were compiled from papers presented at a two-day conference organized by The Wharton Financial Institutions Center, The Wharton School, University of Pennsylvania, in May 1997. The published articles went through the usual scholarly refereeing process, and were also assessed by practitioners to establish that each published article develops our understanding of some aspects of the performance of financial institutions.

Patrick T. Harker, Philadelphia
Stavros A. Zenios, Nicosia and Philadelphia
June 1998

# Part 1

## Introduction

# 1

## What Drives the Performance of Financial Institutions?

Patrick T. Harker[a], Stavros A. Zenios[b]

**Abstract**
While the efficiency of financial markets is widely and extensively studied, little has been done to date to develop our understanding of what drives the performance of the institutions that operate in these markets. Unavoidably, however, the efficient operation of financial intermediaries – banks, insurance and pension fund firms, government agencies, and so on – is instrumental for the efficient functioning of the financial system. In this chapter we present in a coherent framework our current understanding on *what is* and *what drives* performance of financial institutions. The chapter provides the necessary background and the wider context for the remaining chapters of this book.

## 1 Introduction

The financial services sector is perhaps the most significant economic sector in modern societies. In the more advanced service economies – like the United States' – the financial sector employs more people than the manufacturing of apparel, automobiles, computers, pharmaceuticals, and steel combined; 5.4 million people are employed by financial services firms in the U.S. Financial services account for almost 5% of the Gross Domestic Product in the U.S., about 5.5% in Germany, 3.5% in

[a] Department of OPIM, the Wharton School, University of Pennsylvania, Philadelphia, PA 19104-6366. Email: harker@wharton.upenn.edu.
[b] Department of Public and Business Administration, University of Cyprus, Nicosia, CYPRUS; Senior Fellow, the Wharton Financial Institutions Center, University of Pennsylvania, PA. Email: zenioss@ucy.ac.cy.

3

Italy, and similar statistics are found for other European Union economies with highly developed financial intermediaries. The Japanese financial sector accounted for almost 9% of the GDP until 1993 (recently it has experienced severe decline), and the Singapore sector is 6.5% of the GDP. (Data are obtained as the sum of all entries in the rows of Table 5 of Demirguc-Kunt and Levine, 1996.) In smaller economies – especially those that aspire to a significant presence in the international markets through offshore banking activities – the financial services sector could be even more significant. The Swiss financial sector accounts for over 9% of the country's GDP. Cyprus – a small Mediterranean economy offering off-shore banking services to the former Soviet Union states and Eastern European countries – has more than 18% of its GDP arising from financial and business services, and these sectors employ almost 10% of the population. Eighteen percent of the Israeli GDP is due to the combined financial and business services sectors, which employ 10% of the population.

Impressive as these statistics may be, they belie the much larger *indirect* role that this industry plays in the economy. In a nutshell, the financial sector mobilizes savings and allocates credit across space and time. It enables firms and households to cope with economic uncertainties by hedging, pooling, sharing, and pricing risks, thereby facilitating the flow of funds from the ultimate lenders to the ultimate borrowers, improving both the quantity and quality of real investments, and thereby increasing income per capita and raising our standards of living. Herring and Santomero (1991) give a comprehensive contemporary analysis of the role of the financial sector in economic performance.

It is therefore well justified that the performance of the financial sector receives extensive scrutiny from scholars and industry thinkers. While the efficiency of the financial markets has been studied and debated at length, much less has been done in understanding the performance of the institutions that operate in these markets; see, e.g., Merton (1990). Under intense competitive pressures, financial institutions are forced to take a careful look into their performance and the role they are called upon to play in the economies of the 21st century.

Banking institutions face today a dynamic, fast-paced, competitive environment at a global scale. This environment is the catalyst for major restructuring of the industry. Table 1.1 summarizes the changes in the U.S. banking industry over the 15-year period from 1979 – the aftermath of financial deregulation and the collapse of the Bretton-Woods agreement. The total number of banking institutions shrunk by one-third, but more than half of the small banks were eliminated in the process. The

Table 1.1.  *Changes in the U.S. banking industry 1979–1994.*

| Item | 1979 | 1994 |
|---|---|---|
| Total number of banking organizations | 12,463 | 7,926 |
| Number of small banks | 10,014 | 5,636 |
| Industry gross total assets (trillions of 1994 USD) | 3.26 | 4.02 |
|    Industry assets in small banks | 13.9% | 7.0% |
| Total number of employees | 1,396,970 | 1,489,171 |
| Number of automated teller machines | 13,800 | 109,080 |
| Cost (1994 USD) of processing a paper check | 0.0199 | 0.0253 |
| Cost (1994 USD) of an electronic deposit | 0.0910 | 0.0138 |

*Source*:  Berger, Kashyap, and Scalise, 1995.

total number of employees increased by a meager 7% while the number of automated teller machines increased almost ten-fold.

Liberalized domestic regulations in the U.S., financial unification policies in Europe, intensified international competition, rapid innovation in new financial instruments and changing consumer demands, and the explosive growth in information technology fuel these changes. In response, firms are forced to adapt in order to survive, and firm-level innovation brings about more change of the competitive environment. Frei, Harker, and Hunter (1997) discuss various forms of innovation of retail financial institutions in response to these competitive pressures.

Where are the competitive pressures coming from? A recent study on the future of retail banking by Deloitte and Touche (1995) argues that the banking industry is today fragmented due to its inability to exploit *economies of scale and scope*. Before we elaborate on the implications of this argument, we add that studies by Berger and colleagues (see, e.g., Berger and Humphrey, 1991, and Berger, Hancock, and Humphrey, 1993) claim that inefficiencies are far more important than unexploited scale and scope economies. Further work (Berger, Hunter, and Timme, 1993; Soteriou and Zenios, 1999) shows that serious inefficiencies are on the output side, reducing revenues, than on the input side, raising costs. A number of recent indicators lead us to believe that retail banking is increasingly becoming susceptible to scale economies. Declining costs of information technology – hardware and software – and the gradual shift of banking operations from hybrid paper-electronic systems to seamless end-to-end automation lead to restructuring and disaggregation of retail banking. It can be argued that today's mergers and acquisitions do not necessarily add value, but are reactions to competitive threats (Frei, Harker, and Hunter, 1997; Singh and Zollo, 1997). However, evidence is gradually emerging (Pilloff and Santomero, 1997) that consolidation does add value, thus lending credibility to Deloitte and Touche's somewhat speculative study.

The economies of scale that lead to more integrated automation cause further *economies of scope* effects. As financial institutions – in agreement with all other retail services – realize that customer satisfaction and customer loyalty lead to long-term growth, they aim at maximizing the share of customers' wallets that they are servicing. With platform automation, an employee can get a single view of the entire customer relationship; economies of scope can be created when a firm offers suitable product mix to support its client base. Mergers and acquisitions become powerful forces impacting geographical scope and product variety, while also affecting the underlying technological and managerial infrastructures of the institutions. The recent megamerger of Citibank with Travelers Group is a manifestation of economies of scope leading to industry restructuring.

*Technological innovation* adds more competitive pressures. First, it opens up new delivery channels, and while those are not necessarily more cost effective for the firm, consumers get to depend on them and demand access. Whereas in the past the bank branch was the only channel for the distribution of financial services, we see today a variety of channels eroding the branch's dominance.

Furthermore, as banks struggle with the technological issues and complex organizational choices that surround the introduction of, say, PC banking services, they see the emergence of new competitors. Off-the-shelf home finance software – such as Intuit's Quicken and Microsoft's Money – provide some of the services that were traditionally offered by banks, and radically transform the way in which the client interacts with the firm. It is not sufficient for the CEO of Chase Manhattan to be concerned about the competitive strategies of Deutsche Bank or Banque Nacionale de Paris; he also has to ponder whether Microsoft is also a bank. The Deloitte and Touche study argues that technology revolutionizes the moving and storage of money and the distribution of financial products, and more complex software permits more integrated automation. However, the complexities of large software projects create some of the scale effects that reshape the industry. It is likely that new entrants, better equipped with state-of-the-art technology than current banking giants with 1970's technology, can quickly achieve leadership in the retail banking field. Bank executives who wish to maintain their firm's franchise should be aware of Microsoft's and other firms' acquisitions in the area of financial software and network management, and their active interest in possibly buying a bank.

Competitive threats are likely to emerge from more unsuspecting places. Logistics firms, such as Federal Express and UPS, are well equipped to deal with the transfer of goods and information and the management of money. They currently own the process for transferring goods and information; we could expect them to take ownership of the transfer of money as well. The Deloitte and Touche study speculates that "it would not be surprising to see a joint venture between say Deutsche Telecom and Quelle, the large German mail order firm, in which they jointly undertook to design and distribute financial service products." (This hypothetical merger was the subject of a recent article in *The Economist.*)

Perhaps the strongest force of change, however, is the *consumer*. Consumers are demanding anytime-anywhere delivery of financial services, while demonstrating a rapid evolution of their needs and desires. In 1980, almost 40% of the U.S. consumer financial assets were in bank deposits. By 1996 bank deposits accounted for less than 20% of consumers' financial assets with mutual funds and insurance/pension funds absorbing the difference. As a result of changing consumer needs, we have seen an accelerated growth of financial innovation. See, for instance, Allen and Gale (1994) or Consiglio and Zenios (1997) for a discussion of financial innovation and security design. The emergence of new and diverse financial products creates new challenges for financial institutions that now face a host of product-mix and marketing questions along with new competitors. Whereas the typical bank offers a dozen or two different choices of mutual funds, institutions such as Fidelity Investment or Merrill Lynch each offer over 100 different products.

Modern consumers also demand access to more than one delivery channel. While a personal visit to the branch remains the predominant way of doing business, a significant percentage of U.S. households use non-branch channels as well (phone, electronic transfer, ATM); see Figure 1.1.

Some interesting case studies amplify the point we are making on the significant transformation of the banking industry and the challenges facing its institutions. Marks and Spencer, the famous retailer in the United Kingdom, made a significant entry into financial services. By restricting in-store payment to cash, check, or the store's own card, Marks and Spencer has recruited a large number of cardholders. Ana-

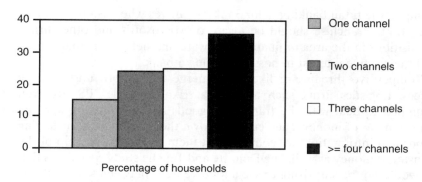

Figure 1.1. Percentage of U.S. households using alternative delivery channels. (Data from Kennickell and Kwast, 1997.)

lyzing the spending patterns of its clients has enabled Marks and Spencer to target these individuals for loans, saving products, pensions, and mutual funds through the mail. The firm now explicitly recognizes that selling financial products forms an increasingly larger part of its corporate strategy.

Smaller and more protected economies of the world run the risk of procrastinating in their liberalization efforts. Behind protective barriers, national retail banks may remain for a while ignorant of the changes that threaten to destroy them. However, this is not a sustainable state of affairs and eventually new entrants will emerge either locally funded or set up by foreign banks. This is precisely what happened in Portugal, where a group of capital providers funded a new start-up bank, Banco Commercial Portugues, which is a new institution revolutionizing the Portuguese banking industry.

Since the late 1970's, banking institutions have been transformed from almost purely *financial intermediaries* to *retail service providers*. Not long ago, banks would entice customers to deposit their money by giving away free coffee makers and toasters for opening new accounts. The management of the customers' money would then drive most of the bank's profits (and pay for the toaster too!). Today banks such as Wells Fargo sublet branch space to Starbucks Coffee, and customers visit the branch to get a large spectrum of retail services – including coffee that is now paid for by the customer! Data from Berger, Kashyap, and Scalise (1995) highlight the magnitude of the shift towards retail servicing: the ratio of noninterest income to operating income rose from 7 in 1979 to 20.9 in 1994 for the large U.S. banks, and from 3.5 to 8.3 for the smaller banks.

As a result of the transformation towards retail servicing and the competitive pressures outlined earlier, retail banking is now focused on the portfolio of interlinked activities that a banking institution may be called upon to perform:

1. Product origination: formulating products such as mortgages or savings for delivery either to clients directly or to intermediaries.
2. Retail servicing: selling and servicing a range of products to individual customers through a range of delivery channels of the customers' choosing.
3. Back office operations: providing the support functions required for the successful and efficient execution of the two primary activities.

The Deloitte and Touche study argues that banking institutions are gradually being reshaped and disaggregated into entities that perform one or more of these activities within a context of strategic partners and alliances, while dealing with a myriad of issues (regulatory barriers to competitive entrants, marketing and product-mix strategies, etc.).

How do we then measure the *performance* of a financial institution in this changing landscape? What drives this performance? What can an institution do to improve it? This is a book of carefully selected, peer-reviewed, scholarly papers that address these questions. It is the product of a two-day international conference held in May 1997 at the Wharton School of the University of Pennsylvania under the auspices of the Wharton Financial Institutions Center. The themes developed in the chapters of this book advance our understanding of what is – and what drives – performance of financial institutions. It is our expectation that the better understanding of performance and its drivers will lead to managerial practices that improve the performance of this significant sector of economic activity.

Measuring performance in our modern world is a challenging problem. In the old economy – where the central feature was mass production and consumption of commodities – "output" or "quantity" measures were adequate indicators of performance. Modern economies are based on production and consumption of increasingly differentiated goods and services. In the case of banking, this increased variety leads to the fragmentation and changing nature of the banking services described above. In this environment, traditional productivity measures are not only extremely difficult to compute, but they also tell us less than they used to; Fornell (1995) and Fornell et al. (1996) discuss these issues at the national and firm level. Griliches (1992) laments the rise of the "unmeasurable" sector of the economy which makes it difficult to measure "performance," however it is defined. Section 2 of this chapter discusses several measures of performance for financial institutions.

A CEO may not rest, however, once he or she understands what is performance and finds ways to measure it. The next challenge is to discover what drives performance so that appropriate managerial actions can be taken. Once more, this is not a simple issue. The drivers of performance are many and are tightly intertwined as their relationships can be quite complex and nonlinear. The complex interactions of various factors that affect performance are exemplified in the study by Roth and van der Velde (1991, 1992), and steps in disentangling and better understanding the relationships are made in Roth and Jackson (1995) and Soteriou and Zenios (1999). In a nutshell, these studies identify the interactions between the design of the operating system and operational efficiency with the quality of the provided services – either from the perspective of internal or external customers – and the ultimate impact of operations and service quality on profitability. Section 3 classifies the drivers of performance in three categories: (*i*) *strategy*, (*ii*) *execution of strategy*, and (*iii*) *the environment*. Within each category we discuss specific drivers.

Section 4 gives a summary of what is currently known on the performance of financial institutions and its drivers. It is not meant to be an exhaustive guide to the literature; the topic of this volume is much too broad to be covered completely in a single volume and summarized in this introductory chapter. Instead, we focus on a few important findings and pay particular emphasis to some of the conclusions of the conference as documented in the papers published herein. Finally Section 5 charts those areas of the bank-performance landscape, where knowledge is scant and where we believe future directions of research should concentrate.

The careful reader must have noticed that while we talk about the performance of financial institutions, in general, most of the discussion in this and other chapters in this book focuses on banking institutions, and on retail banking in particular. By focusing on a single class of financial institutions, we have been able, collectively, to make substantial progress in understanding their performance and its drivers. While not all the findings are applicable to other institutions, commonalities do exist between financial service firms. We hope that the body of knowledge presented here can guide efforts in understanding the performance of other financial institutions as well.

## 2 What Is Performance?

Financial institutions are for-profit organizations, and we can define *performance* to mean economic performance as measured by a host of financial indicators. Price-to-earnings ratios, the firm's stock beta and alpha, and Tobin's $q$-ratios are indicators for short- and long-term financial performance. In particular, Tobin's $q$ – the ratio of market value to replacement cost – is a measure of the firm's incentive to invest and thus is an indicator of its long-term financial performance. For financial institutions where the majority of investments are publicly traded financial assets, the $q$ ratio measures the market capitalization of a firm's franchise value or goodwill. Part, if not all, of this franchise value will be lost in the event of insolvency or substantial increase in financial distress. It is therefore in the best interest of the financial institution to protect its franchise value. But how? Financial indicators (such as $q$) are not actionable: they measure the market's reactions to the institution's actions, but they cannot be directly acted upon.

What can the institution do to improve its $q$? Broadly speaking, a financial institution does two things: (*i*) provides products and services to its clients, and (*ii*) engages in financial intermediation and the management of risk. It turns out that along both of these axes – servicing and intermediation – we can define further measures of performance that have a direct positive impact on financial measures, and that are *actionable*. These are (*i*) quality of the provided services, and (*ii*) efficiency of risk management, respectively.

There is an accumulating body of empirical evidence that quality measures are predictive of future changes in shareholders' value; see Nayyar (1995), Ittner and Larcker (1996), and Fornell, Itner, and Larcker (1996). Why this is the case has been articulated by the proponents of the American Customer Satisfaction Index – ACSI (Fornell et al., 1996):

> For managers and investors, ACSI provides an important measure of the firm's past and current performance, as well as future financial wealth. The ACSI provides a means of measuring one of a firm's most fundamental revenue-generating assets: its customers. Higher customer satisfaction should increase loyalty, reduce price elasticities, insulate current market share from competitors, lower transaction costs and the cost of attracting new customers, and help build a

firm's reputation in the market place. As such, ACSI provides a leading indicator of the firm's future financial health.

A financial institution could jeopardize its franchise value not only by displeasing its customers, but also by undertaking some financial risks that should not have been undertaken, thus mishandling the risk management process. Keeley (1988) demonstrates a clear relation between decreased franchise value and increased risk for commercial banks. Staking and Babbel (1995) establish the negative impact of interest rate risk on the market value of equity for property and liability insurance firms. While empirical evidence on the effects of risk management on banks' financial performance is scant and outdated, there is an extensive body of literature arguing that risk management does matter; see Santomero and Babbel (1997) for a review. While there is to date no consensus on the theory that explains why risk management matters, there is consensus that it does matter and we adopt this point of view herein.

In conclusion, the financial performance of an institution – observable but non-actionable – can be affected by its performance along the axes of service delivery and financial intermediation. The performance along both of those axes is both observable and actionable.

We turn our attention to performance along the axis of service delivery, and attempt to unbundle those factors that drive performance in the delivery of banking services. We do not ask here what drives the performance of financial institutions in the domain of risk management. This question was addressed at two previous conferences of the Wharton Financial Institutions Center, and the proceedings have appeared in special issues of journals: *Journal of Financial Services Research*, 12 (2/3), 1997, publishes the proceedings for bank risk management, and *The Journal of Risk and Insurance*, 64(2), 1997, publishes the proceedings for insurance firms' risk management.

### 3 What Drives Performance?

We classify drivers of performance into three broad classes: (*i*) *strategy*, (*ii*) *execution of strategy*, and (*iii*) *the environment*. Within each category we give details of the various factors that affect performance and provide supporting evidence that these factors do indeed drive performance.

### *3.1 Strategy*

What should a bank do? The articulation of a strategy is a key driver for success and especially so in dynamic, competitive environments such as that in the financial services industry; see, e.g., Boyd (1991) and Capon,

Farley, and Hulbert (1994) for empirical evidence on the *strategic success hypothesis*. In the context of banking institutions, the selection of a strategy primarily involves the decision on how the global banking organization should restructure into the components of the "disaggregated" bank. Here are some of the strategic choices:

1. *Product mix*: Should the bank be a product originator and if so, which portfolio of products should it support? In the United Kingdom, for instance, the Royal Bank of Scotland set up Direct Line as a completely autonomous enterprise to concentrate on consumer automobile insurance. Countrywide Pasadena in the U.S. focuses on a single product: mortgages. Bank of Montreal in Canada has set up a separate, non-branch-based organization called Mbanx that to some extent competes against its branch-based operation.

   It is worth noting that choosing a product mix not only defines the strategy of the institution in providing services, it is also a strategic decision in the context of risk management. Specification of a product mix is equivalent to a choice of the financial risks that the institution plans to manage.

2. *Client mix*: What kind of services does the institution wish to offer to clients? Should it focus on consumer financing or retailing, and which client profile fits best with the bank's line of products? Casework by Deloitte and Touche for a French bank showed that 5% of its clients accounted for 250% of the total profits of this bank's region. The same study found that 20% of the bank's profits were due to clients with low usage of their current accounts, 30% were due to clients that held at least one more product in addition to the current account (these clients account for 14% of the total client base), and only 30% of the client base was profitable. A successful strategic decision then hinges upon matching a targeted client segment with well-priced products.

3. *Geographical location*: Where should a bank operate, locally or internationally? Regulatory restrictions and the choice of product and client mix may determine the geographical scope of the institution. For instance, Countrywide Pasadena operates in California selling mortgage products to local homebuyers. Bank of Cyprus operates branches in New York, Toronto, and London offering full services to wealthy expatriates, and also sells the mutual funds of Swiss Bank Corporation to local clients who want to invest in the international markets. We note once more that the choice of geographical location also implies strategic choices on the risk-management axis of a bank's operations. International operations assume automatically currency exchange risks.

4. *Distribution channels*: As products are differentiated, customer segments are targeted, and geographical locations become dispersed, the choice of suitable distribution channel(s) becomes a crucial linchpin. Successful strategies hinge upon matching a targeted client segment with well-priced products through one or more appropriate delivery

channels. By focusing on one activity, Countrywide Pasadena was able to invest heavily in automation and promote its product through non-traditional media such as advertising, telephone, and print. However, alternative distribution channels are not only a marketing medium, they also provide the means for cost containment. For instance, the cost of an electronic deposit is half that of depositing a paper check, and banks must proactively manage consumers' behavior towards the most cost-effective channels.

5. *Organizational form*: Which organizational form should the bank adopt in the global environment? Should the bank diversify through a multi-bank bank holding company (MBHC) or through a more consolidated structure like an interstate branch-banking network? These issues need to be addressed in conjuction with the strategic choices on geographic location (item 3 above).

Further strategic factors also affect performance in conjunction with the major choices outlined above: the organization of back-office services is currently an integral part of the banks' operations, but gradually may be outsourced to specialized firms; the formation of strategic alliances to support clients in product areas or through delivery channels that are not the bank's primary choice; the choice of a scale of operation that exploits economies of scale without the adverse effects of complexity of scale. Each of these factors on its own is a driver of performance, but the proper *alignment* of these factors is also a driver of performance. Indeed, the Bank Administration Study (Roth and van der Velde, 1992) concluded that best-in-class institutions excel simultaneously in multiple dimensions.

### 3.2 Strategy Execution

The second broad set of performance drivers deals with the execution of a strategy, and the operational decisions that a bank makes in order to achieve its strategic goals. Considering once more *quality of services* as the actionable measure of performance, we identify the factors that drive this particular measure. The study of the Bank Administration Institute (see Roth and van der Velde, 1991, 1992) established that marketing, design of operations, organizational structure, and human resource management are tightly interlinked in a bank's search for excellence. These findings led to the formulation of the service management strategy encapsulated in the triad *operational capabilities–service quality–performance* (C-SQ-P) – see Roth and Jackson (1995). The C-SQ-P triad is, in turn, a focused view of the *service-profit chain* described earlier by Heskett et al. (1994), based on their analysis of successful service organizations; see also Heskett, Sasser, and Schlesinger (1997). Soteriou and

Zenios (1999) develop benchmarking models that formally test several links of the service-profit chain for banking institutions.

The arguments of the service-profit chain proceed as follows: (*i*) profit and growth are stimulated primarily by customer loyalty; (*ii*) loyalty is a direct result of customer satisfaction; (*iii*) satisfaction is largely influenced by the value of services provided to customers; (*iv*) value is created by satisfied, loyal, and productive employees; (*v*) employee satisfaction results primarily from high-quality support services and policies that enable employees to deliver results to customers. Without altering these arguments Soteriou and Zenios (1999) added the design of the operating system – operational practices, policies, and procedures – as a direct driver of satisfaction in links (*iii*) and (*v*).

While this service-profit chain is yet to be fully validated using empirical data – see Heskett et al. (1997), Roth, Chase, and Voss (1997), and Soteriou and Zenios (1999) for current work in this direction – it does provide a framework for identifying those operational and tactical factors that drive performance.

1. *X-efficiency:* Introduced by Leibenstein (1966, 1980) this measure describes all technical and allocative efficiencies of individual firms that are not scale or scope dependent. Thus X-efficiency is a measure of how well management is aligning technology, human resource management, and other resources to produce a given level of output, and it has a positive effect on links (*iii*) and (*iv*) of the service-profit chain.

   This is the most traditional and widely studied driver of performance for financial institutions. It views the bank as a "factory" that consumes various resources to produce several products and establishes the efficiency with which this transformation takes place. Early studies in this direction viewed the bank – usually at the branch level – as a "black box" and attempted to identify those banks branches that excel; see Chapter 2 by Berger and Humphrey for a survey. This line of research has led to the development of models for reducing X-inefficiencies, and such models have been employed in practice by banks as documented in Zenios (1999).

   X-efficiency can be viewed as a driver of performance in the sense that it affects positively some links of the service-profit chain, and a positive correlation exists between our definition of performance in terms of quality and X-efficiency (Soteriou and Zenios, 1998). However, it can also be argued that X-efficiency is not really an action taken in the execution of strategy, but is a result of actions.

   More recent work has focused in prying open the "black box" and understanding what strategy execution actions can be taken to improve X-efficiency; see Chapter 3 by Berger and Mester and Chapter 8 by Frei, Harker, and Hunter. From these efforts stems our further understanding on the drivers of performance, and in particular what drives X-efficiency.

2. *Human resource management*: It covers a number of areas for both managerial and non-managerial employees, such as compensation, hiring and selection, staffing, training, work organization, and employee involvement. Since employee satisfaction is one of the links in the service-profit chain, we may expect human resource management to be a key driver of employee performance and, hence, organizational performance. Indeed, there is solid empirical evidence to support this hypothesis; see Chapter 8 for several references in this direction. Recast in terms of the literature on banking efficiency, these findings imply that some of the inefficiencies in banking may be attributed to the ineffective management of human resources.

Human resource management practices can be viewed at multiple levels. The "architecture" of a human resource management system provides a high-level framework, while policies bring this framework closer to an operational level. System architecture and operational decisions should be properly *aligned* if human resource management is to deliver value added. Furthermore, in large complex organizations such as banks, different subsystems of human resource management govern different groups of employees, and these subsystems should also be properly aligned. The relationship between the CEO and the board – one more dimension of human resource management – with the system architecture and operational decisions of the firm is being studied extensively in executive compensation studies (see, e.g., Lambert, Larcker, and Verrecchia, 1991, or Ittner, Larcker, and Rajan, 1997). However, it has not been recognized as yet another aspect of the broader alignment issue outlined above.

3. *Use of technology*: Large banks in the U.S. spend approximately 20% of non-interest expenses on information technology, and this investment shows no sign of abating. Roth and van der Velde (1991) show that a typical large U.S. bank spends $392K per year on platform automation and an additional $502K on upgrading information and transaction processing. There is substantial evidence that information technology (IT) investments improve productivity – empirical evidence estimates return-on-investment from IT of the order of 50–60%. However, this evidence is available for a broad pool of manufacturing and service firms (Lichtenberg, 1995; Brynjolfsson and Hitt, 1996). Brynjolfsson and Hitt (1995) established the existence of firm effects in IT productivity measures. Although they found that the elasticity of IT remains positive and statistically significant for the firms in their pool, financial services firms were not explicitly included in this analysis. In fact, a recent study by the National Research Council (1994, p. 81) concluded that current productivity measurements are unable to account for improvements in the quality of services offered to customers or for the availability of a much wider array of banking services. Improvements in the speed of credit application processing or the availability of 24-hour banking through call centers and ATMs are not captured as higher banking outputs. The proclaimed benefits of computerization are hard to see in the data, and scholars are still debating this so-called *computer paradox*.

However, while it may still be debatable whether IT investments make banks more profitable, information technology cannot be overlooked as a key driver of performance. As demonstrated earlier in this chapter, customers demand delivery of an increasingly wider array of services, using a variety of delivery channels. Hence, IT becomes an asset in the quest for quality in the delivery of banking services. Furthermore, the cost for transaction processing varies significantly by channel – $1.40 per transaction through a teller, $1.00 through a human-operated call center, $0.15 through an automated voice response unit, and $0.40 through an ATM – and technology is also a key factor in cost containment.

4. *Process design* is the mechanism through which inputs are transformed to outputs; i.e., it is the principles by which work is organized in order to produce a specific set of outputs. Conventional wisdom holds the view that as long as all of the inputs to a service process – human, material, machine, method, management, environment, and measurement system – remain unchanged, the service output will be consistent in their characteristics. In reality, consistency of service performance is a utopia, and Frei, Kalakota, and Marx (1997) provide large-scale evidence from several bank holding companies on the prevalence of process variation.

Reduction of process variability becomes then another driver of performance. Large variation means that more service outputs are closer to the boundary of the range acceptable to the consumer, or even that some outputs are above or below customer specifications if the products are not carefully measured and monitored. In the former case – exceeding customer specifications – the result will be higher-than-expected costs, in the latter – falling short of the specifications – the result will be dissatisfied customers with the negative effects on performance prescribed by the service-profit chain.

5. An overarching factor that drives performance at the level of strategy execution is the *alignment* of human resource management, the use of technology, and the design of processes, with each other and with the institution's strategy. While the value of alignment is still debated – over-alignment may be considered a recipe for competitive failure – Frei, Harker, and Hunter provide in Chapter 4 the first empirical evidence that alignment does matter. They study separately the effects of aligning human resource management practices within diverse units of a bank, the significance of aligning human resource management with IT investments, the significance of aligning production processes, and the significance of aligning inputs with strategy.

Empirical evidence from a large-scale study of bank holding companies (Prassad and Harker, 1997) reveals that the elasticity of IT capital is positive but small, and with very low significance (7%), indicating that there is a very high probability (0.93) that investment in IT has no positive effect on bank productivity. Is this in disagreement with the findings of Lichtenberg (1995) and Brynjolfsson and Hitt (1996), and our arguments above that IT is a driver of performance? Prassad and Harker go further to show that the elasticities of IT labor are both large and significant at the 100% level. Hence, the empirical data seem to indicate that the banks in their sample can reap significant benefits from hiring and training IT labor. IT remains a significant driver of performance, but not so much through IT capital as through IT labor. This is further evidence that alignment is significant – in this case, alignment of IT technology with IT labor.

Further studies on the interaction between information technology, work practices, and wages were undertaken by Hunter and Lafkas (1998). This study, analyzing micro-level data gathered from over 300 U.S. bank branches, established the association between IT and wages for bank employees, and the interaction effects between technology and work practices. For instance, they establish that different work practices are appropriate in the presence of "automating" information technology, and other practices are warranted when IT is "informating" in the sense of creating more information. Informating technologies are associated with higher wages, while automating technologies tend to reduce them. Hence, alignment of work practices with IT is significant, but this alignment is context-dependent and could be quite complicated.

### 3.3 The Environment

We have argued in the introduction to this chapter that changes in the banking industry are the result of changes in the environment: technological, market, regulatory, etc. Environmental factors are indirectly controlled by the banks – through lobbying activities, marketing efforts, research and development – and hence, they can also be viewed as major factors in understanding performance. Which are, then, the environmental factors in explaining performance?

1. *Technology* and, in particular, *information technology* (IT) is the predominant production technology in financial services. We have argued in Section 3.2 that the use of technology is a key driver of performance. In this section we also argue that the technological environment and the changes it is undergoing are also major factors of the performance puzzle. Technological progress has led to quality-adjusted price decline of computers of 20% or more per year (Berndt and Griliches, 1990). Furthermore, from 1978 to 1989 the computer industry had the highest level of research and development intensity of any industry in the manufacturing sector, and its products appear to have exhibited unmatched quality improvements. Technological progress in networking has been equally rapid: the cost of moving data has dropped by a factor of 100 between 1987 and 1993. These developments led to the success of the information superhighway and the World Wide Web. The storage and moving of money are increasingly resembling a small corner of the overall world of telecommunications. These changes are partly responsible for the restructuring of the industry described in the Deloitte and Touche study by creating the so-far elusive economies of scale. The technological developments also facilitate some of the disaggregation

of the industry. For instance, while in the past back-office operations would usually reside in the same physical location where the customer service would take place, it is now conceivable that back-office operations can take place in a centralized firm-wide processing center at a remote location. Back-office operations could very easily take place overseas at a country with a highly skilled labor force, a good telecommunications infrastructure, and lower wages and tax rates. If Japanese automobile manufacturers could produce in the U.S., and U.S. manufacturers in Mexico, it is easy to see banks outsourcing their operations to an Eastern European country with a highly educated work force (but presently a poor telecommunications infrastructure). Conceptually, there is no reason why a bank could not reside on a high-end personal computer. The transmission of data for a simple instruction such as moving money between two accounts is virtually free on the Internet.

The technical changes of IT are only one part of the equation. We also observe increasing access of consumers to IT. The presence of personal computers in households is commonplace and access to the Internet is increasing rapidly. Changing consumer tastes affect the delivery channels that a bank's client is likely to use. The Deloitte and Touche study found that deposits remain the only product for which consumers use traditional delivery channels – the branch – in large percentages (99%), and this number has remained constant. In several other products – consumer loans, housing finance, mutual funds, life insurance – the use of non-traditional delivery channels is much higher, and is continuously gaining ground. How exactly these changes affect performance is unclear; however, they should be recognized as major factors in understanding performance. Banking institutions can take a proactive position in assimilating these changes, as happened for instance with the establishment of the HERMES Laboratory at the Wharton School that studied the developments of high-performance supercomputing for risk-management applications (Zenios, 1991; Worzel and Zenios, 1992). There is evidence (see the Deloitte and Touche study) that the assimilation of new money-moving technologies by banking institutions is a global trend. For instance, cash withdrawals through ATM as compared to the total amount of cash in circulation almost doubled in the U.K. and Italy during the period 1988–1992, and substantial increases were observed in most Western economies.

2. The choice of a client mix was targeted as one of the strategic drivers of performance in Section 3.1. However, *consumer tastes* change and these changes are also major environmental factors in the performance of financial institutions. We have already described some of the changes in the Introduction: the shift of consumer assets from bank deposits to other financial markets and the use of multiple distribution channels. However, consumers are typically conservative in financial matters, and this conservatism has contained a tidal wave of change in the banking industry. Younger people seem more willing to experiment with novel banking products and delivery channels, as well as to switch banks. Half of the banking users in the U.K. in the age group 18–34 use telephone

banking, compared to 40% of those in the 35–45 age group, and less than 10% of the 55+ age group. As the younger group ages, and its share of assets in the economy increases, the banking sector will increasingly feel the effects from this group's changing needs.

3. The banking industry is, in most countries, tightly regulated. However, Europe is moving towards a single market in retail banking and, in the United States, the forces to repeal or substantially weaken the Glass-Steagall Act are stronger than ever. Changing *regulations* is a key environmental factor in understanding performance. First, deregulation allows the fragmentation and reshaping of the industry, while technology facilitates this movement. There is empirical evidence from the United States that deregulation reduced the number of banks and banking companies while increasing their size. Deregulation also brought about reduction in the ratio of non-interest expenses to assets and loan charge-offs, and these reductions were passed on to consumers as cost savings. Post-deregulation periods have also witnessed increases in the market share of high-profit banks.

We note that regulation is imposed along both axes of the banks operations: service delivery and financial intermediation. Presumably regulators do not wish to impose restrictions on a bank's operations unless the services provided affect the financial intermediation process and the depositors' risk exposure. As we argued before, these two primary activities of a bank are tightly intertwined and, in the mind of policymakers, the former is an integral part of the latter. Chapter 13 by Jayaratne and Strahan surveys the effects of regulation on bank performance and provides empirical evidence that deregulation drives performance.

### 4 What Do We Know About Performance and Its Drivers?

The 15 chapters of this book present the state of the art in our understanding of performance and its drivers along the axes described above. The chapters are organized in four logical parts. The first part ("Introduction") contains two survey papers on international studies exploring the efficiency of financial institutions and efforts in understanding differences in efficiency. Efficiency at the operational level (X-efficiency) has been historically the most widely studied topic on the performance of financial institutions. Chapters 2 and 3 aptly summarize the status of international efforts in measuring the efficiency of financial institutions, and our understanding on what drives differences in operational efficiency. This understanding lays the background from which the novel contributions of the Wharton Conference stem. The rest of this volume builds upon and substantially expands the body of knowledge summarized in these two chapters.

The second part ("Drivers of Performance") contains papers concerned with the identification of drivers of performance, the specification and measurement of these drivers, and the measurement and benchmarking of performance per se. These papers focus on the more well understood and widely accepted drivers of performance, such as economies of scale and scope, diversification, alignment, human resource management, etc. The third part ("Environmental Drivers of Performance") deals with technological and regulatory issues and the effects of innovation on performance; these are external drivers of performance due to environmental conditions for which the institution may have little or no control. Finally the two chapters in Part 4, "Performance and Risk Management," make a contribution in bringing together performance and risk management.

### 4.1 Drivers of Performance: Identification, Specification, and Measurement

The most current and comprehensive knowledge on strategic drivers of performance is derived from the Bank Administration Institute study (Roth and van der Velde, 1991, 1992). This study – based on questionnaires administered to the heads of retail banking at all commercial banks in the U.S. with a minimum of $1 billion in assets – identified several success factors: flexibility and responsiveness in operations; ability to understand time-based competition in response to customer needs and expectation; ability to change capacity rapidly and improve customer access; ability to introduce innovative products quickly through superior workforce and systems; and ability to match products to customer expectations effectively. Best-in-class banks were found to excel in marketing, operations, organizational structure, and human resource management simultaneously. This study concluded by proclaiming customer-perceived quality as the key driver for retail banking performance in the 1990's. Some of the case-based findings of the Bank Administration Institute study are further corroborated and expanded upon by the chapters in Part 1.

Klein and Saidenberg and Meador, Ryan, and Schellhorn study economy of scope effects and the advantages of offering multiple products through complex organizational structures. Chapter 4, *Diversification, Organization, and Efficiency: Evidence from Bank Holding Companies*, is concerned with value-added from the recent wave of takeovers, restructuring, and consolidations in the banking industry. Multi-bank bank holding companies (MBHCs) in the U.S. are diversified interstate financial firms that are emerging as a result of the forces of change described in the earlier sections of this chapter. They are also a manifestation of the restructured organizations anticipated by the Deloitte and Touche study. Empirical analysis of data from 412 MBHCs over the period 1990 to 1994 provides evidence that diversification – in product and geographical scope – adds value. Where is this value-added coming from? The authors provide an *efficiency theory* explanation: diversified institutions benefit from opportunities for internal resource allocation and, therefore, can hold less capital and do more lending than more focused institutions. The extra income thus earned is more than adequate in compensating for the increased cost of the complexities of the internal organization. Similar issues are addressed in Chapter 5, *Product Focus Versus Diversification: Estimates of X-Efficiency for the U.S. Life Insurance Industry*. The authors study X-efficiency of 321 insurance firms over the period 1990 to 1995, and test for a relationship between a firm's output choice and measures of X-efficiency. Their analysis establishes that diversification across multiple product lines resulted in greater X-efficiency than more focused product strategies. It is interesting to add to the findings of these two chapters the results of the analysis in Soteriou and Zenios (1999), where they established that economies of scope and product portfolio choices have a much stronger effect than operational choices on X-efficiency. These chapters, collectively, pave the way for evaluating diversified financial providers. As companies from American Express to Sears and Ford Motor Company engage in insurance, financing, and securities underwriting beyond their primary business, the performance of diversified providers becomes a key question for regulators and policymakers. These chapters provide key inputs to managers facing strategic choices on product portfolio.

Chapter 6, *Outperformance: Does Managerial Specialization Pay?*, by P. Eichholtz, H. Op 't Veld, and M. Schweitzer, challenges the universal validity of product diversification. They study the performance of investment trusts, and in particular Real Estate Investment Trusts (REITs). They analyze the performance of 163 equity REITs over the period 1990 to 1996, studying the relationship between trust performance – over and above a broadly defined market index – and specialization by property type and geographic location. They find that companies specializing in a specific type of property outperform the market, whereas geographical specialization results in underperformance. However, the choice of REITs as the data set may limit the applicability of conclusions to real assets or to institutions that are not extensively diversified in the first place: REITs are required to invest up to 75% in real estate. It is within this restrictive investment universe that product specialization appears to pay. The inferences of this paper may not be easily applied to financial institutions which invest in financial assets. Nevertheless, this chapter highlights the need to study economies of scope carefully since they may not always be present, and thus the higher costs of diversification may not be fully justified.

Chapter 7, *Bank Relationships: A Review*, by S. Ongena and D.C. Smith, moves from the bank as a self-contained organization, to the consumer and the relationships of the organization with the consumer. It has long been recognized that relationships between a firm/customer and its bank are significant and lead to benefits accrued through time to both. Relationships take several forms, they have varying effects, and their presence and effects are context dependent. This chapter provides a review of the literature on the duration, scope, control, and density of bank relationships. It summarizes empirical evidence on the benefits and costs of bank relationships, and discusses the complex implications of bank relationships to the economy. As we develop an understanding that customer-perceived quality of services is a strategic driver of performance, this chapter develops our understanding on how to develop relationships with the client, especially when the client is a firm, and how these relationships can affect performance. Relationships are but one means for achieving eventual customer satisfaction with its established positive effects on long-term financial performance.

Chapter 8, *Inside the Black Box: What Makes a Bank Efficient?*, makes the leap from the efficiency measurement studies in Chapters 2 and 3 to an understanding of what drives efficiency at the level of strategy execution. Synthesizing more than 15 years of academic research literature from economics, service management, and operations management, and the empirical results of a four-year research effort by the Wharton Financial Institutions Research Center, Frei, Harker, and Hunter provide a comprehensive paper for the analysis of X-efficiency in financial services. They identify the following drivers of the performance of financial institutions: human resource management (HRM), and the alignment of HRM subsystems within a complex organization with each other and with the organization's strategic goals; capital and, in particular, IT capital and the alignment of IT capital expenditure with investments on IT personnel; and process efficiency and process variability and the alignment of processes with strategy. This chapter provides empirical evidence that these factors do indeed drive performance, at least in the sample of 121 bank holding companies and 135 banks covered by the authors' survey. This survey covers 75% of the total industry as measured by asset size and is the most comprehensive survey of its kind on the retail banking industry to date.

Chapters 9 and 10, by Athanassopoulos and Athanassopoulos, Soteriou, and Zenios, are concerned with the measurment of performance and, in particular, in disentangling several drivers of performance. We have argued at the beginning of this chapter that the relationships between the many drivers of performance are quite complex. These two chapters build on the widely developed methodology of Data Envelopment Analysis to develop models for disentangling the effects of various drivers for financial institutions. Chapter 9 makes the link of capabilities with the quality of services and performance. Chapter 10 succeeds in isolating managerial effects from environmental effects – country specific – on X-efficiency. Empirical results at the branch level from banks in the U.K., Greece, and Cyprus establish measurable effects of service quality on branch performance, and also establish the disadvantages of branches operating in tightly regulated financial regimes over those operating in deregulated environments in economies with highly developed financial sectors.

### 4.2  Environmental Drivers of Performance:
### Innovation, Regulations, and Technology

The revolution in electronic technologies of the 1990's poses special challenges for financial services. This special impact should come as no surprise: information, after all, lies at the heart of successful provision of financial services, and the generation, manipulation, storage, and transmission of information have been at the heart of the electronic revolution. While electronic technologies are not new to banking – "wire transfers" are as old as the telegraph – the technologies of the 1990's do seem different. Older technological changes and innovation focused on production and "back-office" functions, and raised efficiency and outsourcing questions. The recent innovations, while also encompassing vertical integration issues, raise more fundamental questions concerning competition among banks and non-banks, interaction with the consumer, and the delivery of innovative products. Chapter 11, *The Challenges of New Electronic Technologies in Banking: Private Strategies and Public Policies*, by Horvitz and White, discusses four technological innovations – electronic bill-paying, home banking, Internet transactions, and stored-value cards – and uses economic analysis to consider what challenges they pose for bank regulators. With this understanding of the challenges, banks and regulators alike can take cautious and measured steps to avoid the risks of being left behind due to minimalist actions at a time of rapid technological change, or the risks of plunging into the new technologies and subsequently being proven wrong.

Chapter 12, *Technological Change, Financial Innovation, and Financial Regulation in the U.S.*, by White, takes the challenges of technological change to the next level, that of financial innovation. Financial innovation (see, e.g., Allen and Gale, 1994; Consiglio and Zenios, 1997) can place serious strains on the incumbents in a particular industry or sector on which they are focused as well as creating challenges for public policy, especially in heavily regulated industries. While financial innovation is overall beneficial for the economy and the financial system, public policy and regulations have potentially dual impact: they may encourage or inhibit innovation. This chapter presents a classification of financial institutions – *financial intermediaries* and *financial facilitators* – and a classification of regulations – *economic regulations, health-safety-environment regulations*, and *information regulations*. These classifications allow the author to deal with a great variety of issues relating to the complex impacts of regulations on innovation and vice versa. As in the preceding chapter, this analysis can guide policymakers in adopting regulations that do not distort or stifle beneficial innovation, while responding appropriately to the challenges that financial innovation poses.

The broader effects of regulations on bank performance are finally discussed in Chapter 13, *The Effects of Regulation on Bank Performance in the United States*, by Jayaratne and Strahan. Banks in the U.S. and other countries are subjected to a wide range of regulations, including those that limit activities, those related to preserving the safety and soundness of banking institutions, those that constrain pricing, and those that affect banks' ability to expand geographically. Each set of regulations has an effect on the performance of the institution. The authors of Chapter 13 first give a brief overview of several forms of regulation, and focus on geographic restrictions that serve as entry restrictions and hence limit both scope and scale. From studying the literature on this topic and analyzing empirical data between regulated and unregulated regimes – e.g., U.S. versus Canada, and specific states in the U.S. before and after deregulation took place – we gradually come to realize that entry restrictions had a tremendous impact on the industry, and their effects have only recently been fully appreciated. Although individual banks and other parties may have benefited from these restrictions, evidence reveals that geographic restrictions increase bank instability by preventing adequate diversification and reduced industry efficiency. The empirical analysis supports a decline of non-interest-related costs and interest rates after deregulation, increase in market share by the most profitable banks after deregulation, and decrease of the variability in banks' profits after deregulation. Thus, we develop not only an understanding that regulations affect performance, but also of what kind of regulations may be detrimental to performance of the institutions and, hence, against the best interests of the consumer and the economy.

### 4.3 Performance and Risk Management

Although risk management is one of the primary functions of a bank – traditionally it was *the* primary function – very little has been done to date to link risk management with performance. Chapter 14, *Risk and Returns in Relationship and Transactional Banks*, by Dewenter and Hess, provides a sample of the type of research we need to undertake in linking performance with risk management. We surmise that the time is ripe for linking the results of the previous Wharton Financial Institutions Conferences – *Risk Management for Banks* and *Risk Management for Insurers* – with the findings of our conference on *Performance of Financial Institutions*.

Economic studies of bank performance use forward-looking measures, viewing the bank as an ongoing concern and its value as a measure of performance. Backward-looking studies ask why a bank performed the way it did for a specific period of time. Using a bank's economic profit – earnings minus capital charge – as a summary measure of past performance, we may combine risks and returns. Dewenter and Hess study the banks' cost of capital – the risk part of the economic profit that measures the expected rate of return that an investor forgoes by investing in the bank instead of other investments of equal risk – in the context of alternative organizational structures. In particular, they compare transactional and relationship banks. While Chapter 7 reviews bank relationships in general and establishes their effects on performance and general economic activity, Chapter 14 makes the link of relationships with risk. The authors empirically test differences in market risk and default risk exposures between transactional banks – found in the U.S. and the U.K. – and relationship banks – found in Japan and Germany. They find that the market risk of U.S. banks rises during periods of economic contraction, while the market risk of Japanese banks falls during these periods (the market risk of U.K. and German banks does not change over the business cycle). They also find that the returns of only the U.S. and U.K. banks show a significant link to default risk. These results support the idea that relationship banks are more effective monitors than transactional banks, providing some link between organization structures and risk management.

S. Zaheer in Chapter 15, *Acceptable Risk: A Study of Global Currency Trading Rooms in the U.S. and Japan*, takes a look at a different part of the relationship between organizational structures and risk. In particular, she studies the effect of organizational structures on an institution's risk appetite and skill in risk management. Starting from a realization that risk-taking in finance is a precursor to profit-making, this chapter tries to identify those characteristics that affect an organization's ability to take such risks, and therefore drive its performance. In a study of trading rooms – prime specimens of agents that assume risk for the purpose of making profits – in the U.S. and Japan, she investigates the effect of control strategies, norms of acceptable risk, and national culture on risk-taking. Analyzing data from 198 traders in spot and forward foreign-exchange operations in 28 trading rooms of eight Japanese and eight U.S. banks, she identifies the relationship between risk-taking, control strategies, and norms of acceptable risk; however, she finds no significant effects from national culture. These findings are cast not simply in the framework of risk-taking, but in the more relevant metric of *risk transformation* which is the ability to translate higher levels of risk to higher returns.

### 5  What Is Missing? Future Directions . . .

The chapters in this volume are not exhaustive in describing what we know on the performance of financial institutions. However, collectively, they help to fill in the overall performance picture that we have described in this introductory chapter. What is missing from this big picture, and what are the directions where future research efforts should be directed? Each chapter raises several research questions that deserve further investigation. We do not summarize them here. However, some general research themes have emerged at the conference.

First, there is a need to establish the relationship between performance – operational efficiency and quality of services – to long-term growth and market measures of profitability. While there is broad evidence to support the positive correlation of performance with growth from the retail service literature (e.g., the ACSI studies), work is needed to establish this relationship for the particular case of retail banking and financial services. Does this industry segment follow the same patterns of performance-profitability-growth as the whole service industry? Are any of these relationships more or less pronounced? Are there any special lessons to be learnt about these relationships from the financial services industry? These questions are presently open.

Second, we believe that the time is ripe for efforts to study jointly the efficiency of the two major axes along which banks operate: that of the financial intermediary who manages risk, and that of the retail service provider. As banks are restructured, the balance of these two activities in a portfolio may change, and understanding their interrelationship is important for understanding what organizational structures are more efficient. Should financial institutions maintain a balanced mix of financial intermediation together with retail servicing of products? Or should they specialize in either product servicing or risk management and product origination? The issue of enterprise-wide risk management is extremely relevant for retail banks as they move increasingly away from the single role of financial intermediaries (see, e.g., Holmer and Zenios, 1995).

Third, as we gain understanding on the performance of the institutions, we need to move the analysis to a different level and start addressing *interorganizational* issues. We have gradually made the shift from the study of institution as a sequence of functions to that of processes – see the evolution of our thinking of financial institutions from Merton (1990), to Holmer and Zenios (1995), to Frei, Kalakota, and Marx (1997). We now need to understand the process in which these institutions operate. This focus should not be so much the financial intermediation process as it is extensively studied and more or less understood (see, e.g., Herring and Santomero, 1995) but rather, the operational processes that include product origination and sales, payments, transactions processing, product capitalization in the financial markets, and so on. Only then can we fully comprehend the issue of the performance of financial institutions within the financial markets in which they operate, and complete the cycle from financial market efficiency, to institutional efficiency, and back to market efficiency.

The above research questions – although of increasing levels of abstraction – are well posed, and we may conceive of research agendas to address them. However, a grand challenge question remains: What is the role of the financial institution as an intermediary in the age of the information superhighway? As consumers have direct access to capital via the Internet, does the intermediary still have a role? And if the answer is "yes," then what precisely is this role? Tourist agencies are seeing their market share eroding as consumers make directly their own travel arrangements with airline firms and hoteliers. Are financial institutions facing similar challenges? If so, what implications do these challenges have on the structure and efficiency of the industry?

### References

F. Allen and D. Gale. *Financial Innovation and Risk Sharing.* The MIT Press, Cambridge, MA, 1994.

A. N. Berger, D. Hancock, and D. B. Humphrey. Bank efficiency derived from the profit function. *Journal of Banking and Finance*, 17: 317–347, 1993.

A. N. Berger and D. B. Humphrey. The dominance of inefficiencies over scale and product mix economies in banking. *Journal of Monetary Economics*, 28: 117–148, 1991.

A. N. Berger, W. C. Hunter, and S. G. Timme. The efficiency of financial institutions: A review of research past, present and future. *Journal of Banking and Finance*, 17: 221–249, 1993.

A. N. Berger, A. K. Kashyap, and J. M. Scalise. The transformation of the U.S. banking industry: what a long strange trip it's been. *Brookings Papers on Economic Activity*, 2: 55–218, 1995.

E. Berndt and Z. Griliches. Price indexes for microcomputers: an exploratory study: Working paper no. 3378, National Bureau of Economic Research, Washington, DC, 1990.

B. Boyd. Strategic planning and financial performance: A meta-analytical review. *Journal of Management Studies*, 28, 1991.

E. Brynjolfsson and L. Hitt. Information technology as a factor of production: the role of differences among firms. *Economics of Innovation and New Technology*, 3: 183–200, 1995.

E. Brynjolfsson and L. Hitt. Paradox lost? Firm-level evidence of high returns to information systems spending. *Management Science*, 42: 541–558, 1996.

N. Capon, J. Farley, and J. Hulbert. Strategic planning and financial performance: More evidence. *Journal of Management Studies*, 31, 1994.

A. Consiglio and S. A. Zenios. Optimal design of callable bonds using tabu search. *Journal of Economic Dynamics and Control*, 21: 1445–1470, 1997.

Deloitte and Touche Consulting Group. *The Future of Retail Banking: A Global Perspective*. Deloitte Touche Tohmatsue International, Washington, DC, 1995.

A. Demirguc-Kunt and R. Levine. Stock market development and financial intermediaries: stylized facts. *The World Bank Economic Review*, 10: 291–321, 1996.

C. Fornell. Productivity, quality, and customer satisfaction as strategic success indicators at firm and national level. *Advances in Strategic Management*, 11A: 217–229, 1995.

C. Fornell, C. D. Itner, and D. F. Larcker. The valuation consequences of customer satisfaction. Working paper, National Quality Research Center, School of Business Administration, University of Michigan, Ann Arbor, MI, 1996.

C. Fornell, M. D. Johnson, E. W. Anderson, J. Cha, and B. Everitt Bryant. The American customer satisfaction index: nature, purpose, and findings. *Journal of Marketing*, 60: 7–18, 1996.

F. X. Frei, P. T. Harker, and L. W. Hunter. Innovation in retail banking. Report 97–48-b, Financial Institutions Center, the Wharton School, University of Pennsylvania, Philadelphia, PA, 1997.

F. X. Frei, R. Kalakota, and L. M. Marx. Process variation as a determinant of service quality and bank performance: evidence from the retail banking study. Working paper, William E. Simon School of Business, University of Rochester, Rochester, NY, 1997.

Z. Griliches. *Output measurement in the service sector*, National Bureau of Economic Research Studies in Income and Wealth. University of Chicago Press, Chicago, IL, 1992.

R. J. Herring and A. M. Santomero. The role of the financial sector in economic performance. Working paper no. 95–08, the Wharton Financial Institutions Center, University of Pennsylvania, Philadelphia, PA, 1995.

J. L. Heskett, T. O. Jones, G. W. Loveman, W. E. Sasser, and L. A. Schlesinger. Putting the service-profit chain to work. *Harvard Business Review*, 72(2): 164–175, 1994.

J. L. Heskett, W. E. Sasser, and L. A. Schlesinger. *The Service Profit Chain*. The Free Press, New York, 1997.

M. R. Holmer and S. A. Zenios. The productivity of financial intermediation and the technology of financial product management. *Operations Research*, 43(6): 970–982, 1995.

L. W. Hunter and J. J. Lafkas. Information technology, work practices, and wages. Report 98–02, the Wharton Financial Institutions Center, University of Pennsylvania, Philadelphia, PA, 1998.

C. D. Ittner and D. F. Larcker. Measuring the impact of quality initiatives on firm financial performance. *Advances in the Management of Organizational Quality*, 1: 1–37, 1996.

C. D. Ittner, D. F. Larcker, and M. V. Rajan. The choice of performance measures in annual bonus contracts. *Accounting Review*, 72: 231–255, 1997.

M. C. Keeley. Deposit insurance risk and market power in banking. Working paper, Federal Reserve Bank of San Francisco, San Francisco, CA, Sept. 1988.

A. B. Kennickell and M. L. Kwast. Who uses electronic banking? Results from the 1995 survey of consumer finances. Working paper, division of research and statistics, Board of the Governors of the Federal Reserve System, Washington, DC, 1997.

R. A. Lambert, D. F. Larcker, and R. E. Verrecchia. Portfolio considerations in valuing executive compensation. *Journal of Accounting Research*, 29: 129–149, 1991.

H. Leibenstein. Allocative efficiency versus X-inefficiency. *American Economic Review*, 56: 392–415, 1996.

H. Leibenstein. X-efficiency, intrafirm behavior, and growth. In S. Maital and N. Meltz, editors, *Lagging Productivity Growth*, pages 199–220. Ballinger Publishing, Cambridge, MA, 1980.

F. R. Lichtenberg. The output contributions of computer equipment and personnel: a firm-level analysis. *Economics of Innovation and New Technology*, 3: 201–217, 1995.

R. C. Merton. The financial system and economic performance. *Journal of Financial Services Research*, pages 263–300, 1990.

National Research Council. *Information Technology in the Service Society*. National Academy Press, Washington, DC, 1994.

P. R. Nayyar. Stock market reactions to customer service changes. *Strategic Management Journal*, 16: 39–53, 1995.

S. J. Pilloff and A. M. Santomero. The value effects of bank mergers and acquisitions. Working paper no. 97–107, the Wharton Financial Institutions Center, University of Pennsylvania, Philadelphia, PA, 1997.

B. Prasad and P. T. Harker. Examining the contribution of information technology toward productivity and profitability in U.S. retail banking. Report 97–109, the Wharton Financial Institutions Center, University of Pennsylvania, Philadelphia, PA, 1997.

A. V. Roth and W. E. Jackson III. Strategic determinants of service quality and performance: Evidence from the banking industry. *Management Science*, 41: 1720–1733, 1995.

A. V. Roth and M. van der Velde. The retail technology. *Bank Management*, pages 14–19, December 1991.

A. V. Roth and M. van der Velde. *World Class Banking: Benchmarking the Strategies of Retail Banking Leaders*. Bank Administration Institute, 1992.

A. M. Santomero and D. F. Babbel. Financial risk management by insurers: An analysis of the process. *The Journal of Risk and Insurance*, 64: 231–270, 1997.

H. Singh and M. Zollo. Learning to acquire: knowledge accumulation mechanisms and the evolution of post-acquisition integration strategies. Report 97-10-b, the Wharton Financial Institutions Center, University of Pennsylvania, Philadelphia, PA, 1997.

A. Soteriou and S. A. Zenios. Operations, quality, and profitability in the provision of banking services. *Management Science*, 45: 1221-1238, 1999.

K. B. Staking and D. F. Babbel. The relation between capital structure and interest rate sensitivity and market value in the property-liability insurance industry. *The Journal of Risk and Insurance*, 62: 690-718, 1995.

K. Worzel and S. A. Zenios. Parallel- and super-computing in the financial services industry. *Economic & Financial Computing*, 2: 169-184, Oct. 1992.

S. A. Zenios. Massively parallel computations for financial modeling under uncertainty. In J. Mesirov, editor, *Very Large Scale Computing in the 21st Century*, pages 273-294. SIAM, Philadelphia, PA, 1991.

S. A. Zenios, editor, *Data Envelopment Analysis in Banking. Interfaces*. Institute for Operations Research and Management Science, Providence, RI, 29(3), 1999.

# 2

## Efficiency of Financial Institutions: International Survey and Directions for Future Research[1,2]

Allen N. Berger[a,b,*], David B. Humphrey[c]

### Abstract

This chapter surveys 130 studies that apply frontier efficiency analysis to financial institutions in 21 countries. The primary goals are to summarize and critically review empirical estimates of financial institution efficiency and to attempt to arrive at a consensus view. We find that the various efficiency methods do not necessarily yield consistent results and suggest some ways that these methods might be improved to bring about findings that are more consistent, accurate, and useful. Secondary goals are to address the implications of efficiency results for financial institutions in the areas of government policy, research, and managerial performance. Areas needing additional research are also outlined.

### 1 Introduction

The first task in evaluating the performance of financial institutions is to separate those production units that by some standard perform well from

---

[a] Board of Governors of the Federal Reserve System, Washington, DC 20551, USA.
[b] Wharton Financial Institutions Center, University of Pennsyluania, Philadelphia, PA 19104, USA.
[c] Department of Finance, Florida State University, Tallahassee, FL 32306-1042, USA.
[*] Corresponding author. Email: mlanb00@frb.gov.
[1] The opinions expressed do not necessarily reflect those of the Board of Governors or its staff.
[2] Reprinted by permission of the *European Journal of Operational Research*.

those that perform poorly. This is done by applying nonparametric or parametric frontier analysis to firms within the financial industry or to branches within a financial firm. The information obtained can be used either: (1) to inform government policy by assessing the effects of deregulation, mergers, or market structure on efficiency; (2) to address research issues by describing the efficiency of an industry, ranking its firms, or checking how measured efficiency may be related to the different efficiency techniques employed; or (3) to improve managerial performance by identifying "best practices" and "worst practices" associated with high and low measured efficiency, respectively, and encouraging the former practices while discouraging the latter.

At its heart, frontier analysis is essentially a sophisticated way to "benchmark" the relative performance of production units. Most financial institutions, with varying degrees of success, benchmark themselves and/or use industry consultants to perform this task. The power of frontier analysis is twofold. First, it permits individuals with very little institutional knowledge or experience to select "best practice" firms within the industry (or "best practice" branches within the firm), assign numerical efficiency values, broadly identify areas of input overuse and/or output underproduction, and relate these results to questions of government policy or academic research interest. Second, in the hands of individuals with sufficient institutional background, frontier analysis permits management to objectively identify areas of best practice within complex service operations, a determination not always possible with traditional benchmarking techniques due to a lack of a powerful optimizing methodology such as linear programming.

As practiced by academics, frontier analysis will generally tell informed industry participants little they do not already know in a general, qualitative way. While the qualitative "news" may not be new, the quantification of it is. Frontier analysis provides an overall, objectively determined, numerical efficiency value and ranking of firms (also called X-efficiency in the economics literature) that is not otherwise available. This attribute makes frontier analysis particularly valuable in assessing and informing government policy regarding financial institutions, such as determining the efficiency effects of mergers and acquisitions for possible use in antitrust policy. When frontier analysis is more narrowly focused on proprietary transactions data and detailed input use across branches of a financial institution, a firm's internal performance can often be enhanced beyond that possible with its own benchmarking procedures.

There are now enough frontier efficiency studies of financial institutions to make some tentative comparisons of average efficiency levels both across measurement techniques and across countries, as well as outline the primary results of the many applications of efficiency analysis to policy and research issues. Toward this end, we survey and contrast the results of 130 financial institution efficiency studies. This literature has employed at least five major different efficiency techniques, which have been applied to financial institutions in at least 21 countries. We also cover studies of several different types of depository institutions – commercial banks, savings and loans, and credit unions – as well as firms in the insurance industry. We include this large number of nations and wide array of types of financial institutions because the financial markets of the future are likely to become more globalized and have more universal-type institutions offering greater selections of financial services within a single institution.

Section 2 critiques the main nonparametric and parametric efficiency estimation methods. A reasonable familiarity with the various frontier measurement techniques is assumed. Readers wishing to be more fully informed regarding these techniques are referred to the numerous comprehensive methodological surveys which exist (Banker et al., 1989; Bauer, 1990; Seiford and Thrall, 1990; Aly and Seiford, 1993; Greene, 1993; Grosskopf, 1993; Lovell, 1993; Charnes et al., 1994).

In Section 3, the average efficiency and dispersion of efficiency for US commercial banks – the most studied class of financial institutions – are displayed. These data are used to illustrate the differences in efficiency estimates between nonparametric and parametric frontier techniques. As some investigators have already hinted at, the central tendency of the distribution of estimates of average efficiency derived from either type of technique is similar but the degree of dispersion differs. The similarity that exists for average efficiency within an industry across frontier techniques is weaker when rankings of firms by their efficiency value are being compared.

In Section 4, we discuss the similarity of average efficiency estimates across countries and by type of financial institution. We compare the results for 21 nations and four types of financial institutions – banks, S&Ls, credit unions, and insurance firms.

Applications of efficiency analysis are reviewed in Sections 5–7, segmented according to the main purpose of the research. Section 5 reviews studies which provide valuable information for government policy, such as the effects of deregulation, financial institution failure, market structure, and mergers. Section 6 reviews studies that are chiefly concerned with research issues, such as the measurement of efficiency, comparisons of efficiency across international borders, issues of corporate control, risk, and the stability over time of firm-level efficiency. Section 7 analyzes studies that are primarily associated with improving managerial performance, most of which measure the relative efficiencies of individual branches within the *same* firm.

We recognize the somewhat artificial nature of this division of issues into government policy, research, and managerial performance. For example, studies which advance the efficiency research agenda will eventually be useful for studying policy, management, or any other efficiency issue.

Finally, Section 8 concludes, assessing the results of applications of efficiency analysis to financial institutions, and suggesting some new directions for future research. Most of the important suggestions concern finding explanations of efficiency that may help inform government policy, identify the economic conditions that create inefficiency, and improve managerial performance.

## 2 Nonparametric and Parametric Approaches to Measuring Efficiency

Our focus in this article is on frontier efficiency, or how close financial institutions are to a "best-practice" frontier. Since engineering information on the technology of financial institutions is not available, studies of frontier efficiency rely on accounting measures of costs, outputs, inputs, revenues, profits, etc. to impute efficiency relative to the best practice within the available sample. There is a virtual consensus in the literature that differences in frontier efficiency among financial institutions exceed inefficiencies attributable to incorrect scale or scope of output.[3] However, there is really no consensus on the preferred method for determining the best-practice frontier against which relative efficiencies are measured.

At least five different types of approaches have been employed in evaluating the efficiency of financial institutions and branches. These methods differ primarily in the assumptions imposed on the data in terms of (a) the functional form of the best-practice frontier (a more restrictive parametric functional form vs. a less restrictive nonparametric form), (b) whether or not account is taken of random error that may tem-

---

[3] See Berger et al. (1993b) for a review of studies of scale and scope efficiencies of financial institutions and how these compare to frontier efficiencies.

porarily give some production units high or low outputs, inputs, costs, or profits, and (c) if there is random error, the probability distribution assumed for the inefficiencies (e.g., half-normal, truncated normal) used to disentangle the inefficiencies from the random error. Thus, the established approaches to efficiency measurement differ primarily in how much shape is imposed on the frontier and the distributional assumptions imposed on the random error and inefficiency.

### 2.1 Nonparametric Frontiers

Nonparametric approaches, such as much of the work in data envelopment analysis (DEA) and free disposal hull (FDH), put relatively little structure on the specification of the best-practice frontier. DEA is a linear programming technique where the set of best-practice or frontier observations are those for which no other decision making unit or linear combination of units has as much or more of every output (given inputs) or as little or less of every input (given outputs).[4] The DEA frontier is formed as the piecewise linear combinations that connect the set of these best-practice observations, yielding a convex production possibilities set. As such, DEA does not require the explicit specification of the form of the underlying production relationship. The free disposal hull (FDH) approach is a special case of the DEA model where the points on lines connecting the DEA vertices are not included in the frontier. Instead, the FDH production possibilities set is composed only of the DEA vertices and the free disposal hull points interior to these vertices.[5] Because the FDH frontier is either congruent with or interior to the DEA frontier, FDH will typically generate larger estimates of average efficiency than DEA (Tulkens, 1993). Either approach permits efficiency to vary over time and makes no prior assumption regarding the form of the distribution of inefficiencies across observations except that undominated observations are 100% efficient.

---

[4] Developed by Charnes et al. (1978), DEA was originally intended for use in public sector and not-for-profit settings where typical economic behavioral objectives, such as cost minimization or profit maximization, may not apply. Thus, DEA could be used even when conventional cost and profit functions that depend on optimizing reactions to prices could not be justified.

[5] From the perspective of input requirements to produce a given output, DEA presumes that linear substitution is possible between observed input combinations on an isoquant (which is generated from the observations in piecewise linear forms). In contrast, FDH presumes that no substitution is possible so the isoquant looks like a step function formed by the intersection of lines drawn from observed (local) Leontief-type input combinations.

However, a key drawback to these nonparametric approaches is that they generally assume that there is no random error. There is assumed to be: (a) no measurement error in constructing the frontier; (b) no luck that temporarily gives a decision making unit better measured performance one year from the next; and (c) no inaccuracies created by accounting rules that would make measured outputs and inputs deviate from economic outputs and inputs. Any of these errors that did appear in an inefficient unit's data may be reflected as a change in its measured efficiency. What may be more problematical is that any of these errors in one of the units on the efficient frontier may alter the measured efficiency of *all* the units that are compared to this unit or linear combinations involving this unit.

### 2.2 Parametric Frontiers

There are three main parametric frontier approaches. The stochastic frontier approach (SFA) – sometimes also referred to as the econometric frontier approach – specifies a functional form for the cost, profit, or production relationship among inputs, outputs, and environmental factors, and allows for random error. SFA posits a composed error model where inefficiencies are assumed to follow an asymmetric distribution, usually the half-normal, while random errors follow a symmetric distribution, usually the standard normal. The logic is that the inefficiencies must have a truncated distribution because inefficiencies cannot be negative. Both the inefficiencies and the errors are assumed to be orthogonal to the input, output, or environmental variables specified in the estimating equation. The estimated inefficiency for any firm is taken as the conditional mean or mode of the distribution of the inefficiency term, given the observation of the composed error term.

The half-normal assumption for the distribution of inefficiencies is relatively inflexible and presumes that most firms are clustered near full efficiency. In practice, however, other distributions may be more appropriate (Greene, 1990). Some financial institution studies have found that specifying the more general truncated normal distribution for inefficiency yields minor, but statistically significant, different results from the special case of the half-normal (Berger and DeYoung, 1997). A similar result using life insurance data occurred when a gamma distribution, which is also more flexible than the half-normal, was used (Yuengert, 1993). However, this method of allowing for flexibility in the assumed distribution of inefficiency may make it difficult to separate inefficiency from random error in a composed-error framework, since the truncated normal and gamma distributions may be close to the symmetric normal distribution assumed for the random error.

The distribution-free approach (DFA) also specifies a functional form for the frontier, but separates the inefficiencies from random error in a different way. Unlike SFA, DFA makes no strong assumptions regarding the specific distributions of the inefficiencies or random errors. Instead, DFA assumes that the efficiency of each firm is stable over time, whereas random error tends to average out to zero over time. The estimate of inefficiency for each firm in a panel data set is then determined as the difference between its average residual and the average residual of the firm on the frontier, with some truncation performed to account for the failure of the random error to average out to zero fully.[6] With DFA, inefficiencies can follow almost any distribution, even one that is fairly close to symmetric, as long as the inefficiencies are nonnegative.[7] However, if efficiency is shifting over time due to technical change, regulatory reform, the interest rate cycle, or other influences, then DFA describes the average deviation of each firm from the best average-practice frontier, rather than the efficiency at any one point in time.

Lastly, the thick frontier approach (TFA) specifies a functional form and assumes that deviations from predicted performance values within the highest and lowest performance quartiles of observations (stratified by size class) represent random error, while deviations in predicted performance between the highest and lowest quartiles represent inefficiencies. This approach imposes no distributional assumptions on either inefficiency or random error except to assume that inefficiencies differ between the highest and lowest quartiles and that random error exists within these quartiles. TFA itself does not provide point estimates of efficiency for individual firms but is intended instead to provide an estimate of the general level of overall efficiency. The TFA reduces the effect of extreme points in the data, as can DFA when the extreme average residuals are truncated.

---

[6] An alternative way to apply DFA is to use a fixed effects model. In a fixed effects model, a dummy variable is specified for each firm in a panel data set. Differences in the fixed effects estimated across firms represent firm inefficiencies (e.g., Lang and Welzel, 1996). However, Berger (1993) found that the fixed effects were confounded by the differences in scale, which are several thousand times larger in magnitude than differences in efficiency in typical banking data sets.

[7] A plot of an unrestricted distribution of inefficiencies implied by the data in one DFA study determined that the resulting frequency distribution was closer to the shape of a symmetric normal rather than an asymmetric half-normal distribution (Berger, 1993).

### 2.3 Is There a "Best" Frontier Method?

The lack of agreement among researchers regarding a preferred frontier model at present boils down to a difference of opinion regarding the lesser of evils. The parametric approaches commit the sin of imposing a particular functional form (and associated behavioral assumptions) that presupposes the shape of the frontier. If the functional form is misspecified, measured efficiency may be confounded with the specification errors. Usually a local approximation such as the translog is specified, which has been shown to provide poor approximations for banking data that are not near the mean scale and product mix (see McAllister and McManus, 1993; Mitchell and Onvural, 1996). The translog also forces the frontier average cost curve to have a symmetric U-shape in logs.

The nonparametric studies impose less structure on the frontier but commit the sin of not allowing for random error owing to luck, data problems, or other measurement errors. If random error exists, measured efficiency may be confounded with these random deviations from the true efficiency frontier. As seen below, the conflict between the non-parametric and parametric approaches is important because the two types of methods tend to have different degrees of dispersion and rank the same financial institutions somewhat differently.

It is not possible to determine which of the two major approaches dominates the other since the true level of efficiency is unknown. The solution, in our opinion, lies in adding more flexibility to the parametric approaches and introducing a degree of random error into the non-parametric approaches. By addressing the main limitation of each approach, the efficiency results will presumably yield efficiency estimates which are more consistent across the approaches. These processes have already begun. In the parametric approaches, some studies have experimented with specifying more globally flexible forms. To date, this has focused on specifying a Fourier-flexible functional form which adds Fourier trigonometric terms to a standard translog function (Berger and DeYoung, 1997; Berger and Mester, 1997; Berger et al., 1996a, 1997). This greatly increases the flexibility of the frontier by allowing for many inflection points and by including essentially orthogonal trigonometric terms that help fit the frontier to the data wherever it is most needed.[8]

---

[8] The use of the Fourier-flexible form in place of the translog in one case reduced the amount of measured inefficiency by about half – from 10% to 5% of costs – since the more flexible frontier was able to be closer to more of the data (Berger and DeYoung,

In the nonparametric approaches, two research agendas are being pursued.[9] One is analytical, and seeks to provide a statistical foundation for DEA. The other is empirical, and seeks to develop and implement a stochastic version of DEA. The analytical research has demonstrated that, given certain plausible assumptions concerning the structure of technology and the distribution of the "true" efficiencies, (a) the empirical efficiencies calculated from a DEA model provide consistent estimators for the true efficiencies, (b) the DEA estimators can be interpreted as maximum likelihood estimators, and (c) the asymptotic empirical distribution recovers the true distribution under the maintained assumptions. This work thus provides a theoretical foundation for statistical hypothesis testing in a DEA environment (see Banker, 1996, for a summary). However, the fundamental problem is one of specifying the distribution of efficiency across observations (Kneip and Simar, 1996; Simar, 1996). Hypothesis testing can be conducted only after the data generating process has been specified, and in a multidimensional nonparametric setting in which the inefficiencies are one-sided, this is a statistically non-trivial matter. Moreover, the sampling distribution of the DEA efficiency estimators remains unknown, and this observation motivates the second line of research.

A resampling technique, such as bootstrapping, is one way of obtaining an empirical approximation to the underlying sampling distribution of DEA efficiency estimates. Once the underlying distribution is approximated, statistical inference can be conducted. This computer-intensive approach to hypothesis testing, however, requires a careful specification of the data generating process (Simar and Wilson, 1995). A different approach is to apply the techniques of chance-constrained programming to the DEA model (Land et al., 1993; Olesen and Petersen, 1995). Here inequality constraints describing the structure of the nonparametric DEA technology are converted to "chance constraints" which, due to noise in the data, are allowed to be violated by a certain proportion of the observations. If probability distributions are specified for these violations (the data generating process again), the constraints can be converted into certainty equivalents, and a chance-constrained DEA

---

1997). Globally flexible functional forms have also been applied to banking data in non-frontier models of scale economies (McAllister and McManus, 1993; Mitchell and Onvural, 1996).

[9] We thank Knox Lovell for his gracious assistance with this and the following paragraph.

model emerges as a nonlinear programming problem. Although the chance-constrained DEA model remains deterministic, it incorporates noise in the data (see Grosskopf, 1996, for a survey of both empirical approaches).[10]

### 3 Summary of Efficiency Findings by Measurement Method

We now turn to the results of studies of financial institution efficiency. Along the way we will take note of how the efficiency estimates vary by the efficiency approach specified (DEA, FDH, SFA, DFA, TFA) and a number of other facts about the method and sample. Table 2.1 lists the 122 frontier studies we found that apply efficiency analysis to depository financial institutions and notes which of the five frontier methods were used.[11] The eight studies that apply frontier analysis to insurance firms are shown in another table and are discussed later. Table 2.1 also shows the country the analysis was applied to, the author(s) of the study, the average yearly efficiency estimates reported, and the type of institution covered. Overall, there were 69 applications of nonparametric techniques and 60 using parametric approaches (some papers used more than one approach).[12] Studies focusing on US financial institutions were the most numerous, accounting for 66 of the 116 single country studies in Table 2.1.[13]

A frequency distribution of 188 nonparametric and parametric annual average efficiency estimates for US banks from Table 2.1 (excluding

---

[10] An earlier effort to combine parametric and nonparametric approaches has involved using FDH (or DEA) to first "screen the data" in order to identify the set of efficient observations and then use only these observations in a regression-based estimate of a cost frontier (Thiry and Tulkens, 1992; Bauer and Hancock, 1993) or identify these observations with a dummy variable and use all the observations in the regression, circumventing the problem of having too few observations for a large regression (Bardhan et al., 1996). This approach is similar to that of the thick frontier approach except that the criterion used to screen the data is different.

[11] There is also a novel application of DEA efficiency analysis to the performance of mutual funds (Murthi et al., 1997), but it is not listed in our tables.

[12] Of the 69 nonparametric applications, 62 were DEA, 5 were FDH, and 2 were other approaches noted in Table 2.1. The 60 parametric applications were 24 SFA, 20 DFA, and 16 TFA.

[13] Although we have tried hard to be comprehensive, there are undoubtedly some studies we have missed, and we apologize to the authors of those articles. Some that we know we have missed were not written in English or were in journals to which we did not have access.

Table 2.1. *Studies of the efficiency of depository financial institutions.*

| Country | Method[a] | Author (date) | Average annual efficiency estimate | Institution type |
|---|---|---|---|---|
| Belgium | FDH | Tulkens (1993) | 0.97, 0.93 | Branch |
| Belgium | FDH | Tulkens and Malnero (1994) | 0.93 | Branch |
| Canada | DEA | Parkan (1987) | 0.98 | Branch |
| Canada | DEA | Schaffnit et al. (1997) | 0.87 | Branch |
| Cyprus | DEA | Zenios et al.(1999) | 0.89, 0.92, 0.88 | Branch |
| Denmark | DEA | Bukh (1994) | 0.80, 0.85 | Bank |
| Finland | DEA | Kuussaari (1993) | 0.80, 0.86 | Bank |
| Finland | DEA | Kuussaari and Vesala (1995) | 0.86 | Bank |
| France | DFA | Chaffai and Dietsch (1995) | 0.24, 0.33 | Bank |
| France | DFA | Dietsch (1994) | 0.72, 0.71, 0.68, 0.71, 0.69 | Bank |
| Germany | SFA | Altunbas and Molyneux (n.d.) | 0.81, 0.77, 0.77 | Bank |
| Germany | TFA | Lang and Welzel (1995) | 0.93 | Bank |
| Germany | DFA | Lang and Welzel (1996) | 0.54, 0.61 | Bank |
| Greece | DEA, and SFA | Giokas (1991) | 0.87 0.72 | Branch Branch |
| Greece | DEA | Vassiloglou and Giokas (1990) | 0.91 | Branch |
| India | DEA | Bhattacharyya et al. (1997) | 0.86, 0.75, 0.79 | Bank |
| Italy | DEA | Favero and Papi (1995) | 0.88, 0.91, 0.79, 0.84 | Bank |
| Italy | DEA | Ferrier and Hirschberg (1994) | 0.98 | Bank |
| Italy | DEA, and SFA | Resti (1995) | 0.74, 0.76, 0.74, 0.75, 0.73 0.69, 0.70, 0.70, 0.70, 0.70 | Bank Bank |
| Japan | DEA | Fukuyama (1993) | 0.86 | Bank |
| Japan | DEA | Fukuyama (1995) | 0.46, 0.46, 0.44 | Bank |
| Mexico | DEA | Taylor et al. (1997) | 0.75, 0.72, 0.69 | Bank |
| Norway | DEA | Berg (1992) | 0.62, 0.51, 0.57, 0.47, 0.49, 0.68, 0.57 | Bank |
| Norway | DEA | Berg et al. (1991) | 0.81 | Bank |
| Norway | DEA | Berg et al. (1992) | n.a. | Bank |
| Norway | TFA | Berg and Kim (1994) | 0.81, 0.81 | Bank |
| Norway | TFA | Berg and Kim (1996) | 0.89, 0.74 | Bank |
| Saudi Arabia | DEA | Al-Faraj et al. (1993) | 0.87 | Branch |
| Spain | DEA | Grifell-Tatjé and Lovell (1994) | n.a. | S&L |
| Spain | DEA | Grifell-Tatjé and Lovell (1996) | n.a. | Bank, S&L, $\pi$ |
| Spain | DEA | Grifell-Tatjé and Lovell (1997a) | 0.81, 0.85, 0.85, 0.84, 0.83, 0.84, 0.83, 0.87, 0.84, 0.85, 0.84, 0.83, 0.80, 0.82, 0.81, 0.77 | Bank S&L |
| Spain | DEA | Grifell-Tatjé and Lovell (1997b) | 0.76, 0.75, 0.75, 0.80, 0.78, 0.80 | S&L |
| Spain | DEA | Lovell and Pastor (1997) | 0.92, 0.90 | Branch |
| Spain | TFA | Lozano (1995) | 0.90, 0.88, 0.89, 0.88, 0.87, 0.87, 0.87 | Bank |
| Spain | TFA | Lozano (1997) | 0.68, 0.67, 0.66, 0.73, 0.78, 0.81 | S&L, $\pi$ |
| Spain | DEA | Pastor (1995) | 0.87, 0.80 | Branch |
| Spain | DEA | Perez and Quesada (1994) | 0.83 | Bank |

Table 2.1. *(cont.)*

| Country | Method[a] | Author (date) | Average annual efficiency estimate | Institution type |
|---|---|---|---|---|
| Spain | SFA | Maudos (1996a) | 0.81, 0.83, 0.82, 0.81, 0.81, 0.81, 0.81, 0.79, 0.80, 0.82, 0.83, 0.82, 0.80, 0.82, 0.82, 0.81, 0.80, 0.81, 0.85, 0.87, 0.85, 0.81, 0.84, 0.85, 0.84, 0.82, 0.82 | Bank |
| Spain | SFA | Maudos (1996b) | 0.82, 0.83, 0.83 | Bank |
| Sweden | DEA | Hartman and Storbeck (1995) | 0.85, 0.78 | S&L |
| Switzerland | DEA | Sheldon and Haegler (1993) | 0.56 | Bank |
| Tunisia | SFA | Chaffai (1993) | 0.66, 0.65, 0.65, 0.64, 0.63, 0.63 0.62, 0.62, 0.62, 0.61, 0.61, 0.61 | Bank |
| Tunisia | SFA | Chaffai (1997) | n.a. | Bank |
| Turkey | DEA | Oral and Yolalan (1990) | 0.87, 0.53 | Branch |
| Turkey | DEA | Zaim (1995) | 0.83, 0.94 | Bank |
| UK | DEA | Athanassopoulos (1995) | 0.85 | Branch |
| UK | DEA | Athanassopoulos (1997) | 0.90 | Branch |
| UK | DEA | Drake and Howcroft (1997) | 0.93, 0.97 | Branch |
| UK | DEA | Drake and Weyman-Jones (1992) | 0.98 | S&L |
| UK | DEA | Field (1990) | 0.93 | S&L |
| US | DFA | Adams et al. (1999) | 0.64, 0.61, 0.69, 0.64, 0.70, 0.77 | Bank |
| US | DFA | Akhavein et al. (1997a) | 0.24, 0.34 | Bank, $\pi$ |
| US | DFA | Akhavein et al. (1997b) | 0.99, 0.44 | Bank, $\pi$ |
| US | DEA | Aly et al. (1990) | 0.75, 0.81 | Bank |
| US | DEA | Barr et al. (1994) | 0.81, 0.83 | Bank |
| US | SFA, | Bauer et al. (1993) | 0.87, 0.86, 0.86, 0.87, 0.86, 0.88 0.89, 0.87, 0.87, 0.87, 0.85, 0.85 | Bank |
| | DFA, | | 0.86, 0.85, 0.86, 0.86, 0.85, 0.86 0.87, 0.86, 0.86, 0.86, 0.85, 0.85 | Bank |
| | and TFA | | 0.86, 0.90, 0.81, 0.80, 0.84, 0.84 0.86, 0.83, 0.81, 0.82, 0.83, 0.79 | Bank |
| US | DEA | Bauer et al. (1998) | 0.73, 0.71, 0.71, 0.73, 0.75, 0.76 0.74, 0.73, 0.73, 0.70, 0.67, 0.67 | Bank |
| US | DFA | Berger (1993) | 0.85, 0.84, 0.75 | Bank |
| US | DFA | Berger (1995) | n.a. | Bank |
| US | SFA | Berger and De Young (1997) | 0.92, 0.94, 0.95, 0.91, 0.93, 0.91 0.91, 0.91, 0.93, 0.95 | Bank |
| US | DFA | Berger et al. (1993a) | 0.52, 0.65, 0.66 | Bank, $\pi$ |
| US | DFA | Berger and Hannan (1997) | n.a. | Bank |
| US | TFA | Berger and Humphrey (1991) | 0.81, 0.84 | Bank |
| US | TFA | Berger and Humphrey (1992a) | 0.85, 0.81, 0.71, 0.80, 0.84, 0.80 | Bank |
| US | DFA | Berger and Humphrey (1992b) | n.a. | Bank |
| US | DFA | Berger et al. (1997) | 0.94, 0.79 | Branch |
| US | DFA | Berger and Mester (1997) | 0.87 0.55, 0.46 | Bank Bank, $\pi$ |
| US | SFA | Cebenoyan et al. (1993a) | 0.77, 0.83 | S&L |
| US | SFA | Cebenoyan et al. (1993b) | 0.87, 0.86 | S&L |
| US | SFA | Chang et al. (1993) | 0.81 | Bank |
| US | DEA | Charnes et al. (1990) | n.a. | Bank |

43

Table 2.1. *(cont.)*

| Country | Method[a] | Author (date) | Average annual efficiency estimate | Institution type |
|---|---|---|---|---|
| US | TFA | Clark (1996) | 0.73, 0.90 | Bank |
| US | FDH | DeBorger et al. (1995) | 0.94, 0.88, 0.89, 0.80, 0.95, 0.88, 0.89, 0.80, 0.97, 0.95, 0.89, 0.89, 0.77 | Bank |
| US | DEA | Devaney and Weber (1995) | 0.75, 0.75, 0.71 | Bank |
| US | TFA | DeYoung (1994) | n.a. | Bank |
| US | DFA | DeYoung (1997a) | 0.80 | Bank |
| US | TFA | DeYoung (1997b) | 0.82 | Bank |
| US | TFA | DeYoung (1997c) | 0.84, 0.89 | Bank |
| US | DFA | DeYoung and Nolle (1996) | 0.56, 0.73 | Bank, $\pi$ |
| US | DEA, and SFA | Eisenbeis et al. (1996) | 0.72, 0.73, 0.73, 0.78 0.84, 0.87, 0.89, 0.93 | Bank |
| US | SFA | Ellinger et al. (1997) | n.a. | Bank |
| US | DEA | Elyasiani and Mehdian (1990a) | 0.90, 0.78 | Bank |
| US | SFA | Elyasiani and Mehdian (1990b) | 0.88 | Bank |
| US | DEA | Elyasiani and Mehdian (1992) | 0.89 | Bank |
| US | DEA | Elyasiani and Mehdian (1995) | 0.97, 0.95, 0.95, 0.96 | Bank |
| US | DEA | Elyasiani et al. (1994) | 0.86, 0.83 | Bank |
| US | DEA | English et al. (1993) | 0.75, 0.76 | Bank |
| US | DEA | Ferrier et al. (1993) | 0.69, 0.60 | Bank |
| US | DEA | Ferrier et al. (1994) | 0.37, 0.33 | Bank |
| US | DEA, and SFA | Ferrier and Lovell (1990) | 0.83 0.79 | Bank Bank |
| US | IN | Fixler and Zieschang (1993) | n.a. | Bank |
| US | FDH | Fried and Lovell (1994) | 0.93 | CU |
| US | FDH | Fried et al. (1993) | 0.83 | CU |
| US | DEA | Grabowski et al. (1993) | 0.72 | Bank |
| US | SFA, and TFA | Hasan and Hunter (forthcoming) | 0.82, 0.79 0.64, 0.70 | Bank Bank, $\pi$ |
| US | DEA | Hermalin and Wallace (1994) | 0.75, 0.73 | S&L |
| US | TFA | Humphrey and Pulley (1997) | 0.81, 0.82, 0.85 | Bank, $\pi$ |
| US | DFA | Hunter and Timme (1995) | 0.84, 0.77, 0.78 | Bank |
| US | SFA | Kaparakis et al. (1994) | 0.90 | Bank |
| US | SFA | Kwan and Eisenbeis (1994) | 0.88, 0.85, 0.84, 0.84, 0.88, 0.88 | Bank |
| US | TFA | Mahajan et al. (1996) | 0.77, 0.88 | Bank |
| US | SFA | Mester (1993) | 0.92, 0.87 | S&L |
| US | SFA | Mester (1996) | 0.86 | Bank |
| US | SFA | Mester (1997) | 0.93, 0.92, 0.85, 0.87, 0.89, 0.88, 0.86, 0.85 | Bank |
| US | DEA | Miller and Noulas (1996) | 0.97 | Bank, $\pi$ |
| US | DFA | Newman and Shrieves (1993) | n.a. | Bank |
| US | DFA | Peristiani (1997) | 0.79, 0.79, 0.77, 0.81, 0.81, 0.77 | Bank |

44

Table 2.1. *(cont.)*

| Country | Method[a] | Author (date) | Average annual efficiency estimate | Institution type |
|---|---|---|---|---|
| US | SFA | Pi and Timme (1993) | 0.87 | Bank |
| US | DEA | Rangan et al. (1988) | 0.70 | Bank |
| US | DEA | Ray and Mukherjee (1994) | 0.88 | Bank |
| US | DEA | Sherman and Gold (1985) | 0.96 | Branch |
| US | DEA | Sherman and Ladino (1995) | 0.80 | Branch |
| US | DEA | Thompson et al. (1997) | 0.81, 0.69, 0.59, 0.59, 0.54, 0.62 | Bank |
| US | DEA | Thompson et al. (1996b) | 0.53, 0.51, 0.45, 0.39, 0.35, 0.31, 0.46, 0.44, 0.53 | Bank |
| US | DEA | Wheelock and Wilson (1994) | 0.84, 0.77, 0.69, 0.59, 0.59, 0.46, 0.51, 0.42 | Bank |
| US | SFA | Zhu et al. (1997) | 0.88, 0.86, 0.82 | Bank |
| *Multiple countries* | | | | |
| Norway | DEA | Berg et al. (1993) | 0.57 | Bank |
| Sweden | | | 0.78 | Bank |
| Finland | | | 0.53 | Bank |
| Norway | MOS | Bergendahl (1995) | 0.09–1.00; Average = 0.51 | Bank |
| Sweden | | | 0.05–1.00; Average = 0.64 | Bank |
| Finland | | | | |
| Denmark | | | | |
| Norway | DEA | Bukh et al. (1995) | 0.54 | Bank |
| Sweden | | | 0.85 | Bank |
| Finland | | | 0.52 | Bank |
| Denmark | | | 0.78 | Bank |
| 11 OECD countries | DFA | Fecher and Pestieau (1993) | 0.71–0.98; Average = 0.82 | Financial services |
| 8 developed countries | DEA | Pastor et al. (1997) | 0.55–0.95; Average = 0.86 | Bank |
| 15 developed countries | TFA | Ruthenberg and Elias (1996) | 0.55–0.94; Average = 0.70 | Bank |

*Notes*: n.a. indicates either not reported, not comparable, or duplicates earlier estimates.

$\pi$ indicates a profit efficiency measure. The profit efficiency ratios employ a substantially different denominator (maximum or optimal profits), and therefore are not comparable to the other ratios.

In order to make the reported efficiencies as comparable as possible, we try to report only technical efficiency ratios, and exclude scale, scope, and allocative inefficiencies, which are not measured in most studies. In some cases, these other types of inefficiencies could not be separated out. For example, some of the profit efficiency ratios incorporate scale and scope inefficiencies which create deviations from the optimal output point.

[a] IN refers to a nonparametric index number approach. MOS is a mixed optimal strategy where the most efficient "parts" of different banks are combined and used as a frontier, in contrast to DEA and FDH where all parts of an individual bank define the frontier.

*Key*:

Nonparametric: DEA Data envelopment analysis
FDH Free disposal hull
IN Index numbers
MOS Mixed optimal strategy

Parametric: SFA Stochastic frontier approach (composed error)
DFA Distribution free approach (different composed error)
TFA Thick frontier approach

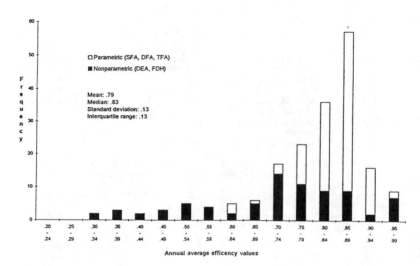

Figure 2.1. Nonparametric and parametric annual average efficiency estimates for U.S. banks (cost and productive efficiency values).

profit efficiency and branch efficiency studies) is shown in Figure 2.1.[14] The 188 annual estimates exceeds the 50 US bank efficiency studies because many of these studies report values for multiple years, techniques, and/or classes of banks, and each is treated as a single observation here.[15] The distribution combines average efficiency estimates of US banks from different time periods, size classes, input–output specifications, and frontier techniques. For DEA-type models, variable returns to scale estimates (if reported) were chosen over efficiency values based on constant returns.

[14] Estimates profit efficiency and branch efficiency are excluded from the display because they are difficult to compare to cost and production efficiencies. Profit efficiency is measured in terms of best-practice profits, which are typically much smaller than the costs, inputs, or output levels used in conventional studies. Branch efficiency is measured relative to the best-practice branch within a firm, which is a very different target than the best firm in a sample.

[15] For example, efficiency estimates obtained by making different assumptions regarding the distribution of inefficiency in SFA composed error models were treated as separate estimates in both Table 2.1 and Figure 2.1. This treatment was also applied to efficiency estimates obtained from banks with different organizational forms or separate samples of banks in states with different branching laws. If semi-annual estimates of efficiency were made, these were averaged into annual figures.

Table 2.2. *Average efficiency of US banks by frontier technique.*

| | Nonparametric techniques | Parametric techniques |
|---|---|---|
| | DEA and FDH[a] (78 observations) | SFA, DFA, and TFA (110 observations) |
| Mean | 0.72 | 0.84 |
| Median | 0.74 | 0.85 |
| Standard deviation | 0.17 | 0.06 |
| Interquartile range | 0.24 | 0.07 |
| Range | 0.31–0.97 | 0.61–0.95 |

[a] Two nonparametric studies (noted as IN and MOS in Table 2.1) have not been included.

The mean of Figure 2.1 using both nonparametric and parametric techniques is 0.79 with median of 0.83, standard deviation of 0.13, range of 0.31 to 0.97, and interquartile range of 0.13. The mean of 0.79 implies an average inefficiency of 27% $[(1 - 0.79)/0.79]$.[16] The interval formed by the mean plus and minus one standard deviation would cover efficiency values from 0.66 to 0.92, and capture 82% of the observations.

The distribution of average efficiency from nonparametric studies of US banks is shown in the dark (bottom) portion of each bar in Figure 2.1 while the light (top) portion indicates the distribution of the parametric results. These separate results are also summarized; see Table 2.2. As seen, the central tendencies of efficiency using these two broad classes of frontier techniques give similar ballpark figures near 80%, with the nonparametric techniques generally giving lower efficiency estimates. The mean and median efficiencies for the nonparametric techniques are 0.72 and 0.74, respectively; the parametric techniques have a mean of 0.84 and median of 0.85. A greater difference between the approaches is that the nonparametric studies suggest a greater dispersion in estimated

---

[16] Efficiency results are typically reported in either of two ways. The 0.79 efficiency figure means that if the average firm were producing on the frontier instead of at its current location, then only 79% of the resources currently being used would be necessary to produce the same output (or meet the same objectives). The 27% inefficiency figure means that the average firm requires 27% more resources to produce the same output (or meet the same objectives) as an efficient firm on the frontier (the relationship is $0.79 = 1/(1 + 0.27)$ or $0.27 = (1 - 0.79)/0.79$).

efficiency ratios. The standard deviation, range, and interquartile range of the nonparametric studies are 0.17, [0.31, 0.97], and 0.24, respectively, which is more dispersed than the 0.06, [0.61, 0.95], and 0.07 values, respectively, for the parametric studies.[17] The dispersion shown in Figure 2.1 and Table 2.2 suggests that the standard errors associated with individual average efficiency estimates may be relatively large, particularly for the nonparametric estimates. As discussed below, this also appears to be the case so far for those studies that have determined confidence intervals for nonparametric bank efficiency estimates using bootstrapping procedures.

### 3.1 Efficiency Rankings for Nonparametric and Parametric Models

Although there is a good deal of information regarding the average efficiency of depository financial institutions by frontier technique, there is only limited information comparing the efficiency rankings of firms across techniques. Based on the few studies that exist, it appears that the similarity of the central tendency of average efficiency estimates evident in Figure 2.1 between nonparametric and parametric techniques does *not* consistently carry over to the rankings of firms within the banking industry. Some studies support a strong relationship between the findings of different techniques, while others find only weak relationships.

Only two studies have compared the efficiency ranking of banking firms between nonparametric and parametric techniques. The Spearman rank correlation coefficient ($R_{RANK}$) between DEA and SFA technical efficiency rankings in one study of smaller US banks for one year was $R_{RANK} = 0.02$ and not significantly different from zero (Ferrier and Lovell, 1990).[18] In another study, using averages over six years, $R_{RANK}$ between DEA and SFA varied from 0.44 to 0.59 across four size classes of larger US banks (Eisenbeis et al., 1996). These bank results are weaker than those obtained for efficiency rankings across nonparametric and parametric frontier techniques for Federal Reserve check processing offices

---

[17] If the extremely low efficiency estimates (0.31 to 0.39 values in Fig. 2.1) from two nonparametric studies are deleted, the mean of the nonparametric studies rises from 0.72 to 0.74 and the standard deviation is reduced from 0.17 to 0.14, slightly closer to the summary statistics for the parametric studies.

[18] Giokas (1991) compared average efficiency results between DEA and a Cobb–Douglas (frontier) econometric estimation for branches of a single bank, not across banks. Although differences in efficiency results between these two techniques were discussed, no rank correlation was reported.

with $R_{RANK}$ values on the order of 0.70 (Bauer and Hancock, 1993) or for insurance firms which yielded $R_{RANK}$ values above 0.50 (Cummins and Zi, 1995) or above 0.72 (Fecher et al., 1993). This is one area where further research would prove useful – determining how the different frontier techniques affect the relative efficiency rankings of individual financial institutions.

There is greater similarity in bank efficiency rankings when, instead of comparing nonparametric with parametric techniques, the comparison is between different techniques within one of these categories. Two parametric techniques – SFA and TFA – were compared when both methods were used to separately identify quartiles of US banks that were, respectively, most or least efficient over a 12 year period. The degree of correspondence was 38% for banks identified by each technique as being in the most efficient quartile (Bauer et al., 1993). A somewhat higher correspondence, at 46%, was found across techniques for banks in the least efficient quartiles. This is compared to an expected 25% correspondence due to chance alone, suggesting a moderate positive relationship between the rankings of the two techniques.

Finally, there are three studies that compared efficiency rankings of banks when different assumptions were applied within a given efficiency approach. One study found that correlation coefficients for efficiency rankings of US banks using four different radial and nonradial technical efficiency measures with a (variable returns to scale) DEA reference technology were relatively large and ranged from 0.87 to 0.99 (Ferrier et al., 1994). A second study undertook a comparison of radial and nonradial technical efficiency measures using both input-based and output-based FDH reference technology and found a wider range of similarity in efficiency rankings, with correlations ranging between 0.32 and 0.96 (DeBorger et al., 1995). A third study reported rank correlation values between 0.86 and 0.99 for SFA efficiency estimates using assumed half-normal, truncated-normal, and exponential distributions of inefficiency (Maudos, 1996a).[19]

Overall, it seems clear that the estimates of mean or median efficiency for an industry may be a more consistently reliable guide for policy and research purposes than are rankings of firms by their efficiency value, especially between nonparametric and parametric approaches. Because the consistency in rankings of individual firms by their efficiency value

---

[19] Rank correlations of these three sets of estimates with a fixed effects and a random effects model ranged from 0.56 to 0.90.

can differ across frontier techniques, it follows that statistical results from the numerous ex post analyses correlating firm-level efficiency estimates with various sets of explanatory variables should be viewed with caution. The use of a different method for determining efficiency may affect the qualitative results when searching for explanations of what makes some firms more efficient. Indeed, SFA efficiency values in one study were significantly associated with differences in market and accounting measures of bank risk and seem to strongly affect bank stock returns while DEA efficiency values were much less informative in this regard (Eisenbeis et al., 1996). This result occurred even though the rankings of banks by their SFA and DEA efficiency values were similar (with rank correlation values of 0.44 to 0.59). Therefore, policy and research issues that rely upon firm-level efficiency estimates (as opposed to industry-wide averages) may be more convincingly addressed if more than one frontier technique is applied to the same set of data to demonstrate the robustness of the explanatory results obtained.

## 4 Average Efficiency Across Countries and by Type of Financial Institution

### 4.1 Average Efficiency Estimates Across Countries
Five studies that have compared efficiency levels across countries are noted at the end of Table 2.1. In one study, a DEA analysis of banks in Norway, Sweden, and Finland was first performed with separate frontiers for each country and then with a "common" frontier. In both the variable and constant returns to scale cases, Sweden was found to be the more efficient of the three (Berg et al., 1993). The robustness of the common frontier results were demonstrated by deleting all banks on the frontier, recomputing efficiency values, and then correlating the new efficiency ranking with the ranking prior to deleting any banks. Even after all the original frontier banks were deleted, the $R_{RANK}$ for the remaining institutions was 0.96, attesting to the robustness of the original DEA rankings with a common frontier and the conclusion that Swedish banks are more efficient. A follow-up analysis, adding Denmark, found broadly similar results (Bukh et al., 1995).[20]

Two other cross-country studies applied DFA and DEA analysis to,

---

[20] The same four countries were covered in another study (Bergendahl, 1995) which sought to develop a composite "reference bank" composed of the most efficient parts of the banks in the sample. This generates higher benchmarks than does DEA and indicates what may be possible rather than only what has been achieved by any one bank alone.

respectively, 11 OECD countries and 8 developed countries.[21] In both cases, the cross-country data are pooled and used to define a common frontier. In the first study, the average efficiency of financial services (banking and insurance) is determined for 11 OECD countries using national accounts data over 1971–1986 (Fecher and Pestieau, 1993). Using a DFA-based fixed effects model, the mean average efficiency value was 0.82 with a range of 0.67 (Denmark) to 0.98 (Japan). Among other results, average efficiency in Sweden (0.76) is found to be lower than that for Norway (0.90), and the US (0.71) had the second lowest efficiency of the 11 countries studied. This result for Sweden is the opposite of that found in the more focused study of Norway, Sweden, and Finland just noted where Swedish banks were the most efficient. In another study, DEA was applied to a cross-section of 427 banks in eight developed countries (Pastor et al., 1997). The mean efficiency value was 0.86 with a range of 0.55 (UK) to 0.95 (France). US banks had the second lowest efficiency value (0.81) in the cross-section, which is consistent with the finding in the previous study that US banks were relatively inefficient. We note that these cross-country comparisons are difficult to interpret because the regulatory and economic environments faced by financial institutions are likely to differ importantly across nations and because the level and quality of service associated with deposits and loans in different countries may differ in ways that are difficult to measure. Such cross-country differences were not specified when a "common" frontier was being estimated and this may affect the cross-country results. Difficult as they may be to perform and interpret, however, cross-country studies can provide valuable information regarding the competitiveness of banks in different countries, a concern of particular importance in the increasingly harmonized European market for banking services and the perhaps more globalized financial markets of the future.

Figure 2.2 shows a frequency distribution for the 131 average efficiency values for banks from 14 non-US countries.[22] The comparability of efficiency estimates for specific countries is limited by the fact that each

---

[21] A different approach would be to contrast individual banks in all countries with only two other banks – one bank with the lowest and another bank with the highest predicted average cost from a standard non-frontier cost function model (Ruthenberg and Elias, 1996). In this analysis the average efficiency was 0.70 for individual banks in 15 (mostly European) countries.

[22] Efficiency comparisons among S&Ls or branches of a single bank, the only information available for six other countries (Belgium, Canada, Cyprus, Greece, Saudi Arabia, and the UK), are discussed below.

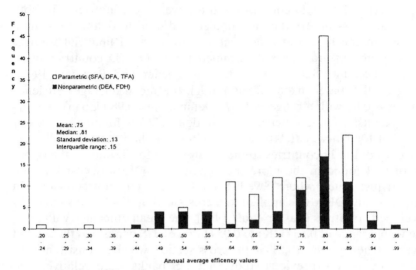

Figure 2.2. Nonparametric and parametric annual average efficiency estimates for non-U.S. banks (cost and productive efficiency values).

country's efficiency estimate is determined relative only to the frontier for that country. Since frontiers may differ across countries, our comparison here can only illustrate (a) the average dispersion of banks in each country away from that country's own measured best-practice frontier, rather than (b) bank efficiency measured relative to any global best-practice frontier. The advantage of (a) is that banks are measured against a frontier that embodies similar levels of service, regulatory treatment, and economic environment. The advantage of (b) would be that a frontier formed from the complete data set across nations would allow for a better comparison across nations, since the banks in each country would be compared against the same standard. Since frontiers likely differ across countries, efficiency measured relative to single-nation frontiers will be overstated relative to what would be measured with a common or global frontier, so (a) will likely show greater overall efficiency than would (b).

With these caveats in mind, the mean annual average efficiency value in Figure 2.2 is 0.75, with median of 0.81, standard deviation of 0.13, range of 0.24 to 0.98, and interquartile range of 0.15. An interval formed by the mean plus and minus one standard deviation would cover efficiency values from 0.62 to 0.88, covering 84% of the observations in Figure 2.2. The mean average efficiency derived from nonparametric (0.75) and parametric (0.76) models is very similar but the standard deviation of the nonparametric model results (0.14) is slightly larger than that for parametric models (0.12).

Strictly speaking, the results of Figures 2.1 and 2.2 are comparable only if all or most of the separate country frontiers would lie close to the same global frontier. We expect this to be an unlikely event and so we cannot draw the conclusion from these figures that US banks are more efficient than banks in other countries. Indeed, the opposite result was found in two of the multiple country studies noted above (where US banks were among the least efficient). Clearly, this is an area where more work is needed, especially the proper specification of country-specific environmental influences that will justify using a common frontier for cross-country comparisons of efficiency.

### 4.2 Average Efficiency of Thrift Institutions

The 14 studies that have focused on savings and loan associations (S&Ls) and credit unions cover the US, UK, Spain, and Sweden. These are listed in Table 2.1. The mean average efficiency level for US S&Ls is 0.83, which is higher than, but close to, the value reported for US banks (0.79) in Figure 2.1. The average efficiency for credit unions, at 0.88, is higher still. The average efficiency of Spanish savings banks, at 0.80, is higher than the mean for banks in other countries in Figure 2.2 (0.75).[23] Similar to the international case above, it is difficult to compare results across industries because no common frontier has been established. Nonetheless, a tentative conclusion is that there is no significant evidence to suggest that there is much of a difference among the average efficiencies of these types of depository financial institutions – banks, S&Ls, and credit unions. A more definitive result will have to await further study.

### 4.3 Average Efficiency of Insurance Firms

The average efficiency for different types of insurance firms is shown in Table 2.3. The mean average annual efficiency for the US insurance firms shown is 0.79 with a standard deviation of 0.15 (profit efficiency excluded). As a central tendency, US insurance firms seem to have an average efficiency close to that for US banks (Figure 2.1). The insurance

---

[23] The remaining S&L studies for Sweden and the UK are branch analyses, which are discussed below.

Table 2.3. *Studies of the efficiency of insurance firms.*

| Country | Method | Author (date) | Average annual efficiency estimate | Institution type |
|---|---|---|---|---|
| France | DEA, and SFA | Fecher et al. (1993) | 0.50, 0.33<br>0.41, 0.24 | Life and non-life<br>Life and non-life |
| Italy | DEA | Cummins et al. (1995a) | 0.71, 0.71, 0.72, 0.76, 0.72, 0.78, 0.77, 0.74 | Life and non-life |
| US | SFA | Cummins and Weiss (1993) | 0.90, 0.79, 0.88 | Property liability |
| US | DFA | Gardner and Grace (1993) | 0.42 | Life |
| US | SFA, and TFA | Yuengert (1993) | 0.75<br>0.63 | Life<br>Life |
| US | DFA | Berger et al. (1997) | 0.74, 0.70<br>0.63, 0.51, 0.68, 0.58 | Property liability<br>Property liability, $\pi$ |
| US | DEA | Cummins et al. (1995b) | 0.88, 0.88, 0.85, 0.86, 0.86, 0.85, 0.85, 0.85, 0.85, 0.85, 0.90, 0.91, 0.88, 0.88, 0.88, 0.87, 0.87, 0.89, 0.88, 0.87 | Property liability |
| US | SFA, and DFA, and DEA, and FDH | Cummins and Zi (1995) | 0.58, 0.63, 0.61, 0.61, 0.63<br>0.47<br>0.56, 0.58, 0.56, 0.61, 0.60<br>0.98, 0.98, 0.98, 0.98, 0.98 | Life<br>Life<br>Life<br>Life |

studies are notable in another respect: rankings of firms by their efficiency level between nonparametric and parametric techniques yielded (as noted earlier) $R_{RANK}$ values above 0.50 (Cummins and Zi, 1995) or above 0.72 (Fecher et al., 1993), showing greater consistency in firm rankings than similar evidence for banks. Cummins and Zi (1995) found even higher correlations for rankings of firms by different nonparametric (DEA and FDH) or different parametric (EFA and DFA) techniques. Thus, consistent with the bank results, there is greater similarity in firm-level efficiency estimates among techniques within the nonparametric or parametric category than there is among techniques between these categories.

A different issue was addressed by Yuengert (1993). This concerned the problem of disentangling the effects of scale inefficiencies from frontier inefficiencies in the presence of heteroscedasticity. The problem arises in cross-section data on US insurance firms and banks where there is a greater dispersion of average costs for smaller firms than for larger ones, but the envelope of lowest-cost firms across all size classes is relatively flat.[24] In such a situation, the *average* of firm average costs for smaller institutions will tend to be higher for smaller institutions than for

---

[24] This result can be seen in scatter diagrams in Yuengert (1993) for insurance firms and Humphrey (1987) for banks.

larger ones. One interpretation is that there are economies of scale and that the greater dispersion in costs for smaller firms is due to heteroscedasticity in the random error. An alternative interpretation is that there are no scale economies, but rather a greater dispersion in efficiency levels for smaller firms than larger ones (reflecting heteroscedasticity of efficiency across firms). Standard composed error models cannot distinguish between these cases or determine which interpretation is more correct.

Yuengert's "solution" to this problem is to permit both the random error term and the inefficiency term to be heteroscedastic and let the data determine the outcome. While this is a useful idea from a theoretical perspective, and could work in very large data sets, it may not be a practical solution when data sets are relatively small as they typically are for most countries. That is, it is very difficult to estimate two types of heteroscedasticity from a single composed error under the best of situations, but it is likely to be even more difficult when data are relatively limited. In practice, it may be best to note the potential for confounding scale with efficiency effects and attempt to judge the potential bias by comparing scale estimates obtained in non-frontier models with frontier scale estimates. If these two sets of scale estimates are very similar, then the bias from "efficiency heteroscedasticity" is likely small, and the measured differences in frontier efficiency across size classes of firms may be relatively accurately estimated. Fortunately, most estimates of average and frontier scale economies in banking are fairly similar, suggesting that this problem of confounding scale economies and inefficiencies due to heteroscedasticity is not substantial.

## 5 Informing Government Policy Toward Financial Institutions

In order to summarize the main findings of efficiency studies of financial institutions, the studies listed in Table 2.1 have been rearranged into three broad categories based upon whether a study's *primary* contribution was to inform government policy, to address general research issues, or to improve managerial performance. These studies are shown in Table 2.4. While many studies have contributed directly to more than one area, and most can be viewed as contributing indirectly to policy makers, researchers, and managers, each study is listed only once.[25] The

---

[25] For example, Giokas (1991) is listed under "Address research issues" because it compares efficiency measurement techniques, but it could have easily been listed under "Improving managerial performance" because it estimates the efficiency of individual bank branches.

Table 2.4. *Applications of efficiency analysis of financial institutions.*

| Application | Country | Method[a] | Author (date) |
|---|---|---|---|
| *Inform government policy:* | | | |
| Deregulation, | Norway | DEA | Berg et al. (1992) |
| financial disruption | US | DEA | Elyasiani and Mehdian (1995) |
| | Japan | DEA | Fukuyama (1995) |
| | Spain | TFA | Lozano (1995) |
| | Turkey | DEA | Zaim (1995) |
| | US | TFA | Humphrey and Pulley (1997) |
| | Spain | DEA | Grifell-Tatjé and Lovell (1997b) |
| Institution failure, | US | TFA | Berger and Humphrey (1992a) |
| risk, problem loans, | | | |
| and management | US | SFA | Ceberoyan et al. (1993a) |
| quality | US | DEA | Berr et al. (1994) |
| | US | DEA | Elyasiani et al. (1994) |
| | US | DEA | Hermelin and Wallace (1994) |
| | US | SFA | Berger and DeYoung (1997) |
| | US | SFA | Mester (1996) |
| | US | SFA | Mester (1997) |
| | US | TFA | DeYoung (1997c) |
| Market structure | Norway | TFA | Berg and Kim (1994) |
| and concentration | US | DFA | Berger (1995) |
| | US | DEA | Devarey and Weber (1995) |
| | Norway | TFA | Berg and Kim (1996) |
| | Spain | SFA | Mandos (1996b) |
| | US | DFA | Berger and Hannan (1997) |
| Mergers | Norway | DEA | Berg (1992) |
| | US | DEA | Berger and Humphrey (1992b) |
| | US | IN | Fixler and Zieschang (1993) |
| | US | DFA | Akhavein et al. (1997a) |
| | US | TFA | DeYoung (1997b) |
| | US | DFA | Peristiani (1997) |
| *Address research issues:* | | | |
| Confidence | Italy | DEA | Ferrier and Hirschberg (1994) |
| intervals | US | DEA | Wheelock and Wilson (1994) |
| Comparing different | US | DEA, SFA | Ferrier and Lovell (1990) |
| efficiency | Greece | DEA, SFA | Giokas (1991) |
| techniques or | US | SFA, DFA, TFA | Bauer et al. (1993) |
| assumptions | US | DEA, SFA | Eisenbeis et al. (1996) |
| | Spain | SFA | Maudos (1996a) |
| | Germany | SFA | Altunbas and Molyneux (n.d.) |
| | US | SFA | Zhu et al. (1997) |
| Comparing different | Norway | DEA | Berg et al. (1991) |
| output measures | Finland | DEA | Kuussaari (1993) |
| | Italy | DEA | Favero and Papi (1995) |
| | US | DFA | Hunter and Timme (1995) |
| | Finland | DEA | Kuussaari and Vesala (1995) |
| Organizational form, | US | DEA | Rangan et al. (1988) |
| corporate control | US | DEA | Aly et al. (1990) |
| issues | US | DEA | Elyasiani and Mehdian (1992) |

Table 2.4. (*cont.*)

| Application | Country | Method[a] | Author (date) |
|---|---|---|---|
| | US | SFA | Cebenoyan et al. (1993b) |
| | US | SFA | Chang et al. (1993) |
| | US | DEA | Grabowski et al. (1993) |
| | US | SFA | Mester (1993) |
| | US | DEA | Newman and Shrieves (1993) |
| | US | SFA | Pi and Timme (1993) |
| | US | DFA | DeYoung and Nolle (1996) |
| | US | TFA | Mahajan et al. (1996) |
| | India | DEA | Bhattacharyya et al. (1997) |
| | US | SFA, TFA | Hasan and Hunter (forthcoming) |
| General level of efficiency | US | DEA | Elyasiani and Mehdian (1990a) |
| | UK | DEA | Field (1990) |
| | UK | DEA | Drake and Weyman-Jones (1992) |
| | Tunisia | SFA | Chaffai (1993) |
| | Japan | DEA | Fukuyama (1993) |
| | Switzerland | DEA | Sheldon and Haegler (1993) |
| | Denmark | DEA | Bukh (1994) |
| | US | SFA | Kaparakis et al. (1994) |
| | Spain | DEA | Perez and Quesada (1994) |
| | Germany | TFA | Lang and Welzel (1995) |
| | Italy | DEA, SFA | Resti (1995) |
| | Germany | DFA | Lang and Welzel (1996) |
| | US | DEA | Miller and Noulas (1996) |
| Intercountry comparisons | Norway Sweden Finland | DEA | Berg et al. (1993) |
| | 11 OECD countries | SFA | Fecher and Pestieau (1993) |
| | 8 developed countries | DEA | Pastor et al. (1997) |
| | Norway Sweden Finland Denmark | DEA | Bukh et al. (1995) |
| | 15 developed countries | TFA | Ruthenberg and Elias (1996) |
| | UK-Greece-Cyprus | DEA | Soteriou et al. (2000) |
| Methodology issues | US | DEA | Charnes et al. (1990) |
| | US | TFA | Berger and Humphrey (1991) |
| | US | DFA | Berger (1993) |
| | Belgium | FDH | Tulkens (1993) |
| | US | DEA | Ferrier et al. (1994) |
| | Spain | DEA | Grifell-Tatjé and Lovell (1994) |
| | Norway Sweden Finland Denmark | MOS | Bergendahl (1995) |

Table 2.4. *(cont.)*

| Application | Country | Method[a] | Author (date) |
|---|---|---|---|
| | US | DFA | Adams et al. (1999) |
| | US | DFA | Akhavein et al. (1997b) |
| | US | FDH | DeBorger et al. (1995) |
| | Spain | DEA | Pastor (1995) |
| | US | DEA | Thompson et al. (1996b) |
| | US | DFA | Berger and Mester (1997) |
| | Tunisia | SFA | Chaffai (1997) |
| | US | DFA | DeYoung (1997a) |
| | Spain | DEA | Grifell-Tatjé and Lovell (1997a) |
| | Spain | DEA | Lovell and Pastor (1997) |
| | Mexico | DEA | Taylor et al. (1997) |
| | US | DEA | Thompson et al. (1997) |
| Opportunity cost, output diversification | US | DEA | Ferrier et al. (1993) |
| | US | TFA | DeYoung (1994) |
| | France | DFA | Dietsch (1994) |
| | France | DFA | Chaffai and Dietsch (1995) |
| | US | TFA | Clark (1996) |
| Profit, revenue | US | SFA | Elyasiani and Mehdian (1990b) |
| | US | DFA | Berger et al. (1993a) |
| | US | DEA | English et al. (1993) |
| | Spain | TFA | Lozano (1997) |
| | Spain | DEA | Grifell-Tatjé and Lovell (1996) |
| | US | SFA | Ellinger et al. (1997) |
| | Cyprus | DEA | Soteriou and Zenios (1999) |
| | Greece | DEA | Athanassopoulos (2000) |
| Stability over time, institution size | US | SFA | Kwan and Eisenbeis (1994) |
| | US | DEA | Ray and Mukherjee (1994) |
| | US | DEA | Bauer et al. (1998) |
| *Improve managerial performance:* | | | |
| Credit unions | US | FDH | Fried et al. (1993) |
| | US | FDH | Fried and Lovell (1994) |
| Bank branch | US | DEA | Sherman and Gold (1985) |
| | Canada | DEA | Parkan (1987) |
| | Turkey | DEA | Oral and Yolalan (1990) |
| | Greece | DEA | Vassiloglou and Giokas (1990) |
| | Saudi Arabia | DEA | Al-Faraj et al. (1993) |
| | Belgium | FDH | Tulkens and Malnero (1994) |
| | UK | DEA | Athanassopoulos (1995) |
| | US | DEA | Sherman and Ladino (1995) |
| | US | DFA | Berger et al. (1997) |
| | Cyprus | DEA | Zenios et al. (1999) |
| | UK | DEA | Athanassopoulos (1997) |
| | Canada | DEA | Schaffnit et al. (1997) |
| | UK | DEA | Drake and Howcroft (1997) |
| S&L branch | Sweden | DEA | Hartman and Storbeck (1995) |

[a] See notes to Table 2.1.

58

discussion of informing government policy toward depository financial institutions is divided into four subcategories: (1) deregulation and financial disruption, (2) institution failure, risk, problem loans, and management quality, (3) market structure and concentration, and (4) the effects of mergers and acquisitions.

### 5.1 Deregulation, Financial Disruption

Deregulation is typically undertaken to improve the performance of the industry being deregulated. If efficiency is raised, the improvement in resource allocation will benefit society and may lead to price reductions and/or service expansion for consumers if competition is sufficient. However, in many cases deregulation is initiated less by a desire to benefit consumers than by a need to improve the competitive viability of the industry. One such example was the removal of interest rate ceilings on deposits paid by US banks in the 1980s, which permitted banks to compete better with money market mutual funds in acquiring funds. Another example is the harmonization and unification of banking markets in Europe – removing restrictions that have limited the ability of banks in one country from aggressively entering markets in other countries.

Given that a primary goal of deregulation has been to improve efficiency, the results have been mixed. Norwegian banks experienced improved efficiency and productivity after deregulation (Berg et al., 1992) as did Turkish institutions in a more liberalized banking environment (Zaim, 1995). In contrast, banking efficiency in the US was relatively unchanged by the deregulation of the early 1980s (Bauer et al., 1993; Elyasiani and Mehdian, 1995). Although measured bank productivity fell (Humphrey, 1993; Humphrey and Pulley, 1997), this was largely because interest rate deregulation induced a competitive scramble to pay higher interest rates on consumer deposits without a corresponding reduction in either banking services or an immediate and fully offsetting increase in deposit fees. Thus productivity benefits which otherwise would have been captured by banks was instead passed on to consumers. Spain experienced deregulation results similar to the US (Grifell-Tatjé and Lovell, 1997b; Lozano, 1995). Lastly, the bursting of the speculative bubble in Japan seemed to have little effect overall on the efficiency of Japanese banks (Fukuyama, 1995), although the bad loans it created clearly had a significant adverse effect on the financial conditions of Japanese banks.

Depending on industry conditions prior to deregulation – such as existing excess loan demand in Norway, a desire to rapidly expand market share in Spain, or competition to pay higher deposit interest rates in the US – the consequences of deregulation may differ across countries. Indeed, in some cases, deregulation appears to have led to a reduction in measured productivity rather than an improvement. The implication for government policy is that the conventional wisdom which holds that deregulation always improves efficiency and productivity may be incorrect. Industry conditions prior to deregulation and other incentives may intervene. Measurement over longer time periods may eventually show a net improvement in both efficiency and productivity but this has not yet been demonstrated.

### 5.2 Institution Failure, Risk, Problem Loans, and Management Quality

A key role of a country's financial institution regulators is to limit systemic risk – the risk that the problems of a few institutions spread to many other institutions that are otherwise solvent and liquid. This protects the money supply and the payment system from being severely disrupted and involves the management of bank failures. Most bank failures are directly related to having a large number of problem loans, a low capital position, a weak or negative cash flow, and poor management quality. It might be expected that institutions would display low efficiency prior to failure and that management quality would be positively related to efficiency. Both of these priors are supported in studies that have looked at these issues.

Banks and S&Ls with low efficiency failed at greater rates than institutions with higher efficiency levels (Berger and Humphrey, 1992a; Cebenoyan et al., 1993a; Hermalin and Wallace, 1994) and this relationship was evident a number of years ahead of eventual failure (Barr et al., 1994). Management quality, as measured by regulatory agency assessments, is positively related to cost efficiency (DeYoung, 1997c) which, in turn, Granger-causes reductions in problem loans (past due and non-accrual, Berger and DeYoung, 1997). As a result, efficiency measures have been shown to improve the predictive accuracy of failure prediction models and thus may represent a useful addition to current modeling efforts by regulatory agencies (as shown by Barr et al., 1994, for banks and Kramer, 1997, for insurance firms).[26]

Problems loans have been included as explanatory variables in some

---

[26] This result is not surprising since it has been shown that information contained in an efficiency measure closely corresponds to that contained in standard financial ratios (Elyasiani et al., 1994).

efficiency studies (e.g., Hughes and Mester, 1993; Mester, 1996, 1997) with the result that slight measured scale diseconomies for larger institutions are altered to economies and efficiency is increased. Whether or not it is appropriate to control for problem loans depends on which is the dominating explanation for the observed negative relationship between measured efficiency and problem loans. If problem loans are generally caused by "bad luck" events exogenous to the bank, such as regional downturns, then measured cost efficiency may be artificially low because of the expenses associated with dealing with these loans (e.g., extra monitoring, negotiating workout arrangements, etc.). Alternatively, problem loans may be related to measured efficiency because "bad management" is poor at controlling both costs and risks. If "bad luck" dominates, then problem loans are mostly exogenous and should be controlled for in efficiency models. If "bad management" dominates, then problem loans are essentially endogenous to financial institution efficiency and should not be controlled for in the analysis of efficiency. To this point, the evidence is mixed, yielding some support for both hypotheses (Berger and DeYoung, 1997). A potential solution to this problem is to control for the problem loan ratio for the state or region of the bank, which should primarily reflect the "bad luck" facing the bank, rather than its own "bad management" (see Berger and Mester, 1997).

### 5.3 Market Structure and Concentration

An important area of government policy concerns antitrust issues. Many studies of financial institutions and other firms have found a positive statistical relationship between market concentration and profitability. This may be due to market-power explanations in which firms in concentrated markets exercise market power in pricing and earn supernormal profits. Alternatively, the efficient-structure paradigm links concentration to high profitability through efficiency (Demsetz, 1973). Under efficient-structure, relatively efficient firms compete more aggressively and gain dominant market shares and also have high profits because of their low costs of production. These different explanations of differences in profitability across firms – market power vs. efficiency – have directly opposing implications for antitrust policy. If high profits are created by market power, then antitrust actions are likely to be socially beneficial, moving prices toward competitive levels and allocating resources more effectively. However, if high efficiency is the explanation for high profits, then breaking up efficient firms that have gained large market shares or disallowing efficient firms to acquire other firms is likely to raise costs and may lead to prices less favorable to consumers. Regulatory agencies have typically followed the market-power paradigm in their antitrust policies.

The evidence comparing market power and efficiency effects is limited, but it suggests that cost efficiency is somewhat more important than market power in explaining profitability. However, as measured by $R^2$'s, neither efficiency nor market power explains much of the observed variance of profitability (Berger, 1995; Maudos, 1996b).

Although concentration is not significantly positively related to profitability after controlling for efficiency, higher concentration is significantly associated with lower deposit interest rates and higher loan rates even after accounting for efficiency differences (Berger and Hannan, 1997). One explanation seems to be that financial institutions with more market power charge higher prices but, instead of enjoying higher than average profits, experience reduced cost efficiency as managers pursue other goals and a "quiet life" (in Hicks' words).[27] The extra costs from "quiet life" inefficiency have been estimated to be several times larger than the traditional welfare triangle costs from the exercise of market power (Berger and Hannan, 1998).

Unfortunately, most of the research on this topic has been on the US banking industry, where the structure of the industry is quite different from the rest of the world. In the US, many financial products such as retail deposits and small business loans are essentially only competed for on a local basis so prices can differ significantly among these markets. Most of the studies have focused on the relationship between local market concentration and measures of bank performance. Although some financial products, such as large certificates of deposit and large wholesale loans, are competed for on a nationwide basis, the US national market is extremely unconcentrated by world standards. For example, it would take over 2000 banking organizations to account for 90% of deposits in the US, while in most other developed countries 90% of deposits would be accounted for by fewer than 10 organizations. It would be of research and policy importance to discover whether the relationships among efficiency, concentration, prices, and profitability found in local US markets obtain in other nations, where banking markets are typically more national in scope and are generally much more highly concentrated.

An alternative approach to examining market structure questions is

---

[27] Some support is found in Devaney and Weber (1995) who determined that rural US banking markets that experience a decrease in concentration appear to have greater efficiency and productivity growth.

to rely on direct estimates of the degree of oligopolistic output inter-dependence among suppliers of financial services. Adopting this approach, a frontier conjectural variations model had been estimated for Norwegian banks (Berg and Kim, 1994). From the view of efficiency analysis, the innovation is that market structure effects are directly accounted for when estimating scale economies and frontier efficiency. This is done by specifying that each firm's cost is a function of its own output as well as the output level of other firms in the same market. While the average of firm frontier cost efficiency estimates is only little affected by including or excluding conjectural variation effects, the scale economy measure moves from indicating constant costs in a standard cost frontier framework to indicating decreasing costs when conjectural variations are added. In a profit function context, however, adding con-jectural variations significantly improves measured profit efficiency, sug-gesting that this aspect of market behavior is likely an important factor in efficiency measurement (Berg and Kim, 1996).

### 5.4 Mergers and Acquisitions

Relative to historical trends, banking industries in a number of countries have been subject to an increased number of mergers and acquisitions. In the US, much of the activity has been spawned by liberalizations of state rules regarding bank and bank holding company expansion both within and between states. In the early 1980s, there was almost no inter-state banking activity, but by the end of 1994, 28% of US banking assets were controlled by out-of-state banking organizations, primarily through regional compacts among nearby states (Berger et al., 1995).

The conventional wisdom among bank consultants and the popular press is that mergers can be and have been successful in improving cost ratios and cost efficiency, at least for a number of firms. However, acad-emic studies usually find no such improvement *on average*. This holds whether simple accounting ratios are compared pre- and post-merger, holding industry effects constant, or in more sophisticated econometric analyses using frontier cost functions (Berg, 1992; Berger and Humphrey, 1992b; Rhoades, 1993; Peristiani, 1997; DeYoung, 1997b).

Although many individual mergers have been quite successful in improving cost performance, many others have worsened their cost ratios or cost efficiency, so that on average there is no significant improvement. This would suggest that government merger policy should not as a rule be influenced by claims of expected cost efficiency benefits from mergers. However, an exception could occur if there existed a reliable precondition that could be used to identify mergers that are very likely to improve cost efficiency. Two plausible preconditions were found, upon testing, to provide little in the way of significant additional information. First, it was expected that a successful merger might be one with a high degree of local market overlap between merging institutions because of the greater potential for eliminating duplicate expenditures on branches and back-office operations. Second, it was thought that mergers would be more successful when the acquiring firm is more cost efficient than the firm being acquired, because the superior management team would gain control and use its (apparently) demonstrated ability to improve the less efficient firm. Upon investigation, neither of these expectations was realized (Berger and Humphrey, 1992b).

The effects of mergers on profit efficiency have been less intensively investigated. However, initial results suggest that profit efficiency improves significantly from mergers of large banks (Akhavein et al., 1997a). The different results experienced for cost and profit efficiency appear to occur because measured cost efficiency changes do not take into account the effects of the changes in output that occur after the merger. Merging banks tend to shift their output mixes away from securities toward loans, which raises profit efficiency because issuing loans creates more value (and usually more risk) than purchasing securities. This shift in mix may occur because merging banks are better able to diversify these risks than the previous management, allowing a higher loan/asset ratio to be held with same amount of capital (see also Benston et al., 1995; Hughes et al., 1996). Further investigation of the profit efficiency vs. cost efficiency effects of mergers represents an area for fruitful additional research.

## 6  Address Research Issues Related to Financial Institutions

Much of the work in efficiency analysis has been focused on methodology and measurement issues. Research issues include the study of: (1) the similarity of efficiency results derived from different frontier models, (2) the sensitivity of efficiency results when different output measures are applied, (3) the association between efficiency and firm organizational structure, (4) different ways to measure efficiency, (5) the effects of incorporating opportunity cost and product diversification in the analysis, (6) the consistency among cost, profit, and production efficiency measures, and (7) the variability of efficiency estimates over time. The general level of efficiency, along with broad comparisons of efficiency levels across different frontier techniques and countries, has been discussed above. The survey that follows will thus focus on the remaining research issues noted in Table 2.4.

### 6.1 Confidence Intervals and Comparing Different Efficiency Techniques or Assumptions

The effect that different frontier approaches can have on estimates of industry average and individual firm efficiency estimates has been noted above.[28] In almost all of these analyses, conclusions have been drawn from only point estimates of efficiency. Thus it is of interest to derive confidence intervals for efficiency estimates in order to determine if the efficiency comparisons being made are meaningful in a statistical sense. Fortunately, bootstrapping methods have become more widely known and available (Efron and Tibshirani, 1993; Hall et al., 1993; Mooney and Duval, 1993; Atkinson and Wilson, 1995). Thus new research in the efficiency area should try to make it a practice to provide confidence intervals for the efficiency estimates they generate. Somewhat similar information may be obtained through sensitivity analysis to examine the robustness of efficiency estimates (Brockett et al., 1995; Thompson et al., 1996a).

When confidence intervals of efficiency estimates have been provided, these intervals appear to be quite large (Simar, 1992; Ferrier and Hirschberg, 1994, Mester, 1996, 1997).[29] When confidence intervals are large, comparisons of efficiency among firms in an industry, or branches within a firm, may be more meaningful when groups of observations, rather than individual values, are being compared. Thus the common practice of regressing point estimates of firm efficiency, or rankings of firms by their efficiency value, on sets of explanatory variables might be improved upon or augmented with a subset analysis. This would involve an additional examination of the data where only subsets of firms with relatively high and relatively low efficiency values are used in a regression (with the middle group of firms excluded) to explore the robustness of the posited relationships. This could also be used to determine if the

---

[28] Additional studies, not mentioned earlier, have examined the stability of efficiency estimates from an SFA model when different efficiency distributions are specified (Altunbas and Molyneux, n.d.) or when different function forms are specified (Zhu et al., 1997).

[29] Confidence intervals are computed for year-to-year changes in efficiency in Wheelock and Wilson (1994).

correspondence of firm-level efficiency estimates among different frontier methods could be improved if only the most important subsets of
observations, rather than all the observations, were used.[30]

### 6.2 Comparing Different Output Measures

There are two main approaches to the choice of how to measure the
flow of services provided by financial institutions. Under the "production" approach, financial institutions are thought of as primarily producing services for account holders. The financial institutions perform
transactions and process documents for customers, such as loan applications, credit reports, checks or other payment instruments, and insurance
policy or claim forms. Under this approach, output is best measured by
the number and type of transactions or documents processed over
a given time period (e.g., Kuussaari and Vesala, 1995). Unfortunately,
such detailed transaction flow data is typically proprietary and not generally available. As a result, data on the stock of the number of deposit
or loan accounts serviced or the number of insurance policies outstanding are sometimes used instead (e.g., Ferrier and Lovell, 1990; Ferrier et
al., 1993). Under the alternative "intermediation" approach, financial
institutions are thought of as primarily intermediating funds between
savers and investors. With this approach, since service flow data are not
usually available, the flows are typically assumed to be proportional to
the stock of financial value in the accounts, such as the numbers of dollars
of loans, deposits, or insurance in force (e.g., Berger and Humphrey,
1991).

These approaches also have implications for which inputs or costs
should be included in the analysis. Under the production approach, only
physical inputs such as labor and capital and their costs should be
included, since only physical inputs are needed to perform transactions
and process financial documents. Under the intermediation approach,
the input of funds and their interest cost should also be included in the
analysis, since funds are the main "raw material" which is transformed
in the financial intermediation process.

Neither of these two approaches is perfect because neither fully
captures the dual roles of financial institutions as (i) providing
transactions/document processing services and (ii) being financial intermediaries that transfer funds from savers to investors. While it would

---

[30] One study where this was done suggested that the improvement may be slight (Bauer
et al., 1993). Even so, it may be useful to see if this result holds up in additional
analyses.

probably be best to employ both approaches to determine whether the results were qualitatively affected by the choice of output metric, sufficient data to implement such a research design are not usually available. Nevertheless, each of the approaches has some advantages. The production approach may be somewhat better for evaluating the efficiencies of branches of financial institutions, because branches primarily process customer documents for the institution as a whole and branch managers typically have little influence over bank funding and investment decisions. The intermediation approach may be more appropriate for evaluating entire financial institutions because this approach is inclusive of interest expenses, which (depending on the phase of the interest rate cycle) often accounts for one-half to two-thirds of total costs. As well, the intermediation approach may be superior for evaluating the importance of frontier efficiency to the profitability of the financial institution, since minimization of total costs, not just production costs, is needed to maximize profits.

One study compared the production and intermediation approaches by applying both to the same data set of bank branches using the same functional form, finding correlations above 0.40 between the frontier efficiency rankings of the two approaches (Berger et al., 1997). Other studies have also compared efficiency results obtained with outputs measured by numbers of accounts vs. the financial values in these accounts. In one case, little difference was found in the distribution of efficiency estimates when these two stock indicators of financial firm output were used (Berg et al., 1991) while in another case, a similar distribution was found but mean efficiency was higher when financial values were specified (Kuussaari, 1993). Although the efficiency estimates had a similar distribution, the rankings of firms within these distributions differed. In Berg et al. (1991), the average $R_{RANK}$ for the two comparisons made was 0.64 while $R_{RANK}$ was 0.32 in Kuussaari (1993). Overall, it appears that inferences regarding efficiency may be importantly affected by how output is measured, a result which is usually less dependent upon investigator choice than availability of data.

Despite the many other differences in assumptions involved in measuring efficiency, there is reasonable agreement about the specification of most of the important inputs and outputs for financial institutions. The asset, user cost, and value-added methods of assigning financial goods to input and output categories all agree that loans and other major assets of financial institutions should count as outputs. However, there is a longstanding controversy whether deposits should count as inputs or outputs. Deposits have input characteristics because they are paid for in part by interest payments, and the funds raised provide the institution with the raw material of investible funds. However, deposits also have output characteristics because they are associated with a substantial amount of liquidity, safekeeping, and payment services provided to depositors.

Some studies resolve this issue with a dual approach that captures *both* the input and output characteristics of deposits. The interest paid on deposits is counted as part of costs, and the rate paid is included as an input price, both consistent with the input of the raw material of investible funds. These same studies specify the quantities of deposits as outputs because these quantities are assumed to be proportionate to the output of depositor services provided (Berger and Humphrey, 1991; Bauer et al., 1993).

Other efficiency studies have first treated deposits as an input and then as an output. These investigations find that efficiency is somewhat higher when deposits are specified as an output. In a DEA model, the $R_{RANK}$ between these two specifications averaged 0.77 (Favero and Papi, 1995), while in a DFA model $R_{RANK} = 0.16$ (Hunter and Timme, 1995). Since the treatment of deposits in efficiency models can affect the efficiency estimates, this aspect of model specification may be of some importance to the outcome.

### 6.3 Organizational Form and Corporate Control Issues

Financial institutions are organized in a number of different ways. Relying on agency theory, some studies have investigated whether organizational form is associated with differences in frontier efficiency. Firms owned by stockholders might be expected to face stronger incentives to control costs and/or enhance profits compared to mutual organizations where depositors or policyholders own the firm. The evidence is mixed. One study found that stock S&Ls were less efficient than mutual S&Ls (Mester, 1993) while another found that efficiency was not significantly related to this difference in ownership (Cebenoyan et al., 1993b). This issue might be somewhat confounded by the fact that so many S&Ls have switched status, possibly creating a sample selection bias if either inefficient or efficient firms switched at a greater pace. Study of frontier efficiency in the US life insurance industry (Gardner and Grace, 1993) and in the US property-liability insurance industry (Berger et al., 1996a) found no significant differences between stocks and mutuals in cost efficiency, but stock firms providing property-liability insurance were sometimes statistically significantly more profit efficient than mutuals, all else held equal.

In the US banking industry, the primary organizational trade-off for large organizations is between a multibank holding company (MBHC) arrangement, where a commonly owned group of banks has separate charters and financial books, vs. an extensive branch banking arrangement where banks have been merged under a single charter within a larger branching network with a consolidated operation. This will likely be an important issue over the next several years in the US, as the Riegle–Neal Interstate Banking and Branching Efficiency Act of 1994 allows widespread interstate branch banking for the first time in many decades. The results of one study suggest that branch banking may lead to greater efficiency than keeping banks separate within an MBHC (Grabowski et al., 1993).[31]

A related issue concerns possible efficiency differences associated with foreign vs. domestic ownership. Four studies have found that foreign-owned banks in the US were significantly less efficient than US-owned banks (Chang et al., 1993; DeYoung and Nolle, 1996; Mahajan et al., 1996; Hasan and Hunter, 1996). In contrast, foreign-owned banks in India were found to be somewhat more efficient than privately owned domestic banks but government-owned banks were more efficient than both (Bhathtacharyya et al., 1997). It has been suggested that foreign-owned banks in the US have in effect traded current profits for rapid expansion of market share. The rapid growth was made possible by relying on purchased funds, which are more expensive than core deposits raised through a network of branches, which takes time to establish.

The evidence is also quite limited on the links between other aspects of corporate governance and frontier efficiency. When the CEO is also the chairman of the board, efficiency has been measured to be lower in one study, and this effect is not offset by having a higher proportion of outside directors on the board (Pi and Timme, 1993). In another study, minority ownership was investigated, but no significant differences were found (Elyasiani and Mehdian, 1992). A different ownership issue concerns possible efficiency differences among banks depending upon holding company status. One study found that being in a holding

---

[31] However, no significant differences in efficiency were found between banks located in branching vs. non-branching (unit banking) states in the US (Rangan et al., 1988; Aly et al., 1990). This result is essentially a weaker test of the branching/separate bank relationship since the separate bank arrangement was important in states that restricted branching while both branching and separate bank arrangements existed in states that permitted branching.

company seemed to confer some cost advantages compared to remaining independent (Newman and Shrieves, 1993), but another study found no difference between one-bank and multibank holding company affiliation (Elyasiani and Mehdian, 1990b). All of these issues will require substantially more future research to resolve.

### 6.4 Methodology Issues

Since our focus in this article is on the application of frontier efficiency techniques to financial institutions, the methodology studies noted here are mostly limited to those in which there has been an application of new methodology to financial institutions. There have been a number of attempts to improve both nonparametric and parametric frontier models and estimation in this field. Improvements and/or alternatives to the standard DEA nonparametric approach concern the development and application of FDH (Fried et al., 1993; Tulkens, 1993; Fried and Lovell, 1994), the polyhedral cone-ratio DEA model (Charnes et al., 1990; Brockett et al., 1997), and the assurance region DEA model (Thompson et al., 1997; Taylor et al., 1997). In addition, the nonparametric Malmquist Index approach to efficiency measurement has been generalized (Grifell-Tatjé and Lovell, 1994), goal programming is being applied (Cooper et al., 1997), and the sensitivity of DEA and FDH efficiency models to different radial and non-radial measurement techniques is being tested (Ferrier et al., 1994; Pastor, 1995; DeBorger et al., 1995). The general conclusion of this work is that the standard DEA model, along with the radial measurement of efficiency, may not be as well suited to distinguishing efficient from inefficient observations as the newer approaches cited here.

From another perspective, two recent additions to the DEA literature promise to extend the analysis in important new directions. First, it has been suggested (Bergendahl, 1995) that perhaps the DEA frontier should be composed of the most efficient *parts* of banks within the sample – forming a composite or representative firm, rather than being composed of separate and individual firms as is now the case. A "composite frontier" would serve to indicate the efficiency that had been achieved within the sample, although not necessarily all at a single institution. Such a frontier more accurately represents what is possible and does not confound efficient results in one specified area of interest with inefficient results from other areas. This "composite frontier" is theoretically similar to the "true" best-practice frontier discussed elsewhere, which would be made up only of branches (and other financial institution units) that are fully efficient (Berger et al., 1997). Both concepts seek to set higher standards for the frontier than any firm in the sample has achieved by looking at the best-practice segments of firms.

A second analysis (Lovell and Pastor, 1997) implements a statistical test of the effect of sequentially reducing the number of constraints in a DEA model. The goal is to provide a method whereby the constraints in the DEA model can be collapsed down to only those that are important to the results obtained. With this approach, extraneous constraints can be discarded and attention focused on only influential constraints. This work, as well as that on cone-ratio and assurance region DEA models which both specify additional *a priori* information, also address the problem where individual bank observations may be 100% efficient by default (due to non-comparability among observations when "too many" constraints are specified). The DEA assurance region model, for example, has consistently reduced the number of bank "self-identified" observations (Taylor et al., 1997; Thompson et al., 1996b, 1997). These techniques should go a long way toward ensuring that extraneous constraints do not "contaminate" the DEA results and thus may generate more consistent efficiency estimates across different studies.[32]

Similar efforts to improve the standard parametric SFA frontier model include the development of two alternatives – the thick frontier approach TFA (Berger and Humphrey, 1991), and distribution-free approach DFA (Berger, 1993), the latter being a modification of earlier work by Schmidt and Sickles (1984). More general parametric estimation procedures have also been attempted. This work has focused on replacing the translog functional form with the more flexible Fourier form (e.g., Berger and Mester, 1997), the use of random coefficient estimation which also provides greater flexibility (Akhavein et al., 1997b), and correcting for situations where the regressors and error are correlated (Adams et al., 1999). In general, greater flexibility has resulted in higher estimates of efficiency. At present, the choice between the various

---

[32] In some cases, the choice of which constraints to discard may be fairly straightforward, such as when some of the constraints essentially contain the same economic information. An example is a DEA model that specifies as bank inputs transactions deposits, nontransactions deposits, total noninterest expenses, and total interest expenses (e.g., Miller and Noulas, 1996, and other papers referenced there). The goal of trying to capture the effects of funding mix (transactions vs. nontransactions deposits) along with the interest rates paid (interest vs. noninterest expenses), while laudable, may be problematic since in cross-section data nontransactions deposits are virtually the sole source of interest expenses while transactions deposits make up the largest segment of noninterest expenses.

parametric models and estimation procedures is based primarily on ease of use and/or the apparent reasonableness of underlying assumptions, rather than on any strong theoretical foundation.

To date, parametric efficiency analysis has essentially assigned all deviations from an estimated efficient frontier to a dependent variable such as total costs or profits. Importantly, the resulting inefficiency value can be made more informative by additionally decomposing it into its technical and allocative components. Further information is obtained when inefficiency can be directly related to specific inputs. This has been done by Kumbhakar (1988) and Chaffai (1997).

### 6.5 Opportunity Cost, Output Diversification

Nonparametric and parametric studies can underestimate efficiency when important cost influences have not been included in the analysis. Two such influences routinely neglected in earlier studies have been the opportunity cost of equity and the expenses undertaken to reduce risk. An expected result would be that including these additional costs may improve efficiency estimates as the cost or profit function would fit the data more closely and less specification error might be counted as inefficiency. Studies incorporating these factors include Dietsch (1994), Clark (1996), Mester (1996, 1997), and Berger and Mester (1997). Clark (1996) and Berger and Mester (1997) compared efficiency estimates that did and did not account for the effects of equity capital; Clark found that accounting for equity raised measured cost efficiency, and Berger and Mester found that it raised estimated profit efficiency substantially. As noted above, there also can be a problem with controlling for problem loans or other variables that may be endogenous to the decisions of the firm being studied.

Extending efficiency analysis in a different direction, some research has been done on the effects on efficiency from output diversification and product diversity. The "optimal scope economies" concept based on the profit function rather than the cost function includes all the revenue effects of output choices as well the cost effects of input choices (Berger et al., 1993a). On the cost side, a measure of diversification more general than the traditional scope concept was applied to US banks (Ferrier et al., 1993). It was found that greater diversification tended to reduce cost efficiency. Similarly, "universal" banks in Europe (who provide a broader mix of services) were found to experience lower cost efficiency than more specialized banks (Chaffai and Dietsch, 1995). A seemingly contrary result was found in an analysis of the effects of shifting from making bank loans to providing a broader mix of services by expanding fee-based services, since the shift was associated with higher (not lower) banking efficiency (DeYoung, 1994).

### 6.6 Profit and Revenue Efficiency

Most of the parametric models applied to financial institutions have focused on cost efficiency while nonparametric models have concentrated on the relationship between inputs and outputs directly. An area only recently attracting interest has been the estimation of profit and revenue efficiency. The techniques are essentially the same but the data are different. Profit efficiency is concerned with both cost and revenue efficiency but only under certain conditions would it be likely that the former will equal the sum of the latter. This is because cost (revenue) efficiency presumes that the observed level of output (input use) is already profit maximizing, which may or may not be the case in practice. In addition, there may be differences in the quality of some financial services that are not captured in the output measures. This may make high-quality producers appear to be cost inefficient because of the extra expenses associated with producing the higher quality output. Such a problem may be ameliorated by the use of a profit function or profit programming orientation because high quality should be rewarded in the marketplace by extra revenues that offset the extra expenses.[33]

A number of the studies cited in Table 1 measure profit efficiency. The mean profit efficiency from studies of US depository institutions is 0.64, so these firms were earning about 64% of their potential profits on average (Berger et al., 1993a; DeYoung and Nolle, 1996; Miller and Noulas, 1996; Akhavein et al., 1997a; Akhavein et al., 1997b; Berger and Mester, 1997; Humphrey and Pulley, 1997; Hasan and Hunter, 1996). Similarly, a study of Spanish depositories found average profit efficiency of 0.72 (Lozano, 1997).[34] Much lower profit efficiency was found for large merging US banking organizations using the DFA method, 0.24 before merger, 0.34 after merger (Akhavein et al., 1997a). This contrasts with a DEA study of large US banks which found profit efficiency of 0.97, with 42% of the firms being 100% technically efficient (Miller and Noulas,

---

[33] The alternative of directly specifying service-level or quality constraints or variables directly in a cost model is usually not possible due to limited and proprietary data.

[34] Profits (and productivity) in the Spanish banking industry have been decomposed into a productivity effect (technical change and operating efficiency), an activity effect (product mix and scale), and a price effect (Grifell-Tatjé and Lovell, 1996, 1997a). Less comprehensively, profits in the US banking industry have been split into an endogenous or management-determined component and a exogenous or external "business conditions" component (Humphrey and Pulley, 1997).

1996). A profit efficiency study of US banks using random coefficients found the average efficiency to be highly dependent upon the choice of subsample (Akhavein et al., 1997b).

A study of insurance companies found average profit efficiencies on the order of about 60% efficient (Berger et al., 1996a). When profit efficiency and cost efficiency results are made comparable by expressing the quantities of inefficiency in terms of a common denominator, cost inefficiency was found to be larger than profit inefficiency, suggesting that cost inefficiency may be overstated because of differences in service quality or other variables not accounted for in the analysis.[35]

Some of these studies employ an alternative profit function in which the firm maximizes profits given output quantities, rather than taking output prices as exogenous (Berger et al., 1996a; Humphrey and Pulley, 1997; Akhavein et al., 1997a; Berger and Mester, 1997; Hasan and Hunter, 1996). In most cases, the alternative profit function provides qualitatively similar results to the standard profit function. The alternative profit function may be useful when one or more of the assumptions underlying the standard cost and profit efficiency models are violated by the data (e.g., competitive imperfections, unmeasured differences in product quality).[36]

Revenue efficiency is essentially the mirror image of cost inefficiency, incorporating errors in the choice of output mix, having too little output, etc. Although few revenue frontier analyses have been undertaken, revenue efficiency estimates (as measured by an output distance function) appear to be similar to those for cost efficiency (English et al., 1993).[37]

### 6.7 Stability over Time
A final research issue concerns the stability of efficiency over time. This refers both to average efficiency levels for an industry and for rankings of firms by their efficiency level. This is an important issue for the DFA

---

[35] In another study of banks, the reverse was found: expressed as a percent of total assets, profit inefficiency was over 10% of asset value while cost inefficiency was between 1% and 3% of asset value (Ellinger et al., 1997). The cost result is possible, since total costs as a percent of assets averages around 7% for banks. However, since profits as a percent of assets are usually only around 1%, it is hard to believe that average inefficiency is 10 times the level of profits.

[36] See Berger and Mester (1997) for further discussion.

[37] Revenue efficiency is expressed as a percent of revenue and, since revenues are typically only a bit larger than costs, revenue efficiency estimates are essentially comparable to those for cost efficiency. An ad hoc revenue frontier approach – essentially a

frontier model since this efficiency measure is based on the assumption that firm efficiency is stable over time and that random error, when averaged, will be close to zero. Several studies have found that efficiency is reasonably persistent over time: two studies computed a series of correlations among firms ranked by their estimated SFA and DEA efficiency level over time (Kwan and Eisenbeis, 1994; Eisenbeis et al., 1996); another looked for consistency in groups of high- and low-cost firms over a number of years (Berger and Humphrey, 1991); and yet another examined the stability of frontier banks over time (Berg, 1992).

Another study tried to determine for DFA the number of years that may be needed to strike a balance between the benefits and costs of the extra information from adding another year of data. The benefits come from having another residual to help average the random error toward zero to get more precise estimates of the inefficiency term, whereas the costs come from the increasing likelihood that the efficiency in the extra year has drifted further away from its level at the point being measured. The study found that the benefits and costs balance out at about six years of US banking data (DeYoung, 1997a).

However, the apparent persistence of relative efficiencies across firms over time does not necessarily carry over to changes in the overall level or distribution of efficiency. Advances and declines in year-to-year efficiency affect banks over time (Bauer et al., 1998). Finally, although numerous studies have commented on how efficiency seems to differ or not differ across size classes of banks (e.g., Ray and Mukherjee, 1994), our view is that these simple contrasts remain unreliable until the issue discussed above of possibly confounding scale economies with inefficiency due to heteroscedasticity in the data is more completely resolved.

### 7 Improving Managerial Performance at Financial Institutions

In principle, virtually *any* efficiency study of financial institutions can be used as a tool by managers to improve performance, as long as there is information in the study on the characteristics or identities of the relatively efficient and inefficient institutions. Management practices or

---

one-year DFA model – found a similar result (Elyasiani and Mehdian, 1990b). Berger et al. (1996b) specified an alternative revenue function, similar to the alternative profit function and found no evidence of revenue economies of scope, suggesting that customers do not value "one-stop banking" or that banks do not have sufficient market power to extract the value that consumers place on this convenience.

characteristics that are found to be relatively common among financial institutions on or near the efficient frontier may be identified as "best practices," which should be adopted if possible. Managers can also adjust their policies and procedures to avoid "worst practices" that are relatively common among institutions that are far from the efficient frontier. In addition, owners and managers of financial institutions may pay particular attention to the relationship between measured frontier efficiency and organizational form, which may suggest managerial arrangements which are more conducive to high performance.

Many frontier efficiency studies perform ex post analyses to identify the most important determinants of firm efficiency. However, to date, the results of these analyses have not been very informative because of a lack of detailed data. Exceptions have been studies that compared and contrasted the performance of individual credit unions (Fried et al., 1993; Fried and Lovell, 1994). The incorporation of price and service variety components into the output of credit unions resulted in more accurate benchmarking of these firms and yielded higher average efficiency values being measured, because certain "high cost" credit unions were found to incur higher costs in order to improve the services they provided. This can be important for mutual and cooperative types of organizations in which the customers are the owners. The customer/owner may prefer an increase is costs which would lower conventionally measured efficiency if the higher costs were in the form of higher interest paid or additional services provided.

Perhaps the best potential use of frontier efficiency methods in improving managerial performance, largely due to the availability of detailed proprietary data, comes from efficiency analysis of the branches of an individual financial institution. A financial institution may use frontier efficiency rankings, along with its own internal measures of performance, to determine where problems lie and help solve them. In the hands of a researcher who has a good institutional understanding of a given industry, frontier analysis can assist management to determine objectively those procedures or branches that may be classified as best practice and worst practice within a firm. The best and worse practices that are discovered can be used to rewrite the policies and procedures book for the branches. In addition, management may use frontier efficiency rankings to determine which branches are in most need of reform, local management replacement, or closure. The measurement and use of frontier efficiency for these purposes may work particularly well in analyzing branches which effectively have the same production function and produce a similar output mix but may differ importantly in productivity and efficiency. While many firms have their own internal benchmarking procedures, they often are composed of relatively simple comparisons or rankings of offices according to a small (or sometimes an overly large) set of partial performance ratios (Colwell and Davis, 1992; Sherman and Ladino, 1995; Lovell and Pastor, 1997). Although informative, such comparisons are not as broadly based as frontier analysis and typically lack a powerful and comprehensive optimizing methodology. As well, the use of simple ratios typically does not account for differences in output mix and input prices faced by the different branches.

However, frontier analysis may not always indicate the remedy for inefficient observations. Internal audits or intensive reviews of procedures are often also needed to uncover the source and nature of the operating and other changes that will likely improve efficiency at less efficient branches.

As shown in Table 2.4, there have been a number of frontier analyses focusing on branch performance within a single banking firm. Only one of these studies used parametric methods, applying DFA (Berger et al., 1997), while all the other studies have relied on nonparametric approaches, DEA or FDH. As proprietary data is often available for these studies, many inputs and outputs can be expressed in physical flow terms (e.g., hours worked by type of labor, numbers of transactions processed) and more accurate measures of stock inputs may be specified (e.g., square footage of office space used). This has been the case for the branch operations of a large Canadian bank (Schaffnit et al., 1997) which permits a detailed and comprehensive efficiency analysis. Regional or seasonal influences, differences in market location or operating environments, office size, or even management style and organization may also be considered (Parkan, 1987; Oral and Yolalan, 1990; Tulkens and Malnero, 1994; Athanassopoulos, 1995, 1997; Sherman and Ladino, 1995; Zenios et al., 1996; Drake and Howcroft, 1997). Less comprehensive studies have to rely on more indirect indicators such as the stock of accounts serviced or the values within various accounts, with little or no information on important customer characteristics or other environmental influences that can importantly affect the outcome.

When detailed transactions and service data are available, they often are grouped into a smaller set of similar categories to be made operational, such as aggregating 60 banking operations into only eight service areas (Tulkens, 1993) or constructing a weighted measure of 4 service categories from 17 of the most common services offered at the branch level (Sherman and Gold, 1985). One reason for partially aggregating the data is that it reduces the number of constraints that have to be specified, and so reduces the number of observations that are determined to be 100% efficient by virtue of having no other observations with which to be compared (self-identifiers). A more appropriate way to do this is through a statistical test which can discriminate between informative and extraneous constraints (Lovell and Pastor, 1997) or applying a cone-ratio or assurance region DEA model (Schaffnit et al., 1997).

The one parametric study finds frontier efficiency of about 0.90 to 0.95 for total branching costs (including interest expenses) or about 0.75 to 0.80 of branch operating costs, consistent with studies of financial institutions generally. In contrast, the nonparametric frontier analyses of branches tend to find a relatively large proportion of branches to be 100% efficient. This may occur in some cases because the number of inputs and outputs is large relative to the number of observations available, making it difficult to find other branches or linear combinations of branches that dominate in every input and output.

## 8 Conclusions and Directions for Future Research

We have outlined the results of 130 studies of financial institution efficiency covering 21 countries that apply five different frontier approaches. The efficiency estimates from nonparametric (DEA and FDH) studies are similar to those from parametric frontier models (SFA, DFA, and TFA), but the nonparametric methods generally yield slightly lower mean efficiency estimates and seem to have greater dispersion than the results of the parametric models. Overall, depository financial institutions (banks, S&Ls, credit unions) in these studies experience an average efficiency of around 77% (median 82%). The similarity in average efficiency values for firms across different frontier models, however, does not strongly carry over to rankings of individual firms by their efficiency values across models. This suggests that estimates of mean efficiency for an industry may be a more reliable guide for policy and research purposes than are the estimated efficiency rankings of firms, and that analyses of the causes or correlates of efficiency should be viewed with caution. The standard deviation of the efficiency estimates, at 13 percentage points, is relatively large. This suggests, and some initial studies confirm, that the confidence intervals surrounding individual firm or branch efficiency estimates may be substantial.

### 8.1 Applications of Efficiency Analysis

In terms of applications, research on financial institution efficiency has largely focused on using institution efficiency estimates: (1) to inform government policy (e.g., by assessing the effects of deregulation, mergers, and market structure on industry efficiency); (2) to address research issues (e.g., by determining how efficiency varies with different frontier approaches, output definitions, and time periods); and (3) to improve managerial performance (e.g., by identifying best-practice and worst-practice branches within a single firm).

Results from these applications suggest the following sets of conclusions. First, the government policy-efficiency literature finds that deregulation of financial institutions can either improve or worsen efficiency, depending upon industry conditions prior to deregulation. In a number of counties, deregulation has led to rapid branch expansion, excessive asset growth, a run-up in bank failures, and reduced efficiency. Although one goal of deregulation has been to improve efficiency, other incentives may intervene.

A similar result applies to mergers and acquisitions: some consolidations improve cost efficiency, whereas others worsen the performance of the combined institution relative to the separate institutions. On average, there appears to be no significant cost improvement. However, profit efficiency may improve with mergers and acquisitions due to altering output mix toward more profitable products (e.g., from securities to loans), rather than improved cost efficiency.

The application of frontier efficiency analysis to the market-power vs. efficient-structure debate about the determinants of profitability also yields mixed results. Cost efficiency is found to be more important than market concentration in explaining financial institution profitability, but both influences together only weakly explain performance variation. Market power does seem to affect the prices of some types of local deposits and loans, but has little apparent effect on profits. One reason may be that the managers of financial institutions with market power appear to take some of the benefits of charging higher prices as a "quiet life" in which they pursue goals other than maximizing efficiency.

The research-efficiency literature on financial institutions generally finds that efficiency rankings differ depending on which frontier approach is used (as noted above) and by how financial institution output is measured – as a transaction-based flow, a stock of numbers of accounts, or a stock of value in these accounts. Once a frontier approach is adopted and an output specification is selected, however, efficiency estimates are fairly stable from year to year, showing persistence. The limited evidence also suggests that the confidence intervals around efficiency estimates may be quite large.

Much of this literature is also concerned with the determinants of efficiency. Firm efficiency appears to be greater for some forms of corporate organization or control than others. However, most of these effects are slight and may not always be economically important, even if they are statistically significant.

There are a number of important methodological developments under way that may help resolve some of the conflicts among methods, make efficiency estimation more accurate, and help find the determinants of efficiency. For the nonparametric techniques, these developments include non-radial measures, the use of "composite" frontiers which embody the best parts of different financial institutions, the use of output distance functions, measurement of confidence intervals, optimization of the number of constraints, finding a statistical basis for the nonstochastic approaches, and resampling to take account of some of the random error in the data. For the parametric techniques, the new developments include the specification of more globally flexible functional forms, the use of less restrictive assumptions on the distributions of inefficiencies, the allowance for heteroscedasticity in the distributions of both inefficiencies and random errors, the measurement of confidence intervals, random coefficient estimation, allowance for correlations between regressors and inefficiencies, measurement of the effects of output mix and diversification, and the development of profit efficiency.

The management performance-efficiency literature on financial institutions is perhaps the least developed of the three types of applications. Some of this research has focused on alternative goals for managers, particularly when the firm is organized on a mutual or cooperative basis, rather than as a value-maximizing enterprise. The burgeoning literature on bank branch efficiency offers an opportunity for researchers to provide managers with information that may help to identify troubled branches and to help rewrite operational policies and procedures books based upon practices that are common among branches with the highest or lowest measured efficiency. Unfortunately, few of these studies have noted in any detail the specific changes implemented to improve performance at inefficient branches.

### 8.2 Directions for Future Research

Finally, it is important to point out shortcomings in existing research that should be addressed, suggest ways in which the existing research may be refocused to fill gaps in the literature, and outline potential areas for future research. Existing research has shown us that financial institutions are less than fully efficient and have quantified the apparent extent of this deficiency. However, little has been offered in terms of the significance of the measured efficiency differences, in determining the specific causes of these differences, and in explaining why they seem to persist in market-based economies.

One problem of frontier analysis is that although the central tendency of average efficiency values for financial institutions is generally similar across frontier techniques, rankings of firms by their measured efficiencies can differ. Since rankings differ depending on the frontier technique used, the common practice of regressing firm efficiency values (or ranks) on other variables of interest may lead to misleading results. If these ex post regressions are to be informative, they should be demonstrated to be robust to efficiency estimates from more than just one class of frontier techniques.

There are also shortcomings in applying both nonparametric and parametric frontier methods. The parametric approaches impose functional forms that restrict the shape of the frontier, and the nonparametric approaches do not allow for random error that may affect measured performance. Attempts to remedy these situations by specifying more globally flexible functional forms in the parametric approaches and trying to implement stochastic versions of the nonparametric approaches should continue. By generalizing both types of approaches, the data will presumably have a better chance to yield results that are more accurate and more consistent across approaches.

Other shortcomings in the two types of approaches are clear as well. For example, the choice among the various parametric models is typically based more on ease of use and/or the apparent reasonableness of the assumptions that underlie the different approaches than on any strong theoretical or empirical foundation. This gap in the literature is being filled for nonparametric models with an attempt to demonstrate that a stronger theoretical foundation exists for FDH than for DEA and that both approaches have a valid statistical foundation. Even so, nonparametric models are often specified in such a manner that many observations turn out to be 100% efficient, and this has been particularly so in the case of bank branches. Financial institutions or branches may be found to be fully efficient either because there truly are no other units that dominate them (even when a small set of important core variables/constraints are specified). Alternatively, these units may be found to be efficient because too many constraints have been specified, leading to excessive numbers of self-identifiers – units which neither dominated any other unit nor were dominated by any other unit or combination of units in every dimension. While this problem is well known, there have been few attempts to solve it. The statistical test applied by Lovell and

Pastor (1997) to identify extraneous constraints, however, may finally address this issue.

In addition, efficiency studies should try to provide confidence intervals for the estimates they generate, as some very recent studies have done. These intervals, when they have been provided, appear to be large relative to the range of efficiency estimates provided. As a result, comparisons of efficiency estimates across observations may be more meaningful if groups of observations, rather than individual observations, were being compared. Attributes associated with the group of observations with relatively high efficiency values can be contrasted with attributes associated with the group with relatively low values (with the middle group excluded entirely). In this context, it would be interesting to see if the imperfect correspondence found for firm-level efficiency estimates among different frontier methods is markedly improved if groups of observations, rather than individual observations, were used.

An area of research also deserving additional attention concerns efficiency comparisons among countries. With so few cross-country comparative efficiency studies to draw upon, the results obtained so far should be taken with caution unless the robustness of an intercountry comparison is demonstrated by finding the same result using different frontier techniques on the same data set. As well, most financial institution efficiency studies have been applied to the US banking industry, which has distinct local markets for many products and is quite unconcentrated by world standards. It is important for research and policy purposes to see if the US results carry over into other nations with banking markets that are more national in scope with much higher levels of concentration.

Finally, there is a considerable lack of information on what the main determinants of efficiency are both across firms within the financial industry and across branches within a single firm. Almost all of the studies which estimate efficiency and then regress it on sets of explanatory variables have been unable to explain more than just a small portion of its total variation. While some differences have been found, little published information exists regarding those influences that are under direct management control, such as the choice of funding sources, wholesale vs. retail orientation, etc. In sum, while there have been improvements made in applying efficiency analysis to financial institutions, there are many areas which deserve further research.

### Acknowledgements

The authors thank Sigbjorn Berg, Bill Cooper, Gary Ferrier, Joaquin Maudos, and Jesus Pastor for insightful comments on earlier drafts, and Knox Lovell for bringing us up to date on stochastic DEA. We also thank Seth Bonime and Emilia Bonaccorsi for outstanding research assistance.

## References

Adams, R., Berger, A. N., and Sickles, R. (1999), "Semiparametric approaches to stochastic panel frontiers with applications in the banking industry", *Journal of Business and Economic Statistics* 17, 349–358.

Akhavein, J. D., Berger, A. N., and Humphrey, D. B. (1997a), "The effects of megamergers on efficiency and prices: Evidence from a bank profit function", *Review of Industrial Organization* 12, 95–130.

Akhavein, J. D., Swamy, P. A. V. B., and Taubman, S. B. (1997b), "A general method of deriving the efficiencies of banks from a profit function", *Journal of Productivity Analysis* 8.

Al-Faraj, T. N., Alidi, A. S., and Bu-Bshait, K. A. (1993), "Evaluation of bank branches by means of Data Envelopment Analysis", *International Journal of Operations and Production Management* 13, 45–52.

Altunbas, Y. and Molyneux, P. (n.d.), "Stochastic estimators, technical efficiency and bank size", Working Paper, University College of North Wales, UK.

Aly, A. I. and Seiford, L. M. (1993), "The Mathematical Programming approach to efficiency analysis", in: H. O. Fried, C. A. K. Lovell, and S. S. Schmidt (eds.), *The Measurement of Productive Efficiency: Techniques and Applications*, Oxford University Press, Oxford, 120–159.

Aly, H. Y., Grabowski, R., Pasurka, C., and Rangan, N. (1990), "Technical, scale, and allocative efficiencies in US banking: An empirical investigation", *Review of Economics and Statistics* 72, 211–218.

Athanassopoulos, A. D. (1995), "Multivariate and frontier analysis for assessing the market and cost efficiency of large scale bank branch networks", Working Paper, University of Warwick, Coventry, UK.

Athanassopoulos, A. D. (1997), "Service quality and operating efficiency synergies for management control in the provision of financial services: Evidence from Greek bank branches", *European Journal of Operational Research* 98, 301–314 (this issue).

Athanassopoulos, A. D. (2000), "An Optimisation Framework of the Triad: Service Capabilities, Customer Satisfaction and Performance," in P. T. Harker and S. A. Zenios (eds.), *Performance of Financial Institutions: Efficiency, Innovation, Regulation*, Cambridge University Press, pp. 312–335.

Atkinson, S. E. and Wilson, P. W. (1995), "Comparing mean efficiency and productivity scores from small samples: A bootstrap methodology", *Journal of Productivity Analysis* 6, 137–152.

Banker, R. D. (1996), "Hypothesis tests using Data Envelopment Analysis", *Journal of Productivity Analysis* 7, 139–159.

Banker, R. D., Charnes, A., Cooper, W. W., Swarts, J., and Thomas, D. A. (1989), "An introduction to Data Envelopment Analysis with some of its models and their uses", in: J. L. Chan and J. M. Patton (eds.), *Research in Governmental and Nonprofit Accounting, Vol. 5*, JAI Press, Greenwich, CT, 125–163.

Bardhan, I. R., Cooper, W. W., Kozmetsky, G., and Kumbhakar, S. C. (1996), "A simulation study of joint uses of Data Envelopment Analysis and statistical regressions for production function estimation and efficiency evaluation", Working Paper, University of Texas, Austin, TX.

Barr, R., Seiford, L., and Siems, T. (1994), "Forecasting bank failure: A non-parametric approach", *Recherches Economiques de Louvain* 60, 411–429.

Bauer, P. W. (1990), "Recent developments in the econometric estimation of frontiers", *Journal of Econometrics* 46, 39–56.

Bauer, P. W., Berger, A. N., Ferrier, G. D., and Humphrey, D. B. (1998), "Consistency Conditions for Regularity Analysis of Financial Institutions: A Comparison of Frontier Efficiency Methods", *Journal of Economics and Business* 50, 85–114.

Bauer, P. W., Berger, A. N., and Humphrey, D. B. (1993), "Efficiency and productivity growth in US banking", in: H. O. Fried, C. A. K. Lovell, and S. S. Schmidt (eds.), *The Measurement of Productive Efficiency: Techniques and Applications*, Oxford University Press, Oxford, 386–413.

Bauer, P. W. and Hancock, D. (1993), "The efficiency of the Federal Reserve in providing check processing services", *Journal of Banking and Finance* 17, 287–311.

Benston, G. J., Hunter, W. C., and Wall, L. D. (1995), "Motivations for bank mergers and acquisitions: Enhancing the deposit insurance put option versus earnings diversification", *Journal of Money, Credit, and Banking* 27, 777–788.

Berg, S. A. (1992), "Mergers, efficiency and productivity growth in banking: The Norwegian experience 1984–1990", Working Paper, Norges Bank, Oslo, Norway.

Berg, S. A., Forsund, F., and Jansen, E. (1991), "Technical efficiency of Norwegian banks: A nonparametric approach to efficiency measurement", *Journal of Productivity Analysis* 2, 127–142.

Berg, S. A., Forsund, F., and Jansen, E. (1992), "Malmquist indices of productivity growth during the deregulation of Norwegian banking, 1980–89", *Scandinavian Journal of Economics* 94 (Supplement), S211–S228.

Berg, S. A., Forsund, F., Hjalmarsson, L., and Suominen, M. (1993), "Banking efficiency in the Nordic countries", *Journal of Banking and Finance* 17, 371–388.

Berg, S. A. and Kim, M. (1994), "Oligopolistic interdependence and the structure of production in banking: An empirical evaluation", *Journal of Money, Credit, and Banking* 26, 309–322.

Berg, S. A. and Kim, M. (1996), "Banks as multioutput oligopolies: An empirical evaluation of the retail and corporate banking markets", Working Paper, Norges Bank, Oslo, Norway.

Bergendahl, G. (1995), "DEA and benchmarks for Nordic banks", Working Paper, Gothenburg University, Gothenburg, Sweden.

Berger, A. N. (1993), "'Distribution-free' estimates of efficiency in the US banking industry and tests of the standard distributional assumptions", *Journal of Productivity Analysis* 4, 261–292.

Berger, A. N. (1995), "The profit-structure relationship in banking-tests of market-power and efficient-structure hypotheses", *Journal of Money, Credit, and Banking* 27, 404–431.

Berger, A. N., Cummins, J. D., and Weiss, M. (1997), "The coexistence of multiple distribution systems for financial services: The case of Property-Liability Insurance", *Journal of Business* 70, 515–546.

Berger, A. N. and DeYoung, R. (1997), "Loan Quality, Risk, and Productive Efficiency in Commercial Banks", *Journal of Banking and Finance* 21, 849–870.

Berger, A. N., Hancock, D., and Humphrey, D. B. (1993a), "Bank efficiency derived from the profit function", *Journal of Banking and Finance* 17, 317–347.

Berger, A. N. and Hannan, T. H. (1998), "The efficiency cost of market power in the banking industry: A test of the 'Quiet Life' and related hypotheses", *Review of Economics and Statistics* 80, 454–465.

Berger, A. N. and Hannan, T. H. (1997), "Using measures of firm efficiency to distinguish among alternative explanations of the structure–performance relationship", *Managerial Finance* 23, 6–31.

Berger, A. N. and Humphrey, D. B. (1991), "The dominance of inefficiencies over scale and product mix economies in banking", *Journal of Monetary Economics* 28, 117–148.

Berger, A. N. and Humphrey, D. B. (1992a), "Measurement and efficiency issues in commercial banking", in: Z. Grilichs (ed.), *Measurement Issues in the Service Sectors*, National Bureau of Economic Research, University of Chicago Press, Chicago, IL, 245–279.

Berger, A. N. and Humphrey, D. B. (1992b), "Megamergers in banking and the use of cost efficiency as an antitrust defense", *Antitrust Bulletin* 33, 541–600.

Berger, A. N., Humphrey, D. B., and Pulley, L. B. (1996b), "Do consumers pay for one-stop banking? Evidence from an alternative revenue function", *Journal of Banking and Finance* 20, 1601–1621.

Berger, A. N., Hunter, W. C., and Timme, S. G. (1993b), "The efficiency of financial institutions: A review and preview of research past, present, and future", *Journal of Banking and Finance* 17, 221–249.

Berger, A. N., Kashyap, A. K., and Scalise, J. M. (1995), "The transformation of the US banking industry: What a long, strange trip it's been", *Brookings Papers on Economic Activity* 2, 55–218.

Berger, A. N. Leusner, J., and Mingo, J. (1997), "The efficiency of bank branches", *Journal of Monetary Economics* 40, 141–162.

Berger, A. N. and Mester, L. J. (1997), "Beyond the black box: What explains differences in the efficiencies of financial institutions?", *Journal of Banking and Finance* 21, 895–947.

Bhattacharyya, A., Lovell, C. A. K., and Sahay, P. (1997), "The impact of liberalization on the productive efficiency of Indian commercial banks", *European Journal of Operational Research* 98, 333–346 (this issue).

Brockett, P. L., Charnes, A., Cooper, W. W., Huang, Z. M., and Sun, D. B. (1997), "Data transformations in DEA cone-ratio envelopment approaches for monitoring bank performances", *European Journal of Operational Research* 98, 251–269 (this issue).

Brockett, P. L., Rousseau, J., and Wang, Y. (1995), "An investigation in the active army recruiting environment post 'Desert Storm'", CCS Research Report No. 777, Graduate School of Business, University of Texas, Austin, TX.

Bukh, P. N. D. (1994), "Efficiency loss in the Danish banking sector: A Data Envelopment approach", Working Paper, University of Aarhus, Denmark.

Bukh, P. N. D., Berg, S. A., and Forsund, F. R. (1995), "Banking efficiency in the Nordic countries: A four-country Malmquist index analysis", Working Paper, University of Aarhus, Denmark.

Cebenoyan, A. S., Cooperman, E. S., and Register, G. A. (1993a), "Firm inefficiency and the regulatory closure of S&Ls: An empirical investigation", *Review of Economics and Statistics* 75, 540–545.

Cebenoyan, A. S., Cooperman, E. S., Register, C. A., and Hudgins, S. (1993b), "The relative efficiency of stock vs. mutual S&Ls: A stochastic cost frontier approach", *Journal of Financial Services Research* 7, 151–170.

Chaffai, M. (1993), "Technical and time variant allocative inefficiency of Tunisian commercial banks: A shadow cost frontier approach using panel data", Working Paper, Faculté des Sciences Economiques, Tunisia.

Chaffai, M. E. (1997), "Estimating input-specific technical inefficiency: The case of the Tunisian banking industry", *European Journal of Operational Research* 98, 315–332.

Chaffai, M. and Dietsch, M. (1995), "Should banks be 'universal'? The relationship between economies of scope and efficiency in the French banking industry", Working Paper, University Robert Schuman of Strasbourg, France.

Chang, C. E., Hasan, I., and Hunter, W. C. (1993), "Efficiency of multinational banks: An empirical investigation", Working Paper, New Jersey Institute of Technology.

Charnes, A., Cooper, W. W., Huang, Z. M., and Sun, D. B. (1990), "Polyhedral cone-ratio DEA models with an illustrative application to large commercial banks", *Journal of Econometrics* 46, 73–91.

Charnes, A., Cooper, W. W., Lewin, A., and Seiford, L. (eds.) (1994), *Data Envelopment Analysis: Theory, Methodology and Applications*, Kluwer Academic Publishers, Boston, MA.

Charnes, A., Cooper, W. W., and Rhodes, E. (1978), "Measuring the efficiency of decision making units", *European Journal of Operational Research* 2, 429–444.

Clark, J. (1996), "Economic cost, scale efficiency and competitive viability in banking", *Journal of Money, Credit, and Banking* 28, 342–364.

Colwell, R. J. and Davis, E. P. (1992), "Output and productivity in banking", *Scandinavian Journal of Economics* 94 (Supplement), S111–S129.

Cooper, W. W., Lelas, V., and Sueyoshi, T. (1997), "Goal programming models and duality relations for use in evaluating security portfolio and regression relations", *European Journal of Operational Research* 98, 432–444.

Cummins, D., Turchetti, G., and Weiss, M. (1995a), "Productivity and technical efficiency in the Italian insurance industry", Working Paper, Wharton Financial Institutions Center, University of Pennsylvania.

Cummins, D. and Weiss, M. (1993), "Measuring cost efficiency in the property – liability insurance industry", *Journal of Banking and Finance* 17, 463–481.

Cummins, D., Weiss, M., and Zi, H. (1995b), "Organizational form and efficiency: An analysis of stock and mutual property – liability insurers", Working Paper, Wharton Financial Institutions Center, University of Pennsylvania.

Cummins, D. and Zi, H. (1995), "Measuring economic efficiency of the US life insurance industry: Econometric and mathematical programming techniques", Working Paper, Wharton Financial Institutions Center, University of Pennsylvania.

DeBorger, B., Ferrier, G., and Kerstens, K. (1995), "The choice of a technical efficiency measure on the free disposal hull reference technology: A comparison using US banking data", Working Paper, University of Arkansas.

Demsetz, H. (1973), "Industry structure, market rivalry, and public policy", *Journal of Law and Economics* 16, 1–9.

Devaney, M. and Weber, W. (1995), "Rural bank efficiency and contestable markets", Working Paper, Southeast Missouri State University.

DeYoung, R. (1994), "Fee-based services and cost efficiency in commercial banks", in: *Proceedings: Conference on Bank Structure and Competition*, Federal Reserve Bank of Chicago, May 1994.

DeYoung, R. (1997a), "A diagnostic test for the distribution-free efficiency estimator: An example using US commercial bank data", *European Journal of Operational Research* 98, 244–250.

DeYoung, R. (1997b), "Bank mergers, X-efficiency, and the market for corporate control", *Managerial Finance* 23.

DeYoung, R. (1997c), "Management quality and X-efficiency in national banks", *Journal of Financial Services Research* 11.

DeYoung, R. and Nolle, D. (1996), "Foreign-owned banks in the US: Earning market share or buying it?", *Journal of Money, Credit, and Banking* 28, 622–636.

Dietsch, M. (1994), "Risk-taking and cost efficiency in French banking industry", Working Paper, Robert Schuman University of Strasbourg, France.

Drake, L. and Howcroft, B. (1997), "A study of the relative efficiency of UK bank branches", *Journal of Banking and Finance*, forthcoming.

Drake, L. and Weyman-Jones, T. (1992), "Technical and scale efficiency in UK building societies", *Applied Financial Economics* 2, 1–9.

Efron, B. and Tibshirani, R. J. (1993), *An Introduction to the Bootstrap*, Chapman & Hall, New York.

Eisenbeis, R. A., Ferrier, G. D., and Kwan, S. H. (1996), "An empirical analysis of the informativeness of programming and SFA efficiency scores: Efficiency and bank performance", Working Paper, University of North Carolina, Chapel Hill, NC.

Ellinger, P., Zhu, S., Shumway, R., and Neff, D. (1997), "Specification of inefficiency in banking: A comparison of cost and profit function approaches", *Journal of Financial Services Research*, forthcoming.

Elyasiani, E. and Mehdian, S. M. (1990a), "A nonparametric approach to measurement of efficiency and technological change: The case of large US commercial banks", *Journal of Financial Services Research* 4, 157–168.

Elyasiani, E. and Mehdian, S. M. (1990b), "Efficiency in the commercial banking industry. A production frontier approach", *Applied Economics* 22, 539–551.

Elyasiani, E. and Mehdian, S. M. (1992), "Productive efficiency performance of minority and nonminority-owned banks: A nonparametric approach", *Journal of Banking and Finance* 16, 933–948.

Elyasiani, E. and Mehdian, S. M. (1995), "The comparative efficiency performance of small and large US commercial banks in the pre- and post-deregulation eras", *Applied Economics* 27, 1069–1079.

Elyasiani, E., Mehdian, S. M., and Rezvanian, R. (1994), "An empirical test of association between production and financial performance", *Applied Financial Economics* 4, 55–59.

English, M., Grosskopf, S., Hayes, K., and Yaisawarng, S. (1993), "Output allocative and technical efficiency of banks", *Journal of Banking and Finance* 17, 349–366.

Favero, C. and Papi, L. (1995), "Technical efficiency and scale efficiency in the Italian banking sector: A non-parametric approach", *Applied Economics* 27, 385–395.

Fecher, F., Kessler, D., Perelman, S., and Pestieau, P. (1993), "Productive performance of the French insurance industry", *Journal of Productivity Analysis* 4, 77–93.

Fecher, F. and Pestieau, P. (1993), "Efficiency and competition in OECD Financial Services", in: H. O. Fried, C. A. K. Lovell, and S. S. Schmidt (eds.), *The Measurement of Productive Efficiency: Techniques and Applications*, Oxford University Press, Oxford, 374–385.

Ferrier, G., Grosskopf, S., Hayes, K., and Yaisawarng, S. (1993), "Economies of diversification in the banking industry: A frontier approach", *Journal of Monetary Economics* 31, 229–249.

Ferrier, G. and Hirschberg, J. (1994), "Bootstrapping confidence intervals for linear programming efficiency scores: With an illustration using Italian banking data", Working Paper, University of Arkansas.

Ferrier, G., Kerstens, K., and Vanden Eeckaut, P. (1994), "Radial and nonradial technical efficiency measures on a DEA reference technology: A comparison using banking data", *Recherches Economiques de Louvain* 60, 449–479.

Ferrier, G. and Lovell, C. A. K. (1990), "Measuring cost efficiency in banking: Econometric and linear programming evidence", *Journal of Econometrics* 46, 229–245.

Field, K. (1990), "Production efficiency of British building societies", *Applied Economics* 22, 415–426.

Fixler, D. and Zieschang, K. (1993), "An index number approach to measuring bank efficiency: An application to mergers", *Journal of Banking and Finance* 17, 437–450.

Fried, H. O. and Lovell, C. A. K. (1994), "Enhancing the performance of credit unions: The evolution of a methodology", *Recherches Economiques de Louvain* 60, 431–447.

Fried, H. O., Lovell, C. A. K., and Vanden Eeckaut, P. (1993), "Evaluating the performance of US credit unions", *Journal of Banking and Finance* 17, 251–265.

Fukuyama, H. (1993), "Technical and scale efficiency of Japanese commercial banks: A non-parametric approach", *Applied Economics* 25, 1101–1112.

Fukuyama, H. (1995), "Measuring efficiency and productivity growth in Japanese banking: A nonparametric frontier approach", *Applied Financial Economics* 5, 95–117.

Gardner, L. and Grace, M. (1993), "X-efficiency in the US life insurance industry", *Journal of Banking and Finance* 17, 497–510.

Giokas, D. (1991), "Bank branch operating efficiency: A comparative application of DEA and the loglinear model", *OMEGA International Journal of Management Science* 19, 549–557.

Grabowski, R., Rangan, N., and Rezvanian, R. (1993), "Organizational forms in banking: An empirical investigation of cost efficiency", *Journal of Banking and Finance* 17, 531–538.

Greene, W. H. (1990), "A gamma-distributed stochastic frontier model", *Journal of Econometrics* 46, 141–163.

Greene, W. H. (1993), "The econometric approach to efficiency analysis", in: H. O. Fried, C. A. K. Lovell, and S. S. Schmidt (eds.), *The Measurement of Productive Efficiency: Techniques and Applications*, Oxford University Press, Oxford, 68–119.

Grifell-Tatjé, E. and Lovell, C. A. K. (1994), "A generalized Malmquist productivity index", Working Paper, University of Georgia, Athens, GA.

Grifell-Tatjé, E. and Lovell, C. A. K. (1996), "Profits and productivity: A theoretical analysis and an empirical application to Spanish banking", Working Paper, University of Barcelona.

Grifell-Tatjé, E. and Lovell, C. A. K. (1997a), "The sources of productivity change in Spanish banking", *European Journal of Operational Research* 98, 365–381.

Grifell-Tatjé, E. and Lovell, C. A. K. (1997b). "Deregulation and productivity decline: The case of Spanish savings banks", *European Economic Review*, forthcoming.

Grosskopf, S. (1993), "Efficiency and productivity", in: H. O. Fried, C. A. K. Lovell, and S. S. Schmidt (eds.), *The Measurement of Productive Efficiency: Techniques and Applications*, Oxford University Press, Oxford, 160–194.

Grosskopf, S. (1996), "Statistical inference and nonparametric efficiency: A selective survey", *Journal of Productivity Analysis* 7, 161–176.

Hall, P., Hardle, W., and Simar, L. (1993), "On the inconsistency of bootstrap estimators", *Computational Statistics and Data Analysis* 16, 11–18.

Hartman, T. and Storbeck, J. E. (1995), "Measuring managerial and program efficiencies in a Swedish savings and loan", Working Paper, Keele University, UK.

Hasan, I. and Hunter, W. C. (1996), "Efficiency of Japanese multinational banks in the US", *Research in Finance*, forthcoming.

Hermalin, B. E. and Wallace, N. E. (1994), "The determinants of efficiency and solvency in savings and loans", *Rand Journal of Economics* 25, 361–381.

Hughes, J. P., Lang, W., Mester, L. J., and Moon, C.-G. (1996), "Efficiency banking under interstate branching", *Journal of Money, Credit, and Banking* 28, 1045–1071.

Hughes, J. P. and Mester, L. J. (1993), "A quality and risk-adjusted cost function for banks: Evidence on the 'too-big-to-fail' doctrine", *Journal of Productivity Analysis* 4, 293–315.

Humphrey, D. B. (1987), "Cost dispersion and the measurement of economies in banking", *Economic Review*, May/June, 24–38.

Humphrey, D. B. (1993), "Cost and technical change: Effects from bank deregulation", *Journal of Productivity Analysis* 4, 5–34.

Humphrey, D. B. and Pulley, L. B. (1997), "Banks' responses to deregulation: Profits, technology, and efficiency", *Journal of Money, Credit, and Banking* 73–93.

Hunter, W. C. and Timme, S. (1995), "Core deposits and physical capital: A reexamination of bank scale economies and efficiency with quasi-fixed inputs", *Journal of Money, Credit, and Banking* 27, 165–185.

Kaparakis, E., Miller, S., and Noulas, A. (1994), "Short-run cost inefficiency of commercial banks: A flexible stochastic frontier approach", *Journal of Money, Credit, and Banking* 26, 875–893.

Kneip, A. and Simar, L. (1996), "A general framework for frontier estimation with panel data", *Journal of Productivity Analysis* 7, 187–212.

Kramer, B. (1997), "N.E.W.S.: A model for the evaluation of non-life insurance companies", *European Journal of Operational Research* 98, 420–431.

Kumbhakar, S. C. (1988), "Estimation of input-specific technical and allocative inefficiency in stochastic frontier models", *Oxford Economic Papers* 40, 535–549.

Kuussaari, H. (1993), "Productive efficiency in Finnish local banking during 1985–1990", Working Paper, Bank of Finland.

Kuussaari, H. and Vesala, J. (1995), "The efficiency of Finnish banks in producing payment and account transactions", Working Paper, Bank of Finland.

Kwan, S. H. and Eisenbeis, R. A. (1994), "An analysis of inefficiencies in banking: A stochastic cost frontier approach", Working Paper, Federal Reserve Bank of San Francisco.

Land, K., Lovell, C. A. K., and Thore, S. (1993), "Chance-constrained Data Envelopment Analysis", *Managerial and Decision Economics* 14, 541–554.

Lang, G. and Welzel, P. (1995), "Technology and cost efficiency in universal banking", Working Paper, University of Augsburg, Germany.

Lang, G. and Welzel, P. (1996), "Efficiency and technical progress in banking: Empirical results for a panel of German banks", *Journal of Banking and Finance* 20, 1003–1023.

Lovell, C. A. K. (1993), "Production frontiers and productive efficiency", in: H. O. Fried, C. A. K. Lovell, and S. S. Schmidt (eds.), *The Measurement of Productive Efficiency: Techniques and Applications*, Oxford University Press, Oxford, 3–67.

Lovell, C. A. K. and Pastor, J. T. (1997), "Target setting: An application to a bank branch network", *European Journal of Operational Research* 98, 291–300.

Lozano, A. (1995), "Efficiency and technical change for Spanish banks", Working Paper, University of Malaga, Spain.

Lozano, A. (1997), "Profit efficiency for Spanish savings banks", *European Journal of Operational Research* 98, 382–395.

Mahajan, A., Rangan, N., and Zardkoohi, A. (1996), "Cost structures in multinational and domestic banking", *Journal of Banking and Finance* 20, 238–306.

Maudos, J. (1996a), "A comparison of different stochastic frontier techniques with panel data: An application for efficiency of Spanish banks", Working Paper, University of Valencia, Spain.

Maudos, J. (1996b), "Market structure and performance in Spanish banking using a direct measure of efficiency", Working Paper, University of Valencia, Spain.

McAllister, P. H. and McManus, D. A. (1993), "Resolving the scale efficiency puzzle in banking", *Journal of Banking and Finance* 17, 389–405.

Mester, L. J. (1993), "Efficiency in the savings and loan industry", *Journal of Banking and Finance* 17, 267–286.

Mester, L. J. (1996), "A study of bank efficiency taking into account risk-preferences", *Journal of Banking and Finance* 20, 1025–1045.

Mester, L. J. (1997), "Measuring efficiency at US banks: Accounting for heterogeneity is important", *European Journal of Operational Research* 98, 230–243.

Miller, S. M. and Noulas, A. G. (1996), "The technical efficiency of large bank production", *Journal of Banking and Finance* 20, 495–509.

Mitchell, K. and Onvural, N. M. (1996), "Economies of scale and scope at large commercial banks: Evidence from the Fourier flexible functional form", *Journal of Money, Credit, and Banking* 28, 178–199.

Mooney, C. Z. and Duval, R. D. (1993), *Bootstrapping: A Nonparametric Approach to Statistical Inference*, Sage, Newbury Park, CA.

Murthi, B. P. S., Choi, Y. K., and Desai, P. (1997), "Efficiency of mutual funds and portfolio performance measurement: A nonparametric approach", *European Journal of Operational Research* 98, 409–419.

Newman, J. and Shrieves, R. (1993), "Multibank holding company effect on cost efficiency in banking", *Journal of Banking and Finance* 17, 709–732.

Olesen, O. B. and Petersen, N. C. (1995), "Chance constrained efficiency evaluation", *Management Science* 41, 442–457.

Oral, M. and Yolalan, R. (1990), "An empirical study on measuring operating efficiency and profitability of bank branches", *European Journal of Operational Research* 46, 282–294.

Parkan, C. (1987), "Measuring the efficiency of service operations: An application to bank branches", *Engineering Costs and Production Economics* 12, 237–242.

Pastor, J. (1995), "How to account for environmental effects in DEA: An application to bank branches", Working Paper, University of Alicante, Spain.

Pastor, J., Perez, F., and Quesada, J. (1997), "Efficiency analysis in banking firms: An international comparison", *European Journal of Operational Research* 98, 396–408.

Perez, F. and Quesada, J. (1994), "Efficiency and banking strategies in Spain", in: D. Fair and R. Raymond (eds.), *The Competitiveness of Financial Institutions and Centres in Europe*, Financial and Monetary Policy Studies, Vol. 28, Kluwer Academic Publishers, Dordrecht, 135–149.

Peristiani, S. (1997), "Do mergers improve the X-efficiency and scale efficiency of US banks? Evidence from the 1980s", *Journal of Money, Credit, and Banking*, 29.

Pi, L. and Timme, S. (1993), "Corporate control and bank efficiency", *Journal of Banking and Finance* 17, 515–530.

Rangan, N., Grabowski, R., Aly, H., and Pasurka, C. (1988), "The technical efficiency of US banks", *Economics Letters* 28, 169–175.

Ray, S. and Mukherjee, K. (1994), "Identifying banks that are too large: A study of size efficiency in US banking", Working Paper, University of Connecticut.

Resti, A. (1995), "Linear programming and econometric methods for bank efficiency evaluation: An empirical comparison based on a panel of Italian banks", Working Paper, University of Bergamo, Italy.

Rhoades, S. A. (1993), "The efficiency effects of horizontal bank mergers", *Journal of Banking and Finance* 17, 411–422.

Ruthenberg, D. and Elias, R. (1996), "Cost economies and interest rate margins in a unified European banking market", *Journal of Economics and Business* 48, 231–249.

Schaffnit, C., Rosen, D., and Paradi, J. C. (1997), "Best practice analysis of bank branches: An application of DEA in a large Canadian bank", *European Journal of Operational Research* 98, 270–290.

Schmidt, P. and Sickles, R. C. (1984), "Production frontiers and panel data", *Journal of Business and Economic Statistics* 2, 367–374.

Seiford, L. M. and Thrall, R. M. (1990), "Recent developments in DEA: The mathematical programming approach to frontier analysis", *Journal of Econometrics* 46, 7–38.

Sheldon, G. and Haegler, U. (1993), "Economies of scale and scope and inefficiencies in Swiss banking", in: N. Blattner, H. Genberg, and A. Swoboda (eds.), *Banking in Switzerland*, Springer-Verlag, New York, 103–140.

Sherman, D. and Gold, F. (1985), "Branch operating efficiency: Evaluation with Data Envelopment Analysis", *Journal of Banking and Finance* 9, 297–315.

Sherman, D. and Ladino, G. (1995), "Managing bank productivity using Data Envelopment Analysis (DEA)", *Interfaces* 25, 60–73.

Simar, L. (1992), "Estimating efficiencies from frontier models with panel data: A comparison of parametric, nonparametric and semiparametric methods with bootstrapping", *Journal of Productivity Analysis* 3, 171–203.

Simar, L. (1996), "Aspects of statistical analysis in DEA-type frontier models", *Journal of Productivity Analysis* 7, 177–185.

Simar, L. and Wilson, P. W. (1995), "Sensitivity analysis of efficiency scores: How to bootstrap in nonparametric frontier models", Working Paper, Institute of Statistics, Université Catholique de Louvain, Belgium.

Soteriou, A., Athanassopoulos, A., Zenios, S. A. (2000), "Disentangling within- and between-country efficiency differences of bank branches", in P. Harker and S. Zenios (eds.), *Performance of Financial Institutions: Efficiency, Innovation, Regulation*, Cambridge University Press, 336–363.

Soteriou, A. and Zenios, S. A. (1999) "Operations, quality and profitability in the provision of banking services", *Management Science* 45, 1221–1238.

Taylor, W. M., Thompson, R. G., Thrall, R. M., and Dharmapala, P. S. (1997), "DEA/AR efficiency and profitability of Mexican banks: A total income model", *European Journal of Operational Research* 98, 347–364.

Thiry, B. and Tulkens, H. (1992), "Allowing for inefficiency in parametric estimates of production functions for urban transit firms", *Journal of Productivity Analysis* 3, 45–66.

Tompson, R. G., Brinkmann, E. J., Dharmapala, P. S., Gonzalez-Lima, M. D., and Thrall, R. M. (1997), "DEA/AR profit-ratios and sensitivity of 100 large US commercial banks", *European Journal of Operational Research* 98, 213–229.

Tompson, R. G., Dharmapala, P. S., Diaz, J., Gonzalez-Lima, M. D., and Thrall, R. M. (1996a), "DEA multiplier analytic center sensitivity with an illustrative application to independent oil companies", *Annals of Operations Research* 66.

Tompson, R. G., Dharmapala, P. S., Humphrey, D. B., Taylor, W. M., and Thrall, R. M. (1996b), "Computing DEA/AR efficiency and profit ratio measures with an illustrative bank application", *Annals of Operations Research* 68.

Tulkens, H. (1993), "On FDH efficiency analysis: Some methodological issues and applications to retail banking, courts, and urban transit", *Journal of Productivity Analysis* 4, 183–210.

Tulkens, H. and Malnero, A. (1994), "Nonparametric approaches to the assessment of the relative efficiency of bank branches", Working Paper, Center for Operations Research and Econometrics, Université Catholique de Louvain, Belgium.

Vassiloglou, M. and Giokas, D. (1990), "A study of the relative efficiency of bank branches: An application of Data Envelopment Analysis", *Journal of the Operational Research Society* 41, 591–597.

Wheelock, D. C. and Wilson, P. W. (1994), "Productivity changes in US banking: 1984–93", Working Paper Federal Reserve Bank of St. Louis.

Yuengert, A. (1993), "The measurement of efficiency in life insurance: Estimates of a mixed Normal – Gamma error model", *Journal of Banking and Finance* 17, 483–496.

Zaim, O. (1995), "The effect of financial liberalization on the efficiency of Turkish commercial banks", *Applied Financial Economics* 5, 257–264.

Zenios, C., Zenios, S., Agathocleous, K., and Soteriou, A. (1999), "Benchmarks of the efficiency of bank branches", *Interfaces* 29(3), 37–51.

Zhu, S., Ellinger, P., and Shumway, R. (1997), "The choice of functional form and estimation of banking efficiency", *Applied Economic Issues*, forthcoming.

# 3

## Inside the Black Box: What Explains Differences in the Efficiencies of Financial Institutions?[1]

Allen N. Berger[a,b,*], Loretta J. Mester[c,d,2]

### Abstract

Over the past several years, substantial research effort has gone into measuring the efficiency of financial institutions. Many studies have found that inefficiencies are quite large, on the order of 20% or more of total banking industry costs and about half of the industry's potential profits. There is no consensus on the sources of the differences in measured efficiency. This chapter examines several possible sources, including differences in efficiency concept, measurement method, and a number of bank, market, and regulatory characteristics. We review the existing literature and provide new evidence using data on US banks over the period 1990–1995.

## 1 Introduction

Over the past several years, substantial research effort has gone into measuring the efficiency of financial institutions, particularly commercial

[a] Board of Governors of the Federal Reserve System, 20th and C Sts. N.W., Mail Stop 153, Washington, DC 20551, USA.

[b] Wharton Financial Institutions Center, Philadelphia, PA 19104, USA.

[c] Federal Reserve Bank of Philadelphia, Philadelphia, PA 19106, USA.

[d] Finance Department, The Wharton School, University of Pennsylvania, Philadelphia, PA 19104, USA.

[*] Corresponding author. Tel.: +202 452 2903; fax: +202 452 5295; e-mail: aberger@frb.gov.

[1] This paper was an invited paper on the occasion of the *Journal of Banking and Finance* 20th anniversary. Reprinted by permission of the *Journal of Banking and Finance*.

[2] Tel.: (215) 574-3807; fax: (215) 574-4364; e-mail: loretta.mester@phil.frb.org.

banks. The focus has been on estimating an efficient frontier and measuring the average differences between observed banks and banks on the frontier. Many studies have found large inefficiencies, on the order of 20% or more of total banking industry costs, and about half of the industry's potential profits. There is no consensus on the sources of the differences in measured efficiency. An obvious next step in the efficiency research program is to determine these sources. This chapter focuses on three sources: (1) differences in the efficiency concept used; (2) differences in measurement methods used to estimate efficiency within the context of these concepts; and (3) potential correlates of efficiency – bank, market, and regulatory characteristics that are at least partially exogenous and may explain some of the efficiency differences that remain after controlling for efficiency concept and measurement method. We review the existing literature on the sources of efficiency of financial institutions and provide new evidence.

Estimates of efficiency often vary substantially across studies according to the data source, as well as the efficiency concepts and measurement methods used in the studies. Berger and Humphrey (1997) documented 130 studies on financial institution efficiency, using data from 21 countries, from multiple time periods, and from various types of institutions including banks, bank branches, savings and loans, credit unions, and insurance companies. These variations in the data sets from which efficiencies are measured make it virtually impossible to determine how important the different efficiency concepts, measurement techniques, and correlates used are to the outcomes of these studies. Put in another way, the sources of differences in efficiency across financial institutions are concealed from view within an opaque "black box" because the individual studies simultaneously differ from one another in so many different dimensions.

Our empirical application tries to get around this problem by employing multiple efficiency concepts, using a number of different measurement methods, and applying a comprehensive set of potential efficiency correlates to a single data set. We estimate the efficiency of almost 6,000 US commercial banks that were in continuous existence over the six-year period 1990–1995 and had no missing or questionable data on any of the variables used. Thus, the differences we observe should reasonably and accurately reflect the effects of changes in the concepts, measurement techniques, and potential correlates that are used, rather than any differences in the data set to which these assumptions are applied.

We employ three distinct economic efficiency concepts – cost, standard profit, and alternative profit efficiencies. We analyze the effects of a number of measurement methods, including use of the distribution-free approach versus the stochastic frontier approach, specification of the Fourier-flexible functional form versus the translog form, and inclusion of problem loans and financial capital in a number of different ways. We find that measured efficiency differs across the three efficiency concepts, and that each adds some independent informational value. A somewhat surprising result is that the choices made concerning efficiency measurement usually make very little difference to our empirical findings in terms of either average industry efficiency or rankings of individual firms, suggesting that the efficiency estimates are fairly robust to differences in methodology. Another surprising result is that we also find substantial unexploited cost scale economies for fairly large sizes of banks in the 1990s, suggesting a change from the 1980s.

Once the conceptual and measurement issues have been controlled for, it is important for the purposes of public policy, research, and managerial performance to explain the remaining differences in efficiency across banks. In a perfectly competitive or contestable market, one would expect inefficient firms to be driven out by efficient firms, so that there would be only a residual level of inefficiency across firms remaining at any given time. An empirical finding of substantial inefficiencies, therefore, raises the question as to whether inefficiencies, which may have been sustainable in the past because of regulatory limits on competition, will continue in the less-regulated future. For antitrust and merger analysis, it is important to know the effects of market concentration and past mergers on banking efficiency. Similarly, it is important to know whether one type of organizational form is more efficient than another, and whether inefficiency manifests itself in the form of poor production decisions, risk management decisions, or both. We review the existing studies that analyzed potential correlates of efficiency, but a comparison across studies is hampered by the fact that different samples, efficiency concepts, and measurement techniques were used. In our empirical analysis, we explore the effects of a number of potential correlates of bank efficiency after controlling for efficiency concept and measurement method. The potential correlates include measures of bank size, organizational form and corporate governance, other bank characteristics, market characteristics, state geographic restrictions, and federal regulator. We find that a number of these factors appear to have independent influences on efficiency, although many expected effects are not present and some of the effects we find are not consistent with expectations.

## 2 The Efficiency Concept – Cost, Standard Profit, and Alternative Profit Efficiency

A fundamental decision in measuring financial institution efficiency is which concept to use. This, of course, depends on the question being addressed. We discuss here what we consider to be the three most important economic efficiency concepts – cost, standard profit, and alternative profit efficiencies. We believe these concepts have the best economic foundation for analyzing the efficiency of financial institutions because they are based on economic optimization in reaction to market prices and competition, rather than being based solely on the use of technology.

### 2.1  Cost Efficiency

Cost efficiency gives a measure of how close a bank's cost is to what a best-practice bank's cost would be for producing the same output bundle under the same conditions. It is derived from a cost function in which variable costs depend on the prices of variable inputs, the quantities of variable outputs and any fixed inputs or outputs, environmental factors, random error, and efficiency. Such a cost function may be written as

$$C = C(w, y, z, v, u_C, \varepsilon_C),\qquad(1)$$

where $C$ measures variable costs, $w$ is the vector of prices of variable inputs, $y$ is the vector of quantities of variable outputs, $z$ indicates the quantities of any fixed netputs (inputs or outputs), which are included to account for the effects of these netputs on variable costs owing to substitutability or complementarity with variable netputs, $v$ is a set of environmental or market variables that may affect performance, $u_C$ denotes an inefficiency factor that may raise costs above the best-practice level, and $\varepsilon_C$ denotes the random error that incorporates measurement error and luck that may temporarily give banks high or low costs. The inefficiency factor $u_C$ incorporates both allocative inefficiencies from failing to react optimally to relative prices of inputs, $w$, and technical inefficiencies from employing too much of the inputs to produce $y$. To simplify the measurement of efficiency, the inefficiency and random term $u_C$ and $\varepsilon_C$ are assumed to be multiplicatively separable from the rest of the cost function, and both sides of (1) are represented in natural logs

$$\ln C = f(w, y, z, v) + \ln u_C + \ln \varepsilon_C,\qquad(2)$$

where $f$ denotes some functional form. The term, $\ln u_C + \ln \varepsilon_C$, is treated as a composite error term, and the various X-efficiency measurement techniques (described in Section 3.1) differ in how they distinguish the inefficiency term, $\ln u_C$, from the random error term, $\ln \varepsilon_C$. We define the cost efficiency of bank $b$ as the estimated cost needed to produce bank $b$'s output vector if the bank were as efficient as the best-practice bank in the sample facing the same exogenous variables $(w,y,z,v)$ divided by the actual cost of bank $b$, adjusted for random error, i.e.,

$$\text{Cost EFF}^b = \frac{\hat{C}^{\min}}{\hat{C}^b} = \frac{\exp[\hat{f}(w^b,y^b,z^b,v^b)] \times \exp[\ln \hat{u}_C^{\min}]}{\exp[\hat{f}(w^b,y^b,z^b,v^b)] \times \exp[\ln \hat{u}_C^b]}$$

$$= \frac{\hat{u}_C^{\min}}{\hat{u}_C^b}, \tag{3}$$

where $\hat{u}_C^{\min}$ is the minimum $\hat{u}_C^b$ across all banks in the sample.

The cost efficiency ratio may be thought of as the proportion of costs or resources that are used efficiently. For example, a bank with Cost EFF of 0.70 is 70% efficient or equivalently wastes 30% of its costs relative to a best-practice firm facing the same conditions. Cost efficiency ranges over $(0,1]$, and equals one for a best-practice firm within the observed data.[3]

### 2.2 Standard Profit Efficiency

Standard profit efficiency measures how close a bank is to producing the maximum possible profit given a particular level of input prices and output prices (and other variables). In contrast to the cost function, the standard profit function specifies variable profits in place of variable costs and takes variable output prices as given, rather than holding all output quantities statistically fixed at their observed, possibly inefficient, levels. That is, the profit dependent variable allows for consideration of revenues that can be earned by varying outputs as well as inputs. Output prices are taken as exogenous, allowing for inefficiencies in the choice of outputs when responding to these prices or to any other arguments of the profit function.

The standard profit function, in log form, is

$$\ln(\pi + \theta) = f(w,p,z,v) + \ln u_\pi + \ln \varepsilon_\pi, \tag{4}$$

---

[3] In applications, efficiency is generally defined relative to the best-practice observed in the industry, rather than to any true minimum costs, since the underlying technology is unknown. (The usual form of the stochastic frontier measurement technique is an exception.) Fortunately, for most economic hypotheses, relative efficiency rather than absolute

where $\pi$ is the variable profits of the firm, which includes all the interest and fee income earned on the variable outputs minus variable costs, $C$, used in the cost function; $\theta$ is a constant added to every firm's profit so that the natural log is taken of a positive number; $p$ is the vector of prices of the variable outputs; $\ln \varepsilon_\pi$ represents random error; and $\ln u_\pi$ represents inefficiency that reduces profits.

We define standard profit efficiency as the ratio of the predicted actual profits to the predicted maximum profits that could be earned if the bank was as efficient as the best bank in the sample, net of random error, or the proportion of maximum profits that are actually earned:

$$\text{Std } \pi \text{ EFF}^b = \frac{\hat{\pi}^b}{\hat{\pi}^{\max}}$$

$$= \frac{\left\{\exp\left[\hat{f}(w^b, p^b, z^b, v^b)\right] \times \exp[\ln \hat{u}_\pi^b]\right\} - \theta}{\left\{\exp\left[\hat{f}(w^b, p^b, z^b, v^b)\right] \times \exp[\ln \hat{u}_\pi^{\max}]\right\} - \theta}, \qquad (5)$$

where $\hat{u}_\pi^{\max}$ is the maximum value of $\hat{u}_\pi$ in the sample.[4]

Standard profit efficiency is the proportion of maximum profits that are earned, so that a Std $\pi$ EFF ratio of 0.70 would indicate that, because of excessive costs, deficient revenues, or both, the firm is losing about 30% of the profits it could be earning. Similar to the cost efficiency ratio, the profit efficiency ratio equals one for a best-practice firm that maximizes profits for its given conditions within the observed data. Unlike cost efficiency, however, profit efficiency can be negative, since firms can throw away more than 100% of their potential profits.

In our opinion, the profit efficiency concept is superior to the cost efficiency concept for evaluating the overall performance of the firm. Profit efficiency accounts for errors on the output side as well as those on the input side, and some prior evidence suggested that inefficiencies on the output side may be as large or larger than those on the input side (e.g., Berger et al., 1993). Profit efficiency is based on the more accepted eco-

---

efficiency is the more appropriate concept. For example, we investigate below whether larger versus smaller banks are more efficient, which requires only comparisons to a consistent frontier.

[4] The profit efficiency does not simplify to a ratio of $\hat{u}_\pi$'s as in the case of cost efficiency because the addition of $\theta$ to the dependent variable before taking logs means that the efficiency factor is not exactly multiplicatively separable in the profit function. A bank's efficiency will vary somewhat with the values of the exogenous variables, so for our efficiency estimates we average the values of the numerator and denominator in (5) over the sample period before dividing to measure the average efficiency of the bank over the sample period.

nomic goal of profit maximization, which requires that the same amount of managerial attention be paid to raising a marginal dollar of revenue as to reducing a marginal dollar of costs. That is, a firm that spends $1 additional to raise revenues by $2, all else held equal, would appropriately be measured as being more profit efficient but might inappropriately be measured as being less cost efficient.

Profit efficiency is based on a comparison with the best-practice point of profit maximization within the data set, whereas cost efficiency evaluates performance holding output constant at its current level, which generally will not correspond to an optimum. A firm that is relatively cost efficient at its current output may or may not be cost efficient at its optimal output, which typically involves a different scale and mix of outputs. Thus, standard profit efficiency may take better account of cost inefficiency than the cost efficiency measure itself, since standard profit efficiency embodies the cost inefficiency deviations from the optimal point.[5]

### 2.3 Alternative Profit Efficiency

An interesting recent development in efficiency analysis is the concept of alternative profit efficiency, which may be helpful when some of the assumptions underlying cost and standard profit efficiency are not met. Efficiency here is measured by how close a bank comes to earning maximum profits given its output levels rather than its output prices. The alternative profit function employs the same dependent variable as the standard profit function and the same exogenous variables as the cost function. Thus, instead of counting deviations from optimal output as inefficiency, as in the standard profit function, variable output is held constant as in the cost function while output prices are free to vary and affect profits. The alternative profit function in log form is

$$\ln(\pi + \theta) = f(w, y, z, v) + \ln u_{a\pi} + \ln \varepsilon_{a\pi}, \tag{6}$$

which is indentical to the standard profit function in (3) except that $y$ replaces $p$ in the function, $f$, yielding different values for the inefficiency and random error terms, $\ln u_{a\pi}$ and $\ln \varepsilon_{a\pi}$, respectively.

---

[5] A few prior papers have studied the standard profit efficiency of US banks (Berger et al., 1993; DeYoung and Nolle, 1996; Akhavein et al., 1997a,b). The measured average profit efficiencies ranged from 24% of potential profits being earned to 67%. Profit function estimation was also used to measure efficiency in terms of the risk-expected return efficient frontier as defined in the finance literature (Hughes and Moon, 1995; Hughes et al., 1996, 1999). A bank with too little expected profit for the amount of risk it is taking

As with standard profit efficiency, alternative profit efficiency is the ratio of predicted actual profits to the predicted maximum profits for a best-practice bank:

$$\text{Alt } \pi \text{ EFF}^b = \frac{a\hat{\pi}^b}{a\hat{\pi}^{\max}}$$

$$= \frac{\left\{\exp[\hat{f}(w^b, y^b, z^b, v^b)] \times \exp[\ln\hat{u}_{a\pi}^b]\right\} - \theta}{\left\{\exp[\hat{f}(w^b, y^b, z^b, v^b)] \times \exp[\ln\hat{u}_{a\pi}^{\max}]\right\} - \theta}. \qquad (7)$$

Here, efficiency values are allowed to vary in an important way with output prices, but errors in choosing output quantities do not affect alternative profit efficiency except through the point of evaluation $\hat{f}(w^b, y^b, z^b, v^b)$ to the extent that the best-practice bank is not operating at the same $(w, y, z, v)$ as bank $b$.

There would be no reason to estimate alternative profit efficiency if the usual assumptions held. Standard profit efficiency and cost efficiency would appropriately measure how well the firm was producing outputs and employing inputs relative to best-practice firms, given the underlying assumptions. However, alternative profit efficiency may provide useful information when one or more of the following conditions hold:

(i)   there are substantial unmeasured differences in the quality of banking services;

(ii)  outputs are not completely variable, so that a bank cannot achieve every output scale and product mix;

(iii) output markets are not perfectly competitive, so that banks have some market power over the prices they charge; and

(iv)  output prices are not accurately measured, so they do not provide accurate guides to opportunities to earn revenues and profits in the standard profit function.

The alternative profit function provides a way of controlling for unmeasured differences in output quality, as in condition (i), since it considers the additional revenue that higher quality output can generate. If output markets are competitive and customers are willing to pay for the additional services provided by some banks, these banks should receive higher revenues that just compensate for their extra costs. Banks would be sorted into market niches that differ by service quality or

on is deemed inefficient. Average efficiency in terms of the percent of expected profit being earned for a given level of risk relative to the best-practice banks was found to be around 85%.

intensity, with customers who need or prefer higher quality or more service paying more per dollar of their loan or deposit. Since the higher interest rates or fees received by the higher quality providers just cover their extra production costs, these banks survive in competitive equilibrium. For example, banks that take on more information-problematic loans should charge higher interest rates or fees to cover their extra origination, monitoring, and control costs than banks that lend to equally risky, but more informationally transparent, borrowers. The alternative profit function essentially replicates the cost function except that it adds revenues to the dependent variable. It accounts for the additional revenue earned by high-quality banks, allowing it to offset their additional costs of providing the higher service levels. So it does not penalize high-quality banks in terms of their efficiency measure, whereas the cost function might. Thus, if banks do not have market power, alternative profit efficiency should be thought of as a better measure of cost efficiency, rather than profit efficiency, since it does not take into account any errors in the quantities of variable outputs.[6] Other methods of controlling for differences in output quality are discussed in Section 3.3.

Alternative profit efficiency might also prove useful if the variable outputs are not completely variable, as in condition (ii) above. Banks differ in size by more than 1000-fold, even within the same local markets. Most banks have fewer than $100 million in assets, yet they operate side-by-side with megabanks with over $100 billion in assets. Clearly, a bank below $100 million cannot reach the size of a megabank except after decades of growth, mergers, and acquisitions, yet the standard profit function essentially treats these large and small banks as if they should have the same variable outputs when facing the same input and output prices, fixed netputs, and environmental variables specified in the standard profit function. Thus, unless the $(w,p,z,v)$ variables give a strong prediction about the size of the bank, a scale bias may occur in the standard profit function, as larger banks have higher profits that are not explained by the exogenous variables. That is, large banks may (arguably mistakenly) be labeled as having higher standard profit efficiency than smaller

---

[6] Differences in output quality may also be partially captured in the standard profit function. However, since it holds output prices fixed, the standard profit function is less able to account for differences in revenue that compensate for differences in product quality, since these revenue differences may be partly reflected in measured prices. Berger et al. (1997a) found that both standard and alternative profit efficiencies helped control for differences in service quality in the property-liability insurance industry.

banks, by virtue of the fact that small banks simply cannot reach the same output levels. This potential problem does not occur to the same degree for the alternative profit function, since outputs are held constant statistically. That is, alternative profit efficiency compares the ability of banks to generate profits for the *same* levels of output and therefore reduces the scale bias that might be present in the standard profit efficiency measure.

The alternative profit efficiency concept may also be helpful in situations in which the firms exercise some market power in setting output prices, as in condition (iii). The standard profit function takes output prices as given and embodies the assumption that the bank can sell as much output as it wishes without having to lower its prices. This can lead to an understatement of standard profit efficiency for firms with output below efficient scale, since these firms might have to reduce their prices to increase output and, therefore, cannot earn as much as maximum potential profits as we measure it.[7]

Under conditions of market power, it may be appropriate to consider output levels as relatively fixed in the short run and allow for efficiency differences in the setting of prices and service quality. That is, an optimizing bank will set each of its prices at the point where the market just clears for its output and choice of service quality. Such a bank will also choose an optimizing service quality niche. Unlike the perfect competition case considered above, a firm with market power may be able to increase revenues more than costs by increasing service quality because there may not be other competitors or potential competitors at that quality niche. It is also possible that the optimizing choice may be to economize on service quality and keep costs relatively low. Alternative profit efficiency measures the extent to which firms are able to optimize in their choices of prices and service quality, as well as their abilities to keep costs low for a given output level. Alternative profit efficiency will also incorporate differences across firms in market power and their abilities to exploit it, which is good for the owners of the bank, but is not a

---

[7] Empirical studies have shown that banks in more concentrated local markets have some control over prices, paying lower rates to small depositors (Berger and Hannan, 1989) and charging higher rates to small borrowers (Hannan, 1991). These results are supported by studies that have tested price-taking versus price-setting behavior for banks, most often finding the latter (Hancock, 1986; Hannan and Liang, 1993; English and Hayes, 1991). Berger et al. (1996) estimated that about 68% of US bank revenues are from products competed for on a local basis and, therefore, could be subject to price-setting behavior. However, it is not known how many of the prices of these products actually do contain significant market power premiums.

social good in the same way that the other efficiencies are. Alternative profit efficiency may be viewed as a robustness check on standard profit efficiency, which takes prices as fixed and allows outputs to be totally variable.

The measurement of alternative profit efficiency may also be motivated in part by inaccuracies in the output price data, as in condition (iv) above. If the output price vector, $p$, is well measured, it should be strongly related to profits and explain a substantial portion of the variance of profits in the standard profit function. If prices are inaccurately measured – as is likely, given the available banking data – the predicted part of the standard profit function, $f$, in (4) would explain less of the variance of profits and yield more error in the estimation of the efficiency term $\ln u_\pi$.[8] In this event, it may be appropriate to try specifying other variables in the profit function that might yield a better fit, such as the output quantity vector, $y$, as in the alternative profit function.[9]

### 3 Efficiency Measurement Methods
Once the efficiency concepts are selected, the next issue is how to go about measuring them. Here we explore four methodological choices – the estimation technique, the functional form specified (assuming a para-

---

[8] There are good reasons to believe that output prices may be inaccurately measured in banking data. Regulatory reports, such as the Call Report form, require accurate figures on balance-sheet quantities, but do not directly measure prices. Rather, prices used in efficiency studies often must be constructed as ratios of revenue flows to stocks of assets, which may incorporate noise due to differences in asset duration, risk, liquidity, collateral, etc., as well as problems in matching revenue flows with the assets and time periods on which they were earned.

[9] One way to examine the problem of inaccurate price data is to determine the extent to which measured prices help predict profits in the profit function. Humphrey and Pulley (1997) specified a bank profit function with both prices, $p$, and quantities, $y$, included. A test of the joint hypothesis that all the $p$ parameters were zero was not rejected by the data, whereas the data did reject the hypothesis that all the $y$ parameters were zero. These results suggest that measured output prices do *not* have the theoretically predicted strong positive relationship with profits, and that output quantities do strongly predict profits, perhaps in part reflecting the scale bias problem discussed above the output quantities are not completely variable over the short term.

Another possible specification of the profit function would be to include *neither* output prices, $p$, nor quantities, $y$. Efficiency would be measured relative to a frontier in which firms optimize over output prices, quantities, and service quality jointly. As argued by Berger et al. (1996) and Humphrey and Pulley (1997), such a specification would likely be too sparse to describe the conditions faced by individual banks and would also be subject to scale biases. It is essentially rejected by the data in the Humphrey and Pulley (1997) test of the $y$ parameters in the profit function.

metric technique is chosen), the treatment of output quality, and the role of financial capital.

### 3.1 Estimation Techniques

The most common efficiency estimation techniques are data envelopment analysis (DEA), free disposable hull analysis, the stochastic frontier approach, the thick frontier approach, and the distribution-free approach.[10] The first two of these are nonparametric techniques and the latter three are parametric methods. Berger and Humphrey (1997) reported roughly an equal split between applications of nonparametric techniques (69 applications) and parametric methods (60 applications) to depository institutions data.

Here, we focus on the parametric techniques primarily because they correspond well with the cost and profit efficiency concepts outlined above. The nonparametric methods generally ignore prices and can, therefore, account only for technical inefficiency in using too many inputs or producing too few outputs. They cannot account for allocative inefficiency in misresponding to relative prices in choosing inputs and outputs, nor can they compare firms that tend to specialize in different inputs or outputs, because there is no way to compare one input or output with another without the benefit of relative prices. In addition, similar to the cost function, there is no way to determine whether the output being produced is optimal without value information on the outputs. Thus, the nonparametric techniques typically focus on *technological* optimization rather than *economic* optimization, and do not correspond to the cost and profit efficiency concepts discussed above. Another drawback of the nonparametric techniques is that they usually do not allow for random error in the data, assuming away measurement error and luck as factors affecting outcomes (although some progress is being made in this regard). In effect, they disentangle efficiency differences from random error by assuming that random error is zero. Studies of US banks that use nonparametric techniques report lower efficiency means on average than those using parametric techniques (an average of 72% vs. 84%) with much greater variation (a standard deviation of 17% vs. 6%), which could, in part, reflect some random error being counted as variations in measured efficiency in these studies (Berger and Humphrey, 1997, Table 3.2).

In the parametric methods, a bank is labeled inefficient if its costs are

---

[10]  See Mester (1994) for further description of these techniques.

higher or profits are lower than the best-practice bank after removing random error – in other words, if the estimated $\ln u_C$, $\ln u_\pi$, $\ln u_{a\pi}$, in Equations (2)–(4), respectively, differ substantially from the best-practice values.[11] The methods differ in the way $\ln u$ is disentangled from the composite error term $\ln u + \ln \varepsilon$. In our study we use both the stochastic frontier approach and the distribution-free approach. As discussed below, the distribution-free approach is our preferred technique.

In the *stochastic frontier approach*, the inefficiency and random error components of the composite error term are disentangled by making explicit assumptions about their distributions. The random error term, $\ln \varepsilon$, is assumed to be two-sided (usually normally distributed), and the inefficiency term, $\ln u$, is assumed to be one-sided (usually half-normally distributed). The parameters of the two distributions are estimated and can be used to obtain estimates of bank-specific inefficiency. The estimated mean of the conditional distribution of $\ln u$ given $\ln u + \ln \varepsilon$, i.e., $\ln \hat{u} \equiv \hat{E}(\ln u \mid \ln u + \ln \varepsilon)$ is usually used to measure inefficiency.

The distributional assumptions of the stochastic frontier approach are fairly arbitrary. Two prior studies found that when the inefficiencies were unconstrained, they behaved much more like symmetric normal distributions than half-normals, which would invalidate the identification of the inefficiencies (Bauer and Hancock, 1993; Berger, 1993).[12] As shown below, the data in the current study are often consistent with the presence of this potential problem – in many cases, the residuals are simply not skewed in the direction predicted by the assumptions of the stochastic frontier approach.

If panel data are available, some of these maintained distributional assumptions can be relaxed, and the *distribution-free approach* may be used. This method assumes that there is a core efficiency or average efficiency for each firm over time. The core inefficiency is distinguished from random error (and any temporary fluctuations in efficiency) by assuming that core inefficiency is persistent over time, while random errors tend to average out over time. In particular, a cost or profit function is

---

[11] In the typical application of the stochastic frontier approach, inefficiency is measured relative to the estimated frontier, $f$, rather than the best-practice bank, i.e., relative to a zero value for $\ln u$, which is not achieved by any firm in the sample. To make our efficiency measures comparable across techniques, we normalize our stochastic frontier efficiency estimates to be deviations from the smallest observed expected value for $\ln u$, so that the most efficient bank in the sample has efficiency of one.

[12] Other distributions have also been used, e.g., normal–truncated normal (Stevenson, 1980; Mester, 1996; Berger and DeYoung, 1997), normal–gamma (Stevenson, 1980; Greene, 1990), and normal–exponential (Mester, 1996).

estimated for each period of a panel data set. The residual in each separate regression is composed of both inefficiency, $\ln u$, and random error,
$\ln \varepsilon$, but the random component, $\ln \varepsilon$, is assumed to average out over time,
so that the average of a bank's residuals from all of the regressions, $\ln \hat{u}$,
will be an estimate of the inefficiency term, $\ln u$. For banks with very
low or very high $\ln \hat{u}$, an adjustment (called truncation) is made to assign
less extreme values of $\ln \hat{u}$ to these banks, since extreme values may indicate that random error, $\ln \varepsilon$, has not been completely purged by averaging. The resulting $\ln \hat{u}$ for each bank is used to compute its core
efficiency.[13]

### 3.2 Functional Forms for the Parametric Methods

We next consider the choice of a functional form for the cost and profit
functions, $f$, when one of the parametric methods is used to estimate efficiency. The most popular form in the literature is the translog; however,
it does not necessarily fit very well data that are far from the mean in
terms of output size or mix. McAllister and McManus (1993), and
Mitchell and Onvural (1996) showed that some of the differences in
results on scale economies across studies may be due to the ill-fit of the
translog function across a wide range of bank sizes, some of which may
be underrepresented in the data.

A more flexible functional form would help to alleviate this problem.
The Fourier-flexible functional form augments the translog by including
Fourier trigonometric terms. It is more flexible than the translog and is
a global approximation to virtually any cost or profit function. Several
studies have shown that it fits the data for US financial institutions better
than the translog.[14] Berger and DeYoung (1997) found that measured
inefficiencies were about twice as large when the translog was specified

---

[13] The reasonableness of these assumptions about the error term components depends on
the length of period studied. If too short a period is chosen, the random errors might
not average out, in which case random error would be attributed to inefficiency
(although truncation can help). If too long a period is chosen, the firm's core efficiency
becomes less meaningful because of changes in management and other events, i.e., it
might not be constant over the time period. Using 1984–1994 data on US commercial
banks and assuming a translog cost model, DeYoung (1997) showed that a six-year time
period, such as we use here, reasonably balanced these concerns.

[14] See McAllister and McManus (1993), Berger et al. (1997a), Berger and DeYoung (1997),
Berger et al. (1997b), and Mitchell and Onvural (1996). McAllister and McManus (1993)
also used kernel regression and spline estimation techniques to obtain better global
properties.

in place of the Fourier-flexible form.[15] Here, we estimate the Fourier-flexible functional form and allow our cost and profit frontiers to vary each year, and also evaluate the effects of switching to the translog by restricting the Fourier terms to be zero.[16]

### 3.3 Output Quality

Theoretically, in comparing one bank's efficiency to another's, the comparison should be between banks producing the *same* output quality. But there are likely to be unmeasured differences in quality because the banking data does not fully capture the heterogeneity in bank output. The amount of service *flow* associated with financial products is by necessity usually assumed to be proportionate to the dollar value of the *stock* of assets or liabilities on the balance sheet, which can result in significant mismeasurement. For example, commercial loans can vary in size, repayment schedule, risk, transparency of information, type of collateral, covenants to be enforced, etc. These differences are likely to affect the costs to the bank of loan origination, ongoing monitoring and control, and financing expense. Unmeasured differences in product quality may be incorrectly measured as differences in cost inefficiency.

We have already discussed how the alternative profit function can help control for unmeasured differences in output quality. Other studies took another approach and included variables intended to control for the quality of bank output. For example, Hughes and Mester (1993), Hughes et al. (1996, 1999), and Mester (1996) included the volume of

---

[15] Other functional forms have also been specified. Mester (1992) estimated a hybrid translog function, and Berger et al. (1993) estimated a Fuss normalized quadratic variable profit function. Hughes et al. (1996, 1999, 1997) estimated a utility-maximization model based on the Almost Ideal Demand System consisting of profit and input share equations. If risk neutrality is imposed on this system, it corresponds to the standard translog cost function and input share equations.

[16] To further increase flexibility, one can allow the parameters being estimated to differ across banks that may be using different production technologies, e.g., banks of different sizes, banks facing different regulatory regimes, banks operating in different time periods, or different types of institutions. Numerous studies have allowed the coefficients to vary according to whether the bank operates in a state that restricts branching or a state that allows intrastate branching (e.g., Berger, 1993). Mester (1993) found a significant difference in both the frontier parameters and parameters of the error term distribution in the stochastic frontier method for mutual and stock-owned savings and loans. Most studies using the distribution-free method allow the frontier parameters to vary over time. Akhavein et al. (1997b) used random coefficient estimation techniques, which allow each bank to have its own parameters.

nonperforming loans as a control for loan quality in studies of US banks, and Berg et al. (1992) included loan losses as an indicator of the quality of loan evaluations in a DEA study of Norwegian bank productivity.

Whether it is appropriate econometrically to include nonperforming loans and loan losses in the bank's cost, standard profit, and alternative profit functions depends on the extent to which these variables are exogenous. Nonperforming loans and loan losses would be exogenous if caused by negative economic shocks ("bad luck"), but they could be endogenous, either because management is inefficient in managing its portfolio ("bad management") or because it has made a conscious decision to reduce short-run expenses by cutting back on loan origination and monitoring resources ("skimping").[17] Berger and DeYoung (1997) tested the bad luck, bad management, and skimping hypotheses and found mixed evidence on the exogeneity of nonperforming loans. In our empirical analysis below we attempt to solve this problem using the ratio of nonperforming loans to total loans in the bank's state. Our state average variable is almost entirely exogenous to any individual bank, but allows us to control for negative shocks that may affect the bank.

### 3.4 The Role of Financial Capital

Another important aspect of efficiency measurement is the treatment of financial capital. A bank's insolvency risk depends on its financial capital available to absorb portfolio losses, as well as on the portfolio risks themselves. Insolvency risk affects bank costs and profits via the risk premium the bank has to pay for uninsured debt, and through the intensity of risk management activities the bank undertakes. For this reason, the financial capital of the bank should be considered when studying efficiency. To some extent, controlling for the interest rates paid on uninsured debt helps account for differences in risk, but these rates are imperfectly measured.

Even apart from risk, a bank's capital level directly affects costs by providing an alternative to deposits as a funding source for loans. Interest paid on debt counts as a cost, but dividends paid do not. On the other

---

[17] Of course, even if the level of nonperforming loans does reflect bank choice to some extent, it could still be appropriate to include it in the cost and profit functions if it is thought to reflect a less frequent decision on the part of the bank (e.g., credit policy) than production decisions. This is the same logic that allows the output levels, which are ultimately endogenous variables chosen by the bank, to be included in the cost and alternative profit functions.

hand, raising equity typically involves higher costs than raising deposits. If the first effect dominates, measured costs will be higher for banks using a higher proportion of debt financing; if the second effect dominates, measured costs will be lower for these banks. Large banks depend more on debt financing to finance their portfolios than small banks do, so a failure to control for equity could yield a scale bias.

The specification of capital in the cost and profit functions also goes part of the way toward accounting for different risk preferences on the parts of banks. The cost, standard profit, and alternative profit efficiency concepts discussed in Section 2 take as given that banks are risk neutral. But if some banks are more risk averse than others, they may hold a higher level of financial capital than maximizes profits or minimizes costs. If financial capital is ignored, the efficiency of these banks would be mismeasured, even though they behave optimally given their risk preferences. Hughes et al. (1996, 1999, 1997) and Hughes and Moon (1995) tested and rejected the assumption of risk neutrality for banks.

Despite these arguments, only a few efficiency studies have included financial capital. Hancock (1985, 1986) conditioned an average-practice profit function on financial capital. Clark (1996) included capital in a model of economic cost and found that it eliminated measured scale diseconomies in production costs alone. The Hughes and Mester (1993, 1998) cost studies and the Hughes et al. (1996, 1997) profit studies incorporated financial capital and found increasing returns to scale at large-asset-size banks, unlike studies that did not incorporate capital. One possible reason is that large size confers diversification benefits that allow large banks to have lower capital ratios than smaller banks. Akhavein et al. (1997a) controlled for equity capital and found that profit efficiency increases as a result of mergers of large banks. Merged banks tend to shift their portfolios toward loans and away from securities for a given level of equity. This could reflect diversification benefits available to merged banks – better diversification would allow the merged bank to manage better the increased portfolio risk with the same amount of equity capital. In the efficiency estimates presented below, we incorporate financial capital in the cost and profit function specifications.

## 4 Efficiency Correlates
Once we have controlled for the efficiency concepts and measurement methods used, and applied these concepts and methods to the same data set, what explains the remaining differences in efficiency across banks?

The answer to this question has important implications for public policy, research, and bank management. A useful first step is to explore the effects of a number of potential correlates of bank efficiency – various bank, market, and regulatory characteristics that are at least partially exogenous to efficiency and so may help explain the observed large differences in efficiency across banks. Several papers have performed analyses along these lines.[18] A two-step procedure is typically used, whereby firm efficiency is estimated using one of the techniques described above and is then regressed on, or tested for correlation with, a set of variables describing the characteristics being investigated.[19]

Some econometric issues make such analyses suggestive but not conclusive. First, the dependent variable in the regressions, efficiency, is an estimate, but the standard error of this estimate is not accounted for in the subsequent regression or correlation analysis. Second, none of the variables used in the regressions is completely exogenous, and the endogeneity of any regressor can bias the coefficient estimates on all the regressors. Even a characteristic like the identity of the bank's primary federal regulator is somewhat endogenous, since banks can change their charters. Endogeneity makes conclusions about causation problematic. As an alternative to regression analysis, simple correlations are provided in some papers to underscore the fact that causation may run in both directions.

The different measurement techniques and efficiency concepts used and time periods and samples studied make it difficult to compare the results of the regression analyses across studies. The potential correlates used in the secondstage regressions also vary substantially across studies, sometimes because each study has a particular focus – e.g., market structure, geographic diversification, or corporate control.

Most studies included the asset size of the institution, but no consistent picture emerges of its relationship with efficiency.[20] Evidence on

---

[18] Bank studies include Aly et al. (1990), Berger et al. (1993), Pi and Timme (1993), Kaparakis et al. (1994), Berger and Hannan (1998), Kwan and Eisenbeis (1995), Spong et al. (1995), Hughes et al. (1996, 1999), and Mester (1996); savings and loan studies include Cebenoyan et al. (1993), Mester (1993), and Hermalin and Wallace (1994).

[19] The regressions are usually linear, but Mester (1993, 1996) used the logistic functional form, as the stochastic frontier inefficiency estimates varied between zero and one.

[20] Hermalin and Wallace (1994) and Kaparakis et al. (1994) found a significant negative relationship; Berger et al. (1993) found a significant positive relationship; and Aly et al. (1990), Berger and Hannan (1998), Cebenoyan et al. (1993), Mester (1993, 1996), and Pi and Timme (1993) found an insignificant relationship.

organizational form was also mixed.[21] There is weak evidence that banks in holding companies are more efficient than independent banks.[22] The relationship between the size of the CEO's stock ownership and efficiency varies across studies.[23] There is limited evidence that banks operating in more concentrated markets are less efficient, supporting the "quiet life" theory that inefficiency has been sustainable in banking because competition has not been robust.[24]

Most of the studies have found that well-capitalized banks and S&Ls are more efficient. This is consistent with moral hazard theory that suggests managers of institutions closer to bankruptcy might be inclined to pursue their own interests. But causation could run the other way – less efficient institutions have lower profits, leading to lower capital ratios. Another fairly general finding among the bank studies is that more efficient banks have lower levels of nonperforming loans, but as described above, nonperforming loans likely have exogenous and endogenous components.[25] As this summary suggests, more work is needed before a complete picture of financial institution efficiency emerges, and this paper tries to help complete the picture.

## 5 Empirical Design for Efficiency Estimation

This section outlines and compares the different econometric models used in the estimations below and the assumptions that these models impose on the data. To facilitate exposition and keep the number of comparisons under control, we choose a "preferred" model and measure the effects of deviations from this model one at a time. That is, we choose what we believe to be the best set of variables, best cost and profit function specification, and best frontier efficiency technique within our data and computational constraints and then estimate the effects of making alternative choices one by one in a controlled experiment. Note that our

---

[21] Cebenoyan et al. (1993) and Hermalin and Wallace (1994) found stock S&Ls more efficient than mutual S&Ls, while Mester (1993) found the reverse, likely because a later sample period was examined.

[22] Mester (1996) found a significant correlation, but Spong et al. (1995) did not.

[23] Pi and Timme (1993) found a significant negative relationship, Berger and Hannan (1998) found an insignificant negative relationship, and Spong et al. (1995) found a positive relationship.

[24] See Berger and Hannan (1998).

[25] We do not include financial capital and nonperforming loans in our analysis of correlates described below, since we control for these in the cost and profit models from which our efficiency measures are derived.

"preferred" model would not be preferred by most or even necessarily many researchers. There is still substantial disagreement over the best methods of estimation, but they do seem to be converging.

We estimate the efficiency of almost 6,000 US commercial banks that were in continuous existence with complete, accurate data over the six-year period 1990–1995.[26] We will discuss here the variables, specification, and estimation method of the preferred model, then briefly mention the alternatives that will be explored in the empirical analysis below.

### 5.1  Variables Included in the Preferred Specifications of the Cost and Profit Functions

Table 3.1 gives the definitions of all the variables specified in the cost, standard profit, and alternative profit functions, as well as their sample means and standard deviations for the most recent year of data, 1995. The variable input prices, $w$, include the interest rates on purchased funds and core deposits as well as the price of labor. Expenditures on these inputs comprise the vast majority of all banking costs. The variable outputs, $y$, include consumer loans, business loans, and securities, the latter category being measured simply as gross total assets less loans and physical capital, so that all financial assets are considered to be outputs. This specification of financial assets as outputs and financial liabilities and physical factors as inputs is consistent with the "intermediation" approach or "asset approach" to modeling bank production (Sealey and Lindley, 1977).[27]

We specify risk-weighted off-balance-sheet items, physical capital, and financial equity capital as fixed netputs, $z$. Off-balance-sheet items are included in the model because they are often effective substitutes for directly issued loans, requiring similar information-gathering costs of origination and ongoing monitoring and control of the counterparties, and presumably similar revenues if these items are competitive substitutes for direct loans. The use of the Basle Accord risk weights implies that these items have approximately the same perceived (according to

---

[26] Between 8,387 and 11,077 banks were used in estimating the cost and profit functions each year 1990–1995, and the restrictions that all the cost and profit function data be complete for all years left 5,949 banks for which we report efficiencies. These banks had about half of the assets of the US banking industry as of December 1995.

[27] In cost function models, deposits may be specified as inputs, or outputs, or as having both input and output attributes. However, we cannot specify deposits as outputs here, since it would be too difficult to measure an output price for deposits for use in the standard profit function. This is because deposit services are often paid for by paying below-market rates on deposits rather than charging a positive price or fee for services.

Table 3.1. *Variables employed in the cost, standard profit, and alternative profit functions, means and standard deviations for 1995 only.*

| Symbol | Definition | Mean | Standard deviation |
|---|---|---|---|
| *Dependent variables* | | | |
| $C$ | Variable operating plus interest costs, includes costs of purchased funds, deposits, and labor | 13,466 | 105,671 |
| $\pi$ | Variable profits, includes revenues from loans and securities less variable costs | 8,628 | 66,767 |
| *Variable input prices* | | | |
| $w_1$ | Price of purchased funds (jumbo CDs, foreign deposits, federal funds purchased, all other liabilities except core deposits) | 0.0410 | 0.0111 |
| $w_2$ | Price of core deposits (domestic transactions accounts, time, and savings) | 0.0284 | 0.0081 |
| $w_3$ | Price of labor (1000's of constant dollars per employee) | 32.5 | 6.8 |
| *Variable output quantities (cost and alternative profit functions only)* | | | |
| $y_1$ | Consumer loans (installment and credit card and related plans) | 38,179 | 298,130 |
| $y_2$ | Business loans (all other loans) | 164,952 | 1,489,552 |
| $y_3$ | Securities (all non-loan financial assets, i.e., Gross Total Assets $- y_1 - y_2 - z_2$) | 114,916 | 838,231 |
| *Variable output prices (standard profit function only)* | | | |
| $p_1$ | Price of consumer loans | 0.0926 | 0.0329 |
| $p_2$ | Price of business loans | 0.0898 | 0.0126 |
| $p_3$ | Price of securities | 0.0468 | 0.0087 |
| *Fixed netput quantities* | | | |
| $z_1$ | Off-balance-sheet items (commitments, letters of credit, derivatives, etc.) measured using Basle Accord risk weights to be risk-equivalent to loans | 26,367 | 445,427 |
| $z_2$ | Physical capital (premises and other fixed assets) | 4,818 | 38,909 |
| $z_3$ | Financial equity capital | 26,686 | 184,880 |

Table 3.1. (cont.)

| Symbol | Definition | Mean | Standard deviation |
|--------|-----------|------|--------------------|
| *Environmental variables* | | | |
| NPL | Nonperforming loans (past due at least 90 days or on nonaccrual basis) divided by total loans | 0.0258 | 0.0217 |
| STNPL | Weighted average of NPL for the state, using proportions of the loans issued by banks in the state as the weights | 0.0220 | 0.0043 |
| Number of observations, cost and alternative profit regressions, 1995 | | 9,002 | |
| Number of observations, standard profit regressions, 1995 | | 8,378 | |

*Note:* All financial variables measured in 1000s of constant 1994 dollars. Prices of financial assets and liabilities are measured as interest rates. All stock values are real quantities as of the December call report and all prices are flows over the year divided by these stocks. Because the price data are subject to error from this procedure, we eliminate observations in which the prices on assets and liabilities (which are interest rates) are more than 2.5 standard deviations from the mean value for that year. Similarly, we eliminate observations in which liability and asset rates are more than 0.10 above and more than 0.50 above the one-year Treasury rate, respectively. The standard profit function uses fewer observations because these procedures eliminated some output price data. We also eliminated observations in which equity was below 1% of gross total assets because the data for such banks are suspicious. From these regressions, efficiency is reported only for the 5,949 observations in which all of these data plus data on other variables in Table 2 are available for every year 1990–1995. All of the continuous variables that can take on the value 0 have 1 added before taking logs in specifying the cost and profit regressions. This applies to the $y$'s, $z$'s, NPL, and STNPL. For $\pi$, an additional adjustment was made because profits can take on negative values (see text).

the Accord) credit risk and, therefore, approximately the same origination, monitoring, and control costs as loans to these same parties. These items are also concentrated in large banks. As a consequence, a scale bias might be present if no account were taken of these items, as larger banks would have disproportionately higher costs relative to their measured outputs. We specify these items as fixed instead of variable primarily because of the difficulty of obtaining accurate output price information for use in specifying the standard profit function.[28]

The treatment of physical capital as a fixed input is relatively standard in efficiency estimation, but specification of equity is not. The reasons for including equity were discussed in Section 3.4. As discussed further in Section 5.2 below, the specification of equity as fixed helps resolve several estimation problems.

Finally, the environmental variables, $v$, are limited to the nonperforming loan to total loan ratio either for the bank (NPL) or for the state in which the bank is located (STNPL). In our preferred specification, we use STNPL, since it is almost entirely exogenous and controls for bad luck in the bank's environment. We are not aware of any previous research in which STNPL has been specified. In principle, $v$ could include other measures of the economic conditions faced by the bank, such as the income growth or unemployment rate of the state where the bank is located, but these variables are closely related to the state's nonperforming loan record and would make interpretation of the coefficients on NPL and STNPL more difficult. Additionally, we could have included regulatory environmental variables such as state restrictions on branching or on bank holding company expansion. We exclude regulatory information from the efficiency estimates because one of our goals is to test how efficiency is related to these laws by treating them as potential correlates of efficiency.

### 5.2 Functional Form of the Preferred Specifications

Our preferred model for estimating efficiency specifies the Fourier-flexible functional form, which is a global approximation that includes a standard translog plus Fourier trigonometric terms. For the cost function we specify

---

[28] A prior study that specified a number of off-balance-sheet activities found that these activities had little effect on cost scale and product mix economies (Jagtiani et al., 1995). However, we are unaware of any frontier efficiency studies of either costs or profits that have taken these activities into account.

$$\ln(C/w_3 z_3) = \alpha + \sum_{i=1}^{2} \beta_i \ln(w_i/w_3)$$

$$+ \frac{1}{2} \sum_{i=1}^{2} \sum_{j=1}^{2} \beta_{ij} \ln(w_i/w_3) \ln(w_j/w_3) + \sum_{k=1}^{3} \gamma_k \ln(y_k/z_3)$$

$$+ \frac{1}{2} \sum_{k=1}^{3} \sum_{m=1}^{3} \gamma_{km} \ln(y_k/z_3) \ln(y_m/z_3) + \sum_{r=1}^{2} \delta_r \ln(z_r/z_3)$$

$$+ \frac{1}{2} \sum_{r=1}^{2} \sum_{s=1}^{2} \delta_{rs} \ln(z_r/z_3) \ln(z_s/z_3)$$

$$+ \sum_{i=1}^{2} \sum_{k=1}^{3} \eta_{ik} \ln(w_i/w_3) \ln(y_k/z_3)$$

$$+ \sum_{i=1}^{2} \sum_{r=1}^{2} \rho_{ir} \ln(w_i/w_3) \ln(z_r/z_3)$$

$$+ \sum_{k=1}^{3} \sum_{r=1}^{2} \tau_{kr} \ln(y_k/z_3) \ln(z_r/z_3) + \sum_{n=1}^{7} [\phi_n \cos(x_n) + w_n \sin(x_n)]$$

$$+ \sum_{n=1}^{7} \sum_{q=n}^{7} [\phi_{nq} \cos(x_n + x_q) + \omega_{nq} \sin(x_n + x_q)]$$

$$+ \sum_{n=1}^{7} [\phi_{nnn} \cos(x_n + x_n + x_n) + \omega_{nnn} \sin(x_n + x_n + x_n)]$$

$$+ v_1 \ln(\text{STNPL}) + \frac{1}{2} v_{11} [\ln(\text{STNPL})]^2 + \ln u_C + \ln \varepsilon_C, \tag{8}$$

where $(y_k/z_3)$, $(z_r/z_3)$, and the STNPL variables have 1 added for every firm in order to avoid taking the natural log of zero, the $x_n$ terms, $n = 1, \ldots, 7$ are rescaled values of the $\ln(w_i/w_3)$, $i = 1, 2$, $\ln(y_k/z_3)$, $k = 1, 2, 3$, and $\ln(z_r/z_3)$, $r = 1, 2$, such that each of the $x_n$ is in the interval $[0,2\pi]$ and $\pi$ refers to the number of radians here (not profits), and the standard symmetry restrictions apply to the translog portion of the function (i.e., $\beta_{ij} = \beta_{ji}$, $y_{km} = y_{mk}$, $\delta_{rs} = \delta_{sr}$).[29]

---

[29] We cut 10% off each end of the $[0,2\pi]$ interval so that the $x_n$ span $[0.1 \times 2\pi, 0.9 \times 2\pi]$ to reduce approximation problems near the endpoints. The formula for $x_n$ is $0.2\pi - \mu \times a + \mu \times$ variable, where $[a,b]$ is the range of the variable being transformed, and $\mu \equiv (0.9 \times 2\pi - 0.1 \times 2\pi)/(b - a)$. We limit the third-order Fourier terms to include just the interactions of the own terms because of computational limitations in applying the stochastic frontier approach below. The model as shown includes 122 net free parameters after imposing symmetry. We exclude consideration of factor share equations embodying

The standard and alternative profit functions use essentially the same specification with a few changes. First, the dependent variable for the profit functions replaces $\ln(C/w_3 z_3)$ with $\ln[(\pi/w_3 z_3) = |(\pi/w_3 z_3)^{\min}| + 1]$, where $|(\pi/w_3 z_3)^{\min}|$ indicates the absolute value of the minimum value of $(\pi/w_3 z_3)$ over all banks for the same year. Thus, the constant $\theta = |(\pi/w_3 z_3)^{\min}| + 1$ is added to every firm's dependent variable in the profit functions so that the natural log is taken of a positive number, since the minimum profits are typically negative. Thus, for the firm with the lowest value of $(\pi/w_3 z_3)$ for that year, the dependent variable will be $\ln(1) = 0$. For the alternative profit function, this is the only change in specification (other than relabelling the composite error term as $\ln u_{a\pi} + \ln \varepsilon_{a\pi}$), since the exogenous variables are identical to those for the cost function. For the standard profit function, the terms containing the variable output quantities, $\ln(y_k/z_3)$, and their trigonometric $x_n$ terms are replaced by the corresponding output prices, $\ln(p_k/w_3)$, and their $x_n$ trigonometric terms.

The Fourier-flexible form is a global approximation because the $\cos x_n$, $\sin x_n$, $\cos 2x_n$, $\sin 2x_n$, etc., terms are mutually orthogonal over the $[0,2\pi]$ interval, so that each additional term can make the approximating function closer to the true path of the data wherever it is most needed.[30] A good fit of the data for the estimated efficient frontier is important in estimating efficiency, because inefficiencies are measured as deviations from this frontier.

As shown in Equation (8), all of the cost, profit, input price, and output price terms – including the Fourier terms for prices before transformation – are normalized by the last input price, $w_3$, in order to impose linear homogeneity on the model. That is, on the efficient frontier, a doubling of all input prices exactly doubles costs, and a doubling of all input and output prices doubles standard profits.[31] This normalization is the only way to impose homogeneity on the Fourier-flexible specification, since unlike the translog terms, the Fourier terms are not multiplicative.

We specify all of the cost, profit, variable output quantities, and other fixed netput quantities as ratios to the fixed equity capital input, $z_3$, to control for heteroskedasticity, to help control for scale biases in estima-

Shephard's Lemma or Hotelling's Lemma restrictions because this would impose the undesirable assumption of no allocative inefficiencies.

[30] The orthogonality is perfect only if the data are evenly distributed over the $[0,2\pi]$ interval, but in practice the Fourier terms have improved the fit of the data in every application of which we are aware.

[31] The homogeneity restriction does not have to be imposed on the alternative profit function, but it is imposed to keep the functional forms equivalent.

tion, and to give the models more economic interpretation. Since the costs and profits of the largest firms are many times larger than those of the smallest firms, large firms undoubtedly would have random errors with much larger variances in the absence of the normalization. In contrast, firms of different sizes have ratios of costs or profits to equity that typically vary only by a few-fold. This is particularly important because the inefficiency terms $\ln \hat{u}_C$, $\ln \hat{u}_\pi$, and $\ln \hat{u}_{a\pi}$ are derived from the composite residuals, which might make the variance of the efficiencies dependent on bank size in the absence of normalization. Similarly, the normalization of the variable output and fixed netput quantities keep these variables from being very skewed for the large banks, so that the dependent and independent variables are roughly of the same order of magnitude.

Normalization by equity also reduces the scale bias discussed in Section 2.3 that is likely to be present, particularly in the standard profit function. Large banks will tend to have higher profits for a given set of prices, primarily because they were able to gain size over a period of decades, a feat that small banks cannot achieve in the short run. However, the profits per dollar of equity and assets per dollar of equity of large banks are well within the achievable range for small banks. Moreover, even in the short run, equity is often the variable that limits bank size. Regulators and market participants generally tie the allowable size of the bank, especially its loan portfolio, to its quantity of equity capital available to absorb loan losses. Normalization by equity makes the dependent variable reasonably equally achievable for all banks.

Normalization by equity also has a particular economic meaning. The dependent variable in the profit functions in essentially the return on equity, or ROE, achieved by the bank (normalized by prices and with a constant added), or a measure of how well the bank is using its scarce financial capital.[32] This measure may be closer to the goal of the bank than maximizing the level of profits, particularly in banking, which is one of the most highly financially leveraged industries. Shareholders are interested in their rate of return on equity, which is approximated by ROE, and most debtholders do not put much pressure on banks to earn profits because their returns are guaranteed by deposit insurance.

*5.3 Preferred Frontier Efficiency Estimation Technique*
Our preferred method of estimating efficiency is the distribution-free approach, which disentangles the inefficiency term, $\ln u$, from the random

---

[32] Unfortunately, our accounting measure of equity does not perfectly correspond to the market value of the bank, but market values are unavailable for most banks.

error term, ln $\varepsilon$, in Equations (2)–(4) and (6) by assuming that inefficiencies are relatively stable over time and random errors tend to average out over time.

We briefly sketch the procedure as it is applied here. The cost, standard profit, and alternative profit equations are estimated separately for each year, 1990–1995, allowing the coefficients to vary to reflect changes in technology, regulation, and market environment. The average residual for each bank $b$ is formed, which is an estimate of ln $u_C^b$, ln $u_\pi^b$, or ln $u_{a\pi}^b$, depending on the equation. Despite the assumption that random error averages out to zero over time, we realize that the extreme values of these inefficiency estimates may reflect substantial random components. Thus, we use truncation to reassign less extreme values to banks with the most extreme values in each of 10 bank size categories. We assign to each bank in the top and bottom 5% of the distribution of the average residuals in a size category the value for the bank that is just at the 5th or 95th percentile, respectively. (Other degrees of truncation are also tried, as discussed below.) Truncation is performed within size class deciles (by gross total assets) to reduce the effects of persistently good or bad luck for these banks relative to firms of their size (DeYoung and Nolle, 1996). The resulting estimates of the inefficiency terms, ln $\hat{u}_C^b$, ln $\hat{u}_\pi^b$, and ln $\hat{u}_{a\pi}^b$, along with their minimum or maximum values ln $\hat{u}_C^{min}$, ln $\hat{u}_\pi^{max}$, and ln $\hat{u}_{a\pi}^{max}$, are then substituted into Equations (3), (5), and (7), and the numerators and denominators are summed over the six years to estimate the efficiency ratios.[33]

The distribution-free method gives a single set of cost, standard profit, and alternative profit efficiency measures for each bank over the entire six-year period, 1990–1995. Since it is likely that relative efficiencies among the different banks shift somewhat over time because of changes in management, technical change, regulatory reform, the interest rate cycle, and other influences, this method describes the average deviation of each firm from the best-average-practice frontier. That is, our core efficiency estimates how well a bank tends to do relative to its competitors over a range of conditions over time, rather than a firm's relative efficiency at any one point in time. Besides the fact that this method uses less arbitrary assumptions to disentangle inefficiencies from random

---

[33] Because the costs and profits in the dependent variables are expressed in terms of ratios to $w_3z_3$, the $\exp(\hat{f}(\cdot))$ terms in the efficiency ratios are replaced by $w_3z_3 \times \exp(\hat{f}(\cdot))$, where $\hat{f}(\cdot)$ is the predicted part of the cost or profit function. In order to offset the nonlinearities introduced by exponentiating and including the $\theta$ terms, all the predicted costs and profits are multiplicatively adjusted so that the average predicted cost or profit for each year equals the average actual cost or profit for the same year.

error, we believe that by averaging over a number of conditions, this method gives a better indication of a bank's longer-term performance and how it is likely to perform in the future than any method that relies on a bank's performance under a single set of circumstances.

### 5.4 Deviations from Our Preferred Efficiency Measurement Methods

We measure the effects of several deviations from our preferred methods for measuring efficiency to determine the effects of some of the assumptions commonly employed in the efficiency literature. By changing just one assumption at a time, but leaving the data set and all other assumptions unchanged, we aim to isolate the individual effects. The deviations we try are: (1) specifying the translog functional form in place of the preferred Fourier-flexible specification, (2) trying several different specifications of the nonperforming loan ratios (NPL and STNPL), (3) removing equity capital from the model, and (4) using the stochastic frontier approach in place of the distribution-free approach.

## 6 The Empirical Results Pertaining to the Efficiency Concepts and Measurement Methods

Table 3.2 shows the means and standard deviations of the efficiencies estimated in the preferred model and in each variation, along with the rank-order correlations of the efficiencies from each variation with those from the preferred model. The means and standard deviations are weighted by the denominators of the efficiency ratios (estimated cost or potential profits) to represent the proportion of the entire sample's resources that are used efficiently or potential profits that are earned.[34]

### 6.1 Efficiency Estimates from the Preferred Model

The mean cost efficiency from the preferred model of 0.868 suggests that about 13.2% of costs are wasted on average relative to a best-practice firm. The 0.868 figure is within the range found in the literature, but is slightly higher than the most typical finding of about 80% cost efficiency. The slightly higher figure might be explained by the fact that we are

---

[34] The cost, standard profit, and alternative profit function coefficient estimates are available upon request from the authors.

Table 3.2. *Measured bank X-efficiency using various econometric models, US banks 1990–1995 (weighted mean efficiencies, standard deviations in parentheses, correlations).*

| Model specification | Cost efficiency | Standard profit efficiency | Alternative profit efficiency |
|---|---|---|---|
| Preferred model: Distribution-free approach, Fourier-flexible specification, Includes state average nonperforming loan ratios and equity capital | 0.868 (0.062) | 0.549 (0.208) | 0.463 (0.195) |
| Same as preferred model, except uses translog specification in place of Fourier-flexible specification | 0.860 (0.063) | 0.539 (0.207) | 0.452 (0.194) |
| Rank-order correlation with preferred model: | 0.979 | 0.995 | 0.995 |
| Same as preferred model, except includes bank's own NPL ratio instead of state average STNPL | 0.866 (0.062) | 0.550 (0.209) | 0.469 (0.198) |
| Rank-order correlation with preferred model: | 0.992 | 0.999 | 0.997 |
| Same as preferred model, except includes bank's own NPL ratio in addition to state average STNPL | 0.866 (0.062) | 0.550 (0.208) | 0.471 (0.197) |
| Rank-order correlation with preferred model: | 0.992 | 0.999 | 0.999 |
| Same as preferred model, except excludes both STNPL and NPL | 0.869 (0.061) | 0.546 (0.207) | 0.461 (0.196) |
| Rank-order correlation with preferred model: | 0.999 | 0.9999 | 0.998 |
| Same as preferred model, except excludes equity capital | 0.869 (0.062) | 0.088 (0.287) | 0.106 (0.301) |
| Rank-order correlation with preferred model: | 0.834 | 0.215 | 0.425 |

Table 3.2. *(cont.)*

| Model specification | Cost efficiency | Standard profit efficiency | Alternative profit efficiency |
|---|---|---|---|
| Same as preferred model, except stochastic frontier approach, half-normal distribution[a] | 0.942 (0.023) | — — | 0.351[b] (0.709) |
| Rank-order correlation with preferred model: | 0.988 | — | 0.912 |
| Number of observations: | 5,949 | 5,949 | 5,949 |

*Note*:
[a] For the stochastic frontier approach to yield meaningful efficiency estimates, the cost or profit residuals must have the correct skew (rightward for cost, leftward for profit). In some cases this did not occur, including standard profit efficiency in all six years, cost efficiency in 1992, and alternative profit efficiency in 1994 and 1995. The stochastic frontier cost efficiency estimate is therefore based on data from 1990, 1991, 1993, 1994, and 1995 only, and alternative profit efficiency is based on data from 1990–1993. To be consistent with the distribution-free approach, the stochastic frontier efficiencies were calculated by comparing firms to the best observed expected value of ln $u$ so that the best-practice firm has an efficiency of 1.
[b] Three banks were eliminated from this calculation because they had negative potential profits, and the profit efficiency ratios are meaningless in these cases. This leaves a sample size of 5,946.

examining data from the first six years of the 1990s, rather than the 1980s, the period of study for most earlier work.[35]

The mean efficiencies for the standard and alternative profit functions are similar to each other, both showing that about half of the potential profits that could be earned by a best-practice firm are lost to inefficiency. These figures are also well within the observed range from the few other profit efficiency studies. The standard deviations of the profit efficiencies

[35] The reported efficiency estimates are based on 5% truncation of the average residuals, but other degrees of truncation were also tried. The average measured cost efficiencies at the 0%, 1%, 5%, and 10% truncation levels were 0.689, 0.784, 0.868, and 0.901 respectively. Thus, measured efficiency increases considerably when the degree of truncation rises up to 5% but the increase tapers off after this point. This suggests that 5% truncation removes most of the random error not already eliminated by averaging over time. Moreover, further truncation would not change the efficiency estimates by any economically meaningful amount. Similar results obtained for the measured profit efficiencies.

are about 20 percentage points, suggesting that these efficiencies are quite dispersed, with many firms earning considerably more or less than the average figure. By contrast, the cost efficiencies are more tightly distributed with a standard deviation of 6.2 percentage points.

We also note that the alternative profit function does not fit the data nearly as well as the standard profit function. The average adjusted $R^2$ (not shown) of the cost, standard profit, and alternative profit functions across the six years were 0.931, 0.607, and 0.329 respectively. Apparently, the measured prices of the loan and security outputs are more closely related to the profit dependent variable than are the quantities of these outputs. While a full investigation is beyond the scope of this paper, it seems likely that at least part of the explanation may lie in differing degrees of service quality or market power. That is, if some banks are providing service qualities that are more in demand and, therefore, are able to charge higher prices, or if some banks are able to exercise market power to raise profits substantially through higher loan prices, this would yield higher explanatory power for the standard profit function.

It is also noteworthy that the alternative profit efficiency ratios are lower on average than the standard profit efficiency ratios. This finding again could be explained by service quality or market power considerations. If, on average, banks are making poor service quality choices relative to the best-practice banks, and these choices are reflected in lower output prices and revenues, the alternative profit efficiency measures would correctly capture this source of inefficiency. Standard profit efficiency is less able to capture the effects of service quality because it takes output prices as given (although they are imperfectly measured). Similarly, if market power in setting output prices tends to explain profitability, the dispersion from the alternative profit frontier may be greater than from the standard profit frontier, because the alternative frontier does not control for output prices whereas the standard frontier does. Some evidence in favor of these explanations is that the alternative profit efficiency ratio is much more highly correlated with output prices than the standard profit efficiency ratio.[36] Thus, the firms measured as alternative profit inefficient receive relatively low prices for their outputs, perhaps reflecting either low service quality or lack of market power.

---

[36] Specifically, the correlations of Alt $\pi$ EFF with $p_1, p_2$, and $p_3$ are 0.288, 0.528, and 0.593, respectively, whereas the corresponding correlations for Std $\pi$ EFF are 0.198, 0.325, and 0.260, respectively. All are statistically significant at the 1% level.

## 6.2 Efficiency Estimates from Variations in
## Measurement Technique

In the first variation on our preferred model, the translog functional form is substituted for the preferred Fourier-flexible specification by restricting the coefficients of all the trigonometric terms (the $x$'s in Equation (8) above) to be zero.[37] The results here suggest only a small difference in average efficiencies and very little difference in efficiency dispersion or rank from using the more restricted specification. The average efficiencies are lower by about 1% of costs or potential profits in each case, with about the same degree of dispersion, and rank order correlations of 0.979 or higher with the preferred specification.

Formal statistical tests indicate that the coefficients on the Fourier terms are jointly significant at the 1% level in all 18 cases – the cost, standard profit, and alternative profit functions in all six years. However, the average improvement in goodness of fit or adjusted $R^2$ is relatively small. Thus, while the null hypothesis of the translog form is rejected from a statistical viewpoint and the Fourier-flexible efficiency estimates are likely more accurate, the improvement in fit is not significant from an economic viewpoint. Both functional forms yield essentially the same average level and dispersion of measured efficiency, and both rank the individual banks in almost the same order.

The next three variations in the table contain alternative specifications of nonperforming loans. In contrast to our preferred model, which specifies the state's nonperforming loan ratio in first- and second-order logged terms [ln STNPL and 1/2 (ln STNPL)$^2$], the next three specifications: (1) replace these terms with the bank's own ln NPL and 1/2 (ln NPL)$^2$; (2) include all of the STNPL and NPL terms; and (3) include none of the STNPL or NPL terms. The efficiency estimates are strikingly similar across the four specifications (including the preferred specification). The average efficiencies are all within 1 percentage point of each other, the measured dispersion is virtually identical, and rank-order correlations are all over 99%. Apparently, given the rest of our specification, the treatment of nonperforming loans is not materially important to the efficiency estimates.

Nonetheless, the coefficients of the STNPL and NPL variables in the

---

[37] If one of the specifications fits the data better than the other, it does not necessarily imply that measured efficiency will either increase or decrease. See Berger and DeYoung (1997) for more discussion. They found that the Fourier-flexible specification fit the data better and registered higher measured efficiency, but the efficiencies from both specifications were highly correlated.

cost and profit functions (not shown) did yield some insights as to which of the main hypotheses about the effects of nonperforming loans – bad luck, bad management, or skimping – is most consistent with the data. For each of the cost and profit equations, we formed the derivatives of the dependent variable with respect to STNPL and/or NPL evaluated at the mean values of the data (not shown). The data primarily supported the bad management hypothesis – i.e., that firms that are inefficient at managing their operations are also poor at managing their loan portfolios. In almost every case, the derivative with respect to NPL was unfavorable (positive for costs, negative for profits) and statistically significant at the 1% level. That is, firms with loan performance problems also tended to have high costs and low profits, consistent with the bad management hypothesis. This occurred whether STNPL was specified in the same equation, which should remove much of any bad luck effect. The derivative with respect to STNPL was often statistically significant in the predicted direction at the 1% or 5% level, but was not as consistent as the results for NPL. Thus, the bad luck hypothesis – under which exogenous conditions cause loan performance problems that raise costs received more limited support than the bad management hypothesis. The skimping hypothesis – under which nonperforming loans may be associated with *low* costs from choosing to put less effort into loan monitoring and control – was generally not supported by the data, or the hypothesis' consequences were overwhelmed by bad management effects. These results support our choice of specifying STNPL in the cost and profit functions and excluding NPL. STNPL appears to be a useful control variable for the bank's economic environment and is almost completely exogenous, whereas the inclusion of NPL likely adds an endogenous efficiency factor that should not be controlled for when estimating efficiency.

In the next variation, the equity capital fixed input $z_3$ is eliminated from the cost and profit functions. There is little effect on the average level or dispersion of cost efficiency, although the firms are ranked slightly differently, with a rank order correlation of 0.834 with the preferred model. More important, the average profit efficiencies fell from means of about 50% of potential profits earned on average to about 10%, with a much higher standard deviation and much lower rank-order correlation with the estimates from the preferred specification. This is not unexpected. As discussed above, the specification of equity as a fixed input in the preferred model reduces the scale bias that may be created by the fact that the equity capital of small banks cannot be expanded to match that of large banks and allow them to expand their asset portfolios greatly except after a period of decades. The dependent variable in this variation depends on the level of profits, which can be much higher for large banks, as opposed to our preferred specification, where the dependent variable is a function of the rate of return on equity, which is more comparable across size classes.

A breakdown of the measured profit efficiencies by size class when equity is removed (not shown) is consistent with these arguments. Banks with gross total assets below $50 million had mean measured standard and alternative profit efficiencies of –0.068 and 0.020, respectively, whereas the corresponding efficiencies for banks with over $10 billion were 0.768 and 0.783. Clearly, the removal of the equity control variable rewards large banks that have high levels of profits by virtue of their equity positions that have been built up over time, but these firms generally do not have particularly high rates of return on their equity. The evidence from this variation strongly supports our specification of equity capital as fixed in the preferred model.

The final variation shown in Table 3.2 uses the stochastic frontier approach where the inefficiencies are assumed to be half-normally distributed. The data, however, do not appear to fit that distribution very well. As described in the table, the skew of the data was not consistent with the half-normal assumptions in a number of cases. As a result, we do not have any standard profit efficiency estimates, and the cost and alternative efficiencies must be based on partial samples.

Despite these difficulties, the efficiencies estimated by the stochastic frontier approach are reasonably consistent with those of the preferred distribution-free approach. The average cost efficiency is somewhat higher with less dispersion, and the average alternative profit efficiency is somewhat lower with more dispersion, but in both cases, the rank-order correlations with the distribution-free method are over 90%.

Overall, the results of Table 3.2 suggest that variations in methodology usually do not affect measured efficiency substantially, except that profit efficiencies may be significantly scale biased when equity capital is excluded. For the most part, the findings support the choices made in our preferred approach and give us confidence to proceed from this point forward only with the estimates derived from the preferred model.

### 6.3 Cost Scale Economies in the Preferred Model

Table 3.3 shows cost ray scale efficiency by size class and breaks out the X-efficiency by size class as well. Scale efficiency is defined as the ratio of predicted minimum average costs to actual average costs, both adjusted to be on the X-efficient frontier (i.e., setting $\ln u_C$ to the

Table 3.3. *Cost scale and X-efficiency estimates by size class (weighted means).*

| Bank size (GTA) | # of banks | Scale efficiency | % Below efficient scale | $t^*$ | X-efficiency | Total cost efficiency | C/GTA |
|---|---|---|---|---|---|---|---|
| 0–$50M | 2,218 | 0.856 | 94.3 | 2.200 | 0.851 | 0.728 | 0.0482 |
| $50M–$100M | 1,794 | 0.842 | 96.5 | 2.363 | 0.870 | 0.733 | 0.0473 |
| $100M–$300M | 1,344 | 0.818 | 97.3 | 2.523 | 0.873 | 0.715 | 0.0466 |
| $300M–$1B | 392 | 0.786 | 99.8 | 2.815 | 0.876 | 0.688 | 0.0453 |
| $1B–$10B | 171 | 0.782 | 99.8 | 2.986 | 0.860 | 0.671 | 0.0436 |
| >$10B | 30 | 0.782 | 94.4 | 2.673 | 0.872 | 0.680 | 0.0427 |
| Total | 5,949 | 0.795 | 97.3 | 2.723 | 0.868 | 0.689 | 0.0443 |

*Note*: All figures (except C/GTA, which is weighted by GTA) are weighted by each bank's predicted costs; consequently the efficiencies indicate the proportion of the sample banks' costs that are used efficiently, with respect to scale efficiency, frontier efficiency, and total cost efficiency (the product of scale and frontier efficiency).

The percent below efficient scale refers to the percentage of banking costs that are incurred by firms below efficient scale.

$t^*$ is the bank's ratio of the cost-efficient size to its actual size, so that $t^* > 1$ indicates unexploited scale economies, and $t^* < 1$ indicates diseconomies of scale.

C/GTA is average cost or total cost divided by gross total assets, and is included as a raw-data version of cost efficiency. It has an unweighted mean of 0.0473 and a standard deviation of 0.0050.

Because the Fourier-flexible form has numerous local minima and maxima, the scale-efficient point for each bank's product mix was discovered by means of grid search over the interval [0.5, 5.0]. We limit the interval in order to avoid extrapolating too far from the observed data, but this interval should allow for any realistic short-term expansion or contraction prospects. Fortunately the limits on the interval were generally non-binding, as only 3 banks out of 5,949 had $t^*$ values at one of the endpoints (see Berger et al. (1997b) for more details on this method).

minimum in the sample and $\ln \varepsilon_C$ to zero). Total cost efficiency is the product of the scale and X-efficiency ratios.[38] The variable $t^*$ is the ratio of efficient scale to actual scale.

The basic result shown in Table 3.3 is that in every size class, the typical bank shows unexploited ray scale economies – i.e., that the bank's product mix could be produced at lower average cost by increasing the scale of output. The mean scale efficiencies are around 80%, suggesting

[38] The standard profit efficiencies are already inclusive of scale efficiency. We do not compute scale efficiencies for the alternative profit function because they would include economies on the consumer side, and would not be comparable (see Berger et al., 1996).

that approximately equal amounts of resources are lost because of scale and X-inefficiencies. In every size class more than 90% of firms are operating below efficient scale, and the mean $t*$ is between 2 and 3 for each size class, suggesting that the typical bank would have to be two to three times larger in order to maximize cost scale efficiency for its product mix and input prices.[39]

To ensure that our scale economies estimates reflect the shape of the frontier and are not simply the consequence of correlation between the X-inefficiencies and scale, we re-estimated the Fourier-flexible cost model using only relatively efficient banks. We divided the banks into asset size deciles, chose the top 25% of the distribution in terms of efficiency scores in each size class, re-estimated the cost frontier model using these banks, and then recomputed the scale measures. We got very similar results to those shown in Table 3.3.[40]

These findings differ from most of those found using 1980s data, in which large banks were typically found to be operating at constant returns to scale or with slight cost diseconomies of scale. In almost all cases, cost scale economies were exhausted well below $10 billion in assets.[41] The difference could have occurred because of some of the differences in specification between our cost function and those typically employed in the literature. One candidate is our use of the Fourier-flexible function form in place of the more common translog specification. The translog forces a symmetric U-shape in logs on the ray average cost frontier, which could force measured scale diseconomies on the large banks as the imposed reflection of the scale economies found for small banks. However, this does not appear to be the case here. We re-estimated the scale economies using the translog (not shown) and found that, if anything, the measured scale economies for the larger banks were even greater. Another candidate is our use of equity capital. Failure to control for equity could give a bias toward finding cost scale diseconomies, because large banks tend to have lower equity ratios and pay interest on higher portions of their funds. Re-estimation without specifying equity capital (not shown) did reduce our measured scale

---

[39] As shown in Table 3.3, unexploited scale economies are actually somewhat larger for banks in the larger size classes. This would be consistent with the hypothesis that larger banks choose product mixes that are more conducive to large scale.

[40] The weighted average scale efficiency across all banks in this estimation was 0.815, the weighted average $t*$ was 1.854 (significantly greater than 1), and a weighted average of 93.5% of bank costs were incurred by banks that were operating below efficient scale.

[41] Exceptions include Hunter and Timme (1986), Shaffer and David (1991), Shaffer (1994), Hughes et al. (1996, 1997), and Hughes and Mester (1998).

economies for large banks, consistent with the expected bias, but it did not eliminate them. The last column of Table 3.3 reports the results of another robustness check of these scale economy findings. We examined the raw data without imposing a specification. The ratio C/GTA, average cost per dollar of assets, falls consistently when moving into larger size classes. This simple measure is, if anything, biased against the larger banks, which typically have more off-balance-sheet items and more loans per dollar of assets, which should raise average costs. The finding of declining cost per dollar of assets by size class strongly supports our scale economy findings. Moreover, an examination of the ratio C/GTA for banks over the 1980s reveals mild scale economies for asset levels below $1 billion and diseconomies for larger banks, which is consistent with the prior scale economies literature. This suggests that the 1990s are indeed different, and that our methodology has not created the result.

An important caveat to the scale efficiency findings is that they may not hold for the very largest banks. We group the data from all banks with GTA greater than $10 billion into a single size class in Table 3.3 because there are few very large banks in the US to form credible size subclasses of this largest size class, and our data exclusion rules exacerbated the problem by dropping several of these banks. To try to ameliorate this problem, we recalculated the C/GTA ratio in the last column of Table 3.3 including all US banks (regardless of our data exclusion rules), and segmented the largest size class into $10 billion–$25 billion, $25 billion–$50 billion, and above $50 billion ranges. We find average costs to be decreasing in all size classes up through $25 billion, with an increase in average costs thereafter. Thus, we still find relatively robust evidence of scale economies well beyond the region usually found in studies using the 1980s data. Serious estimates of scale economies for US banks over $25 billion will likely have to wait for the consolidation of the industry to create enough of these large banks to yield reasonable estimates.

Our scale economy results suggest that some conditions changed between the 1980s and 1990s that substantially raised the cost-efficient scale of US banks. While a complete investigation is beyond the scope of this paper, three explanations seem plausible. First, open-market interest rates have been relatively low recently – the one-year US Treasury rate averaged 9.74% in the 1980s and 5.39% over our sample period of 1990–1995. It is quite likely that these low rates reduced interest rate expenses (which account for most of costs) proportionally more for large banks than small banks, because a greater proportion of large banks' liabilities tend to be market-sensitive. Large banks often rely on wholesale purchased funds that pay market rates, whereas small banks typically rely more on core deposits with rates that do not vary one-for-one with open-market rates. Under this explanation, the scale economies of the early 1990s may be a temporary phenomenon that will disappear if and when market rates rise substantially. To partially check this explanation, we reevaluated each bank's scale economies as if interest rates were at their levels in the 1980s.[42] We still find scale economies (although they are slightly lower), suggesting that a rise in interest rates back to the higher levels of the 1980s would not eliminate the scale economies. We acknowledge, however, that our interest-rate experiment is subject to the Lucas critique. Namely, the cost function was estimated for the low interest rate environment of the 1990s. Because rates are low, banks might be paying less attention to optimizing with respect to interest rates. As interest rates rise, the parameters of the cost function could change in a way that affects scale economies significantly.

A second possible explanation for our scale economies result is that recent regulatory changes may have tended to favor large banks relative to small banks. In particular, the elimination of geographic restrictions on bank branching and holding company expansion during the 1980s and into the early 1990s may have removed some scale diseconomies and made it less costly to become large. For example, in the extreme case of unit banking, there are very severe diseconomies to becoming large without being able to have any branch offices to collect deposits, and such diseconomies would be removed by allowing statewide branching.[43] Similarly, the removal of interest rate ceilings on core deposits during the 1980s likely raised costs more for small banks, which rely more on core deposits for their funding.

Finally, improvements in technology and applied finance may have reduced costs more for large banks than for small banks. Improvements in information processing and credit scoring may have reduced the costs

[42] In particular, for each bank in the sample that had at least nine years of data for the 1980s, we calculated the average interest rate the bank paid on purchased funds and core deposits in the 1980s and the average interest rates it paid for these funding sources in the 1990s, and found the differences in average rates paid. We then added each bank's difference to its core deposit rate in each year in the 1990s and recalculated the bank's scale economies at this new evaluation point. On average, this added 2.55% to the purchased funds rate and 2.50% to the core deposit rate.

[43] Jayaratne and Strahan (1998) found that bank performance measured several different ways improved after within-state branching restrictions were removed, although they did not separate the improvement into scale and $X$-efficiency effects.

Table 3.4. *Correlations among the efficiency measures and raw-data measures of performance*[a].

|  | Cost efficiency | Standard profit efficiency | Alternative profit efficiency | C/GTA | ROA |
|---|---|---|---|---|---|
| Standard profit efficiency | 0.019 (0.145) | | | | |
| Alternative profit efficiency | −0.167 (0.000) | 0.794 (0.000) | | | |
| C/GTA | −0.206 (0.000) | −0.119 (0.000) | −0.235 (0.000) | | |
| ROA | 0.247 (0.000) | 0.122 (0.000) | 0.177 (0.000) | −0.279 (0.000) | |
| ROE | 0.205 (0.000) | 0.469 (0.000) | 0.334 (0.000) | −0.220 (0.000) | 0.726 (0.000) |

*Notes:* [a] Spearman correlation coefficients with $p$-values of the tests for zero correlation in parentheses.
C/GTA is average cost, i.e., total cost divided by gross total assets, a raw-data version of cost efficiency. It has an unweighted mean of 0.047 and a standard deviation of 0.005 over 1990–1995.
ROA is return on assets, i.e., net income divided by gross total assets. It has a mean of 0.011 and a standard deviation of 0.004 over 1990–1995.
ROE is return on equity, i.e., net income divided by equity. It has a mean of 0.016 and a standard deviation of 0.047 over 1990–1995.

of extending small business loans and credit card loans more for larger banks. Similarly, improved automation may have allowed large banks to expand faster and at lower cost by setting up ATM machines in place of adding more expensive brick-and-mortar branch offices. Large banks may have also been better positioned to take advantage of the new tools of financial engineering, such as derivative contracts and other off-balance-sheet activities.

### 6.4 Comparison of Efficiency Across Concepts

Table 3.4 shows the rank-order correlations among the different X-efficiency measures and some other commonly used financial ratios that may be considered raw-data measures of performance. Standard and alternative profit efficiency are highly positively and statistically significantly correlated with each other ($\rho = 0.794$), as expected. Perhaps surprisingly, however, measured cost efficiency is essentially uncorrelated with standard profit efficiency and it is negatively correlated with alternative profit efficiency.

One possible explanation is that cost and revenue inefficiencies may be negatively related, so that firms with low cost efficiency tend to have high revenue efficiency that offsets it. This could occur because of competitive pressures if, for example, firms with highly valued product mixes or high revenue efficiency feel less market discipline to control their costs.

An alternative explanation is that much of what are measured as cost inefficiencies are actually unmeasured differences in product quality that required additional costs to create. As discussed above, the alternative profit function and to a lesser extent the standard profit function tend to control for product quality implicitly by letting revenues received for higher quality offset the extra costs of creating the quality. We will explore this possibility more in the next table, where we compare cost and profit inefficiencies.

The correlations between the efficiencies and each of the raw-data measures follow the expected pattern – efficiency by any definition is negatively and significantly correlated with the standard average cost ratio C/GTA and positively and significantly correlated with the standard profitability ratios ROA and ROE. These findings suggest that our efficiency measures are robust and are not simply the consequences of our specifications or methods.

As measured, the cost and profit efficiency ratios are not directly comparable because they are reported in terms of different denominators (predicted actual costs vs. potential profits). In Table 3.5, we report the dollar values of the cost, standard profit, and alternative profit inefficiencies divided by the same denominators – potential profits, gross total assets, and equity. The meanings of these ratios are the proportions of potential profits lost, the loss of return on assets (ROA), and the loss of return on equity (ROE), respectively, because of inefficiency. These ratios may provide evidence on the extent to which the measured cost inefficiencies incorporate unmeasured differences in product quality. If markets are competitive so that differences in product quality are rewarded with higher revenues that cover the costs, the alternative profit inefficiency essentially just improves on cost efficiency by offsetting the extra costs of producing higher quality with higher revenues. In this event, the alternative profit inefficiency ratios measured here would be expected to be smaller than the cost inefficiency ratios. If, instead, the effects of market power in pricing bank outputs are more important, alternative profit inefficiency may be larger than both cost inefficiency and standard profit inefficiency, as firms with the most market power are measured as much more alternative-profit efficient than the average bank.

Table 3.5. Cost, standard profit, and alternative profit X-inefficiencies relative to potential profits,[a] gross total assets, and equity.

| Bank size (GTA) | # of banks | Inefficiency/potential profits | | | Inefficiency/GTA | | | Inefficiency/equity | | |
|---|---|---|---|---|---|---|---|---|---|---|
| | | Cost[b] | Standard profit[c] | Alternative profit[c] | Cost[b] | Standard profit[c] | Alternative profit[c] | Cost[b] | Standard profit[c] | Alternative profit[c] |
| 0–$50 M | 2,218 | 0.165 (0.085) | 0.414 (0.157) | 0.412 (0.217) | 0.007 (0.003) | 0.018 (0.011) | 0.018 (0.011) | 0.074 (0.039) | 0.185 (0.071) | 0.184 (0.090) |
| $50 M–$100 M | 1,794 | 0.143 (0.074) | 0.382 (0.140) | 0.362 (0.188) | 0.006 (0.003) | 0.016 (0.009) | 0.015 (0.009) | 0.065 (0.034) | 0.173 (0.065) | 0.164 (0.078) |
| $100 M–$300 M | 1,344 | 0.182 (0.092) | 0.472 (0.220) | 0.732 (0.276) | 0.006 (0.003) | 0.015 (0.008) | 0.023 (0.010) | 0.066 (0.034) | 0.172 (0.072) | 0.267 (0.102) |
| $300 M–$1 B | 392 | 0.184 (0.107) | 0.449 (0.229) | 0.775 (0.311) | 0.006 (0.003) | 0.013 (0.008) | 0.023 (0.009) | 0.068 (0.039) | 0.167 (0.089) | 0.288 (0.101) |
| $1 B–$10 B | 171 | 0.204 (0.113) | 0.456 (0.224) | 0.694 (0.276) | 0.006 (0.003) | 0.013 (0.008) | 0.020 (0.009) | 0.082 (0.045) | 0.182 (0.092) | 0.278 (0.104) |
| >$10 B | 30 | 0.184 (0.135) | 0.468 (0.200) | 0.628 (0.248) | 0.005 (0.003) | 0.014 (0.005) | 0.018 (0.006) | 0.078 (0.051) | 0.199 (0.073) | 0.267 (0.084) |
| Total | 5,949 | 0.185 (0.114) | 0.451 (0.208) | 0.639 (0.303) | 0.006 (0.003) | 0.014 (0.008) | 0.020 (0.009) | 0.075 (0.044) | 0.183 (0.081) | 0.259 (0.102) |

*Note*: All figures are weighted averages of the values for all banks in the sample. If an individual bank's value is given by $x/z$, then the figures in the table are $\sum x_i / \sum z_i$. Numbers in parentheses are standard deviations.
[a] The potential profits denominator in the first set of comparisons is calculated using the standard profit function. Using the alternative profit function yields similar results.
[b] Cost inefficiency is predicted cost minus minimum cost.
[c] Profit efficiency is potential profits minus predicted profits.

The empirical results suggest that this market power paradigm appears to dominate any effects of unmeasured differences in product quality on measured efficiency. Alternative profit inefficiency is larger than are both cost and standard profit inefficiencies. This does not suggest that unmeasured differences in product quality are unimportant, just perhaps less important than market power considerations in determining bank profits. These results also suggest that the standard assumption of perfect competition in setting output prices maintained for measuring standard profit efficiency may be violated by the data.

### 7 Empirical Investigation of the Potential Correlates of Efficiency

The last part of our analysis relates our efficiency estimates to various aspects of the banks, their markets, and their regulation that are potential correlates of efficiency, i.e., factors that are at least partially exogenous and may explain some of the efficiency differences that remain after controlling for efficiency concept and measurement method. Here, we use the three distribution-free X-efficiency measures estimated for the 1990–1995 period and the average values of the bank, market, and regulatory characteristics over 1990–1995. Similar to what we did when estimating efficiency, we also investigate a few alternative specifications of the potential correlates to check robustness.

The characteristics we investigate are given in Table 3.6, where we show their definitions, means, and standard deviations over 1990–1995. These variables fall into six broad categories: *bank size, organizational form and corporate governance, other bank characteristics, market characteristics, state geographic restrictions on competition*, and *primary federal regulator*.

We performed both multiple regressions and single variable regressions. Including an endogenous variable in a multiple regression can bias the coefficients even on the exogenous variables, and perhaps all of our variables are partly endogenous and partly exogenous. Thus, in addition to the multiple regressions, we also ran regressions that each included a constant term and a single explanatory variable. These single-variable regression coefficients are proportional to correlation coefficients. A disadvantage of these single-variable regressions is that any significant correlation found might be spurious, with both efficiency and the included variable being significantly related to a third, omitted factor. Because each of the multiple and single regression analyses has advantages and disadvantages, we will be conservative and tend to draw conclusions only when the coefficients in both are statistically significant and of the same sign. These results are shown in Table 3.7.

Table 3.6. *Variables employed as potential correlates of efficiency (one observation per bank averaged over 1990–1995 unless otherwise indicated). (All financial variables measured in 1,000's of constant 1,994 dollars).*

| Symbol | Definition | Mean | Standard deviation |
|---|---|---|---|
| *Bank size variables* | | | |
| SMLBANK | Dummy, equals one if bank has GTA below $100 million. Excluded from the regressions as the base case | 0.673 | 0.449 |
| MEDBANK | Dummy, equals one if bank has GTA of $100 million to $1 billion | 0.293 | 0.432 |
| LARBANK | Dummy, equals one if bank has GTA of $1 billion to $10 billion | 0.028 | 0.157 |
| HUGBANK | Dummy, equals one if bank has GTA over $10 billion | 0.005 | 0.067 |
| *Organizational form/governance* | | | |
| MERGED | Dummy, equals one if bank survived one or more bank-level mergers during the period (i.e., absorbed the assets of one or more other banks) | 0.132 | 0.338 |
| ACQUIRED | Dummy, equals one if bank was acquired by a new high holder bank holding company during the period | 0.108 | 0.310 |
| INBHC | Dummy, equals one if bank is owned by a bank holding company | 0.761 | 0.407 |
| MUL_LAY | Dummy, equals one if the bank is in multiple-layered BHC, i.e., the direct holder is not the high holder | 0.087 | 0.251 |
| OUTST | Dummy variable, equals one if bank's high holder is located in another state | 0.055 | 0.211 |
| PUB_TRADED | Dummy, equals one if the bank's high holder is registered with the SEC for public trading | 0.228 | 0.407 |
| INSIDE | Proportion of stock owned by board members and their relatives. Reported only for banks with over 50% of the banking assets of publicly traded organizations (126 observations). | 0.159 | 0.187 |
| OUTSIDE | Proportion of stock owned by outside owners with share blocks greater than 5%. Same restrictions as INSIDE (126 observations). | 0.058 | 0.083 |

Table 3.6. *(cont.)*

| Symbol | Definition | Mean | Standard deviation |
|--------|------------|------|--------------------|
| *Other bank characteristics* | | | |
| AGE | Number of years the bank existed before 1990 | 67.6 | 33.6 |
| LOAN/GTA | Loans divided by gross total assets (GTA) | 0.532 | 0.130 |
| SUB_DER | Dummy, equals one if the total notional value of the bank's swaps, forwards, futures, and similar contracts exceeds 5% of GTA | 0.025 | 0.155 |
| PF/GTA | Purchased funds (deposits >$100,000, foreign deposits, federal funds purchased, subordinated debt, other non-deposit liabilities) to GTA ratio | 0.119 | 0.061 |
| SDROA | Standard deviation over time of the bank's annual return on assets | 0.003 | 0.003 |
| SDROE | Standard deviation over time of the bank's annual return on equity (used only in robustness checks to substitute for SDROA) | 0.036 | 0.043 |
| *Market characteristics* | | | |
| HERF | Herfindahl index of local market concentration | 0.248 | 0.155 |
| SHARE | Bank's share of local market deposits (used only in robustness checks to substitute for HERF) | 0.175 | 0.197 |
| INMSA | Dummy, equals one if the bank is in a Metropolitan Statistical Area | 0.361 | 0.472 |
| STGROW | Real state income growth (decimal) | 0.007 | 0.002 |
| STUNEMP | State unemployment rate (decimal) (used only in robustness checks to substitute for STGROW) | 0.065 | 0.013 |
| *State geographic restrictions on competition* | | | |
| UNITB | Dummy, equals one for unit banking states (the six-year average will be at most 0.167, there are no UNIT banking states after 1990) | 0.010 | 0.040 |
| LIMITB | Dummy, equals one for limited branching states | 0.473 | 0.468 |
| STATEB | Dummy, equals one for statewide branching states. Excluded from the multiple regressions as the base case | 0.516 | 0.462 |

Table 3.6. *(cont.)*

| Symbol | Definition | Mean | Standard deviation |
|---|---|---|---|
| LIMITBHC | Dummy, equals one for states with limits on expansions of multibank holding companies. As of 1990, all states permitted some multibank holding company activity, so the excluded case is that the state allows statewide holding company powers | 0.518 | 0.500 |
| NOINTST | Dummy, equals one for states that do not allow interstate expansions of multibank holding companies | 0.032 | 0.095 |
| ACCESS | Proportion of nation's banking assets in states that are allowed to enter the state (equals proportion of national assets in the state for states that do not allow interstate banking) | 0.503 | 0.276 |
| *Primary federal regulator* | | | |
| FED | Dummy, equals one if the bank's primary federal regulator is the Federal Reserve | 0.085 | 0.268 |
| FDIC | Dummy, equals one if the bank's primary federal regulator is the FDIC | 0.608 | 0.481 |
| OCC | Dummy, equals one if the bank's primary federal regulator is the OCC. Excluded from the multiple regressions as the base case | 0.307 | 0.455 |
| *Raw data measures of performance*[a] | | | |
| C/GTA | Total cost divided by gross total assets, a raw-data version of cost efficiency | 0.047 | 0.005 |
| ROA | Return on assets: ratio of net income to gross total assets | 0.011 | 0.004 |
| ROE | Return on equity: ratio of net income to equity | 0.116 | 0.047 |
| Number of observations | | | 5,949 |

*Note*: [a] The raw data measures of performance are included in the analysis as alternative measures of efficiency for robustness checks of the more complicated frontier efficiency estimates. They are included in a separate correlation analysis but are excluded from the regression analysis as being completely endogenous.

Table 3.7. *Regression analysis of the potential correlates of efficiency*[a].

| Dep var | Cost efficiency | | Standard profit efficiency | | Alternative profit efficiency | |
|---|---|---|---|---|---|---|
| | (1) | (2) | (3) | (4) | (5) | (6) |
| *Bank size variables* | | | | | | |
| SMLBANK | 0.883** | −0.021** | 0.184** | 0.083** | 0.375** | 0.206** |
| | (137.355) | (−12.682) | (10.929) | (15.799) | (19.890) | (38.908) |
| MEDBANK | 0.902** | 0.021** | 0.036* | −0.083** | 0.117** | −0.200** |
| | (132.626) | (12.118) | (1.994) | (−15.099) | (5.885) | (−35.778) |
| LARBANK | 0.899** | 0.012* | 0.009 | −0.038* | 0.077** | −0.147** |
| | (97.130) | (2.536) | (0.358) | (−2.444) | (2.859) | (−8.708) |
| HUGBANK | 0.908** | 0.009 | −0.040 | −0.089** | 0.093* | −0.132** |
| | (60.940) | (0.773) | (−1.028) | (−2.492) | (2.133) | (−3.349) |
| *Organizational form/governance* | | | | | | |
| MERGED | −0.004 | 0.007** | 0.023** | 0.004 | 0.031** | −0.052** |
| | (−1.532) | (3.168) | (3.606) | (0.511) | (4.303) | (−6.631) |
| ACQUIRED | 0.006* | 0.010** | −0.002 | 0.019* | 0.007 | 0.013 |
| | (2.223) | (3.989) | (−0.335) | (2.387) | (1.005) | (1.508) |
| INBHC | 0.004* | 0.012** | 0.055** | 0.079** | 0.057** | 0.039** |
| | (2.062) | (6.318) | (10.549) | (13.609) | (9.909) | (5.974) |
| MUL_LAY | 0.011** | 0.020** | 0.040** | 0.032** | 0.031** | −0.017 |
| | (3.303) | (6.709) | (4.525) | (3.314) | (3.201) | (−1.561) |
| OUTST | 0.010* | 0.021** | −0.006 | 0.015 | −0.011 | −0.046** |
| | (2.562) | (5.996) | (−0.529) | (1.273) | (−0.960) | (−3.687) |
| PUB_TRADED | 0.008** | 0.017** | 0.025** | 0.032** | 0.013* | −0.038** |
| | (3.691) | (9.064) | (4.433) | (5.448) | (2.114) | (−5.825) |

*Other bank characteristics*

| | (1) | (2) | (3) | (4) | (5) | (6) |
|---|---|---|---|---|---|---|
| AGE | 0.00003 | 0.0001** | −0.0006** | −0.0008** | −0.0009** | −0.001** |
| | (0.900) | (4.283) | (−9.776) | (−10.734) | (−12.373) | (−13.256) |
| LOAN/GTA | −0.019** | 0.005** | 0.755** | 0.656** | 0.426** | 0.260** |
| | (−2.943) | (0.867) | (45.731) | (39.678) | (23.059) | (12.860) |
| SUB_DER | −0.019** | 0.004 | 0.015 | −0.013 | 0.053** | −0.084** |
| | (−3.128) | (0.771) | (0.930) | (−0.856) | (2.924) | (−4.917) |
| PF/GTA | 0.024 | 0.032** | −0.143** | −0.131** | −0.224** | −0.404** |
| | (1.771) | (2.620) | (−3.970) | (−3.335) | (−5.558) | (−9.396) |
| SDROA | −2.517** | −2.905** | −2.89** | 0.258 | −3.876** | 1.718 |
| | (−9.120) | (−10.788) | (−3.995) | (0.299) | (−4.796) | (1.805) |
| *Market characteristics* | | | | | | |
| HERF | −0.015** | −0.018** | 0.023 | 0.035** | 0.067** | 0.130** |
| | (−2.610) | (−3.614) | (1.527) | (2.243) | (4.039) | (7.572) |
| INMSA | −0.007** | 0.001 | 0.003 | −0.008 | 0.021** | −0.042** |
| | (−3.368) | (0.926) | (0.491) | (−1.474) | (3.665) | (−7.405) |
| STGROW | −1.610** | −1.640** | 4.172** | 1.843 | 6.038** | 8.967** |
| | (−3.220) | (3.602) | (3.185) | (1.274) | (4.125) | (5.632) |
| *State geographic restrictions on competition* | | | | | | |
| UNITB | −0.058** | −0.059** | 0.337** | 0.450** | 0.426** | 0.603** |
| | (−2.768) | (−3.106) | (6.115) | (7.547) | (6.922) | (9.196) |
| LIMITB | 0.008** | 0.005** | −0.013** | −0.020** | −0.041** | −0.006 |
| | (4.450) | (3.146) | (−2.641) | (−3.912) | (−7.449) | (−1.131) |
| STATEB | — | 0.005** | — | 0.017** | — | 0.002 |
| | | (−2.911) | | (3.300) | | (0.349) |
| LIMITBHC | −0.0008 | −0.004* | 0.032** | 0.007 | 0.032** | 0.030** |
| | (−0.462) | (−2.380) | (6.737) | (1.442) | (6.064) | (5.730) |
| NOINTST | −0.046** | −0.036** | −0.028 | −0.089** | −0.039 | −0.047 |
| | (−4.745) | (−4.497) | (−1.053) | (−3.536) | (−1.374) | (−1.682) |

Table 3.7. (*cont.*)

| Dep var | Cost efficiency | | Standard profit efficiency | | Alternative profit efficiency | |
|---|---|---|---|---|---|---|
| | (1) | (2) | (3) | (4) | (5) | (6) |
| ACCESS | -0.011** | 0.0009 | 0.054** | -0.027** | 0.079** | -0.006 |
| | (-3.090) | (0.315) | (6.008) | (-3.080) | (7.891) | (-0.593) |
| *Primary federal regulator* | | | | | | |
| FED | 0.008* | 0.008** | -0.003 | 0.002 | -0.013 | -0.015 |
| | (2.559) | (2.947) | (-0.412) | (0.252) | (-1.433) | (-1.536) |
| FDIC | -0.0006 | -0.007** | -0.008 | 0.018** | -0.019** | 0.031 |
| | (-0.340) | (-4.193) | (-1.784) | (3.514) | (-3.808) | (5.544) |
| OCC | — | 0.004** | — | -0.020** | — | -0.029** |
| | | (2.696) | | (-3.863) | | (-4.953) |
| Adj $R$-sq[b] | 0.067 | | 0.364 | | 0.348 | |
| Number of banks | 5,949 | 5,949 | 5,949 | 5,949 | 5,949 | 5,949 |

*Note:*

[a] Columns (1), (3), and (5) report multivariate regression coefficients with $t$-statistics in parentheses. Note that the OCC and STATEB dummy variables and a constant term are omitted from the multivariate regressions to avoid perfect collinearity. Columns (2), (4), and (6) report univariate regression coefficients, where each regression included the variable and an intercept term, with $t$-statistics in parentheses.

[b] The adjusted $R$-squared is computed as $1 - [(N-1)/(N-K)](1-R^2)$ where $N$ = number of observations, $K$ = number of parameters, $R^2$ = sum of squared errors from the regression/sum of squared deviations of the dependent variable from its mean. This adjusted $R$-squared is equivalent to that obtained from the model in which SMLBANK is replaced with an intercept term.

* Significant at the 5% level; ** significant at the 1% level.

### 7.1 Bank Size

The bank size variables (SMLBANK, MEDBANK, LARBANK, and HUGBANK) are measured with dummy variables to allow for nonmonotonicity and nonlinearities in the relationship between bank size and efficiency. We specified our multiple regression equation without a constant term and included all four of these size variables.[44] As shown in Table 3.7, the cost efficiency estimates do not vary much across size classes – holding everything else equal, the cost efficiency is about 2.5% higher at the largest banks (with assets over $10 billion) than the smallest banks (with assets under $100 million). But in terms of profit efficiency (both standard and alternative), small banks show the greatest level of efficiency. This result suggests that our profit efficiency measures display very little of the potential scale biases favoring larger firms discussed above (as long as equity capital is specified). The cost and profit efficiency results together seem to imply that as banks grow larger, they are equally able to control costs, but it becomes harder to create revenues efficiently. This is consistent with conventional wisdom and the historical fact that small banks typically have higher profitability ratios. It also helps explain the lack of a positive correlation between cost efficiency and profit efficiency discussed above.

### 7.2 Organizational Form and Corporate Governance

The banking industry is consolidating at a rapid pace, so it is important to determine the efficiency effects of bank mergers and acquisitions. Our results indicate that, with everything else equal, banks that have survived at least one merger over our sample period (MERGED) have higher standard and alternative profit efficiency than other banks, which is consistent with prior findings discussed above. This result is not confirmed, however, in the single-variable regressions, where alternative profit efficiency is significantly lower for banks that have been involved in mergers. This is perhaps because being involved in a merger is correlated with bank size, and size is negatively related to alternative profit efficiency. On the other hand, being acquired by another holding company (ACQUIRED) does not appear to be associated with profit efficiency, but is associated with higher cost efficiency. All in all, these results are fairly mixed.

Banks with complicated organizational forms or internal management

---

[44] We excluded one of the state branching dummy variables (STATEB) and one of the primary federal regulator dummy variables (OCC) to avoid perfect collinearity in the multiple regressions.

structures could be less efficient, but a holding company structure might also impose some discipline on banks, so we explored the relationships between efficiency and whether the bank is in a bank holding company (INBHC), whether the holding company is multilayered (MUL_LAY) and whether the top-tier holding company is located out of state (OUTST), which could make control more difficult. Banks in holding companies tend to have higher levels of profit efficiency (both standard and alternative) than independent banks, and their cost efficiency is significantly greater as well, consistent with some previous cost efficiency studies. If the holding company has multiple layers, this means even higher levels of profit and cost efficiency. Thus, the more complex structure of multilayered holding companies does not appear to be harming bank efficiency. Having the highest holding company owner from out of state also is associated with higher, not lower, cost efficiency. A potential explanation for these results may be a form of the efficient structure hypothesis (Demsetz, 1973) – more efficient banking organizations may tend to acquire other banks, and the multilayer, multistate holding company is the vehicle that allows them to do it.

We also included a variable indicating whether the bank's highest holder is registered with the SEC for public trading (PUB_TRADED). To the extent that outside shareholders can exert control over bank management, we might expect publicly traded banks to be more efficient, all else equal, and this is indeed what our results indicate. Publicly traded firms tend to have both higher cost and standard profit efficiencies.

For 126 of the banks we have information from 1987–1988 on the proportion of stock owned by insiders, i.e., board members and their relatives (INSIDE) and the proportion of stock owned by outsiders who had more than 5% of the outstanding shares (OUTSIDE).[45] So in an alternative specification with the more limited number of observations (not shown in Table 3.7), we also included the first- and second-order terms of these two variables [INSIDE, 1/2 INSIDE$^2$, OUTSIDE, and 1/2 OUTSIDE$^2$]. We included the second-order terms because Gorton and Rosen (1995) predict a U-shaped relationship between insiders' stock holdings and efficiency. At low levels of inside ownership, a negative relationship would be consistent with managers who have greater control pursuing their own interests, which may involve inefficiencies. However, at higher stakes, an increase in insider ownership may serve to align management's objectives with those of owners, yielding greater efficiency. We include the OUTSIDE variables, since outside investors can be a controlling influence, and the more stock in the hands of large, outside investors, the more

[45] We thank Gary Gorton and Rich Rosen for providing these data.

control these investors can be expected to exert and the more efficient the bank might become. However, in none of our regressions are any of these governance variables significantly related to efficiency.

### 7.3 Other Bank Characteristics

We also explored the effects of other characteristics of the bank. A bank's age (AGE) might be related to efficiency since bank production might involve "learning by doing" (Mester, 1996). While significantly different from zero in our profit efficiency regressions, the coefficient on AGE is very small in all the regressions.

We included several variables to control for the strategic niche of the bank, including proxies for the amount of risk the bank is taking on. Banks with higher loan-to-asset ratios (LOAN/GTA) tend to have higher profit efficiency. This might reflect that banks' loan product is more highly valued than securities, or it could reflect the higher market power that exists in loan markets compared to the other product markets in which banks operate. Whether a bank is heavily using derivative contracts, such as swaps, forwards, and futures (SUB_DER), does not appear to be consistently related to its efficiency. This might be because of heterogeneity in the uses of these instruments, which can be used for both hedging and speculative purposes. Reliance on purchased funds (PF/GTA) could also be related to efficiency, since the cost of purchased funds differs from that of core deposits over the business cycle. We find that banks that use more of these funds tend to have lower profit efficiencies than other banks.

As a direct measure of bank risk, we included the standard deviation of return on assets (SDROA). To the extent that we are not adequately controlling for risk taking in our profit models, riskier banks may be more profit efficient if they are trading off between risk and return. Alternatively, banks that are poor at operations might also be poor at risk management, which would imply a positive relationship between profit and/or cost efficiency and risk. The evidence suggests that banks with more variable returns tend to have lower profit efficiencies (in the multiple regressions) and also lower cost efficiencies, consistent with the notion that bad managers are poor at both operations and risk management. A negative relationship with cost efficiency was also found when we replaced SDROA with the standard deviation of the return on book equity (SDROE) as a robustness check.

### 7.4 Market Characteristics

The next set of variables characterizes the competitive conditions of the markets in which the banks operate. The Herfindahl index (HERF) measures the degree of local deposit market concentration and proxies for the bank's market power. As might be expected, market power is negatively related to cost efficiency but positively related to alternative profit efficiency. Banks in less competitive markets can charge higher prices for their services but might feel less pressure to keep costs down (i.e., enjoy the "quiet life").[46] We included two other variables related to market competition. INMSA indicates whether the bank is located in a metropolitan area, which may be more competitive than a rural area. The results are not consistent across the multiple and single variable regressions, because INMSA is likely correlated with other aspects of the bank, like its size, merger activity, etc. State income growth (STGROW) proxies for the growth of market demand for banking services. Greater demand might allow for less cost-efficient production, at least in the short run before new competitors enter, but more profit efficiency, since it means greater opportunity to make profit. This is what our estimates show.[47]

### 7.5 State Geographic Restrictions on Competition

Geographic restrictions on bank expansion, which differ across states, can also limit the competitive forces banks face. We included variables to control for the degree of branching restrictions (UNITB, LIMITB, STATEB), the degree of in-state holding company expansion permitted (LIMITBHC), whether out-of-state holding company expansion is allowed or not (NOINTST), and the proportion of the banking industry's assets held in any state that are allowed to enter (ACCESS). These variables are meant to control for the degree of competition or contestability of the bank's market. Perhaps the most surprising finding here is that the relationship between branching restrictions and efficiency does not appear to be monotonic in the severity of the restrictions. We find some support that banks in states with limited branching restrictions have higher cost efficiency and lower profit efficiency than banks in either unit banking states or state without branching restrictions; banks in unit banking states appear to be the least cost efficient but most profit efficient. The other variables included to measure geographic restrictions

---

[46] However, this result is not robust to replacing HERF with SHARE, the bank's share of local market deposits, as SHARE is significantly positively related to cost efficiency.

[47] For a robustness check, we replaced STGROW with the state unemployment rate (STUNEMP), which is negatively related to market demand. Here the results are much weaker, and the signs on STUNEMP in the profit regressions are positive, indicating a negative relationship between market demand and profit efficiency.

produce no consistently significant results, except that banks in states that prohibit interstate expansions (NOINTST) appear to be less cost efficient than banks in states that permit such expansions. In summary, efficiency does seem to be related to limits on geographic expansion, but the findings are somewhat inconsistent.

### 7.6 Federal Bank Regulator

Our last group of variables – the identity of the bank's primary federal regulator – helps account for the regulatory regime banks are facing. The regulator, like the market, exerts some control over the bank and thus might be related to bank efficiency. Also, the bank's primary federal regulator (FED, OCC, or FDIC) varies depending on the type of charter the bank has; thus, the variables might reflect differences in banks with different charters. We find only weak relationships between regulator identity and our three efficiency measures, with banks overseen by the Federal Reserve tending to be more cost efficient than banks overseen by the OCC or FDIC.

### 7.7 Fit of the Correlates Equations

A final observation from Table 3.7 is that the adjusted $R^2$s suggest that we have not explained most of the variance in measured efficiency. Our 25 explanatory variables are able to explain about 7% of the variance of measured cost efficiency and about 35% of the variance of the two types of measured profit efficiency. We make no judgment as to whether these figures are high or low, but simply note that most of the variance in measured efficiency after controlling for efficiency concept and measurement methods remains unexplained. It may be due to essentially unmeasurable factors, such as differences in managerial ability, to potential correlates of efficiency that we could have included but failed to do so, or to measurement error in the dependent variable due to the many difficulties in measuring efficiency. Further investigation is beyond the scope of this paper.

## 8 Conclusion

Despite the very significant research effort that has been mounted over the last few years examining the efficiency of financial institutions, there is as yet little information and no consensus on the sources of the substantial variation in measured efficiency, i.e., these sources remain a "black box." Here, we focus on getting inside the box by examining a number of sources, holding the data set constant. We examine three types of sources: (1) differences in the efficiency concept used, (2) differences in efficiency measurement methodology within the context of these concepts, and (3) the potential correlates of efficiency that may explain some of the efficiency differences that remain after controlling for efficiency concept and measurement method. We review the literature on the sources of efficiency at commercial banks and provide new evidence using a large data set of almost 6,000 US commercial banks that were in continuous operation over the six-year period 1990–1995.

We examine three economic efficiency concepts – cost, standard profit, and alternative profit efficiencies. Each corresponds to how well a firm performs relative to a different economic optimization program, and so each may provide different insights about firm efficiency. Consistent with this expectation, we find that measurement of each of the efficiency concepts does add some independent informational value. In fact, the measures of profit efficiency are not positively correlated with cost efficiency, even though all three efficiency measures are positively related to some raw-data measures of performance. As well, a number of the potential correlates had different relationships with the three different efficiency measures, again suggesting that each is measuring a different type of optimization. These results suggest that future researchers might consider measuring all three concepts to be sure that any conclusions about which firms are most efficient or which potential correlates succeed in "explaining" efficiency are robust with respect to all three economic efficiency concepts.

We explore the effects of a number of different efficiency measurement methods on each of the three efficiency concepts. These methods include the use of different measurement techniques, different functional forms, and various treatments of output quality and financial capital. The results for each of the efficiency concepts are quite robust. We find that the choices made concerning measurement technique, functional form, and other variables usually make very little difference in terms of either average industry efficiency or the rankings of individual firms in our data set. An exception is the treatment of equity capital. Failure to account for the equity position of a bank seems to yield a strong scale bias, making large banks appear to be more profit efficient than small banks by virtue of the equity they have built up over time.

We also find substantial unexploited cost scale economies for our 1990s data up to bank sizes much larger than typically found in the past. This might have occurred because the decline in interest rates, regulatory changes such as the liberalization of intrastate and interstate banking, and improvements in technology and applied finance since the 1980s may have tended to favor large banks over small banks.

Our analysis of the potential correlates of bank efficiency cover a number of bank, market, and regulatory characteristics using multiple- and single-variable regressions. The results are quite mixed. Some of the potential correlates of efficiency have the predicted sign and statistical significance; others have little independent influence on efficiency; and some have unexpected or mixed signs. Importantly, most of the variance in measured efficiency for each of the efficiency concepts remains unexplained, because of unmeasured factors such as differences in managerial ability, potential correlates that were inadvertently excluded from the analysis, or measurement error in the efficiency dependent variables. We leave to future research the task of better explaining efficiency or determining that not much more can be explained.

We close with a caveat that the empirical results of this study should not be taken too seriously unless confirmed by future research. To our knowledge, this is the first study of the efficiencies of the first six years of the 1990s, the first to compare cost, standard profit, and alternative profit efficiency of banks using a single data set and consistent specifications, the first to evaluate the effects of so many differences in methodology, and the first to use such a comprehensive set of potential correlates of efficiency. It is quite likely that some of these results will differ in future studies of these data that use different sets of assumptions.

### Acknowledgements

The views expressed in this chapter do not necessarily represent those of the Federal Reserve Bank of Philadelphia, of the Board of Governors of the Federal Reserve System, or of the Federal Reserve System. The authors thank Emilia Bonaccorsi, Dave Humphrey, and audience participants at the Federal Reserve Bank of New York, the Wharton School, and the Atlantic Economic Society meetings for helpful comments, and Seth Bonime, Margaret Kyle, and Joe Scalise for excellent research assistance.

### References

Akhavein, J. D., Berger, A. N., and Humphrey, D. B., 1997a. The effects of megamergers on efficiency and prices: Evidence from a bank profit function. Review of industrial Organization 12, 95–139.

Akhavein, J. D., Swamy, P. A. V. B., Taubman, S. B., and Singamsetti, R. N., 1997b. A general method of deriving the efficiencies of banks from a profit function. Journal of Productivity Analysis 8, 71–93.

Aly, H. Y., Grabowski, R., Pasurka, C., and Rangan, N., 1990. Technical, scale, and allocative efficiencies in U.S. banking: An empirical investigation. Review of Economics and Statistics 72, 211–218.

Bauer, P. W. and Hancock, D., 1993. The efficiency of the Federal Reserve in providing check processing services. Journal of Banking and Finance 17, 287–311.

Berg, S. A., Førsund, F. R., and Jansen, E. S., 1992. Malmquist indices of productivity growth during the deregulation of Norwegian banking, 1980–89. Scandinavian Journal of Economics 94, S211–S228.

Berger, A. N., 1993. Distribution-free estimates of efficiency in the U.S. banking industry and tests of the standard distributional assumptions. Journal of Productivity Analysis 4, 261–292.

Berger, A. N., Cummins, D., and Weiss, M., 1997a. The coexistence of multiple distribution systems for financial services: The case of property-liability insurance. Journal of Business 70.

Berger, A. N. and DeYoung, R., 1997. Problem loans and cost efficiency in commercial banks. Journal of Banking and Finance 21, 849–870.

Berger, A. N., Hancock, D., and Humphrey, D. B., 1993. Bank efficiency derived from the profit function. Journal of Banking and Finance 17, 317–347.

Berger, A. N. and Hannan, T. H., 1989. The price-concentration relationship in banking. Review of Economics and Statistics 71, 291–299.

Berger, A. N. and Hannan, T. H., 1998. The efficiency cost of market power in the banking industry: A test of the "quiet life" and related hypotheses. Review of Economics and Statistics 80, 454–465.

Berger, A. N. and Humphrey, D. B., 1997. Efficiency of financial institutions: International survey and directions for future research. European Journal of Operational Research 98, 175–212.

Berger, A. N., Humphrey, D. B., and Pulley, L. B., 1996. Do consumers pay for one-stop banking? Evidence from an alternative revenue function. Journal of Banking and Finance 20, 1601–1621.

Berger, A. N., Leusner, J. H., and Mingo, J., 1997b. The efficiency of bank branches. Journal of Monetary Economics 40.

Cebenoyan, A. S., Cooperman, E. S., Register, C. A., and Hudgins, S. C., 1993. The relative efficiency of stock vs. mutual S&Ls: A stochastic frontier approach. Journal of Financial Services Research 7, 151–170.

Clark, J., 1996. Economic cost, scale efficiency and competitive viability in banking. Journal of Money, Credit, and Banking 28, 342–364.

Demsetz, H., 1973. Industry structure, market rivalry, and public policy. Journal of Law and Economics 16, 1–9.

DeYoung, R., 1997. A diagnostic test for the distribution-free efficiency estimator: An example using US commercial bank data. European Journal of Operational Research 98, 243–249.

DeYoung, R. and Nolle, D., 1996. Foreign-owned banks in the US: Earning market share or buying it? Journal of Money, Credit, and Banking 28, 622–636.

English, M. and Hayes, K., 1991. A simple test of market power. Working paper, Southern Methodist University.

Gorton, G. and Rosen, R., 1995. Corporate control, portfolio choice and the decline of banking. Journal of Finance 50, 1377–1420.

Greene, W. H., 1990. A gamma-distributed stochastic frontier model. Journal of Econometrics 46, 141–163.

Hancock, D., 1985. The financial firm: Production with monetary and nonmonetary goods. Journal of Political Economy 93, 859–880.

Hancock, D., 1986. A model of the financial firm with imperfect asset and deposit elasticities. Journal of Banking and Finance 10, 37–54.

Hannan, T. H., 1991. Bank commercial loan markets and the role of market structure: Evidence from the survey of commercial lending. Journal of Banking and Finance 15, 133–149.

Hannan, T. H. and Liang, N., 1993. Inferring market power from time-series data: The case of the banking firm. International Journal of Industrial Organization 11, 205–218.

Hermalin, B. E. and Wallace, N. E., 1994. The determinants of efficiency and solvency in savings and loans. Rand Journal of Economics 25, 361–381.

Hughes, J. P., Lang, W., Mester, L. J., and Moon, C.-G., 1996. Efficient banking under interstate branching. Journal of Money, Credit, and Banking 28, 1045–1071.

Hughes, J. P., Lang, W., Mester, L. J., and Moon, C.-G., 1999. The dollars and sense of bank consolidation. Journal of Banking and Finance 23, 291–324.

Hughes, J. P., Lang, W., Mester, L. J., and Moon, C.-G., 1997. Recovering risky technologies using the almost ideal demand system: An application to U.S. banking. Working paper no. 97–8, Federal Reserve Bank of Philadelphia.

Hughes, J. and Mester, L. J., 1993. A quality and risk-adjusted cost function for banks: Evidence on the too-big-to-fail doctrine. Journal of Productivity Analysis 4, 293–315.

Hughes, J. and Mester, L. J., 1998. Bank capitalization and cost: Evidence of scale economies in risk management and signaling. Review of Economics and Statistics 80, 314–325.

Hughes, J. and Moon, C.-G., 1995. Measuring bank efficiency when managers trade return for reduced risk. Working paper, Department of Economics, Rutgers University.

Humphrey, D. B. and Pulley, L. B., 1997. Banks' responses to deregulation: Profits, technology, and efficiency. Journal of Money, Credit, and Banking 29, 73–93.

Hunter, W. C. and Timme, S. G., 1986. Technical change, organizational form, and the structure of bank production. Journal of Money, Credit, and Banking 18, 152–166.

Jagtiani, J., Nathan, A., and Sick, G., 1995. Scale economies and cost complementarities in commercial banks: On- and off-balance sheet activities. Journal of Banking and Finance 19, 1175–1189.

Jayaratne, J. and Strahan, P. E., 1998. Entry restrictions, industry evolution, and dynamic efficiency: Evidence from commercial banking. Journal of Law and Economics 41, 239–273.

Kaparakis, E. I., Miller, S. M., Noulas, A. G., 1994. Short-run cost inefficiency of commercial banks: A flexible stochastic frontier approach. Journal of Money, Credit, and Banking 26, 875–893.

Kwan S. H. and Eisenbeis, R. A., 1995. An analysis of inefficiency in banking: A stochastic cost frontier approach. Working paper, Working Papers in Applied Economics, Federal Reserve Bank of San Francisco.

McAllister, P. H. and McManus, D., 1993. Resolving the scale efficiency puzzle in banking. Journal of Banking and Finance 17, 389–405.

Mester, L. J., 1992. Traditional and nontraditional banking: An information-theoretic approach. Journal of Banking and Finance 16, 545–566.

Mester, L. J., 1993. Efficiency in the savings and loan industry. Journal of Banking and Finance 17, 267–286.

Mester, L. J., 1994. How efficient are Third District banks? Business Review, Federal Reserve Bank of Philadelphia, pp. 3–18.

Mester, L. J., 1996. A study of bank efficiency taking into account risk preferences. Journal of Banking and Finance 20, 1025–1045.

Mitchell, K. and Onvural, N. M., 1996. Economies of scale and scope at large commercial banks: Evidence from the Fourier flexible functional form. Journal of Money, Credit, and Banking 28, 178–199.

Pi, L. and Timme, S. G., 1993. Corporate control and bank efficiency. Journal of Banking and Finance 17, 515–530.

Sealey, C. and Lindley, J., 1977. Inputs, outputs, and a theory of production and cost at depository financial institutions. Journal of Finance 32, 1251–1266.

Shaffer, S., 1994. A revenue-restricted cost study of 100 large banks. Applied Financial Economics 4, 193–205.

Shaffer, S. and David, E., 1991. Economies of superscale in commercial banking. Applied Economics 23, 283–293.

Spong, K., Sullivan, R., and DeYoung, R., 1995. What makes a bank efficient? A look at financial characteristics and bank management and ownership structure. Financial and Industry Perspectives, Federal Reserve Bank of Kansas City.

Stevenson, R. E., 1980. Likelihood functions for generalized stochastic frontier estimation. Journal of Econometrics 13, 57–66.

# Part 2

## Drivers of Performance: Identification, Specification, and Measurement

# 4

## Diversification, Organization, and Efficiency: Evidence from Bank Holding Companies[a]

Peter G. Klein[b], Marc R. Saidenberg[c]

**Abstract**
We use a portfolio-simulation technique to estimate the value added from diversification by bank holding companies. Using a sample of multi-bank bank holding companies (MBHCs) from 1990 to 1994, we construct pro forma benchmark portfolios for each MBHC composed of shares of single banks, weighted to correspond to be MBHC's distribution of activities across size and state. We then compare the performance and characteristics of the MBHCs with those of their pro forma benchmarks. We find that diversification within the holding-company structure does bring benefits: the MBHCs hold less capital and do more lending, on average, than their pro forma benchmarks. They also earn enough income to compensate for the administrative costs of internal organization. These findings are consistent with an efficiency explanation for diversification stressing internal-capital-market advantages, rather than an empire-building explanation.

## 1 Introduction

The current wave of takeovers, restructurings, and consolidations in the banking industry raises new questions about the efficient scale and scope

[a] The opinions expressed in this paper do not necessarily reflect those of the Federal Reserve Bank of New York or the Federal Reserve System.
[b] Department of Economics, University of Georgia, Athens, GA 30602-6254, (706) 542-3697 (voice), (706) 542-3376 (fax), pklein@terry.uga.edu.
[c] Federal Reserve Bank of New York, 33 Liberty Street, New York, NY 10045, (212) 720-5968 (voice), (212) 720-8363 (fax), Marc.Saidenberg@ny.frb.org.

of the firm in the financial-services industry. Until recently, the size, product range, and internal organization of banks were prescribed within fairly narrow boundaries. Beginning in the early 1980s, however, changes in state-level banking laws gave rise to new institutions such as the diversified, interstate, multi-bank bank holding company (MBHC). Are diversified financial services firms more efficient than traditional, narrowly focused banks, insurance firms, and securities underwriters? Do these new forms of organization create efficiencies, or merely build banking empires? These are particularly important questions now that the Riegle–Neal Act allows geographically diversified MBHCs to shed their holding-company structures and branch across state lines.

Moreover, some observers argue that banks should be allowed to engage in non-bank activities directly, diversifying internally rather than through the holding-company structure (see Whalen, 1997, for example). It is important, then, to know if the holding-company structure itself has advantages, beyond those of asset diversification per se. We address this issue by comparing MBHCs to portfolios of assets that are similarly diversified, yet without the holding-company structure. In this way we separate the effects of diversification and organizational form.

We use a portfolio test to evaluate the efficiency of diversified bank holding companies. Efficiency studies in banking are usually carried out at the level of the individual bank, comparing banks to an industry-specific "best-practice" frontier.[1] Instead, we focus on the holding company itself. We compare MBHCs with pure-play portfolios composed of single banks, chosen and weighted to match the size and location of the MBHC's subsidiaries. These pro forma holding companies ("pro forma BHCs") capture the risk-smoothing benefits of diversification, thus providing performance benchmarks for each MBHC. By comparing the performance of the MBHCs to that of the pure-play benchmarks, we measure the effect of organizational form, controlling for size and geographic diversification. The comparison assesses the benefits of diversifying within a holding company independent of the benefits of diversification per se. From this we can see if MBHCs perform like simple collections of smaller banks, or if they generate organization-wide synergies.

MBHCs have at least two built-in disadvantages compared to portfolios of assets. First, the placement of multiple business units within a single firm must carry with it some additional administrative or "bureaucratic" costs (otherwise we are back to Coase's [1937] question: why isn't

---

[1] See Berger and Humphrey, 1997, for a recent survey.

all production carried on within a single firm?). Second, adding or removing additional business units from a banking conglomerate should incur higher transaction costs than those associated with changing the composition of a portfolio; buying and selling shares is easier than acquiring or spinning off subsidiaries. For these reasons, if MBHCs perform as well as, or better than, pure-play portfolios of independent banks, then there must be synergies that exceed the bureaucratic and transactional disadvantages of firm-level diversification. If the MBHCs perform worse than their corresponding portfolios, then there are no such efficiencies, or the efficiencies are smaller than the transaction costs, and an empire-building explanation should be preferred.

Our sample contains 412 observations on MBHCs from 1990 to 1994. For each MBHC in each year, we match its subsidiaries to randomly selected independent banks, matched by size and state, and aggregate these single banks into a pro forma BHC. We then compute weighted-average balance-sheet and income statistics for the pro forma BHCs and the corresponding MBHCs. We find that MBHCs act as unified banking institutions and not merely portfolios of assets: on average, the MBHCs do significantly more lending, and hold significantly less capital, than their pro forma benchmarks. Furthermore, we find no evidence for empire building: the MBHCs earn about the same income as their corresponding portfolios, suggesting that they earn enough additional income to compensate for the higher transaction costs of internal organization.

How can diversified MBHCs hold less capital and do more lending than their pure-play benchmarks? We suggest that these organizations benefit not only from diversification, but also from access to an "internal capital market" that reallocates resources within the firm. If this internal capital market can provide funds to subsidiaries more easily than the external financial markets can provide funds to independent banks, then a diversified MBHC made up of such subsidiaries can hold less capital than a similar collection of independent banks. Similarly, if the internal capital market can channel funds quickly and efficiently toward high-yield projects available to a particular subsidiary, then a diversified MBHC can do more lending than a similar collection of independent banks.

Because of these desirable balance-sheet characteristics, the MBHCs can generate additional income to offset the transaction costs of internal organization. We do find that MBHCs have higher non-interest incomes, on average, than their benchmark portfolios. This might suggest that their additional incomes derive from participation in different activities, rather than any internal-capital-market advantages. However, the MBHCs also have higher non-interest expenses (salaries and benefits as well as premises and fixed assets), so the mix of activities alone cannot explain the income results. On the whole, our results imply that banks benefit from geographic diversification and access to internal capital markets. We show, more generally, that organizational form is important, and that further research on the effects of organizational form on behavior and performance is needed.

The remainder of the chapter is organized as follows. Section 2 reviews the literature on diversification and organizational form and argues that access to internal capital markets provides a compelling efficiency rationale for diversification. Section 3 describes our data and our procedure for estimating the benefits of diversification within the holding company. Results and discussion are presented in Section 4. Section 5 concludes and suggests directions for future research.

## 2  Why Do Firms Diversify?

The demise of the single-product firm and the rise of the large, diversified organization are two of the greatest changes in the American corporate sector over the postwar period. Rumelt (1982, p. 361) reports that the percentage of Fortune 500 firms classified as "single business" fell from 42.0 in 1949 to 22.8 in 1959, and again to 14.4 in 1974, while the percentage of "unrelated business" firms rose from 4.1 in 1949, to 7.3 in 1959, to 20.7 by 1974. Servaes (1996), using Standard Industrial Classification codes to measure diversification, finds a similar pattern throughout this period. Among firms making acquisitions, the trend is even stronger: pure conglomerate or unrelated-business mergers, as defined by the FTC, jumped from 3.2% of all mergers in 1948–53 to 15.9% in 1956–63, to 33.2% in 1963–72, and then to 49.2% in 1973–77 (Federal Trade Commission, 1981).

Today despite evidence of de-diversification or "refocus" during the 1980s (Lichtenberg, 1992; Liebeskind and Opler, 1995; Comment and Jarrell, 1995), major U.S. corporations continue to be diversified. Montgomery (1994) reports that for each of the years 1985, 1989, and 1992, over two-thirds of the Fortune 500 companies were active in at least five distinct lines of business (defined by four-digit SIC codes). As she reminds us, "While the popular press and some researchers have highlighted recent divestiture activity among [the largest U.S.] firms, claiming a 'return to the core,' some changes at the margin must not obscure the fact that these firms remain remarkably diversified" (p. 163).

There is no consensus on why this transformation has taken place. Indeed, we lack a generally accepted theory of the rationale for diversification or of when the efficient boundary of the firm extends across multiple product lines. Here we review briefly some common explanations for diversification, particularly as applied to the provision of financial services. Both efficiency and agency explanations appear in the literature. For our purposes, two of the explanations are the most plausible: the "internal-capital-market" advantages of the diversified, divisionalized firm (an efficiency explanation), and managerial entrenchment (an agency explanation). If MBHCs are better performers than their pure-play benchmarks, then internal-capital-market advantages are implied. If they are worse performers, then these advantages must not obtain, and diversification implies entrenchment.

### 2.1 Efficiency

In the efficiency view, product and market diversification allows banks to reduce firm-specific risk by holding a greater variety of assets and offering a greater variety of services (Saunders, Strock, and Travlos, 1990). However, risk reduction alone is not a complete efficiency rationale for diversification. For publicly traded banks, at least, shareholders can reduce their risk by holding a diversified portfolio of non-diversified banks, gaining the risk-reducing advantages of diversification without incurring the costs of managing a large organization (Levy and Sarnat, 1970). Risk pooling at the level of the firm should actually be more costly than risk pooling at the level of the individual investor, since the transaction costs of buying or selling stock are presumably lower than the transaction costs of adding or liquidating a division (Williamson, 1975, p. 144). Diversification to reduce risk does, of course, benefit managers, who may try to reduce their own "employment risk" at the expense of the value of the firm (Amihud and Lev, 1981). For this reason, diversification is thought to be beneficial only if it also provides economies of scope.

There are at least two potential sources of scope economies in financial services: "internal" or cost economies of scope, in joint production and marketing, and "external" or revenue economies of scope in consumption. Internal economies of scope may come from excess capacity in computer and telecommunications equipment that can be used for a variety of products, or from customer information (credit histories, ratings, and the like) that can be used jointly to produce multiple outputs (Clark, 1988; Mester, 1987). External economies of scope exist if there are benefits to the consumer of "one-stop shopping" for various financial services (Berger, Humphrey, and Pulley, 1996).

Undoubtedly, scale and scope economies are important determinants of bank structure and conduct (see Berger, Hunter, and Timme, 1993, for an overview). However, these properties of cost and revenue functions do not fully account for the size and shape of the firm as a legal entity. Economies of scope imply joint production, but the joint production need not take place within a single firm. Absent contracting costs, two separate banks could simply contract to share the inputs, facilities, or whatever accounts for the relevant scope economies (Teece, 1980, 1982). The cost-saving advantages of joint production and marketing, for example, could be achieved by two separate firms contracting to share facilities, customer data, and marketing information. For the consumer, the advantages of one-stop shopping for bank, insurance, and securities transactions can also be realized by contractual agreements among the various providers. In neither case is organizational integration necessary, unless the costs of writing or enforcing the relevant contracts are greater than the benefits from joint production. Whether the firms will integrate thus depends primarily on the comparative costs and benefits of contracting, not on the underlying production function.[2]

Alchian (1969), Williamson (1975, pp. 155–75), and more recently Gertner, Scharfstein, and Stein (1994) and Stein (1997) offer an explanation for the multi-product firm based on intra-firm capital allocation. In this theory, the diversified firm is best understood as an alternative resource-allocation mechanism. Capital markets act to allocate resources between single-product firms. In the diversified, multidivisional firm, by contrast, resources are allocated via an internal capital market: funds are distributed among profit-center divisions by the central headquarters of the firm (HQ). This miniature capital market replicates the allocative and disciplinary roles of the financial markets, ideally shifting resources toward more profitable activities.[3] For a diversified bank, the internal

---

[2] There is a large empirical literature adopting this "comparative contracting" approach. Following Coase (1937), Williamson (1975, 1985), Klein, Crawford, and Alchian (1978), and Grossman and Hart (1986), this research seeks to explain firm boundaries as responses to contracting hazards brought about by relationship-specific assets, uncertainty, frequency, and other conditions of trade. For a survey of the empirical literature, see Shelanski and Klein (1995).

[3] Such a process is described explicitly in the annual reports of some conglomerates from the 1960s and 1970s. Fuqua Industries, a conglomerate with interests in lawn and garden equipment, sports and recreation, entertainment, photofinishing, transportation, housing, and food and beverages, reports that its corporate strategy is "to allocate resources into business segments having prospects of the highest return on investment and to extract resources from areas where the future return on investment does not meet our ongoing requirements. . . . The same principle of expanding areas of high return and shrinking

capital market could shift funds to subsidiaries with sudden capital requirements, or to subsidiaries with access to particularly attractive lending opportunities.

According to the internal capital markets theory, diversified institutions arise when imperfections in the external capital market permit internal management to allocate and manage funds more efficiently than the external capital market. These efficiencies may come from several sources. First, HQ typically has access to information unavailable to external parties, which it extracts through its own internal auditing and reporting procedures (Williamson, 1975, pp. 145–47).[4] Second, managers inside the firm may also be more willing to reveal information to HQ than to outsiders, since revealing the same information to the capital market would also reveal it to rivals, potentially hurting the firm's competitive position.[5] Third, HQ can intervene selectively, making marginal changes to divisional operating procedures, whereas the external market can discipline a division only by raising or lowering the share price of the entire firm. Fourth, HQ has residual rights of control that providers of outside finance do not have, making it easier to redeploy the assets of poorly performing divisions (Gertner, Scharfstein, and Stein, 1994). More generally, these control rights allow HQ to add value by engaging in "winner picking" among competing projects when credit to the firm as a whole is constrained (Stein, 1997). Fifth, the internal capital market may react more "rationally" to new information: those who dispense the funds need only take into account their own expectations about the returns to a particular investment, and not their expectations about other investors' expectations. Hence there would be no speculative bubbles or waves.

Bhide (1990) uses the internal-capital-markets framework to explain both the 1960s and 1980s merger waves, regarding these developments as responses to changes in the relative efficiencies of internal and exter-

---

areas of low return is constantly extended to product lines and markets within individual Fuqua operations. Only with a diversified business structure is the application of this modern fundamental business investment policy practical" (1977 *Annual Report*).

Another conglomerate, Bangor Punta Corporation, explained that the role of its corporate HQ is "to act as a central bank supplying operating units with working capital and capital funds" (1966 *Annual Report*).

[4] Myers and Majluf (1984) show that if the information asymmetry between a stand-alone firm and potential outside investors is large enough, the firm may forego investments with positive net present value rather than issue risky securities to finance them.

[5] Bhattacharya and Ritter (1983) model the trade-off between the benefits of external finance and the loss of firm value from revealing private information to rivals. They find that limited revelation to outside parties can be sustained in equilibrium.

nal finance. For instance, the re-specialization or "refocus" of the 1980s can be explained as a consequence of the rise of takeovers by tender offer rather than by proxy contest, the emergence of new financial techniques and instruments like leveraged buyouts and high-yield bonds, and the appearance of takeover and breakup specialists like Kohlberg Kravis Roberts which themselves performed many functions of the conglomerate HQ (Williamson, 1992). Furthermore, the emergence of the conglomerate in the 1960s can itself be traced to the emergence of the multidivisional corporation. Because the multidivisional structure treats business units as semi-independent profit centers, it is much easier for a multidivisional corporation to expand via acquisition than it is for the older unitary structure. New acquisitions can be integrated smoothly when they can preserve much of their internal structure and retain control over day-to-day operations. In this sense, the conglomerate could emerge only after the innovation of the multidivisional firm had diffused widely throughout the corporate sector.

### 2.2 Agency

Not all explanations for diversification claim efficiency. In the agency or entrenchment view, managers diversify, especially by acquisition, primarily to increase their compensation, job security, or span of control (Amihud and Lev, 1981; Born, Eisenbeis, and Harris, 1988). Managers may entrench themselves by investing in projects for which they have specialized expertise – an idiosyncratic filing system, for example (Shleifer and Vishny, 1989) – or by investing in projects with noisier returns (Edlin and Stiglitz, 1995). Diversification may allow cross-subsidization of unprofitable divisions, whose losses do not appear on consolidated balance sheets. Diversification via acquisition can also be a form of "empire building," if expansion into particular industries is a key to rapid growth.[6]

Even if diversification via acquisition merely facilitated empire building by managers of bidding firms, there could still be net efficiency gains if it were the case that these takeovers disciplined the managers of target firms. Evidence on the disciplinary effect of the takeover wave of the late

---

[6] Aron (1988) and Hermalin and Katz (1993) suggest, by contrast, that diversification may itself be a form of corporate governance, in that multiple product lines facilitate multiple measures of managerial performance. However, diversification is a costly way of getting additional performance measures, since multiple measures are typically available for the single-business firm as well – share price, earnings, return on equity, and so on.

1960s and early 1970s is mixed. Curbing managerial slack may well have been an important contributing factor.[7]

On the whole, however, the entrenchment literature suggests that diversification, particularly via expansion, reduces shareholder value. In that case we expect MBHCs to perform poorly relative to similarly diversified groups of assets that are not organized as banking conglomerates.

### 2.3 A Summing Up

We have identified two candidate explanations for the diversified firm: (1) internal-capital-market advantages (an efficiency explanation) and (2) entrenchment (an agency explanation). Each offers different predictions about the characteristics of MBHCs relative to their pure-play benchmarks. Recall that organizing activities within a diversified MBHC incurs administrative costs not borne by diversification within a portfolio. Absent internal-capital-market efficiencies, then, a banking conglomerate should perform worse than a portfolio of independent banks. This allows a simple test between our two candidate explanations. A profit-maximizing bank will diversify only if the benefits of creating an internal capital market are at least as great as the costs of internal organization. An inefficient bank run by empire-building managers will diversify even if the benefits do not exceed the costs. Thus if our MBHCs perform as well as, or better than, their benchmark portfolios, diversification reflects efficiency considerations. If the MBHCs perform worse than the benchmarks, then diversification mainly reflects empire building.

Because we try to measure organizational, not technological, economies of scope, our approach differs from those used in the efficiency literature (Humphrey, 1985; Berger, Hanweck, and Humphrey, 1987; Berger and Humphrey, 1991; Aly, Grabowski, Pasurka, and Rangan, 1990; Ferrier, Grosskopf, Hayes, and Yaisawarng, 1993). Frontier models test for scale and scope economies *within* multi-product banks. We look for scope

---

[7] Ravenscraft and Scherer (1987) argue that this disciplinary motive cannot explain most of the mergers in the late 1960s and early 1970s, because targets tended to be profitable, well-managed firms. Their study of 634 mergers from 1968, 1971, and 1974 finds that the target firms had average profit rates twice those of the industry averages. However, Ravenscraft and Scherer's sample pools both large public targets and small private ones, whereas the disciplinary motive would explain only takeovers of large, publicly held firms. Matsusaka (1993) examines an expanded version of Ravenscraft and Scherer's sample, distinguishing between publicly and privately held targets. He finds that while both types of target tended to be more profitable than their industry averages, the average pre-merger profitability of the public targets was significantly lower than that of the private targets.

economies *between* the subsidiaries of a multi-bank bank holding company. Because we choose our matches according to characteristics of the subsidiaries, we take no position in the debate between the "production approach" and the "intermediation approach."[8] In the production approach, banks are seen as transforming stocks of capital and labor into stocks of accounts (loans and deposits), measured by the number of accounts (see, for example, Ferrier and Lovell, 1990; Ferrier, Grosskopf, Hayes, and Yaisawarng, 1993). In the intermediation approach, banks are seen as intermediaries transforming flows of deposits into interest-earning assets (loans), measured in dollar values (see, for example, Berger and Humphrey, 1991). In either approach, economies of scope are due to the combined use of some input(s). Our study looks for economies of scope due to organizational form, not technology.

### 3  Data and Methods

We distinguish the internal-capital-market hypothesis from the entrenchment hypothesis by examining the efficiency of the diversified banking structure. One way to estimate the effects of diversification is to compare the average income or profit of diversified banks with that of specialized banks. However, if the subsidiaries of a diversified bank systematically operate at a more efficient scale, or are systematically located in more prosperous states, then such a comparison will lead to the conclusion that diversification enhances profitability even though the positive relation between diversification and profit has nothing to do with diversification itself. To eliminate this problem, we compare the profits of MBHCs with the profits they would have if the profit of each subsidiary were the profit of a randomly selected independent bank from the same state and about the same size. This comparison assesses the benefits of diversification within the holding company independent of the benefits of diversification per se. Following Lang and Stulz (1994), we call this hypothetical profit the pure-play profit or the industry-adjusted profit. If diversification adds value, then the profit of MBHCs should exceed the pure-play profit. If the MBHC profit is less than the pure-play profit, then bank performance could presumably be improved by dismantling the holding company into a group of independent banks.

### 3.1  Matching Procedure

Data are taken from the quarterly Statements of Income and Condition (Call Reports) filed by commercial banks. We begin by considering all

---

[8]  See Humphrey (1985) for the distinction.

holding companies meeting the following two criteria. First, the holding company must have two or more commercial bank subsidiaries. Second, these commercial bank subsidiaries cannot all be located in the same state. Over the 1990–94 period (fourth quarters), this includes 952 MBHC observations with a total of 7,400 commercial-bank subsidiaries. For each of these 7,400 subsidiaries, we then search for single banks (including subsidiaries of one-bank holding companies) that, during the same year, operated in the same state as the MBHC subsidiary and were within 25% of the MBHC subsidiary in total assets. With these criteria we can identify, on average, 21.7 potential matches per MBHC subsidiary.[9]

We also experimented with different matching criteria, exploring the trade-off between the "tightness" of the criterion (e.g., asset size) and the ability to generate a reasonable sample. For instance, a fairly loose matching criterion (±50% in assets) generates matches for all but 207 of the 1,499 MBHC subsidiaries for 1994 (87%), giving us 121 MBHC observations for that year with all subsidiaries matched. A tighter criterion (±10%) matches only 1,077 of the 1,499 unit banks (72%), giving only 77 MBHC observations with all subsidiaries matched. We choose ±25% as an intermediate criterion.

We then randomly select, from the set of potential matches identified above, a matched pair for each MBHC subsidiary. We can match 5,949 of the 7,400 subsidiaries.[10] The final sample include only MBHCs in a given year for which we could match each subsidiary; this leaves 418 MBHC observations with all subsidiaries matched. Subsequently, 6 of the 418 were dropped due to missing balance-sheet data. Using the matched pairs for the subsidiaries of each MBHC, we construct a pro forma BHC as a pure-play benchmark for its corresponding MBHC. Our final sample contains 412 multi-state, multi-bank bank holding companies and 412 matching pro forma holding companies.[11]

---

[9] The median number of matches was 11, with a minimum of 0 and a maximum of 217.

[10] In general, the subsidiaries that failed to match were the very largest and the very smallest.

[11] Note that we treat each MBHC-year as a separate observation; we do not construct a set of pro forma BHCs for 1990 and then track them for five years. This yearly resampling raises the concern that a particular single bank could be matched repeatedly to make up a given pro forma BHC. However, of the 1,521 single banks constituting the matched pairs for the five-year period, one was selected four times, five were selected three times, 74 were selected twice, and the remaining 1,354 were selected only once. None of the banks that appeared three or four times were among the very largest or very smallest banks.

Similar studies of diversification in manufacturing choose matched pairs by industry and year. Lang and Stulz (1994) and Rajan, Servaes, and Zingales (2000) match by three-digit SIC code and year; Klein (1998) matches by two-digit SIC code, year, and size. Because we are looking within a single industry, we match not by SIC code, but by state – state proxies for the environment and activities in which a bank is involved.[12] We thus use state, year, and size as matching criteria. Of course, these criteria do not ensure that all relevant characteristics of the MBHC subsidiaries are controlled for in the matching procedure. Our MBHC subsidiaries could be systematically different from their potential matched pairs in output mix, relative risk, or efficiency. However, including additional matching criteria in this type of study may not be warranted, for several reasons. First, given the difficulties of generating a usable sample when matching by size and state alone, adding further restrictions to the matching routine would leave too few potential matched pairs to draw truly random matches. Second, as we explain below, the MBHCs and the pro forma BHCs we construct while matching by size and state do turn out to have similar mixes of output and risk, so we do not believe differences in activities between the MBHC subsidiaries and the matching independent banks are driving our results.

Third and most important, we do not match by efficiency level because this would exclude the possibility that efficiency is itself a function of organizational form. In our framework, the unit of observation is the holding company, not the individual bank; we take bank-level efficiency to be endogenous. Suppose, for example, that one of our MBHCs is more efficient than its pure-play alternative because its subsidiaries were highly efficient. This means either that the holding company has systematically targeted more efficient banks for acquisition, or that governance from the parent holding company has caused the member banks to become collectively more efficient. In either case, the source of the efficiency gain is organizational form.

### 3.2 Descriptive Statistics

Table 4.1 provides descriptive statistics about the MBHCs and the pro forma BHCs. As is apparent from the table, the matching process produces pro forma BHCs with characteristics very similar to those of the MBHCs. The MBHCs average $750.173 million in assets and cover a fairly wide range from $19 million to $9.8 billion. Similarly, the pro forma

---

[12] Because regulation varies by state, not locality, we use state rather than a finer measure such as MSA (Metropolitan Statistical Area).

Table 4.1. *Descriptive statistics for MBHCs and pro forma BHCs, 1990–94.*

| | $n$ | Mean | Standard deviation | Minimum | Maximum |
|---|---|---|---|---|---|
| Total assets, MBHCs | 412 | 750,173 | 1,426,344 | 19,643 | 9,854,872 |
| Total assets, pro forma BHCs | 412 | 720,395 | 1,388,230 | 17,992 | 10,300,000 |
| Number of banks (subsidiaries) | 412 | 3.6578 | 3.5166 | 2 | 33 |
| Number of states | 412 | 2.0922 | 0.3363 | 2 | 5 |

*Note*: Assets in thousands of US dollars.

BHCs average $720.395 million in assets, ranging from $17 million to $10.3 billion. For both the sample of MBHCs and the sample of pro forma BHCs, the number of states ranges from two to five, and the number of bank subsidiaries ranges from two to 33.

For each of the MBHCs and pro forma BHCs, we examine balance-sheet and income ratios. We calculate these ratios for each MBHC, and then calculate a weighted average for each corresponding pro forma BHC. (The ratios for each MBHC were constructed, similarly, as a weighted average of its commercial bank subsidiaries.) Finally, for each of these performance measures, we then compare each bank's performance to that of its pure-play counterpart by testing the hypothesis that the sample means of the two groups, MBHCs and pro forma BHCs, are significantly different.

## 4 Results

### 4.1 Capital and Lending

We begin by looking at two balance-sheet characteristics, capital-asset ratio (equity capital/total assets) and lending activity (total loans/total assets). Results of the matched pairs tests are given in Tables 4.2 and 4.3. As evident from Table 4.2, the MBHCs hold, on average, almost one percentage point less capital relative to total assets than do the pro forma BHCs (statistically significant at the 1% level). For a bank holding company this is economically meaningful as well as statistically significant. Likewise, the MBHCs have lending-to-asset ratios over three percentage points higher than their pure-play benchmarks (also statistically significant at the 1% level).

Table 4.2. *Balance-sheet characteristics of MBHCs and pro forma BHCs.*

|  | MBHCs | Pro Forma BHCs | Difference |
|---|---|---|---|
| Capital-asset ratio | 0.08388 | 0.09236 | −0.00848** |
| (equity capital/total assets) | (0.00141) | (0.00109) | |
| Lending activity | 0.59195 | 0.55949 | 0.03246** |
| (total loans/total assets) | (0.00596) | (0.00565) | |

*Note*: ** Significant at the 1% level.
* Significant at the 5% level.
Standard errors are in parentheses. Significance is determined by a paired *t*-test.

We interpret this finding as evidence that MBHCs enjoy the benefits of both geographic diversification and access to internal capital markets. When a particular subsidiary needs additional funds, it can draw those funds from another subsidiary within the holding company. This allows each subsidiary to hold less capital than an independent bank with similar asset size and geographic characteristics. A holding company will thus tend to hold less capital in the aggregate than a pro forma benchmark holding company. Similarly, the MBHC subsidiaries can rely on the internal capital market for loanable funds when high-yield projects become available. Since the MBHCs do make more lending in the aggregate than their pure-play benchmarks, this internal capital market must have advantages relative to the external financial markets.

Our finding here is consistent with several other recent studies of MBHC behavior. Demsetz (1996) finds that MBHC subsidiaries are both more likely to engage in loan sales, and more likely to engage in loan purchases, than banks that are not part of a holding company. For sales and purchases between banks within the same holding company, there are at least two reasons that MBHC subsidiaries would appear to be more active in the secondary market for loans. If the subsidiaries are acting independently, then membership in the same holding company makes it easier to develop a reputation for truthful disclosure, helping to overcome the adverse-selection problem associated with such transactions. Alternatively, the holding company itself could be acting as a single agent, using the loan sale as a means of shifting resources from one part of the organization to another. In either case, the resulting benefits would be aspects of the internal-capital-market advantages described in Section 2 above.

Table 4.3. *Income characteristics of MBHCs and pro forma BHCs.*

|                                         | MBHCs      | Pro forma BHCs | Difference |
| --------------------------------------- | ---------- | -------------- | ---------- |
| Return on equity                        | 0.10859    | 0.09863        | 0.00996    |
| (net income/total equity)               | (0.00911)  | (0.00534)      |            |
| Return on assets                        | 0.01011    | 0.00952        | 0.00060    |
| (net income/total assets)               | (0.00052)  | (0.00034)      |            |

*Note*: ** Significant at the 1% level.
* Significant at the 5% level.
Standard errors are in parentheses. Significance is determined by a paired *t*-test.

In a more direct test, Houston, James, and Marcus (1997) study the relationship between lending and cash flows at the MBHC subsidiary level. They find that loan growth at MBHC subsidiaries is more sensitive to the holding company's cash flow and capital position than to the bank's own cash flow and capital. They also find that bank loan growth is negatively related to loan growth among the other subsidiaries in the holding company. This suggests that MBHCs do in fact use internal capital markets to allocate funds within their organizations. Similarly, Berger, Saunders, Scalise, and Udell (1998) find that banks tend to do more lending following a merger. Our results suggest that this may be because the bank now has access to funds taken from within the larger, merged entity.

### 4.2 Income

Despite the transaction costs of internal organization, our MBHCs earn about the same incomes as their pure-play counterparts. This is shown in Table 4.3, which compares two income measures, return on equity (net income/total capital) and return on assets (net income/total assets). As seen in the table, the MBHCs average a return on equity of 10.9%, compared with 9.9% for the pro forma BHCs, but this difference is not statistically significant. The MBHCs average a 1.01% return on assets, compared with 0.95% for the pro forma BHCs, but again the difference is not statistically significant. As before, the matching process controls for size and geographic diversification. Evidently, the benefits of lower capital holdings and higher lending ratios associated with internal capital markets allow the MBHCs to generate income sufficient to overcome their additional administrative expenses.

Table 4.4. *Components of lending for MBHCs and pro forma BHCs (all amounts as a fraction of total assets).*

|  | MBHCs | Pro forma BHCs | Difference |
|---|---|---|---|
| Commercial and industrial | 0.09823 (0.00274) | 0.09346 (0.00109) | 0.00477 |
| Real estate | 0.32297 (0.00617) | 0.30860 (0.00581) | 0.01437* |
| Agriculture | 0.04616 (0.00371) | 0.04278 (0.00331) | 0.00338 |
| Consumer | 0.10494 (0.00524) | 0.10019 (0.00517) | 0.00475 |

*Note*: ** Significant at the 1% level.
* Significant at the 5% level.
Standard errors are in parentheses. Significance is determined by a paired *t*-test.

### 4.3 Output Mix, Risk, and Efficiency

As discussed above, because we match by size and state, our MBHC subsidiaries could be systematically different from their potential matched pairs in output mix, relative risk, and technical efficiency. To see if such differences are driving our results, we separated both lending activity and income into components. Table 4.4 gives the value of total loans (as a fraction of total assets) by both the MBHCs and the pro forma BHCs in each of four categories: commercial-and-industrial loans, real-estate loans, agricultural loans, and consumer loans. The MBHCs do more lending in each of the four categories (the difference is statistically significant only for real-estate loans). Apparently, the MBHCs' ability to channel funds to high-yield projects is not specific to a particular sector. Furthermore, to the extent the overall risk of the organization is correlated with the composition of its lending, the MBHCs and the pro forma BHCs have similar levels of risk.

We also broke down the income results into components. Table 4.5 shows interest income, interest expense, non-interest income, and non-interest expense for the MBHCs and pro forma BHCs. Non-interest expense is also broken down into salaries and benefits and premises and fixed assets. Interestingly, the MBHCs as a group have significantly higher non-interest expenses, both for salaries and benefits and for premises and fixed assets. This may reflect additional overhead associated with being a subsidiary of a holding company rather than an independent bank. (Since our MBHC data are aggregated from

Table 4.5. *Components of income for MBHCs and pro forma BHCs*
*(all amounts as a fraction of total assets).*

|  | MBHCs | Pro forma BHCs | Difference |
|---|---|---|---|
| Interest income | 0.07785 | 0.07745 | 0.00040 |
|  | (0.00071) | (0.00073) |  |
| Interest expense | 0.03668 | 0.03679 | −0.00011 |
|  | (0.00059) | (0.00056) |  |
| Non-interest income | 0.01538 | 0.00902 | 0.00636** |
|  | (0.00183) | (0.00057) |  |
| Non-interest expense | 0.03765 | 0.03245 | 0.00521** |
|  | (0.00145) | (0.00059) |  |
| Salaries and benefits | 0.01691 | 0.01543 | 0.00148** |
|  | (0.00051) | (0.00021) |  |
| Premises and fixed assets | 0.00488 | 0.00438 | 0.00050** |
|  | (0.00013) | (0.00008) |  |

*Note*: ** Significant at the 1% level.
* Significant at the 5% level.
Standard errors are in parentheses. Significance is determined by a paired $t$-test.

the MBHC's member banks, these are not expenses for an independent central office.) However, the MBHCs also have significantly higher non-interest income, so the additional administrative expense should be offset by additional revenues. The MBHCs have about the same interest income and interest expense as the pro forma BHCs. Thus, the MBHCs' inability to translate their increased lending into higher income is not due to an obvious difference in activities or administrative expenses.

### 4.4 Robustness Tests

How robust are these findings? There are at least two general areas of concern. The first is that we measure the performance of each MBHC as a weighted average of the performance of its commercial bank subsidiaries, rather than using consolidated balance-sheet and income data. Second, we pool a large number of banks over a five-year period, possibly obscuring differences between large and small MBHCs and differences across time. We address these concerns below.

A potential weakness of our analysis is the omission of an MBHC's nonbank subsidiaries. In constructing our pure-play benchmarks, we match only the commercial bank subsidiaries of each MBHC. This is because we do not have a suitable pool of independent trading companies, leasing operations, and check processing firms from which to draw matches for the nonbank subsidiaries. Consequently, we compute the performance ratios for each MBHC as weighted averages of the performance ratios of its commercial bank subsidiaries. An alternative would be to compute the same ratios for the MBHCs using consolidated financial statements (Y-9C forms), which include nonbank subsidiaries. To check that the exclusion of nonbank subsidiaries is not driving our findings, we recomputed these ratios using the Y-9C data and re-did our balance-sheet and income comparisons. All our qualitative conclusions held: the MBHCs hold less capital and do more lending, on average, than their pure-play alternatives, while earning about the same levels of income (by both income measures).

Next, we split the sample by year to see if our findings were consistent across time. We tried two splits, 1990–92 and 1993–94, and then 1990–91 and 1992–94. With either split, the balance-sheet results are the same in both periods; the income results are the same in the first period and slightly stronger in the second period (for the 1993–94 and 1992–94 periods, the MBHCs earn significantly higher returns on equity than the pro forma portfolios). Our results do not seem particularly sensitive to the period under consideration.

We also divided the sample into size quartiles to see if the results were limited to very large or very small MBHCs. The findings were roughly consistent across quartiles, though the capital and lending results are weaker for the largest banks. In the smallest two quartiles (defined by asset size), the results were the same as our aggregate result: the MBHCs hold less capital and do more lending than the pro forma benchmarks (significant at the 1% level), and there are no statistically significant differences in return on assets (ROA) or return on equity (ROE). In the third and fourth quartiles, the capital and lending results are similar, but weaker: the MBHCs still hold less capital and do more lending than their benchmarks, but the differences are generally not significant. However, the income results are now stronger: the MBHCs now have higher returns on equity (significant at the 5% level in the third quartile and the 1% level in the fourth quartile) and higher returns on assets (significant at the 5% level in the fourth quartile).

This suggests that internal-capital-market advantages are smaller for larger MBHCs. But this is a sensible result: larger MBHCs tend to have larger subsidiaries, so the independent banks making up their pro forma BHCs will tend to be larger. Because large banks have access to their own internal capital market, the gains from combining these large banks into an MBHC will tend to be smaller. That is, the banks in the benchmark portfolios for the largest MBHCs will also be enjoying the internal-capital-market advantages available to the corresponding MBHCs. Furthermore, larger independent banks will tend to have less costly access to external funds, so the relative advantages of the internal finance available within larger MBHCs will be smaller.

## 5 Conclusions

Our chapter distinguishes between two explanations for MBHC diversification, an efficiency explanation based on internal-capital-market advantages, and an agency explanation based on managerial entrenchment. We find support for the efficiency explanation: banks benefit from geographic diversification and the resulting opportunities for internal resource allocation. Specifically, we show that diversified MBHCs can hold less capital and do more lending than pure-play portfolios. Moreover, these MBHCs can earn enough income to compensate for the costs of internal organization, costs not borne by the portfolio benchmarks. Consistent with our thesis, we find that internal-capital-market advantages are smaller for larger MBHCs; larger MBHCs tend to have larger subsidiaries which are more likely to have access to their own internal capital markets. More generally, we show that MBHCs act as unified banking organizations, not merely portfolios of assets. For these reasons, we expect that banks will continue to expand to enjoy the benefits of geographic diversification and access to internal capital markets.

Besides the comparison of MBHCs to pure-play portfolios of nondiversified banks, our technique could be used to evaluate other kinds of diversified financial-services providers. Companies ranging from American Express to Sears, Roebuck to Ford Motor Company engage in insurance, financing, and securities underwriting beyond their primary businesses. A key question in bank regulation and deregulation is whether banks are potentially better providers of such services than these firms whose core businesses are in seemingly unrelated areas. Our approach should prove useful in a future study that includes these nonbank institutions as well.

### Acknowledgments

We thank Rebecca Demsetz, Scott Frame, Beverly Hirtle, Knox Lovell, Joe Sinkey, Philip Strahan, Ron Warren, two anonymous referees, and participants at Wharton's Performance of Financial Institutions Conference for helpful comments and JoAnne Collins, Paul Cowgill, and Yih-Pin Tang for research assistance. The first author thanks the University of Georgia Research Foundation for financial support.

## References

Alchian, Armen A. 1969. "Corporate Management and Property Rights." In Henry Manne, ed., *Economic Policy and the Regulation of Corporate Securities*. Washington, D.C.: American Enterprise Institute, pp. 337–360.

Aly, Hassan Y., Richard Grabowski, Carl A. Pasurka, and Nanda Rangan. 1990. "Technical, Scale, and Allocative Efficiencies in US Banking: An Empirical Investigation." *Review of Economics and Statistics* 72 (May): 211–218.

Amihud, Yakov and Baruch Lev. 1981. "Risk Reduction and a Managerial Motive for Conglomerate Merger." *Bell Journal of Economics* 12 (Autumn): 605–617.

Aron, Debra J. 1988. "Ability, Moral Hazard, Firm Size, and Diversification." *Rand Journal of Economics* 19, no. 1 (Spring): 72–87.

Berger, Allen N., Gerald A. Hanweck, and David B. Humphrey. 1987. "Competitive Viability in Banking: Scale, Scope, and Product Mix Economies." *Journal of Monetary Economics* 20, no. 3 (December): 501–520.

Berger, Allen N. and David B. Humphrey. 1991. "The Dominance of Inefficiencies over Scale and Product Mix Economies in Banking." *Journal of Monetary Economics* 28 (August): 117–148.

Berger, Allen N. and David B. Humphrey. 1997. "Efficiency of Financial Institutions: International Survey and Directions for Future Research." *European Journal of Operations Research*, 98, no. 2 (April): 175–212.

Berger, Allen N., David B. Humphrey, and Lawrence B. Pulley. 1996. "Do Consumers Pay for One-Stop Banking? Evidence from an Alternative Revenue Function." *Journal of Banking and Finance* 20, no. 9 (November): 1601–1621.

Berger, Allen N., William C. Hunter, and Stephen G. Timme. 1993. "The Efficiency of Financial Institutions: A Review and Preview of Research Past, Present, and Future." *Journal of Banking and Finance* 17, nos. 2–3 (April): 221–249.

Berger, Allen N., Anthony Saunders, Joseph M. Scalise, and Gregory S. Udell. 1998. "The Effects of Bank Mergers and Acquisitions on Small Business Lending." *Journal of Financial Economics* 50, no. 2: 187–229.

Bhattacharya, Sudipto and Jay R. Ritter. 1983. "Innovation and Communication: Signalling with Partial Disclosure." *Review of Economic Studies* 50, no. 2 (April): 331–346.

Bhide, Amar. 1990. "Reversing Corporate Diversification." *Journal of Applied Corporate Finance* 3, no. 2: 70–81.

Born, Jeffrey A., Robert A. Eisenbeis, and Robert Harris. 1988. "The Benefits of Geographical and Product Expansion in the Financial Service Industries." *Journal of Financial Services Research* 1 (January): 161–182.

Clark, Jeffrey A. 1988. "Economies of Scale and Scope at Depository Financial Institutions: A Review of the Literature." Federal Reserve Bank of Kansas City, *Economic Review* (September–October): 16–33.

Coase, Ronald H. 1937. "The Nature of the Firm." In idem, *The Firm, the Market, and the Law*. Chicago: University of Chicago Press, 1988.

Comment, Robert and Gregg A. Jarrell. 1995. "Corporate Focus and Stock Returns." *Journal of Financial Economics* 37 (January): 67–87.

Demsetz, Rebecca. 1996. "Bank Loan Sales: New Evidence Regarding the Comparative Advantage Hypothesis." Mimeo, Banking Studies Department, Federal Reserve Bank of New York.

Edlin, Aaron S. and Joseph E. Stiglitz. 1995. "Discouraging Rivals: Managerial Rent-Seeking and Economic Inefficiencies." *American Economic Review* 85, no. 5 (December): 1301–1312.

Federal Trade Commission, Bureau of Economics. 1981. *Statistical Report on Mergers and Acquisitions, 1979*. Washington, D.C.: U.S. Government Printing Office.

Ferrier, Gary D., Shawna Grosskopf, Kathy Hayes, and Suthathip Yaisawarng. 1993. "Economies of Diversification in the Banking Industry: A Frontier Approach." *Journal of Monetary Economics* 31 (April): 229–249.

Ferrier, Gary D. and C. A. Knox Lovell. 1990. "Measuring Cost Efficiency in Banking: Econometric and Linear Programming Evidence." *Journal of Econometrics* 46 (October–November): 229–245.

Gertner, Robert H, David S. Scharfstein, and Jeremy C. Stein. 1994. "Internal Versus External Capital Markets." *Quarterly Journal of Economics* 109 (November): 1211–1230.

Grossman, Sanford J. and Oliver H. Hart. 1986. "The Costs and Benefits of Ownership: A Theory of Vertical and Lateral Intergration." *Journal of Political Economy* 94 (August): 691–719.

Hermalin, Benjamin E. and Michael L. Katz. 1993. "Corporate Diversification and Agency." Mimeo, Department of Economics, University of California, Berkeley.

Houston, Joel, Christopher James, and David Marcus. 1997. "Capital Market Frictions and the Role of Internal Capital Markets in Banking." *Journal of Financial Economics* 46 (November): 135–164.

Humphrey, David B. 1985. "Costs and Scale Economies in Bank Intermediation." In R. C. Aspinwall and Robert A. Eisenbeis, eds., *Handbook for Banking Strategy*. New York: Wiley & Sons.

Klein, Benjamin, Robert A. Crawford, and Armen A. Alchian. 1978. "Vertical Integration, Appropriable Rents, and the Competitive Contracting Process." *Journal of Law and Economics* 21 (October): 297–326.

Klein, Peter G. 1998. "Were the Acquisitive Conglomerates Inefficient? A Reconsideration." Mimeo, Department of Economics, University of Georgia.

Lang, Larry H. P. and René M. Stulz. 1994. "Tobin's *Q*, Corporate Diversification, and Firm Performance." *Journal of Political Economy* 102 (December): 1248–1280.

Levy, H. and M. Sarnat. 1970. "Diversification, Portfolio Analysis, and the Uneasy Case for Conglomerate Mergers." *Journal of Finance* 25 (September): 795–802.

Lichtenberg, Frank. 1992. "Industrial De-diversification and Its Consequences for Productivity." *Journal of Economic Behavior and Organization* 18 (August): 427–438.

Liebeskind, Julia P. and Tim C. Opler. 1995. "The Causes of Corporate Refocusing: Evidence from the 1980s." Mimeo, Fisher College of Business, Ohio State University.

Litan, Robert E. 1987. *What Should Banks Do?* Washington, D.C.: Brookings Institution.

Matsusaka, John G. 1993. "Target Profits and Managerial Discipline During the Conglomerate Merger Wave." *Journal of Industrial Economics* 41, no. 2 (June): 179–189.

Mester, Loretta J. 1987. "Efficient Production of Financial Services: Scale and Scope Economies." Federal Reserve Bank of Philadelphia, *Business Review* (January–February): 15–25.

Montgomery, Cynthia A. 1994. "Corporate Diversification." *Journal of Economic Perspectives* 8 (Summer): 163–178.

Myers, Stewart C. and Nicholas S. Majluf. 1984. "Corporate Financing and Investment Decisions When Firms Have Information That Investors Do Not Have." *Journal of Financial Economics* 13, no. 2 (June): 187–221.

Rajan, Raghuram, Henri Servaes, and Luigi Zingales. 2000. "The Costs of Diversity: The Diversification Discount and Inefficient Investment." *Journal of Finance*, forthcoming.

Ravenscraft, David and F. M. Scherer. 1987. *Mergers, Sell-Offs, and Economic Efficiency*. Washington, D.C.: Brookings Institution.

Rumelt, Richard P. 1982. "Diversification Strategy and Profitability." *Strategic Management Journal* 3, no. 4 (October): 359–369.

Saunders, Anthony, Elizabeth Strock, and Nickolaos G. Travlos. 1990. "Ownership Structure, Deregulation, and Bank Risk Taking." *Journal of Finance* 45 (June): 643–654.

Servaes, Henri. 1996. "The Value of Diversification During the Conglomerate Merger Wave." *Journal of Finance* 51 (September): 1201–1225.

Shelanski, Howard A. and Peter G. Klein. 1995. "Empirical Research in Transaction Cost Economics: A Review and Assessment." *Journal of Law, Economics, and Organization* 11, no. 2 (October): 335–361.

Shleifer, Andrei and Robert W. Vishny. 1989. "Management Entrenchment: The Case of Manager-Specific Investments." *Journal of Financial Economics* 25, no. 1 (November): 123–139.

Siems, Thomas F. 1996. "Bank Mergers and Shareholder Wealth: Evidence from 1995's Megamerger Deals." Federal Reserve Bank of Dallas *Financial Industry Studies* (August): 1–12.

Stein, Jeremy C. 1997. "Internal Capital Markets and the Competition for Corporate Resources." *Journal of Finance* 52, no. 1 (March): 111–133.

Teece, David J. 1980. "Economies of Scope and the Scope of the Enterprise." *Journal of Economic Behavior and Organization* 1, no. 3: 223–247.

Teece, David J. 1982. "Towards an Economic Theory of the Multi-Product Firm." *Journal of Economic Behavior and Organization* 3: 39–64.

Whalen, Gary. 1997. "Bank Organizational Form and the Risks of Expanded Activities." Office of the Comptroller of the Currency Economics, Working Paper, 97–101.

Williamson, Oliver E. 1975. *Markets and Hierarchies: Analysis and Antitrust Implications.* New York: Free Press.

Williamson, Oliver E. 1985. *The Economic Institutions of Capitalism.* New York: Free Press.

Williamson, Oliver E. 1992. "Markets, Hierarchies, and the Modern Corporation: An Unfolding Perspective." *Journal of Economic Behavior and Organization* 17, no. 3 (May): 335–352.

# 5

# Product Focus Versus Diversification: Estimates of X-Efficiency for the U.S. Life Insurance Industry

Joseph W. Meador[a], Harley E. Ryan, Jr.[b],
Carolin D. Schellhorn[c]

## Abstract

Using data for the life insurance industry during 1990–1995, we empirically test for a relationship between a firm's output choice and measures of X-efficiency. Our empirical evidence suggests that diversification across multiple product lines resulted in greater X-efficiency than a more focused product strategy. The analysis in this article is consistent with the proposition that managers of multiproduct firms are able to achieve greater cost efficiencies than their counterparts in more focused firms by sharing inputs and efficiently allocating resources across product lines in response to changing industry conditions. Our findings are important since they help explain the existence of multiproduct firms in the absence of cost complementarities and identify product diversification as a source of cost efficiency in the life insurance industry that should be recognized by managers, policyholders, and regulators.

## 1 Introduction

Increased competition, consolidation, and a changing regulatory environment have characterized the life insurance industry in recent years.

[a] College of Business Administration, Finance Group, 413 Hayden, Northeastern University, Boston, MA 02115, 617-373-4713 (voice), 617-373-8798 (fax).
[b] E. J. Ourso College of Business Administration, Louisiana State University, Baton Rouge, LA 70803-6308, 225-388-6258 (voice), 225-388-6366 (fax).
[c] Department of Finance and Law, College of Business and Economics, Lehigh University, Bethlehem, PA 18015, 610-758-4533 (voice), 610-758-6429 (fax).

Profit margins have come under pressure as mutual funds, commercial banks, and independent investment advisors have begun to compete with insurance companies for the same customers.[1] Insurance companies have responded by aggressively marketing products that offer competitive rates of return, such as variable annuities and guaranteed investment contracts. Meanwhile, the National Association of Insurance Commissioners (NAIC) has coordinated a tightening of solvency standards among state insurance regulators, which culminated in the adoption of risk-based capital standards in 1993. These standards require many firms to improve the quality of their assets. Further, increased mergers and acquisitions have led to significant consolidation in the industry [Cummins, Tennyson, and Weiss (1997)]. Inevitably, these developments have intensified financial economists' interests in the "best practices" of efficient firms.

A firm's efficiency is typically affected by managerial decisions regarding the scale and scope of the firm's operation. Recent studies of the life insurance industry document both economies and diseconomies of scale [e.g., Grace and Timme (1992), Yuengert (1993), and Cummins and Zi (1997)] but find little evidence of economies of scope [e.g., Kellner and Mathewson (1983), Fields (1988), and Grace and Timme (1992)]. Despite the apparent lack of cost complementarities, multiproduct firms continue to thrive. One possible reason is that the multiproduct firm offers managers greater opportunities for cost savings from input allocation decisions.[2] The purpose of this chapter is to examine whether a manager's product choices (a diversified versus a focused product offering) influence the firm's X-efficiency.[3] Utilizing Berger's (1993) distribution free

---

[1] For example, non-insurance financial service providers have attracted assets away from insurance companies by offering products that compete directly with annuities and insurance policies that have a savings component.

[2] Another possibility is that multiproduct firms have market advantages leading to higher revenues. Efficiency studies for life insurance companies are limited to an analysis of costs, because the measurement of revenue efficiencies requires estimation of a profit function. While profit function models have been specified for banks [Berger, Hancock, and Humphrey (1993)] and for property-casualty insurers [Berger, Cummins, and Weiss (1997)], researchers are unable to do the same for life insurers, because the available data do not yield credible proxies for the prices of the firm's netputs.

[3] For a definition of X-efficiency that is consistent with the original definition of Leibenstein (1966), see Berger (1993), p. 264:

> X-efficiency is defined as the ratio of the minimum costs that could have been expended to produce a given output bundle to the actual costs expended, and varies between 0 and 100 percent. X-efficiency includes both technical inefficiency, or errors that result in general overuse of inputs, and allocative inefficiency, or errors in choosing an input mix that is consistent with relative prices.

approach (DFA) and a firm-specific product Herfindahl index, we document that diversified life insurance firms are more cost efficient than focused providers. The main contributions of this chapter are: (i) we identify product diversification as a source of efficiency in the life insurance industry, (ii) we update the DFA efficiency estimates reported in Cummins and Zi (1997), and (iii) we provide new evidence on the cross-sectional determinants of X-efficiency in the life insurance industry examined by Gardner and Grace (1993). Our results are important for the managers, policyholders, and regulators of life insurance companies, because they suggest the existence of cost advantages for multiproduct firms. Further, these results should be of interest to the managers and regulators of other financial institutions (e.g., banks) that have become serious competitors of life insurance companies.

Most studies in the recent literature that estimate cost efficiencies for life insurance firms use econometric techniques.[4] Yuengert (1993), for instance, analyzes the measurement of X-efficiency and finds that estimates vary widely. Gardner and Grace (1993) suggest that X-efficiencies are related to rent-seeking activities and external (but not internal) monitoring. Grace and Timme (1992) document the existence of scale economies, but find little evidence of scope economies for multiproduct firms. This result is surprising given the well-publicized trend toward diversified product offerings in the financial services industry. In the absence of cost complementarities, the authors conclude that multiproduct firms may exist to reap the benefits from diversification, or the cost savings from sharing inputs across independent product lines.

We support this conjecture by providing empirical evidence that X-efficiencies are greater for life insurance firms with a diversified product mix compared to firms that focus on a relatively narrow range of outputs. Our results are consistent with variations in X-efficiency due to differences in managers' ability to respond effectively to rapidly changing industry conditions. Compared to their counterparts in more narrowly focused firms, the managers of diversified firms appear better able to contain costs by reallocating inputs among independent product lines when adjusting to shifts in product demands.

Subjecting our data for 1990–1995 to cross-sectional analyses, we test two hypotheses regarding the effect of a life insurer's output choice on estimates of its X-efficiency.

---

[4] An exception is Cummins and Zi (1997), who compare econometric and mathematical programming approaches and find that the choice of estimation methodology may affect the life insurance company efficiency rankings.

1.  *Diversification Hypothesis: X-efficiency increases when managers make resource-allocation decisions for a broader range of distinct, but related, outputs.*

    The outputs of life insurance companies are related in that, to varying degrees, they all involve risk bearing/risk pooling and intermediation. They are distinct in that they address different contingent risks (e.g., health insurance versus life insurance), have different investment characteristics (e.g., an annuity versus life insurance), and are targeted toward different markets (e.g., groups versus individuals). Managers' abilities to reduce costs by sharing inputs and efficiently allocating resources across these product lines may result in greater efficiency. Hence, life insurance companies that offer multiple products may prove more X-efficient than firms that specialize.

2.  *Concentration Hypothesis: X-efficiency increases when managers focus on a particular area of expertise and a small number of product lines.*

    Managers generate cost savings by concentrating their financial and human resources in a single area of expertise. Hence, life insurance companies that focus on a limited product offering may prove more X-efficient than firms that compete in multiple product market segments.

It is possible to test these hypotheses for the life insurance industry since reporting requirements disclose the manager's output choices (individual or group life insurance, health and accident insurance, and individual or group annuity products) and provide sufficient data to estimate X-efficiencies. To estimate X-efficiency, we use the distribution free method, an approach originally suggested in Schmidt and Sickles (1984) and developed by Berger (1993). To measure product focus, we calculate a firm-specific Herfindahl index across each insurance firm's product line premiums. We then perform two independent tests of our hypotheses. First, we conduct an univariate comparison of means and medians for focused (high Herfindahl) versus diversified (low Herfindahl) firms over 1990–1995. Second, we estimate a multivariate fixed effects model over the same time period to control for other firm-specific and environmental factors that have been identified in previous studies of insurer efficiency. Analyzing a sample of 321 life insurance decision-making units (DMUs),[5] we find that multiproduct insurance DMUs are more X-efficient than their more focused counterparts.

The scope of our analysis is also related to research in corporate finance that analyzes the influence of business focus on the value and performance of publicly traded industrial firms. These studies generally

---

[5] An insurance decision-making unit is defined as a group of affiliated insurance firms or an independent insurance firm that is not affiliated with a group. Major decisions for insurance groups are typically made at the group level.

conclude that greater focus leads to increased shareholder wealth. For example, Hite, Owers, and Rogers (1987) find that asset sales by firms increase their value, while John and Ofek (1995) present evidence that asset sales lead to improved operating performance. Results reported by Wernerfelt and Montgomery (1988) suggest that Tobin's q, the market value of a firm's assets divided by their replacement value, is negatively related to the number of industries in which a firm operates.[6] There are two fundamental differences, however, between these studies and our paper. First, our analysis of life insurance companies addresses the *intra-industry* characteristics of diversified versus focused *financial service* providers, while these industrial studies primarily analyze the effects of *inter-industry* diversification for manufacturing firms. Second, we examine cost efficiency, not stock market performance. Our results regarding the impact of a firm's product choices on its cost efficiency provide important information for managers and regulators who must weigh the benefits and costs of the continuing trend toward increased diversification of financial service providers.

The remainder of our chapter is organized as follows. Section 2 explains our data and estimation methodology. In Section 3, we present X-efficiency estimates and regression results. Section 4 summarizes and concludes the study.

## 2 Data and Estimation Methodology

### 2.1 Data

Most of the cross-sectional data required for this study were obtained from the NAIC data tapes. State wage information and consumer price indices were obtained from the Bureau of Labor Statistics, and GNP deflators and implicit price deflators were obtained from the *Survey of Current Business* of the Bureau of Economic Analysis. Information on firm distribution systems was collected from the *Best's Insurance Reports*. The data were collected for individual firms and then aggregated for any affiliated insurers within a given group.[7] The group, or the unaffiliated firm, is chosen as the relevant DMU, so as to minimize the impact on the results of allocations and transfers among the members within a group. To be included in our sample, an insurance firm's data had to be

---

[6] Further support for the notion that greater corporate focus is consistent with shareholder wealth maximization in publicly traded industrial firms is provided by Berger and Ofek (1995) and Comment and Jarrell (1995).

[7] See, for example, Yuengert (1993) and Cummins and Zi (1997).

available for six consecutive years (1990–1995) on the NAIC tapes. Since Yuengert (1993) finds that very small firms are a major source of heteroscedasticity in cost function residuals, we follow Cummins and Zi (1997) in deleting firms with assets below $10 million. The final sample consists of 321 DMUs.[8]

### 2.2 Variable Definitions

*2.2.1 Outputs, Input Prices, and Total Cost.* We follow Cummins and Zi (1997) in specifying six outputs and deflate the current year numbers by the consumer price index (CPI) to the base year of 1990. Five of the outputs proxy for the risk bearing/risk pooling function of life insurers: incurred benefit payments in 1) individual life insurance $(Y_1)$, 2) group life insurance $(Y_2)$, 3) individual annuities $(Y_3)$, 4) group annuities $(Y_4)$, and 5) accident and health insurance $(Y_5)$. The sixth output, additions-to-reserves $(Y_6)$, proxies for the DMU's intermediation service.[9]

Our specification of three inputs (labor, financial capital, and materials), and the assumptions we make to compute the required input prices, are consistent with Cummins and Zi (1997). All input prices vary across DMUs and over time. The price of labor $(w_1)$ equals the weighted sum of the price of administrative labor and the price of agent labor. The price of administrative labor is a premium weighted index calculated as the product of the average weekly wage per employee in life insurance (SIC 6311) by state and the portion of insurance business written in the state. The price of agent labor is a premium weighted index calculated as the product of the average weekly wage per employee in life insurance agencies (SIC 6411) by state and the portion of insurance business

---

[8] Our sample represents 89.5% of industry assets (as of 1992), which is very close to the "nearly 90%" reported in a study of 445 life insurance DMUs from 1988–1992 by Cummins and Zi (1997). The smaller number of DMUs in our sample is consistent with the well-documented concentration trend in the insurance industry during this period [Cummins, Tennyson, and Weiss (1997)]. Hence, the sample in this study is representative of the life insurance industry.

[9] Grace and Timme (1992) and Gardner and Grace (1993) use premiums as measures of life insurers' outputs. Premiums, however, do not measure output quantity but rather price times quantity. In contrast, incurred benefit payments, which were first suggested as output proxies by Doherty (1981), and additions-to-reserves, first employed by Yuengert (1993), are relatively independent of product pricing and, thus, dominate premiums as measures of the quantity of insurance output. We also estimate efficiencies using a specification similar to that of Gardner and Grace. Although the average efficiency estimates differ, the relationship between efficiency and product focus is qualitatively the same as the relationship reported in this paper.

written in the state.[10] The weights applied when summing the prices of administrative and agent labor are determined by the proportion of total wages and benefits paid to administrative employees versus agents in each firm.

Financial capital is a major input for life insurance companies. Economic market models commonly used to estimate the price of capital (e.g., the capital asset pricing model) cannot be applied to the estimation of the cost of capital for insurance companies since many insurers are mutual organizations or closely held stock firms. Following Cummins and Zi (1997), we define the price of financial capital ($w_2$) as the three-year moving average of the rate of return on capital (average income divided by the sum of equity and borrowed funds). A challenge associated with estimating the cost of capital with accounting data is the treatment of extreme values – negative returns that cannot be used as proxies for the price of capital and very high positive rates of return that might overstate the market price of capital in any given year. To address this challenge, we employ the following two-step procedure. First, we examine the distribution of positive rates of return on capital and determine the 5th and 95th percentiles. We then impose these percentages as the maximum and minimum estimates for our entire sample.[11] The maximum cost of capital for the DMUs in our sample equals 33.12%, the sample minimum is 1.81%, and the average is 11.2%.[12]

The price of materials ($w_3$) is a weighted average of component price indices for 11 items identified by Cummins and Zi (1997).[13] The weights

---

[10] Average weekly wages for administrative employees and agents in the life insurance industry were obtained from the Bureau of Labor Statistics of the U.S. Department of Labor.

[11] This procedure is one of several possible solutions to the problem of dealing with negative prices for financial capital. Cummins and Zi (1997) set negative returns to 1% and Cummins and Weiss (1993) set negative values to the industry average. No one solution appears to dominate all others. To our knowledge, we are the first to truncate the upper tail of the distribution. Not truncating the upper tail results in a maximum cost of capital estimate greater than 100%.

[12] In comparison, Cummins and Zi (1997) report an average of 12%, a minimum of 1%, and a maximum of 102%.

[13] Specifically, we deflate advertising by the GNP implicit deflator for communications; books, printing, and stationery by the CPI for reading materials; bureau and association fees by the GNP deflator for wholesale trade, and legal fees by the CPI for legal services; capital equipment by the implicit price deflator for capital stock; accounting and claim settlement fees, etc., by the GNP deflator for business services; medical exam fees by the CPI index for medical care; insurance purchased by a fixed weight price index for insurance; travel expenses by the CPI for food consumed away from home; rental expenses by the GNP deflator for tenant rental of non-farm dwellings; and miscellaneous expenses by the overall CPI.

Table 5.1.  *Sample summary statistics: 1990–1995*
*(321 insurance DMUs).*

| Variable | Mean | Median | Minimum | Maximum | Coefficient of Variation |
|---|---|---|---|---|---|
| Total Assets[a] | 6,373,400,000 | 311,340,000 | 10,280,557 | 374,000,000,000 | 3.52 |
| Total Cost[a] | 515,850,000 | 66,427,491 | 1,551,358 | 18,020,000,000 | 2.59 |
| *Outputs*[a] | | | | | |
| $Y_{IL}$ | 73,424,400 | 5,814,460 | 0 | 3,371,000,000 | 3.27 |
| $Y_{GL}$ | 47,130,234 | 326,777 | 0 | 10,110,000,000 | 8.39 |
| $Y_{IA}$ | 39,178,132 | 1,076,707 | 0 | 1,903,100,000 | 3.27 |
| $Y_{GA}$ | 78,609,468 | 0 | 0 | 7,343,100,000 | 5.56 |
| $Y_{AH}$ | 172,980,000 | 7,022,146 | 0 | 9,421,200,000 | 3.31 |
| $Y_{AR}$ | 655,920,000 | 40,000,727 | 0 | 23,800,000,000 | 3.11 |
| *Input Prices* | | | | | |
| $P_L$[a] | 597.90 | 598.71 | 436.00 | 818.00 | 0.09 |
| $P_C$ | 11.20% | 9.68% | 1.81% | 33.12% | 0.66 |
| $P_M$ | 1.11 | 1.11 | 1.01 | 1.30 | 0.05 |

*Note*: 1) Definitions:
$Y_{IL}$ = Incurred benefits from individual life insurance
$Y_{GL}$ = Incurred benefits from group life insurance
$Y_{IA}$ = Incurred benefits from individual annuities
$Y_{GA}$ = Incurred benefits from group annuities
$Y_{AH}$ = Incurred benefits from accident and health insurance
$Y_{AR}$ = Additions to reserves
$P_L$ = Unit price of labor input (composite average weekly wage)
$P_C$ = Unit price of financial capital input (three-year moving average return on capital)
$P_M$ = Unit price of materials input (ratio of nominal to real miscellaneous expenditures)
Outputs and total costs are expressed in constant 1990 dollars.
DMU = Decision Making Unit, defined as an insurance group or unaffiliated independent insurance firm.
2) Notes:
[a] Expressed in dollars.

for the component price indices vary across DMUs and over time with the proportion of expenditures a DMU allocates to each item. Total cost (C) is the sum of labor, financial capital, and materials expenses. Summary statistics for the sample are reported in Table 5.1.

*2.2.2 Focus Proxy.* We use a firm-specific product Herfindahl index (FOCUS) calculated across the output premiums (individual life, individual annuities, group life, group annuities, and accident and health) to measure the extent to which a DMU chooses to focus versus diversify its output across multiple product lines. A DMU that exclusively

Table 5.2. *Summary statistics for the focus proxy for 321 insurance DMUs 1990–1995.*

| Year | Mean | Median | Minimum | Maximum | Coefficient of Variation |
|------|------|--------|---------|---------|--------------------------|
| 1990[a] | 0.6233 | 0.5754 | 0.2330 | 1.000 | 0.3499 |
| 1991[a] | 0.6280 | 0.5809 | 0.2399 | 1.000 | 0.3496 |
| 1992[a] | 0.6320 | 0.5834 | 0.2551 | 1.000 | 0.3455 |
| 1993[a] | 0.6359 | 0.5861 | 0.2552 | 1.000 | 0.3420 |
| 1994[a] | 0.6359 | 0.5947 | 0.2558 | 1.000 | 0.3366 |
| 1995[a] | 0.6379 | 0.5902 | 0.2503 | 1.000 | 0.3367 |
| 1990–95[b] | 0.6204 | 0.5783 | 0.2541 | 1.000 | 0.3441 |

*Note*: Definitions:
[a] Herfindahl index based on premiums from this year. This index is used to create a panel data set in order to estimate a six-year fixed effects model.
[b] Herfindahl index based on six years of summed premiums.

$$\text{FOCUS} = \frac{P_{IL}^2 + P_{IA}^2 + P_{GL}^2 + P_{GA}^2 + P_{AH}^2}{[P_{IL} + P_{IA} + P_{GL} + P_{GA} + P_{AH}]^2}$$

$P_{IL}$ = Premiums from individual life insurance
$P_{IA}$ = Premiums from individual annuities
$P_{GL}$ = Premiums from group life insurance
$P_{GA}$ = Premiums from group annuities
$P_{AH}$ = Premiums from accident and health insurance
DMU = Decision Making Unit, defined as an insurance group or unaffiliated independent insurance firm.

focuses on the production of any one of the outputs defined above has a Herfindahl index of one, while a DMU that offers a broader range of product lines would have a lower Herfindahl index.[14]

Table 5.2 reports summary statistics for the focus proxy used in our analysis. On average, life insurers have a focus proxy of 0.6204 for the entire time period. The focus metric ranges from a low of 0.2330 to a maximum of 1. Thus, we have a wide range of output choices in our sample. This dispersion makes our sample suitable for an analysis of the relationship between a DMU's X-efficiency and its product choice.

[14] Other measures of product focus can be constructed. In addition to the measure reported, we used a Herfindahl index based on incurred benefits and the number of product lines marketed (e.g., 1–5) with similar results.

### 2.3 Control Variable Definitions

Previous studies have identified numerous firm-specific and environmental factors that influence X-efficiency. We control for these factors in our fixed effects model by including the same vector of variables as Gardner and Grace (1993) in our multivariate test of the relationship between firm X-efficiency and product focus. These control variables and their proxies are discussed below.

### 2.3.1 New York Regulation.

Boose (1990) argues that the higher regulatory standards imposed by New York on all life insurance companies writing insurance in the state (regardless of state of domicile) should increase the efficiency of these firms relative to the efficiency of "non-New York" firms. We include a 0/1 dummy variable ($D_{NY}$) to control for the New York regulatory influence. The dummy equals 1 if a DMU wrote any business in New York and 0 otherwise.

### 2.3.2 Organizational Form.

Mayers and Smith (1981, 1986, and 1988) use agency-theoretic arguments to derive two testable hypotheses regarding insurance efficiency and organizational form. The managerial discretion hypothesis contends that mutual and stock insurers sort themselves into product market segments where they have a comparative advantage in minimizing costs. Mutual life insurers are more likely to succeed in less risky product lines where the degree of managerial discretion and the costs of monitoring managers are relatively low, particularly if the potential for policyholder-owner conflict is relatively high. Stock life insurers should have a comparative advantage in more risky product lines, as their form of ownership allows market discipline, and is thus better able to control owner-manager problems that tend to arise when managers have relatively more discretion. If the managerial discretion hypothesis is correct, firms will sort themselves into different product market segments based on their abilities to minimize cost. In this case, one would expect any remaining differences in cost efficiency between mutual and stock insurance firms to be explained by factors other than ownership structure [Cummins, Weiss, and Zi (1997)]. For instance, mutual firms may prove more efficient than stock firms, if the operating costs associated with less risky product lines are lower compared to the operating costs associated with more complex product offerings. Expense-preference arguments, on the other hand, suggest that mutual firms are less efficient than stock companies due to the relatively greater consumption of perquisites resulting from the lack of effective monitoring of managers by shareholders [see, e.g., Mester (1989, 1991)].

The empirical evidence in the literature for life insurance firms is mixed [Fields (1988), Grace and Timme (1992), Gardner and Grace (1993), and Cummins and Zi (1997)]. We include a 0/1 dummy variable ($D_{MUTUAL}$) to control for the influence of organizational structure on efficiency.

*2.3.3 Distribution System.* Life insurance companies distribute their products through either an exclusive agency system or through independent brokers. We posit that building an exclusive agency system is more expensive for life insurance firms than using independent brokers since all costs must be absorbed by one insurer rather than several. If this is the case, then one would expect DMUs using broker-ages to be relatively more cost efficient. However, DMUs using exclusive agents may be able to offset the relatively greater expense with higher revenues and profits, so that the integration of the production and distribution functions may be advantageous despite the relatively higher cost.[15] Again, prior empirical evidence for life insurers regarding effects of the distribution system choice on cost efficiency is ambiguous [Grace and Timme (1992), and Gardner and Grace (1993)]. To control for the choice of distribution system, we include a dummy variable ($D_{AGENCY}$) that is 1 if a DMU uses an exclusive agency system and 0 if the DMU utilizes independent brokers.

*2.3.4 Rent-Seeking Activities.* Gardner and Grace (1993) hypothesize that life insurers trying to build barriers to entry in an effort to seek economic rents will, ceteris paribus, spend more on bureau and agency fees, litigation, and advertising. To control for the possibility of rent-seeking by life insurance companies, we include bureau and agency fees as a percentage of net premiums (BUREAU), legal expenses unrelated to claims as a percentage of net premiums (LEGLFEE), and advertising expenditures as a percentage of net premiums (ADVERT).

*2.3.5 Non-Admitted Assets.* Non-admitted assets represent relatively less productive assets. These assets may lack liquidity, be excessively risky, or have value that is very specific to the firm. For instance, firms with cash flow problems resulting from large accounts receivable balances tend to have relatively higher levels of non-admitted assets. Thus, non-admitted assets may be more highly correlated to a firm's profit efficiency than its cost efficiency. Nonetheless, to control for a

---

[15] As previously stated, the data do not allow researchers to estimate credibly a profit function for life insurers. For an analysis of how the choice of distribution system affects both the cost efficiency and the profit efficiency of property-liability insurers, see Berger, Cummins, and Weiss (1997).

possible effect of non-admitted assets on cost, we use non-classified aggregate write-ins as a percentage of total assets (AGWRITES) in our regressions.

 *2.3.6 Capital Structure, Market Share, and Firm Size.* Since we use financial capital as an input, DMUs with relatively more equity funds are expected to be less cost efficient than DMUs with less equity funds. We use the ratio of equity to total assets (CAP) to control for the effect of differences in capital ratios on cost.[16] DMUs that serve a large percentage of the market tend to have market power. Percentage market share based on total premiums (MSHR) is included to control for this possibility. Cummins and Zi (1997) find both decreasing and increasing returns to scale with average efficiencies initially decreasing with size and ultimately increasing for the very largest DMUs. We include the natural logarithm of total assets (SIZE) as a proxy for firm size and the square of this term (SIZE$^2$) to account for the nonlinear size-efficiency relationship documented by Cummins and Zi.

 *2.4 Methodology*

We use Berger's (1993) distribution free approach to estimate X-efficiency in order to avoid having to impose an arbitrary distribution on cost residuals. We specify the translog cost function for the six outputs and three inputs described above. Firm and time subscripts s and t are suppressed in Equation 1 for expositional ease:

$$\ln C = \alpha + \sum_{j=1}^{6} \beta_j g(Y_j) + \frac{1}{2} \sum_{j=1}^{6} \sum_{k=1}^{6} \beta_{jk} g(Y_j) g(Y_k) + \sum_{n=1}^{3} \gamma_n \ln \omega_n$$

$$+ \frac{1}{2} \sum_{n=1}^{3} \sum_{p=1}^{3} \gamma_{np} \ln \omega_n \ln \omega_p + \sum_{j=1}^{6} \sum_{n=1}^{3} \rho_{jn} g(Y_j) \ln \omega_n + \ln \varepsilon \quad (1)$$

The $Y_j$ represent dollar amounts of outputs, and the $\omega_n$ denote input prices. Since many DMUs have zero outputs, we add 1 to all outputs prior to taking the logarithm; thus $g(Y_j) = \ln(Y_j + 1)$.

 The error term $\ln \varepsilon_{st}$ consists of two components: the persistent error $(\ln u_{st})$ and the random disturbance $(\ln x_{st})$, which averages over time to equal zero. To compute an average efficiency ratio for each DMU during 1990–1995, we estimate the cost function (with the usual symmetry and

[16] Again, due to the lack of data, we cannot test for a relationship between capital ratios and profit efficiencies. If higher capital ratios imply lower default probabilities, then DMUs that use relatively more capital may be compensated for their reduced cost efficiencies with higher revenues or profits.

homogeneity restrictions in prices) for each of the years 1990–1995. Given estimates of six cost functions, we determine the residual $\ln \varepsilon_{st}$ for each DMU s in year t. We then average across a DMU's residuals to determine the DMU's mean residual, which we take to be our estimate of the DMU's persistent error for the sample period, $\ln \bar{u}_{st}$. We identify a benchmark efficiency measure by selecting the DMU with the lowest persistent error, $\ln \bar{u}_{st}^{\min}$. Our efficiency measure thus corresponds to the formula developed in Berger (1993):

$$XEFF_{st} = \exp(\ln \bar{u}_{st}^{\min} - \ln \bar{u}_{st}.). \tag{2}$$

The most efficient DMU obtains an average X-efficiency estimate of 1, while X-efficiency is bounded from below at 0.[17]

### 3 Estimation and Results

#### 3.1 Estimation

We estimate Equation 1 using the maximum likelihood method. We scale all variables by their sample means to obtain unbiased hypothesis tests [Spitzer (1985)]. X-efficiency for each DMU is calculated in two different ways. Average efficiency measures for the period are based on the average of residuals over the entire six years. This estimate is used for univariate comparisons and tests. Second, we create a six-year panel data set of efficiency estimates to be used as the dependent variable in a fixed effects regression model. These efficiencies are estimated using the method of Gardner and Grace (1993) by averaging residuals over five years, excluding a different year of the six-year period for each time series observation. For example, a DMU's panel data X-efficiency estimate, omitting the 1990 data, is calculated as:

$$\ln \bar{u}_{90} = (\ln \varepsilon_{91} + \ln \varepsilon_{92} + \ln \varepsilon_{93} + \ln \varepsilon_{94} + \ln \varepsilon_{95})/5 \tag{3}$$

and

$$XEFF_{90} = \exp(\ln \bar{u}_{90}^{\min} - \ln \bar{u}_{90}). \tag{4}$$

This process is repeated for all six years. We denote these estimates by the year of the omitted data for lack of a better notation. The reader should not interpret these estimates as efficiencies for any given year. This method allows us to make full use of the information contained in the explanatory variables over the entire six-year period. As recom-

---

[17] Note that this is a relative efficiency measure since there is no guarantee that the minimum residual firm is operating on the efficient frontier.

Table 5.3.  *Distribution free estimates of X-efficiency (5% truncation)*
*for 321 insurance DMUs 1990–1995.*

| Year | Mean | Median | Minimum | Maximum | Coefficient of Variation |
|------|------|--------|---------|---------|--------------------------|
| 1990[a] | 57.71% | 54.94% | 22.97% | 100.00% | 0.3749 |
| 1991[a] | 54.29% | 50.76% | 20.57% | 100.00% | 0.3890 |
| 1992[a] | 55.22% | 52.41% | 21.14% | 100.00% | 0.3800 |
| 1993[a] | 56.68% | 54.13% | 22.63% | 100.00% | 0.3749 |
| 1994[a] | 57.23% | 54.79% | 22.23% | 100.00% | 0.3773 |
| 1995[a] | 56.48% | 54.31% | 22.23% | 100.00% | 0.3791 |
| 1990–95[b] | 54.92% | 52.24% | 21.59% | 100.00% | 0.3815 |

*Notes*:
Definitions:
[a] The X-efficiency estimate ($XEFF_i$) is calculated using the averaged residuals from five of the six years, following the method of Gardner and Grace (1993). This measure is used to create a cross-sectional and time series panel data set in order to estimate a six-year fixed effects model. These estimates are denoted 1990 through 1995 for lack of a better notation and should not be misconstrued as year-specific X-efficiency estimates.
[b] The X-efficiency estimate (XEFF) is based on the averaged residuals over six years. This measure is used for mean and median comparisons over the sample period.
DMU = Decision Making Unit, defined as an insurance group or unaffiliated independent insurance firm.

mended by Berger (1993), we used 5% truncations on both tails of the distribution of the average residuals since all random noise does not average out over the estimation period.

Table 5.3 contains summary statistics of the X-efficiency estimates based on a 5% truncation. Using six years of data spanning the overall time period, we estimate an average X-efficiency of 54.92%. X-efficiency ranges from a low of 21.59% to a maximum of 100%. The median estimate is 52.24%. Gardner and Grace (1993) report a DFA X-efficiency estimate using a 5% truncation for 1985–1990 of 42%, while Cummins and Zi (1997) report an untruncated DFA estimate of 47% for 1988–1992. Our specification is more similar to the specification proposed by Cummins and Zi using incurred benefits than to the premium-based approach of Gardner and Grace. Furthermore, the sample period in Cummins and Zi (1988–1992) has some overlap with our sample period (1990–1995). Given the overlap in time periods and the similarity in specifications, it is not surprising that our estimates correspond more closely to those of Cummins and Zi.[18]

### 3.2 Univariate Tests of X-Efficiency and Product Focus

Univariate comparisons of X-efficiency by quartiles of the product focus proxy (FOCUS) using mean t-tests and non-parametric Wilcoxon tests are presented in Panel A of Table 5.4. Means are presented on the left side of the table and medians on the right. In general, diversified firms (Q1 + Q2) are more X-efficient (59.55% versus 50.26%, T = 4.06) than focused firms (Q3 + Q4). This difference is also significant when we compare the first quartile with Q3 and Q4 respectively (T = 2.62 and T = 3.84), or the second quartile with Q3 and Q4 respectively (T = 1.91 and T = 3.11). Although not all quartile pairs are statistically different, the average X-efficiency estimates decrease monotonically as one moves from each lower quartile to a higher quartile of FOCUS. The results for medians are similarly compelling. All differences between median X-efficiencies across quartiles have statistically significant Wilcoxon statistics except for the difference between the medians of the two most diversified groups (Q1 versus Q2).

These results provide evidence that life insurers offering a diversified product mix have achieved greater average X-efficiency than focused DMUs. Firm size, however, is negatively correlated ($\rho = -0.26$) with the Herfindahl index. To control for the possibility that scale economies and not product diversification drive the results, we partition our sample into four different classes by asset size. These results are presented in Panel B. In each size class, we compare the X-efficiencies of the diversified DMUs with those of the focused DMUs. For means and medians in all four size classes, we find that the X-efficiency estimates of the diversified DMUs exceed the X-efficiency estimates of the focused DMUs. All results are statistically significant at the 5% or, in some cases, the 1% level. These results provide strong evidence that insurance companies with a diversified product mix achieve greater cost efficiencies than their focused counterparts.[19]

---

[18] Non-truncated estimates of X-efficiency averaged 31.8%. For a 1% truncation, the average was 39.0%, the average for a 6% truncation was 58.1%, and the average estimate for a 10% truncation was 63.3%.

[19] Another possibility is that participation in a particular line is the source of the efficiency differences. To check for this possibility, we segregated the sample into firms that generate some premiums from a particular product line and firms with zero premiums from this product. This was done for each of the product lines (e.g., individual life insurance, individual annuities, etc.). We did not find any statistical differences in the efficiencies of these subsamples. Hence, it is doubtful that a particular product is the source of the observed difference in efficiencies.

Table 5.4. Comparison of X-efficiency by level of product focus for 321 life insurance DMUs (1990–1995).

| | Means | | | Medians | | |
|---|---|---|---|---|---|---|
| | Diversified | Non-diversified | T-statistic | Diversified | Non-diversified | Wilcoxon |
| *Panel A. Comparison of X-efficiency by FOCUS[a]* | | | | | | |
| (Q1[b] + Q2[c]) versus (Q3[d] + Q4[e]) | 59.55% (N = 161) | 50.26% (N = 160) | 4.06*** | 57.51% (N = 161) | 47.43% (N = 160) | 4.06*** |
| Q1[b] versus Q4[e] | 60.36% (N = 81) | 47.98% (N = 80) | 3.84*** | 56.48% (N = 81) | 45.07% (N = 80) | 4.06*** |
| Q2[c] versus Q3[d] | 58.73% (N = 80) | 52.54% (N = 80) | 1.91* | 58.08% (N = 80) | 51.05% (N = 80) | 1.70* |
| Q2[c] versus Q4[e] | 58.73% (N = 80) | 47.98% (N = 80) | 3.11*** | 58.08% (N = 80) | 45.07% (N = 80) | 3.27*** |
| Q3[d] versus Q4[e] | 52.54% (N = 80) | 47.98% (N = 80) | 1.41 | 51.05% (N = 80) | 45.07% (N = 80) | 1.84* |
| Q1[b] versus Q3[d] | 60.36% (N = 81) | 52.54% (N = 80) | 2.62*** | 56.48% (N = 81) | 51.05% (N = 80) | 2.43** |
| Q1[b] versus Q2[c] | 60.36% (N = 81) | 58.73% (N = 80) | 0.51 | 56.48% (N = 81) | 58.08% (N = 80) | 0.50 |

*Panel B. Comparison of X-efficiency by FOCUS[a] within asset size classes*

| | Q1[b] + Q2[c] | Q3[d] + Q4[e] | | Q1[b] + Q2[c] | Q3[d] + Q4[e] | |
|---|---|---|---|---|---|---|
| Assets ≤ $343M (bottom quartile) <br> (Q1[b] + Q2[c]) versus (Q3[d] + Q4[e]) | 71.21% <br> (N = 28) | 57.39% <br> (N = 53) | 2.56** | 70.68% <br> (N = 28) | 57.32% <br> (N = 53) | 2.34** |
| $343M < Assets < $2.04B (second quartile) <br> (Q1[b] + Q2[c]) versus (Q3[d] + Q4[e]) | 64.19% <br> (N = 35) | 51.32% <br> (N = 45) | 2.87*** | 65.68% <br> (N = 35) | 48.07% <br> (N = 45) | 2.75** |
| $2.04B < Assets < $16.82B (third quartile) <br> (Q1[b] + Q2[c]) versus (Q3[d] + Q4[e]) | 56.62% <br> (N = 38) | 43.32% <br> (N = 42) | 3.34*** | 58.06% <br> (N = 38) | 43.97% <br> (N = 42) | 3.41*** |
| Assets > $16.82B (top quartile) <br> (Q1[b] + Q2[c]) versus (Q3[d] + Q4[e]) | 53.25% <br> (N = 60) | 43.60% <br> (N = 20) | 2.18** | 50.99% <br> (N = 60) | 41.26% <br> (N = 20) | 2.13** |

*Note:*

Definitions:

[a] $$\text{FOCUS} = \frac{P_{IL}^2 + P_{IA}^2 + P_{GL}^2 + P_{GA}^2 + P_{AH}^2}{[P_{IL} + P_{IA} + P_{GL} + P_{GA} + P_{AH}]^2}$$

$P_{IL}$ = Premiums from individual life insurance.

$P_{IA}$ = Premiums from individual annuities.

$P_{GL}$ = Premiums from group life insurance.

$P_{GA}$ = Premiums from group annuities.

$P_{AH}$ = Premiums from accident and health insurance.

[b] The set of firms in the first (bottom) quartile of FOCUS.

[c] The set of firms in the second quartile of FOCUS.

[d] The set of firms in the third quartile of FOCUS.

[e] The set of firms in the fourth (top) quartile of FOCUS.

DMU = Decision Making Unit, defined as an insurance group or unaffiliated independent insurance firm.

*** Significant at the 1% level.

** Significant at the 5% level.

* Significant at the 10% level.

To control for firm characteristics other than asset size that might be driving the results, we estimate a fixed effects model on pooled cross-section and time series data using the control variables previously described. This analysis is presented in the next subsection.

### 3.3 Fixed Effects Model Using Pooled Cross-Section and Time Series Panel Data

The regression of a pooled cross-section and time series panel data set of efficiency measures is a daunting econometric task. Pooled time series data are often both heteroscedastic and autoregressive [Kmenta (1986)], efficiency measures have been identified as heteroscedastic [Yuengert (1993)], and the efficiency measure is truncated at 1 providing a limited dependent variable. It is difficult to control for all of these issues using a single method. Thus, we estimate a fixed effects model using ordinary least squares, and generalized least squares with adjustments for heteroscedasticity and autoregression, but assuming cross-sectional independence [see Kmenta (1986) p. 618] and Tobit regressions. Dummy intercept variables (D91–D95) allow for a different intercept in each year. The results are presented in Table 5.5.

Table 5.5. *Fixed effects models of U.S. life insurer efficiency (X-efficiency, 5% truncation) 1990–1995.*

| Explanatory variable | OLS ($t$-statistic) | GLS ($t$-statistic) | Tobit ($\chi^2$ statistic) |
|---|---|---|---|
| Intercept | 5.1570 | 3.3871 | 9.2733 |
|  | (15.46)*** | (11.28)*** | (199.30)*** |
| D91 | −0.0251 | −0.0295 | −0.0487 |
|  | (−1.96)** | (−2.84)*** | (3.81)* |
| D92 | −0.0077 | −0.0132 | −0.0116 |
|  | (−0.60) | (−1.27) | (0.22) |
| D93 | 0.0174 | 0.0097 | 0.0385 |
|  | (1.36) | (0.93) | (2.36) |
| D94 | 0.0140 | 0.0082 | 0.0241 |
|  | (1.08) | (0.78) | (0.91) |
| D95 | 0.0122 | 0.0048 | 0.0205 |
|  | (0.94) | (0.46) | (0.65) |
| $D_{MUTUAL}$ | 0.0440 | 0.0441 | 0.0910 |
|  | (4.79)*** | (5.75)*** | (25.69)*** |
| $D_{NY}$ | −0.0208 | −0.0568 | −0.0292 |
|  | (−2.11)** | (−6.84)*** | (2.30) |
| $D_{AGENCY}$ | −0.0223 | −0.0129 | −0.0308 |
|  | (−1.94)* | (−1.37) | (1.89) |

Table 5.5. *(cont.)*

| Explanatory variable | OLS (*t*-statistic) | GLS (*t*-statistic) | Tobit ($\chi^2$ statistic) |
|---|---|---|---|
| AGWRITES | 0.0025 | 0.0079 | 0.0017 |
|  | (0.48) | (1.55) | (0.03) |
| LEGLFEE | −0.0073 | −0.0048 | −0.0129 |
|  | (−2.75)*** | (−2.90)*** | (6.21)** |
| BUREAU | −0.0269 | −0.0360 | −0.0891 |
|  | (−1.39) | (−2.21)** | (5.58)** |
| ADVERT | −0.0044 | −0.0053 | −0.0068 |
|  | (−2.36)** | (−3.67)*** | (3.58)* |
| SIZE | −0.3609 | −0.2091 | −0.07941 |
|  | (−10.85)*** | (−7.01)*** | (147.45)*** |
| SIZE$^2$ | 0.0073 | 0.0040 | 0.0164 |
|  | (8.79)*** | (5.45)*** | (101.32)*** |
| CAP | −0.7792 | −0.6452 | −1.6149 |
|  | (−26.99)*** | (−27.22)*** | (809.01)*** |
| MSHR | 0.0283 | 0.0245 | 0.0433 |
|  | (3.25)*** | (2.79)*** | (6.56)** |
| FOCUS | −0.2720 | −0.2179 | −0.5745 |
|  | (−14.43)*** | (−13.83)*** | (242.82)*** |
| R$^2$/Likelihood Ratio Index | 0.4285 | 0.4205 | 0.4961 |
| Adj. R$^2$/Likelihood Ratio Index | 0.4234 | 0.4153 | 0.4916 |

*Note*: Fixed effect models are estimated on a vector of explanatory variables for 321 insurance decision-making units (DMU) over a six-year panel data set (1,926 observations). D91–D95 are 0/1 dummy variables allowing for differing intercepts by year, $D_{MUTUAL}$ is 1 if the DMU is a mutual firm and 0 if not, $D_{NY}$ is 1 if the DMU conducted business in New York and 0 if not, $D_{AGENCY}$ is 1 if the DMU uses a captive agent sales force and 0 if not, AGWRITES is non-classified aggregate write-in non-admitted assets as a percentage of total assets, LEGLFEE is legal expenses unrelated to claims, as a percentage of net premiums, BUREAU is bureau and association expense as a percentage of net premiums, ADVERT is advertising expense as a percentage of net premiums, SIZE is the natural logarithm of total admitted assets, CAP is equity divided by total admitted assets, MSHR is percentage market share, and FOCUS is a firm-specific Herfindahl index calculated across the insurance company's sources of premiums. The model is estimated using (1) ordinary least squares (OLS), (2) generalized least squares (GLS) corrected for heteroscedasticity and autocorrelation, and (3) using a Tobit regression for a dependent variable truncated on the right tail at 1. T-statistics are in parentheses for the OLS and GLS regressions and $\chi^2$ statistics are in parentheses for the Tobit regression.
*** Significant at the 1% level.
** Significant at the 5% level.
* Significant at the 10% level.

*3.3.1 Product Focus and X-Efficiency.* For the purpose of testing our hypotheses, the most important result is that the coefficient on FOCUS is negative and significant at the 1% level regardless of the regression technique used. This finding confirms that the results of the univariate tests are robust to the inclusion of other known influences on X-efficiency.

*3.3.2 Firm-Specific and Environmental Influences.* Consistent with the results reported by Cummins and Zi (1997), we estimate a negative coefficient on the natural logarithm of total assets (SIZE), and a positive coefficient on its square (SIZE$^2$), suggesting that DMUs of approximately medium size are relatively less X-efficient. These coefficient estimates are significant at the 1% level for OLS, GLS, and Tobit regressions. The relationships with rent-seeking activities (ADVERT, BUREAU, and LEGLFEE) are all negative and significant, except for the OLS coefficient estimate of BUREAU, which is negative but insignificant. These results appear reasonable given our measures of *cost* efficiencies, not *profit* efficiencies, and are consistent with the notion that firms accept lower cost efficiencies in order to build barriers to competition and accrue economic rents [Gardner and Grace (1993)].

We document a negative relationship between X-efficiency and the NY dummy variable ($D_{NY}$), which is significant for OLS and GLS, but not for Tobit. This result stands in contrast to the significantly positive sign reported by Gardner and Grace (1993). The increased concentration of the industry between the two sample periods provides a possible explanation for this difference in findings. As some DMUs not subject to New York regulation have merged with DMUs subject to New York regulation, the relative efficiency of "non New York" insurers has likely changed. There is some evidence in support of this possibility in our data. In 1990, only 23% of all DMUs reporting to the NAIC wrote business in New York, while 70% of the DMUs that met the six-consecutive-year requirement were subject to New York regulation. In any event, our finding suggests that additional analysis of the influence of New York regulation on X-efficiency is warranted.

The coefficient of market share (MSHR) is positive and significant regardless of the regression method used. Similarly, the sign of $D_{MUTUAL}$ is significantly positive with OLS, GLS, and Tobit regressions, providing support for the managerial discretion hypothesis. Consistent with the prediction that exclusive agency systems are more expensive, we find a negative sign on $D_{AGENCY}$, but it is significant only in the OLS regression. The coefficient of non-admitted assets (AGWRITES) is insignificant in all regressions. This finding is not surprising since we have previously argued that non-admitted assets are more likely to be correlated with revenues than with cost efficiency. The sign on the capital ratio (CAP) is consistently negative and significant, implying reduced cost efficiency with greater use of equity funds. This result is as expected given that financial capital is used as one of the inputs in the cost function specification.[20]

As a final check on the validity of our tests, we examine the survivorship of insurance DMUs during our time period. Since diversification leads to greater efficiency, one would expect that diversified DMUs are more likely than focused DMUs to meet the six-year criterion. We explore this possibility by comparing the Herfindahl index (number of product lines) of DMUs in our sample to the Herfindahl index (number of product lines) of DMUs that did not meet the six-year requirement. To ensure that our comparison captures the maximum number of firms that failed the data screen, this comparison is conducted as of 1990. As expected, surviving DMUs are more diversified on average (FOCUS = 0.62 versus 0.67, t = 2.68) and offer more product lines (3.79 versus 3.31, t = 4.61). These results are consistent with the notion that offering multiple products is, at least on average, a "best practice" in the life insurance industry. Diversified firms are, on average, more efficient and more likely to survive.

### 4 Summary and Conclusion

Using data for the life insurance industry during 1990–1995, we empirically test for a relationship between a firm's output choice and measures of X-efficiency. We introduce a firm-specific Herfindahl index (FOCUS) across premiums from different market segments as a proxy for product focus in the life insurance industry. Our empirical evidence suggests that product diversification across multiple insurance and investment product

---

[20] There is some slight to moderate pair-wise collinearity among the independent variables. The maximum correlation is between market share and size ($\rho = 0.59$). No other correlation is greater than 0.50 and most are less than 0.20. The univariate correlations between X-efficiency and the independent variables confirm the signs in the multivariate regressions. To control for possible group-wise collinearity, we estimate each regression omitting one independent variable at a time. Except for AGWRITES, there are no changes in the signs of the estimated coefficients. AGWRITES is significantly negative without controlling for capital structure (CAP). The two variables are only slightly positively correlated ($\rho = 0.11$). Hence it would appear that this change in sign is a result of the absence of a direct control for capital structure, and not a statistical anomaly resulting from multicollinearity.

lines resulted in greater X-efficiency than a more focused product choice. These results are robust to the inclusion of previously examined firm-specific and environmental control variables and to the application of OLS, GLS, and Tobit regression techniques. In addition to the positive relationship between X-efficiency and product diversification, we document a U-shaped relationship between X-efficiency and size, positive relationships with mutual organization and market share, negative relationships between X-efficiency and economic rent-seeking activities, and a negative relationship with New York regulation. We thus update evidence from earlier time periods on the influence of these firm-specific and environmental factors, while introducing a firm's product choice as an important determinant of cost efficiency.

The analysis in this chapter is consistent with the proposition that managers of multiproduct firms are able to achieve greater cost efficiencies than their counterparts in more focused firms by sharing inputs and efficiently allocating financial capital, human resources, and materials across product lines in response to changing industry conditions. As the demand for life insurance products has declined, while investors increasingly require fund management services in order to provide for their own retirement, the ability to reallocate resources and adapt the firm's product mix to the market's changing needs has emerged as an important competitive advantage. Our findings thus help explain the existence of multiproduct firms in the absence of cost complementarities, and identify product diversification as a source of cost efficiency in the life insurance industry that should be recognized by managers, policyholders, and regulators.

Recent times have seen an increasing number of financial service providers offering multiple, yet related, products to their clienteles. As a result, life insurance companies find themselves competing with mutual funds to manage investment portfolios while banks have begun to market life insurance. This trend toward "financial supermarkets" has continued despite the apparent lack of significant cost complementarities between the product lines. Our findings suggest that the trend toward multiproduct financial service providers may be driven by efficiency gains which, in turn, likely result from greater managerial flexibility in adapting to changing market conditions. Regulators and policymakers who are evaluating the desirability of functional barriers in the financial services industry should carefully consider this point. On the other hand, regulators are charged with protecting the stability of the financial system. Thus, our results on X-efficiency should not be viewed independently of safety and soundness considerations.

Future research might also test the limits of cost savings from diversification. It is conceivable that X-efficiencies decline once firms move beyond an "optimal" degree of diversification and offer a product mix that is too diverse. In this case, it may become impractical or impossible to share inputs across different production processes because each process requires product-specific inputs. Furthermore, managers may find it increasingly difficult to identify cost-efficient reallocations of their companies' resources. In recent years, life insurance companies have restricted the breadth of their offerings to life insurance products and annuities, a product mix apparently homogeneous enough to be impervious to diseconomies from excessive diversification. The continued trend to dismantle functional barriers in the financial services industry may require a reexamination of the result that X-efficiency increases with greater product diversification.

### Acknowledgments
We thank Marty Grace, Richard Phillips, Joan Lamm-Tennant, David Cummins, and two anonymous referees for helpful comments. All errors remain the responsibility of the authors.

### References

Berger, Allen N., "'Distribution free' Estimates of Efficiency of the U.S. Banking Industry and Tests of the Standard Distributional Assumptions," *Journal of Productivity Analysis*, Vol. 4, 1993, pp. 261–292.

Berger, Allen N., J. David Cummins, and Mary A. Weiss, "The Coexistence of Multiple Distribution Systems for Financial Services: The Case of Property-Liability Insurance," *Journal of Business*, Vol. 70, No. 4, 1997, pp. 515–546.

Berger, Allen N., Diana Hancock, and David B. Humphrey, "Bank Efficiency Derived from the Profit Function," *Journal of Banking and Finance*, Vol. 17, 1993, pp. 317–347.

Berger, Philip G. and Eli Ofek, "Diversification's Effect on Firm Value," *Journal of Financial Economics*, Vol. 37, No.1, 1995, pp. 39–65.

Boose, M. A., "Agency Theory and Alternative Predictions for Life Insurers: An Empirical Test," *Journal of Risk and Insurance*, Vol. 57, 1990, pp. 499–518.

Comment, Robert and Gregg A. Jarrell, "Corporate Focus and Stock Returns," *Journal of Financial Economics*, Vol. 37, No. 1, 1995, pp. 67–87.

Cummins, J. David, Sharon L. Tennyson, and Mary A. Weiss, "Efficiency, Scale Economies, and Consolidation in the U.S. Life Insurance Industry," S. S. Huebner Foundation for Insurance Education Working Paper, University of Pennsylvania, November 14, 1997.

Cummins, J. David and Mary A. Weiss, "Measuring Cost Efficiencies in the Property-Liability Insurance Industry," *Journal of Banking and Finance*, 1993.

Cummins, J. David, Mary A. Weiss, and Hongmin Zi, "Organizational Form and Efficiency: An Analysis of Stock and Mutual Property-Liability Insurers," Working Paper 97–02, *Wharton Financial Institutions Center*, University of Pennsylvania, 1997.

Cummins, J. David and Hongmin Zi, "Measuring Cost Efficiency in the U.S. Life Insurance Industry: Econometric and Mathematical Programming Approaches," S. S. Huebner Foundation for Insurance Education Working Paper, University of Pennsylvania, July 15, 1997.

Doherty, Neil A., "The Measurement of Output and Economies of Scale in Property-Liability Insurance," *Journal of Risk and Insurance*, Vol. 48, pp. 391–402.

Fields, Joseph A., "Expense Preference Behavior in Mutual Life Insurers," *Journal of Financial Services Research*, Vol. 1, 1988, pp. 113–129.

Gardner, Lisa A. and Martin F. Grace, "X-Efficiency in the U.S. Life Insurance Industry," *Journal of Banking and Finance*, Vol. 17, 1993, pp. 497–510.

Grace, Martin F. and Stephen Timme, "An Examination of Cost Economies in the United States Life Insurance Industry," *Journal of Risk and Insurance*, Vol. 59, 1992, pp. 72–103.

Hite, Gailen L., James E. Owers, and Ronald C. Rogers, "The Market for Interfirm Assets Sales: Partial Sell-offs and Total Liquidations," *Journal of Financial Economics*, Vol. 18, 1987, pp. 229–252.

John, Kose and Eli Ofek, "Asset Sales and Increase in Focus," *Journal of Financial Economics*, Vol. 37, No. 1, 1995, pp. 105–126.

Kellner, S. and G. Frank Mathewson, "Entry Size Distribution, Scale and Scope Economies in the Life Insurance Industry," *Journal of Business*, Vol. 56, 1983, pp. 23–44.

Kmenta, Jan, *Elements of Econometrics* (Macmillan, New York), 1986.

Leibenstein, Harvey, "Allocative Efficiency versus 'X-Efficiency'," *American Economic Review*, Vol. 56, 1966, pp. 392–415.

Mayers, David and Clifford W. Smith, Jr., "Contractual Provisions, Organizational Structure, and Conflict Control in Insurance Markets," *Journal of Business*, Vol. 54, 1981, pp. 407–434.

Mayers, David and Clifford W. Smith, Jr., "Ownership Structure and Control: The Mutualization of Stock Life Insurance Companies," *Journal of Financial Economics*, Vol. 16, 1986, pp. 73–98.

Mayers, David and Clifford W. Smith, Jr., "Ownership Structure across Lines of Property-Casualty Insurance," *Journal of Law and Economics*, Vol. 31, 1988, pp. 351–378.

Mester, Loretta, "Testing for Expense Preference Behavior: Mutual versus Stock Savings and Loans," *Rand Journal of Economics*, Vol. 20, 1989, pp. 483–498.

Mester, Loretta, "Agency Costs among Savings and Loans," *Journal of Financial Intermediation*, Vol. 1, 1991, pp. 257–278.

Schmidt, Peter and Robin C. Sickles, "Production Frontiers and Panel Data," *Journal of Business and Economic Statistics*, Vol. 2, 1984, pp. 367–374.

Spitzer, John J., "Variance Estimates of Models with Box-Cox Transformations: Implications for Estimation and Hypothesis Testing," *Review of Economics and Statistics*, Vol. 66, 1985, pp. 645–652.

Wernerfelt, Birger and Cynthia A. Montgomery, "Tobin's q and the Importance of Focus in Firm Performance," *American Economic Review*, Vol. 78, No. 1, March 1988, pp. 246–250.

Yuengert, Andrew M., "The Measurement of Efficiency in Life Insurance: Estimates of a Mixed Normal-Gamma Error Model," *Journal of Banking and Finance*, Vol. 17, pp. 483–496.

# 6

# REIT Performance: Does Managerial Specialization Pay?

Piet Eichholtz, Hans Op 't Veld, Mark Schweitzer[a]

**Abstract**

In this study, we investigate whether managerial specialization explains the performance of investment trusts. One of the unsolved puzzles in the literature regarding the performance of mutual funds concerns the persistence of this performance. We argue that specialization is one of the factors determining this persistence. We use data on US Real Estate Investment Trusts (REITs) since managerial specialization of these companies can be measured in a straightforward way. We look at the effects of specialization by property type and by geographic region and find that property specialization leads indeed to outperformance of the market by property companies, whereas geographical specialization leads to underperformance.

## 1 Introduction

In this chapter we investigate whether managerial specialization explains performance in investment portfolios. We are combining two strands of

[a] Eichholtz is at the Limburg Institute of Financial Economics (LIFE) of Maastricht University, at University of Amsterdam, and at Global Property Research (GPR). Op 't Veld and Schweitzer are both at GPR. We would like to thank Kees Koedijk, Patricia Rudolph, Lynne Sagalyn, Peter Schotman, the referee, and participants to the 1997 meeting "Performance of Financial Institutions" at the Wharton Business School in Philadelphia, to the 1997 ERES conference in Berlin, to the 1997 international meeting of the FMA in Honolulu, and to the 1998 AREUEA conference in Chicago for their valuable comments. Furthermore, Auke Schilder is thanked for valuable research assistance. All errors remain the responsibility of the authors. Correspondence: Mark Schweitzer LIFE/Maastricht University PO Box 616, 6200 MD MAASTRICHT, The Netherlands. Email: m.schweitzer@gpr.nl.

the literature. To study the causes of out- and underperformance, we first look at the literature concerning financial performance measurement and then at the literature about managerial specialization or focus.

The literature about the performance measurement of mutual funds is quite extensive. Most studies use measures derived from the Capital Asset Pricing Model to determine the performance of a fund relative to a benchmark, which corrects for priced and unpriced risk. Studies like Lehmann and Modest (1987), Grinblatt and Titman (1989), Malkiel (1995), Coggin, Fabozzi, and Rahman (1993), Grinblatt and Titman (1994), Brown and Goetzmann (1995) and Ferson and Schadt (1996) define outperformance as the deviation of the mutual funds' return from the security market line. This measure of outperformance is the well-known Jensen $\alpha$ (Jensen (1969)). In an informationally efficient capital market, $\alpha$ should not be significantly greater than zero since no fund manager should be able to outperform the market consistently. In that case, having superior information or specialized knowledge is irrelevant for performance. However, most of the empirical studies mentioned above have found significant $\alpha$'s.

The literature trying to explain the empirically observed outperformance of mutual funds has two main branches. One branch starts from the premise that the observed outperformance is due to measurement error and tries to find the causes for this error. The other branch builds on the notion that consistent outperformance is really possible, and tries to find economic explanations for outperformance. We will briefly discuss both strands of the literature.

Malkiel (1995) investigates whether outperformance is due to survivorship bias: the fact that the well-performing funds survive whereas the bad performers disappear. He concludes that the outperformance found in previous studies is indeed influenced by survivorship bias. He also concludes that persistence in outperformance is period-specific. The choice of the performance benchmark is another source of measurement error. This issue is discussed and tested for mutual funds by Lehmann and Modest (1987). They do not find any significant benchmark sensitivity.

An example of a study in which mutual fund performance is explained by economic variables is Ferson and Schadt (1996), which shows that performance is influenced by changing economic conditions. These can change the calculated $\beta$'s and thus also the $\alpha$'s, the measure for outperformance. Selection and timing ability of the fund managers are discussed by Grinblatt and Titman (1989, 1994, and 1995). They find evidence of timing ability of the mutual funds in their sample. Brown and Goetzmann (1995) discuss persistence in outperformance. They show that outperformance in one year makes outperformance in the next year more likely. This indicates that there are indeed some structural factors affecting the performance of mutual funds. This issue is regarded as a venue for further research by Grinblatt and Titman (1995) and Brown and Goetzmann (1995).

More insights in these structural factors can be found in the literature about managerial focus and specialization of industrials firms. Whereas in the past usually the potential benefits of diversification were discussed, more recently the potential costs of diversification get more attention. Berger and Ofek (1995), Comment and Jarrell (1995), John and Ofek (1995), and Denis, Denis, and Sarin (1997) are recent examples of this. One of the main questions these studies address is why firms are still diversifying when agency problems preclude them from fully realizing the diversification potential. It seems that diversification enables managers to accrue private benefits which do not translate into firm value or stock returns.

In our chapter we test whether managerial specialization can explain persistence in performance in the investment industry. Instead of looking at cost and profit functions of financial institutions, we measure performance by looking at excess stock returns. Our study will validate the hypothesis that managerial specialization affects investment performance. Measuring specialization and comparing performance between companies in general is difficult, as branch and individual firm characteristics disturb empirical tests. In empirical studies, which are limited to one particular branch, the sample size is usually quite small. We believe we can get around these problems by using data of United States Real Estate Investment Trusts (REITs). REITs are hybrid financial institutions with characteristics of both mutual funds and corporations. They manage money like mutual funds, but invest in real assets like common corporations. This makes them eminently suitable to investigate the effects of managerial specialization. REITs also have the advantage that the level of managerial specialization can be measured in a straightforward way by looking at the investment portfolio. Furthermore, since all companies in our sample have a similar structure to qualify as a REIT and since they own and manage their properties themselves, it is possible to compare them and test the significance of managerial specialization in an effective way.

The combination of management style and performance has not yet received a lot of attention in the literature. Coggin, Fabozzi, and Rahman (1993) find that the investment styles of money managers affect performance. Shukla and Van Inwegen (1995) show that local fund managers outperform foreign managers, which suggests that specialized knowledge can help to outperform the market. Ito, Lyons, and Melvin (1997) reveal that even on the foreign exchange market, traders do have some private information which they can use to their benefit. It is likely that traders and fund managers will have more private information when they specialize. As REITs invest in assets through private markets, our study directly investigates the effects of private information and managerial specialization. We expect a specialized firm to have this private information, which it can use to outperform the market persistently. For the international context, Eichholtz, Koedijk, and Schweitzer (1996) have already shown that domestic property companies, with better access to non-public information, have a better performance than international property companies. This indicates that specialization gives access to private information, which enables managers to generate persistent outperformance.

The chapter is organized as follows: In Section 2 we discuss the data we use regarding the performance and portfolio compositions of REITs. Section 3 deals with the way we measure specialization, while Section 4 concerns the measurement of performance. In Section 5 we present the results of a regression model in which specialization is directly linked to performance. This model is expanded in Section 6 to include other variables which may affect performance. In that section we employ a panel methodology to test our hypothesis in a more robust way. Section 7 concludes the study and gives some suggestions for further research.

## 2 Data Description

REITs have existed since the signing of the Real Estate Investment Trust Tax Provisions Act in 1960, but only since the beginning of the 1990's has the number and total market value of listed REITs increased dramatically. In the beginning of 1990, some 53 equity REITs existed with a total market value of $8.5 billion dollars (in 1996 dollars), whereas at the end of 1996 150 equity REITs had a combined market value of $69.6 billion.[1]

In order to qualify as a REIT, a real estate investment company has to meet strict criteria like a minimum of 100 shareholders, a payout ratio

---

[1] This only represents the number of REITs we use in our sample. The total REIT market consists of almost 300 listed REITs at the end of 1996, but those include mortgage REITs as well. Furthermore the REIT market expanded as many initial public offerings (IPOs) took place in 1996, which we did not include either.

of 95% of earnings, and at least 75% of total assets in real estate. The main benefit is that the REITs don't pay corporate taxes.

All REITs are members of the National Association of Real Estate Investment Trusts (NAREIT). This association collects information about different characteristics of all REITs and publishes it annually in a handbook. The information distributed by NAREIT includes details regarding the balance sheets and the character of all listed REITs. Most important for us is that it indicates for each REIT the size and composition of the real estate portfolio, by giving the number of properties in the different states and real estate categories. We use the handbooks of 1990–1996 to accumulate data about the level of specialization by property type and by state. Besides this information, we collect the book value of total assets, total equity, and leverage ratio annually. As we include all equity REITs mentioned in any one of the handbooks, our sample is largely free of survivorship bias. In Appendix A, we present a list of all 150 equity REITs we use. We checked the collected information about portfolio construction with figures from company reports, and the information for capital structure with data from Datastream.

We collect returns, dividends, and market capitalization for all REITs. For this, we use the Real Estate Securities Database of Global Property Research and collect total monthly returns from January 1990 through December 1996. Again, we checked the collected data with the annual reports, other company publications, and Datastream.

We use two performance benchmarks. The first is a market-weighted index based on all REITs in our sample, and the second is the Standard & Poor (S&P) 500 Composite total return index. As a proxy for the risk-free rate, we take the one-month Treasury Bill rate. Table 6.1 and Figure 6.1 give insight in the performance of the REITs in our sample and the S&P 500. Figure 6.1 shows that both indices follow similar patterns in time, but differ somewhat in value. While both indices are set at 100 at December 1988, our REIT index ends with a value of 284 in December 1996, and the S&P 500 total return index with a value of 257.

Table 6.1 gives the summary statistics for the whole period and two equal sub-periods. The table puts the figure a bit more into perspective. Over the complete sample period, the stock index has a lower return and a lower standard deviation than the REIT index. In the last sub-period, stocks have a higher average return: 16.87% versus 14.53% for the REITs. Their standard deviation is lower in both sub-periods, which suggests that an investment in common stocks is less risky than an investment in real estate investment companies. Over the whole period, the correlation between the monthly returns on the two indices is 0.47.

Table 6.1. *Summary statistics.*

|  |  | REITs | S&P 500 |
|---|---|---|---|
| 1990:1–1996:12 | $\mu$ | 14.92 | 13.46 |
|  | $\sigma$ | 12.37 | 10.61 |
| 1990:1–1993:6 | $\mu$ | 15.32 | 10.06 |
|  | $\sigma$ | 14.37 | 12.22 |
| 1993:7–1996:12 | $\mu$ | 14.53 | 16.87 |
|  | $\sigma$ | 10.16 | 8.75 |

*Note*: The table gives average annualized logarithmic total returns and standard deviations for the whole period and two 42-month sub-periods for the REIT index and the S&P 500 composite index.

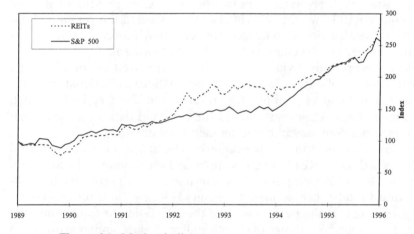

Figure 6.1.  Market indices.

These numbers give information regarding the performance of the REIT market as a whole and about REIT performance relative to the stock market in general. Within the REIT market, we expect the specialized REITs to be better risk-adjusted performers than the diversified REITs. In order to find out more about that, we first have to measure specialization. In the next section, we explain how we do that.

### 3 Measuring Specialization
Financial institutions, like all corporations, can diversify in product and geographic dimensions. As we noted in the introduction, measuring the

level of specialization and diversification and their effects on performance may be hard for financial institutions in general. For REITs, however, that is not the case, as their diversification strategy and their performance are clearly measurable.

In the case of real estate, property type and geographic region are meaningful ways to measure specialization. First of all, the different property types are heterogeneous and require different managerial skills. For example, the retail sector is quite different from the residential sector regarding rental contracts. In the residential sector, the rents are fixed for some time and tenants are flexible in moving away. This is in contrast to the retail sector, where in some occasions rents are dependent on the total sales of the store and tenants cannot move out of a building during the duration of the lease without incurring costs. Other major differences are in the scale and nature of properties, the type of tenants, the type of locations, and the degree of landlord involvement in the management of the properties. In other words, the economics of property investment are to a large extent determined by property type. This implies that specialized knowledge regarding a certain property type could be important in owning and managing properties and that, consequently, there may be information costs involved in operating in several sectors. Similarly, geography is an important driver of property performance. Real estate returns are strongly influenced by locational factors, and real estate markets show important regional differences. For example, the timing of cyclical developments in the real estate markets differs considerably across regions. Again, this implies potential benefits of managerial focus and costs related to diversification.

On the other hand, we know from the literature that there are indeed diversification benefits to be gained through investment in different sectors and regions. Miles and McCue (1984) and Hartzell, Hekman, and Miles (1986) are examples of studies which show how beneficial diversification over these two dimensions can be. Therefore, there is a trade-off between the costs and the benefits of diversification, both through property type and through region.

We rank the REITs by specialization using the Herfindahl index. We calculate Herfindahl indices for each individual REIT and for two dimensions of specialization: geographical and property type.[2] In

---

[2] The Herfindahl index is defined as: $H_{it1,2} = \sum_{i=1}^{n} (S_{jr})^2$, in which $H_{it1,2}$ are the Herfindahl indices at time $t$ for REIT $i$, $j$ is the state or the property type in which REIT $i$ invests, $n$ is either the total number of states or the number of property types in which REIT $i$

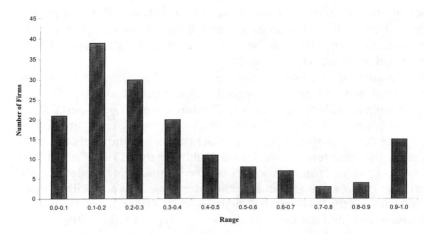

Figure 6.2. Histogram geographical Herfindahl.

line with NAREIT, we distinguish seven property types: retail, residential, office, hotel, healthcare, industrial, and other. With respect to the geographical specialization, measure we distinguish 50 different states.[3]

In Figures 6.2 and 6.3, we present the frequency diagrams for the average Herfindahl indices for the complete sample period. Figure 6.2 shows that the REITs are geographically diversified, with 61% of the REITs having an index value below 0.35. In contrast, Figure 6.3 reveals that most REITs are specialized in property type, since 56% of the companies have an index value between 0.90 and 1.00.[4]

Figure 6.4 shows that the Herfindahl indices were relatively stable in

---

invests, and $S_{jr} = X_{jn}/X_j$, where $X_{jn}$ is either the number of properties in a specific state or the number of properties in one class of property type, and $X_j$ is the total number of states or property types.

[3] The fact that we use the state as the geographical distinction is mainly driven by the availability of information regarding REIT portfolios. Some regions, like New England, may share similar characteristics across several states, whereas some states like California may consist of several different property markets.

[4] REITs that specialize in a certain property type usually remain invested in that same property type during our sample period. We find specialized REITs in all property categories, which is necessary to investigate the effects of specialization. If all specialized REITs would be invested in offices, for example, we would not measure the effect of specialization but rather the performance of the office market.

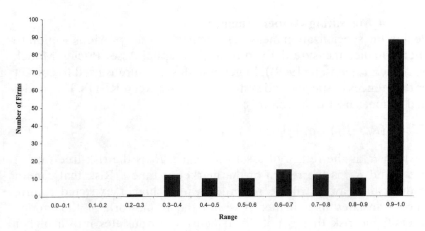

Figure 6.3. Histogram property type Herfindahl.

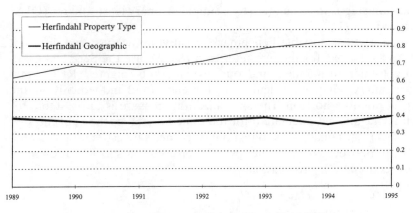

Figure 6.4. Time series of average Herfindahl indices.

time. The annual averages over all Herfindahl indices in the sample indicate a slight upward trend for the property type specialization of the REIT industry. Between 1989 and 1995, the average sector Herfindahl increased from 0.63 to 0.82. The pattern for the geograpical Herfindahl is more stable, indicating that the level of regional specialization has remained rather constant in the sample period.

## 4 Measuring Outperformance

We link the specialization measures calculated in the previous section to a performance measure derived from the Capital Asset Pricing Model: the Jensen $\alpha$ (Jensen (1969)). In general, this measure is used to correct for differences in specific and systematic risk between REITs. The model used to measure the Jensen $\alpha$ is:

$$(R_{it} - R_{ft}) = \alpha_i + \beta_i(R_{mt} - R_{ft}) + \varepsilon_{it} \tag{1}$$

in which $R_{it}$ is the return of asset $i$ in year $t$, $R_{ft}$ is the risk-free rate at time $t$, and $R_{mt}$ is the return of the market at time $t$. Risk that cannot be diversified away will be rewarded with a higher expected return, which translates in a higher $\beta_i$ within the framework of the model. Diversifiable risk that is not diversified away translates into a higher noise term $\varepsilon_{it}$. Within the framework of an informationally efficient capital market, the fund managers are not expected to out- or under-perform the market. This means that the expected value of $\alpha_i$ is zero. In the case of outperformance, the $\alpha_i$ will be positive. Therefore, the first important step is to calculate $\alpha$ by a simple ordinary least squares (OLS) regression of (1).

To correct for possible benchmark sensitivities, we use two different indices as a proxy for the market return $R_{mt}$. We use the S&P 500 Composite total return index, and our own market-weighted REIT total return index. First, we calculate $\alpha_i$ for each fund individually at the longest possible horizon. The specialization measure is fairly stable for each REIT and we calculate it for the same horizon as the $\alpha_i$ of the specific REIT. This enables us to test our hypothesis by estimating the relationship between $\alpha_i$ and the two dimensions of specialization in a cross-sectional OLS regression.

$$\alpha_i = \gamma_0 + \gamma_{geo}H_{geo} + \gamma_{prop}H_{prop} + \eta_i \tag{2}$$

in which $\alpha_i$ is the Jensen $\alpha$ of REIT $i$ and $\gamma_0$ is a constant, which is expected to be zero if the model is correctly specified and there are no omitted variables. $H_{geo}$ and $H_{prop}$ are the Herfindahl measures of geographical and property type specialization, $\gamma_{geo}, \gamma_{prop}$ the coefficients to be estimated, and $\eta_i$ the error term. We also estimate whether the significance of $\alpha_i$ influences the results by regressing the t-statistic of $\alpha_i$ on the factors. Using this method, we correct for the significance of $\alpha_i$, as a significant $\alpha_i$ gets more weight. The next section presents the results of the empirical estimation of the relationship between specialization and outperformance.

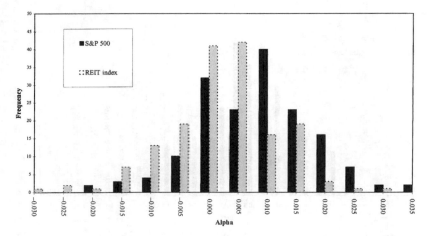

Figure 6.5. Distribution of alpha.

## 5 Results

We start by briefly presenting the results of the estimation of (1). Thereafter we discuss the relation between the estimated $\alpha_i$ and the specialization measures.

As said before, we run the regression twice; once with the S&P 500, and once with a market-weighted index of all REITs we have in our sample. We limit ourselves to just presenting Figures 6.5, 6.6, and 6.7, which give the distributions of $\alpha$ and $\beta$ and the significance of $\alpha$. Figure 6.5 shows that both $\alpha_i$-estimates give the same pattern for the S&P 500 and the REIT index. The average $\alpha$ estimated with the S&P gives an annual outperformance of 5.74%, and estimated with the REIT index an outperformance of –0.40%.

The result that the S&P is outperformed by the individual REITs is quite surprising when we compare it with the summary statistics in Table 6.1. This result is explained when looking at Figure 6.6, in which we show the distribution of the $\beta$'s estimated with the S&P. This figure tells us that the lower $\beta_i$'s were responsible for the higher $\alpha_i$'s. Figure 6.7 shows that only 13 REITs significantly out- or underperform the market.

We now turn to the relationship between $\alpha_i$ and the Herfindahl indices. We start in Table 6.2 by presenting the correlation coefficients between them. For each benchmark, we present four figures: the correlation between the two Herfindahl indices on the one hand and the $\alpha_i$ and the

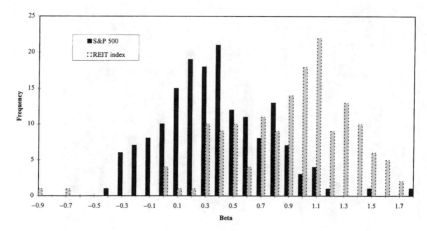

Figure 6.6.  Distribution of beta.

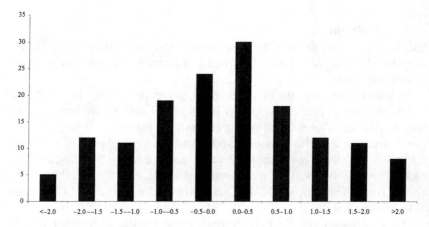

Figure 6.7.  Distribution of t-statistics (estimated with the REIT index).

t-statistic of $\alpha_i$ on the other.[5] It becomes immediately clear that specialization into a specific state does not pay. The correlation between the $\alpha_i$ and the geographical Herfindahl index is negative. On the other hand, property type specialization does seem to be a strategy to obtain out-

[5] We use the t-statistics to control for possible outliers in the performance measure which might drive the results.

Table 6.2. *Correlation: Herfindahl and outperformance.*

|  |  | Geographical Herfindahl | Property type Herfindahl |
|---|---|---|---|
| S&P 500 | $\alpha_i$ | −0.14* | 0.18** |
|  | $T_{\alpha i}$ | −0.18** | 0.16* |
| REITs | $\alpha_i$ | −0.13* | 0.15* |
|  | $T_{\alpha i}$ | −0.13* | 0.13* |

*Note*: This table gives the correlation coefficients between the average Herfindahl index and the measure for outperformance using two benchmarks. These figures are calculated individually for each REIT over the maximum sample size of 150. The ** denotes coefficients significantly different from zero at the 5% confidence level ($1.96/\sqrt{150} = 0.16$) and * denotes significance at the 10% level ($1.65/\sqrt{150} = 0.13$).

performance since it has a positive correlation in all occasions. Some of these results are confirmed in the real estate literature. See, for example, Goetzmann and Wachter (1995) and Capozza and Seguin (1997). Table 6.2 shows that only in two instances the correlation coefficient is significantly different from zero. These results are both obtained when the test is performed with the S&P 500. This is probably a result of the higher average $\alpha_i$'s when the S&P is used as a benchmark. It is clear that the results are not sensitive whether the test is performed with $\alpha_i$ or with the t-statistic of $\alpha_i$.

In Table 6.3, we give the results of the more formal hypothesis test: the OLS regression of (2). We have repeated the regression four times: two regressions for each benchmark – one for $\alpha_i$, and one for the t-value of $\alpha_i$. The results confirm the patterns found in the correlation coefficients presented in the previous table. The coefficients measuring the effect of geographical specialization have a negative sign, and the coefficients for the effect of specialization by property index a positive sign. This suggests that specialization by property type pays, whereas geographical specialization does not. To correct for a possible heteroskedasticity problem, we calculate normal and White (1980) standard errors and present the latter in Table 6.3. Heteroskedasticity in the regression residuals does not seem to be present since the conventional and White standard errors are virtually the same.

Besides the results for $\gamma_{geo}$ and $\gamma_{prop}$, we see that the constant $\gamma_0$ is not significantly different from zero, which suggests that our regression is

Table 6.3. *Specialization and performance.*

$$\alpha_i = \gamma_0 + \gamma_{geo}H_{geo} + \gamma_{prop}H_{prop} + \eta_i$$

|  |  | $\gamma_0{}^*$ | $\gamma_{geo}{}^*$ | $\gamma_{prop}{}^*$ | $R^2$(adj) |
|---|---|---|---|---|---|
| S&P 500 | $\alpha_i$ | 0.08 | −0.43 | 0.68 | 0.04 |
|  |  | (0.31) | (−1.57) | (2.20) |  |
|  | $T_{\alpha i}$ | 28.12 | −69.40 | 70.24 | 0.05 |
|  |  | (0.95) | (−2.35) | (2.02) |  |
| REIT index | $\alpha_i$ | −0.02 | −0.36 | 0.47 | 0.03 |
|  |  | (−1.11) | (−1.53) | (1.67) |  |
|  | $T_{\alpha i}$ | −23.22 | −56.55 | 58.55 | 0.03 |
|  |  | (−0.79) | (−1.80) | (1.63) |  |

*Note*: This table gives the basic results of the estimation of Equation 3, for the two specialization factors. $\alpha_i$ refers to the Jensen $\alpha$ estimated with Equation 2, and $T_{\alpha i}$ refers to the t-statistic of the $\alpha_i$ estimate. The number in parentheses represents the t-statistic based on White (1980) standard errors of the estimated $\gamma$ coefficient. The estimated coefficients are presented as percentages and the sample size is 150.

correctly specified. Nevertheless, the adjusted $R^2$ is relatively low. To improve the analysis, we will expand the regression model to include factors which have been found to have an effect on stock returns. In the next section, we will present the method and discuss the results at the same time.

## 6 Other Factors Generating Performance

In the finance literature, a debate has been going on whether other factors besides the market return influence the performance of an individual stock. (See, for example, Fama and French (1992)). The question whether those factors represent priced risk factors or anomalies is beyond the focus of this paper, but since we are interested to know whether it is specialization that drives performance or the other factors studied in the literature, it is important to include those factors and the degree of specialization in the same model. The factors we incorporate are the book-to-market ratio, the price/earnings ratio, firm size, and leverage. As these factors are not constant in time, we cannot simply include them in (2) and estimate the equation using average factor values over the complete sample period for each REIT. The factors mentioned have a high variance around their average values, which might bias the estimation. For this reason, we use a panel model that enables us to use the data in an efficient way. We use a one-step procedure in which the $\alpha$, the effects of the specialization measures, and the effects of the time-series anomalies studied in the literature are simultaneously estimated. The factors have a monthly frequency, and since the Herfindahl measures are only available at an annual basis, we use a constant Herfindahl index for the 12 months after the month it is measured. In formal terms, we use an OLS regression to estimate the following equation:

$$(R_{it} - R_{ft}) = \alpha + \beta_i(R_{mt} - R_{ft}) + \gamma_1 F_{1it} + \ldots + \gamma_k F_{kit} + \varepsilon_{it} \tag{3}$$

In this setup, $\alpha$ is expected to be zero since we assume that all determinants of firm performance are included in the model. The $\beta_i$ coefficient measures the sensitivity of the individual firm to market developments, and the $\gamma_{1..k}$ measures the effect of firm characteristics. In line with Fama and French (1992), we use fixed $\gamma$'s to measure factor sensitivities. $F_{1it} \ldots F_{kit}$ are the factors that we employ in a particular estimation. All these factors are measured at the end of the month, and are related to excess returns obtained in the next month. Each time we perform the regression, we utilize different combinations of factors, but we always include the Herfindahl measures. For possible multicollinearity reasons, we both perform the regression for individual factors and for all factors combined. Furthermore we assume that there is no autocorrelation in the error term over $t$, which is confirmed by the autocorrelation coefficients, which are insignificantly different from zero. The coefficients are presented in the last column of Table 6.4.[6]

Table 6.4 presents the results of the panel model.[7] As we first look at the estimation of the effect of the geographical Herfindahl, we see that the coefficient is negative in all occasions and that it is significant at a

---

[6] To estimate the significance and the t-statistic of the estimated coefficients, we have to estimate the variance of the coefficients as well. We do this by using the following equation:

$$Var(\alpha, \beta_i, \gamma) = \left( \frac{1}{it - k - i} \sum_i \sum_t \varepsilon_{it}^2 \right)(X'X)^{-1}$$

in which $i$ is the number of REITs, $t$ is the number of months, $k$ is the number of factors that we include, and $X$ is a matrix including all data on explanatory variables, which we also used to estimate the coefficients.

[7] We have estimated the model using the S&P 500 index and the REIT index. As the results are very similar, we present only those for the REIT index.

Table 6.4. *Results of the panel model.*

$(R_{it} - R_{ft}) = \alpha + \beta_i(R_{mt} - R_{ft}) + \gamma_1 F_{1it} + \ldots + \gamma_k F_{1it} + \varepsilon_{it}$

| # | $\alpha$ | $\gamma_{btm}$ | $\gamma_{pe}$ | $\gamma_{size}$ | $\gamma_{leverage}$ | $\gamma_{geo}$ | $\gamma_{prop}$ | $R^2$ | $\rho$ |
|---|---|---|---|---|---|---|---|---|---|
| 1 | −1.13 | — | — | — | — | −6.55 | 3.70 | 0.24 | −0.15 |
|   | (−0.79) |   |   |   |   | (−2.44) | (1.85) |   |   |
| 2 | −1.12 | 0.00 | — | — | — | −6.55 | 3.70 | 0.24 | −0.15 |
|   | (−0.78) | (0.01) |   |   |   | (−2.44) | (1.85) |   |   |
| 3 | −1.01 | — | −0.01 | — | — | −6.45 | 3.75 | 0.24 | −0.15 |
|   | (−0.70) |   | (−0.80) |   |   | (−2.40) | (1.87) |   |   |
| 5 | 6.17 | — | — | −1.77 | — | −7.24 | 5.54 | 0.24 | −0.15 |
|   | (2.32) |   |   | (−3.27) |   | (2.67) | (2.66) |   |   |
| 6 | 0.40 | — | — | — | −4.87 | −5.92 | 4.13 | 0.24 | −0.15 |
|   | (0.24) |   |   |   | (−1.80) | (−2.19) | (2.04) |   |   |
| 7 | 7.07 | 0.05 | −0.01 | −1.67 | −3.93 | −6.64 | 5.82 | 0.24 | −0.14 |
|   | (2.61) | (0.32) | (−0.69) | (−3.07) | (−1.44) | (−2.45) | (2.78) |   |   |

*Note*: This table shows the results of the panel regressions. The columns present the estimated coefficients and the t-statistic between parentheses. The — indicates that the factor was not used in the regression. We use the following symbols to indicate the factors: $\gamma_{btm}$ is the book-to-market, $\gamma_{pe}$ is the price earnings, $\gamma_{size}$ is the market value of the company, $\gamma_{leverage}$ is the ratio debt to total assets, $\gamma_{geo}$ is the geographic Herfindahl, and $\gamma_{prop}$ is the property type Herfindahl. All factors are presented in percentages at an annual basis. The $R^2$ gives the average individual $R^2$. The $\rho$ gives the average autocorrelation for each individual company.

95% confidence interval. The results confirm our earlier results that geographical specialization does not pay. It also tells us that possible distortion caused by values as leverage and book-to-market does not really disturb the estimation of the specialization effects. The same story holds for the property type Herfindahl index. In each regression, the coefficient is positive and almost always significant at a 95% confidence interval, which indicates that property type specialization is indeed positively related to risk-adjusted returns.

Even though the other factors do not influence the effect of specialization very much, we will briefly discuss them next. First, we see that the book-to-market coefficient is positive, which is in line with the literature. A higher book-to-market value will give a higher return in the future. The price-earnings ratio shows a negative relationship with future returns, which confirms earlier results as well. The well-known size effect is also statistically significant in our sample. The negative coefficient implies that the small firms outperform large firms. The only finding that seems to contradict the literature is the sign of the leverage coefficient. It is negative, indicating that more debt is related to lower performance. However, this may be explained by the fact that REITs don't pay corporate taxes and are therefore not able to benefit from tax shields. Thus, the negative sign can be explained by arguing that more debt indicates more risk and a higher interest rate on the outstanding debt and thus a lower performance.

### 7 Conclusion

The results we find in this chapter are straightforward. Building on the literature regarding mutual fund performance measurement and managerial focus, we argue that specialization may be related to the persistent outperformance of investment funds. We study the Real Estate Investment Trust industry in the United States since it comprises a unique sample of 150 companies working in the same industry, all having a comparable structure. Managerial specialization can easily be measured by looking at the portfolio of each REIT. We find companies that specialize in a specific property type to outperform the market, whereas geographically specialized companies underperform on average. This indicates that the question whether the cost of diversification can outweigh the benefits depends on the dimension along which the diversification takes place.

The results suggest that real estate investors should specialize in one property type, and diversify across regions. Investors who also want to diversify across property types can do so by buying the shares of different REITs, each specialized in a different property type. The property companies should use this knowledge and diversify their portfolios geographically, and focus on one property type only. In fact, the current average portfolio composition of the REITs in our sample shows that they already do this.

Besides these practical implications for investors, this study also makes a major contribution to the literature regarding focus and managerial specialization. It shows that the way specialization is measured is crucial for the question whether specialization pays or not. We measure specialization in two ways and find opposite effects. This suggests that the trade-off between the costs and the benefits of specialization or diversification should be investigated very carefully, and that researchers are well advised to look at various ways to measure specialization. This issue is a worthwhile venue for further research.

## Appendix A. REITs in Sample

| Name | First month | Last month | Name | First month | Last month |
|---|---|---|---|---|---|
| Agree Realty Corporation | Jun 94 | Dec 96 | Crescent Real Estate Equities | Jun 94 | Dec 96 |
| Alexander Haagen | Feb 94 | Dec 96 | CROCKER REAL.INV | Mar 93 | Jul 95 |
| Alexander's Inc. | Jan 90 | Dec 96 | Crown American Realty Tr. | Oct 93 | Dec 96 |
| Ambassador Apartments (= Prime Residential) | Oct 94 | Dec 96 | Developers Diversified Realty | Apr 93 | Dec 96 |
| America First REIT | Jul 93 | Jul 95 | Duke Realty Investments | Jan 90 | Dec 96 |
| American Health Properties Inc. | Jan 90 | Dec 96 | Eastgroup Properties | Jan 90 | Dec 96 |
| American Industrial Properties REIT | Jan 90 | Dec 96 | EQK REALTY INVESTORS | Jan 90 | Dec 96 |
| American Real Estate Inv. | Jan 94 | Dec 96 | Equity Inns | Apr 94 | Dec 96 |
| AMLI RESIDENTIAL PROPS.TST.SHBI | Apr 94 | Dec 96 | Equity Res. Prop Trst | Oct 93 | Dec 96 |
| Apartment Investment and Management Company | Sep 94 | Dec 96 | Essex Property Trust | Aug 94 | Dec 96 |
| Arbor Properties | Jan 90 | Dec 96 | Evans Withycombe Residential | Oct 94 | Dec 96 |
| ASR INVS.CORP.COM.NEW | Jan 90 | Dec 96 | Excel Realty Trust | Oct 93 | Dec 96 |
| Associated Estates Realty Corp | Jan 94 | Dec 96 | Factory Stores of America | Aug 93 | Dec 96 |
| Avalon Properties Inc. | Jan 94 | Dec 96 | Fed. Realty Inv. Trust | Jan 90 | Dec 96 |
| BANYAN STGC.TST.SHBI | Jan 90 | Dec 96 | Felcor Suite Hotels | Sep 94 | Dec 96 |
| Bay Appartment Communities | May 94 | Dec 96 | First Industrial Realty Trust | Aug 94 | Dec 96 |
| Beacon Properties Inc. | Jul 94 | Dec 96 | First Union Real Estate Investments | Jan 90 | Dec 96 |
| BEDFORD PROPS.INVS.PAR | Jan 90 | Dec 96 | FIRST WASH RYLT.TR.INC.COM. | Aug 95 | Dec 96 |
| Berkshire Realty | Aug 91 | Dec 96 | Franchise Finance Corporation of America | Aug 94 | Dec 96 |
| Boddie-Noell Properties Inc. | Jan 90 | Dec 96 | G & L Realty Corporation | Feb 94 | Dec 96 |
| BRADLEY REAL EST. | Jan 90 | Dec 96 | Gables Residential Trust | Mar 94 | Dec 96 |
| Brandywine Realty Trust | Jan 90 | Dec 96 | General Growth Prop. | Jun 93 | Dec 96 |

| Company | Start | End |
|---|---|---|
| BRE Properties | Jan 90 | Dec 96 |
| Burnham Pacific Prop. | Jan 90 | Dec 96 |
| Cali Realty Corp | Oct 94 | Dec 96 |
| California Jockey Club | Jan 90 | Dec 96 |
| Camden Prop. Trust | Sep 93 | Dec 96 |
| Capstone Capital Corporation | Aug 94 | Dec 96 |
| CarrAmerica Realty Corp. | Apr 93 | Dec 96 |
| CBL & Associates | Dec 93 | Dec 96 |
| Cedar Income Fund | Jan 90 | Jan 93 |
| Centerpoint Prop. | Feb 94 | Dec 96 |
| Charles E. Smith Residential Realty | Aug 94 | Dec 96 |
| Chateau Prop. | Jan 94 | Dec 96 |
| Chelsea GCA Realty | Dec 93 | Dec 96 |
| Chicago Dock and Canal Trust | Jan 90 | Dec 96 |
| Colonial Properties Trust | Nov 93 | Dec 96 |
| Columbus Realty Trust | Feb 94 | Dec 96 |
| Commercial Net Lease Realty | Jan 90 | Dec 96 |
| Continental Mortgages & Equity Trust | Jan 90 | Dec 96 |
| COPLEY PROPS. | Jan 90 | Jul 96 |
| Koger Equity | Jan 90 | Dec 96 |
| Kranzco Realty | Jan 93 | Dec 96 |
| Lexington Corp. Prop. | Dec 93 | Dec 96 |
| Liberty Property Trust | Aug 94 | Dec 96 |

| Company | Start | End |
|---|---|---|
| GLENBOROUGH RLTY TST. | Apr 96 | Dec 96 |
| Glimcher Realty Trust | Mar 94 | Dec 96 |
| GROVE REAL ESTATE AS. | Aug 94 | Dec 96 |
| Health and Retirement Properties Trust | Jan 90 | Dec 96 |
| Health Care Prop. Inv | Jan 90 | Dec 96 |
| Healthcare Realty Trust | Aug 93 | Dec 96 |
| Highwoods | Aug 94 | Dec 96 |
| HMG COURTLAND PROPS. | Jan 90 | Dec 96 |
| Home Properties of New York Inc. | Sep 94 | Dec 96 |
| Horizon Outlet Cent. | Jan 94 | Dec 96 |
| HOSPITALITY PROPS. TST.SHRE.BENL.INT. | Oct 95 | Dec 96 |
| Host Funding | Jun 96 | Dec 96 |
| HRE Properties | Jan 90 | Dec 96 |
| Imkeepers USA Trust | Nov 94 | Dec 96 |
| IRT Prop. Comp | Jan 90 | Dec 96 |
| JAMESON | Apr 94 | Dec 96 |
| JDN Realty Corporation | May 94 | Dec 96 |
| JP Realty, Inc. | Mar 94 | Dec 96 |
| Kimco Realty Corp. | Jan 92 | Dec 96 |
| Regency Realty Corp. | Dec 93 | Dec 96 |
| RFS Hotel Investors | Oct 93 | Dec 96 |
| ROC Communities | Oct 93 | Dec 96 |
| ROYALE INVS. | Feb 92 | Dec 96 |

Appendix A. *(cont.)*

| Name | First month | Last month | Name | First month | Last month |
|---|---|---|---|---|---|
| Macerich Company, The | May 94 | Dec 96 | Santa Anita | Jan 90 | Dec 96 |
| Malan Realty Investors | Aug 94 | Dec 96 | Saul Centers | Oct 93 | Dec 96 |
| Manufactured Home Communities | Apr 93 | Dec 96 | Security Capital Industrial Trust | May 94 | Dec 96 |
| Mark Centers Trust | Jul 93 | Dec 96 | Security Capital Pacific Trust | Jan 90 | Dec 96 |
| MERIDIAN INDL.TST. | Apr 96 | Dec 96 | Shurgard Storage Centers Inc. | May 94 | Dec 96 |
| Merry Land & Inv. Co. | Jan 90 | Dec 96 | Simon Property Group | Feb 94 | Dec 96 |
| MGI Properties | Jan 90 | Dec 96 | Sizeler Property Investors | Jan 90 | Dec 96 |
| Mid-America Realty Inv. | Jan 90 | Dec 96 | South West Property Trust | Jul 93 | Dec 96 |
| Mills Corporation, The | Jun 94 | Dec 96 | Sovran Self Storage | Aug 95 | Dec 96 |
| MONMOUTH REIT | Jan 90 | Dec 96 | Starwood Lodging Tr. | Jan 90 | Dec 96 |
| National Golf Properties | Oct 93 | Dec 96 | STORAGE PROPERTIES | Nov 90 | Jul 96 |
| National Income Realty Trust | Jan 90 | Dec 96 | STORAGE TST.REALTY SHBI | Jan 95 | Dec 96 |
| Nationwide Health Properties | Jan 90 | Dec 96 | Storage USA | May 94 | Dec 96 |
| New Plan Realty Tr. | Jan 90 | Dec 96 | Summit Properties | Apr 94 | Dec 96 |
| Oasis Residential | Dec 93 | Dec 96 | Sun Communities | Feb 94 | Dec 96 |
| Pacific Gulf Properties | Apr 94 | Dec 96 | Sunstone Hotel Inv. | Oct 95 | Dec 96 |
| Paragon Group | Sep 94 | Dec 96 | Tanger Factory Outlet Centers | Jul 93 | Dec 96 |

| Company | | |
|---|---|---|
| Partners Preferred Yield I | Jan 92 | Dec 96 |
| Partners Preferred Yield II | Jan 92 | Dec 96 |
| Partners Preferred Yield III | Jan 92 | Dec 96 |
| Patriot American Hospitality | Nov 95 | Dec 96 |
| Pennsylvania REIT | Jan 90 | Dec 96 |
| Pittsburgh & West Virginia Railroad | Jan 90 | Dec 96 |
| Post Properties | Sep 93 | Dec 96 |
| Price REIT, class B | Oct 93 | Dec 96 |
| Prime Retail | May 94 | Dec 96 |
| Property Capital Trust | Jan 90 | Dec 96 |
| Public Storage Inc. | Jan 90 | Dec 96 |
| PUBLIC STRG.PROPS. X | May 91 | Oct 96 |
| PUBLIC STRG.PROPS. XI | May 91 | Dec 96 |
| PUBLIC STRG.PROPS. XII | May 91 | Oct 96 |
| Public Storage Prop. XIX | Jan 92 | Dec 96 |
| Public Storage Prop. XV | Nov 91 | Dec 96 |
| Public Storage Prop. XVII | Nov 91 | Dec 96 |
| Public Storage Prop. XVIII | Nov 91 | Dec 96 |
| Realty Income Corporation | Dec 94 | Dec 96 |
| RECKSON ASSOCS.RLTY CORP | Jul 95 | Dec 96 |
| Taubman Centers Inc. | Jan 93 | Dec 96 |
| Town and Country Trust, The | Oct 93 | Dec 96 |
| Transcontinental Realty Investors | Jan 90 | Dec 96 |
| Trinet Corporate Realty Trust | Jul 93 | Dec 96 |
| United Dominion Realty Trust | Jan 90 | Dec 96 |
| United Mobile Homes | Jan 90 | Dec 96 |
| Universal Health Realty | Mar 95 | Dec 96 |
| Urban Shopping Centers | Dec 93 | Dec 96 |
| USP REIT | Jan 90 | Dec 96 |
| Vornado Realty Trust | Jan 90 | Dec 96 |
| Walden Residential Properties | Apr 94 | Dec 96 |
| Washington REIT | Jan 90 | Dec 96 |
| Weeks Corporation | Oct 94 | Dec 96 |
| Weingarten Realty Inv. | Jan 90 | Dec 96 |
| WELLINGTON PROPS. TST.SHRANL.INT. | Jun 96 | Dec 96 |
| Wellsford Res. Prop. Tr. | Jan 93 | Dec 96 |
| Western Inv. Real Estate | Jan 90 | Dec 96 |
| Wetterau Properties | Jan 90 | Jun 94 |
| Winston Hotels | Jul 94 | Dec 96 |

219

## References

Berger, P. G. and E. Ofek, "Diversification's Effect on Firm Value", *Journal of Financial Economics* 37, 1995, 39–65.

Brown, S. J. and W. N. Goetzmann, "Performance Persistence", *Journal of Finance* 50, No. 2, 1995.

Capozza, D. R. and P. S. Seguin, "Why Focus Matters", *working paper*, 1997.

Coggin, T. D., F. J. Fabozzi, and S. Rahman, "The Investment Performance of U.S. Equity Pension Fund Managers: An Empirical Investigation", *Journal of Finance* 48, No. 3, 1993.

Comment, R. and G. A. Jarrell, "Corporate Focus and Stock Returns", *Journal of Financial Economics* 37, 1995, 67–87.

Denis, D. J., D. K. Denis, and A. Sarin, "Agency Problems, Equity Owership, and Corporate Diversification", *Journal of Finance* 52, No. 1, 1997.

Eichholtz, P. M. A., C. G. Koedijk, and M. Schweitzer, "Testing International Real Estate Investment Strategies", *LIFE working paper*, 1996.

Fama, E. F. and K. R. French, "The Cross-Section of Expected Returns", *Journal of Finance* 47, No. 2, 1992, 427–465.

Ferson, W. E. and R. W. Schadt, "Measuring Fund Strategy and Performance in Changing Economic Conditions", *Journal of Finance* 51, No. 2, 1996, 425–461.

Goetzmann, W. N. and S. M. Wachter, "Clustering Methods for Real Estate Portfolios", *Real Estate Economics* 23, No. 3, 1995, 273–310.

Grinblatt, M. and S. Titman, "Portfolio Performance Evaluation: Old Issues and New Insights", *Review of Financial Studies* 2, No. 3, 1989, 393–421.

Grinblatt, M. and S. Titman, "A Study of Monthly Mutual Fund Returns and Performance Evaluation Techniques", *Journal of Financial and Quantitative Analysis* 29, 1994, 419–444.

Grinblatt, M. and S. Titman, "Performance Evaluation", *Handbooks in Operations Research and Management Science* 9, R. A. Jarrow, V. Maksimovic, and W. T. Ziemba, 1995.

Hartzell, D., J. Hekman, and M. Miles, "Diversification Categories in Investment Real Estate", *AREUEA Journal* 14, No. 2, 1986, 230–254.

Ito, T., R. K. Lyons, and M.T. Melvin, "Is There Private Information in the FX Market? The Tokyo Experiment", *Working Paper*, 1997.

Jensen, M. C., " Risk, the Pricing of Capital Assets, and the Evaluation of Investment Portfolios," *Journal of Business* 42, No. 2, 1969, 167–247.

John, K. and E. Ofek, "Asset Sales and Increase in Focus", *Journal of Financial Economics* 37, 1995, 105–126.

Lehmann, B. and D. Modest, "Mutual Fund Performance Evaluation: A Comparison of Benchmarks and Benchmark Comparisons", *Journal of Finance* 42, No. 2, 1987, 233–265.

Malkiel, B. G., "Returns from Investing in Equity Mutual Funds 1971 to 1991", *Journal of Finance* 50, No. 2, 1995, 549–572.

Miles, M. and T. McCue, "Diversification in the Real Estate Portfolio", *Journal of Financial Research* 7, No. 1, 1984, 57–68.

Shukla, R. K. and G. B. Van Inwegen, "Do Locals Perform Better Than Foreigners?: An Analysis of UK and US Mutual Fund Managers", *Journal of Economics and Business* 47, 1995, 241–254.

White, H., "A Heteroskedasticity-Consistent Covariance Matrix Estimator and a Direct Test for Heteroskedasticity", *Econometrica* 48, 1980, 817–838.

# 7

## Bank Relationships: A Review[a]

Steven Ongena[b], David C. Smith[c]

> *The banker . . . is not so much primarily a middleman in the commodity "purchasing power" as a producer of this commodity. He is essentially a phenomenon of development (and) makes possible the carrying out of new combinations, authorizes people, in the name of society as it were, to form them.*
>
> Joseph Schumpeter (1934), *The Theory of Economic Development*
>
> *The right relationship is everything.*
>
> Corporate slogan, Chase Manhattan Bank

### 1 Introduction

As a bank provides an array of services through time to a customer, it gains substantial knowledge about its customer's financial needs. The bank can use this knowledge to establish a close kinship with the customer. This kinship can, in turn, lead to benefits for both the customer and the bank. For example, as a bank learns more about a customer's

[a] Mark Flannery, Joel Houston, Stavros A. Zenios, and three anonymous referees made comments that greatly helped to improve this chapter. All remaining errors and omissions are our own.

[b] Department of Finance, Tilburg University, PO Box 90153, 5000 LE Tilburg, the Netherlands. Email: steven.ongena@kub.nl.

[c] Warrington College of Business Administration, University of Florida, PO Box 117168, Gainesville, FL 32611-7168 and Department of Financial Economics, Norwegian School of Management – BI, PO Box 580 N-1301 Sandvika, Norway. Email: smithdc@dale.cba.ufl.edu.

payment habits, it can tailor contracts to directly suit the financial requirements of the customer. A loyal customer will be more willing to purchase all of its financial services from the bank it trusts, aiding the bank in the marketing of profitable new products. Indeed, as the Chase Manhattan slogan suggests, bankers often perceive the creation of strong customer *relationships* to be a core element of the services they offer. Irwin Teich, president of Fleet Capital Corporation, mirrors this view: "the marketing philosophy of customer satisfaction, based on long-term relationships, must permeate all of the (bank's) functions. Relationship-building is a specific process we go through with our customers" (Teich, 1997, p. 12).

Despite the perception of its importance, the value in a modern economy of a close relationship between the bank and customer is unclear. Many of today's financial transactions are executed via automated, anonymous markets that require little relationship-building. For instance, the total dollar value of deposits into U.S. money market mutual funds in December 1997 was 1.5 times greater than the value of all demand and checkable deposits (Federal Reserve Bulletin, 1998). During the same period, the total value of commercial paper and corporate bond issues in the U.S. exceeded consumer and industrial bank loans by a factor of 1.21 (Federal Reserve Bulletin, 1998). The global trends toward deregulation, disintermediation, and securitization appear only to accelerate the transition from relationship-intensive services to more market- or transactions-oriented financial products. Yet relationship-intensive financing may be a fundamental ingredient in the nurturing of developing firms and economies.

This chapter of the volume reviews the existing evidence from the financial economics literature on the value of bank relationships. In so doing, the chapter attempts to answer the following questions: What measured benefits accrue to banks and their customers via a relationship? How does competition influence the services provided by banks? What types of customers gain the most from a close relationship with their bank? And finally, what impact do bank relationships have on the macroeconomy? Following the financial economics literature, our review does not emphasize retail bank relationships, but instead focuses on commercial bank relationships with firms as customers.

Early research into the value of bank relationships by Hodgman (1963), Kane and Malkiel (1965), and Wood (1975) emphasizes the influence of the relationship on the credit channel through which monetary policy affects the economy. The motivation for the more recent research originates from the observation by Fama (1985) and James (1987) that bank loans to companies possess unique characteristics, compared to alternative forms of financing. Fama (1985) conjectures that a bank's role as an "insider" distinguishes bank loans from market loans. James (1987) documents the curious result that stock prices increase on the announcement of company financing by a bank loan, but decrease on the announcement of public financing.

Research interest into bank relationships has grown to include several different strands of literature. One area concentrates on the value of bank relationships to small firm financing, because small firms typically have difficulty obtaining investment funds from public sources (see Berger and Udell, 1998, for a comprehensive overview of small firm financing). Another line of research focuses on evaluating the cross-sectional differences in financial systems. Some financial systems, such as those in Germany and Japan, are said to be *relationship-intensive* because they are dominated by long-term bank relationships. Following the original works by Hodgman (1961), Kane and Malkiel (1965), and Wood (1975), a third area is devoted to examining the role of bank relationships in transmitting monetary policy. We draw on research from all of these areas because they share a common emphasis on quantifying the value of bank relationships.

In this review, we strive not to duplicate the work available in other reviews on the existence, nature, and role of financial intermediaries. Berlin (1996), for example, provides a perceptive introduction to the bank relationship literature using three hypothetical case studies, while Bhattacharya and Thakor (1993), Bernanke (1993), and Freixas and Rochet (1997) contain broader coverages of current research issues in banking. Our review is organized into seven sections. Section 2 begins by defining a bank relationship. This discussion is followed by an introduction to the early theoretical papers that have prompted much of the current academic interest in bank relationships. Section 3 focuses on the impact a bank relationship has on the performance of the firm as customer. We examine both the impact of bank loan announcements on the owner's wealth and the influence of the bank relationship on firm financing, corporate control, and the confidentiality of information. In Section 4, we turn to measures of the strength of a bank relationship and its impact on bank performance. We focus on three areas emphasized by the literature: duration, scope, and extended bank relationships. Section 5 is devoted to multiple bank relationships and credit market concentration. We round out our review in Section 6 with a look at how bank relationships influence the macroeconomy. This section also touches upon the influence of bank mergers and bank defaults on bank relationships. Section 7 summarizes and discusses some outstanding issues that warrant further research.

## 2  Introduction to Bank Relationships

### 2.1  Definition of a Bank Relationship

In its most basic form, a *bank* is an institution whose primary activities are the granting of loans and the taking of deposits from the public. As an intermediary between individuals wishing to save and those who need to borrow, a bank is similar to a securities market. The bank creates and exchanges financial contracts to facilitate the movement of funds between savers and borrowers. Historically speaking, a bank has also provided liquidity and safety not available through securities markets. As Carey (1817), an advocate for improved banking practices in 19th century America, writes,

> In times of distress and difficulty, and stagnation of trade and commerce, policy, as well as humanity, dictates an extension of accommodation, and of course in the most imperious manner forbids Banks to press upon their debtors (p. 11).

A bank is expected to "lean against the wind" and accommodate its debtors during difficult financial times. Such flexibility is not available in an anonymous securities market. To ensure its credibility as a savings institution, a bank is also counted on to redeem deposits quickly to savers *on demand*. Rajan (1996, 1998) argues this ability to offer liquidity continuously to both borrowers and savers distinguishes a bank from "arm's-length" securities markets.

In providing such financial flexibility, a bank requires a close association with each of its customers. Such an association can be termed a relationship. In its most general form, we define a bank relationship to be *the connection between a bank and customer that goes beyond the execution of simple, anonymous, financial transactions*. The benefits of a relationship may include the transfer of proprietary information, a commitment to continue doing business together through financially tough times, or the offer and delivery of services at prices different from costs. A bank relationship can be more specifically defined along two dimensions. The first is time. The importance of a relationship will depend on the length or *duration* of the interaction between the customer and bank. Wood (1975), for example, believes a loan customer relationship exists when "the current quantity of loans extended affects the strength of future loan demand" (p. 11), and Rajan (1997) explains that "relationships may evolve in situations where explicit contracts are inadequate, but a long term interaction between two parties is mutually beneficial" (p. 12). The second dimension is *scope*, which pertains to the breadth of services offered by the bank to its customer. Hodgman (1963) asserts that a customer relationship is, "that strategic nexus of customer service, loans, and deposits which gives to commercial banks their unique character" (p. 113).

Maintaining a relationship often means that the customer and bank are willing to make temporary sacrifices in favor of obtaining future benefits. For example, a bank may attract borrowers by offering up-front interest rates that are below cost, with the hope of charging higher rates to the same customers later to recoup initial losses. Conversely, a firm may be willing initially to accept above-cost interest loans, if a long relationship promises a lower permanent rate in the future. Such pricing decisions will influence the expected duration of the bank relationship. The bank could also offer below-cost loans to a customer, with the hope of recovering the losses through customer purchases of other services from the bank. Such pricing decisions then impact the scope of the relationship.

A bank relationship will be influenced by a variety of external factors, including the competitive environment of the banking system, the level of development of arm's-length securities markets, the types of regulation faced by investors, and the degree of technological development. Throughout this chapter, we discuss the influence of these factors directly on the bank relationship and indirectly on the performance of the firm-customer and bank. We now turn to a discussion of the early research on bank relationships.

### 2.2 Theories on Bank Relationships

Drawing on a comprehensive survey of senior managers at 18 commercial banks, Hodgman (1960, 1961, 1963) is the first to investigate the importance of customer relationships in banking. Hodgman focuses on *deposit* relationships. He hypothesizes that the value of a deposit relationship arises in response to competition between banks. Competition forces rents earned from lending to be passed on to the suppliers of loanable funds – the depositors. Since the interest directly paid on deposits (for example, demand deposits) is capped by regulation, banks compensate loyal depositors by offering below-cost loans. Therefore, a deposit relationship leads to a customer receiving more favorable loan conditions than non-depositors.

Kane and Malkiel (1965) build on the intuition in Hodgman to argue that strong deposit relationships also reduce the variability in loanable funds, which in turn increases the return per unit of risk of the bank's loan portfolio. A key point made by Kane and Malkiel (1965) is that an incumbent bank gains an *informational advantage* over competitors by privately observing the payment behavior of its depositors. This leads the incumbent bank to offer below-cost loans to its best depositors – those customers with the most stable deposits. The cheap loan preempts competing loan offers from drawing away the stable depositors because competing banks are unable to offer the same loan rates without also attracting unprofitable, poor depositors.

Wood (1975) recognizes that a *lending* relationship may develop independently of a customer's deposit behavior because, "current accommodation of prospective borrowers by a bank influences future demands for credit from the bank" (p. 11). He notes that a bank may find it profitable to offer easy or low-cost credit in one period in hopes of charging higher rates to a customer in the future. In order for the bank to have the ability to charge higher rates in the future, some mechanism must lock the customer into the current relationship. Wood (1975) conjectures that such "holdup" problems may occur when the borrower faces search costs for transferring business to a competing lender.

Leland and Pyle (1977), Diamond (1984), Ramakrishnan and Thakor (1984), Fama (1985), and Boyd and Prescott (1986) argue that it is a bank's ability to reduce information asymmetries between borrowers and savers that makes a bank unique relative to other financial institutions. We motivate the intuition behind these theories using Fama's argument. Fama points out a paradox. He observes that firms willingly borrow from a bank, although they must bear an additional cost – the opportunity cost of non-interest bearing reserves held by the bank against certificates of deposit (CDs) – that is absent from non-bank lending sources. Like Kane and Malkiel (1965), Fama reasons that a bank gains proprietary knowledge of its firm-customer through deposit services. Fama also recognizes that a bank learns a substantial amount of information when it initially screens the borrower for the loan, has the ability to monitor the behavior of firm management closely over the course of the loan, and can even influence decisions made by management. The fact that the bank has such wide access to private information about its borrowers leads Fama to term the bank an "inside debtholder."

Fama (1985) alludes to the importance of the firm-bank relationship as it affects a firm's ability to raise capital, both from within the bank and through other non-bank sources. His reasoning is as follows. Bank loans are typically short term. Each time a bank renews a short-term loan contract, the renewal acts as an accreditation of the ability for the firm to meet the bank obligation. This renewal creates two positive externalities. It enables other providers of financing to avoid duplicating the evaluation process of the bank, and it provides accreditation to the public that the firm will be able to produce enough cash flows in the future to meet its fixed obligation. Periodic evaluation and subsequent renewals are features of a developing firm-bank relationship.

### 3 Bank Relationships and Firm Performance

Given the short theoretical introduction in Section 2, we begin this section with a review of studies that measure the impact on a firm's stock price when it publicly reveals information about a bank relationship. The information released may be related to new debt financing from the bank, a loan renewal, or a backing of other firm activities. Some of the evidence is summarized in Table 7.1. We return to the theoretical literature to analyze the benefits and costs of a bank relationship as they could impact firm performance.

### 3.1 Shareholder Wealth Effects of
### Bank Loan Announcements

Motivated by Fama's conjectures regarding the uniqueness of bank loans, James (1987) studies the average stock price reaction of firms that publicly announce a bank loan agreement or renewal. Such an "event study" measures the perceived impact on firm value of a loan, as measured by changes in stockholder wealth on the announcement date. A positive, abnormal price reaction indicates that the bank loan will either lead to future increases in firm cash flows, or it reveals positive information about the future value of the firm (see Chapter 4 of Campbell, Lo, and MacKinlay, 1997, for a discussion of event study methodology). James (1987) compares the stock price reaction to announcements of both privately placed and publicly issued debt. Investors in private placements share some of the characteristics of a bank, since they also have the opportunity to obtain inside information from the borrowing company.

The results in James (1987) are interesting. The first row of Table 7.1 summarizes his findings. He finds that bank loan announcements are associated with *positive* and statistically significant stock price reactions, while announcements of privately placed and public issues of debt experience zero or negative stock price reactions. This result holds independently of the type of loan and the default risk and size of the borrower. The positive stock-price reaction supports the Fama (1985) argument

Table 7.1. *Evidence on bank relationships: event studies.*

| Paper | Sample period | Average (median) firm size | Announcement (number of events) | Two-day, −1 and 0, mean abnormal return (is difference significant?) |
|---|---|---|---|---|
| James (1987) | 1974–1983 | Liabilities: 675 (212) | Bank loan agreement (80) | 1.93*** |
| Slovin et al. (1988) | 1982–1985 | 7,303 | Commercial paper offering (35) through note issuance facility (18) or letter of credit backed (17) | 1.39** |
| Lummer and McConnell (1989) | 1976–1986 | n/a | Bank credit agreements (728) Revised (357) / new (371) | 0.61*** 1.24*** / −0.01 (n/a) |
| Best and Zhang (1993) | 1977–1989 | n/a | Bank credit agreement (491) Renewals (304) / new (187) Renewals and noisy[a] (156) / new and accurate[a] (187) | 0.32** 1.97** / 0.26 (no) 0.60** / −0.05 (*) |
| Billett et al. (1995) | 1980–1989 | Equity market: 316 (79) | Loan (626) Renewals (187) / new banks (51) Banks' rating: AAA (78) / <BAA (29) | 0.68*** 1.09** / 0.64* (no) 0.63** / −0.57 (no) |
| Hadlock and James (1997) | 1980–1993 | Assets: 2,181 (238) 3,252 (485) / 315 (143) | Bank loan (120) Public debt: with (64) / without (56) | 0.91*** 1.50* / 0.19 (*) |
| Shockley and Thakor (1998) | 1989–1990 | n/a | Loan commitments purchases (189) Usage fees: with (137) / without (52) | 1.95*** 2.47*** / 0.54 (***) |
| Kracaw and Zenner (1998) | 1980–1989 | Equity market: 296 (65) | Bank loan (378) Clear and potential strong interlocks (32) / no (346) | n/a −0.89 / 0.96 (*) |

*Note:* Average (median) firm size is the size of the firms in millions of U.S. dollars in the last year of the sample. [a] Prediction. *** Significant at 1%, ** significant at 5%, * significant at 10%.

that a bank loan provides accreditation for a firm's ability to generate a certain level of cash flows in the future.

The results in James (1987) also suggest that the value added by a bank relationship goes beyond simply being an inside lender. Although holders of privately placed debt also have access to inside information from the firm, James (1987) finds a negative, though insignificant, price reaction on the announcement of the private placement. More recent research has produced results that conflict with this finding from James (1987). Once they control for the credit rating of the lender, Billett, Flannery, and Garfinkel (1995) find the price reaction of private placements to be similar to bank loans. Moreover, Carey, Post, and Sharpe (1998) use loan-specific data to demonstrate that differences between privately placed loans to non-bank finance companies and loans by banks are due to variations in the riskiness of the loans, not to information-related differences.

Numerous other event studies have expanded on the results in James (1987). For example, Slovin, Sushka, and Hudson (1988) show that announcements of public commercial paper issues backed by standby letters of credit from a bank have a positive and significant impact on the share price of the borrowing firm. James and Wier (1990) and Slovin and Young (1990) find that initial public offerings (IPOs) of firms with an existing bank lending relationship are significantly less underpriced than IPOs for firms with no bank relationship. Similarly, in Hirshey, Slovin, and Zaima (1990), announcement of a corporate divestiture decision by a firm with bank debt results in positive announcement-day abnormal returns while a sell-off by a firm with little bank debt does not result in abnormal returns.

More recently, Billett et al. (1995) study the relationship between lender quality and loan announcement-day returns. They conjecture that loans from high-quality lenders are more likely to be viewed as positive news by stockholders than loans from low-quality lenders. Consistent with their conjecture, Billett et al. (1995) find that loans from higher-quality lenders, as proxied by the institution's credit rating from Moody's, are associated with positive and statistically significant price reactions, while loan announcements from lower-rated institutions are associated with negative, though insignificant, returns. Shockley and Thakor (1998) find the announcement of bank loan *commitments* to be positive and statistically significant only for those firms that pay up-front usage fees. Hadlock and James (1997) argue that a positive price response to a bank loan announcement should be largest for undervalued firms that also have public financing as a viable option. Consistent with this prediction,

Hadlock and James (1997) find the two-day abnormal return around a bank loan announcement to be larger when a firm already has public debt in its capital structure and when the ex ante likelihood of borrowing from a bank is low.

### 3.2 Bank Loan Announcements and Bank Relationships

Lummer and McConnell (1989) divide bank loan announcements into first-time loan initiations and follow-up loan renewals. Because loan initiations are loans to new customers while renewals are loans to established customers, the difference in stock price reactions between the two categories should act as a measure of the value of an established relationship. Consistent with this argument, Lummer and McConnell (1989) find that stock price reactions to bank loan announcements are driven by renewals. The event period abnormal returns associated with announcements of initiations are not statistically different from zero, while favorable renewals are positive and statistically significant.

The results in Lummer and McConnell (1989), however, have been difficult to duplicate. Slovin, Johnson, and Glascock (1992), Wansley, Elayan, and Collins (1992), Best and Zhang (1993), and Billett et al. (1995) document positive and significant price reactions to both initiation and renewal announcements and find little difference in price reactions between the two categories. Best and Zhang (1993) do find that price reactions to renewal announcements are significantly larger than initiations when analyst uncertainty about the loan customer is high. In their study, Billett et al. (1995) argue that the Lummer and McConnell (1989) results may be driven by their system for classifying loans into initiation and renewal categories. Lummer and McConnell (1989) classify any loan announcement that does not mention "renewal" as an initiation. Overall, the evidence on the differential wealth effects of loan renewals versus initiations is inconclusive.

Another important event study containing direct evidence on the value of the bank relationship is Slovin, Sushka, and Polonchek (1993). They examine the influence of the 1984 impending insolvency of Continental Illinois on the stock price of firms with an ongoing lending relationship with the bank. Slovin et al. (1993) report an average abnormal two-day return of −4.2 percent around the insolvency announcement and an abnormal increase of 2.0 percent upon the announcement of the FDIC rescue. They argue that such large price changes are estimates of the potential value tied directly to the firm-bank relationship. The existence of these quasi-rents implies that borrowers are bank stakeholders.

Motivated by the potential holdup problems of a strong bank relationship (see Section 3.4), Kracaw and Zenner (1998) examine the influence of interlocking directorships on loan announcement returns. An interlocking directorship occurs when either a senior officer of a lending bank sits on the customer's board of directors ("strong interlock"), a representative from the borrowing firm sits on the bank's board ("weak interlock"), or the borrowing firm and lending institution share a common board member ("weak interlock"). Kracaw and Zenner (1998) find that loan announcement abnormal returns for strong interlocks are reliably negative, while weak interlocks are associated with positive or zero abnormal returns. They argue their evidence suggests that firm-bank relationships that are "too strong" can actually harm firms.

### 3.3 Benefits and Cost to the Firm of a Bank Relationship

The event studies suggest that stockholders in publicly traded firms view bank lending and, more generally, contact with a bank as value-increasing activities. Announcements of bank loans convey positive information to other investors, reducing the firm's cost of capital from public sources. There are also circumstances where firms will choose bank or inside financing to the exclusion of public, arm's-length financing. Financing through public capital markets may be so expensive for some firms that a relationship with a bank is the only way to obtain capital. In this section, we introduce four reasons that bank relationships improve financing possibilities, create value, and ultimately improve firm performance. Bank relationships improve contracting flexibility between the customer and bank, reduce agency problems through increased control, enable reputation-building, and ensure confidentiality. We also discuss in this section one potential cost of a strong relationship, the so-called "holdup" problem.

Armed with the information it privately observes, a bank can exploit the length of a relationship to increase ex ante loan contracting flexibility. Boot and Thakor (1994) derive a framework where firms optimally choose to enter an infinite-period lending contract with a bank rather than borrow directly from the capital market. In their equilibrium, a bank offers a contract that initially requires the firm to pledge a high amount of collateral and to pay above-cost interest rates. However, the contract also stipulates that once the bank has privately observed successful completion of a financed project, the bank reduces both the interest charged and required collateral on the project. Von Thadden (1995) investigates the relationship between debt contract flexibility and the firm's investment horizon. The study shows that a debt contract resembling a line of credit, which requires periodic monitoring and contains a clause allowing the lender to deny continuation, induces firms to avoid myopic investment behavior. Such myopia is present in public market contracts.

Bank relationships not only allow for more flexible ex ante contracting, they also increase the ease with which contracts can be renegotiated ex post. For a firm experiencing difficulty meeting contracted loan payments, a bank can re-adjust the terms of the contract and either accommodate the firm with new lending or refuse future lending, conditional on actions taken by the firm during and after the distress period. Thus, banks have the ability to exert control over the management of firm assets. In Rajan (1992), bank debt is beneficial exactly because of this corporate control feature: a bank's threat to withdraw funding induces the firm manager to accept positive net present value (NPV) projects. Longhofer and Santos (1998) conjecture that bank debt seniority may play an important role in encouraging the formation of ongoing bank-firm relationships. As senior creditors, banks will benefit first from additional investment in a distressed firm. Hence banks will have incentives to build relationships that allow them to determine the value of such investment.

Since repeated lending from a bank provides credible certification of payment ability, borrowers may establish a relationship in order to gain a reputation for making timely loan payments. Reputational concerns can therefore influence a firm's choice between bank financing and arm's-length financing. Diamond (1991) argues that reputation building through bank borrowing serves as a means for establishing enough credibility to eventually borrow through public markets. Higher-quality firms care most about establishing a reputation and find it therefore most costly to default on a monitored bank loan. Eventually, a high-quality firm's reputation grows to such an extent that the cost of default – through loss of reputation – is so high that the firm can seek unmonitored, public debt. In Hoshi, Kashyap, and Scharfstein (1993), only firms with low investment opportunities bond themselves by choosing to be monitored by a bank. High-growth firms require no such bonding and instead finance using public debt.

Finally, bank relationships also enable a firm to obtain financing without disclosing valuable information to the public. Campbell (1979) is the first to recognize that inside debt contracts are preferable when a firm manager wants to maintain confidentiality. Bhattacharya and Chiesa (1995) argue that the confidentiality of bank lending protects proprietary information and facilitates screening and monitoring. In their model, the improved confidentiality encourages investment in research and development (R&D), when public disclosure of accumulated R&D knowledge creates a free-rider problem. Yosha (1995) argues that high-quality firms will choose bilateral bank financing to avoid information leakage through multilateral or public financing. Hence, confidentiality of the bilateral bank-firm relationship encourages the flow of information.

### 3.4 The Holdup Problem

The ability for a bank to privately observe proprietary information and maintain a close relationship with its customer can also impose costs on the customer. Sharpe (1990) argues that long-term bank relationships arise in a competitive loan market because an incumbent bank has the ability to offer only above-cost loans to its best customers and to hold up customers from receiving competitive financing elsewhere. The incumbent bank gains this monopoly power through its informational advantage over competitors. A high-quality firm that tries to switch to a competing uninformed bank gets pooled with low-quality firms and is offered an even worse, breakeven interest rate. Motivated by the suggestion in Wood (1975), Greenbaum, Kanatas, and Venezia (1989) model the holdup problem by assuming that firms must invest resources in searching for competing bank offers. The fixed search cost creates an option-like feature in the bank's profit function. As the bank gleans more information from its customers through time, uncertainty about a given customer's cash flow declines, mitigating the holdup problem. Holdup costs are also present in the model of Rajan (1992), since the bank has the power to withdraw financing when it perceives the firm to be inadequately managing the financed assets. This degree of control can be costly because it reduces the incentives of the firm manager to exert effort.

The extent to which any one bank can exploit an information monopoly is unclear. Sharpe (1990) predicts that an incumbent bank's monopoly power will be mitigated by accurate public signals of the firm's ability to pay. Greenbaum et al. (1989) argue that the value of the holdup rents declines in the length of the relationship. Similarly, repeated borrowing from one inside bank may increase the firm's reputation for payment ability, allowing for easier access to public markets (Diamond, 1991). Schmeits (1997) argues that the potential for moral hazard problems associated with asset substitution increases as the bank charges higher interest rates, thus limiting the bank's monopoly power. The information monopoly rents of the inside bank may also be contained by loan commitments (Houston and Venkataraman, 1994) or eroded through market-driven information leaks and information-sharing sources like credit registers (Padilla and Pagano [1997], Van Cayseele, Bouckaert, and Degryse [1994]).

One seemingly simple solution to the holdup problem is for a firm to establish more than one inside bank relationship and have the banks compete away the monopoly rents. Rajan (1992), however, warns that such competition can be a "double-edged sword." Any outside lender that competes with an existing inside bank by offering a lower interest rate at an interim stage of financing will suffer from a winner's curse problem. The inside bank will offer a competitive bid for good firms while allowing bad firms to take the outside lender's offer (a similar point is made by von Thadden, 1998). When competition ensues between more symmetrically informed banks, monopoly rents can be eliminated, but only at the expense of reduced control over firm investment behavior. Hence competition at the outset between an insider and outsider has the benefit of reducing the monopoly rent one bank can charge, but also reduces its ability to control the investment behavior of the firm. Moreover, Petersen, and Rajan (1995) reason that credit market competition reduces the availability of credit to firms that benefit most from relationship lending. We address the issue of competition from multiple banks in more detail in Section 5.

The costs arising from holdup problems may also be tempered by the bank's reputation. Sharpe (1990) argues that banks build valuable reputations by refraining from extracting monopoly holdup rents. In Chemmanur and Fulghieri (1994), banks use the ability to renegotiate as a means of acquiring a valuable reputation, and reputation building provides the bank with an incentive to establish a relationship with a firm. In this study's model, banks have the choice between liquidating the firm when distressed or renegotiating the loan contract. Banks wishing to establish a reputation for financing productive firms monitor the firms more intensively, which in turn leads to more efficient continuation decisions in renegotiation. If bank reputation is positively correlated with a credit rating, then the results in Billett et al. (1995) are consistent with the theory in Chemmanur and Fulghieri (1994). Firms that are financed by more reputable banks experience the largest positive value increases upon announcement of the loan.

In the next section, we introduce measures of the strength of a bank relationship and relate empirical estimates of strength to the performance of banks.

**4 Measures of Relationship Strength and
the Performance of Banks**

We begin this section by investigating two measures of relationship strength: duration and scope. We then examine the influence of relationships between bank and customer that extend beyond the standard services provided by a bank.

*4.1 The Duration of a Relationship*

An important observable measure of the strength of a bank relationship is its *duration*. As the duration of a bank relationship lengthens, the bank has the opportunity to observe, learn, and utilize the private information about its customer, has more flexibility in writing, committing to, and enforcing contracts, and can credibly build a reputation for quality service. The ability for a given bank to preserve a relationship will depend on the price and quality of services offered, the quality of the customer, and the competitive environment in which the bank operates.

Table 7.2 summarizes the international evidence from recent papers on the average length of bank relationships. At first glance, Table 7.2 suggests that the duration of Japanese and continental European bank relationships tends to be greater than their counterparts in the U.S. This pattern is consistent with the idea that Japan and continental European countries tend to be bank-dominated economies, where relationship-based financing plays a dominant role (see, for example, Cable, 1985, and Aoki and Patrick, 1994). Elsas and Krahnen (1998) estimate the mean duration of a bank relationship in their sample of German companies to be 20 years, while in Horiuchi, Packer, and Fukuda (1988), the estimate for Japanese firms is between 21 and 30 years. The estimates from Norway and Sweden are of the same order of magnitude. In contrast, most of the U.S. estimates of duration are less than ten years. Cole (1998), for example, finds the mean duration of U.S. firms in his sample to be seven years.

However, the estimates in Table 7.2 are deceiving because the cross-country data vary greatly according to the characteristics of the sample firms and by how duration is estimated. For example, the size of the firms from all of the available U.S. studies is comparatively small. Petersen and Rajan (1994), Berger and Udell (1995), and Cole (1998) all use data from the National Survey of Small Business Finances (NSSBF), a data set collected for the U.S. Small Business Administration and limited to firms with less than 500 employees. By contrast, Elsas and Krahnen (1998) and

Table 7.2. *Evidence on bank relationships: duration.*

| Paper | Country | Sample years(s) | Sample size | Average (median) firm size | Average (median) duration |
|---|---|---|---|---|---|
| Cole (1998) | U.S. | 1993 | 5,356 | Book assets: 1.63 | 7.03 |
| Blackwell and Winters (1997) | U.S. | 1988 | 174 | Book assets: 13.5 | 9.01 |
| Petersen and Rajan (1995) | U.S. | 1987 | 3,404 | Book assets: 1.05 (0.3) Employees: 26 (5) | 10.8 |
| Angelini et al. (1998) | Italy | 1995 | 1,858 | Employees: 10.3 | 14.0 |
| Harhoff and Körting (1998b) | Germany | 1997 | 994 | Employees: ±40 (10) | ±12 |
| Elsas and Krahnen (1998) | Germany | 1992–1996 | 125 / year | Turnover: (30–150) | 22.2 |
| Ongena and Smith (1998a) | Norway | 1979–1995 | 111 / year | Market equity: 150 | (15.8–18.1) |
| Zineldin (1995) | Sweden | 1994 | 179 | Employees: (<49) | (>5) |
| Sjögren (1994) | Sweden | 1916–1947 | 50 | Largest firms | >20 (5–29) |
| Degryse and Van Cayseele (1998) | Belgium | 1997 | 17,776 loans | Employees: (1) | 7.82 |
| Horiuchi et al. (1988) | Japan | 1972–1983 | 668 | Largest firms | (30) |

*Note:* Sample size is the number of firms (unless indicated otherwise). Average (median) firm size is the size of the firms in millions of U.S. dollars in the last year of the sample or, if indicated, the number of employees. Average (median) duration is the duration of bank relationships in years.

Horiuchi et al. (1988) employ a sample of large industrial firms. A German study that utilizes a data set comparable to the NSSBF data is Harhoff and Körting (1998b). They report the average duration of a bank relationship to be around 12 years – an estimate of the same magnitude as the estimate from the U.S. data.

A second problem with the duration estimates in Table 7.2 is censoring. Censoring induces inconsistent estimates of duration and occurs when either the beginning of the relationship, end of the relationship, or both is not observed by the empiricist. A simple illustration of the censoring problem can be made using the NSSBF cross-sectional data. Firms surveyed at one point in time about their incumbent bank relationship cannot provide information about when the relationship will end. The duration of the firms is thus "right-censored" since the maximum length of the relationship is limited by the survey year. Moreover, the duration is limited by the age of the firm. The average age of a firm is 11 years in the 1988 NSSBF survey and 12 years in the 1993 survey, limiting the maximum duration of the bank relationship for each firm to a relatively short time span.

Ongena and Smith (1998a) use a panel data of connections between Oslo Stock Exchange–listed firms and their banks for the period 1979–1995, enabling them to observe the entire evolution of some of the bank relationships in their sample. Still, 75 percent of their observations are censored. Many of the bank relationships began before 1979 or continued after 1995, censoring the maximum observable duration to 16 years. Firms also list and delist during the sample period, compounding the censoring problem. To obtain consistent estimates of relationship duration, Ongena and Smith (1998a) adopt censored-robust estimators of the *hazard function*. A hazard function measures the likelihood of ending a bank relationship conditional on its duration. The influence of censoring is clear in the data set used by Ongena and Smith (1998a). The mean length of an observed bank relationship with no adjustment for censoring is six years. After adjusting for censoring, the estimate of mean duration varies between 15 and 21 years.

Ongena and Smith (1998a) is also the only study listed in Table 7.2 that investigates the determinants of bank relationship duration. Using a sample of 386 bank relationships observed over the period 1979–1995, Ongena and Smith (1998a) find that longstanding bank relationships are more likely to be terminated than shorter relationships. Such behavior is consistent with the conjecture in Greenbaum et al. (1989) that the value to the bank of a relationship decreases as the relationship lengthens. Ongena and Smith (1998a) also report that bank relationships tend to be shorter for small, young, and relatively high-leveraged firms, suggesting that those firms most in need of bank financing maintain relationships for relatively shorter periods of time. Moreover, Ongena and Smith (1998a) report that firms that maintain multiple simultaneous bank relationships end a given bank relationship sooner than a firm with one bank relationship.

Consistent with the results reported in Ongena and Smith (1998a), recent U.S. evidence suggests that the benefits from a bank relationship may accrue only in the earlier part of the relationship. In a study updating the Petersen and Rajan (1994) and Berger and Udell (1995) papers, Cole (1998) uses the 1993 NSSBF survey to show that credit availability increases in the length of the relationship over its first year, but does not increase thereafter.

Petersen and Rajan (1994) investigate the impact of relationship duration on the terms offered by the bank to its customer, enabling them to measure the value of a "strong" relationship for the credit policy of a bank. Petersen and Rajan (1994) study a sample of over 3,000 firms from the 1987 NSSBF survey. The NSSBF study is unique because it contains detailed information on the financing behavior of the sample firms, including information on the source and type of all outstanding loans, as well as detailed contract information on a firm's most recent loan. Petersen and Rajan (1994) find that the reported duration of the relationship has no statistically significant influence on the loan rate offered by a bank to the firm. Instead, Petersen and Rajan (1994) find that firm age is the most important explanatory variable in explaining cross-sectional variation in loan rates, with older firms receiving more favorable terms. However, duration does appear to influence positively the availability of bank credit to customers. Firms with longer bank relationships tend to rely less on expensive trade credit than firms with shorter bank relationships.

In a follow-up paper using the same data set, Berger and Udell (1995) argue that Petersen and Rajan (1994) fail to find a relation between interest rates and duration because they do not focus on the most important form of commercial bank lending, the line of credit. Berger and Udell (1995) find that the interest rates charged on lines of credit fall as time in a relationship lengthens. In addition, firms in longer bank relationships are less likely to pledge collateral against the loan. Berger and Udell (1995) argue that their results are consistent with the idea that a bank relationship involves revelation of valuable private information that improves contracting terms for the firm and that banks themselves appear not to price a loan as if they had monopoly power. Blackwell and

Winters (1997) also find in a sample of small firm loan contracts from six U.S. banks that longer relationships lead to lower monitoring frequency, and lower cost of credit.

The results reported by Berger and Udell (1995) and Blackwell and Winters (1997) do not appear to carry over to European data (see also Table 7.3) Elsas and Krahnen (1998), drawing from credit file data from large German "house" banks, and Harhoff and Körting (1998b), using data from a survey of German firms similar to those in the NSSBF survey, also study rates charged on lines of credit, but find no significant impact of duration on cost of credit. From a sample of nearly 18,000 loans from one Belgian bank, Degryse and Van Cayseele (1998) document a *positive* relation between relationship length and contract interest rate, implying the bank is able to earn monopoly rents through holdup. Angelini, Di Salvo, and Ferri (1998) obtain similar results using a small firm survey from Italy. Moreover, Degryse and Van Cayseele (1998) are unable to uncover a relation between duration and the probability of pledging collateral in Belgian firms.

The European studies do, however, broadly confirm the U.S. results on credit availability. For example, Harhoff and Körting (1998b) and Angelini et al. (1998) show that credit availability for small firms typically increases with the length of the relationships, and Elsas and Krahnen (1998) find that German house banks continue to lend to customers after deterioration in the customer's credit rating.

### 4.2 Scope of the Relationship

The strength of a bank relationship may also be measured by its *scope* at one point in time. Scope is defined in terms of the breadth of services offered by the bank and utilized by the firm. In addition to lending, a U.S. bank relationship can currently include deposit and investment activities, check clearing, cash management, and currency exchange services. In many other countries and through holding companies in the U.S., a bank can also provide investment banking, brokerage, insurance, and other financial services. The use of these services gives a bank the opportunity to learn more about a firm's loan payment ability, provides the bank with additional contracting flexibility, and allows the bank to set pricing policies across different services. Following the early emphasis by Hodgman (1961), Hodgman (1963), Kane and Malkiel (1965), Wood (1975), and Black (1975), Nakamura (1993), Vale (1993), and Rajan (1998) argue that it is the special information received through checking account transactions that enables a bank to be an informed and efficient lender. If the bank provides most of the firm's payment services,

Table 7.3. *Duration and number of bank relationships and cost and availability of credit.*

| | | Cost of credit | | | Availability of credit | | |
|---|---|---|---|---|---|---|---|
| | | | Impact on the cost of credit of | | | Impact on the availability of credit of | |
| | Data source (firm size) | Measure | Duration | Number | Measure | Duration | Number |
| Cole (1998) | 1993 NSSBF (small) | | | | Extension of credit | Positive | Negative |
| Blackwell and Winters (1997) | 6 banks (small) | Spread revolver/ prime rate | No | No | | | |
| Berger and Udell (1995) | 1987 NSSBF (small) | Spread line of credit/ prime rate | Negative | Negative | No collateral | Positive | |
| Petersen and Rajan (1994) | 1987 NSSBF (small) | Most recent loan rate (prime on RHS) | No | Positive | Trade credit paid on time – % | Positive | Negative |
| Harhoff and Körting (1998b) | German survey (small) | Line of credit | No | No | No collateral | Positive | Negative |
| Elsas and Krahnen (1998) | 5 German banks (larger) | Spread line of credit/ FIBOR | No | No | | | |
| Degryse and Van Cayseele (1998) | 1 Belgian bank (mostly small) | Loan yield till next revision | Positive | | No collateral | No | |
| Angelini et al. (1998) | Italian survey (small) | Line of credit | Positive (non-CCB) negative (CCB member) | Negative | No rationing | Positive | Negative |

*Note:* CCB: Italian Cooperative Bank. NSSBF: National Survey of Small Business Finances. RHS: Right Hand Side.

the bank can draw an adequate and reliable picture of the firm's operational and financial activities, which may assist in deciding on the firm's current or future loan applications.

There is little evidence documenting the influence of the scope of a bank relationship on the performance of banks or firms. The primary reason for the paucity of evidence stems from the data demands analysis of scope requires. Detailed financial data at the service level is typically proprietary and unavailable. Even more aggregated estimates of scope efficiency appear to be unreliable (Berger, Hunter, and Timme, 1993).

In his survey of managers at top commercial banks, Hodgman (1963) finds that managers consider the quality of a deposit relationship to be the most important criterion in deciding whether or not to extend a loan. Petersen and Rajan (1994) control for whether a firm maintains deposits or purchases other non-lending services from its bank in their interest cost and credit availability regressions. They are unable to uncover a relation between the scope variables and contracted interest costs, but do find that firms that purchase other services from the bank are less credit constrained. Berlin and Mester (1998) present results to suggest that banks with strong market power in deposits are more accommodative with lending. Banks holding a large proportion of a region's core deposits maintain loan contracts that are less sensitive to economic fluctuations. Cole (1998), however, finds the dependence between the purchase of financial services and credit availability to be negative. Degryse and Van Cayseele (1998) find that the purchase of other information-sensitive services from a bank lowers the interest rate charged to the customer, and Angelini et al. (1998) find that members of cooperative (mutual) banks obtain easier access to credit at lower interest rates than non-members.

### 4.3 Extended Bank Relationships

A bank-customer relationship can extend beyond the usual banking activities of deposit-taking, lending, and related ancillary financial services. For example, a bank can exert direct, ownership-type control over a firm by participating in an external supervisory role or by holding voting equity in the firm. The relationship-based banking systems of Germany and Japan are often defined in terms of this close control.

Board-of-director interlocks, where firms and banks share common board members, provide an extra mechanism for the bank to facilitate information transfer and control managerial decision-making. This degree of control may enhance the benefits of the relationship by, for example, strengthening a bank's commitment to be accommodative during difficult financial times, but may also accentuate a bank's monopoly power over the firm. Kracaw and Zenner (1998) examine stock price reactions to 378 U.S. bank loan announcements over the period 1980–1989 for firms that have interlocking directorates with their banks. They find lower stock price reactions at the announcement of a bank loan for "strong" interlocks. This result is especially strong for smaller firms. They interpret their results as implying that strong board interlocks intensify holdup problems. Berglöf and Sjögren (1995) find that Swedish firms maintaining interlocking directorates (and that are partly and indirectly owned by banks) rarely switch banks. Van Ees and Garretsen (1994) examine a panel of 76 larger Dutch firms between 1984 and 1990 and find that sharing of board members, which link about half the sample firms to a "main" bank, reduces liquidity constraints.

Bank equity ownership of German firms is found by Elston (1995) and Harm (1996) to decrease the sensitivity of investment to internal liquidity constraints. But the positive impact of equity-holding banks on the performance of German firms has decreased through time in sync with the decline in the frequency of block holding (Gorton and Schmid, 1996).

Overall, banks are often conjectured to play a much less dominant role in corporate finance in the U.S., Canada, and the U.K. than in Continental Europe and Japan. A growing literature describes and dissects the merits and drawbacks of the Anglo-Saxon, transactions-based financial system relative to the Continental European and Japanese relationship-based systems. (For example, see Macey and Miller, 1995, or the Winter 1997 issue of the *Journal of Applied Corporate Finance* for recent published debates on the subject. Edwards and Fisher, 1994, and Corbett and Jenkinson, 1997, question whether there actually is a large distinction between the different countries.)

The studies place particular emphasis on the so-called "main" banks in Japan and "house" banks in Germany. A Japanese main bank is defined by Hoshi, Kashyap, and Scharfstein (1990) to be a bank that "provides debt financing to the firm, owns some of its equity, and may even place bank executives in top management positions" (p. 68). A German house bank is defined by Elsas and Krahnen (1998) as "the premier lender of a firm, being equipped with more relevant and more timely information than any 'normal', non-house bank" (p. 1). Both definitions emphasize the strength of the relationship between the bank and firm.

A relatively large literature exists exploring the influence of Japanese main banks. Japanese main bank ties are reported to reduce the cost of firm financial distress (Hoshi et al., 1990), debt capacity constraints

(Fukuda and Hirota, 1996), investment sensitivity to liquidity (Hoshi, Kashyap, and Scharfstein, 1991), managerial entrenchment (Kang and Shivdasani, 1995; Kaplan, 1994; Kaplan and Minton, 1994), inflexibility in restructuring (Kang and Shivdasani, 1997), and capital constraints (Weinstein and Yafeh, 1998). Weinstein and Yafeh (1998) report, however, that firms with main bank relationships face higher interest charges and experience slower growth rates than non-main bank firms. In addition, Kang and Stulz (1997) find that firms with close banking relationships performed worse during and after the 1990–1993 deflation of the Japanese stock market because banks themselves were facing financial problems. Using data from the period 1994–1995, Gibson (1997b) reports that bank-dependent firms invest significantly less when their main bank is rated low.

Elsas and Krahnen (1998) compare the contract terms and credit availability of house banks versus normal banks in Germany. They find that the loan pricing practices of house banks are indistinguishable from normal banks. However, they also provide evidence that house banks follow relatively more accommodative policies to customers facing rating downgrades.

### 5 Multiple Bank Relationships and Credit Market Concentration

In this section, we explore two related extensions of the study of bank relationships to the competitive environment in which banks and firms interact. The first area relates to the observation that many firms maintain multiple-bank relationships. When a firm maintains multiple bank relationships, it can improve the terms of its financial contracts by forcing banks to compete. The second area focuses on the degree to which a few banks dominate the banking industry in a particular market. The first area relates to concentration of banking at the firm level, while the second concerns bank concentration at the market level. The two measures of concentration are related, because more concentrated bank markets imply fewer bank relationships per firm, though less concentrated markets need not imply more bank relationships per firm. Before discussing these two issues separately, we first present some summary evidence on the number of bank relationships and market concentration across different countries and data sets.

### 5.1 International Summary Statistics

Table 7.4 assimilates estimates of average number of bank relationships per firm across a variety of countries and data sets. We list details on the

Table 7.4. *Evidence on bank relationships: number and concentration.*

| Paper | Country | Sample year(s) | Sample size | Average (median) firm size | Average (median) number | Concentration ratio |
|---|---|---|---|---|---|---|
| *Ongena and Smith (1998b)* | *Average 20 countries* | *1996* | *1,129* | *Sales: 750* | *5.6* | |
| | *Italy* | | *70* | *1,500* | *15.2* | *35.9* |
| Detragiache et al. (1997) | Italy | 1989–1993 | ±1,000 / year | Employees: 926 (293) | 16.4 (13) | |
| Pagano, Panetta, and Zingales (1998) | Italy | 1982–1992 | 19,274 | Employees: 737 (258) | 13.9 (11) | |
| Rossignoli and Chesini (1995) | Italy | 1993 | 1,527 | | 14.8 | |
| Angelini et al. (1998) | Italy | 1995 | 1,858 | Employees: 10.3 | 2.4 | |
| Cesarini (1994) | Italy | 1993 | 263,376 | Credit line: <1 bln. Lira | 1.6 | |
| | | | | Credit line: >500 bln. Lira | 33.2 | |
| | *Portugal* | | *43* | *750* | *11.5* | *38.1* |
| | *France* | | *25* | *1,500* | *11.3* | *63.6* |
| | *Belgium* | | *10* | *3,500* | *11.1* | *44.4* |
| | *Spain* | | *68* | *1,500* | *9.7* | *50.1* |
| | *Germany* | | *67* | *3,500* | *8.1* | *89.5* |
| Elsas and Krahnen (1998) | Germany | 1992–1996 | 125 / year | Turnover: (30–150) | 6.0 (5.0) | |
| Harhoff and Körting (1998a) | Germany | 1997 | 994 | Employees: ±40 (10) | 1.8 (1 or 2) | |
| | *Greece* | | *41* | *750* | *7.4* | *98.3* |
| | *Austria* | | *37* | *1,500* | *5.2* | *61.4* |
| | *Luxembourg* | | *8* | *375* | *5.0* | |
| | *Czech Republic* | | *59* | *<100* | *4.7* | *17.2* |

| Study | Country | Year | Sample size | Firm size | Average (median) | Concentration ratio |
|---|---|---|---|---|---|---|
| | *Hungary* | | 44 | 175 | 4.0 | 93.8 |
| | *Finland* | | 89 | 750 | 3.6 | 79.8 |
| | *Switzerland* | | 39 | 3,500 | 3.6 | 63.7 |
| | *Denmark* | | 51 | 750 | 3.5 | |
| | *Netherlands* | | 49 | 1,500 | 3.5 | 59.0 |
| | *Poland* | | 13 | 175 | 3.3 | |
| | *Ireland* | | 67 | 750 | 3.2 | 93.6 |
| | *U.K.* | | 142 | 1,500 | 2.9 | 29.1 |
| | *Sweden* | | 50 | 1,500 | 2.5 | 86.6 |
| Zineldin (1995) | Sweden | 1994 | 179 | Employees: (<49) | (1) | |
| Berglöf and Sjögren (1995) | Sweden | 84, 90, 93 | ±30 / year | Large firms | (1) | |
| | Norway | | 41 | 750 | 2.3 | 48.8 |
| Ongena and Smith (1998a) | Norway | 1979–1995 | 111 / year | Market equity: 150 | 1.4 (1) | |
| Horiuchi (1993), | Japan | 1990 | 126 / 309 | Employees: <300 / >300 | 3.4 / 7.7 | 28.3 |
| Horiuchi (1994) | | 1992 | 175 / 189 | Employees: <10 / >10 | 2.9 (3) / 3.1 (3) | |
| Petersen and Rajan (1995), Berger and Udell (1995) | U.S. | 1987 | 3,404 | Book assets: 1.05 (0.3) Employees: 26 (5) | 1.6 (1) | 13.3 |
| Houston and James (1996) | U.S. | 80–85–90 | ±250 / year | Market assets: 1,502 (112) | 5.22 | |

*Note:* Sample size is the number of firms (unless indicated otherwise). Average (median) firm size is the size of the firms in millions of U.S. dollars in the last year of the sample or, if indicated, the number of employees. Average (median) number is the number of bank relationships. The Concentration ratio is the percentage of total banking system assets accounted for by the largest three banks in 1993. *Source:* for Norway: Nordal and Nærland (1995), Table 2b; for all other countries: Barth, Nolle, and Rice (1997), Table 3.

sample period, sample size, country of origin, and average size of the firm within each sample. For the 20 European countries covered in Ongena and Smith (1998b), we also list the proportion of the country's bank assets owned by the three largest banks. This provides a measure of country-level credit market concentration.

There is large variation across data sets in the average number of bank relationships per bank, though multiple-bank relationships are a common feature to nearly all of the data sets. The first thing to note from the table is that multiple bank relationships are common across almost all the data sets. Small firms tend to maintain fewer bank relationships than large firms. For example, U.S. studies using the NSSBF data estimate the mean number of banks per firm to be two and the median to be one. There also appears to be a strong country effect. Firms in the U.K., Norway, and Sweden maintain relatively few bank relationships – fewer than three on average – while firms in Italy, Portugal, Belgium, and Spain maintain on average ten or more bank relationships. Ongena and Smith (1998a) show that the relative rankings in Table 7.4 of the European countries hold after controlling for firm size (along with other firm characteristics). Thus, although firm size is important in describing the number of bank relationships per firm, the size of firms within a country does not alone explain the variation in average number of bank relationships across countries.

The third thing to note in Table 7.4 is the negative correlation between number of bank relationships and credit market concentration. Firms in markets where a few banks own a relatively large proportion of total bank assets tend to maintain fewer bank relationships.

*5.2 Single Versus Multiple-Bank Relationships*

Why do we observe few bank relationships as the norm in some data sets and multiple bank relationships as the norm in others? In Diamond (1984), a single bank arises as the optimal mechanism for channeling loans from investors to firms when costly information asymmetries exist between the investors and project insiders. Many of the other information-based theories of banking build on the similar idea that by *coordinating* investors, a bank can efficiently reduce information asymmetries and improve the flexibility in writing and renegotiating loan contracts. These theories imply that a firm should only borrow from one bank, since borrowing from more than one bank implies duplication of information production or increased costs of contracting.

By inviting competition from other banks, a firm can reduce the possibility for its incumbent bank to extract monopoly rents. Thus, in the presence of holdup costs, one bank relationship may no longer be optimal. However, competition among banks may actually harm a borrower if competition forces rents to the point where it is no longer profitable for either bank to lend to the firm. Petersen and Rajan (1995) model the dependency of a firm's ability to borrow on the market power of the lending bank. They show that borrowing from banks with large market power facilitates intertemporal sharing of rent surplus and hence increases the value of a single relationship, while competition in the credit markets hinders such accommodative policies. Such intertemporal surplus sharing is crucial for smaller or younger firms, which Petersen and Rajan (1995) argue are most in need of bank financing.

Evidence on the impact of multiple-bank relationships on credit availability, contract pricing, and firm performance is mixed. Petersen and Rajan (1994) find those firms that maintain multiple-bank relationships face *higher* interest payments and are more credit constrained than single-bank firms are. In line with the results in Petersen and Rajan (1994), Cole (1998) finds multiple-bank firms are denied credit more frequently than single-bank firms, and Harhoff and Körting (1998b) document lower availability of credit to multiple-bank firms.

On the other hand, Houston and James (1996) demonstrate that, for their sample, a single-bank firm's reliance on bank debt is negatively correlated with future growth potential, while the relation between bank debt level and growth for multiple-bank firms is positive. Houston and James (1995) find that single-bank firms are more sensitive to investment cash flow constraints, hold larger stocks of liquid assets, and pay lower dividends. Overall, Houston and James (1995) conclude that single-bank firms are *more* credit constrained than multiple-bank firms. Ongena and Smith (1998a) show that firms with multiple-bank relationships end a bank relationship sooner than single-bank firms, suggesting that a given bank relationship is less valuable to multiple-bank firms.

### 5.3 Credit Market Concentration

Petersen and Rajan (1994) show that small firm borrowing in the U.S. is highly concentrated. Even when firms have multiple lending sources, they tend to concentrate their borrowing from one source. This pattern becomes less apparent as the size of the firm grows. The level of credit market concentration, measured by the Herfindahl index of lenders within a firm's region, is found by Petersen and Rajan (1994) to be positively related to credit availability. This latter result is studied in greater detail (using the same data set) in Petersen and Rajan (1995). In this paper, they find that young firms are more likely to obtain bank financing in concentrated credit markets, while older firms borrow less from institutions and are less influenced by the concentration of the market. With respect to the cost of lending, Petersen and Rajan (1995) find that young firms pay lower interest rates in concentrated markets, while older firms receive better rates in competitive markets.

### 5.4  More on Multiple-Bank Relationships

Multiple-bank relationships may be beneficial for reasons other than reducing the holdup rents accruing to one bank. First, if there exists an exogenous chance that a firm will lose a valuable bank relationship, firms may invest in establishing multiple-bank relationships to "diversify" the risk of losing their connection to a bank. Second, there may arise situations in which *lack of coordination* among lenders aids in resolving information asymmetries.

An example of the diversification argument is Detragiache, Garella, and Guiso (1997). They study an economy where inside bank relationships are valuable, but banks are also susceptible to exogenous liquidity shocks. When a liquidity shock occurs, the bank cuts off financing to the firm, forcing a single-bank firm to borrow from expensive, outside lending sources. Firms have an incentive to insure themselves against a bank loss by investing in more than one bank relationship. In Detragiache et al. (1997), the optimal choice of number of bank relationships is shown to be a function of the fragility of a country's banking system and the efficiency of its bankruptcy process.

Dewatripont and Maskin (1995) compare the impact of centralized versus decentralized concentrated banking systems on the incentives of borrowers within the system. Decentralized economies inhibit bank commitments to finance unprofitable, long-term projects because dispersed banks with limited capital find it costly to communicate or coordinate actions. Knowledge of such renegotiation costs induce firm managers to make efficient accept-reject decisions on long-term projects. Bolton and Scharfstein (1996) argue that borrowing from multiple lenders decreases the incentive for a firm manager to default strategically and "take the money and run," since the manager must coordinate a restructuring plan with multiple claimants. Borrowing from multiple sources also increases the cost of renegotiation in cases where a firm requires project refinancing. The choice of optimal number of lenders balances the benefits from disciplining the borrower with the increased inefficiencies that arise when liquidity is required to continue a positive NPV project. Bolton and Scharfstein (1996) predict that the number of lenders should be *decreasing* in the default risk of the firm, in the complementarity of firm assets, and in the liquidation value of the firm's assets.

Ongena and Smith (1998b) study the determinants of multiple bank relationships using survey evidence from 1,129 firms in 20 European countries. Their most interesting results come from the exploration of the cross-country variation in average number of bank relationships. They find that, after controlling for firm- and industry-specific characteristics, the average number of bank relationships per firm is related to the fragility of a country's banking system, though in the opposite direction than hypothesized by Detragiache et al. (1997), and negatively related to the efficiency of its bankruptcy process and enforcement of creditor rights. In addition, they find that concentration of the banking system and the degree of stock market development reduce the number of bank relationships, while public bond markets have a complementary effect and increase the average number of banks per firm.

## 6 Importance of Bank Relationships in the Macroeconomy

Following the original motivation of Kane and Malkiel (1965) and Wood (1975), Bernanke and Blinder (1988) argue that monetary policy influences real output through a so-called "credit channel"; for example, decreasing the money supply reduces the volume of bank credit. In Kashyap, Stein, and Wilcox (1993), this model is further enriched by modeling a bank relationship benefit, which depends on the total amount that firms borrow from banks. In such a model, monetary policy consequently has implications for the firms' financial structure, providing testable hypotheses about the importance and strength of the credit channel. In Gibson (1997a), a bank's optimal policy is to drop long-term customers following contractionary monetary policy, especially when the fraction of a bank's assets devoted to loans is high. Hence, this model links the strength of the bank lending channel to the composition of bank assets.

Bank relationships can also directly impact the macroeconomy when relationships are lost in bank default. When default occurs, it disrupts lending to loan customers. Single-bank firms that rely only on bank lending may have to reduce real investments. More generally, increased risk in the banking sector may decrease the expected benefits firms can derive from their bank relationship, increasing the expected cost of corporate finance, and reducing the level and growth of real activity (Gray and Ongena, 1996).

In addition, bank defaults may create deadweight costs when customer reputations gained through the relationship are lost and future borrowing is hampered (de Lange, 1992). Stiglitz (1992) argues that uninformed banks that choose to lend to one of a failed bank's customers must bear the cost of becoming informed. Loss of financing to firms after a default could also exert excess pressure on other banks in the system. For example, Gale (1993) conjectures that bank failures may accelerate market collapse, as the influx of cut-off firms seeking financing from other banks may congest the available reduced information processing capacity. On the other hand, the existence of bank relationships may lessen the likelihood of bank default. If bank relationships create franchise value for the bank (Demsetz, Saidenberg, and Strahan, 1996), banks managing many strong relationships with their customers will operate more conservatively and will be less likely to default (Keeley, 1990).

Besides bank liquidation, formal actions (see, for example, Peek and Rosengren, 1995), dispositions of failed or failing banks, and voluntary bank mergers will also cause temporary disruptions in banking services. Armed with contract-specific information on lending relationships of Italian firms, Sapienza (1998) argues that the impact of a merger on a bank relationship depends on the market share of the consolidated banks and on the size of the firm-customer. Both Berger, Saunders, Scalise, and Udell (1998) and Sapienza (1998) find that loan contracts to smaller firms become less attractive after a merger and that small firms are more likely to leave their bank after a merger.

### 7 Concluding Remarks

We conclude here with a summary and discussion of future research ideas. According to both practitioner beliefs and recent theoretical papers in banking, it is through the close relationship formed with its customers that a bank distinguishes itself as an independently important, functioning intermediary between savers and users of funds. A relationship can facilitate the screening and pruning of loan customers, reveal information important to establishing future credit terms, and be an integral part of controlling the behavior of firm managers. The strength of a relationship can be measured by the duration of the relationship through time, and by the scope of services offered by the bank to its customer.

Several empirical patterns stand out from the growing evidence on bank relationships. First, announcements by companies of bank loan agreements, as well as other private lending arrangements, generate positive abnormal stock returns. In contrast, announcements of public debt offerings are associated with zero or negative abnormal returns. The reasons for this pattern are unclear. Early evidence reported by James (1987) and Lummer and McConnell (1989) suggested that announcements by *banks* with *established lending relationships* were responsible for the high abnormal returns. Later studies, however, are unable to uncover meaningful differences between banks and other private lenders and question the result that established relationships generate higher abnormal returns than new ones. Still, the investigation of the underlying causes of these price reactions is in its infancy. The increasing availability of detailed, contract-specific information will allow for more powerful tests to distinguish between competing hypotheses. New international data will help to relate the features of a loan contract more closely to the event-day abnormal return.

Second, small private firms and family-owned businesses, which rely primarily on banks for external financing, appear to be less credit constrained when they maintain a one bank relationship over relatively long periods of time. Petersen and Rajan (1995) find that small and young U.S. firms tend also to be less credit constrained and to receive better lending rates when they borrow from one bank and operate in a concentrated credit market. The Petersen and Rajan (1995) results therefore suggest that competition between banks hurts small and young borrowers. By contrast, the results in Houston and James (1996) demonstrate that large, exchange-listed U.S. firms benefit from multiple-bank relationships and are hindered by single-bank lending. In line with the evidence in Houston and James (1996), Ongena and Smith (1998a) find that exchange-listed Norwegian firms with multiple bank relationships are more active in ending a given bank relationship than a single-bank firm. Ongena and Smith (1998a) also document that small, exchange-listed firms do not value long-term relationships. Instead, small firms are more likely to end a bank relationship than larger, exchange-listed firms.

Third, multiple-bank relationships are quite common in the cross-section of countries for which relationship data are available, and the average number of bank relationships across these countries varies considerably. In many countries, even small firms maintain multiple-bank relationships. This observation makes it unlikely that these firms suffer from large holdup problems. The differences in average number of bank relationships across countries is related to factors such as the fragility of the banking system, the efficiency of the bankruptcy process and legal system, the degree of development of public capital markets, and the level of bank concentration within an economy. Because these characteristics are certainly interrelated, causal judgments are difficult. For example, if the level of bank concentration within a country is exogenously determined (by regulation, for example), then the observed relation suggests that multiple-bank relationships and competitive, unconcentrated markets are optimal in an unregulated environment.

There are several questions related to the strength and value of bank relationships that have received very little attention in the existing literature. These questions can be usefully grouped according to their focus on firm, bank, or aggregate economy.

First, more evidence on the relation between the decision to switch banks and subsequent *firm performance* could be useful. Large firms may actually screen and monitor the performance of their banks. They do so by choosing only highly reputable banks with the intent of maximizing their own reputational effects (Hadlock and James, 1997). These same firms will shy away from low-rated banks as they fear the considerable disruptions to business caused by bank default.

Second, we need to better understand the impact of bank relationships on *bank performance*. Is it profitable, as the Chase Manhattan motto suggests, for banks to engage in intensive relationship-building? Or should banks focus on becoming multi-faceted "transactions centers"?

Third, we know very little about the impact of relationship scope on either the firm or the bank. To what extent does the scope of the entire bank relationship determine the characteristics of the lending relationship? Or is the importance of the lending relationship subordinate to other services (deposit, clearing, cash management) offered by the bank? And how does cross-selling of services work?

Fourth, we need more evidence on cross-border bank relationships to aid in understanding how deepening global integration of the financial service sector may affect banks, firms, and regulators. How do international bank relationships differ from domestic bank relationships? Are cross-border bank relationships as durable and numerous as their domestic counterparts? What types of firms and banks engage in cross-border relationships? And, do factors such as financial fragility and judicial efficiency, which may play a role in the firm's decision regarding the number of domestic bank relationships, also affect the choice of the country of origin of the banks the firm engages?

Finally, a better understanding is required of how banks and bank relationships fit into the operation of financial systems as a whole and how the performance of the financial sector determines aggregate economic growth. The average number of bank relationships across different countries reported here is but one indication of the variation present in financial systems around the world. There is anecdotal evidence that the close relationships between firm and bank have created and exacerbated the financial problems in Japan. Some argue that relationships have been "too cozy," leading to a vast misallocation of credit in a number of other East Asian countries. As more and more previously underdeveloped or heavily regulated countries adopt lower regulations and freer markets, the understanding of how to develop a well-functioning financial system becomes more pertinent.

## References

P. Angelini, R. Di Salvo, and G. Ferri. Availability and Cost of Credit for Small Businesses: Customer Relationships and Credit Cooperatives. *Journal of Banking and Finance* 22: 925–954, 1998.

M. Aoki and H. Patrick. *The Japanese Main Bank System*. Oxford University Press, Oxford, 1994.

J. Barth, D. Nolle, and T. Rice. Commercial Banking Structure, Regulation, and Performance: an International Comparison. Economics Working Paper, Office of the Comptroller of the Currency, 1997.

A. N. Berger, W. C. Hunter, and S. G. Timme. The Efficiency of Financial Institutions: a Review and Preview of Research Past, Present, and Future. *Journal of Banking and Finance* 17: 221–249, 1993.

A. N. Berger, A. Saunders, J. M. Scalise, and G. F. Udell. The Effects of Bank Mergers and Acquisitions on Small Business Lending. *Journal of Financial Economics* 50: 187–230, 1998.

A. N. Berger and G. F. Udell. Relationship Lending and Lines of Credit in Small Firm Finance. *Journal of Business* 68: 351–381, 1995.

A. N. Berger and G. F. Udell. The Economics of Small Business Finance: The Roles of Private Equity and Debt Markets in the Financial Growth Cycle. *Journal of Banking and Finance* 22: 613–673, 1998.

E. Berglöf and H. Sjögren. Combining Arm's-Length and Control Oriented Finance – Evidence from Main Bank Relationships in Sweden. Mimeo, Stockholm University, 1995.

M. Berlin. For Better and for Worse: Three Lending Relationships. *Federal Reserve Bank of Philadelphia Business Review* November: 3–12, 1996.

M. Berlin and L. J. Mester. Why Is the Banking Sector Shrinking? Core Deposits and Relationship Lending. Working Paper, Federal Reserve Bank of Philadelphia, 1998.

B. S. Bernanke. Credit in the Macroeconomy. *Federal Reserve Bank of New York Quarterly Review* 18: 50–70, 1993.

B. S. Bernanke and A. S. Blinder. Money, Credit and Aggregate Demand. *American Economic Review* 82: 901–921, 1988.

R. Best and H. Zhang. Alternative Information Sources and the Information Content of Bank Loans. *Journal of Finance* 48: 1507–1522, 1993.

S. Bhattacharya and G. Chiesa. Proprietary Information, Financial Intermediation, and Research Incentives. *Journal of Financial Intermediation* 4: 328–357, 1995.

S. Bhattacharya and A. V. Thakor. Contemporary Banking Theory. *Journal of Financial Intermediation* 3: 2–50, 1993.

M. T. Billett, M. J. Flannery, and J. A. Garfinkel. The Effect of Lender Identity on a Borrowing Firm's Equity Return. *Journal of Finance* 50: 699–718, 1995.

F. Black. Bank Funds Management in an Efficient Market. *Journal of Financial Economics* 2: 323–339, 1975.

D. W. Blackwell and D. B. Winters. Banking Relationships and the Effect of Monitoring on Loan Pricing. *Journal of Financial Research* 20: 275–289, 1997.

P. Bolton and D. S. Scharfstein. Optimal Debt Structure and the Number of Creditors. *Journal of Political Economy* 104: 1–25, 1996.

A. W. A. Boot and A. V. Thakor. Moral Hazard and Secured Lending in an Infinitely Repeated Credit Market Game. *International Economic Review* 35: 899–920, 1994.

J. H. Boyd and E. C. Prescott. Financial Intermediary Coalitions. *Journal of Economic Theory* 38: 211–232, 1986.

J. R. Cable. Capital Market Information and Industrial Performance: The Role of West German Banks. *Economic Journal* 95: 118–132, 1985.

J. Y. Campbell, A. W. Lo, and A. C. MacKinlay. *The Econometrics of Financial Markets*. Princeton University Press, Princeton, NJ, 1997.

T. S. Campbell. Optimal Investment Financing Decisions and the Value of Confidentiality. *Journal of Financial and Quantitative Analysis* 14: 232–257, 1979.

M. Carey. *Reflections on the Present System on Banking, in the City of Philadelphia with a Plan to Revive Confidence, Trade, and Commerce, and to Facilitate the Resumption of Specie Payments*. Philadelphia, 1817.

M. Carey, M. Post, and S. Sharpe. Does Corporate Lending by Banks and Finance Companies Differ? Evidence on Specialization in Private Debt Contracting. *Journal of Finance* 53: 845–878, 1998.

F. Cesarini. The Relationship between Banks and Firms in Italy: A Banker's View. *Review of Economic Conditions in Italy* 29–50, 1994.

T. J. Chemmanur and P. Fulghieri. Reputation, Renegotiation and the Choice between Bank Loans and Publicly Traded Debt. *Review of Financial Studies* 7: 475–506, 1994.

R. Cole. The Importance of Relationships to the Availability of Credit. *Journal of Banking and Finance* 22: 959–977, 1998.

J. Corbett and T. Jenkinson. How Is Investment Financed? A Study of Germany, Japan, the United Kingdom, and the United States. *Manchester School of Economic and Social Studies* 65: 69–93, 1997.

M. de Lange. Essays on the Theory of Financial Intermediation: Market Imperfections, the Allocation of Credit, Deposit Insurance and the Transmission of External Shocks. Research Series 26. Tinbergen Institute, 1992.

H. Degryse and P. Van Cayseele. Relationship Lending within a Bank-Based System: Evidence from European Small Business Data. Mimeo, Tilburg University, 1998.

R. S. Demsetz, M. R. Saidenberg, and P. E. Strahan. Banks with Something to Lose: The Disciplinary Role of Franchise Value. *Federal Reserve Bank of New York Economic Policy Review* 2: 1–14, 1996.

E. Detragiache, P. G. Garella, and L. Guiso. Multiple versus Single Banking Relationships. Discussion Paper 1649. Centre for Economic Policy Research, 1997.

M. Dewatripont and E. Maskin. Credit and Efficiency in Centralized and Decentralized Economies. *Review of Economic Studies* 62: 541–555, 1995.

D. Diamond. Financial Intermediation and Delegated Monitoring. *Review of Economic Studies* 51: 393–414, 1984.

D. Diamond. Monitoring and Reputation: The Choice between Bank Loans and Privately Placed Debt. *Journal of Political Economy* 99: 689–721, 1991.

J. Edwards and K. Fisher. *Banks, Finance, and Investment in Germany*. Cambridge University Press, Cambridge, 1994.

R. Elsas and J. P. Krahnen. Is Relationship Lending Special? Evidence from Credit-File Data in Germany. *Journal of Banking and Finance* 22: 1283–1316, 1998.

J. A. Elston. Investment, Liquidity Constraints and Bank Relationships: Evidence from German Manufacturing Firms. Discussion Paper 1329. Centre for Economic Policy Research, 1995.

E. F. Fama. What's Different about Banks? *Journal of Monetary Economics* 15: 5–29, 1985.

X. Freixas and J. C. Rochet. *Microeconomics of Banking*. Massachusetts Institute of Technology Press, Cambridge MA, 1997.

A. Fukuda and S. Hirota. Main Bank Relationships and Capital Structures in Japan. *Journal of the Japanese and International Economies* 10: 250–261, 1996.

D. Gale. Informational Capacity and Financial Collapse. In C. Mayer and X. Vives, Eds., *Capital Markets and Financial Intermediation*, pp. 117–155. Cambridge University Press, Cambridge, 1993.

M. S. Gibson. The Bank Lending Channel of Monetary Policy Transmission: Evidence from a Model of Bank Behavior That Incorporates Long-Term Customer Relationships. International Finance Discussion Paper 584. Board of Governors of the Federal Reserve System, 1997a.

M. S. Gibson. More Evidence on the Link between Bank Health and Investment in Japan. *Journal of Japanese International Economics* 11: 29–49, 1997b.

G. Gorton and F. A. Schmid. Universal Banking and the Performance of German Firms. Working Paper 5453. National Bureau for Economic Research, 1996.

J. A. Gray and S. Ongena. Bank Relationship Benefits, Bank Risk and the Paper-Bill Spread. Mimeo, University of Oregon, 1996.

S. I. Greenbaum, G. Kanatas, and I. Venezia. Equilibrium Loan Price under the Bank-Client Relationship. *Journal of Banking and Finance* 13: 221–235, 1989.

C. Hadlock and C. James. Bank Lending and the Menu of Financing Options. Mimeo, University of Florida, 1997.

D. Harhoff and T. Körting. How Many Creditors Does It Take to Tango? Mimeo, Wissenschaftszentrum, Berlin, 1998a.

D. Harhoff and T. Körting. Lending Relationships in Germany – Empirical Evidence from Survey Data. *Journal of Banking and Finance* 22: 1317–1353, 1998b.

C. Harm. Investments, Liquidity, and Bank Lending in Germany. Mimeo, New York University, 1996.

M. Hirshey, M. B. Slovin, and J. K. Zaima. Bank Debt, Insider Trading and the Return to Corporate Selloffs. *Journal of Banking and Finance* 14: 85–98, 1990.

D. R. Hodgman. The Deposit Relationship and Commercial Bank Investment Behavior. *Review of Economics and Statistics* 41: 257–261, 1961.

D. R. Hodgman. *Commercial Bank Loan and Investment Policy*. Bureau of Economic and Business Research, University of Illinois, Urbana-Champaign, 1963.

T. Horiuchi. An Empirical Overview of the Japanese Main Bank Relationship in Relation to Firm Size. *Rivista Internationale di Scienze Economiche e Commerciale* 40: 997–1018, 1993.

T. Horiuchi. The Effect of Firm Status on Banking Relationships and Loan Syndication. In M. Aoki and H. Patrick, Eds., *The Japanese Main Bank System*, pp. 258–294, Oxford, 1994. Oxford University Press.

T. Horiuchi, F. Packer, and S. Fukuda. What Role Has the "Main Bank" Played in Japan? *Journal of Japanese and International Economies* 2: 159–180, 1988.

T. Hoshi, A. Kashyap, and D. Scharfstein. The Role of Banks in Reducing the Costs of Financial Distress in Japan. *Journal of Financial Economics* 27: 67–88, 1990.

T. Hoshi, A. Kashyap, and D. Scharfstein. Corporate Structure, Liquidity and Investment: Evidence from Japanese Industrial Groups. *Quarterly Journal of Economics* 106: 33–60, 1991.

T. Hoshi, A. Kashyap, and D. Scharfstein. The Choice Between Public and Private Debt: An Analysis of Post-Deregulation Corporate Financing in Japan. Working Paper 4421. National Bureau for Economic Research, 1993.

J. Houston, and C. James. Bank Information Monopolies and the Mix of Private and Public Debt Claims. *Journal of Finance* 51: 1863–1889, 1996.

J. F. Houston and C. James. Banking Relationships, Financial Constraints and Investment: Are Bank Dependent Borrowers More Financially Constrained. Mimeo, University of Florida, 1995.

J. F. Houston and S. Venkataraman. Information Revelation, Lock-In, and Bank Loan Commitments. *Journal of Financial Intermediation* 3: 355–378, 1994.

C. James. Some Evidence on the Uniqueness of Bank Loans. *Journal of Financial Economics* 19: 217–235, 1987.

C. James and P. Wier. Borrowing Relationships, Intermediation and the Cost of Issuing Public Securities. *Journal of Financial Economics* 28: 149–171, 1990.

E. J. Kane and B. G. Malkiel. Bank Portfolio Allocation, Deposit Variability, and the Availability Doctrine. *Quarterly Journal of Economics* 79: 257–261, 1965.

J. K. Kang and A. Shivdasani. Firm Performance, Corporate Governance, and Top Executive Turnover in Japan. *Journal of Financial Economics* 38: 29–58, 1995.

J. K. Kang and A. Shivdasani. Corporate Restructuring during Performance Declines in Japan, *Journal of Financial Economics* 46: 29–65, 1997.

J. K. Kang and R. Stulz. Is Bank-Centered Corporate Governance Worth It? A Cross-Sectional Analysis of the Performance of Japanese Firms during the Asset Price Deflation. Mimeo, Ohio State University, 1997.

S. N. Kaplan. Top Executive Rewards and Firm Performance: A Comparison of Japan and the United States. *Journal of Political Economy* 102: 510–546, 1994.

S. N. Kaplan and B. A. Minton. Appointments of Outsiders to Japanese Boards: Determinants and Implications for Managers. *Journal of Financial Economics* 36: 225–258, 1994.

A. K. Kashyap, J. C. Stein, and D. W. Wilcox. Monetary Policy and Credit Conditions: Evidence from the Composition of External Finance. *American Economic Review* 83: 78–98, 1993.

M. C. Keeley. Deposit Insurance Risk and Market Power in Banking. *American Economic Review* 80: 1183–1200, 1990.

W. A. Kracaw and M. Zenner. Bankers in the Boardroom: Good News or Bad News. Mimeo, University of North Carolina, 1998.

H. E. Leland and D. H. Pyle. Informational Asymmetries, Financial Structure, and Financial Intermediation. *Journal of Finance* 32: 371–387, 1977.

S. D. Longhofer and J. A. C. Santos. The Importance of Bank Seniority for Relationship Lending. Mimeo, Bank for International Settlements, 1998.

S. L. Lummer and J. J. McConnell. Further Evidence on the Bank Lending Process and the Capital Market Response to Bank Loan Agreements. *Journal of Financial Economics* 25: 99–122, 1989.

J. R. Macey and G. P. Miller. Corporate Governance and Commercial Banking: A Comparative Examination of Germany, Japan, and the United States. *Stanford Law Review* 48: 73–112, 1995.

L. I. Nakamura. Monitoring Loan Quality via Checking Account Analysis. *Journal of Retail Banking* 14: 16–34, 1993.

I. A. Nordal and M. Nærland. Financial Institutions in 1994. *Economic Bulletin of the Central Bank of Norway* 95: 69–97, 1995.

S. Ongena and D. C. Smith. The Duration of Bank Relationships. Mimeo, Norwegian School of Management, 1998a.

S. Ongena and D. C. Smith. What Determines the Number of Bank Relationships? Cross-Country Evidence. Mimeo, Norwegian School of Management, 1998b.

A. J. Padilla and M. Pagano. Endogenous Communication among Lenders and Entrepreneurial Incentives. *Review of Financial Studies* 10: 205–236, 1997.

M. Pagano, F. Panetta, and L. Zingales. Why Do Companies Go Public? An Empirical Analysis. *Journal of Finance* 53: 27–64, 1998.

J. Peek and E. S. Rosengren. Bank Regulatory Agreements in New England. *New England Economic Review* 95: 15–24, 1995.

M. A. Petersen and R. G. Rajan. The Benefits of Lending Relationships: Evidence from Small Business Data. *Journal of Finance* 49: 3–37, 1994.

M. A. Petersen and R. G. Rajan. The Effect of Credit Market Competition on Lending Relationships. *Quarterly Journal of Economics* 110: 406–443, 1995.

R. G. Rajan. Insiders and Outsiders: the Choice between Informed and Arm's-length Debt. *Journal of Finance* 47: 1367–1400, 1992.

R. G. Rajan. Is There a Future in Banking? Towards a New Theory of the Commercial Bank. *Journal of Applied Corporate Finance* 2: 115–132, 1996.

R. G. Rajan. The Past and Future of Commercial Banking Viewed through an Incomplete Contract Lens. *Journal of Money, Credit and Banking* 30: 524–550, 1998.

R. T. S. Ramakrishnan and A. V. Thakor. Information Reliability and a Theory of Financial Intermediation. *Review of Economic Studies* 51: 415–432, 1984.

B. Rossignoli and G. Chesini. Multi-Banking and Customer Relationships in the Italian Banking System. *Research Papers in Banking and Finance* 17. Institute of European Finance, 1995.

P. Sapienza. The Effects of Banking Mergers on Loan Contracts. Mimeo, Harvard University, 1998.

A. Schmeits. Discretion in Bank Contracts and the Firm's Funding Source Choice Between Bank and Financial Market Financing. Mimeo, Tilburg University, 1997.

S. A. Sharpe. Asymmetric Information, Bank Lending and Implicit Contracts: A Stylized Model of Customer Relationships. *Journal of Finance* 45: 1069–1087, 1990.

R. Shockley and A. V. Thakor. Bank Loan Commitment Contracts: Data, Theory, and Tests. *Journal of Money, Credit, and Banking* 29: 517–534, 1998.

H. Sjögren. Long-Term Financial Contracts in the Bank-Oriented Financial System. *Scandinavian Journal of Management* 10: 315–330, 1994.

M. B. Slovin, S. A. Johnson, and J. L. Glascock. Firm Size and the Information Content of Bank Loan Announcements. *Journal of Banking and Finance* 16: 35–49, 1992.

M. B. Slovin, M. E. Sushka, and C. D. Hudson. Corporate Commercial Paper, Note Issuance Facilities, and Shareholder Wealth. *Journal of International Money and Finance* 7: 289–302, 1988.

M. B. Slovin, M. E. Sushka, and J. A. Polonchek. The Value of Bank Durability: Borrowers as Bank Stakeholders. *Journal of Finance* 48: 289–302, 1993.

M. B. Slovin and J. E. Young. Bank Lending and Initial Public Offerings. *Journal of Banking and Finance* 14: 729–740, 1990.

J. E. Stiglitz. Capital Markets and Economic Fluctuations in Capitalist Economies. *European Economic Review* 36: 269–306, 1992.

I. Teich. Holding on to Customers: The Bottom-line Benefits of Relationship Building. *Bank Marketing* 2: 12–16, 1997.

B. Vale. The Dual Role of Demand Deposits under Asymmetric Information. *Scandinavian Journal of Economics* 95: 77–95, 1993.

P. Van Cayseele, J. Bouckaert, and H. Degryse. Credit Market Structure and Information Sharing Mechanisms. In V. Witteloostuyen, Ed., *Studies in Industrial Organization*, pp. 129–143. Kluwer Academic Publishers, Dordrecht, 1994.

H. Van Ees and H. Garretsen. Liquidity and Business Investment: Evidence from Dutch Panel Data. *Journal of Macroeconomics* 16: 613–627, 1994.

E. L. von Thadden. Long-term Contracts, Short-term Investment, and Monitoring. *Review of Economic Studies* 62: 557–575, 1995.

E. L. von Thadden. Asymmetric Information, Bank Lending, and Implicit Contracts: The Winner's Curse. Mimeo, University of Lausanne (DEEP), 1998.

J. W. Wansley, F. A. Elayan, and M. C. Collins. Investment Opportunities and Firm Quality: An Empirical Investigation of the Information in Bank Lines of Credit. Working Paper, University of Tennessee, 1992.

D. E. Weinstein and Y. Yafeh. On the Costs of a Bank Centered Financial System: Evidence from the Changing Main Bank Relations in Japan. *Journal of Finance* 53: 635–672, 1998.

J. H. Wood. *Commercial Bank Loan and Investment Behavior*. Wiley, New York, 1975.

O. Yosha. Information Disclosure Costs and the Choice of Financing Source. *Journal of Financial Intermediation* 4: 3–20, 1995.

M. Zineldin. Bank-Company Interactions and Relationships: Some Empirical Evidence. *International Journal of Bank Marketing* 13: 30–40, 1995.

# 8

## Inside the Black Box: What Makes a Bank Efficient?

Frances X. Frei[a], Patrick T. Harker[b], Larry W. Hunter[b]

**Abstract**

A decade of econometric research has shown that X-efficiency dominates scale and scope as the drivers of inefficiency in the U.S. banking industry. However, this research falls short in explaining the causes of the high degree of X-efficiency in the industry. This paper summarizes a four-year research effort to understand the drivers of this inefficiency. Key findings from this research, based on the most comprehensive studies to date of management practices in the retail banking industry, give insight into the drivers of X-efficiency. The paper provides a comprehensive framework for the analysis of X-efficiency in financial services.

### 1 Opening the Black Box

A vast literature addresses the causes of inefficiency in financial services, particularly in banking. The typical study assumes that the bank is a "black box"; that is, the production function of the organization is a simple relationship between inputs and outputs. The goal of many of these studies is to ascertain whether scale or scope economies exist in banking. In addition to these traditional economic explanations of performance differences among firms, recent studies have focused on the notion of *X-efficiency* (Leibenstein, 1966, 1980), a measure of the performance of an organization relative to the best practice in that

[a] Harvard University.
[b] The Wharton School, University of Pennsylvania.

industry. More precisely, X-efficiency describes all technical and allocative efficiencies of individual firms that are not scale/scope dependent. Thus X-efficiency is a measure of how well management is aligning technology, human resources, and other assets to produce a given level of outputs. Summarizing this research, Berger, Hunter et al. (1993) state:

> The one result upon which there is virtual consensus is that X-efficiency differences across banks are relatively large and dominate scale and scope efficiencies.

Other results, such as those reported by Fried, Lovell et al. (1993), in the context of credit unions, add additional weight to the importance of X-efficiency by providing evidence that it is a dominant factor in both large and small institutions.

Based on this evidence, it is clear that scale and scope economies are not the driving factor in explaining firm-level efficiency. The explanation of variance in firm-level efficiency is incomplete so long as it treats X-efficiency as an unexplained residual. Our goal herein is to begin to build toward the understanding of variance in X-efficiency in financial institutions. *That is, we seek to understand how technology, human resources, and process management methods vary across these organizations and how this variation affects performance.* Put another way, our goal is to pry open the "black box" of the organization in order to ascertain what drives X-efficiency in the industry. In so doing, we are attempting to address the concern raised by Berger, Hancock, and Humphrey (1993) at the conclusion of their profit efficiency study of banks:

> Our results suggest that inefficiencies in U.S. banking are quite large – the industry appears to lose about half of its potential variable profits to inefficiency. Not surprisingly, technical inefficiencies dominate allocative inefficiencies, suggesting that banks are not particularly poor at choosing input and output plans, but rather are poor at carrying out these plans.

What is inside this "black box"? Several attempts have been made to understand the role of management and managerial decisions in the efficiency of organizations (see, e.g., Chapter 1 in this volume). Hoch (1962) and Mundlak (1961) view management as the explanatory variable for the residuals in a production function estimation. While simple to operationalize, equating the residuals with management practices does not provide any theoretical basis for why such management practices matter. To address this concern, Mefford (1986) attempts to internalize these management practices in a production function as follows:

$$Q = f(K^*, L^*, MGMT)$$

where $K^*$ is quality-adjusted capital, $L^*$ is quality-adjusted labor, and MGMT are management control variables that attempt to measure the relative quality of the management talent in the organization. The quality-adjusted inputs are equal to the raw capital and labor inputs to the firm, adjusted for the relative skill/functionality levels of the capital and labor. While this approach can be operationalized using existing production function methods, it too lacks a firm theoretical basis for why such adjustments matter.

Nelson and Winter (1982) provide a theoretical basis for the role of management as the definers and modifiers of the "routines" used by the organization. That is, management's role is to shape the processes by which goods and services are produced; i.e., their "technological regime." This view of management as the "process engineers" has been the subject of numerous studies and extensions in recent years (see, for example, Morroni, 1992). Out of this work has emerged the view that the role of management is more than a control variable in the estimation of a production function. Management integrates people, technology, and routines/processes to define the production function of the organization (Scazzieri, 1993). Thus, the management of the organization is intricately related to the production technology and subsequent productivity of the organization.

To provide some rigor to the role of management in defining an organization's productivity and hence to understand the drivers of X-efficiency, consider an industry where S products or services are produced. Let $O_s$ denote the level of output for service $s \varepsilon S$, and define $O \varepsilon R^{|S|}$ to be the vector of outputs for the firm. Given this vector of outputs, let $v(O)$ denote the revenue or value created for the firm by the production of the outputs O. Note that, particularly in services, this linkage between the outputs and the revenue or value generated for the firm is more complex than a simple multiplication of the price of each output by the quantity produced. In the recent study by the National Research Council (1994) on services, the linkage problem in the context of banking is summarized as follows:

> ... [existing approaches for productivity measurement are not]
> able to account for improvements in the quality of service
> offered to customers or for the availability of a much wider
> array of banking services. For example, the speed with which
> the processing of a loan application is completed is an
> indicator of service that is important to the applicant, as is the

24-hour availability through automated teller machines (ATMs) of many deposit and withdrawal services previously accessible only during bank hours. Neither of these services is captured as higher banking output at the macroeconomic level.

The linkage between output and value is complex. Let us consider one small, straightforward, and important example drawn from our work in retail banking: the quality of the service provided, as proxied by a simple metric such as waiting time in a bank branch or on the telephone. It is clear that this quality plays a major role in the acquisition of new business along with the retention of existing accounts (Rust and Metters, 1996). Furthermore, this quality output is the result of a series of decisions on the part of management (e.g., by deciding on the staffing levels in a bank branch, management has decided upon the level of service to offer to the average customer). However, the linkage between such quality measures and revenues is much more complex than assigning a dollar figure to a unit of quality; such relationships are highly nonlinear in nature (Rust, Zahorik, and Keiningham, 1995). The role of management is to discover these relationships between outputs and value, i.e., to discover, either through deliberate decisions or through the development of emergent strategies, the linkage of outputs to value creation for the firm. Further, we might note that this measure of quality does not adjust for the accuracy of any information provided or tasks completed, or for the accompanying emotional aspects of the service transaction (Rust, Zahorik, and Keiningham, 1995; Soteriou and Zenios, 1999). Such attributes may also generate value for the bank, and these are also the result of managerial decisions regarding the allocation of resources.

Foremost of the decisions facing management is the choice of the production function itself. Either through incremental change (Rosenberg, 1982) or through discontinuous learning (Schumpeter, 1939), management "chooses" the production technology for the firm. Conceptually, let us define P as the set of all possible production functions/routines/technologies, and let $F_p$ be the production function associated with $p \varepsilon P$. Given the choice of $p \varepsilon P$, the choices for capital and labor inputs are severely constrained (Morroni, 1992). For example, if I choose a branch-based delivery system, I must staff the branch with a certain number of tellers in order to deliver a given level of quality (e.g., waiting time). If, however, I choose a production technology that is a mix of branch, phone, and ATM machines, my choices for meeting this same level of service are greatly expanded. Therefore, by the choice of $p \varepsilon P$, the firm constrains its choice of labor $L_p$, capital $K_p$, and information technology (IT) $T_p$. (note that throughout this paper, IT and non-IT capital are kept separate due to the increasing importance of IT capital in financial services).

While the input choices are oftentimes limited, as noted by Mefford (1986), managerial decisions play a vital role in the creation of effective inputs. That is, the purchase of a computer in and of itself adds nothing to the productive capability of an organization. It is only after this computer has been integrated into the production technology of the firm that it adds value. The same is true of labor and other capital inputs. Without the proper training, additional labor adds no value to the firm. Thus, management plays a crucial role in transforming "raw" inputs into useful/effective inputs for the firm.

Consider the management of human resources. Studies in manufacturing have clearly shown the effects of different ways of managing employees on performance outcomes such as productivity (MacDuffie, 1991; Ichniowski, Shaw, and Prennushi, 1994) and quality (Arthur, 1994; MacDuffie, 1995). Considerable anecdotal evidence suggests that the management of people in financial services may also affect performance outcomes (see, for example, Long, 1988; Beatty and Gup, 1989; Roth and van der Velde, 1991a). Yet careful empirical studies considering the role of human resources in financial services have taken one of two tacks. Much of the solid econometric work on efficiency of financial service organizations considers crude aggregate measures of labor as an input (labor cost, hours worked, or number of employees) without attention to the management of labor. And work that considers management practices focuses on high-level managers (see, for example, Donnelly et al., 1989; Sellers, 1992; Blackwell et al., 1994), but does not address the bulk of the workforce involved in delivering financial services to customers. Neither of these two approaches allows for the possibility that banks may gain competitive advantage from effective management of the broader workforce. One study, however, suggests that top performing Finnish banks are leaders with respect to training and employee empowerment (Tainio et al., 1991), a result consistent with the manufacturing studies cited above.

Technology also plays a key role in the performance of firms in this industry. Roth and van der Velde (1991b; Figure 3) show that $392,000 per bank ($2.1 million for banks with more than $3 billion assets) is spent annually on platform automation, and $502,000 ($3.2 million for the larger banks) is spent on upgrading information and transaction processing. Even with these large investments, it is still difficult to ascertain the payoffs associated with these projects. In manufacturing, recent studies (Brynjolfsson and Hitt, 1993; Lichtenberg, 1995) have found large payoffs in IT investments, both in terms of equipment and personnel. For example, Lichtenberg (1995) states that "the estimated marginal rate of substitution between IT and non-IT employees, evaluated at the sample mean, is six: one IT employee can substitute for six non-IT employees without affecting output." Unfortunately, similar results for financial services are not available, mainly due to the problems of accurately measuring IT investment and outputs.

Thus, the firm selects the levels of labor (L), capital (K), and information technology (T) to deploy in a given production process in addition to the methods for managing these "raw" inputs to create useful productive assets for the firm. That is, the firm transforms these inputs into "effective" inputs through the choice (deliberate or emergent) of the transformation functions $g_i$ for each input $i \varepsilon K$, L, and T:

$$L^* = g_L(L)$$

$$K^* = g_K(K)$$

$$T^* = g_T(T)$$

Lastly, the firm is faced with a cost function c(L,K,T) for the inputs. Note that this function is again more complex than the simple summation of costs and input levels due to the presence of cost complementarities (Milgrom and Roberts, 1990, 1995).

Given this framework, the problem facing the management of a firm can be stated as:

$$\text{maximize } v(O) - c(K,L,T)$$

by selecting:

- the levels of inputs K, L, and T;
- the input transformation functions $g_i$;
- the production technology/function for the organization $p \varepsilon P$; and
- the mix of outputs $O_S$ that will derive the value $v(O)$.

The key decisions facing the firm are the last three in the sense that the input levels are derived from the latter decisions.

Therefore, the management qualities that generate differential X-efficiencies are defined by their ability to (1) align the outputs of the firm with strategic directions that are profitable today and tomorrow; (2) align the production function/technology of the organization in the most efficient manner to produce these outputs; and (3) align/transform the raw inputs into effective human resources, capital, and technology for the given production technology. That is, management must *align* strategy with the design of the production processes of the organization and the inputs in order to become effective and efficient.

### 1.1 This Chapter

This chapter summarizes a four-year research effort aimed at understanding this alignment of strategy, process, people, and technology in the retail banking industry. Rather than reviewing any one managerial action or explanation of the drivers of efficiency in detail, the current paper synthesizes the detailed research in several papers by the authors with the results of our field-based research investigations. While not providing definitive answers in the form of a full estimation of the conceptual model described above, this paper presents evidence (both statistical and case-based) on the drivers of efficiency and effectiveness in the choices of human resource practices, technology management, and the design of the production processes. Based on the most comprehensive data collection effort ever undertaken in the retail banking industry (see Appendix A for details), the aim of this paper is to provide insights into what drives X-efficiency in this industry. In this sense, our goal is to fulfill the desire expressed by Griliches (1992, p. 7) in his review of the state-of-knowledge on service-sector productivity:

... the necessary economic-engineering research that would tell us which of the characteristics and training levels are important for their successful performance has not been done. We are thus lacking the scientific base for the desired measurement procedures.

Through the synthesis of detailed operational, human resource, technology, process, and strategy data, our purpose is to build a base of knowledge for the banking industry. The plan of the remainder of this paper is as follows: the next section reviews the overall design of the retail banking study. Sections 3 and 4 then explore the results of previous research on the data described in Appendix A by the authors on the effectiveness of management practices to deal with human resources and capital (especially information technology), respectively. The issue of selection/alignment of production processes is explored in Section 5, and the question of aligning these practices with strategy is dealt with in Section 6. The paper concludes in Section 7 with a discussion of our view as to what drives efficiency in retail banking as well as describing a set of research questions that emerge from this analysis.

## 2  Study Design

The focus of all of the research reported herein is on the products and services provided by the banking industry to the consumer marketplace. Given the fact that the retail operations of a typical bank are only a portion of its overall enterprise, why focus solely on the consumer market? And, given this choice of focus, what data problems arise?

Each of the studies reviewed in the following sections relies on a set of data collected by the authors. We describe this data collection effort here. In the field-based portion of the data collection (see Appendix A for details), interviews with industry executives clearly surfaced the increasing emphasis they are placing on the retail consumer. The growth of non-bank competitors and the advent of new distribution channels enabled by advances in information technology are rapidly changing the competitive landscape of consumer financial services. Banks are responding to this challenge with a variety of choices of delivery systems, human resource changes, and massive technology investments. Thus, the retail banking operations of the industry provide a significant "natural variation" that can be used to study the impact of process, technology, and human resource practices on performance. In other words, the field-based interviews with industry executives led us to conclude that a significant cause of the variation in X-efficiency lies in the consumer operations of a typical bank.[1] In addition, it is precisely this variation that is of interest to industry executives. Given the detailed data requested from the banks in the study, including several confidential pieces of information, it was vital that senior executives found the results of interest in order to participate. By focusing on the retail business, a data set was developed that covers almost 80% of the industry (by asset size); see Appendix A for detail. Therefore, by limiting the focus to retail banking, a very rich set of strategy, operational, and performance data was created for the industry. Again, each of the studies summarized herein analyzes this data set.

The focus on the retail side of the banking industry does limit the data in several ways. It is very hard, even for the banks in the study, to clearly separate, in terms of financial and operating data, the retail and non-retail portions of their business. For example, the expenditure of technology on the retail business versus on the bank as a whole is often impossible to discover. To deal with this inability to disentangle the retail

---

[1] This conclusion is based on our observation that each of our seven pilot institutions stressed their opinion that consumer operations were in fact a large cause of inefficiency.

business from the overall bank operations, an elaborate data collection effort was undertaken in this study. Specific data have been collected, per the advice found in Griliches (1992). The data consist of micro-level details on the operations of the retail bank (number of full-time equivalent employees [FTE], the actual functionality of the technology deployed in the branch system, etc.) in addition to cost and revenue figures. While the financial data is suspect due to the reasons listed above, we are very confident in the quality of the micro-level/"engineering" data that were collected.

Thus, using this combination of bank-level financial data and the detailed "engineering" data, the studies discussed below were able to undertake analyses of retail bank efficiency at a variety of levels: from the efficiency of the bank as a whole, using the financial data collected despite its limitations, to detailed analyses of the efficiency of key service delivery processes in the bank. While none of these analyses is without its limitations due to the data collected, it is the combination of all of these analyses that begins to paint a picture of what drives X-efficiency in this industry. It is in the combination of these studies that this current paper makes its contribution. Ideally, there would be similar data on the other parts of the banking establishments (wholesale, commercial, off-balance sheet activities, etc.) to be used to create a full and consistent data set for the bank; this is left for future research. At this point, the studies focus only on the retail bank. While limited, this focus does uncover interesting patterns of efficient versus inefficient organizations; it is these patterns across the studies that are the focus of this paper.

### 2.1 The Inputs and Outputs Considered in the Studies

As described above (and more fully in Frei, Harker, and Hunter, 1994), the choices of human resource, technology, and process management techniques and their impact on the quality, cost, and convenience of the services provided by the financial institutions are vital drivers of efficiency. The three studies that we will synthesize address each of these factors in detail:

1. *Human resource management practices* are considered in a number of areas: compensation, hiring and selection, staffing, training, work organization, and employee involvement. Further, these practices are analyzed as they govern both managerial and non-managerial employees. Both groups play important roles. In branches of retail banks, for example, employees from the manager's office to the teller window sell products and support selling at previously unprecedented levels.

Practices in successful retail banks must reinforce the ability of the organization to compete for investment dollars, to solve customers' problems, and to complete transactions quickly and accurately (Hunter, 1997).

2. *Technology* in banking (IT) is considered at two basic levels within a bank: overall investment in IT, and the functionality of the technology deployed in the production/service delivery processes in the branch and phone delivery systems. Thus, technology is viewed at both a macro level in terms of investment, and at a micro level in terms of its ability to perform certain functions within the organization. In addition, the management of IT, both in terms of the selection of projects and their management, is a crucial factor in transforming the investment T into effective technology T*. The key technological thrusts found in the retail banking survey conducted by Roth and van der Velde (1992) suggest that major technology investments are under way to integrate the traditional front- and back-office systems into a seamless service delivery process. These and many other studies of information technology suggest that IT is best able to add value when it *informates*, creating new sources of information in an organization, rather than simply automating existing processes (Zuboff, 1985). In banking, this trend manifests itself in the desire to provide expertise and information to the people who are in closest contact with customers (Prasad and Harker, 1997).

3. In order to understand how a bank interacts with its customers, we examine a subset of the *product and service delivery processes* across five representative products of the *core* retail bank. The products include consumer checking, certificates of deposit (CDs), home equity loans, small business loans, and mutual funds. For each of these products, typical transactions, such as opening an account, as well as error resolution transactions, such as double-posting a check, were analyzed. Variation in work-steps and available tools can affect the characteristics of processes. For example, more sophisticated technology may speed up a process through automation. At the same time, technology may lengthen process time by increasing the information available to the bank or the customer. Similarly, staffing a particular process with a highly experienced employee may increase speed or accuracy, but also may increase the amount of time introducing the customer to additional appropriate products (cross-selling). Combining different levels of technology and human resources has different effects, and there are trade-offs in results associated with different process designs. In addition, customers have co-productive effects on processes. As an integral part of the process, the customer is a resource just as the platform representative's time is a resource. In fact, the time required of the customer may be a consideration in particular process designs. Some processes may waste the customer's time, others will not; some processes will take advantage of interaction with the customer to increase sales or the information available to the bank (Frei and Harker, 1999a, Frei et al., 1999).

As described above, the limitations of the data collected as part of this study restrict our ability to link management practices definitively to overall profitability of the retail bank for two reasons. The first reason lies in the inability to disentangle the financial data of the retail bank from the overall organization. Ideally, a longitudinal data set would permit one to decouple the retail and non-retail portions of the bank. However, the current data is cross-section in nature and thus it must be assumed that the overall profitability of the organization is highly correlated with its retail bank performance. While this assumption seems reasonable given the prominence the retail bank is given both organizationally and in terms of managerial resources dedicated to it, only a panel data set would permit one to test this hypothesis formally; this is left for future research. Second, the bank provides a variety of outputs, such as quality, that are crucial in growing the business, but are difficult to link to overall value. There is significant theoretical and anecdotal evidence to suggest that outputs such as quality, convenience, etc., are linked to value creation; the exact form of this transformation function, $v(O)$, however, can only be discovered with a longitudinal data set. Thus, the cross-sectional operational data somewhat limits our analysis.

To overcome these limitations, analyses across these studies have been performed at three levels: overall profitability, performance in terms of quality, and detailed process-level performance of the organizations. As stated above, none of these analyses lead to definitive results by themselves. However, when viewed together along with the results of our field-based interviews, they begin to surface the key drivers of efficiency in the banking industry.

Thus, the outputs of the retail bank are viewed at three levels. For aggregate analyses comparing one bank to another, Return On Assets (ROA) is used as the financial performance metric. While this measure is aggregate in nature and, hence, suffers from the fact that the retail franchise is only a portion of the overall bank, it does provide some insight into the payoff of various investments and management practices. Thus, these aggregate analyses focus on overall profitability, $v(O) - c(K,L,T)$.

Finally, the detailed process-level data collected creates the ability to study the drivers of profitability and satisfaction in terms of the convenience, precision, and adaptability of the retail bank:

1. *Customer convenience.* Historically, consumers chose financial services based largely on availability and location. With advances in technology and innovations in human resource practices, the concept of

convenience has been extended well beyond availability and location to imply easy access to a wide range of products and services available at any time, from any place. Rapid turnaround time of customer product and service requests also is increasingly important. For example, customers expect firms to be capable of moving money instantly between investment product options and accounts. Equally important is the amount of time required of the customer in these co-productive processes. Whether it is standing in the teller line, filling out a loan application, or coming to the branch for a loan closing, the demands placed on the customer must be measured and made mutually beneficial.

2. *Precision.* While customers may make many choices based on convenience, they also expect quality in the delivery of financial services and products. The customer defines quality as a broad range of tangible and intangible attributes. Examples include error-free statements, checks printed correctly, and the operational soundness of all delivery channels. Consumers and shareholders also want the firm to be able to make good business decisions, which requires operating precision from the bank. First, the source information, which forms the basis for any decision, must be accurate. Second, the institution must have the tools that enable accurate interpretation of the source information. For example, making good lending decisions requires accurate information from the consumer, a detailed understanding of the economic environment, and tools such as credit scoring models to facilitate the analysis process. While these decisions may occur without the benefit of sophisticated tools, the bank's ability to increase precision even slightly on an individual credit analysis might translate into systemic improvements.

3. *Adaptability.* The first indication of an organization's adaptability is its willingness to adapt to the demands of the customer. Pricing flexibility may evidence this willingness. It also surfaces in the concept of mass *customization* of services (Pine, 1993). Customers have individual needs that are not easily satisfied by standard products and services. Not surprisingly, the need to customize products and services underlies much of the IT investment in banking. In addition to responding to the customer, financial institutions display adaptability in their ability to respond to the marketplace. In competition with non-bank financial institutions, the bank's challenge is to create competitive products and introduce them effectively to protect or enhance the firm's relative competitive position. Changes in products or the IT infrastructure require the institution to change business processes. Organizations and processes should be able to withstand and plan for change.

Appendix A describes the survey methodology that was used to capture data on all of these elements of the banking industry's performance listed above. This data was then analyzed in the previous studies using a variety of statistical and linear programming-based methods; Appendix B summarizes the analytical methodology used in most of these studies. Rather than focusing on the detailed results of these analyses, which are described in the papers cited herein, the remainder of the paper turns to the question of what these analyses say with respect to uncovering the drivers of X-efficiency in the banking industry. That is, what do the various levels of analyses and field-based interviews with those in the industry, both in the boardroom and in the bank lobby, say about what makes a retail bank efficient?

We begin with a discussion of human resources in banking.

### 3 Aligning Labor

There is solid empirical evidence that human resource management (HRM) contributes to organizational performance (Arthur, 1994; Cutcher-Gershenfeld, 1991; Delery and Doty, 1996; Huselid, 1995; Huselid and Becker, 1996; Ichniowski, Shaw, and Prennushi, 1994; Mac-Duffie, 1995). Recast in terms of the literature on banking efficiency, this implies that some of the inefficiencies in banking may be attributable to ineffective management of human resources.

Understanding of the management of human resources may be cast at multiple levels (Becker and Gerhart, 1996). The "architecture" of a human resource system provides a high-level framework and guiding principles for HRM, while policies bring this framework down closer to an operational level. At these levels, the limited evidence suggests there may be some *best practices* in HRM (Pfeffer, 1994; Huselid, 1995; Milgrom and Roberts, 1995). Such evidence raises the question of why firms do not adopt these architectural characteristics and policies (such as valuing employee performance, developing employee skills, and encouraging commitment and involvement). There are, however, both in-firm and external impediments to such adoption (see Levine, 1995, for more on this argument). The result is that effective HRM may be difficult to adopt or imitate. HRM may therefore serve as a source of competitive advantage in the resource-based sense (Barney, 1991; Lado and Wilson, 1994; Pfeffer, 1994). This seems to be at least partially true in banking. Delery and Doty (1996), for example, find that the existence of HRM policies favoring profit-sharing and results-oriented performance appraisals for lending officers is significantly related to return on average assets and return on equity for U.S. commercial banks.

At increasingly specific levels below HRM architecture and policy lies the implementation of particular HRM practices. It is at these levels that HRM practices might actually create value. Practices, as organizational structures, attract and retain employees, reinforce employee behaviors, and develop employee skills (Wright and McMahan, 1992). One open question is the extent to which these practices are inimitable and therefore the potential source of performance differences. The appropriate alignment of these practices toward the solution of particular sets of business problems (such as effective customer service, cost minimization, revenue generation, and the like) under a broader architecture may be quite idiosyncratic and could therefore represent such a source (Becker and Gerhart, 1996).

In complex organizations such as banks, different groups of employees are governed by different "subsystems" of HRM practice (Osterman, 1987). Each subsystem may have its own distinct logic and appropriate accompanying set of HRM practices. For example, branch-level employees may be embedded in one subsystem and governed by one set of practices, telephone center employees may work in another subsystem, corporate lenders in another, and traders in another. Each employment subsystem in a bank generates multiple outcomes. Each subsystem may contribute to the overall efficiency of the bank independently and may make contributions that are complementary (Milgrom and Roberts, 1990) to the contributions of other groups.

Alignment of HRM practices in these subsystems can contribute to efficiency in a number of ways. First of all, where practices within a subsystem are aligned with one another toward key goals, that subsystem performs more efficiently. For example, bundles of lean-production HRM practices in auto assembly production facilities lead to higher levels of productivity and quality (MacDuffie, 1995). Further, the alignment of HRM practices within one subsystem with those in other subsystems may produce further efficiency benefits; these may be in addition to or traded off against those benefits within the subsystem in question. And it is clear that the problems of alignment in complex organizations are themselves computationally complex, requiring considerable information; as the number of choice parameters and the strength of complementarities grow, the problem of selecting among policies becomes more difficult (Milgrom and Roberts, 1990).

This discussion has so far had a fairly abstract character. Our work in banking, however, enables us to make a start on understanding the relationships between HRM and efficiency by considering the effects of alignment of HRM practices within and across particular subsystems. We start by considering the subsystem of HRM practices governing branch employees. As we noted in the earlier discussion of measures of value creation, branches have a number of subordinate goals that might in turn contribute to organizational efficiency: provision of services in ways that customers find convenient; precision in the provision, collection, and analysis of financial information (which in turn contributes to risk minimization and fraud detection); cost control and efficient sub-processes; adaptability to the demands of customers (particularly those customers with whom it is profitable for the bank to maintain relationships); and high-quality customer service leading to satisfaction and increased sales. In a previous study of this data, it was found that branches with HRM practices aligned toward particular sets of goals perform better than those that do not have such alignment. Where HRM practices develop skills and reward behaviors in line with these subordinate goals, performance on a given dimension is typically superior to performance in other units where such practices are not so aligned (Hunter, 1997).

Because each bank may have its own weighting scheme for valuing outcomes, aligned sets of practices – even in efficient banks – may look somewhat different. For example, a bank that values streamlined processes quite highly may have practices (such as training, incentives, and job design) that encourage employees to move customers swiftly through such exercises as checking account openings. A bank that values sales more highly may have differently designed training practices, reward structures, and jobs. This raises two questions, separable in principle. First, the mixes of outcomes banks obtain from different sets of HRM practices may represent more or less efficient performance. Second, banks may have HRM practices more or less effectively aligned toward the production of a given mix of outcomes. The first question is, in principle, a more strategic decision (based on the value weightings banks assign to sub-outcomes). The second question is more oriented toward implementation, asking whether banks have optimal HRM practices for the achievement of particular outcomes. (Empirically, however, separating these two questions is more difficult since variance in value weightings of outcomes across banks may in part derive from the cost of implementing the HRM practices necessary to achieve those outcomes.)

Taking this to an increasingly specific level, and again with application to the branch subsystem, two different trends have been identified (see Table 8.1) guiding the re-shaping of employment practice in leading American retail banks (Hunter, 1997). Both trends involve a departure from the traditional, bureaucratically organized bank branch, in which jobs were narrowly defined, linked in a hierarchical ladder, and governed by a set of restrictive rules over behaviors.

The *inclusive* strategy involves investment in the entire retail workforce. In this model, tellers' jobs are enriched to include sales responsibility and cross-training to platform functions. All employees are to some extent responsible for initiating and maintaining customer contact.

Table 8.1. *Two models of employment practice for bank branches.*

| HRM practice | Inclusive model | Segmented model |
| --- | --- | --- |
| Selection criteria | High school, some college Trainability Customer focus | College required for platform High school for tellers |
| Training emphasis | Broadly cast | Focused on platform |
| Compensation | At or above market Incentives for team/group Returns to tenure | Above market for key platform employees Low for others Individual incentives |
| Job design | Broad cross-training Teamwork | Narrow, specialized Autonomy within specific tasks |
| Use of part-timers | For "retention" reasons | Use where possible, cost-control-oriented |
| Role of local manager | Facilitator/trainer Customer relations Generalist | Supervisor and scheduler Facilitator to platform Product specialist |
| Organizing logic of worksite | Team of generalists | Collection of specialists |

Tellers focus on the provision of basic services, while platform employees engage in relationship management and active selling, but either employee may be expected to cover the duties of the other. An ideal-typical inclusive system couples relatively high wages with incentive pay for effective sales and sales referrals. The model also includes elements of teamwork within the branch, cross-functional cooperation between different job families, and branch or unit-based performance bonuses. The role of the branch manager in this environment is one of a team facilitator and customer-relations expert, with a wider array of knowledge about products and services, and overall responsibility for the performance of the unit.

An alternative ideal-typical strategy for organizing the branch, the *segmentation* approach, focuses chiefly on cost containment in the mass market, with specialized services for an elite segment of customers. In this model, banks attempt to match different kinds of employees to sharply distinct roles. A few specialized employees – branch managers, product specialists, and "personal bankers" on the platform – are responsible for managing relationships between the bank and qualified customers. Ideally these are customers with high-profit potential such as upper-income professionals and owners of small businesses. The employees responsible for serving these customers are carefully screened, typically college-educated, and, increasingly, licensed to sell investment products. They are well paid, and embedded in the internal labor market of the bank, with opportunities for advancement and access to training. These employees also have considerable range for discretionary decision-making; they are charged with using this autonomy to enhance the relationship between the bank and its customers. In this model, however, the majority of branch and telephone center employees receive considerably less compensation and training. They are often employed on a part-time basis and their compensation may not include benefits. Typically, they are shut off from promotion opportunities unless they acquire an external credential such as a college degree. The positions, typically, tend to be high-turnover and to have relatively flat wage profiles. Further, the distinctions between the jobs are quite sharp: cross-training is scant and there are few cross-functional responsibilities. In this model, the role of the branch manager is less that of a facilitator and more that of a traditional supervisor.

The two models for organizing work are neither entirely orthogonal to one another, nor do they represent different ends of a unidimensional continuum. Most branches feature some aspects of segmentation and other aspects of inclusion. On some dimensions of practice (cross-training of tellers, for example), a choice between the two models is required: more inclusion necessarily implies less segmentation. On other dimensions (incentive pay, for example), it is possible to have aspects of the segmented model (with its focus on individual incentives), aspects of the inclusive model (with group pay incentives), both, or neither.

Both branches with more inclusive HRM practices and those that employ segmentation may be effective in some dimensions. Inclusive HRM practices in branches are significantly and positively related to customer satisfaction measured at the bank level (Hunter, 1996b), for example. Further kinds of effectiveness are contingent on the consistency with which the model of HRM is applied. Consider key branch-level outcomes such as rates of "cross-selling" (as measured by the average number of standard retail products held per customer) and basic productivity (as measured by customers served in a branch, per full-time equivalent employee). Analyses controlling for other plausible determinants of performance, such as characteristics of local markets, show that branches which employ either high levels of cross-training from teller to platform and vice versa, or high levels of employee autonomy, significantly outperform those with branches which take neither approach and those which have both cross-training and high autonomy (Hunter and Hitt, 1997).

Effectiveness is also contingent upon the role the branch plays in the strategic direction of the bank. If pure process efficiency, for example, rather than customer satisfaction, is a target, then inclusive models are less desirable. Alignment of practices in an inclusive direction has a negative and statistically significant relationship to measures of process efficiency (Frei, 1996). Further, while banks that feature low levels of cross-training and low levels of employee autonomy – in short, those traditional bureaucracies comprising narrow and constrained jobs – do not perform well on sales or straight productivity outcomes, these same banks actually appear to have lower levels of branch-level losses as measured by branch "out-of-balance" figures (Hunter and Hitt, 1997). These results suggest that the question of which kinds of HRM practices in bank branches are most efficient remains open and may depend upon the cost of implementing such practices (something we need more data on), as well as on the varying values different banks place on the different outcomes (sales versus traditional productivity versus process efficiency versus losses, for example). It is also worth noting here that there is no direct evidence that HRM practices in branches are associated with performance with respect to risk beyond simple losses due to error or fraud (for example, poor lending decisions). The HRM data are cross-sectional and, presumably, the effects of HRM practices on risk-related outcomes would take a considerably longer period of time to emerge.

The above discussion covers the effects of HRM on performance outcomes within a single subsystem. There may also be important effects on efficiency that depend upon alignment of practices *across* subsystems. Here, consider the examples of either multiple branch subsystems, or branch and telephone center subsystems. HRM subsystems may be locally aligned yet have negative effects on efficiency if those subsystems have negative effects on the efficiency of other subsystems. To take one example, HRM practices in a single branch might contribute positively to improved sales or customer convenience at that branch, but negatively to customers' willingness to use alternative delivery channels (such as telephone banking) which themselves have higher rates of sales conversion or more streamlined processes.

From the point of the view of the bank, aggregate efficiency depends upon the proper aggregation of HRM effects not only within but also across subsystems. The cross-channel evidence is more circumstantial than our within-unit evidence. However, fieldwork in one leading U.S.

bank is suggestive here. The bank is implementing a variety of segmentation-oriented HRM practices, coupled with decreased levels of employee autonomy driven by process reengineering. Consistent with our broader work, we find that the adoption of these practices contributes negatively to a variety of sales- and service-related performance outcomes at the branch level. However, the same practices contribute positively to customers' willingness to transact in other channels that the bank *believes* to be more efficient in serving customers. If the HRM subsystem in the telephone call center of this bank is designed appropriately, the net effect of both subsystems on efficiency could well be positive.

### 4 Aligning Capital

The preceding section argued that evidence suggests that the way in which labor is managed may be closely related to X-efficiency in banking. Similar considerations apply to capital; that is, while capital itself may serve as an input in the construction of efficiency measures, the management of capital contributes to the explanation of the sources of X-efficiency in the industry. More specifically, consider the role of information technology (IT). Financial services are the largest consumer of IT in the economy. It has been a matter of much debate whether or not investment in IT provides improvements in productivity and business efficiency. For several years, scholars and policymakers lacked conclusive evidence that the high levels of spending on IT by businesses improved their productivity, leading to the coining of the term *IT Productivity Paradox*. Morrison and Berndt (1990) concluded that additional IT investments contributed negatively to productivity, arguing that "estimated marginal benefits of investment [in IT] are less than the estimated marginal costs." Others, such as Loveman (1994) and Baily et al. (1991), posit that there is no conclusive evidence to refute the hypothesis that IT investment is inconsequential to productivity. Of late, researchers working with firm-level data have found significant contributions from IT toward productivity (Lichtenberg, 1995, and Brynjolfsson and Hitt, 1996, for example). Most of these firm-level studies have been restricted to the manufacturing sector, in large part owing to lack of firm-level data from the service sector.

Prasad and Harker (1997) take an aggregate approach to consider the effects of IT on productivity in the retail-banking industry in the United States using the data described in Appendix A. This section summarizes the results of this analysis.

Using a Cobb-Douglas production function as in Loveman (1994),

Lichtenberg (1995), and Brynjolfsson and Hitt (1996), Prasad and Harker (1997) estimate the following equation using the data described in Appendix B:

$$Q = e^{\beta_0} C^{\beta_1} K^{\beta_2} S^{\beta_3} L^{\beta_4} \tag{1}$$

where

Q = output of the firm
C = IT capital investment
K = non-IT capital investment
S = IT labor expenses
L = non-IT labor expenses

and $\beta_1$, $\beta_2$, $\beta_3$, and $\beta_4$ are the associated output elasticities.

Using this function, the following hypotheses were tested:

H1:   IT investment makes a positive contribution to output (i.e., the gross marginal product is positive).
H2:   IT investment makes a positive contribution to output after deductions for depreciation and labor expenses (i.e., the net marginal product is positive).
H3:   IT investment makes zero contribution to profits or the stock market value of the firm.

Studies of productivity in the banking industry struggle with the issue of what constitutes the *output* of a bank. The various approaches chosen to evaluate the output of banks may be classified into three broad categories: the assets approach, the user-cost approach, and the value-added approach (Berger and Humphrey, 1992). As a result, various measures of output were tested in Prasad and Harker (1997). Benston, Hanweck, and Humphrey (1982) posit that "output should be measured in terms of what banks do that cause operating expenses to be incurred." Prasad and Harker (1997) look at a wide variety of output measures, both financial and customer satisfaction (i.e., the first two levels of analysis described in Section 2). The most meaningful results from this analysis arise when Total Loan + Deposits is used as the output of the institution; these results are summarized in Table 8.2.

From this table, it can be seen that the elasticities (the coefficients) associated with IT capital and labor are positive. However, the low significance associated with the IT capital coefficient implies that there is a high probability (0.93) that the elasticity of IT capital is zero. Thus, there is not sufficient evidence to support Hypothesis H1 for IT capital (i.e., that IT capital produces positive returns in productivity). It is interesting to note that the elasticity of non-IT capital is, at best, zero (being not significantly different from zero), implying that IT capital investment is

Table 8.2. *Output = (total loans + total deposits).*

| Parameter | Coefficient | Standard error | t-statistic | t-statistic: significance | Ratio to output | Marginal product |
|---|---|---|---|---|---|---|
| IT capital | 0.00116 | 0.013 | 0.089 | 7% | 0.000452 | 2.56 |
| IT labor | 0.25989 | 0.031 | 8.34 | 100% | 0.0006 | 449.75 |
| Non IT capital | −0.02071 | 0.026 | −0.79 | 57% | 0.00428 | −4.84 |
| Non IT labor | 0.53244 | 0.059 | 8.95 | 100% | 0.01475 | 36.10 |

*Note*: $R^2 = 41\%$ (OLS); 99% (2-step WLS).

relatively better than investment in non-IT capital. However, the results show that H1 cannot be rejected for IT labor, and since the marginal product of IT labor is \$449.75, it can be concluded that IT labor is associated with a high increase in the output of the bank.

Since H1 cannot be supported for IT capital, the discussion of the stronger hypothesis, H2, is restricted to the IT labor results. First, it can be seen that the marginal product for IT labor is very high. Since IT labor is a flow variable, then every dollar of IT labor costs a dollar. In view of this, the excess returns from IT labor can be computed to be \$(449.75–1), or \$448.75. Thus, H2 cannot be rejected for IT labor. For H3, one has

$$\beta_3 - (\text{IT Labor Expenses} / \text{Non-IT Labor Expenses}) * \beta_4 = 0.2390 > 0.$$

Thus, there is support for H3 for IT labor.

As far as H3 is concerned for capital expenses, it can be seen that the marginal product of non-IT capital is negative. Further, given the standard errors of the estimation, it is asserted that IT capital is more likely to yield either slightly positive or no benefits, whereas non-IT capital will most probably have a negative effect, decreasing productivity. More formally,

$$\beta_1 - (\text{IT Capital Expenses} / \text{Non-IT Capital Expenses}) * \beta_2 = 0.00334 > 0.$$

Given the significance associated with the IT capital estimate, however, H3 failed to be rejected.

Thus, these results from Prasad and Harker (1997) show that IT capital makes zero, and perhaps even a slightly negative, contribution to output. This result is significantly different from previous studies in the manufacturing sector (Lichtenberg, 1995; Brynjolfsson and Hitt, 1996), and seems to be more in conformity with those obtained in Parsons et al. (1993), the only formal study on IT in banking to date. While Parsons et al. report slightly positive contribution to IT investment, this analysis demonstrates zero or slightly negative contributions. It should be noted that the production function used in Prasad and Harker (1997) is assumed to be separable and that if this is not the case, then these results may not hold.

IT labor presents a very different picture than does IT capital. IT labor contributes significantly to output; its marginal product is at least 10 times as much as that of non-IT labor (Prasad and Harker, 1997). Rather than make the simplistic conclusion from this that a single IT person is equivalent to 10 non-IT persons, it is better perhaps to speculate that this may simply reflect the fact that there is significant difference between the types of personnel involved in IT and non-IT functions. It is more interesting to compare the marginal product of IT capital versus IT labor. It is striking that while IT labor contributes significantly to productivity increases, IT capital does not. Thus, these results state that while banks may have over-invested in IT capital, there is significant benefit in hiring and retaining IT labor (Prasad and Harker, 1997).

This result and interpretation is consistent with the idea that aligning capital, rather than throwing technology at problems, is what affects efficiency. IT personnel are likely to be much more effective at ensuring that the implementation of technology does what it is meant to do. That is, it is our opinion that the management of IT has profound effects on efficiency. Banks that are able to manage their IT effectively are likely to be efficient, a finding that is consistent with our fieldwork experiences. This is also consistent with the fact that today's high demand for IT personnel is unprecedented in U.S. labor history. Figures from the Bureau of Labor Statistics show that while the overall job growth in the U.S. economy was 1.6% between 1987 and 1994, software employment grew in these years at 9.6% every year, and "cranked up to 11.5% in 1995"; the prediction is that over the next decade, we will see further growth in software jobs at 6.4% every year (Rebello, 1996).

The problems are actually likely to be subtler than these measures suggest. For example, IT personnel, while evidently valuable, may not be equally valuable. The point was driven home to us in a series of interviews in a major New York bank. A Senior Vice President there lamented the fact that, "The skills mix of the IT staff doesn't match the current strategy of the bank," and said that he "didn't know what to do about it." At the same bank, the Vice President in charge of IT claimed, "Our current IT training isn't working. We never spend anywhere near our training budget." IT labor is in very short supply, and issues as basic as re-skilling the workforce cannot be addressed given the lack of sufficient IT labor in banking.

Other researchers have observed this dependence and under-investment in human capital in technologically intensive environments. To quote Gunn's (1987) work in manufacturing, "Time and again, the major impediment to [technological] implementation . . . is people: their lack of knowledge, their resistance to change, or simply their lack of ability to quickly absorb the vast multitude of new technologies, philosophies, ideas, and practices, that have come about in manufacturing over the last five to ten years." Another observation about the transitions firms need to make to gain from technology, again in the manufacturing context, comes from Reich (1984): ". . . the transition also requires a massive change in the skills of American labor, requiring investments in human capital beyond the capital of any individual firm."

The evidence also suggests that the effects of management of IT are also being felt more broadly. Consider the *inclusive* model for managing branches, discussed in the preceding section. In this model, information technology and process redesign (popularly, *reengineering*) combine to remove from employees as many basic servicing tasks as possible. These tasks – simple inquiries, transactions, and movement of funds – can be automated or turned over to customers. Reengineering frees employees to concentrate more effort on activities that have potentially higher added value: customized transactions, and the provision of financial advice coupled with sales efforts. Second, information technology gives to each employee a full picture of each customer's financial position and potential; this enhances sales efforts, enabling tellers and customer service representatives to suggest a fit between customers and services, and to refer the customers to employee-teammates with particular expertise in a product if that should become necessary. Challenges under the *segmented* model are less acute, yet still present. In this model, technology is used to simplify the majority of the jobs, to make them easier to learn and, therefore, to make turnover less costly. Only the high value-added, personal banking jobs have access to the broad range of information that might be useful in generating sales leads and opportunities.

In order for either model to function effectively, those responsible for designing IT must understand not only the purposes of the technology, but the capabilities and propensities of the workforce, and the likely effects of different choices in technology on employee and customer behavior. Further, IT staff must be able to assess the likely effects of different configurations of technologies and employment systems if they are to be able to contribute to strategic decisions around the deployment of IT.

Thus, these results are very consistent with Osterman's (1996) conclusion that "... as IT Capital prices fall, production becomes increasingly information-worker intensive." The results described in this section seem to confirm this: banks have over-invested in IT capital, and investment in IT labor has become necessary. Further, IT labor is the most profitable of all four types of investment – IT and non-IT capital and labor available to the bank. That is, the biggest challenge facing banks with respect to aligning capital lies not in the technology, but in people.

### 5 Aligning Production Processes

As stated in Section 1, production processes are often seen as "black boxes." If labor and capital are the contents of the "black box," then production processes define its architecture. After a particular production technology is chosen, the choices of capital and labor are severely constrained. However, it is not enough simply to choose the appropriate level of inputs for a process, but rather it is necessary to figure out how to use these inputs effectively; i.e., how to design the box itself. It is in the design of the production process that these inputs are transformed into effective inputs and then aligned with the output goals of the organization.

The intent of this section is to review the analysis of the data described in Appendix A in order to understand the role of production processes in the transformation of capital and labor into value for the firm. The preceding sections argued that the way in which labor and capital are managed independently may be closely related to X-efficiency in banking. The purpose in this section is to understand the role production processes have in the cause of this inefficiency.

Before we present the analysis, we give a formal description of a production process. A production process is the way in which work is organized and inputs are consumed in order to accomplish a specified task of producing outputs. For example, a process might be the way in which a checking account is opened. The inputs consumed are the labor (platform representative) and capital (information technology), and the outputs produced are the opening of the account in a way that is convenient for the customer (in terms of customer time involved and when they have access to their money). In order to understand, for example, the process of opening a checking account, there must be knowledge of the steps involved, the order of these steps, the way in which people are involved, and the role of technology. The process-level analysis looked at a process as the transforming mechanism from inputs to outputs and identified the critical design issues that lead to greater value (Frei and Harker, 1999a; Frei et al., 1999). This section uses the definition of process efficiency in the context of retail banking; the next section will analyze two case studies in order to highlight and "give life" to the general conclusions regarding process efficiency discussed herein.

Before exploring the efficiency with which processes transform capital and labor into value for the customer and the bank, it is important to understand the role process design has on value creation. That is, processes can be designed to affect explicitly one or more value measures. For example, in order to improve the convenience of a process, the design can be altered to remove or shorten as many steps as possible. However, these adjustments might be at the expense of other value measures. Alternatively, a process can be designed to consume the least inputs (cost focus) even at the expense of decreasing market penetration and, hence, revenue. The point is that process design in and of itself can affect value creation. It is the intent of this section to review the research which addresses the extent to which process performance affects value creation for the data described in Appendix A – that is, to understand the combination of the design and the efficiency with which that design transforms inputs to outputs.

The data analyzed in Frei and Harker (1999a) and Frei et al. (1999) consisted of details on 11 processes that represent the bulk of the work that occurs at a typical retail bank's branch. These processes span five products and represent opening of accounts, error correction on the part of the bank, and error correction on the part of the consumer. The intent of using these 11 processes was to reflect the bulk of the work performed in the branch environment. In choosing the five most typical products and their account opening and an exception (such as correcting a check posted twice), the aim was to capture enough data so as to reflect the branch's overall process performance. It should be clearly stated that the process metrics are for a subset of the overall set of work performed by the branch, albeit a representative subset as confirmed by discussions with many industry participants.

For each of the 11 processes, an efficiency score was determined using the analysis described in Frei and Harker (1999a) and summarized in Appendix B. This analysis determines the efficiency with which each bank produces a set of outputs from a set of inputs. The categories of inputs and outputs for each process are shown in Table 8.3. For each process, the banks were ranked according to their efficiency score and

Table 8.3. *Summary of process inputs and outputs.*

| Process | Inputs | Outputs |
|---|---|---|
| *Open checking account* | Activity time: The amount of time bank personnel spend in the process | Customer time: The amount of time the customer spends in the process |
| | Checking IT functionality: The level of IT used in the process as indicated by a relative score | Check cycle time: The elapsed time from the start of the process until the customer receives his or her checks |
| | | ATM cycle time: The elapsed time from the start of the process until the customer receives his or her ATM card |
| *Open small business* | Activity time | Customer time |
| *Loan account* | IT functionality | Approval cycle time: The elapsed time from the start of the process until the customer hears about the approval |
| | | Money cycle time: The elapsed time from the start of the process until the customer receives his or her money |
| *Open certificate of deposit* | Activity time IT functionality | Customer time |
| *Open mutual fund* | Activity time IT functionality | Customer time |
| *Open home equity loan account* | Activity time IT functionality | Customer time Approval cycle time Money cycle time |
| *Correct a checking double post* | Activity time IT functionality | Customer time Correct cycle time: The elapsed time from the start of the process until the correction is completed |

Table 8.3. *(cont.)*

| Process | Inputs | Outputs |
|---|---|---|
| *Correct a home equity* | Activity time | Customer time |
| *Loan double post* | IT functionality | Post cycle time: The elapsed time from the start of the process until the correction is posted<br>Notify cycle time: The elapsed time from the start of the process until the customer is notified about the correction |
| *Correct a small business* | Activity time | Customer time |
| *Loan double post* | IT functionality | Post cycle time<br>Notify cycle time |
| *Redeem a premature certificate of deposit* | Activity time<br>IT functionality | Customer time<br>Redeem cycle time: The elapsed time from the start of the process until the redemption is completed |
| *Stop payment on a check* | Activity time<br>IT functionality | Customer time |
| *Replace a lost ATM card* | Activity time<br>IT functionality | Customer time<br>Replace cycle time: The elapsed time from the start of the process until the customer receives his or her new ATM card |

thus each bank had up to 11 rankings (Frei and Harker, 1999a). These individual process ranks were then aggregated to a single process performance metric using the methodology described in Frei and Harker (1999b) and summarized in Appendix B. The resultant process performance metric serves as an institutional aggregate process efficiency score. The aggregated score is then used to analyze the role of process efficiency in describing the X-efficiency of a bank.

As can be seen in Table 8.3, the outputs for each process are convenience measures (time) and the inputs are related to cost (labor time and technology functionality). These are the only two value-creation

Table 8.4. *Firm size, process performance, and financial performance.*

| Dependent variable | Constant | Assets (log) | Aggregate process rank | Adjusted $R^2$ |
|---|---|---|---|---|
| ROA | 1.01 | 0.02 | −0.02*** | 0.134 |

*Note*: *** Indicates significance at the 1% level.

measures represented in the individual process analysis, as they are the only process-level measures that we were able to collect data on. The other value-creation measures such as financial performance are at the bank level and thus are correlated with the aggregate process performance.

### 5.1 Does Process Efficiency Matter?

While there is a significant body of theoretical (Morroni, 1992) and anecdotal (Davenport and Short, 1990) evidence on the importance of process management, there is very little statistical evidence that process management matters with respect to the "bottom line" of the institution. Using the language of Section 1, does the choice of a process $p \varepsilon P$ matter? The previous research shows that, while no individual process is correlated with firm performance, the aggregate measure of process performance affects firm performance (Frei et al., 1999, Table 8.4). In an attempt to determine the causes of the relation between process performance and firm financial performance, the previous study tested whether the consistency (i.e., the alignment) of process performance is more important than performance in and of itself.[2] To address this hypothesis, process variability was considered, i.e., the variability of the bundle of processes that are offered to the customers of the institution.

### 5.2 Process Variation

When an institution performs a set of processes for a customer, there is undoubtedly going to be variation in the level of inputs consumed and the value provided to the customer. Process variation is defined as the

---

[2] The previous study does not argue that consistently poor performance is a good strategy but rather evidence is presented in terms of an analytical model and empirical data that suggests that if there is an additional resource to be invested in a firm, then the investment should go to improving consistency rather than to moving a single process towards best in class (Frei et al., 1997).

Table 8.5. *Firm size, process performance, process variation, and financial performance.*

| Dependent variable | Constant | Assets (log) | Aggregate process rank | Process variation | Adjusted $R^2$ |
|---|---|---|---|---|---|
| ROA | 0.92 | 0.03 | −0.01* | −0.03** | 0.244 |

*Note*: *Indicates significance at the 10% level.

variation in performance across the 11 individual process performance scores for each bank. The fundamental question addressed in Frei et al. (1999) is which is more important for a bank, to do a few things well and, hence, to do other things not so well, or to provide a reasonably consistent set of service delivery processes to the customer? What ultimately matters, occasional excellence or consistency? To address this question, the model from Table 8.4 was expanded to include process variation, as shown in Table 8.5. As can be seen from these tables, the measure of process variation is also correlated with firm financial performance.

With the demonstrated relation between process performance, process variation, and financial performance, Frei et al. (1999) next tested whether process variation is more important than process performance, with respect to financial performance. To test this, banks were defined to have *good processes* if they had better than average aggregate process performance, and banks were defined to have *consistent processes* if they had lower than average process variation. Then dummy variables were introduced for *good* process performance and *consistent* process performance. Using these dummy variables instead of the continuous measures, the question of which matter more (in terms of financial performance), *continuous* processes or *good* processes, could be addressed. By comparing the coefficients on *good* and *consistent* processes in Table 8.6, it was found that the coefficient on *consistent* is significantly greater than the coefficient on *good*. This analysis reinforced the analytical model presented in Frei et al. (1999) by showing that when analyzing the relation between the process measures and firm performance, there tends to be a stronger financial return for banks with *consistent* processes than for banks with *good* processes. That is, on the margin, consistency may be more important than aggregate performance, but the analysis also clearly demonstrates the positive impact of improving along both

Table 8.6. *The effect of good and consistent processes on financial performance.*

| Dependent variable | Constant | Assets (log) | Dummy variable for aggregate process rank | Dummy variable for process variation | Interaction term for process variables | Adjusted $R^2$ |
|---|---|---|---|---|---|---|
| ROA | 0.73 | 0.01 | 0.15* | 0.28*** | –0.18 | 0.239 |

*Note*: * Indicates significance at the 10% level.
** Indicates significance at the 5% level.
*** Indicates significance at the 1% level.

lines. Considering both the analytical model and the data, it is concluded that process variability is a compelling contributor to overall firm performance. In addition, this is considered strong evidence to support the claim that for firms where customers interact across a bundle of processes, it is imperative not to take a single-process view (along the best-practices theme), but rather these processes need to be considered collectively when undergoing process improvement. This result is consistent with the argument in the service quality literature (Rust, Zahorik, and Keiningham, 1995; Soteriou and Zenios, 1999) that firms that set expectations and consistently meet them have more satisfied customers and are more profitable.

### 5.3 What Drives Process Efficiency?
To address the question of what drives process efficiency, one must first look at the characteristics of the banks with better process performance. From our fieldwork, we hypothesize that banks have better process performance when they have one person or a small group of people dedicated to managing across all of the processes "touched" by the consumer. That is, banks with a sort of "industrial engineering" function that spans the traditional business unit boundaries are, by definition, more likely to have a *process focus*. Smaller banks are more likely to have this person since their operations are typically not as sprawling either geographically or in terms of span of control as the larger institutions. In larger banks, there was typically no such person, which explains some of the lower process performance (Frei, 1996). Recalling Section 4, where we discussed the returns on capital, it was determined that there were significant positive returns on IT labor and that the types of labor offering this return were the system integrators. It is precisely this position, serving the role of the "industrial engineer," that will help create a process focus

in the organization. Thus, we posit that one of the explanatory factors for the positive returns on IT labor is the increased efficiencies that can be gained through a process focus.

From the data, we know that smaller banks tend to have slightly better aggregate process performance and significantly more consistent processes (Frei, 1996). We have already mentioned the existence of the system integrator with a process focus in small banks as a partial explanation for this performance. In addition, small banks have not likely undergone as many mergers or made as many technology upgrades and thus have had a chance to have their processes develop in a coherent, consistent manner.

Beyond the role of a systems integrator or systems architect, another hypothesis for what drives process efficiency lies in the degree of technological sophistication of the organization. By analyzing the correlation of technology functionality with process performance, we would expect that increased functionality would lead to improved process performance. However, just the opposite result is found (Frei, 1996). This counter-intuitive result is due to the fact that functionality was used as an input for each of the process performance models (see Table 8.3 and Frei and Harker, 1999a) and, since a process is more efficient if it consumes fewer inputs, there will be a negative relationship between functionality and process performance. However, there is a competing effect at work, because we also expect that processes that use more technology will have better outputs (e.g., cycle time) as a result. The data show that the net effect of these two competing forces is a significantly negative relationship between technology and process performance (Frei, 1996). Our interpretation of this result is that, on average, banks are not utilizing their technology as effectively as they can, in terms of enhanced value for the customer. This will be further evidenced in the next section, where we show an example of a bank that uses very little of its available technology functionality in its process design.

In summary, it has been shown that the alignment of production processes, similar to labor and capital management, clearly affects firm performance. Specifically, the relationship between a collection of customer service delivery processes and firm performance has been demonstrated. Thus, we conclude that the way in which a firm chooses its production process $p \varepsilon P$, and the way in which it manages the transformation of inputs into effective inputs, will affect firm performance. That is, much of the success of the efficient banks in the sample may not be due to clever strategies, creative human resource practices, or exotic technology. Rather, it is our opinion that it is the basic "blocking and tackling" of aligning the service delivery systems with the chosen strategy of the bank and effectively creating the inputs needed for this bundle of processes that distinguish the high from low achievers. Thus, in our opinion, the "devil" seems truly to be in the "details." The next section describes two case studies of banks in our sample that illustrate this point.

## 6 Aligning Inputs with Strategy

The previous three sections have summarized research that demonstrates the role of alignment (i.e., consistent management practices) in explaining the relative efficiency of retail banks. It has been our experience that the best performing banks are those in which their management practices are aligned with their strategy.[3] Ideally, we would have been able to develop a fully specified version of the model presented in Section 1 to estimate the impact of alignment on overall performance of the bank. However, such a model would require a panel data set in order to generate any results of significance; this work is left for future research as we develop a deeper set of data for the industry. At the present time, our only recourse is to explore this relationship by considering the patterns that emerged through statistical analysis of the cross-sectional data along with the results of the extensive field-based studies. Two case studies are used as representative examples to illustrate how the alignment of management practices occurs and why it matters.

Porter (1980) suggests that there are two generic strategies that can be pursued: differentiation and cost control. From our fieldwork, we have found that banks are either leaning towards a total sales environment where every action is geared toward knowing the customer and determining how to best fulfill his or her needs, or towards the mass-market approach which emphasizes highly standardized practices for customer segments. The first strategy typically involves greater cost but also produces greater revenue than the second. In this section, we will show how the management practices ideally interact for each strategy and then conclude with two case studies that illustrate the effect of this interaction.

### 6.1 Differentiated Strategy

As mentioned above, the differentiated strategy that we found in our fieldwork consisted of an empowered workforce, enabled with the infor-

---

[3] It is interesting to note that we found no dominant strategies in our fieldwork. Thus, it is not a single strategy that affects performance but rather, the way in which a particular strategy is implemented which affects performance.

mation necessary to satisfy the needs of its customers. In terms of labor practices, the implementation of this strategy clearly benefits from the inclusive labor model, which requires training focused on the customer, broad cross-training across job categories, incentives for group performance, and enhanced discretion in terms of interacting with the customer. Not surprisingly, when employees are given greater flexibility to emphasize the customer, there is greater customer satisfaction and higher cross-sell ratios (see Section 3).

How do these labor practices interact with capital and the choice of production processes? To empower employees who have been trained to emphasize the customer's needs, a bank must provide its employees with relationship information on the customer. If the customer has several accounts with the bank, some of which reside on different information systems, the employee needs the ability to take a holistic view of the customer's accounts. No matter how empowered an employee is, without the necessary information technology, he or she will have a difficult time understanding the customer's full relationship with the bank. In addition, in order for the bank to make use of its technology investment, it needs to ensure that the employees are effectively using the available information; this requires a process design that takes advantage of the available labor and technology. However, the process design must also take into account what the customer values, which is typically convenience in terms of time required for the customer to complete the transaction. The best way to allow for customer convenience is to determine the steps that do not add value to the customer, and to perform these steps when the customer is no longer immediately involved in the process.

### 6.2 Cost Containment Strategy

The cost containment strategy that we found in our fieldwork consisted of a specialized workforce focused on operational efficiencies. In terms of labor practices, this strategy clearly benefits from a segmented labor model that requires training focused on the tasks an employee performs, incentives for individual performance, and limited discretion in terms of interacting with the customer. This strategy emphasizes the need to perform repetitive tasks efficiently.

How do these labor practices interact with capital and process designs to enforce the cost containment strategy? When a bank is training the employees for the tasks they will be performing, the employees need technological support for as many of the open-ended tasks as possible. For example, if an employee is required to attempt a cross-sell to a customer after completing the account opening process, the bank cannot rely on the employee's feel for the customer's situation, but rather needs to support the employee with cross-selling prompts that will guide any employee through the process. Not only does this ensure consistent sales processes, but it also allows any employee to serve any customer. By supporting the employees with the necessary technology, banks can limit the amount of training necessary and can avoid the drain on resources that specialization requires.

Under the cost containment approach, banks design their production processes with the efficient use of the employees in mind. This focus on labor efficiency means that there is more than likely the specialization of tasks and thus more hand-offs than in the differentiated model. However, such "Taylorism" also produces greater utilization of the employees. Firms utilizing this approach will require less labor and will have processes that do not emphasize relationship building to the extent of the differentiated strategy. We expect this approach to require less cost, but to produce less revenue as it is the relationship building that typically leads to cross-selling.

We have described the ideal settings in order for banks to implement two of the more popular strategies noted by Porter (1980). Consider now two banks that have chosen a cost and differentiation strategy, respectively. The first bank has attempted to implement the differentiation strategy and has been very successful. We will illustrate the specific design issues and management practices that have led to this success. The second case study is of a bank attempting to implement the cost containment strategy but has fallen short in its implementation across a number of dimensions. We will isolate some of the problems in the bank's implementation and show how these problems ultimately relate to the misalignment of labor, capital, and service delivery processes with the bank's chosen strategy. The relevant relative metrics for each of these banks are described in Table 8.7.

*6.2.1 Bank A.* The indications of success for Bank A are the above average measures of financial performance, customer satisfaction, and cross-sell ratios. The bank utilized an average amount of technology in order to produce these results. The first indication of how the bank went about achieving these results is that it had well above average aggregate process performance. That is, when looking at the bank's collection of customer service delivery processes, Bank A was one of the most efficient banks in terms of producing value for the customer at the encounter level. Even more importantly, the bank achieved this high aggregate process performance by having consistently good practices.

Table 8.7. *Bank performance metrics.*

| Performance dimension | Bank A | Bank B |
|---|---|---|
| IT functionality | Average | Better than average |
| Aggregate process performance | Better than average | Worse than average |
| Process noise | Better than average | Better than average |
| Customer satisfaction | Better than average | Worse than average |
| Financial performance | Better than average | Worse than average |
| Cross-sell ratio | Better than average | Worse than average |

That is, Bank A did not have some great processes and some mediocre ones, but rather had a consistently high level of service.

In order to illustrate how Bank A managed this consistent level of service, we have reproduced the open checking account process map in Figure 8.1. This process is quite representative throughout our sample of the type of "process thinking" that occurs in the banks. Each of the steps in the process is either a square or an oval, which represents that a step was performed manually or was performed with a computer (what we call an on-line step), respectively. Although this bank has an average level of technology functionality available, Bank A has an above average number of on-line steps in its process. That is, the bank is better at using its available functionality than most banks. In addition, by inspecting all 11 of the bank's processes, we note that a consistent level of technology is used throughout each process. Thus, Bank A efficiently used its available technology across all processes.

In addition to Bank A being much better than average at effectively using its information technology, the bank also was very cognizant of how much of the customer's time is required in the process. For example, when opening a checking account (Figure 8.1), the bank can complete several steps after the customer leaves, as they do not require the customer's involvement nor do they add value to the customer. An example of a step in a process that does not add value is sending the check order to the vendor. Every bank needs to do this, but from the perspective of the customer, there was no value added by performing this task in his or her presence (and thus potentially wasting his or her time). For the open checking account process, these non-value-added steps include writing a thank you card, sending the checks and ATM orders to the appropriate vendors, recording the sales credit, and filing documents. To perform these steps while the customer is in the branch does not benefit the

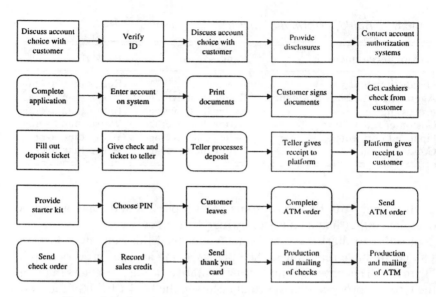

Figure 8.1. Open checking account process for Bank A.

customer. In most banks that we studied, there seemed to be an almost random decision as to when these steps were performed. That is, for most banks, some of these steps were performed before the customer left for one process, but after the customer left for another process. Clearly, if a step provides no benefit or potential benefit to the customer, then it should be performed after the customer leaves the branch. The only argument against this type of process design is that there may be a potential benefit to the customer staying in the branch as long as possible in order to extract more information from him or her and/or to sell the customer an additional product as a result of this greater understanding; however, we found no evidence of such a benefit in the analysis of the cross-sell numbers in our data set. As can be seen in Figure 8.1, Bank A performs all of these non-customer-value-added steps after the customer has left the bank, and thus is cognizant of its customer's time.

In addition to Bank A's efficient use of technology and customer's time, the bank's model of employment practices most closely resembles the inclusive model. That is, the employees were empowered to satisfy their customers (e.g., to waive checking fees), were cross-trained to cover all the needs of the customer, and received training focusing specifically on satisfying their customer's needs (as opposed to focusing on the tasks they needed to perform). It is the combination of the efficient and consistent uses of technology, processes, and labor practices that produced the above average results for this bank.

*6.2.2 Bank B.* In contrast to the situation in Bank A, where the management practices were aligned with the strategy to produce above average results, Bank B is an example of a bank with below average results. All three of the outcomes – financial performance, customer satisfaction, and cross-sell measures – were below average. We again look at the areas of technology, processes, and labor to see if there is an explanation for this poor performance. In terms of technology, we again found a consistent use of technology (a similar proportion of on-line steps in each process), but the proportion of on-line steps was quite small (see Figure 8.2 for an example). This is troublesome considering the fact that this bank actually has more technology available than Bank A (see Table 8.7). Thus, by not making use of its available technology, Bank B is effectively under-utilizing its resources, thus providing a partial explanation for its poor financial performance.

While Bank B has better than average process consistency, it is consistently of a very low quality (see the low aggregate process performance in Table 8.7). While we have found that consistent processes are very important in terms of driving performance, it is still necessary to have an acceptable level of quality in these practices. To illustrate the specific management practices that are causing the bank's poor process performance, consider the way in which Bank B managed the customer's time in the open checking account process, as depicted in Figure 8.2. Four of the five non-value-added steps (described above as writing a thank you card, sending the checks and ATM orders to the appropriate vendors, recording the sales credit, and filing documents) are performed before the customer leaves the bank. By performing these steps in the presence of the customer, the bank is either assuming that it will gain some benefit from keeping the customer in the office longer or, more likely, has not carefully thought out the precise role of the customer in the process. The most common argument for keeping a customer in the office longer is so that the bank has an ability to sell more of its products. However, it is not clear that if customers are waiting for documents to be filed that they will be more likely to buy additional products. However, due to the very low cross-sell ratio of Bank B, we suspect that rather than attempting to add value to the customer through performing these steps in the presence of the customer, the bank has not given much thought to the customer's involvement in the process. This inattention to process design will ensure that regardless of which strategy a

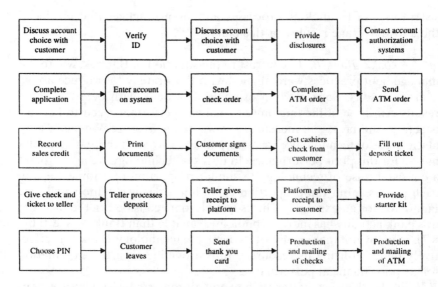

Figure 8.2. Open checking account process for Bank B.

bank is attempting to follow, it will have a difficult time aligning its management practices to match the strategy.

In addition to Bank B's inefficient use of its technology and poor management of customer time, the bank also did not have evidence of a clear approach for creating an effective labor force. That is, there was evidence of both the inclusive as well as segmented model which, in effect, means that neither model was present. Specifically, this bank emphasized a great deal of cross-training even though its employees were given highly specialized tasks and were afforded little empowerment. Thus, the bank did not exhibit a clear alignment of labor practices with its strategy. In addition, while there was a great deal of technology functionality available, it was not of the sales-support type (e.g., cross-sell prompts) that we would expect for a specialized group of workers. After viewing the technology implementation, process design, and human resource practices, it is not surprising that Bank B has poor overall performance.

Therefore, these two banks illustrate the importance and challenge in aligning labor, capital, and production processes with the overall strategy of the institution. These banks were carefully selected to represent common themes that we saw across all of the banks in our sample. That is, we saw strong evidence of the connection between the management of a firm's resources and the strategy the firm was apparently trying to

Table 8.8. *Elements of a carefully aligned strategy.*

Technology
- Consistent use of technology across processes
- Processes effectively use the available IT functionality
- Available functionality was appropriate for the given strategy

Process Design
- Consistent process performance in terms of individual process efficiency
- High level of aggregate process performance
- Non-value-added steps performed after the customer has left

Human Resources
- Consistent employment model
- Appropriate employment model for the given strategy

implement. If these practices were aligned with the strategy, as was the case with Bank A, then the bank's performance was generally very good. If these management practices were not aligned with the strategy, as was the case with Bank B, then there was typically poor performance.

Table 8.8 summarizes the findings from comparing these two representative banks. What is both striking and disturbing is the simplicity of these findings. No one strategy, labor management practice, or technological breakthrough is the cause of X-efficiency. Rather, it is the basic "blocking and tackling" of management. What seems to separate the good and bad performers is simple: *the ability of management to create and execute a set of HRM, IT, and process design practices that are aligned with the overall strategy of the institution.*

### 7 What Makes a Bank Efficient?

This paper, through a review of previous analyses of retail banking efficiency (all using the common data set described in Appendix A), paints a picture of what drives X-efficiency in this industry. The good news (or bad news, depending on your perspective) is that is there is simply no "silver bullet," no one set of management practices, capital investments, and strategies that lead to success. Rather, it appears that the "devil" is truly in the details. The alignment of technology, HRM, and capital investments with an appropriate production "technology," as depicted in Figure 8.3, appears to be the key to efficiency in this industry. To achieve this alignment, banks need to invest in a cadre of "organizational architects" that are capable of integrating these varied pieces together to form a coherent structure. In fact, several leading

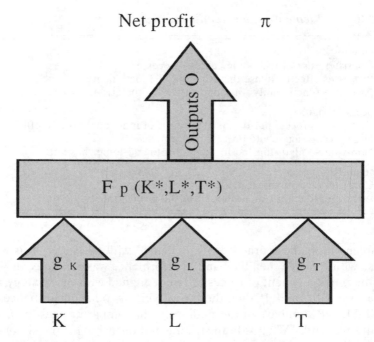

Figure 8.3. Alignment of practices given a strategy.

financial services firms have realized the need for such talents and are investing heavily in senior managers from outside the industry (most notably, from manufacturing enterprises) to drive this alignment of technology, HRM, and strategy.

The challenge, therefore, is not to undertake any one set of practices, but rather to develop senior management talent that is capable of this alignment of practices. Unfortunately, this task is quite complex. As described in Section 1, bank management faces discrete choices of production processes and the input transformation functions. In seems that these choices are far from "convex"; a little more technology, a mix of HRM practices, etc., seem to have little effect. As illustrated by the differences between Banks A and B in the previous section, one must choose very carefully among all of the components depicted in Figure 8.4, or fall behind.

While this alignment may be a problem for those currently in the industry, a longer-term and broader perspective may ask, "So what?" With the increasing deregulation of the financial services industry, those

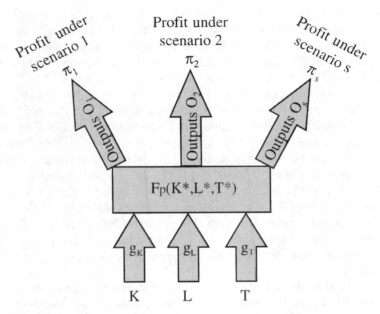

Figure 8.4. Alignment of practices given multiple strategies.

that are capable of successfully aligning business practices will succeed, and others will perish. In the end, the results reported herein have nothing to add to the current policy debates concerning the future of this industry.

The problem with this argument is depicted in Figure 8.4; the rapid pace of evolution in the banking industry – fueled by deregulation, technological innovation, and changing consumer tastes – creates a complex dynamic system. The many and varied future scenarios concerning deregulation and technological innovation lead to the inability to focus on alignment; on which scenario or scenarios should one focus? If one could settle on a given strategy, then, sooner or later, well-managed firms will achieve the alignment depicted in Figure 8.4. However, the future direction of the industry is subject to a tremendous degree of uncertainty. For example, we collected a variety of strategy-related data as part of this study. As described by Hunter (1996a) in the context of human resources, most banks simply could not articulate a consistent and coherent strategy for the future. In numerous visits with the banks that were a part of the study, we would feed back the data they had given to us in order to check their validity. When we would come to the strategy-related questions in the survey, someone in the bank, usually at a senior management level, would state something like, "This is wrong; this CAN'T be our strategy!" We would then tell them who provided these data (always another senior manager), and we would become embroiled in a real-time debate over defining the strategy of the bank!

The tension we experienced in the banks over forming a strategy for the future reflects the tension between investing in the perfection of the alignment of labor, capital, and production processes for today's strategy versus the investment in a portfolio of alternative future strategies. This tension is both quite typical and quite real in the banking industry. Given the inability to control the use of the varied distribution channels (ATMs, branches, etc.), banks are either investing in all channels simultaneously or undertaking fairly radical changes to their service offerings in order to deal with this proliferation of services. Thus, bank managers face a crucial decision as to missing the "correct" strategy for the future versus living with misaligned systems that they know to be inefficient.

Given this uncertainty, the removal of inefficient firms may take quite a while to occur. Furthermore, if we are correct in our assessment that a major cause of X-efficiency in the industry is the misalignment of management practices, and given that X-efficiency is a major cause of inefficiency in banking in general, the necessity for integrated financial services organizations to "hedge their bets" on the future may be a major cause of persistent inefficiency in the banking industry. Clearly, alignment would be simpler and occur more rapidly in a industry made up of many "niche" players, each focusing on a likely future scenario, as shown in Figure 8.5. Such movement to dis-integrate financial services are already under way in most banking organizations when one considers how business units like credit cards and trusts are run as completely separate operations.

Thus, the alignment hypothesis is a crucial link in understanding the potential benefits of industry restructuring. If alignment is as difficult as it appears from the current study, it is possible that increased mergers of dissimilar businesses, as measured by their misalignment of the production processes of the organization, may increase X-efficiency. However, the reverse is possible. The only way to know for sure is to develop, based on the cross-sectional data set described in Appendix A, a panel data set that can be used to assess how organizations are adapting their management practices to align themselves with the future of the industry; this is the goal of our future research.

For now, the results of this research can be summarized with reference

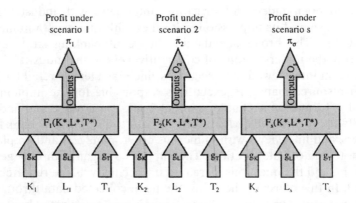

Figure 8.5. Multiple alignments of multiple strategies.

to the wisdom of the ages. For a banker, like an architect, the following advice holds:

Three things are to be looked to in a building:
that it stand on the right spot;
that it be securely founded;
that it be successfully executed.[4]

### Acknowledgments

This research was supported by the Wharton Financial Institutions Center through a grant from the Sloan Foundation. The comments of Tony Santomero, Kathleen (Holmes) McClave, Erik Brynjolfsson, Lorin Hitt, and many others on all or portions of the research reported herein are warmly acknowledged. Of course, all errors and omissions are the responsibility of the authors.

### Appendix A: Structure of the Wharton/Sloan Retail Banking Study

The retail banking study is an interdisciplinary research effort at the Wharton Financial Institutions Center aimed at understanding the drivers of competitiveness in the industry, where competitiveness means not simply firm performance but the relationship between industry trends and the experiences of the retail banking labor force. In the exploratory first phase of a study of the United States retail banking industry during Summer 1993 through Fall 1994, a research team

---

[4] Johann Wolfgang von Goethe, *Elective Affinities* (1808), Book I, Chapter 9.

conducted open-ended and structured interviews with industry informants, and shared its impressions with these informants at a number of
conferences. The broad agenda for the retail banking study entails
furthering the understanding of competitiveness in the industry.

The team interviewed top executives, line managers in retail banking,
human resource managers, executives responsible for the implementation of information technology, retail bank employees, and industry
consultants. The first phase featured site visits to 13 U.S. retail bank headquarters, and interviews with numerous other managers and employees
in remote and off-site locations. The interviews began with very general
questions, and the questions increased in specificity as the research progressed. In this phase of the study, the team collected data through the
use of two waves of structured questionnaires in seven retail banks. The
team's analysis of the data in these questionnaires was then presented
to management teams in six of the seven banks, and used as the basis for
the second phase, a large-sample survey.

The second phase of the study entailed a detailed survey of technology, work practices, organizational strategy, and performance in 135 U.S.
retail banks. The team sought to survey a group of banks that could yield
the broadest coverage of trends in human resources, technology, and
competitiveness in the industry. The survey focused on the largest banks
in the country and was not intended as a random sample of all U.S. banks.
In the end, the approach gained the participation of banks holding over
75% of the total assets in the industry in 1994. The process began by com-
piling a list of the 400 largest bank holding companies (BHCs) in
America at the beginning of 1994. Merger activity, and the fact that a
number of BHCs had no retail banking organization (defined as an entity
that provides financial services to individual consumers), reduced the
possible sample to 335 BHCs. Participation in the study was confidential, but not anonymous, enabling the team to match survey data with
data from publicly available sources.

Participation in the study required substantial time and effort on the
part of organizations. Therefore, commitment to participation was sought
by approaching the 70 largest U.S. BHCs directly, and, in the second half
of 1994, the participation of one retail banking entity from each BHC
was requested. Fifty-seven BHCs agreed to participate. Of these, seven
BHCs engaged the participation of two or more retail banks in the BHC,
giving us a total of 64 participating retail banks. Multiple questionnaires
were delivered to each organization in this sample. Questionnaires
ranged from 10 to 30 pages, and were designed to target the "most
informed respondent" (Huber and Power, 1985) in the bank in a number

of areas, including business strategy, technology, human resource management and operations, and the design of business processes. The team made a telephone help line available to respondents who were unsure of the meaning of particular questions. Questionnaires to four top managers were delivered: the head of the retail bank, the top finance officer, the top marketing officer, and the top manager responsible for technology and information systems. These banks received questionnaires for one manager of a bank telephone center, and for one branch manager and one customer service representative (CSR) in the bank's "head office" branch, defined as the branch closest to the bank's headquarters. In addition, an on-site researcher gathered data about all business process flows in the head-office branch. Identical questionnaires were mailed to five more branch managers; the instructions to the bank were to choose the sample branches so that, if possible, data were received from two rural, two urban, and two suburban branches. Questionnaires were also mailed to CSRs in those branches. In these questionnaires, the CSRs themselves mapped processes associated with home equity loans, checking accounts, certificates of deposit, mutual fund accounts, and small business loans.

In order to facilitate the creation of process maps via the mailed survey, a worksheet was developed for the CSRs to fill out. These worksheets, a sample of which is shown in Frei (1996), list the majority of potential steps required in the process so that the CSR need only indicate the order of the step, the person responsible for its execution, the type of technology involved, and the amount of time the step takes. Adequate space was provided for the addition of steps unique to an institution.

In late 1994, survey questionnaires were mailed to top executives of the 265 next largest BHCs, and followed with a telephone call requesting the participation of one of their retail banking organizations. Sixty-four of these BHCs agreed to participate in the study, and four of these engaged the participation of two or more retail banks in the BHC, so a total of 71 retail banks participated in the mailed survey. For this group of banks, the head of the retail bank was surveyed, and many of the questions directed to the other top managers were consolidated into this survey. Prior interviews had suggested that for banks of this size, the head of retail was able to answer this broader set of questions accurately. For this sample, questionnaires were mailed to one telephone center manager, one branch manager, and one CSR in the head office branch. The telephone help line was also available to respondents in this sample.

All together, the entire survey of retail banking covers 121 BHCs and 135 banks, which together comprise over 75% of the total industry, as measured by asset size. The scope and scale of this survey make it the most comprehensive survey to date on the retail banking industry.

### Appendix B: Analytical Approach for the Study

One way of understanding the goal in the process analysis performed on the data in Appendix A project is to view it as an attempt to use a process view as the basis for understanding how IT and human resources interact to move firms to the boundary of the performance frontier. When estimating the performance of processes, the first consequence to note is that there are usually multiple outputs. These multiple outputs preclude the use of standard statistical regressions involving a single dependent variable. The estimation methods used in the previous analysis and referenced in this paper deal with these multiple outputs by using deterministic frontier estimation. Specifically, Data Envelopment Analysis (DEA) is used to determine relative performance amidst multiple inputs and outputs. Charnes, Cooper, and Rhodes (1978) introduced DEA as a new way to measure efficiency of decision-making units (DMUs). Since then, there have been over 400 articles that have used variations of DEA in analyzing performance (see Seiford, 1990). See Fare, Grosskopf, and Knox Lovell (1994) for an introduction to DEA.

The original DEA method determines the relative efficiency measure for a DMU by maximizing the ratio of weighted outputs to inputs subject to the condition that similar ratios for every DMU not exceed one. The result is a set of efficiency scores between zero and one as well as a set of reference DMUs whose performance is better than the existing DMUs using the same scale. This method has come to be known as the output-oriented method, as its efficiency score is determined by holding inputs constant and assessing to what extent outputs could potentially be improved. The input-oriented DEA is identical to the output-oriented method except that the objective is to minimize the ratio of weighted inputs to outputs subject to the condition that similar ratios for every DMU not go lower than one. The result is a set of efficiency scores greater than or equal to one. In this case, an inefficient DMU has a score determined by the amount that inputs can potentially be decreased without changing the outputs. Many extensions have been made to the oriented methods described above, including multiplier weight flexibility (Dyson and Thanassoulis, 1988), stochastic frontier (Sueyoshi, 1994; Land, Knox Lovell, and Thore, 1993), categorical outputs (Rousseau and Semple, 1993), and non-linear frontier estimation (Sengupta, 1989;

Charnes et al., 1982). A third method was developed by Ali and Seiford (1993) which actually builds the efficient frontier in its solution and determines its relative efficiency score by the distance that a DMU is from its associated hyperplane. Again a single linear program is required for each DMU; rather than optimizing a ratio of inputs and outputs, the objective is to determine the coefficients of the hyperplane that will get closest to the current DMU without moving past any other DMU. The result is a distance of each DMU from its associated hyperplane, with a distance of zero implying that it is on the frontier. Each of the above methods is described in detail in Frei and Harker (1999a).

The limitations of the oriented methods are precisely in their orientation. That is, they apply only in instances when it is reasonable to hold either inputs or outputs constant. The limitation of the hyperplane method is that the distance measure is taken from a DMU to its associated hyperplane even if that hyperplane is not the closest point on the frontier. The method extends the hyperplane method by determining the shortest distance from a DMU to the entire frontier. In addition, the concept of the observable portion of the frontier is introduced which yields efficiency scores based on the distance from the section of the frontier in which the associated scale has actually been realized.

To overcome these limitations, Frei and Harker (1999a) have introduced new DEA-like methods for the calculation of process efficiency. Their methods allow the comparison of both the quality and cost of a process. Thus, a high-quality, high-cost and a low-quality, low-cost process can both be considered efficient using this method. These efficiency metrics can then be studied in relation to the HR and IT practices in the banks to ascertain their relative efficiency. Thus, this frontier estimation technique, along with standard data analysis/statistical methods, provides the analytic backbone for our investigation.

In determining an institution's composite process performance in the studies referenced in this paper, we considered each process as a round of competition between institutions. Thus when one bank performed better than another for a given process, that bank had won one round of head-to-head competition. By viewing process performance across institutions, we used a "tournament" ranking scheme as the basis for evaluation. The tournament is a set of head-to-head competitions between institutions where a head-to-head competition consists of performance across a common process. Two difficulties arise when viewing processes as competitions between banks. First, if two banks have no processes in common, then they are not competing against one another and thus there is "missing data" in the tournament ranking methodology. Fortunately, this situation has appeared in the literature and is easily overcome by using the missing data correction developed by Harker (1987). The second problem, however, is far more complicated and has not been previously addressed in the literature. That is, what happens when one bank is better than another in all rounds of competition? In the existing literature, there is always an assumption that if participants compete against each other, then they each win at least one of the matches. This has in it the assumption that each participant has a positive probability or chance of winning a future match. However, in the situation evaluated in the referenced studies, these scores do not reflect a future probability of winning, but rather represent past performance. Thus, in the existing methods there is no likelihood of one institution "winning" all of the matches, as there always is a positive probability of an institution winning a future match. However, in the retail-banking situation, it is quite likely that one institution will dominate another across all of their common processes and thus this needs to be accommodated. A methodological extension to existing methods was developed to achieve this in Frei and Harker (1999b).

The methodology in Frei and Harker (1999b) allows the generation, for each institution, of a composite process performance score by comparing processes. This composite score determines which institutions have better process performance and allows for analysis to determine what drives this performance. The use of this composite score as the measure of an institution's process performance indicates that the institution is viewed as a collection of processes. The collected data on a representative sample of these processes lead to the assumption that the performance of this sample is representative of the performance of the institution as a whole. The result of this methodology is an ordinal rank of each institution which then allows for the comparison of one institution with another based on relative aggregate process performance.

### References

Ali, A. I. and L. M. Seiford (1993), "The mathematical programming approach to efficiency analysis," in H. O. Fried, C. A. Knox Lovell, and S. S. Schmidt (eds.), *The Measurement of Productive Efficiency* (New York: Oxford University Press).

Arthur, J. (1994), "Effects of human resources system on manufacturing performance and turnover," *Academy of Management Journal 37(3)*, 670–687.

Baily, B. A., C. Kriebel, and T. Mukhopadhyay (1991), "Information technology and business value: an analytical and empirical investigation," University of Texas at Austin, Working Paper (Austin, TX).

Barney, J. (1991), "Firm resources and sustained competitive advantage," *Journal of Management 17*, 99–120.

Beatty, S. E. and B. E. Gup (1989), "A guide to building a customer service orientation," *Journal of Retail Banking 11(2)*, 15–22.

Becker, B. and B. Gerhart (1996), "The impact of human resource management on organizational performance: progress and prospects," *Academy of Management Journal 39*, 779–801.

Benston, G. J., G. A. Hanweck, and D. B. Humphrey (1982), "Scale economies in banking: a restructuring and reassessment," *Journal of Money, Credit and Banking 14*, 435–450.

Berger, A. N., D. Hancock, and D. B. Humphrey (1993), "Bank efficiency derived from the profit function," *Journal of Banking and Finance 17*, 317–348.

Berger, A. N. and D. B. Humphrey (1992), "Measurement and efficiency issues in commercial banking," in Z. Griliches (ed.), *Output Measurement in the Services Sector: National Bureau of Economic Research Studies in Income and Wealth* (Chicago, IL: University of Chicago Press).

Berger, A. N., W. C. Hunter, et al. (1993), "The efficiency of financial institutions: a review and preview of research past, present and future," *Journal of Banking and Finance 17*, 221–250.

Blackwell, D. W., J. A. Brickley, et al. (1994), "Accounting information and internal performance evaluation: Evidence from Texas banks," *Journal of Accounting and Economics 17(3)*, 331–358.

Bohn, R. (1995), "Noise and learning in semiconductor manufacturing," *Management Science 41*, 31–42.

Brynjolfsson, E. (1993), "The productivity paradox of information technology," *Communications of the ACM 35*, 66–67.

Brynjolfsson, E. and L. Hitt (1993), "Is information systems spending productive? New evidence and new results," Working Paper, Coordination Laboratory, Massachusetts Institute of Technology (Cambridge, MA).

Brynjolfsson, E. and L. Hitt (1996), "Paradox lost? Firm-level evidence on the returns to information systems spending," *Management Science 42*, 541–558.

Charnes, A., W. W. Cooper, and E. Rhodes (1978), "Measuring the efficiency of decision making units," *European Journal of Operational Research 2*, 429–444.

Charnes, A., W. W. Cooper, L. Seiford, and J. Stutz (1982), "A multiplicative model for efficiency analysis," *Socio-Economic Planning Sciences 16*, 223–224.

Cutcher-Gershenfeld, J. (1991), "The impact on economic performance of a transformation in workplace relations," *Industrial and Labor Relations Review 44*, 241–260.

Davenport, T. H. and J. E. Short (1990), "The new Industrial Engineering: information technology and business process redesign," *Sloan Management Review 31*, 11–27.

Delaunay, J. C. and J. Gadrey (1992), *Services in Economic Thought: Three Centuries of Debate* (Boston, Kluwer).

Delery, J. and H. Doty (1996), "Modes of theorizing in strategic human resource management: Tests of universalistic, contingency, and configurational performance predictions," *Academy of Management Journal 39*, 802–835.

Donnelly, J., H. James, J. L. Gibson, et al. (1989), "The behaviors of effective bank managers," *Journal of Retail Banking 10(4)*, 29–37.

Dyson, R. G. and E. Thanassoulis (1988), "Reducing weight flexibility in data envelopment analysis," *Journal of the Operational Research Society 39*, 563–576.

Fare, R., S. Grosskopf, and C. A. Knox Lovell (1994), *Production Frontiers* (Cambridge, England: Cambridge University Press).

Frei, F. X. (1996), *The Role of Process Designs in Efficiency Analysis: An Empirical Inves-*

*tigation of the Retail Banking*, unpublished Ph.D. dissertation, the Wharton School, University of Pennsylvania (Philadelphia, PA).

Frei, F. X. and P. T. Harker (1999a), "Projections onto efficient frontiers: theoretical and computational extensions to DEA," *Journal of Productivity Analysis 11:5*, 275–300.

Frei, F. X. and P. T. Harker (1999b), "Measuring aggregate process performance using AHP," *European Journal of Operational Research 116*, 436–442.

Frei, F. X., P. T. Harker, and L. W. Hunter (1994), "Performance in consumer financial services organizations: framework and results from the pilot study," Working Paper, Wharton Financial Institutions Center, the Wharton School, University of Pennsylvania (Philadelphia, PA).

Frei, F. X., R. Kalakota, A. Leone, and L. Marx (1999), "Process variation as a determinant of bank performance: Evidence from the retail banking study," *Management Science 4:9*, 1210–1220.

Fried, H. O., C. A. K. Lovell, et al. (1993), "Evaluating the performance of U.S. credit unions," *Journal of Banking and Finance 17*, 251–266.

Griliches, Z. (1992), *Output Measurement in the Services Sector: National Bureau of Economic Research Studies in Income and Wealth* (Chicago, IL: University of Chicago Press).

Gunn, T. G. (1987), *Manufacturing for Competitive Advantage* (Cambridge, MA: Bollinger).

Hancock, D. (1991), *A Theory of Production for the Financial Firm* (Boston, MA: Kluwer Academic Press).

Harker, P. T. (1987), "Incomplete comparisons in the Analytic Hierarchy Process," *Mathematical Modeling 9*, 837–848.

Hitt, L. and E. Brynjolfsson (1996), "Productivity, business profitability, and consumer surplus: three different measures of information technology value," *MIS Quarterly* (June), 121–142.

Hoch, I. (1962), "Estimation of production function parameters combining time-series and cross-section data," *Econometrica 30*, 34–53.

Huber, G. P. and D. J. Power (1985), "Retrospective reports of strategic-level managers: guidelines for increasing their accuracy," *Strategic Management Journal 6*, 171–180.

Hunter, L. W. (1996a), "When fit doesn't happen: The limits of business strategy as an explanation for variety in human resource management practices," presented at the Academy of Management Annual Meeting, Cincinnati, OH, August 1996.

Hunter, L. W. (1996b), "Lousy jobs: why do organizations choose human resource practices that reinforce the position of the working poor?" presented at the Academy of Management Annual Meeting, Cincinnati, OH, August 1996.

Hunter, L. W. (1997), "Transforming retail banking: Inclusion and segmentation in service work," Working Paper, Wharton Financial Institutions Center, the Wharton School (Philadelphia, PA).

Hunter, L. W. and L. Hitt (1997), "Technology, human resources, and productivity in bank branches," Working Paper, Wharton Financial Institutions Center, the Wharton School (Philadelphia, PA).

Huselid, M. A. (1995), "The impact of human resource management practices on turnover, productivity, and corporate financial performance," *Academy of Management Journal 38*, 635–672.

Huselid, M. A. and Brian E. Becker (1996), "Methodological issues in cross-sectional and panel estimates of the human resource – firm performance link," *Industrial Relations 35*, 400–423.

Ichniowski, C. (1992), "Human resource practices and productive labor-management relations," in D. Lewin, O. S. Mitchell, and P. D. Sherer (eds.), *Research Frontiers in Industrial Relations and Human Resources* (Madison, WI: IRRA).

Ichniowski, C., K. Shaw, and G. Prennushi (1994), "The impact of human resource management on productivity." Working Paper No. 5333, National Bureau of Economic Research (Cambridge, MA).

Lado, A. A. and M. C. Wilson (1994), "Human resource systems and sustained competitive advantage: a competency-based perspective," *Academy of Management Review 19,* 699–727.

Land, K. C., C. A. Knox Lovell, and S. Thore (1993), "Chance-constrained data envelopment analysis," *Managerial and Decision Economics 14,* 541–554.

Leibenstein, H. (1966), "Allocative efficiency versus 'X-inefficiency," *American Economic Review 56,* 392–415.

Leibenstein, H. (1980), "X-efficiency, intrafirm behavior, and growth," in S. Maital and N. Meltz (eds.), *Lagging Productivity Growth* (Cambridge, MA: Bollinger Publishing), 199–220.

Levine, D. I. (1995), *Reinventing the workplace: how business and employees both win* (Washington, DC: Brookings Institution).

Lichtenberg, F. R. (1995), "The output contributions of computer equipment and personnel: a firm-level analysis," *Economics of Innovation and New Technology 3,* 201–217.

Long, R. H. (1988), "High-performance bank culture," *Journal of Retail Banking 10(3),* 13–22.

Loveman, G. W. (1994), "An assessment of the productivity impact of information technologies," in T. J. Allen and M. S. Scott Morton (eds.), *Information Technology and the Corporation of the 1990s: Research Studies* (Cambridge, MA: MIT Press).

MacDuffie, J. P. (1991), "*Beyond mass production: flexible production systems and manufacturing performance in the world auto industry,*" unpublished Ph.D. dissertation, Massachusetts Institute of Technology (Cambridge, MA).

MacDuffie, J. P. (1995), "Human resource bundles and manufacturing performance: organizational logic and flexible production systems in the world auto industry," *Industrial and Labor Relations Review 48(2),* 197–221.

MacDuffie, J. P. and T. A. Kochan (1991), "Does the U.S. underinvest in human resources? Determinants of training in the world auto industry," *Fifty-First Annual Meeting of the Academy of Management,* Miami Beach, FL.

Mefford, R. N. (1986), "Introducing management into the production function," *The Review of Economics and Statistics 68,* 96–104.

Mester, L. (1987), "A multiproduct cost study of savings and loans," *The Journal of Finance 42,* 423–445.

Milgrom, P. and J. Roberts (1990), "The economics of modern manufacturing: technology, strategy, and organization," *American Economic Review 80,* 511–528.

Milgrom, P. and J. Roberts (1995), "Complementarities and fit: strategy, structure, and organizational change in manufacturing," *Journal of Accounting and Economics 19,* 179–208.

Morrison, C. J. and E. R. Berndt (1990), "Assessing the productivity of information technology equipment in the U.S. manufacturing industries," National Bureau of Economic Research, Working Paper 3582.

Morroni, M. (1992), *Production Process and Technical Change* (Cambridge, United Kingdom: Cambridge University Press).

Mundluk, Y. (1961), "Empirical production function free of management bias," *Journal of Farm Economics 43,* 44–56.

National Research Council (1994), *Information Technology in the Service Society* (Washington, DC, National Academy Press).

Nelson, R. and S. Winter (1982), *An Evolutionary Theory of Economic Change* (Cambridge, MA: Harvard University Press).

Osterman, P. (1986), "The impact of computers on the employment of clerks and managers," *Industrial and Labor Relations Review 39*, 175–186.

Osterman, P. (1987), "Choice of employment systems in internal labor markets," *Industrial Relations 26*, 46–67.

Osterman, P. (1994), "How common is workplace transformation and who adopts it?" *Industrial and Labor Relations Review 47(2)*, 173–188.

Parsons, C. K., R. C. Liden, et al. (1991), "Employee response to technologically-driven change: the implementation of office automation in a service organization," *Human Relations 44*, 1331–1356.

Parsons, D., C. C. Gotlieb, and M. Denny (1993), "Productivity and computers in Canadian banking," in Z. Griliches and J. Mairesse (eds.), *Productivity Issues in Services at the Micro Level* (Boston, MA: Kluwer Academic Press).

Pfeffer, J. (1994), *Competitive Advantage Through People* (Boston, MA: Harvard Business School Press).

Pine, B. J. (1993), *Mass Customization: The New Frontier in Business Competition* (Boston, Harvard Business School Press).

Porter, M. E. (1980), *Competitive Strategy: Techniques for Analyzing Industries and Competition* (New York: Free Press).

Prasad, B. and P. T. Harker (1997), "Examining the contribution of information technology toward productivity and profitability in U.S. retail banking," Working Paper, Financial Institutions Center, the Wharton School, University of Pennsylvania (Philadelphia, PA).

Rebello, K. (1996), "We humbly beg you to take this job. Please.," *Business Week* (June).

Reich, R. B. (1984), *The Next American Frontier* (New York: Penguin Books).

Rosenberg, N. (1982), *Inside the Black Box: Technology and Economics* (Cambridge University Press, Cambridge, United Kingdom).

Roth, A. V. and M. van der Velde (1991a), "Customer-perceived quality drives retail banking in the '90s," *Bank Management* (November), 29–35.

Roth, A. V. and M. van der Velde (1991b), "The retail technology," *Bank Management* (December), 14–19.

Roth, A. V. and M. van der Velde (1992), *World Class Banking: Benchmarking the Strategies of Retail Banking Leaders* (Chicago, IL: Center for Banking Excellence, Bank Administration Institute).

Rousseau, J. J. and J. H. Semple (1993), "Categorical outputs in data envelopment analysis," *Management Science 39*, 384–386.

Rust, R. T. and R. Metters, "Mathematical models of service," *European Journal of Operational Research 91*, 427–439.

Rust, R. T., A. J. Zahorik, and T. L. Keiningham (1995), "Return on quality (ROQ): Making service quality financially accountable," *Journal of Marketing 59*, 58–70.

Scazzieri, R. (1993), *A Theory of Production* (Oxford, United Kingdom: Clarenden Press).

Schumpeter, J. A. (1939), *Business Cycles* (New York: McGraw-Hill).

Seiford, L. M. (1990), "A bibliography of Data Envelopment Analysis," Working Paper, Department of IEOR, University of Massachusetts at Amherst (Amherst, MA).

Sellers, B. L. (1992), "The bonus onus: devising a fair plan," *Bankers Monthly 109(5)*, 27–29.

Sengupta, J. K. (1989), "Nonlinear measures of technical efficiency," *Computers & Operations Research 16*, 55–65.

Soteriou, A. and S. A. Zenios (1999), Operations, Quality and Profitability in the Provision of Banking Services, *Management Science 45*, 1221–1238.

Steiner, T. D. and D. B. Teixeira (1990), *Technology in Banking: Creating Value and Destroying Profits* (Homewood, IL: Irwin).

Sueyoshi, T. (1994), "Stochastic frontier production analysis: measuring performance of public telecommunications in 24 OECD countries," *European Journal of Operational Research 74*, 466–478.

Tainio, R., P. J. Korhonen, et al. (1991), "In search of explanations for bank performance – some Finnish data," *Organization Studies 12(3)*, 426–450.

Walton, R. E. (1985), "From control to commitment in the workplace," *Harvard Business Review 63*, 76–84.

Wright, P. M. and G. C. McMahan (1992), "Theoretical perspectives for strategic human resource management," *Journal of Management 18*, 295–320.

Zuboff, S. (1985), "Automate/informate: the two faces of intelligent technology," *Organizational Dynamics* (Fall), 5–18.

# 9

# An Optimisation Framework of the Triad: Service Capabilities, Customer Satisfaction, and Performance

Antreas D. Athanassopoulos[a]

**Abstract**
This chapter focuses on the strategic marketing triad among firm capabilities, service quality, and performance. It is recognised that this relatively new concept about service provision effectiveness offers useful insights regarding the accountability of service quality on firm performance. We discuss critical aspects involving service quality and its interaction with operating efficiency. An optimisation framework regarding the capabilities-service quality-performance triad is then proposed which is based on a two-stage data envelopment analysis model. Empirical results from the theoretical model are drawn from a sample of 60 retail bank branches in Greece. The empirical results succeeded in accounting measurable effects of service quality adequacy on bank branch outcomes.

## 1 Introduction

The introduction of quality in the managerial agenda has progressed gradually from being an organisational function to the more recent and ambitious goal of describing the characteristics of quality-oriented organisations. The "quality revolution" has been promoted within the manufacturing and service industries because management realised that customer retention and market share growth are highly dependent upon the quality of the products/services provided, Deming (1986). Quality has

[a] Athens Laboratory of Business Administration (ALBA), Athinas Avenue & Areos Str. 2A, 166 71 Vouliagmeni, Greece, and London Business School, London, UK. E-mail: athan@bpm.gr.

312

been described as "the single most important force leading to the economic growth of companies in international markets," by Feigenbaum (1982). The increased importance given to quality by managers has been confirmed in the survey by Zeithaml et al. (1990), where service and product quality were ranked as the most important challenges that U.S. business faces. Finally, Chase and Heskett (1995) argue for the need to modify old models and/or to develop new ones in order to accommodate the different character of services. In a special issue of *Management Science* (1995), the editors acknowledged the need for interdisciplinary research on the pursuit of service-tailored modelling.

Diminishing returns from the efforts made to increase quality standards in both products and services are a well-accepted proposition. Quality initiatives are well received in manufacturing organisations, where improved quality usually leads to reduced costs (defect repair and inspection costs). The hypothesis that higher product quality will lead to higher costs (see Porter, 1980) has been defeated by empirical studies on corporate firm performance (see Phillips, 1983). Quality in services, however, has a very strong intangible component that is driven by the interactions between management employees and customers. This is a difficult relationship which acts as a cost driver rather than a cost saver process while the benefits from increased service quality have an imprecise and lagged payoff period. Service provider firms, especially those involved in mass customisation, are seeking to exploit economies of scale in order to minimise costs which create trade-offs with the maximisation of service quality, Anderson et al. (1994).

The main criticism against the justification of quality-related expenditure is its lack of accountability regarding measurable benefits towards business objectives, Rust et al. (1994) and (1995). This statement is representative of previous research studies which sought to establish measurable linkages between service quality and business performance. Buzzell and Gale (1987) provided evidence of a positive association between quality and firm profitability, based, however, on firm data reported into the Profit Impact on Market Strategy (PIMS) databases. The representation of firm performance has taken the form of market share, Anderson et al. (1994); repurchasing intentions, Kordupleski et al. (1993); customer retention, Rust and Zahorik (1993); profitability, Rust et al. (1995); and cost position, Philips et al. (1983). These elements of firm performance, however, cannot be seen as independent entities, and thus the question of definition/selection of firm performance metrics should be emphasised along with the definition of the service quality area of assessment.

The focus on recognition of service quality and performance measurement has promoted their positioning as critical aspects of firms' sustained competitive advantage. This led to the development of a new strategic marketing paradigm based on the triad of capabilities, service quality, and performance (C-SQ-P). Arguably the development of this triad stemmed from the industrial organisation economics prototype of market structure, conduct, and performance (S-C-P), Shaferr (1994). The theoretical underpinnings of the C-SQ-P paradigm are discussed by Bullard et al. (1993) and Roth and Jackson (1995) while it is also recognised to be devoid of empirical insights.

In this research, the banking industry is selected and the C-SQ-P paradigm is used to extend Athanassopoulos' (1997) and (1998a) research, which advocates the need to bridge the arbitration between service performance and quality towards a global view about service provision effectiveness. In a more general context, research on banking productivity attracts significant (see Berger and Humphrey, 1997) and innovative (see Frei and Harker, 1996, and Schaffnit et al., 1997) research effort; see also chapter 1 in this volume. The constructs and measures of the performance of banking institutions find increasing use in the literature as an explanatory variable of classical economic hypotheses. For instance, Berger (1995) uses measures of scale and X-efficiency in order to test the market-structure hypothesis within the banking industry in the USA. Berger et al. (1995) attributed the performance differentials between the alternative distribution systems of the insurance industry to the different levels of service quality between these systems. Faulhaber (1995) proposed an integrated framework for examining the interactions between productivity, risk management, and customer satisfaction at the level of corporate banking. In his empirical results, Faulhaber (1995) found that greater customer satisfaction correlates with greater profitability. However, the basic modelling premise had been that customer satisfaction should be treated in the short run as a characteristic of a bank rather than as a choice the bank makes.

Prior research achievements that seek to open the connection between service quality, efficiency, and profitability can be found in Athanassopoulos (1997), who proposed an effort effectiveness function, where the production and intermediation efficiency of bank branches is linked directly to the dimensions of service quality. In this research, however, service quality was treated as a control variable in order to facilitate the estimation of attainable efficiency targets for individual bank branches. More recently, Soteriou and Zenios (1999) have operationalised the triad capabilities, service quality, and performance within an optimisation framework that resembles the one proposed in this research. Aside from the differences between the two research efforts, the present study and the work by Soteriou and Zenios (1999) opened a research enquiry that seeks to operationalise the service profit chain conceptual framework, Heskett et al. (1994).

The rest of the chapter is organised as follows. The next section contains some critical aspects of service quality and its antecedents on the business process, such as pricing and operating efficiency. The paper will then propose an optimisation framework regarding the capabilities, service quality, and performance triad in service organisations based on a two-phase data envelopment analysis model. Empirical results from the theoretical model are drawn from a sample of 60 retail bank branches in Greece.

## 2 Firm Capabilities, Service Quality, and Performance (C-SQ-P)

Chase and Hayes (1992) have proposed a typology upon which Roth and Jackson (1995) based their C-SQ-P paradigm. This typology recognises technology, people, and processes as the drivers of service quality and performance. These drivers are also encapsulated into four operational capabilities such as technological innovations, human resources development, business process integration, and the achievement of factor productivity, Roth and van der Velde (1989 and 1991). The relative importance of these capabilities, however, is affected by the nature of the service environment concerned. For example, in retail banking institutions with very high customer contact and repeated purchasing processes, the staff has a leading role in the capabilities mix. The positive effect of the employees' capabilities is highly recognised by Schneider (1980) and (1991), who referred to them as the human assets within the service delivery process. Schneider, in a series of contributions (Schneider et al. (1980), Schneider and Bowen (1985 and 1995)), emphasised the importance of employees' perceptions as reliable predictors of service quality provision within retail bank branches. Emphasis on the positive role of the service employee has also been given by Kelley (1993), who advocated employee discretion as a factor that can enhance service quality.

We use four propositions in order to set the scheme of the proposed C-SQ-P framework:

> PROPOSITION 1. *In a retail banking environment, firm capabilities will be given strong human and process orientation*, Schneider et al. (1980) and Kelley (1993).

PROPOSITION 2. *Service quality is considered to be an outcome of the strategic choices made by the firm to invest in human capital and also develop appropriate processes. Our C-SQ-P framework will seek to estimate the best level of SQ that corresponds to given levels of firm capabilities.*

PROPOSITION 3. *Performance is a multidimensional construct and thus it will be assessed by using a multi-input-output representation of the operating process of individual branches. The definition of performance has, thereby, an X-efficiency[1] rationale whereby branches will be considered efficient if for a given bundle of inputs they maximise their bundle of outputs and/or for a given bundle of outputs produced they minimise their bundle of inputs used,* Mahajan (1991) and Berger (1995).

PROPOSITION 4. *The effect of firm capabilities on service quality is assumed to be supportive while there is no predetermined assumption as to whether service quality has positive or negative effect on performance,[2]* Schneider (1991).

Our proposed C-SQ-P framework can be represented mathematically with the Equations (1) and (2).

$$ServiceQuality = F(\text{Capabilities, Size of activity}) \tag{1}$$

$$Performance_{rj} = F(ServiceQuality, \text{Branch size, Cost,} \\ \text{Outputs, Workload}) \tag{2}$$

Service quality and performance are represented in (1) and (2) as multi-attribute value functions. The set of equations in (1) seek to estimate a branch-specific level of service quality which has, however, a latent unobserved nature. Following that, service quality is given a direct role on the estimated branch performance in (2). The set of equations in (1) and (2) suggests, similarly to Rust et al. (1995), that service quality is seen as a resource level which should be capitalised in the form of expanding the value creation of individual branches. The latter, however, can be monitored by a controlled framework where performance gains will not be detrimental to service quality, as is often reported in the literature (see Anderson et al. (1994)).

The multiattribute value expressions about service quality and per-

---

[1] We have adopted the term X-efficiency in order to differentiate the concept of performance from the more traditional economic notions of cost, revenue, and profit efficiencies. In the management science literature, the concept of X-efficiency is often called "technical" efficiency and there are numerous extensions that the interested reader can find discussed in Charnes et al. (1994).

[2] As we shall see later, the operationalisation of the particular proposition requires specific modelling assumptions that predetermine the exact linkage between service quality and performance.

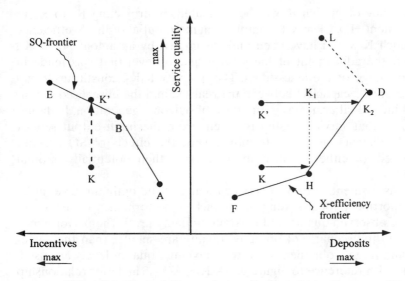

Figure 9.1. Embodying service quality into the performance frontier.

formance, as illustrated in (1) and (2), constitute objective functions to be maximised. Service quality, albeit an input in the assessment of performance, is the direct outcome of the resource commitment of individual branches, as described in (1). The mechanism of this two-stage process of assessing the effectiveness of bank branch operations is graphically illustrated in Figure 9.1.

Figure 9.1 shows a pictorial representation of a two-stage process that is proposed for operationalising the triad C-SQ-P. The left part of Figure 9.1 represents the assessment of service quality, while the right part concerns the subsequent assessment of branch efficiency. Service quality is given a multidimensional representation which is affected by the *incentives* given to the employees of the branches (capabilities). In the second phase, SQ becomes an input in the maximisation of branch output.

The service-quality efficiency of branch K is assessed by projecting it onto the EB segment of the service quality (SQ)-frontier (under variable returns to scale). The efficient position K′ shows the service-quality score of branch K had it fully utilised its corresponding capabilities. The efficient level K′ is used as an input into the assessment of the X-efficiency of branch K as illustrated on the right part of the frontier. The

X-efficiency of branch K will be estimated by projecting $K'$ to $K_2$ of the segment HD. Clearly, the improvement potential of the X-efficiency of branch K would have been underestimated by an amount of $K_1K_2$, without the adjustment of the service quality level that was made in the first stage of the assessment. The quantity $K_1K_2$, constitutes a gap (unrecognised capacity) between the realised and the unrealised potential of individual branches in the form of outcome generation. It should be noted that service quality is absent from the input-output sets of typical efficiency assessment studies. Thus the effects of SQ are not accounted for either at their observed or at their potentially optimal levels.

The assessment of branch service quality at the optimum level gives the opportunity for assessing the branches' performance under a scenario of observed quality and maximum-quality level. The performance targets in the scenario of observed quality are smaller than the corresponding targets obtained when the maximum-quality levels are used. That is, with reference to Figure 9.1, $K'K_1 \leq K'K_2$. The latter relationship draws upon a fundamental assumption of isotonicity that drives DEA under which, for efficient operations, higher levels of resources will lead to higher or the same levels of outputs. Furthermore, the current DEA framework adopted in the study induces strong output disposability assumptions and thus the observation at point L should not be considered an efficient observation.

In summary, the rationale behind the pre-estimation of maximum attainable levels of service quality is twofold. We seek to estimate the maximum attainable level of service quality after controlling for the internal characteristics of each branch. This process will eliminate the inconsistencies that might exist between the perceptions of different management across the branch network. The second stage of the assessment will focus on the X-efficiency of individual branches having controlled for the maximum level of service quality that should be provided in the first place. The latter can be used as the basis of modifying the form of the equation in (2) by (3).

$$Performance_{rj} = F(\text{Max}[ServiceQuality], \text{Branch size},$$
$$\text{Cost, Outputs, Workload}) \qquad (3)$$

The substitution of service quality with the corresponding maximum feasible level will be used as the basis for assessing the impact of service quality on performance (see (2)) and also the opportunity cost arising from not providing appropriate levels of service quality (see (3)). The modelling implications of the C-SQ-P triad can be addressed using decision calculus from the field of mathematical programming.

### 2.1 Mathematical Formulation of C-SQ-P Assessment

Let us consider a set of $j = 1, \ldots, n$ bank branches. This set of branches uses a set of discretionary inputs $D \in \mathfrak{R}_+^m$ with $x_{ij}$ the input i of branch j; has discretionary internal factors $I \in \mathfrak{R}_+^b$ with $t_{ij}$ the internal factor of branch j; has service-quality features $Q \in \mathfrak{R}_+^a$ with $q_{rj}$ the quality factor r of branch j; yields output quantities $O \in \mathfrak{R}_+^s$ with $y_{rj}$ the output r of branch j; and also has non-discretionary outputs $F \in \mathfrak{R}_+^d$ with $z_{pj}$ the output p of branch j. The two-stage efficiency assessment of the bank branches is pursued at the multi-input/output dimensions using the optimisation models in (4) and (5). Equation (4) shows the first stage, service-quality maximisation; Equation (5) shows the second stage, performance assessment.

$$\underset{\phi_r, v_i, \lambda_j}{Max} \sum_r \omega_r \phi_r - \sum_i \omega_i v_i \qquad (5.0)$$

$$\underset{\theta_r, \kappa_j}{Max} \sum_r P_r \theta_{rk} \qquad (4)$$

$$\sum_{j=1}^n \lambda_j x_{ij} - v_i x_{ik} = 0 \qquad i \in D \quad (5.1)$$

$$\sum_{j=1}^n \mu_j t_{ij} \le t_{ik} \quad i \in I$$

$$\sum_{j=1}^n \lambda_j y_{rj} - \phi_r y_{rk} = 0 \qquad r \in O \quad (5.2)$$

$$\sum_{j=1}^n \mu_j q_{rj} = \theta_{rk} q_{rk} \quad r \in Q$$

$$\sum_{j=1}^n \lambda_j z_{pj} = z_{pk} \qquad p \in F \quad (5.3)$$

$$\sum_{j=1}^n \mu_j = 1$$

$$\sum_{j=1}^n \lambda_j \theta_{rj} q_{rj} \le \theta_{rk} q_{rk} \quad r \in Q \quad (5.4)$$

$$\sum_{j=1}^n \lambda_j = 1$$

$$\theta_{rk} \ge 1, \mu_j \ge 0$$

$$\phi_r \ge 1, v_i \le 1, \lambda_j \ge 0$$

The linear programming formulations in (4) and (5) are employed in order to obtain estimates of maximum levels of service quality and its ensuing implications on branch performance. The models (4) and (5) represent an instance of the assessment for branch k under variable returns to scale assumptions. The two formulations in (4) and (5) belong to the family of non-radial efficiency models (see Athanassopoulos (1996)). That is, the optimal solution in (4) and (5) yields improvement rates for individual inputs and outputs according to their representation in the objective functions. An assessed branch k is relatively efficient if $\theta^*_{rk} = 1$ $\forall r \in Q$ in (4) and[3] $\phi^*_{rk} = 1$ $\forall r \in O$ *and* $v^*_{ik} = 1$ $\forall i \in D$ in (5). The objective functions in (4) and (5) contain preferences $P_r$, $\omega_r$, $\omega_i$ over inputs and outputs respectively regarding decision makers' priorities on the rate of improvement of the inputs/outputs. Setting these priorities to unity, the assessment does not imply any preferential treatment over individual inputs/outputs. In the current empirical study, the priority levels were set either at level 1 or 0, simply to indicate the preference over controllable and non-controllable inputs and outputs.

The first stage of the assessment in (4) yields the efficient service-quality level $(\theta^*_{rk}q_{rk}$ $\forall(r, k))$ for each branch. Service quality is given a multidimensional nature and thus the model in (4) has a non-radial nature so that targets will be estimated for all service-quality dimensions. The second phase of the assessment yields performance targets for controllable inputs and outputs of the branches (see (5.1) and (5.2)). Furthermore, the model incorporates control variables (5.3) that correspond to production attributes, such as queue length, whereby they are not treated as controllable factors in the context of the current study. Finally, the equations in (5.4) reflect factors that represent the service-quality attributes included in the model. In the context of the present empirical application, service quality is given an explicit input behaviour in the formulation of model (5.4). Thus, as was illustrated in Figure 9.1, higher levels of service quality should lead to higher levels of output performance.

In the current formulation of (5), the service quality is represented by its maximum feasible levels as estimated by (4). Different results will be obtained, in the case when service quality is represented using observed instead of estimated management perceptions. Furthermore, the optimisation framework in (5) does not include any *a priori* assumptions as to whether service quality should be considered to have a positive, neutral, or negative effect on branch performance. The lack of such assumption is facilitated via the equality constraints in (5.4), where service quality is given a weakly disposable character. This option has been found necessary as there seem to be different theoretical arguments as well as empirical findings regarding the effect of quality on the generation of outputs.

---

[3] The optimal solution of the two models is by no means related and thus branches may be efficient in terms of quality maximisation and inefficient in terms of X-efficiency or *vice versa*.

## 2.2 Opportunity Gap Due to Service-Quality Underprovision

One important by-product of the two-stage assessment in (4) and (5) is the opportunity to obtain measurable effects of the underprovision of service quality on the performance outcomes of individual branches. To derive an estimate from this X-efficiency gap, one will have to re-estimate the outcome targets in (5), using the observed levels of service quality in (5.4) instead of using its maximum obtainable amounts. Let us assume that the rate of improvement of controllable output r of branch k is estimated as $\phi_{rk}^*$. A similar but different in magnitude rate of improvement ($\hat{\phi}_{rk}^*$) will be obtained if the model in (5) is resolved by using the observed levels of service quality instead of the efficient ones. It can be shown that the rate of improvement as obtained from (5) for output r will always be greater than or equal to the corresponding value obtained from the revised solution[4] ($\phi_{rk}^* \geq \hat{\phi}_{rk}^* \geq 1$). The relationship between the two types of efficiency indices holds due to the isotonicity and strong-output disposability assumptions that hold in model (2).

The quality gap in the performance targets of output r of branch k is then estimated by $SQG_{rk} = \phi_{rk}^* \Big/ \hat{\phi}_{rk}^*$, which takes values greater than one in the case of service quality underprovision and one if the service quality has no incremental impact on the branch outcomes. Similarly, the X-efficiency quality gap of input i of branch k can be estimated by $SQG_{ik} = v_{ik}^* \Big/ \hat{v}_{ik}^*$, where ($\hat{v}_{ik}^*$), and ($v_{ik}^*$) give the rate of improvement for input i of branch k, when the corresponding observed and efficient levels of service quality are used in the solution of model (5). It must be noted that the rates of improvement for input i as obtained from the two alternative versions of model (5), ($\hat{v}_{ik}^*$), and ($v_{ik}^*$) do not have a predetermined relationship. This is due to the fact that the increased level of service quality in (5.4) may imply that its achievement will incur incremental operating costs for individual branches. The latter is a very important observation which adds further complexity to the role and demanding nature of service quality and customer satisfaction and their effects on the cost elements of branch operations.

---

[4] Under the assumption that we keep unchanged the priorities in the objective function of (4).

### 3  Empirical Results

The empirical results of the paper were derived from a set of 60 bank branches that operate in the city of Athens, which is the capital of Greece. Information was drawn both from the quantitative databases of the bank and the responses to a detailed questionnaire by branch management. The representation of the judgmental variables was obtained from groups of questions that were included in the survey. The quantification of individual variables was pursued by aggregating the responses from particular groups of questions. Details regarding the construction of the qualitative variables are included in the appendix.

The representation of service quality constitutes a key element of the modelling framework. The service marketing literature discusses extensively the advantages and disadvantages of alternative theoretical constructs that capture the dimensions of service quality. In this study, we adopt the Lehtinen and Lehtinen (1991) framework where service quality is considered along with *physical, corporate,* and *interactive* quality. The adequacy of the three-dimensional construct has been confirmed in previous empirical research by Oakland (1986) and Athanassopoulos (1998b). The empirical assessment of service-quality dimensions was derived from using the branch managers' responses on a series of service-related questions (see the appendix). The decision to incorporate these responses to single-dimension variables by averaging their response along with the three dimensions was verified by means of assessing the internal validity and structure of the responses.

The score on physical quality is based on the average score from three question-items (Cronbach's alpha score 0.85 and the first factor captured 72% of the responses' variation). The score on interactive quality is based on seven question-items (Cronbach's alpha score 0.90 and the first factor captured 69% of the responses' variation). The score on corporate quality is based on nine question-items (Cronbach's validity score 0.88 and the first factor captured 60% of the responses' variation). Finally, the variable concerning the managers' motivation also has a composite nature with six questions (Cronbach's alpha score 0.82 and the first factor captured 59% of the responses' variation). The decision for a single factor representative from each question was further verified by the significant chi-squared tests that were obtained from the maximum likelihood method used to produce the factor analysis results.

Having described the conceptual basis of assessing the performance of bank branches, we propose an operational framework summarised in Table 9.1.

Table 9.1. *Optimal levels of service quality.*

| Input-output (no. of questions*) | | Branch (min) level | | Branch (average) level | | Branch (max) level | |
|---|---|---|---|---|---|---|---|
| | | Observed | Target | Observed | Target | Observed | Target |
| Management motivation | (8) | 19 | 19 | 31 | 30 | 40 | 40 |
| Employee flexibility | (2) | 0 | 0 | 4 | 2 | 11 | 11 |
| Employee motivation | (2) | 0 | 0 | 5 | 4 | 14 | 9 |
| Manager's experience | (1) | 10 | 10 | 23 | 21 | 37 | 25 |
| % of employees with university degree | | 6 | 4 | 30 | 20 | 62 | 45 |
| Number of employees | | 4 | 4 | 24 | 23 | 190 | 190 |
| Corporate quality | (9) | 20 | 32 | 39 | 42 | 43 | 45 |
| Interactive quality | (7) | 18 | 23 | 34 | 39 | 42 | 43 |
| Physical quality | (3) | 6 | 11 | 13 | 16 | 18 | 18 |

*Note*: * In parentheses, we note the number of question items included in each dimension.

Bank branch performance is pursued in two phases as shown in Figure 9.2. In the first stage, we seek to find, at the branch level, the maximum obtainable level of service quality given the branch's operating profile. The inputs and outputs of this stage have a highly judgmental character as they are derived from survey responses. In the second phase we seek to assess the X-efficiency having controlled for the maximum service-quality level of the individual branches.

- *Service-quality assessment*
  This part of the assessment is pursued on the basis of the branch managers' perceived levels of branch capabilities and service-quality achievements. On the input side, we use a bundle of branch attributes that encapsulate their internal capabilities (the question-items included on each capability attribute are explained in the appendix). The number of employees is used as a control variable that accounts for the effects of branch size on the quality outcomes. On the output side, we include subjective scores regarding the scores of physical, corporate, and inter-active quality at the branch level. These three outcomes are sought to be maximised (under variable returns to scale) using the model in (3).
- *Performance assessment*
  In the second phase, branch performance is assessed having controlled

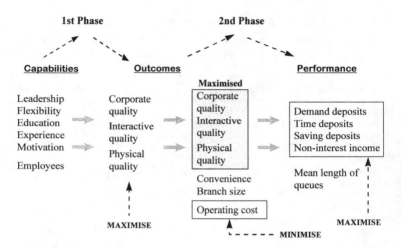

Figure 9.2. Netput framework of the operations of bank branches.

for the maximum levels of service quality. On the input side, we include as latent variables the target levels of the three service-quality dimensions obtained from the first stage of the assessment. The remaining inputs constitute variables regarding the convenience of individual branches, the branch size, and the branches' operating costs. The input-output construct draws upon the definitions of intermediation efficiency being suitably adjusted for the purpose of this study, Berger et al. (1995). We use as outputs the non-interest income, time deposit accounts, savings deposit accounts, and current deposit accounts. We have adopted the Doukas and Switzer (1991) structure of intermediation efficiency, whereas on the input side we only include operating costs and the physical size of bank branches. Note that the sales of loans at the branch level have been excluded as the individual branches have limited control over these outputs, and furthermore there is very strong spatial variation as to which branches have a demand for selling loans.[5]

The proposed input-output set also includes control variables,[6] in order to encapsulate the effects of service quality and the volume of workload

---

[5] This type of analysis would be appropriate if we had information concerning the market conditions in the surrounding area of each branch. As a consequence, in the operating expenditure input variable, the costs associated with personnel managing the loans function were excluded.

[6] Recall here that the optimisation model about performance measurement does not adjust the observed quantity levels of the control variables. Therefore, the mean queue length is not treated, in the present formulation, as a factor from which we seek to gain any reductions.

on the assessment of the branches' performance. The volume of work-load is represented via the mean queue length in front of the tellers of each bank branch. This variable is also used to capture the volume of work done by individual branches which is, in effect, an indication of the effort that individual branches need to produce in order to satisfy their customers. The variable also carries surrogate information on the location and surrounding characteristics of individual branches. For example, sites in the city centre attract a higher number of customer transactions, which consume employee effort in the provision of adequate levels of service quality. Carmon et al. (1995) showed that consumers' final dis-satisfaction from waiting for service is highly correlated with their global retrospective (dis)satisfaction judgments. Bank branch performance is accomplished using model (4), where controllable factors were operat-ing costs (minimised), three types of deposits, and non-interest income (maximised). The rationale can be stated as follows: Given the level of maximum service quality and given the average queue lengths of each branch, assess each branch's X-efficiency. In any case, it is worth men-tioning that the queue levels should be treated as a controllable variable provided that there is adequate information for assessing the particular performance dimension of the branch. That is, the minimisation of the queue levels would require extra resources (e.g. tellers and ATMs) and also different ways of organising branch activities.

### 3.1 Maximising Branch-Specific Service Quality
As mentioned earlier, the combined assessment of service quality and X-efficiency in the provision of financial services is defined via two inter-connected steps. The identification of the maximum level of service-quality provision, given the profile of the branch, is the first stage of this assessment, and a summary of these results is given in Figure 9.3.

The box-plot in Figure 9.3 summarises the distribution of the rate of improvement necessary for each dimension of service quality in order to attain optimal levels. These improvements were obtained from relative comparisons between branches with similar resource profiles in order to identify best practices in the provision of service quality. The analysis has shown that most branches are deficient on their corporate quality mix. This observation should send important messages to the bank's senior management. Improvements have also been identified for the interactive and physical quality components which can be controlled by the man-agement of individual branches. The degree of controllability associated with each service-quality dimension is worth noting. Undoubtedly, cor-porate quality is outside of the control of individual branch managers,

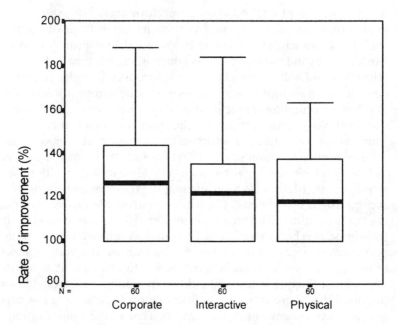

Figure 9.3. Box-plot of the rate of improvement of the three quality components.

and physical quality requires considerable time for its adjustment, while interactive quality is mainly controlled by individual branches. The degree of controllability sends clear messages as to which service-quality dimensions need to be prioritised. This option can be accommodated by the optimisation tool in (3) with appropriate priorities in the objective function of the model.

Service-quality target assessment is elaborated further in Table 9.1, where we list the input-output profile of three extreme cases.

The input-output mix of the branches listed in Table 9.1 does not relate to any actually observed branch in the study. The three cases correspond to the minimum, average, and maximum observed level of each input/output and their corresponding level of improvement. The first six rows in Table 9.1 correspond to input factors to the assessment which were not given any priority in improving their levels in the objective function of (4). The reduction that is proposed for some of these inputs, therefore, corresponds to potential (slack) improvements that identify areas where particular branches are over-resourced. Without losing track of the main objective of the assessment, which is clearly the maximum level of service quality, the model can be used to spot candidates for resource reallocation in terms of input resources used. For example, the targets for the branch with the highest score of employee motivation (reduction from 14 to 9) indicate that the branch could generate similar output levels with less than the observed employee motivation. For the bank's management, the policy implication is that the bank could transfer "less motivated" staff to this branch and vice versa such that the bank will improve the long-term motivation of the entire branch network. The latter, however, is not straightforward since the motivation of a team of employees is a complicated issue affected by both individual and group dynamics. Furthermore, the slack targets regarding management experience have shown that the very high levels of experience may be taken as an ageing profile of branches' management. The proposed reduction of managers' maximum experience from 37 to 25 years is an indicator of the need to inject more motivated managers in the network of branches.

On the service-quality side, the estimation of targets reveals the extent to which service quality can improve within individual branches without altering their capabilities in terms of resources provided. The assumption of variable returns to scale has prevented the model from yielding targets that exceed the maximum feasible score for each question. Thus, only moderate targets were assessed for the branches with high observed service-quality values. This is in accordance with the theoretical conception of the model and previous research work which advocates the presence of decreasing marginal returns in terms of service quality when the level of resources committed exceeds certain levels.

### 3.2 Output Targets with the Maximum Level of Service Quality

Having estimated the efficient levels of service quality for individual branches, the next step is to use these estimates to derive output augmentation targets. This was performed using the formulation in (5), the results of which are summarised in the box-plot shown in Figure 9.4.

The results in Figure 9.4 yield information about the rate of improvement of the inputs-outputs in the formulation of model (4). Therefore, the rate of output improvement takes values greater than or equal to 100%, while the opposite holds for the non-interest costs of the branches. The median of the efficiency components takes high values, while the demand deposits show the greatest variability with some branches having an expected range of improvement that exceeds 250%. This is a

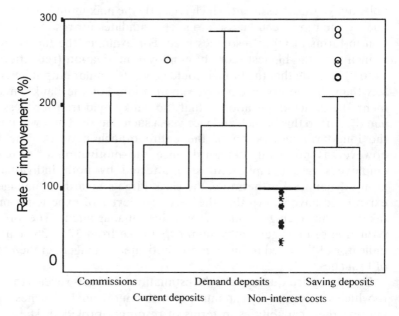

Figure 9.4. Box-plot of the rates of improvement of banking inputs-outputs.

case that indicates that bank branches do specialise. Since we do not have information concerning the profile of the market in which the branches operate, the targets constitute a reflection of the diversity that branches exhibit on their specialisation towards banking products. The specialisation is not always a result of rational choices since there are factors of convenience and culture that may affect the performance profile of each branch.

The statistics for the non-interest costs have shown relatively high values of efficiency with only a small fraction of extreme cases (represented by an "*" in Figure 9.3) with reduction rates. The overall picture drawn from the results in Figure 9.3 is that the targets are directed primarily towards the augmentation of outputs and not to the reduction of inputs. As was mentioned in the formulation of the optimisation models, alternative target scenarios can be implemented, and explicit preferences towards the reduction of inputs can be accommodated. The results concerning the X-efficiency assessment are further elaborated in Table 9.2.

Table 9.2. *X-efficiency targets (in thousands or Drachmas) having controlled for maximum service quality.*

| Input-output | Branch (min) level | | Branch (average) level | | Branch (max) level | |
|---|---|---|---|---|---|---|
| | Observed | Target | Observed | Target | Observed | Target |
| Saving deposits | 160,300 | 160,300 | 2,987,510 | 4,009,238 | 8,412,000 | 8,412,000 |
| Demand deposits | 38,980 | 38,980 | 1,034,434 | 1,448,207 | 3,880,000 | 3,880,000 |
| Time deposits | 400,000 | 696,007 | 824,387 | 1,030,484 | 7,808,000 | 7,808,000 |
| Commissions | 17,240 | 35,212 | 214,981 | 277,325 | 4,987,000 | 4,987,000 |
| Non-interest costs | 12,970 | 12,970 | 168,389 | 153,234 | 835,000 | 835,000 |
| +Branch size | 80 | | 355 | | 3,500 | |
| +Convenience | 3 | | 6 | | 12 | |
| +Mean queue length | 1 | | 4 | | 17 | |
| Corporate quality | 32 | | 42 | | 45 | |
| Interactive quality | 23 | | 39 | | 42 | |
| Physical quality | 11 | | 16 | | 18 | |

*Note*: + Non-controllable input/output factors.

The input-output mix of the examples in Table 9.2 does not relate to any directly observed branch of the study. The three cases correspond to the minimum, average, and maximum observed level of each input/output and their corresponding efficient targets. The first five rows correspond to the four outputs and one input that were given controllable nature in the assessment of the X-efficiency of the branches. The level of the remaining inputs such as the maximum service quality, the branch size, and the mean queue length is also listed in the remaining rows of Table 9.2. The information listed in Table 9.2 shows how diverse the profiles of the branches are in terms of their size. For those branches with large operating scales, the assessment did not provide any substantial targets for improvement in either the output or the cost side. The latter is a result of the variable returns to scale assumption that was adopted in the particular model. That is, large-scale bank branches tended to be self-evaluating branches and thus were rated as efficient in the absence of other, more efficient comparators. Furthermore, performance variations were exhibited among the medium- and small-sized branches while larger branches exhibited a more uniform performance profile.

The X-efficiency targets can be qualified further by assessing the extent to which the lack of service quality creates opportunity costs for individual branches – that is, by identifying the extent to which the

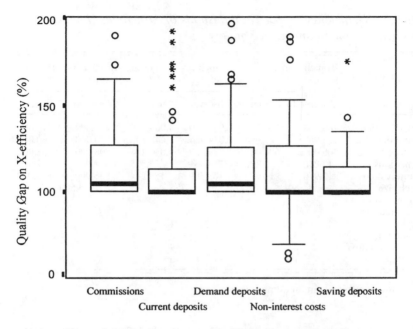

Figure 9.5. Quality-gap on the X-efficiency of branches.

adjusted levels of service quality lead to substantially different targets for the branch outcomes. Following the methodological tools explained in the previous section (the SQG formulae), we have estimated the quality-gap rate of improvement for each controllable input-output of the study, which is summarised in the box-plots of Figure 9.5.

The results concerning the quality-gap on the X-efficiency targets give evidence that the service quality under-utilisation creates considerable opportunity costs for individual branches. The quality gap is defined as the ratio between the rate of improvement of individual inputs/outputs using the optimal and the observed level of service quality, respectively. For the four bank outputs, this ratio takes values greater than or equal to 100% since the optimal level of service quality is higher than or equal to its corresponding observed level. Commissions and demand deposits seem to be the outputs most affected by the under-provision of service quality by some branches since the corresponding quality gap on the particular outputs has taken the highest values. These two branch outputs belong to the non-traditional products of the bank portfolio with considerably higher profitability. The message for branch management is that the provision of services of maximum quality has profound positive implications on product innovation success.

The room for output improvement as indicated by the efficiency index $\hat{\phi}^*$ decreases by half when the actual quality levels are used instead of the theoretical ones. Thus, the relative efficiency of the branches looks relatively higher when we look at their observed quality levels, and this provides some evidence that quality excellence should be rewarded by productivity returns. On the other hand, branches failing to excel in quality levels should not be expected to increase their productivity in any significant way. The evidence obtained from the analysis supports the view about the complementary and non-competing relationship between service quality and branch performance.

In the case of non-interest costs, however, the corresponding quality-gap ratio takes values lesser or greater than 100%. This is due to the fact that the non-interest costs are treated as a controllable input factor which is sought to be minimised. Thus, quality-gap magnitudes on non-interest costs lower than 100% imply that the estimated rate of improvement using the observed level of service quality is lower than the rate obtained using the optimal level of service quality (i.e. $v^*_{\cos t} < \hat{v}^*_{\cos t}$). This case shows that the particular branch will incur incremental costs in order to retain the optimal levels of service quality which in turn leads to higher outputs. Thus, the quality gap, in terms of outcome generation, can be sustained only if the branch sacrifices some of its potential to reduce costs.

### 4 Conclusions

The main premise of this chapter has been to propose a modelling framework that will facilitate the integration between the internal characteristics of service-providing units, the provision of service quality, and the assessment of efficiency. The chapter has proposed a two-stage framework in which service quality is sought to be maximised in the first stage and then in the second stage the outcomes and costs of individual branches are sought to be optimised taking into account the service-quality standards. The assessment of X-efficiency, including observed and optimal levels of service quality, has enabled opportunity-cost measurement. That is, sub-optimal levels of service quality bring an extra component into the quality-gap literature.

The synergy between service quality and the various forms of operating efficiency at the branch level lies within the general framework of investigation of the potential effects of service quality upon the firms' performance. The advances in the area of performance measurement and also the assessment of service quality at the branch level create a unique opportunity for the development of operational models that will accommodate the interactions between service quality and efficiency. This development has profound marketing management implications since the typical conflicts between marketing strategies for higher service quality and cost saving strategies for reducing operating costs will be brought together in order to explore their implications in response to the need to generate maximum outcomes.

The proposed research framework can be extended into a number of alternate directions. The empirical application concerning the case of financial services should be enhanced by considering the synergy between service quality and alternate characteristics of bank branch performance. These characteristics include: marketing efficiency, which includes interactions with the market conditions of each branch; transaction efficiency, which focuses on the transacting mission of the branch; and finally, process efficiency, which focuses on individual functions undertaken at the branch level and their unique interactions with service quality at the branch level.

### Appendix

The attributes used to represent branch capabilities and service-quality dimensions were derived from branch managers' responses to a survey. The survey instrument was based on questions regarding management's perceptions of the services provided to the managers. Their responses were mapped onto a five-degree Likert scale responding to questions such as, "How do you perceive the level of . . . service provided to your customers?" Similar questions were also included regarding the internal characteristics profiles of each branch (e.g., "How do you perceive the internal communications between the employees of your branch?").

> *Corporate* quality: {Product variety, new products, product flexibility to customer needs, product uniqueness, size of branch network, collaboration with other banks, bank's prestige, promotion strategy, discretion offered}
> *Physical* quality: {Telephone transactions, hours of operation, presence of ATM machine}
> *Interactive* quality: {Lack of bureaucracy, personnel courtesy, personnel relation to customers, provision of financial advice, error-free transactions, response on requests, service time}
> *Convenience*: {Distance from home, distance from work, location on central place}
> *Management's working experience* in financial services measured in years

*Management's motivation*: {Type of job, salary, relationship with upper management, relationships with employees, responsibilities, workload}
*Employees' motivation* in the branch: {Degree of horizontal communication among employees, perceived staff motivation}
*Branch flexibility:* {Extent to which management roles change within the branch, in order to adapt to varying levels of demand for services, supervision, and guidance regarding the provision of solutions to uncommon problems}
*Percentage of employees with higher education degree*
*Mean queue length per teller machine.* This variable's estimation was based on a sequential measurement of the queue length in individual branches. The assessment was pursued in a series of measurements that were realised systematically at different times and days.

## References

Anderson, E. W., C. Fornell, and D. R. Lehman (1994), Customer Satisfaction, Market Share, and Profitability: Findings from Sweden, *Journal of Marketing*, Vol. 58 (July), 53–66.

Athanassopoulos, A. D. (1996), Assessing comparative spatial disadvantage of regions in the European Union using non-radial data envelopment analysis models, *European Journal of Operational Research*, Vol. 94, 439–452.

Athanassopoulos, A. D. (1997), Embodying service quality into operating efficiency for assessing the effort effectiveness in the provision of financial services, *European Journal of Operational Research*, Vol. 98, 300–313.

Athanassopoulos, A. D. (1997), Another look into the agenda of customer satisfaction: focusing on service providers' own and perceived viewpoints, *International Journal of Bank Marketing*, Vol. 15, No. 7, 264–279.

Athanassopoulos, A. D. (1998), Multivariate and frontier analysis for assessing the market and cost efficiency of large scale bank branch networks, *Journal of Money and Credit Banking*, Vol. 30, No. 2 (May), 30–51.

Berger, A. (1995), The profit-structure relationship in banking – Tests of market-power and efficient structure hypothesis, *Journal of Money, Credit and Banking*, Vol. 27, No. 2, 404–431.

Berger, A., J. David, and M. Weiss (1995), The coexistence of multiple distribution systems for financial services: the case of property-liability insurance, Wharton Financial Institutions Research Center, Working paper.

Berger, A. and D. Humphrey (1997), Efficiency and financial institutions: International survey and directions for future research, *European Journal of Operational Research*, Vol. 30, No. 2, 1–25.

Bullard, W., J. Cronin, and D. Shemwell (1993), The effect of strategic consumer service levels on corporate performance, in *Service superiority: the design and delivery of effective service operations*, R. Johnston and N. Slack (eds.), Warwick, UK.

Carmon, Z., G. Shanthikumar, and T. Carmon (1995), A physiological perspective on service segmentation models: The significance of accounting for consumers' perceptions of waiting and service, *Management Science*, Vol. 41, 1806–1815.

Chase, R. and R. Hayes (1992), Beefing up operations in service firms, *Sloan Management Review*, 15–26.

Chase, R. and J. Heskett (1995), Introduction to the focused issue on service management, *Management Science*, Vol. 41, No. 11, 1717–1719.

Deming, E. (1986), *Out of the Crisis*, Boston: MIT Center for Advanced Engineering Study.

Doukas J. and L. Switzer (1991), Economies of scale and scope in Canadian branch banking, *Journal of International Financial Markets Institutions and Money*, 1, 61–84.

Faulhaber, G. R. (1995), Banking markets: Productivity, Risk and Customer Satisfaction, Wharton Financial Institutions Center, No. 95–14.

Feigenbaum, A. V. (1982), Quality and business growth today, *Quality Progress*, Vol. 15(11), 22–25.

Frei, F. and P. Harker (1996), Measuring the efficiency of service delivery processes: With application to Retail Banking, Wharton Financial Institutions Center, No. 96–31.

Heskett, J., T. Jones, G. Loveman, W. Sasser, and L. Schlesinger (1994), Putting the service-profit chain to work, *Harvard Business Review*, 164–174.

Kelley, S. (1993), Discretion and the service employee, *Journal of Retailing*, 69, 104–125.

Kordupleski, R., R. Rust, and A. Zahorik (1993), Why improving quality doesn't improve quality, *California Management Review*, 35, 82–95.

Lehtinen, U. and J. R. Lehtinen (1991), Two Approaches to Service Quality Dimensions, *The Service Industries Journal*, Vol. 11, No. 3 (July), 287–303.

Mahajan, J. (1991), A data envelopment analysis model for assessing the relative efficiency of the selling function, *European Journal of Operational Research*, 53(2), 189–205.

Oakland, J. (1986), Systematic quality management in banking, *The Service Industries Journal*, Vol. 6(2), 193–204.

Philiphs, L., D. Chang, and R. Buzzell (1983), Product quality, cost position and business performance: a test and some key hypotheses, *Journal of Marketing*, 47, 26–43.

Porter, M. (1980), *Competitive Strategy*, New York: Free Press.

Roth, A. and W. Jackson (1995), Strategic determinants of service quality and performance: Evidence from the banking industry, *Management Science*, Vol. 41(11), 1720–1733.

Roth, A. and M. Van der Velde (1989), Investing in retail delivery systems technology, *Journal of Retail Banking*, 11, 2, 23–34.

Roth, A. and M. van der Velde (1991), Operations as marketing: a competitive service strategy, *Journal of Operations Management*, 10, 3, 303–328.

Rust, R. and A. Zahorik (1993), Customer satisfaction, customer retention and market share, *Journal of Retailing*, 69, 193–215.

Rust, R., A. Zahorik, and T. Keiningham (1994), *Return on quality: Measuring the financial impact of your company's quest for quality*, Cambridge: Probus Publishing.

Rust, R., A. Zahorik, and T. Keiningham (1995), Return on quality (ROQ): Making service quality financially accountable, *Journal of Marketing*, Vol. 59, 58–70.

Schaffnit, C., D. Rosen, and J. Paradi (1997), Best practice analysis of bank branches: an application of DEA in a large Canadian bank, *European Journal of Operational Research*, Vol. 98(2), 269–289.

Schneider, B. (1991), Service quality and profits: can you have your cake and eat it, too?, *Human Resource Planning*, 14, 2, 151–157.

Schneider, B. and D. Bowen (1985), Employee and customer perceptions of service in banks: replication and extension, *Journal of Applied Psychology*, 70, 423–433.

Schneider, B. and D. Bowen (1993), The service organisation: Human resources management is crucial, *Organisational Dynamics*, Spring, 39–52.

Schneider, B. and D. Bowen (1995), *Winning the Service Game*, Boston: Harvard Business School Press.

Schneider, B., J. Parkington, and V. Buxton (1980), Employee and customer perceptions of service in banks, *Administrative Science Quarterly*, 25, 252–267.

Soteriou, A. and S. Zenios (1999), Efficiency, Profitability and Quality in the Provision of Banking Services, *Management Science*, (in print).

Zeithaml, V., A. Parasuraman, and L. Berry (1990), *Delivering quality service*, New York: Free Press.

# 10

## Disentangling Within- and Between-Country Efficiency Differences of Bank Branches[a]

Antreas D. Athanassopoulos[b], Andreas C. Soteriou[c], Stavros A. Zenios[d]

### Abstract

In this chapter, we propose a framework to assess the efficiency of bank branch networks operating in different financial environments. The framework can be used to disentangle within country from between-country performance differences. The framework is *constructive* in that it identifies operational aspects responsible for superior performance and suggests guidelines for branch improvement. We report results from three bank branch networks in the UK, Greece, and Cyprus, and demonstrate how branch networks can benefit from such international comparisons.

## 1 Introduction

The assessment of the performance of financial institutions has been given unprecedented publicity over the last years, for reasons related to

[a] The authors would like to thank the two anonymous reviewers for their helpful comments, the Center of Banking and Financial Institution, University of Cyprus, for partially supporting this research, and Emmy Gabriel for research assistance. The authors are also grateful to the banks from the UK, Greece, and Cyprus, which provided the data necessary for this study.

[b] Athens Laboratory of Business Administration (ALBA), Athinas Ave. 2A, 166 71 Vouliagmeni, Greece, and London Business School, London, UK.

[c] Department of Public and Business Administration, University of Cyprus, Kallipoleos 75, P.O. Box 537, CY 1678, Nicosia, Cyprus.

[d] Department of Public and Business Administration, University of Cyprus, Kallipoleos 75, P.O. Box 537, CY 1678, Nicosia, Cyprus, and senior fellow, the Wharton Financial Institutions Center, University of Pennsylvania, USA. Email: zenioss@ucy.ac.cy.

stringent market conditions, competitive pressures, the emergence of substitute channels of distribution, consumer demand, and technological progress. Bank management is under constant pressure to improve the competitiveness of its operations, which includes issues of financing, product development, innovation, marketing, and human resource management. Recently, the redefinition of distribution channels and service provision, a role historically played by bank branch networks, has resulted in new management challenges for large-scale networks.

The proliferation and commercialization of new technologies provided additional management challenges and brought up serious questions regarding the role of branch networks as an aid to banks' strategies. These issues are further complicated when examining branch networks operating in different financial environments, at different levels of development. In the developed economy of the UK, for example, the impact of new technologies led to a reduction in the number of bank branches by 35%, in the period 1981 to 1996. During the same time period, the number of bank branches in Greece increased by 48%, as a result of the deregulation and growth of the financial services industry.

Irrespective of the context of assessment, bank branches are the front line of the corporate bank servicing existing customers and selling new products. Thus, due to the universal role of banking, one would expect some congruence between the operating features of bank branches across different markets. Homogeneity of operations is also maintained due to the presence of foreign banks in different countries. Such operational homogeneity, however, does not imply similar performance among competing banks. Differentiation can result from a number of other operational aspects such as technology utilization, human resource investment, etc.

Despite the information asymmetries and incompatibilities across banking institutions from different countries, we have been witnessing the development of a culture which lends itself to international performance comparisons, manifested by the increased number of international comparisons of banking institutions, see Berg et al. (1993) and Allen and Rai (1996). The scope of most of these comparisons has, thus far, focused on the corporate banking level seeking to measure different aspects of X-efficiency (e.g. cost minimization and economies of scale and scope). Less attention has given to lower levels of analysis, such as the bank branch level or the process level.

In this chapter, we propose a framework for assessing the efficiency of bank branches operating in different countries. Our modeling approach allows us to disentangle within- from between-country performance differences. This chapter concludes that country performance differences do exist among the UK, Greek, and Cypriot bank branches that were included in our assessment, with the UK branch network demonstrating higher levels of efficiency when compared to the other two branch networks. This conclusion may be considered trivial, since the more advanced stage of development of the UK banking and financial system, vis-à-vis the Greek and Cypriot systems, is well known to the average observer. However, the framework we develop is constructive, and as such it indicates those aspects of the branches' operations that are the source of superior performance, thus providing improvement guidelines for the less efficient branches. Furthermore, in spite of the overall lower efficiency ratings, the Greek and Cypriot networks contain mechanisms that can be used by the UK branches in order to improve their efficiency further. A final, surprising observation is that the Cypriot branch network is not, on average, less efficient than the Greek one, in spite of the fact that it operates in a highly regulated environment.

The remainder of the chapter is organized as follows. In Section 2 we present a brief discussion on the strategic role of bank branch networks. International comparisons are briefly discussed along with our main thesis that is further investigated using the framework developed in the next section. Section 3 presents bank branch efficiency studies relevant to this research, and develops the framework which disentangles within- from between-country efficiencies. An application of the framework is described for three national branch networks in Section 4. Section 5 discusses the insights that were obtained from the application of the framework. Concluding remarks are given in Section 6.

## 2 The Strategic Role of Branch Networks and International Comparisons

### 2.1 The Strategic Role of the Branch

In the rapidly changing world of financial services, many scholars have sought to examine the strategic role of branch networks. Carroll (1991) argues that bank branch management practices should resolve issues of profitability and efficiency measurement, location appropriateness, and marketing conduct prior to embarking into areas of service quality and customer retention. McCormick and Rose (1994) suggest that the continuous decline of the role of branches in US banking is attributable to the products sold, the markets targeted, and the distribution network. Rose (1992) argues that the demand for bank credit and liability products has a sluggish growth while on the other hand the supply of these products will increase rapidly. Critical issues for retail intermediaries will prove to be their decision to refine their management practices in terms of cross-selling efforts, effective branch location, and customer targeting.

There is widespread agreement among academics (Berger and Humphrey, 1997) and practitioners (Pihl and Whitmyer, 1994) on the strategic relevance of performance measurement in bank branch networks. The universal message from both academia and industry advocates the use of non-financial measures of performance, and also the need for global performance assessment of individual branches. The focus on the branch performance level exerts particular measurement problems because of the need for accurate and informative measures. Recent research concerning branch-related performance measurement yardsticks has revealed the need for branch-level customized methods of efficiency assessment. Furthermore, the strong process component in the operations of bank branches has inspired the use of benchmarking methodologies focusing on the efficiency of particular processes (e.g. the lending process) on the overall efficiency of the branch (Frei and Harker, 1996).

### 2.2 International Comparisons

Empirical studies regarding international performance comparisons have been presented in the literature. Berg et al. (1993), for example, studied 799 banks from the Nordic countries, while Allen and Rai (1966) examined 194 banks from 15 countries during a five-year period. In both cases the assessment was based on corporate banking performance, and the studies were intended to examine the presence of technical inefficiency among the banks. Despite the limitations imposed by data availability, the two empirical studies demonstrated evidence on performance differences between banks at either the national or international level. For example, Berg et al. (1993) reported the dominance of Swedish banks compared to those of Finland and Norway when production efficiency was examined. The more detailed study by Allen and Rai (1996) led to a number of important conclusions regarding performance differences among banks of different countries and of different sizes. Their results provide evidence that the existence of national barriers causes non-optimal cost behavior. Global banking institutions exhibit the highest efficiency with particular strong banks emanating from Japan, Austria, Australia, Denmark, Sweden, and Canada. Banks in France, Italy, the UK, and the US were found less efficient.

In most international comparison studies, the level of the analysis is the bank. Focusing on branch performance, however, can yield particularly useful information on the need to control and manage branch operations (Berger et al., 1994). Branch performance assessment must incorporate information from different branch networks operating in the same or different markets. Comparisons between branches competing even in the same local markets are difficult to carry out due to limited access to bank branch data from competing banks. Furthermore, the regulating bodies of each country do not consider the performance of branch networks as part of their monitoring activities and, as a result, do not collect any relevant information. Therefore, empirical studies in the literature regarding branch performance are typically based on individual branch networks and not on cross-network comparisons.

The international dimension of institutional performance is gaining increasing importance in the banking sector, as international barriers collapse and many bank branch networks find themselves operating in different types of financial environments. These can be more or less liberalized, have rigid or more loose control mechanisms, with high or no competition at all. Following the recent socioeconomic developments in Europe, for example, a number of banks, such as Eastern European banks, have found themselves operating in less restrictive and more competitive environments. Others, such as the Czech Republic, Hungary, Poland, Slovene, Cyprus, etc., are also preparing for such liberalized regimes as the European Union (EU) expands.

The modeling framework we propose in this study can shed light onto a number of issues which are difficult to address at the corporate level of a bank. In the US, a positive relationship between market share and performance has often been reported (Rhoades, 1982). Hypotheses such as the efficient-structure (ES) hypothesis were formulated (Smirlock, 1985). ES states that large market share is the result of the efficient operations of the firms. On the other hand, the structure-conduct-performance (SCP) hypothesis (Stigler, 1964) states that better performance is due to anti-competitive price settings. Although no conclusive evidence on the structure-conduct-performance relationship exists (Osborne and Wendel, 1982), if the SCP hypothesis is adopted, then branch networks operating in highly concentrated markets need not be efficient. They can improve further via the comparative assessment of bank branches which operate in more competitive environments. That is, the assessment of the efficiency of a bank branch from a single network can lead to "myopic" results due to the absence of more competitive comparators from branches which belong to different networks. Such comparative assessment can yield information regarding performance gaps that need to be eliminated, not only for branch networks operating in less dynamic environments, but also for branch networks operating in more dynamic financial markets.

In the next section, we develop a framework which can shed light onto the above issues. The framework can be used to disentangle within- from between-country differences. As a result, important observations regarding the resulting within-country efficiency distributions can be made. One would expect, for example, that bank branch networks which operate into markets that exert high internal controls, or are characterized by close geographical proximity, would exhibit a homogenous picture of their performance profile. That is, such branch networks are expected to exhibit low variability in their efficiency compared to branch networks that operate under less organized controls, or in dispersed environments. In such environments, the manager's ability to cross-validate management behavior and practices may decrease. The proposed framework can shed light on the above issues and provide direction for improvement.

### 3 Theoretical Framework Development

*3.1 Bank Branch Network Efficiency*
The research literature concerning the efficiency of banking institutions has experienced a phenomenal growth in the nineties which was translated into a considerable volume of theoretical and empirical research (see, for example, the special issue of the *Journal of Productivity Analysis* (1993), *Journal of Banking and Finance* (1993), *European Journal of Operational Research* (1997) and *Interfaces* (1999)). One of the interesting aspects of this research volume is the gradual increase of the non-US dimension of banking efficiency. The notable European dimension emanates from the financial integration of EU countries followed by deregulation and reorganization of traditional financial services' structures.

A growing research trend in banking includes micro-efficiency studies focusing on the branch level (Schaffnit et al., 1997; Zenios et al., 1998; Athanassopoulos, 1997), or the branch-processes level (Frei and Harker, 1996). The empirical evidence of these studies is heretofore drawn from country-specific studies that do not offer any insights on bank branch competitiveness in a global environment. The present empirical evidence about branch efficiency indicates that there are significant cost gains that can be achieved by individual bank branches at a level that often exceeds

Table 10.1. *Branch-specific efficiency definitions.*

| Activity | Efficiency | Description | Objective |
|---|---|---|---|
| Transaction | Technical, scale | Inputs: operating costs and technology<br>Outputs: volume of transactions | Minimize operating costs |
| Production | Technical, scale | Inputs: operating costs and technology<br>Outputs: volume and/or number of accounts | Minimize operating costs |
| Intermediation | Technical, scale, allocative | Inputs: interest and non interest costs<br>Outputs: volume and non-interest income | Minimize total costs |

20% of current costs. The relevant branch performance literature (reviewed by Berger and Humphrey, 1997) indicates a wide spectrum of models that are used to assess the efficiency of branch operations. These models are partly driven by the different functions – selling, servicing, intermediation – that coexist within each branch, and by data availability differences which constrain research aspirations.

A summary of the main definitions used in the branch-efficiency literature is given in Table 10.1.

The information in Table 10.1 summarizes the three main activities analyzed in studies of branch efficiency. The assessment of technical and scale efficiency is prevalent in all three cases while in the intermediation models there also exist examples of input-mix efficiency (allocative). It is noteworthy that even within the previous classification of efficiency measures, there are incompatibilities concerning the way particular variables are measured. For example, the transactions of individual branches can appear in the form of raw numbers or alternatively the time equivalent that corresponds to them. Furthermore, the volume of deposit accounts can either be considered as an input or as an output to the intermediation models (see Berger et al., 1994).

### 3.2 A Modeling Framework Based on Data Envelopment Analysis

The assessment of bank branch efficiency can be undertaken by means of examining financial activities which emphasize the aspects of revenue generation from intermediating funds and assuming risks (see Holmer and Zenios, 1995). Of equal importance are also the operating aspects of their performance which focus on the cost of servicing the customers of each branch. In this paper we concentrate on the use of Data Envelopment Analysis as a method of assessing the operating efficiency of bank branches. The method was initially applied by Sherman and Gold (1985) for assessing the efficiency of bank branches, and it thereafter proved a promising tool for monitoring efficiency in banking (see Berger and Humphrey, 1997).

Data Envelopment Analysis is a linear programming-based method originally suggested by Charnes, Cooper, and Rhodes (1978). Given a set of Decision Making Units (DMUs) $j = 1, 2, \ldots, n$, utilizing quantities of inputs $X \in \Re^m_+$ to produce quantities of outputs $Y \in \Re^s_+$, we can denote $x_{ij}$ the amount of the $i^{th}$ input used by the $j^{th}$ DMU, and $y_{rj}$ the amount of the $r^{th}$ output produced by the $j^{th}$ DMU. The mathematical programming model (weights model) and its dual (envelopment model) for assessing the efficiency of unit $k$ under the assumption of constant returns to scale (CRS) are stated as follows:

| Weights model | Envelopment model |
|---|---|
| $\displaystyle \text{Maximise}_{v_i, u_r} \sum_{r=1}^{s} u_r y_{rk}$ | $\displaystyle \text{Minimise}_{\lambda_j, h} h_k = h - \varepsilon\left(\sum_i s_i^- + \sum_r s_r^+\right)$ |
| $\displaystyle \sum_{i=1}^{m} v_i x_{ij} = 1$ | $\displaystyle \sum_{j=1}^{n} \lambda_j x_{ij} + s_i^- = h x_{ik} \quad i = 1, \ldots, m$ |
| $\displaystyle \sum_{r=1}^{s} u_r y_{rj} - \sum_{i=1}^{m} v_i x_{ij} \leq 0 \; \forall j$ | $\displaystyle \sum_{j=1}^{n} \lambda_j y_{rj} - s_r^+ = y_{rk} \quad r = 1, \ldots, s$ |
| $v_i, u_r \geq \varepsilon,$ | $h$ free and $\lambda_j \geq 0, \; \forall j$ |
| $0 < \varepsilon \ll 1$ | $s_i^-, s_r^+ \geq 0, 0 < \varepsilon \ll 1.$ |

where

$v_i, u_r$  are weight factors for the input $i$ and output $r$ of each assessed branch obtained from the solution to the weight's model,

$\lambda_j$  is the intensity factor showing the contribution of branch $j$ in the derivation of the efficiency of branch $k$ in the envelopment model,

$h$  is the radial efficiency factor showing the rate of reduction to the input levels of branch $k$,

$s_i^-, s_r^+$  are slack variables accounting for extra savings in input $i$ and extra gains in output r,

$\varepsilon$  is a very small positive number used as a lower bound to input/output weights; it is also used to scale the input/output slacks in the envelopment model. Commercial DEA software implements two-phase optimization routines to avoid problems associated with the specific value of $\varepsilon$.

A sequence of linear programming problems needs to be solved, one for each DMU $j = 1, \ldots, n$ to assess their relative efficiency. DMUs with solution $h_k^* = \Sigma_{r=1}^s u_r^* y_{rk} = 1$ are characterized as relatively efficient or as benchmark DMUs. In any other case, $h_k^*$ gives the maximum proportionate reduction to the inputs of DMU $k$ that must be achieved in order to become efficient.

The assessment of performance is often associated with the need to contrast alternative policies that characterize various subgroups of the branches included in the assessment. In the first study of this nature, Charnes et al. (1981) describe an approach to isolate and evaluate school program efficiency. Other examples drawn from banking are reported in the literature by Banker and Morey (1986), Athanassopoulos and Thanassoulis (1995), Zenios et al. (1999), Brockett and Golany (1996), and Berg et al. (1993). In this study the presence of three national networks motivates an organized multi-stage comparison of performance. This includes assessing each branch network separately and then pooling the branches into a single sample, but only after their inputs-outputs were adjusted at their within-country efficient level. This analysis will yield within- and between-country efficiency indices that can enhance our understanding about the competitiveness of national branch networks in different financial environments.

The modeling framework we propose for benchmarking branch networks operating in different countries proceeds in three steps:

1. Apply DEA to each network separately to examine efficiency differences within a country. Insights can be obtained regarding different management practices in different financial environments.
2. Remove managerial inefficiencies observed within the financial environment in which branches operate, as identified in Step 1. This is done by projecting inefficient branches onto their efficient frontier.[1] A set of virtual branches is constructed for each branch network.[2]

---

[1] In this research, a radial projection method has been used to project inefficient DMUs on the frontier. This approach does not yield any situations where inefficient DMUs use unobserved parts of the frontier for their projection. Alternative projection methods can be adopted, namely the non-radial methods (Thanassoulis and Dyson, 1992; Athanassopoulos, 1996) or the minimum distance methods (Frei and Harker, 1995), but caution should be exercised to avoid projecting inefficient DMUs on segments of the frontier that were not observed in practice.

[2] We point out that it may not be appropriate to include in a country's frontier branches which find themselves on the frontier but not in the reference set of any other branches. Further investigation into the impact of such "outlier" branches on the results of the analysis may be necessary, as excluding such branches from the analysis could provide a more appropriate frontier for each country. In the empirical study described in the next

3. Apply DEA to the pooled data set consisting of all efficient and virtual branches from all branch networks under consideration. Between-country differences can now be examined. Information can be obtained on how branches can benefit from management practices observed in branches operating in different financial environments.

Following the original assessment of bank branches at both national and international levels, one can focus on some by-products of the method to gain additional insights.

- The assumption of CRS may not be applicable, and thus the branch networks were also assessed under the variable returns to scale (VRS) assumption. In operational terms, this would imply the use of an extra free variable in the formulation of the weights model or the use of an extra constraint ($\Sigma_{j=1}^{n}\lambda_j = 1$) in the formulation of the envelopment model. Banker and Thrall (1992) provide more details on economies of scale and their identification. A combination of CRS and VRS efficiency indices for each branch $k$, $E_k^{CRS}$, and $E_k^{VRS}$, respectively, can be used as the basis for estimating the *scale efficiency* ($E_k^{Scale} = E_k^{CRS}/E_k^{VRS}$) of each branch. Scale economies can also be assessed based on the sign of the dual variable on the convexity constraint.
- A follow-up of the assessment of the scale efficiency of individual branches is to investigate the extent to which this is due to increasing or decreasing returns to scale. We implement the method suggested by Banker and Thrall (1994) whereby we examine the sign of the variable returns to scale factor.
- In assessing the efficiency profile of the branch networks, we also focus upon their input-output mix. In the absence of unit prices, we study the relative importance given by each inefficient branch to its inputs and/or outputs when assessed for its efficiency. This information is obtained from the disaggregation of the composite weighted input/output factors in the solution of the weights DEA model. That is, $u_r y_{rk}/\Sigma_{r=1}^{s}u_r y_{rk}$ and $v_i x_{ik}$ give, respectively, the relative importance of output $r$ and input $i$ when the efficiency of branch $k$ is assessed. Due to the presence of multiple optimal sets of weights ($v_i$ *and* $u_r$) in efficient branches, this analysis is applied mainly to inefficient branches. Analyzing the distribution of weights, we obtain information on the effect of pooling the national branch networks under one common frontier denominator as compared to the case of conducting separate assessments for each country network.

We next demonstrate the applicability of this framework using data from three bank branch networks operating in the UK, Greece, and Cyprus.

---

section, only 6 out of 507 branches were reported as such. The analysis was repeated after these branches were removed from the data set but no significant changes in the results were observed.

Table 10.2. *Differences between financial environments of the UK, Greece, and Cyprus.*

| | Number of commercial banks | Number of branches | Concentration ratio (deposits of largest 3 banks/ total deposits) | Total deposits | Government control | Interest rates |
|---|---|---|---|---|---|---|
| Cyprus | 9 | 500+ | 0.89 | US$ 11 billion | High | Fixed |
| Greece | 41 | 2,500+ | 0.72 | US$ 80 billion | Medium-low[§] | Variable (long term 17.5%) |
| UK | 68 | 12,000 | 0.60 | US$ 1,198 billion | Low | Variable 6.5% (official) |

*Note*: [§] In the post-1991 period.

## 4 Application to Three National Branch Networks

### 4.1 Description of the National Branch Networks

Each of the branch networks we studied represents a distinct and different market environment which varies from the highly competitive conditions of the UK and the emerging competitive environment of Greece, to the more segmented in size and scope environment of Cyprus. All three countries, however, share the vision of a common European market. Table 10.2 presents a basic profile of the banking system of the three branch networks.

In the UK, for example, there has been a considerable decline in bank branch numbers over the last decade. This trend, which still continues today, has resulted into 100,000 job cuts since the early nineties, and industry experts predicted a further reduction up to 15% of the total number of branches before the end of 1998. The overbranching signs experienced in various developed economies are undoubtedly accelerated by the rapid commercialization of new technologies such as the Internet and Virtual and Home Banking, and by the entrance of non-banking institutions that have capabilities to support retail financial services.

The UK branch network we examine has a regional base in Central England and belongs to one of the five largest clearing banks in the UK. The particular bank competes in all aspects of retail and commercial banking in the UK and its branches have full-scale responsibility to market and service the bank's product base.

In Greece, a dismantling of the administrative controls in the banking sector in 1987 was soon followed by the creation of new market segments, the appearance of new business opportunities, and the entrance of new competitors into the Greek banking market. The resulting intensified competition has not as yet affected the state controlled banks, which still hold over 75% of the total assets with 50% concentrated in the big five banking institutions. The foreign representation of banks in Greece includes 21 institutions (e.g. Citibank, Barclays, Natwest, Amex) with a total network of 100 (out of a total of 2,500) branches and holding 17% of the loans and 6% of the total deposits. The banking sector in Greece is currently undertaking large-scale technology infrastructure projects varying from the development of ATM facilities to the modernization of the computer platforms of its branches. The optimistic prospects of financial services in Greece are associated with a phenomenal expansion of the number of bank branches. Branch management administration varies from aggressive expansion of the newer private banks to efforts for cost containment and consolidation from the large networks of traditional public sector banks.

The Greek bank branch network examined contains a large sample of branches from one of the largest five banks in Greece with full-scale commercial operations. The bank itself is not considered a market leader. Noticeable aspects of its profile include the large asset and depository base, the relative small credit and non-banking activities, and the lack of sufficient computerized facilities evident at its branch network.

The financial environment in Cyprus is characterized by tight government regulations and fixed interest rates. During 1994, interest rates in Cyprus, for example, were kept at the same level and so was competition. This is at best an oligopolistic environment where two banks alone hold more than 75% of the market share, the remaining 25% of which is shared by less than ten banks. Cyprus belongs, however, to the group of potential European Union partners (membership negotiations were expected to begin within 1998). As a result, the banking environment in Cyprus is anticipating a major change towards a more liberalized regime, resulting in the removal of restrictions on interest rates and competition. Most banks, including the one we studied, have initiated a number of programs targeting the improvement of efficiency and performance, in order to be able to survive and successfully compete in the new environment.

Finally, the branch network we considered in Cyprus forms the largest single network in the country, with approximately a 45% share of local market deposits. Its total assets in 1994, the year during which the study took place, were CYP 2.03B (1 CYP ≈ 2 USD), and the before-tax earnings for the same period were CYP 20.3M. A full range of retail banking services is offered to commercial clients and individuals in more than 140 branches. These branches are scattered among the four major cities of the country and among various villages and tourist resorts. A total of 83 branches are located in urban areas, 41 are located in rural areas, and 20 branches operate near tourist resorts along the coast of the island. All branches offer a full range of services: personal savings, company, and credit application accounts.

### 4.2  Comparing the Three Networks

As Table 10.2 suggests, the three branch networks described above operate in three different financial environments. On one side of the spectrum we find the UK environment, characterized by low concentration ratio, highly variable interest rates, and low government control. On the other side, we find the Cyprus environment with tight government control, fixed interest rates, and high concentration ratio. The Greek environment finds itself somewhere in between the two, still probably closer to the one of Cyprus in spite of the changes Greece underwent during the last few years.

Based on the discussion of Section 2.2 and on the SCP hypothesis, networks operating in highly concentrated markets may not be efficient. Thus, we would expect UK branches to exhibit higher efficiency ratings compared to those in Greece and Cyprus. In a similar fashion, the Greek branches operating in an environment where competition is higher than that of Cyprus, are expected to exhibit higher efficiency ratings compared to those observed in Cyprus. Furthermore, the differences between the competitive structure of the financial environments are expected to force the branch networks to place different importance on different product mix and resource structure, in their attempt to appear as efficient as possible. Finally, if a negative relationship between market concentration and efficiency does exist, then we should expect that UK branches will appear more frequently in the peer group of inefficient branches when a common frontier for all branches is constructed. The issues outlined in this section are investigated empirically using the framework developed in the next section.

### 4.3  Specification of Input and Output Sets

The branch networks were assessed by focusing on their production activities. The selection of inputs and outputs for this assessment was affected by the need for identical measurements and representation

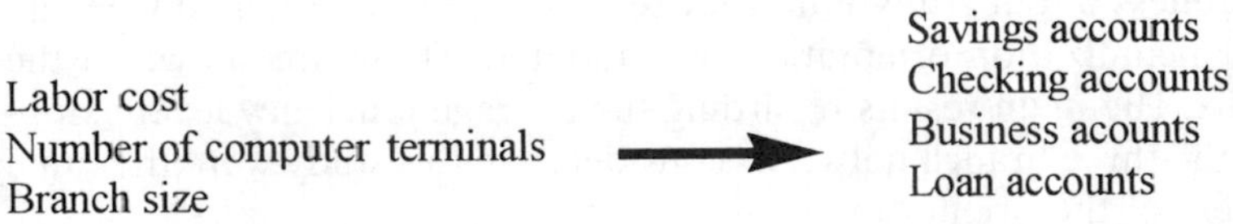

Labor cost
Number of computer terminals  ⟶
Branch size

Savings accounts
Checking accounts
Business acounts
Loan accounts

Figure 10.1.  Input-output sets for assessing branch operating efficiency.

across the three branch networks. Similar problems were also encountered in previous cross-national empirical studies, Berg et al. (1993). The input-output set used for assessing production efficiency is shown in Figure 10.1. Production efficiency is assessed in order to capture the nature of the bank branch as a service producer. Three cost-related factors that represent branch operations were used as inputs. They include the resources available to the bank branch: the space measured in square meters, the number of computer terminals, and the total employee compensation (see Sherman and Gold, 1985, and Vassiloglou and Giokas, 1990, for a more detailed discussion on the choice of inputs). On the output side, the branch products were grouped into four different types of accounts: savings, current, business, and loan accounts.[3] The definition of the input-output set is compatible with previous research (Berger et al., 1994). The main objective of this assessment is to compare the cost structure of the three networks concerning the number of accounts they manage.[4]

Depending on the type of information available, an input minimization or an output maximization orientation can be adopted. In the rest of the paper, we present results from an input minimization orientation, since no market information about the environment the branches operate in (such as competition, consumer demographics, etc.) was available. Thus, branches are assessed on how efficiently they use their resources given the current volume of sales and services. However, for

---

[3] The number of accounts as a proxy for the non-easily obtainable number of transactions has been used extensively in the literature.

[4] An alternate model which included the volume of the different accounts in the output set was also considered. Such a model focuses on the effect that small or large accounts might have on the cost efficiency of branches. Other models based on the intermediation approach, accounting for interest costs and revenue per branch, can also be utilized. The focus of this paper is to demonstrate the framework to disentangle efficiency differences in operational efficiency; thus, we only report results from the production approach model.

completeness of our study, efficiency results were also obtained when an output maximization orientation was adopted. These are shown in the appendix. The main results regarding the average efficiency level exhibited by the three branch networks considered in this study were the same regardless of the orientation chosen.[5]

Detailed information on the branches of the three banks described above was obtained for the period January–December 1994. More specifically, data on 126 branches from the Cyprus bank, 185 from the Greek bank, and 196 branches from the UK bank were collected. The data sets used in this study were constructed directly from performance information provided to us by the banks. Thus, they are likely to be cleaner and more accurate compared to data obtained from regulatory sources which vary among different economic and regulatory environments.

One of the problems in cross-country comparisons is that data, such as costs and other dollar-denominated variables – product volumes, etc. – are not comparable. Data, for example, were made available to us in Cyprus pounds, British pounds, and Greek drachmas. To overcome this problem, data were first converted to a common currency (US$) and then adjusted using the "average cost of a basket of goods" described in the Prices and Earnings around the Globe, issued by the Union Bank of Switzerland, for 1994.[6] This conversion of the dollar denominated variables to "number of baskets" made such variables comparable across countries. Table 10.3 presents descriptive information on the variables used for the three networks.

### 4.4 Benchmarking Within-Country Branch Efficiencies

We now present the empirical results obtained from analyzing the three branch networks described above. First, each of the three networks was examined separately. The Warwick DEA (Thanassoulis, 1994) software was utilized for the analysis. Table 10.4 outlines some descriptive statistics on the input-minimization efficiency ratings obtained when a

---

[5] We point out, however, that when using an output maximization orientation to assess branch efficiency, market information regarding the environment that branches operate in can be useful, especially if we are to provide branch managers with specific guidelines for improvement.

[6] The basket of goods is typically used to determine living costs and contains 111 different goods and services, chosen based on the average monthly needs of a European family of three. Food products accounted for 20%, beverage products for 5%, clothing for 7%, rent for 18%, heat and electricity 5%, household appliances 7%, personal care products 7%, transport 14%, and miscellaneous services 17%.

Table 10.3. *Mean values of the variables included in the model.*

| Variables | UK branches | Greek branches | Cyprus branches |
|---|---|---|---|
| **Inputs** | | | |
| Cost of personnel | | | |
| (number of baskets) | 195.1 | 271.7 | 135.16 |
| Space (m²) | 446.5 | 429.3 | 140.52 |
| Number of computers | 5.1 | 1.5 | 3.9 |
| **Outputs** | | | |
| Current accounts | 13,425 | 6,858 | 352.4 |
| Savings accounts | 1,381.4 | 962.5 | 1,657 |
| Company accounts | 306.5 | 63.41 | 139.5 |
| Credit accounts | 2,168 | 1,419.6 | 345.7 |

Table 10.4. *Descriptive statistics on efficiency ratings obtained (separate frontiers for each branch network, input minimization, and VRS).*

| | Number of branches | Mean | Median | Standard deviation | Minimum | Maximum |
|---|---|---|---|---|---|---|
| Cyprus branches | 126 | 88.89 | 92.89 | 11.93 | 54.65 | 100 |
| Greek branches | 185 | 74.28 | 73.83 | 19.82 | 33.36 | 100 |
| UK branches | 196 | 78.77 | 78.57 | 21.03 | 28.58 | 100 |

separate frontier was constructed for each branch network, under a VRS assumption.

In agreement with previous empirical studies, our results indicate the presence of considerable cost inefficiencies even when comparing branches within each country. Clearly, cost efficiency is not the sole driver in the management of branch networks. This may provide some explanation for the presence of such large inefficiencies. Our production efficiency estimates are close to previous empirical results (Berger et al., 1994, from the US; Tulkens, 1993, from Belgium, and Athanassopoulos, 1996, from the UK) that indicate average levels of cost efficiency below 80%.

Since the resulting efficiency distributions are not normal, non-parametric tests were used to investigate them further. A non-parametric Kruskal-Wallis test was used to test the null hypothesis that

Table 10.5. *Number of branches exhibiting different efficiency levels (separate frontiers for each branch network, input minimization, and VRS).*

| Efficiency range – % | Cyprus branches (total 126) | Greek branches (total 185) | U.K. branches (total 196) |
|---|---|---|---|
| 98–100 | 49 | 39 | 79 |
| 90–98 | 18 | 18 | 8 |
| 80–90 | 27 | 20 | 11 |
| 65–80 | 27 | 39 | 26 |
| less than 65 | 5 | 69 | 72 |

all three networks follow the same efficiency distribution. This null was rejected ($p < 0.001$). Non-parametric Mann-Whitney tests were then used to test differences between pairs of the resulting efficiency distributions. Cyprus branches find themselves, on average, closer to their efficient frontier compared to how far the Greek and the UK branches are from their own efficient frontier ($p < 0.001$). This is also evident in Table 10.5, which demonstrates that a great proportion of Greek and UK branches fall in the lower category of efficiency ratings of less than 0.65.

The branches from the Cyprus network exhibit a uniform within-country performance profile. This can be attributed to the tight management controls that exist within the Cyprus banking system, and the geographical proximity of the branches. The lower efficiency distributions of the Greek and UK branches can be attributed to fundamentally different strategic choices. In the UK, the demanding competitive environment has driven all retail banks towards a battle for market share. Their commercial presence is sustained in some trade areas of low potential or stiff competition and, thus, a poor customer base and not cost management can be blamed for low cost efficiency. The lack of internal controls can provide some explanation for observed variability in the assessed efficiencies of the Greek network. In addition, the wide local proximity of the particular branch network further reduces opportunities for organizational learning via informal flows between branches.

### 4.5 Benchmarking Between-Country Branch Efficiencies

The assessment of the within-country efficiency indices can lead to useful conclusions about branch performance within each network. A more

Table 10.6. *Descriptive statistics on efficiency ratings obtained (single frontier on pooled data set, input minimization, and VRS).*

|  | Number of branches | Mean | Median | Standard deviation | Minimum | Maximum |
|---|---|---|---|---|---|---|
| Cyprus branches | 126 | 91.21 | 94.98 | 10.69 | 43.03 | 100 |
| Greek branches | 185 | 84.16 | 88.16 | 17.55 | 19.44 | 100 |
| UK branches | 196 | 96.63 | 98.99 | 5.38 | 66.37 | 100 |

Table 10.7. *Number of branches exhibiting different efficiency levels (single frontier for all countries, VRS, and input minimization).*

| Efficiency range – % | Cyprus branches (total 126) | Greek branches (total 185) | U.K. branches (total 196) |
|---|---|---|---|
| 98–100 | 31 | 83 | 121 |
| 90–98 | 58 | 7 | 55 |
| 80–90 | 20 | 24 | 18 |
| 65–80 | 13 | 36 | 2 |
| less than 65 | 4 | 35 | 0 |

challenging question, however, is the assessment of branch performance using as a reference base the best practices across all three branch networks. Here, we make an implicit assumption that the three branch networks operate within a global competitive market, after managerial inefficiencies at the country level have been removed.

We follow the three-step framework presented in Section 3 to construct a common frontier for all networks and isolate efficiency differences that can be attributed to differences in the environment in which the branches operate. First, the model for each branch network is run separately and all inefficient branches are projected on their corresponding frontier. We then pool all efficient and virtual units and run the analysis again. Tables 10.6 and 10.7 present descriptive statistics on the efficiency ratings, and information on the efficiency distributions, respectively.

A Kruskal-Wallis test was conducted to test the null hypothesis that efficiency distributions from the three different networks are identical. This null was rejected ($p < 0.001$). Additional Mann-Whitney tests were used to examine efficiency differences between pairs of branch networks. The mean efficiency of the UK branches was higher than that of the Greek and the Cyprus networks ($p < 0.05$), suggesting that the average efficiency of the UK branches does indeed outperform the average efficiency of the branches in Greece and Cyprus. However, the null hypothesis that the average efficiency of Greek branches will, on average, dominate that of the Cyprus branches was rejected ($p < 0.05$). This result is surprising, as it suggests that the Greek branches have not, on average, demonstrated efficiency superiority over the Cyprus branches, even though they operate in a more favorable, more competitive European Union environment. This can, of course, be attributed to the poor management practices of the particular bank. As can be seen in Table 10.3, the particular bank in Greece lacks, for example, sufficient computer support. We also know that even though this particular bank is one of the largest in the country, it is not considered a market leader.

However, irrespective of the context of the environment, all inefficient branches can benefit by carefully examining best practices by branches in their peer groups. In Section 4.2, we speculate that the average efficiency dominance of the UK branches would also result in peer groups dominated by UK branches. We conducted a $\chi^2$ test to test this. More specifically, the null hypothesis was that the peer branch proportion from each country will equal the proportion of the branches from each country included in the data set. This null was not rejected ($p > 0.05$).

A more careful examination of the country of origin of peer groups further confirms the suggestions which can be made based on this result: In spite of the efficiency dominance of the UK branches, best practice units include branches from Cyprus and Greece which can serve as role models even for UK inefficient branches. A more detailed examination can reveal the management practices in such yardstick branches which can provide direction for improvement to inefficient branches, irrespective of the context of the environment.

## 5 A Closer Look into the Performance Profile of the Three Networks

In this section, we address a number of questions related to the performance results obtained from the within- and between-country efficiency results.

### 5.1 Technology Profile on the Assessment of Efficiency

By examining the virtual weights of the inputs and outputs, we can extract important information on the product or resource structure of

Table 10.8. *Mean virtual weights of inefficient branches (separate frontiers for each branch network, VRS, and input minimization).*

|  | Cyprus branches (total inefficient 65%) | Greek branches (total inefficient 80%) | U.K. branches (total inefficient 60%) |
|---|---|---|---|
| **Inputs** | | | |
| Space | 9.36 | 20.62 | 10.92 |
| Personnel cost | 72.86 | 59.39 | 29.47 |
| Computers | 17.78 | 19.99 | 59.61 |
| **Outputs** | | | |
| Current accounts | 21.61 | 2.95 | 5.93 |
| Savings accounts | 24.07 | 31.16 | 55.98 |
| Company accounts | 12.79 | 22.19 | 2.05 |
| Credit accounts | 41.53 | 43.70 | 36.07 |

the different branch networks. For example, we can gain insights on the product structure which deems the branches of a network more efficient than others. Table 10.8 presents descriptive statistics on the average relative importance for the different inputs and outputs of inefficient units, when the DEA model was run separately for the branches of each bank.[7] (We look at the weights of inefficient units because efficient units have multiple weight solutions, and furthermore the choice of the weights of inefficient units will still leave the efficient units on their corresponding frontier.)

Mann-Whitney tests were conducted to assess differences in the mean weights within each frontier. As Table 10.8 suggests, the UK branches appear to place more emphasis on technology compared to their space and personnel ($p < 0.001$). On the other hand, the branches in Greece and Cyprus place more emphasis on their personnel compared to other inputs ($p < 0.001$), in their attempt to appear as efficient as possible within their network. These results are not surprising considering that UK branches enjoy the benefits of better technology (see also Table 10.3). Furthermore, Greek and Cypriot branches appear to emphasize a similar product mix and resource structure.

[7] In the input minimization case, the relative importance of the inputs corresponds to their virtual weights, since they must all sum up to one. To obtain the relative importance of each output, we divided the virtual weight of the output by the total efficiency obtained by the virtual weights of the remaining outputs.

Table 10.9. *Mean virtual weights of inefficient branches (VRS, input minimization, and single frontier for all countries).*

|  | Cyprus branches (total inefficient 86%) | Greek branches (total inefficient 77%) | U.K. branches (total inefficient 69%) |
|---|---|---|---|
| **Inputs** | | | |
| Space | 26.75 | 23.87 | 13.39 |
| Personnel cost | 58.92 | 50.31 | 51.48 |
| Computers | 14.32 | 25.83 | 35.12 |
| **Outputs** | | | |
| Current accounts | 2.28 | 7.42 | 13.84 |
| Savings accounts | 84.03 | 44.49 | 36.72 |
| Company accounts | 8.90 | 2.44 | 10.07 |
| Credit accounts | 4.70 | 45.64 | 39.35 |

Next, we examined whether the importance given on product mix and resource structure changed when branches from different countries were pooled in the analysis, and a common frontier for all countries was constructed. Mann-Whitney tests were also conducted for assessing the mean weights differences shown in Table 10.9, which presents the resulting average relative importance given to inputs and outputs.

On the input side, the most interesting observation is that now that the UK branches "compete" with branches from Greece and Cyprus, they increase the emphasis they place on personnel cost and decrease the emphasis on technology. One explanation for this could be that UK branches are now being compared directly to branches which are more labor cost efficient because, for example, they operate in environments where labor is less expensive. Nevertheless, the importance given by UK branches on technology still remains higher than what is observed by the branches in Greece and Cyprus ($p < 0.01$); this is also one of the main drivers of their efficiency superiority. Overall, the UK branches demonstrate greater flexibility regarding their efficient input mix. That is, it was possible for them to lower the emphasis from technology to labor cost items and still remain dominant during the efficiency comparisons. Furthermore, although the UK branches place more emphasis on credit accounts, no single output is over- or underemphasized. Both the Cypriot and Greek branches, on the contrary, have given most emphasis on their savings, and savings and credit accounts, respectively.

Table 10.10. *Scale efficiency descriptive statistics.*

|  | Number of branches | Mean | Median | Standard deviation | Minimum | Maximum |
|---|---|---|---|---|---|---|
|  | Separate frontier for each country | | | | | |
| Cyprus branches | 126 | 83.07 | 94.01 | 22.04 | 17.45 | 100 |
| Greek branches | 185 | 92.37 | 97.20 | 11.29 | 38.86 | 100 |
| UK branches | 196 | 80.29 | 83.84 | 17.99 | 27.72 | 100 |
|  | Single frontier for all countries | | | | | |
| Cyprus branches | 126 | 77.79 | 85.71 | 19.45 | 27.81 | 100 |
| Greek branches | 185 | 90.92 | 95.30 | 11.65 | 38.85 | 100 |
| UK branches | 196 | 94.49 | 97.34 | 6.95 | 58.51 | 100 |

### 5.2 Within- and Between-Country Scale Efficiency and Returns to Scale Effects

Scale efficiency can be assessed by comparing the efficiency ratings $E_k^{CRS}$ and $E_k^{VRS}$ obtained under CRS and VRS, respectively. Scale inefficiencies are observed in all three branch networks. Table 10.10 presents within- and between-country scale efficiency results ($E_k^{Scale} = E_k^{CRS}/E_k^{VRS}$).

When separate frontiers are considered for each country, the UK network exhibits high scale inefficiencies, compared to the branches in Cyprus and Greece. Table 10.10 suggests that when a single frontier is constructed for all branch networks, the scale efficiency of the Cyprus branches, on average, further drops. The UK branches retain their overall efficiency dominance even in the case of scale inefficiencies, while the Greek branches exhibit a similar scale efficiency pattern in both the within- and between-country assessment. In all cases, the magnitude of the scale inefficiencies needs to be explored further by considering whether these correspond to increasing or decreasing returns to scale.

We next proceed in analyzing returns to scale effects. In Data Envelopment Analysis, the assessment of economies of scale effects is a frontier property regarding the position of scale inefficient branches on the VRS efficient frontier. Therefore, one characterizes returns to scale for branches located on the VRS efficient frontier that are also inefficient under the CRS assumption. Results related to the three branch networks in the study are listed in Table 10.11.

A $\chi^2$ statistic rejected the hypothesis of independence between returns

Table 10.11. *Number of branches exhibiting returns to scale in the within- and between-country comparisons.*

|  | Increasing returns (number of branches) | | Decreasing returns (number of branches) | | Constant returns (number of branches) | |
|---|---|---|---|---|---|---|
|  | Within* | Between** | Within | Between | Within | Between |
| Cyprus branches | 54 | 41 | 6 | 16 | 36 | 6 |
| Greek branches | 34 | 35 | 34 | 41 | 37 | 16 |
| UK branches | 104 | 53 | 1 | 25 | 48 | 24 |

*Note*: * Within-country returns to scale effects.
** Between-country returns to scale effects.

to scale and country membership in both the case of between- and also within-country efficiency ($p < 0.05$). That is,

- Economies of scale for the Cyprus branches lie in the area of increasing returns, which indicates that larger-sized branches outperform the smaller ones. A similar picture also holds in the case of the between-country assessment, which enforces the previous indication of local increasing returns to scale.
- A balanced picture between local increasing and decreasing returns to scale appears in the case of the Greek branches. This case is slightly enforced in favor of the decreasing returns to scale in the case of the between-country efficiency assessment. The message here is that there is great variability in size and performance in the Greek branches and thus different sized branches performed at high- and/or low-performance levels.
- For the UK branches, the within-country assessment revealed strong increasing returns to scale effects. That is, larger branches (in this case, city center branches) perform better in terms of cost productivity. The noticeable effect is that in the between-country results, we have a relatively higher proportion of UK branches operating under local decreasing returns to scale. The latter indicates the presence of Greek and Cypriot efficient branches of small size which outperform some large UK branches. This phenomenon is attributable to the different local markets' sizes, suggesting that city center (mostly productive) branches from Greece and Cyprus having relatively smaller size outperform the corresponding larger UK branches.[8]

---

[8] It is reminded that the efficiency assessment is conducted exclusively on a productivity basis, ignoring differences in service quality or customer satisfaction.

Overall, the scale of a branch's operations hinges upon many exogenous factors, primarily related to space and target markets. The selection of branch sites is not always discretional due to the difficulty of finding available sites with desirable location and size characteristics. Furthermore, the capital required to maintain branch positions (at a given level of depreciation or rent) is highly variable even for branches with similar market profile. The lack of full control on the size of individual branches also has operational bearings since a very large branch will need to be staffed appropriately if it is to provide adequate service levels. Finally, the question of returns to scale has a dynamic character; anticipated future market prospects in the vicinity of each branch must be evaluated before conclusive judgments are made regarding its scale size viability.

### 6 Concluding Remarks

In this chapter we present a modeling framework which is focused on international efficiency comparisons of bank branches. This framework is able to disentagle within- from between-country efficiency differences and provides an empirical benchmark upon which banking institutions can assess their performance. The methodological requirements for this type of analysis are discussed and the applicability of the framework is demonstrated using data from major banks in three countries operating in different financial environments.

Clearly, one of the limitations of this study is that the individual branch networks used may not provide a fair representation of the industry structure of each country. The banks, however, operate within particular market conditions and are therefore expected to comply with some general expectations as discussed in the previous sections of the paper.

International studies, such as the one carried out here, can provide useful insights and directions for improvement to the bank's management. For example, branch networks operating in highly protected markets with centralized regulatory regimes, such as the Cyprus branch network, may exhibit high internal consistency due to the internal capabilities of the bank and its internal controls. The source of disadvantage for these banks is the local market structure and limited competition under which they operate. Benchmarking bank branch networks operating in such restrictive regimes against branch networks in more liberalized financial environments is extremely important. This is especially true for banks operating in countries expecting changes in their financial environments. Examples include Eastern European and Mediterranean countries anticipating entrance to the European Union. We point out, however, that although some of the operational suggestions obtained by such international comparisons are difficult to implement, they can provide the means to prepare for the forthcoming changes at a strategic level. Bank management, for example, may not learn precisely how to improve the bank's efficiency, but can get a clear picture about how far away the bank is from the efficiency standards set by global leaders, against which it may soon find itself competing. Thus, the merit of this framework lies in identifying strategic shortcomings rather than providing specific ways to address such shortcomings.

### Appendix

In this appendix, efficiency results from an output orientation are presented. We point out, however, that the choice of an input minimization or output orientation towards the assessment of operating efficiency requires different information considerations and can provide different management insights. Efficiency information obtained through an input orientation, for example, can provide valuable information to the central management of a branch network. More often than not, decisions regarding human resources, location, technology, etc., are not made at the branch level, as branch networks are managed centrally. Thus, two relevant issues for central management include: (a) whether cost is effectively controlled throughout the branch network, and (b) whether branches realize expected sales. The input orientation adopted throughout the paper provides useful information towards addressing the former, and can provide cost efficiency insights on overall branch network performance.

The output orientation results listed below can provide a complimentary view to the reader regarding the efficiency of the three networks of our study, especially regarding the second issue mentioned above. Since no information regarding the market conditions in which a branch operates is available, output maximization results will probably not be of direct interest to a specific branch manager but can be of interest to central management. Output orientation efficiency indices may provide insights as to the mismatch between capital allocated to each branch and the ultimate conversion into measurable outcomes.

Finally we would also like to point out that under a CRS assumption, the efficiency indices obtained through an input or output orientation approach are identical. Differences only occur under a VRS assumption.

By examining Tables 10.12 through 10.15, we observe that the overall

Table 10.12. *Descriptive statistics on efficiency ratings obtained (separate frontiers for each branch network, output maximization, and VRS).*

| | Number of branches | Mean | Median | Standard deviation | Minimum | Maximum |
|---|---|---|---|---|---|---|
| Cypriot branches | 126 | 79.53 | 88.57 | 22.95 | 18.63 | 100 |
| Greek branches | 185 | 74.50 | 74.43 | 20.54 | 24.21 | 100 |
| UK branches | 196 | 68.50 | 66.09 | 21.27 | 23.55 | 100 |

Table 10.13. *Number of branches exhibiting different efficiency levels (separate frontiers for each branch network, and output maximization).*

| Efficiency range: VRS – % | Cypriot branches (total 126) | Greek branches (total 185) | U.K. branches (total 196) |
|---|---|---|---|
| 98–100 | 43 | 40 | 32 |
| 90–98 | 18 | 15 | 12 |
| 80–90 | 12 | 29 | 17 |
| 65–80 | 21 | 38 | 40 |
| Less than 65 | 32 | 63 | 95 |

Table 10.14. *Descriptive statistics on efficiency ratings obtained (single frontier on pooled data set, output maximization, and VRS).*

| | Number of branches | Mean | Median | Standard deviation | Minimum | Maximum |
|---|---|---|---|---|---|---|
| Cypriot branches | 126 | 86.27 | 89.87 | 13.53 | 32.15 | 100 |
| Greek branches | 185 | 86.73 | 94.30 | 16.79 | 37.79 | 100 |
| UK branches | 196 | 96.68 | 99.48 | 6.35 | 51.95 | 100 |

picture is similar to the one observed when an input orientation is used. That is, when we consider separate frontiers, the Cyprus branch network finds itself closer to its efficient frontier than the other two networks. Also similar to the input minimization case, the average efficiency level of the UK branches outperforms the average efficiency level of the other two branch networks when a single frontier is considered.

Table 10.15.  *Number of branches exhibiting different efficiency levels (single frontier for all countries, VRS, and output maximization).*

| Efficiency range – % | Cypriot branches (total 126) | Greek branches (total 185) | U.K. branches (total 196) |
|---|---|---|---|
| 98–100 | 24 | 87 | 124 |
| 90–98 | 39 | 18 | 52 |
| 80–90 | 31 | 28 | 15 |
| 65–80 | 24 | 24 | 3 |
| less than 65 | 8 | 28 | 2 |

## References

Allen, L. and A. Rai (1996), "Operational efficiency in banking: An international comparison", *Journal of Banking and Finance*, Vol. 20, pp. 655–672.

Athanassopoulos, A. D. (1996), "Assessing the Comparative Spatial Disadvantage (CSD) of Regions in the European Community Using Non-Radial Data Envelopment Analysis Models", *European Journal of Operational Research*, Vol. 94, pp. 439–452.

Athanassopoulos, A. D. (1997), "Embodying service quality into operating efficiency for assessing the effort effectiveness in the provision of financial services", *European Journal of Operational Research*, Vol. 98, pp. 300–313.

Athanassopoulos, A. D., "Multivariate and frontier analysis for assessing the market and cost efficiency of large scale bank branch networks", *Journal of Money, Credit and Banking*, forthcoming.

Athanassopoulos, A. and E. Thanassoulis (1995), "Separating market efficiency from profitability and its implications for planning", *Journal of the Operational Research Society*, Vol. 46, pp. 20–34.

Banker, R. D. and R. C. Morey (1986), "The use of categorical variables in Data Envelopment Analysis", *Management Science*, Vol. 32(12), pp. 1613–1627.

Banker, R. D. and R. Thrall (1992), "Estimation of returns to scale using Data Envelopment Analysis", *European Journal of Operational Research*, Vol. 17, pp. 74–84.

Berg, S., F. Forsund, L. Hjalmarsson, and M. Suominen (1993), "Banking efficiency in the Nordic countries", *Journal of Banking and Finance*, Vol. 17, pp. 371–388.

Berger, A. and D. Humphrey (1997), "Efficiency and financial institutions: International survey and directions for future research", *European Journal of Operational Research*, Vol. 98, pp. 1–20.

Berger A., J. Leusner, and J. Mingo (1994), "The efficiency of bank branches", paper presented in the 3rd Productivity Workshop in Georgia.

Brockett, P. L. and B. Golany (1996), "Using rank statistics for determining programmatic efficiency differences in DEA", *Management Science*, Vol. 42, No. 3, pp. 466–472.

Carroll, P. (1991), "Rethinking the basics of retail banking", *Journal of Retail Banking*, Vol. 13(3), pp. 5–18.

Charnes A., W. W. Cooper, and E. Rhodes (1981), "Evaluating program and managerial efficiency: An application of Data Envelopment Analysis to program follow through", *Management Science*, Vol. 27, pp. 668–697.

Frei, F. and P. Harker (1995), "Projections onto Efficient Frontiers: Theoretical and Computational Extensions to DEA", Wharton Financial Institutions Center, Report No. 95–22.

Frei, F. and P. Harker (1996), "Measuring the efficiency of service delivery processes", Wharton Financial Institutions Center, Report No. 96–31.

Holmer, M. and S. A. Zenios (1995), "The productivity of financial intermediation and the technology of financial product management", *Operations Research*, Vol. 43(6), pp. 970–982.

McCormick, J. and S. Rose (1994), "Restoring relevance to retail banking", *Journal of Retail Banking*, Vol. 16(1), pp. 5–10.

Osborne, D. K. and J. Wendel (1982), "A critical review of empirical research in banking competition 1964–1979", unpublished manuscript, Oklahoma State University.

Pihl, W. and L. Whitmyer (1994), "Making branch performance relevant in a new competitive era", *Bank Management*, August, Vol. 70(4), pp. 58–64.

Rhoades, S. (1982), "Structure-performance studies in banking: An updated summary and evaluation", Staff Study #119, Board of Governors of the Federal Reserve System.

Rose, S. (1992), "What's ahead for retail intermediation", *Journal of Retail Banking*, Vol. 14(3), pp. 5–16.

Schaffnit, C., D. Rosen, and J. C. Paradi (1997), "Best practice analysis of bank branches: An application of DEA in a large Canadian bank", *European Journal of Operational Research*, Vol. 98 (2), pp. 269–289.

Sherman, H. D. and F. Gold (1985), "Bank branch operating efficiency: evaluation with data envelopment analysis", *Journal of Banking and Finance*, Vol. 9, pp. 297–315.

Smirlock, M. (1985), "Evidence on the (non) relationship between concentration and profitability in banking", *Journal of Money, Credit and Banking*, Vol. 17, pp. 69–83.

Soteriou, A. C. and S. A. Zenios (1999), "On the costing of bank products", *European Journal of Operational Research*, Vol. 114, pp. 234–248.

Stigler, G. J. (1964), "A theory of oligopoly", *Journal of Political Economy*, Vol. 72 (February), pp. 44–61.

Thanassoulis, E. (1994), DEA Software Version 5.1. Operations Research and Systems Group, Warwick Business School, University of Warwick.

Thanassoulis, E. and R. G. Dyson (1992), "Estimating Preferred Target Input-Output Levels Using Data Envelopment Analysis", *European Journal of Operational Research*, Vol. 56(1), pp. 80–98.

Tulkens, H. (1993), "On FDH efficiency analysis: some methodological issues and applications to retail banking, courts and urban transit", *Journal of Productivity Analysis*, Vol. 4(1–2), pp. 183–210.

Vassiloglou, M. and D. Giogas (1990), "A study of the relative efficiency of bank branches: an application of Data Envelopment Analysis", *Journal of Operations Research Society*, Vol. 41(7), pp. 591–597.

Zenios, C. V., S. A. Zenios, K. Agathocleous, and A. C. Soteriou (1999), "Benchmarks of the efficiency of bank branches", *Interfaces*, Vol. 29(3), pp. 37–51.

# Part 3

**Environmental Drivers of Performance: Innovation, Regulations, and Technology**

# 11

## The Challenges of the New Electronic Technologies in Banking: Private Strategies and Public Policies

Paul M. Horvitz[a], Lawrence J. White[b]

### 1 Introduction

The revolution in electronic technologies that has swept through the U.S. economy in the past decade has posed special challenges for the financial services sector. This special impact should come as no surprise: Information, after all, lies at the heart of the successful provision of financial services; and information – its generation, manipulation, storage, and transmission – has been at the heart of the electronic revolution. Rapid changes in the financial services environment would naturally have substantial consequences for the actors in that environment.

Commercial banks[1] have been especially prominent in the discussions of the consequences of the revolution (see also Chapter 1 in this volume). Again, this should come as no surprise: Banks are numerous: As of year-end 1997 there were about 9,000 separately chartered commercial banks in the U.S., with almost 70,000 banking offices (i.e., home offices plus branches). Despite the continuing decline of banks' share of financial assets in the U.S. economy (Litan, 1987; Cadette, 1996; Edwards, 1996; Kroszner, 1996), banks are still collectively the plurality group in the financial services sector. Virtually all enterprises and most individuals have

[a] Department of Finance, University of Houston.
[b] Stern School of Business, New York University.
    The authors wish to thank Gerald Hanweck, Larry Mote, Daniel Orlow, Myron Uretsky, and two anonymous referees for their comments and suggestions on an earlier draft of this paper.
[1] This paper will largely focus on and refer to commercial banks; but the discussion is equally applicable to other depository institutions – i.e., savings and loan associations, savings banks, and credit unions.

some financial connection to a bank. And banks continue to be at the center of the money creation and payment mechanisms of the economy. Federal and state regulation of banks – a rough indicator of the public's special focus on and concern about banks – remains extensive, even in an era of deregulation. In short, banks continue to be prominent in the public consciousness of the financial services sector.

Accordingly, a discussion of technology's impact on banking can and should maintain a broader perspective – on the industry *and* on the public policies that surround the industry – than would be applicable to many other industries. This chapter will follow that course.[2] In Section 2 we will specify and briefly describe the new technologies and innovations that pose special challenges for banks and their regulators. Section 3 will focus on the challenges for the banks; Section 4 will focus on public policy. And Section 5 will offer a brief conclusion.

## 2 The New Electronic Technologies

### 2.1 The Technologies

In an important sense, electronic technologies are not new to banking. "Wire transfers" are surely almost as old as the telegraph[3]; later in the 19th century, the first commercial use of the telephone was by two bankers (Brooks, 1975, p. 53), and "on-line" balance inquiries were then possible; the FedWire began shortly after the establishment of the Federal Reserve system, though the Clearing House Interbank Payment System (CHIPS) began only in 1970; bank credit cards have been in existence for about 40 years; automated teller machines (ATMs) have been in place for over 20 years.

Nevertheless, the burgeoning electronic technologies of the 1990s do seem different and worthy of notice and discussion. Unlike many of the older technological changes and innovations, which focused on production and "back office" functions,[4] many of the new technologies involve banks' retail transactions and contacts with their customers.[5] The older

---

[2] This is the course followed also in the Congressional Budget Office (CBO) 1996 report.

[3] Also, as Garbade and Silber (1978) illustrate, an early use of the telegraph was to transmit financial price information and thus to facilitate arbitrage.

[4] Credit scoring, for example, as a means of improving banks' credit judgments on mortgage loans, credit card loans, and (more recently) small-business loans, is heavily electronic in its use and manipulation of data, but is largely a "behind-the-scenes" technology.

[5] This was also true in the past for bank credit cards, debit cards, and ATMs; and, at least for credit cards, many of the same retail competition questions that we raise in Section 3 have been applicable.

innovations raised efficiency and "outsourcing" (vertical integration and disintegration) questions; the newer innovations, while also encompassing vertical integration issues, raise more fundamental questions concerning competition among banks and between banks and non-banks. Further, an important economic aspect of these technological developments is that they are occurring in an environment in which bank costs, and changes in those costs, may be more rapidly reflected in the prices that banks charge to their customers than was true in the pre–1980s world of Regulation Q.

Specifically, we believe that because of their potential for widespread consumer acceptance and cost savings, four of the newer innovations merit deeper discussion:

1. *Electronic bill-paying.* By this we mean a system – based on a personal computer (PC) and a modem, or a "smart" telephone and a screen, or an interactive TV system – whereby individuals (through appropriate software) can direct that bills be paid electronically, on either a one-at-a-time or a recurring basis, thereby substituting electronic transfers for check writing and sending.
2. *Home banking.* By this we mean an expanded system that involves direct, on-line connections between an individual and his/her bank and encompasses a wider range of transactions than just bill-paying, including balance inquiries, transfers among bank accounts, the purchase and sale of other financial instruments, and perhaps even the arranging of a loan or mortgage through the provision of sufficient information that would allow the bank to use credit scoring or other methods to make rapid credit decisions.
3. *Internet transactions.* By this we mean banking and other transactions that are conducted directly on and through the Internet.
4. *Stored-value cards and smart cards.* By these we mean a system of electronic cards (with information encoded on a magnetic strip or a microchip) and readers, whereby an institution creates liabilities on itself by issuing cards with encoded values that can then be used as payments (via a card reader) in subsequent transactions.[6] This includes disposable cards that may be used for limited purposes (e.g., phone calls or transit fares) or in a more open environment, as well as reusable cards in which values can be restored by telephone, PC, or ATM. While the alternative forms of stored-value cards may seem very similar to the consumer, they may have very different implications for banks and for regulation.

### 2.2 The Diffusion of These Technologies

As of the late 1990s these technologies are still in their nascent stages; diffusion has been slow. It is estimated that only 7% of banks offer

---

[6] These cards are sometimes also called "electronic purses" (Wenninger and Laster, 1995).

on-line banking services; only 2% of households engage in home banking, and only a fraction of them do their banking through the Internet (GAO, 1998; Luhby, 1998). Even banks that are considered to be substantially ahead of their peers in promoting home banking have less than 5% of their households involved in home banking ("Huntington Claims . . . ," 1998). (By contrast, about 40% of homes have a PC, and about half of those have an Internet connection.) Of the estimated 20 billion consumer bill payments made annually, only 268 million transactions occurred through home banking or telephone bill payment services (Marjanovic, 1998).

In the area of smart cards, less than 500,000 have been issued in the U.S., and most of those are found in controlled environments such as university campuses and military bases; by contrast, in France alone banks have issued 25 million smart cards (Pae and Spurgeon, 1998; Kutler and Coulton, 1998; Coulton, 1998).

Even electronic transactions through an automated clearing house (ACH) – e.g., direct deposit of paychecks, automatic payment of utility or credit-card bills – have been surprisingly slow in being adopted. Only 55% of private-sector workers are paid through direct deposit.[7] Of the 20 billion annual consumer bill payments, only 1 billion occurred through an ACH. Even the bulk of business-to-business payments continues to occur outside the ACH.

Indeed, despite over 30 years of forecasts of a "checkless society" and the replacement of checks with electronic payments systems, the annual volume of paper checks written has continued to mount, reaching a record 62 *billion* in 1997.

### 2.3 Why Has Diffusion Been So Slow?

Though we are not sociologists, we have little doubt that cultural factors, technophobia, fear of the unfamiliar, and inertia are part of the reasons for the persistence of the paper check and the slow diffusion of the new electronic technologies. But we believe that there are also important economics-based explanations for these patterns.

First, the application of electronic technologies themselves to the paper check – specifically, magnetic ink coding and computerized reading

---

[7] And even in those firms and institutions where the employer has a direct deposit arrangement for wages and salaries, any employee requests for expense reimbursement almost always lead to a paper check being written.

of checks – has helped contain the costs of processing these huge volumes of checks. Second, a pricing structure that has not been linked to costs – specifically, the traditional (Regulation-Q-based) pricing of demand deposit accounts, in which zero interest was combined with a zero marginal price for checks written and processed – has been a continuing factor in this growth of check volume. Also, the check as proof of payment in the event of disputes is often an important factor for a continuing preference for checks.

With respect to stored-value and smart cards, the high quality and low cost of using the U.S. telephone system have allowed merchants quickly to verify credit card and debit card validity and thus to encourage their usage; in this environment, the advantages of stored-value and smart cards appear to be modest at best. By contrast, in Europe where telephone charges are substantially higher, merchants would understandably be more receptive to stored-value and smart cards, in which the value transfer occurs off-line and does not require a costly telephone call for verification.

Finally, an important feature of all four of the technological innovations under discussion is their system or "network" characteristics (Katz and Shapiro, 1994; Besen and Farrell, 1994; Liebowitz and Margolis, 1994; Economides, 1996; White, 1999); i.e., each innovation involves a combination of hardware and software, and permits the bank customer to conduct transactions with others, outside of the physical confines of a bank. Accordingly, issues of compatibility among transactors, so as to permit the smooth flow of transactions, and the related issues of the technical standards that enable and enforce compatibility, are important for these innovations. Further, the value of these innovations to customers increases as the numbers of other actual or potential transactors in a system increases; thus, there are positive externalities to an individual's use of the innovation. Finally, the electronic technologies themselves often involve economies of scale: There are large fixed costs to set up a system and very low (but not zero) marginal costs of putting additional transactions through the system; because the fixed costs of the systems are readily spread over larger volumes of transactions, average unit costs are lower when volumes are higher. This may provide an established provider of services with a substantial cost advantage that is difficult to dislodge, even by a technically superior system.

All of these systems/network characteristics imply that adoption of the technologies would be expected to be slow and halting.

### 3 The Challenges for Banks

#### 3.1 Some General Observations

*3.1.1 The "Inevitability" of These Innovations.* The siren songs of "technologists" and "futurologists" can be beguiling indeed. The descriptions of the beauty and efficiency – and inevitability – of new technologies are often seductive.

But, "if you build it, they will come," is not a theorem, let alone an iron law. New technologies must ultimately earn their place in the market through real and demonstrated practicability, convenience, and efficiency – not just promises.[8] Many, if not most, industries have experienced the promises of "revolutionary" technologies and innovations that have failed to survive the rigors of the marketplace. As we discussed in Section 2 above, the "checkless payment system" has been a just-over-the-horizon promise for over three decades, and the adoption of the new technologies has been slow.

The pace of adoption is likely to increase in the first decade of the 21st century, for economics-based as well as cultural-based reasons. Beyond some critical points, the systems/networks aspects of these technologies will operate in the direction of their adoption, as will consumers' greater familiarity with them and the wider distribution of home PCs and Internet access. Also, the federal government's push to handle its payments electronically by 1999 will surely hasten the process. But the specific forms, standards, and hardware/software combinations that will eventually prevail will continue to be difficult to predict *a priori*.

In sum, banking executives should be properly suspicious of *anyone's* claim as to the inevitability, and especially the imminence, of any technology. This statement ought not to be interpreted as a Luddite call for foot-dragging, complacency, and "doing things the way we've always done them." There are substantial dangers – especially in competitive markets, which increasingly characterize banking – to being slow to embrace the successful technologies that have already been adopted by one's rivals and thereby experiencing cost and/or product disadvantages. But "successful" is an *ex post* rather than *ex ante* concept, and there are

---

[8] A qualification to this statement involves the network aspects of these technologies and the consequent possibilities for tipping and momentum phenomena, as is discussed in the text below.

also substantial dangers to investing large sums in technologies that subsequently prove to be impractical and inappropriate. Being the first bank in the market to offer interactive TV as the gateway to home banking services could be very profitable if that turns out to be the approach chosen by most consumers. But if the telephone or the PC turn out to be the preferred devices, an investment in TV can be a total loss. (As we argue in Section 4, the dangers of misjudging the success of a particular technology apply to regulators as well as to bankers.)

   *3.1.2 The "Front End" Nature of the New Technologies.* As we stated in Section 2, the new technologies that are the focus of this paper are on the retail or "front end" of the financial transactions with a bank's customers. They involve direct contact with the bank's customers and entail the customers' having more choices as to how they conduct their financial transactions. These are not simply "back office" processing innovations.[9]

Though these innovations may bring greater efficiency and new services – always a healthy development for an industry – they are also likely to pose major competitive challenges to *incumbent* banks. This will occur because the innovations are likely to bring with them new firms that are the immediate providers of the new retail services and to whom the bank's customers may shift their loyalties. With respect to electronic bill-paying and home banking, for example, the loyalties of the users of these services may well attach to the provider of the software and/or specialized equipment that facilitate the service. If the bank is not the provider – if, for example, the provider is a software company (such as Intuit or Microsoft, or an on-line service provider, such as America Online) – then the power of the bank's brand name vis-a-vis those customers has diminished, and the non-bank company may well be in a position to extract rents and "steer" its customers to its preferred banks. In essence, the bank's products and services become yet more like commodities (which is already true, to a great extent, for standardized products such as certificates of deposit, residential mortgages, and auto loans), and banks are forced to become yet more competitive in their pursuit of the business of the "steerers." This would place banks increasingly in a

---

[9] It should be noted, however, that the success of these innovations is dependent on the efficient functioning of the back end. The consumer attracted by the convenience and cost advantages of electronic bill payment must be confident that payments will be made correctly. Low-cost electronic systems with high reliability are not yet in place for bill paying.

position similar to that of the insurance companies that sell their policies through "independent" agents.[10]

Further, to the extent that incumbent banks (and their customers) currently benefit from the banks' ability to provide locational convenience, that source of competitive advantage will be substantially eroded by developments that allow consumers convenient access to financial services without regard to the physical location of the provider.

The dilemma for banks in this respect is that they are not software or equipment specialists. Banks may be able to buy the software or equipment "wholesale" and then keep their brand names attached and prominent for users; but scale effects and the banks' expertise limitations may make this a risky and costly strategy. They may be able to form consortia or joint ventures of banks to buy the software or equipment,[11] thus easing the scale problems and possibly even their expertise problems.[12] Otherwise, individual banks may face the unpleasant choice of either watching third-party branded entities gain some of the contact with and subsequent loyalties of their customers or risking the total loss of their customers if they do not provide the new service at all while other banks (or non-banks) are providing it.

*3.1.3 Network Effects.* As we noted in Section 2, the new technologies have important network effects, and the development of tech-

---

[10] Again, the sale of goods and services through independent retailers may well be the course of greater efficiency. Manufacturers typically arrange for the sale of consumer goods through independent retailers, such as supermarkets and department stores, thereby gaining widespread distribution; it seems unlikely that the H.J. Heinz Co., for example, would benefit from trying to sell its ketchup and pickles exclusively through its own retail outlets. There is no magic or inherent efficiency in greater (or lesser) vertical integration as a general rule; the efficient extent of vertical integration is idiosyncratic to the technologies and managerial capabilities of individual industries and even individual companies. But the *transition* for firms that have been accustomed to direct contact with their retail customers, along with the potential diminution of the power of their brand names, could be wrenching indeed.

[11] This has been done successfully in the case of ATMs and medium-successfully in credit cards. The problem in the latter area is that non-banks (e.g., AT&T) have been allowed to join the consortia and thus offer extra competition to banks. In 1995 Nations Bank and Bank of America purchased MECA from H&R Block. MECA's principal product is Managing Your Money, a personal finance software system that is competitive with Intuit's Quicken and Microsoft's Money. Several other large banks have since acquired equity interests in the company. It remains to be seen whether this joint venture will be financially successful, but it clearly reduces the vulnerability of the participants to competitive pressure from non-bank competitors.

[12] But consortia may present their own problems of coordination and strategic behavior (Jorde and Teece, 1990; Ordover, 1991).

nical standards – so as to ensure widespread compatibility among users, and thus to obtain scale and usage benefits – is an important phenomenon for networks.[13] At the early stages of development of technologies, competing providers may offer competing and incompatible approaches. Investing in one of the approaches can be risky and costly, if that approach does not survive. (But, again, holding back and not committing may also be risky and costly in a competitive market.) Over time, as technologies mature, standards may arise in a *de facto* manner, if a third party's software or hardware becomes the dominant means of providing the service, or industry consortia may be the vehicle for coordinating and achieving a set of standards.

Standards are important in all of the innovations we are considering. Merchants may be willing to accept stored-value cards issued by many different banks or non-banks, but not if they need a different terminal for each card. Utilities and other billers who accept electronic payments find that these payments are much more expensive to handle than paper checks because of the lack of standardization in formats.

The importance of standardization, the increased value for each participant in a system as the number of participants increases, and the low marginal costs of system operation together result in markets with increasing returns to scale. That is, the larger is the system, the lower are its unit costs, the greater is its value to new participants, and hence the greater is its potential profitability. Such markets are subject to "tipping" – "the tendency of one system to pull away from its rivals in popularity once it has gained an initial edge" (Katz and Shapiro, 1994, p. 106).

*3.1.4 Synergies Among the Electronic Innovations.* There are likely to be synergies among these electronic innovations. For example, if stored-value or smart cards can be replenished at a home PC through a telephone or Internet process, both the use of the cards and the use of the Internet or telephone channels for home banking are likely to be greater than would be the case if there were totally separate technologies.

---

[13] It is important to note that incompatibility among systems may sometimes be bridged easily through low-cost modifications to equipment or through software applications. For example, "incompatible" 33-1/3, 45, and 78 rpm records could all be played on most record players through modest gear adjustments on turntable motors, and Macintosh PCs can now be equipped with software that will allow them to read otherwise incompatible Windows-Intel programs and files. On the other hand, no one ever invented a low-cost VCR that could "read" both Beta and VHS formats.

*3.1.5 Capturing Customer Information.* The new technologies are likely to allow banks more effectively to capture substantially more transactions information about their customers. In principle, some of this information (e.g., where a bank customer conducts many of his/her retail transactions) is currently available from checks and credit card information; but extracting the information in usable form, especially from checks, is currently unwieldy. With better and cheaper electronics, however, and with electronic bill-paying, smart cards,[14] and credit cards, a bank customer could leave an extensive electronic trail of where, when, and what he/she buys.

This information could then be used by the bank directly in its "cross-marketing" of other goods and services.[15] And the information could be valuable if sold to other marketers. But many bank customers may react strongly and negatively if they discover that their transactions are being tracked in great detail and that this information is then being sold and used by others.[16] The best long-run strategy to maintain the loyalty of its customers is probably for the bank to disclose its policies with respect to information collection, usage, and sale and (on the assumption that the transactions costs would not be large) to provide opt-in and/or opt-out choices for their customers.[17]

### 3.2 Some Specific Observations

*3.2.1 Electronic Bill-Paying and Home Banking.* These technologies are still at stages that are far from mature. With "electronic" bill-paying programs, for example, over half of the payments are still made by paper check issued by a third-party bill-payer (e.g., because the payment recipient is not connected electronically to the system); these systems are not yet providing the reductions in transactions

---

[14] And even a stored-value card that is issued specifically to a user and has the user's identification on it would allow the capture of information. The capture of information will not occur, however, for anonymous stored-value cards, as is currently the case for transit cards and telephone cards.

[15] This advantage for banks is reminiscent of the argument that banks that make loans to small businesses are better able to monitor those loans by being able to monitor those firms' checking accounts (Nakamura, 1993).

[16] Will bank customers react as strongly if they discover that the information is being used by other parts of the bank? What about bank subsidiaries? Or sister subsidiaries of the bank's holding company?

[17] We expect that the cost consequences of a customer's choices would be reflected in the prices charged the customer for the bank's services.

costs that seem possible. Further, because of problems of formats, account numbers, and the absence of payment coupons or stubs to accompany the electronic payment (or even the electronically initiated paper check), payments can be misrecorded or otherwise go awry, to the displeasure and unhappiness of the original bank customer (Hansell, 1996a, 1996b; Weber, 1996; Geldard, 1996) and increased costs to the payment recipient; that is, the potential for error makes the value of the service to the consumer lower than its potential. These problems could become worse as home banking systems attempt to provide more functions and services.

The numbers of users of home banking services are currently quite small, and even large annual percentage increases for a few years would still imply small absolute numbers.[18] Though there are risks to banks from allowing an Intuit or a Microsoft to become the exclusive or dominant provider of these services, there are also the risks of unhappy customers if banks become overly identified with ill-performing systems. Cautious movement forward – through bank consortia, if possible – appears to be the best strategy for banks.

*3.2.2 The Internet.* The most promising short-term use of the Internet appears to be as an advertising and information vehicle. The providers of standardized financial products – such as CDs, auto loans, and residential mortgages – may be able to advertise their prices and availability in a low-cost and effective manner, thereby increasing the intensity of competition for the products.

The use of the Internet to effect payments still appears to be hampered by concerns about security and fears that criminal hackers could intercept messages and gain access to credit card numbers[19] and/or shift funds out of an individual's account. Until these security problems are solved to the satisfaction of risk-averse bank customers (and/or adequate indemnification or reimbursement arrangements are in place), the

---

[18] Discussions of the problems in these systems can be found in Hoenig (1995) and Horvitz (1996).

[19] At first glance, the security problems of credit card numbers over the Internet would appear to be no worse than those of everyday usage of credit cards, whereby individuals regularly give their cards or card numbers to store personnel, restaurant waiters, and telephone sales personnel, who could easily transcribe the numbers for future use. But credit card system managers are confident that they could spot and control such illicit uses of card numbers, whereas they are currently concerned about their abilities to trace hackers' lifting of the information.

Internet's use for financial transactions is likely to remain limited.[20] Again, cautious movement through bank consortia appears to be the sensible route.

    *3.2.3 Stored-Value and Smart Cards.* Banks may face an interesting political-economy strategic choice. They might try to lobby for regulatory restrictions, such that banks are the only entities that are permitted to issue these types of cards.[21] But the cards would then be encumbered with the restraints of regulation, which banks are generally trying to minimize. Alternatively, they could accept a non-regulated environment for the cards; but they must then be concerned about whether they can successfully compete with efficient non-banks (e.g., AT&T, GE Capital) in that environment. The proliferation of stored-value cards – by telephone companies, transit systems, universities, etc. – may have proceeded so far, however, that the former strategy may not currently be a realistic option,[22] and banks may have to do the best that they can in the latter environment.

    Stored-value and smart cards may be a convenient substitute for cash in small transactions – this is the route that is being pursued by a number of universities with respect to the on-campus purchases of their students – or they could be a substitute for travelers' checks (and be useful for trips, including those that require foreign currencies).[23] Both functions, of course, are possible. Also, smart cards have the advantage that they can be replenished and can carry other information that might be useful in transactions (e.g., frequent flier numbers, medical histories, etc.).

    A uniform format – so that users do not have to purchase and carry

---

[20] Announcements of the development of secure payments systems for the Internet have been invariably followed by successful efforts to break the security system by amateurs viewing the announcement as an intellectual challenge. The developers of the system promptly fix the weakness. Because there is no significant volume of transactions on the Internet, we have not yet had incentives for well-financed, organized, criminal groups to pierce the security of Internet payments systems. If they are successful, they are unlikely to call a press conference to relate how they did it and where the bugs in the system are.

[21] This is the direction that the European Union (EU) appears to be heading.

[22] If stored-value and/or smart cards were to attain widespread usage *and* there were some notorious failures of card issuers, the political system might re-open the question of who should be permitted to issue these cards. See our discussion in Section 4.

[23] In principle, since the issuing bank's identification would have to be part of the encoded information on a stored-value card or a smart card (so that the recipient of the electronic "dollars" in a transaction could ultimately redeem them from the issuer), the replacement-if-lost feature of travelers' checks would also be possible.

multiple cards and merchants do not have to maintain multiple readers – will clearly enhance the cards' usefulness and acceptance.

## 4 Public Policy

Just as the new electronic technologies present challenges for banks, they also present challenges for the public policies that surround banks. Those policies can be broadly described as "regulation" and "antitrust." Included in the former category are three federal agencies (the Federal Reserve, the Office of the Comptroller of the Currency, and the Federal Deposit Insurance Corporation) and 50 state agencies and a wide range of goals (including maintaining the safety and soundness of banks and thus the safety of their deposits, ensuring that their customers are adequately informed about the terms of their financial transactions, and preventing abuses based on market power or information asymmetries).[24] In the latter category are two federal agencies (the Antitrust Division of the U.S. Department of Justice, and the Federal Trade Commission) and 50 state attorneys general[25] and the more specific goals of maintaining competitive market structures and preventing the exercise of market power.

These regulatory and antitrust agencies do have roles to play with respect to the emerging technologies. But, in an environment of rapidly changing technologies, cautious movement is generally the recommended course. Regulatory actions affect the relative costs (and even the feasibility) of alternative technologies and services. An incorrect regulatory action may preclude banks from following what may turn out to be the optimum path. We believe that the regulatory agencies should eschew action in the absence of a clear and present danger to bank safety and soundness, and the Federal Reserve should not attempt to shape technological developments on the basis of what is the most convenient for the conduct of monetary policy.

### 4.1 Some General Observations

*4.1.1 Safety-and-Soundness Considerations.* Because banks play a crucial role in the payments system of the U.S. and because they are an important repository for the savings of individuals who are likely to

---

[24] For an overview of U.S. financial regulation and its relationship to technological innovation, see White (1999).

[25] Also, private parties can bring civil suits under the federal antitrust laws and, if successful in winning and demonstrating injury, gain treble damages.

be poorly informed about their financial institution's solvency, safety-and-soundness regulation can serve legitimate, market-enhancing purposes (Diamond and Dybvig, 1983; Postlewaite and Vives, 1987). Further, the need for such regulation is likely to be greatest when banks come under stress – when their operating margins become thinner and when operating and/or capital losses cause their capital (or net worth) to be relatively thin. It is at such times that bank owners and managers face the greatest ("moral hazard") temptations to undertake risky strategies, since the legal principles of limited liability for corporate owners imply that they are unlikely to suffer the "downside" consequences of large losses from risk-taking, while they will be the beneficiaries of the "upside" gains.

The new technologies are likely to increase the competitive pressures felt by banks, as well as giving them more opportunities to make costly strategic mistakes, at a time when competitive pressures on banks will be greater anyway (e.g., because of changes in state and federal laws that permit more widespread branching by banks, and because improved telecommunications and data processing technologies generally are allowing non-banks to provide many of the products and services that were previously the preserve of banks). In this environment, the scrutiny of safety-and-soundness regulators should be enhanced, the balance-sheet information available to them should be based on up-to-date values,[26] and minimum capital requirements must be enforced vigorously and appropriately to the underlying risks embedded in the regulated institutions. This should not, however, be an excuse for major increases in bank regulation or for restrictions on banks' financial activities.

*4.1.2 Networks and Standards.* As we have noted a number of times in this paper, the new technologies have important networks aspects, which make issues of compatibility and technical standards to achieve that compatibility important. Public policy can play a role here in at least two ways.

First, antitrust enforcement can prevent dominant firms from using their market power to establish and enforce standards that may raise barriers to entry and inhibit competition.[27] Similarly, antitrust can

---

[26] I.e., on market value accounting information.

[27] The Justice Department's successful challenge of the proposed purchase of Intuit by Microsoft appeared to be based on the fear that the combined entity would possess such market power, with these consequences, in the home banking area (Horvitz, 1996).

prevent coalitions of firms from using their collective market power to establish standards that freeze out rivals, especially aggressive "mavericks." There are extensive dangers here, however, of actually discouraging competition in the name of enhancing it. Firms that develop systems and the supporting standards may well be reluctant to share them with rivals, and antitrust decisions that force such sharing may discourage the investment in and development of such systems in the first place – because the system developers may believe that they cannot receive an adequate return on their investment and efforts, and because firms generally may come to believe that they can readily join other systems and hence need not make the effort to develop their own.

Similar issues were faced in the development of ATM systems. The general regulatory approach has been to treat ATM networks as an "essential facility" and require that deployers of ATMs make them available on reasonable terms to all banks. While there may have been legitimate concerns about protecting small banks, the result is that competition among ATM systems is now virtually nonexistent (Baker, 1996).[28]

Second, regulatory agencies can be the vehicle for the achievement of technical standards. They can take a completely "hands off" stance; or they can provide a forum and informal encouragement for industry members to reach agreements among themselves; or they can establish the technical standards through regulatory edict.[29] There are always risks, however, that the regulatory process may force an agreement too soon in the development process and/or that the regulatory edict settles on an inappropriate or inefficient standard. Because of the tipping problem, mistakes may be very difficult to reverse.

In sum, the right course of action for public policy in the field of technical standards is extremely difficult to distill *ex ante*. Delay of action may allow the entrenchment of market power; premature action may stifle development and competition. And determining the right point in the trade-off between the benefits of compatibility and ubiquity, on the

---

[28] The attempt to protect small banks in this way may have backfired as surcharging for ATM transactions has become more common. If there were competing ATM systems, competition with respect to surcharges would give bank customers more choice. Under current circumstances, large banks can attract customers from small banks by offering widespread ATM convenience that is free of surcharges.

[29] For example, the Federal Communications Commission, which has been in the middle of standard-setting processes in telecommunications, has at various times adopted all of these strategies (Besen and Johnson, 1986).

one hand, and of competition between systems, on the other, is difficult indeed.[30]

### 4.1.3 Timing.

In public policy, as in sports, timing is often crucial. As we have discussed above, in a field experiencing rapid technological change, premature public policy actions may stifle, retard, or distort important developments;[31] but excessively delayed policy actions may allow the entrenchment of market power. *Ex ante*, these timing questions have no easy answers.

### 4.2 Some Specific Observations

### 4.2.1 Electronic-Bill Paying and Home Banking.

To the extent that electronic payments by bank customers do become popular and add to the already quite large bank-to-bank electronic funds transfer (EFT) flows (through the FedWire and CHIPS), the "daylight overdraft" problems of systemic risk among banks may be exacerbated.[32] These problems arise when a bank promises to transfer funds to another bank early in a business day but actually transfers the funds later in the day. In essence, the latter bank is extending a loan to the former bank during the intervening period. If a major bank were to fail during such an intervening period and thus be unable to honor its obligations, either there could be major systemic and cascading effects among banks, or (more likely) the Federal Reserve would have to assume and satisfy the failed bank's obligations (Humphrey, 1986, 1989). In the latter scenario, the Federal Reserve has become the guarantor of banks' intra-day obligations. To deal with this problem, the Federal Reserve has informally discouraged large daylight overdraft positions and has recently begun charging very small interest fees on daylight overdraft positions on the FedWire.

---

[30]  For an argument that antitrust policy in the area of ATMs has been too tolerant of claims of required access to and too tolerant of mergers among ATM networks and thus has excessively favored ubiquity at the expense of competition, see Baker (1996).

[31]  For example, the Federal Reserve has proposed differential regulatory treatment for stored-value and smart cards that are above and below $100. The lighter restrictions on the lesser-valued cards may well cause banks to focus their product development efforts on these lesser-valued cards. But, if the major use of these cards is eventually as a substitute for travelers' checks (rather than as a substitute for cash in small transactions), this regulatory distinction may well be premature and misguided.

[32]  The dollar volume of retail payments that may ultimately flow electronically, while large in absolute amount, would nevertheless be much less than the existing volume of payments now flowing over the FedWire.

4.2.2 *Stored-Value and Smart Cards.* Should bank regulators treat these as "money"? An immediate implication of such treatment would be either that only banks should be permitted to issue them or that other issuers should be subject to financial suitability requirements, such as capital or collateralization requirements.[33]

To address this question, it is worth reviewing the arguments favoring special regulatory (i.e., safety-and-soundness) treatment of banks.[34] The specialness arguments usually have two alternative strands: First, since banks' deposit liabilities are generally much more liquid (thus making them money or near-money) than their assets, they are susceptible to runs by nervous or ill-informed depositors, and the runs could be contagious and costly, forcing the premature closure of or suspension of deposit liquidity by even solvent banks (Diamond and Dybvig, 1983; Postlewaite and Vives, 1987). Second, banks' depositors are likely to be ill-equipped to monitor the financial dealings and financial health of their institutions and thus to protect themselves, while their losses in the event of their bank's failure could involve significant fractions of their savings.[35]

These are weak arguments for restrictive regulatory treatment of stored-value or smart cards at this stage in their development. It seems unlikely that card issuers would be subject to serious runs by card holders. And, though the holders of these cards are likely to be in a poor position to monitor the financial health of the card issuers, the sums involved for any card holder are likely to be relatively small.[36] Further, there will be merchants who will accrue substantial claims against the issuers of electronic money. They will have an incentive to monitor and police the credit quality of card issuers and to accept only the cards

---

[33] Other issues would include whether FDIC insurance should be available for these liabilities and whether banks would be required to hold reserves at the Federal Reserve against them. The FDIC has recently concluded that, depending on how a bank arranges these accounts, deposit insurance may or may not be available; see *Federal Register*, 61 (August 2, 1996), pp. 40490–40494.

[34] The arguments also justify deposit insurance. It is worth noting, however, that the special safety-and-soundness treatment of banks by the states and by the federal government long pre-dates the institution of federal deposit insurance.

[35] This second strand also provides the justification for special safety-and-soundness treatment for insurance companies and defined-benefit pension funds and for the government insurance and indemnification arrangements that have surrounded these institutions.

[36] Indeed, the individual holders of purchased-but-not-yet-used airline tickets are likely to lose larger sums from the financial failure of an airline than would the individual holders of these cards.

issued by credit-worthy issuers. Though consumers are unlikely to do their own credit analysis, they will tend to buy the cards that will be accepted by merchants.

In sum, despite these cards' use as a medium of exchange and facilitator of transactions and thus as a form of money, we believe that the wisest regulatory course at present would be one of benign neglect.[37] If these instruments should flourish and become so popular that the arguments for special treatment then become persuasive, there should still be adequate opportunity for bank regulators to revisit the issue and take appropriate actions.[38]

*4.2.3 Privacy.* As we indicated in Section 3, the new electronic technologies will provide banks with the ability to capture extensive transactions information about their customers. It is easy to see how some bank customers (and their governmental representatives) could fear potential abuse of this information and thus demand regulatory prohibitions on such abuse.

In principle, a well-functioning competitive market should solve such potential problems without the need for regulatory intervention. Individual banks would establish and announce their policies with respect to the use of this information. Some banks might proudly announce, "We promise that this information will never be used, even by other subsidiaries of the bank!" Others might promise only that the information might never be sold to third parties. Yet others would acknowledge that the information would be sold but that the gains would be passed to the bank's customers through lower prices for services. Or some banks would offer the choice of any of these possibilities to their customers. Bank customers would thus have a set of price-quality alternatives available to them and could choose among those alternatives. The absence of any

---

[37] There have been a few financial failures of relatively small issuers of pre-paid (stored-value) telephone cards, leaving the card holders with modest losses (Naik, 1996). A major failure could well generate widespread newspaper and television news stories, including interviews with the unfortunate holders of the suddenly worthless cards. Legislators may then hold hearings and ask why regulators had not anticipated these events and issued regulations to forestall them. Despite the likelihood of *ex post* thunderings, we nevertheless believe that the best *ex ante* course of action is that of no action.

[38] It has been suggested to us that banks' heavy load of regulation places them at a competitive disadvantage vis-a-vis non-bank issuers of these cards and that this disadvantage creates a reason for restricting issuance to banks. Though a "second best" argument can be created here, we are unconvinced as to the strength of its merits (and we shudder to think of the implications of the argument for other financial products offered by both banks and non-banks).

announced policy by a bank would likely cause its customers to believe the worst about its policies and to make their choices accordingly.

Nevertheless, to forestall potential opportunistic behavior by some banks, a minimalist but prudent regulatory stance would be to require that banks establish clear policies with respect to the use of their customers' transactions information and announce their policies to their customers.[39] A regulatory requirement that banks also offer opt-in and/or opt-out alternatives to their customers does not seem warranted. If the transactions costs of offering these alternatives are low, banks in a competitive market structure will offer them; if the transactions costs are high, then the net gain from their being required could well be negative.

## 5  Conclusion

The new electronic technologies will clearly pose interesting and important challenges for banks and for their regulators. On both sides of the private/public interface, there is the trade-off between the danger of being left behind and the danger of choosing the wrong technology. Value-maximizing private-sector firms face these choices frequently and have developed techniques for making investment decisions; we have little new advice for them. On the public-policy side, we see greater danger from regulation that is too soon or too heavy-handed than from regulation that is too tardy.

### References

Baker, Donald I., "Shared ATM Networks – The Antitrust Dimension," *Antitrust Bulletin*, 41 (Summer 1996), pp. 399–425.

Besen, Stanley M. and Joseph Farrell, "Choosing How to Compete: Strategies and Tactics in Standardization," *Journal of Economic Perspectives*, 8 (Spring 1994), pp. 117–131.

Besen Stanley M. and Leland L. Johnson, *Compatibility Standards, Competition, and Innovation in the Broadcasting Industry*. Washington, D.C.: Rand, 1986.

Brooks, John, *Telephone: The First Hundred Years*. New York: Harper & Row, 1975.

Cadette, Walter, "Universal Banking: A U.S. Perspective," in Anthony Saunders and Ingo Walter, eds., *Universal Banking: Financial System Design Reconsidered*. Chicago: Irwin, 1996, pp. 696–715.

Congressional Budget Office, *Emerging Electronic Methods for Making Retail Payments*, (June 1996).

Coulton, Antoinette, "Gemplus Marketing More in Nonbank Directions," *American Banker*, March 25, 1998.

---

[39] The rationale for regulation is enhanced by the potential for broadened services provided by banks. The potential for cross-selling, and the use of customer information, are increased in an organization such as the proposed Citicorp-Travelers combination.

Diamond, Douglas W. and Philip H. Dybvig, "Bank Runs, Deposit Insurance, and Liquidity," *Journal of Political Economy*, 91 (June 1983), pp. 401–419.

Economides, Nicholas, "The Economics of Networks," *International Journal of Industrial Organization*, 14 (October 1996), pp. 673–699.

Edwards, Franklin R., *The New Finance: Regulation and Financial Stability*. Washington, D.C.: American Enterprise Institute, 1996.

Geldard, Richard G., "I'd Rather Use a Checkbook," *New York Times*, February 11, 1996, pp. 3–13.

General Accounting Office, "Electronic Banking: Experiences Reported by Banks in Implementing On-line Banking," GAO/GGD-98-34, January 15, 1998.

Hansell, Saul, "Banking at Home: Once More, with Feeling," *New York Times*, February 25, 1996a, pp. 3–1.

Hansell, Saul, "Finding Your Glitch in Banking on Your PC," *New York Times*, February 5, 1996b, pp. 3–9.

Hoenig, Thomas M., "The Evolution of the Payments System: A U.S. Perspective," *Economic Review* (Federal Reserve Bank of Kansas City), 80 (Third Quarter 1995), pp. 5–9.

Horvitz, Paul M., "Efficiency and Antitrust Considerations in Home Banking: The Proposed Microsoft-Intuit Merger," *Antitrust Bulletin*, 41 (Summer 1996), pp. 427–446.

Humphrey, David B., "Payments Finality and Risk of Settlement Failure," in Anthony Saunders and Lawrence J. White, eds., *Technology and the Regulation of Financial Markets: Securities, Futures, and Banking*. Lexington, Mass.: Heath, 1986, pp. 97–120.

Humphrey, David B., "Market Responses to Pricing Fedwire Daylight Overdrafts," *Economic Review* (Federal Reserve Bank of Richmond) 75, (May/June 1989), pp. 23–34.

"Huntington Claims 100,000 Web Accounts," *American Banker*, May 14, 1998, p. 17.

Jorde, Thomas and David Teece, "Innovation and Cooperation: Implications for Competition and Antitrust," *Journal of Economic Perspectives*, 4 (Summer 1990), pp. 75–96.

Katz, Michael L. and Carl Shapiro, "Systems Competition and Network Effects," *Journal of Economic Perspectives*, 8 (Spring 1994), pp. 93–115.

Kroszner, Randall S., "The Evolution of Universal Banking and Its Regulation in Twentieth Century America," in Anthony Saunders and Ingo Walter, eds., *Universal Banking: Financial System Design Reconsidered*. Chicago: Irwin, 1996, pp. 70–99.

Kutler, Jeffrey and Antoinette Coulton, "Industry Inertia Subdues Conference Mood," *American Banker*, May 6, 1998, p. 14.

Liebowitz, S. J. and Stephen E. Margolis, "Network Externality: An Uncommon Tragedy," *Journal of Economics Perspectives*, 8 (Spring 1994), pp. 133–150.

Litan, Robert E., *What Should Banks Do?* Washington, D.C.: Brookings Institution, 1987.

Luhby, Tami, "National Commerce Demonstrating Home Banking Software in Branches," *American Banker*, April 2, 1998, p. 18.

Marjanovic, Steven, "37% of Households Using ACH Bill Payment," *American Banker*, May 15, 1998, p. 10.

Nakamura, Leonard I., "Commercial Bank Information: Implications for the Structure of Banking," in Michael Klausner and Lawrence J. White, eds., *Structural Change in Banking*, Homewood, Ill.: Business One Irwin, 1993, pp. 131–160.

Naik, Gautam, "Sorry, Your Prepaid Phone Card Has Been Deactivated," *Wall Street Journal*, July 16, 1996, p. B1.

Ordover, Janusz A., "A Patent System for Both Diffusion and Exclusion," *Journal of Economic Perspectives*, 5 (Winter 1991), pp. 43–60.

Pae, Peter and Devon Spurgeon, "Smart Cards Get off to a Slow Start," *Washington Post*, March 21, 1998, p. D1.

Postlewaite, Andrew and Xavier Vives, "Bank Runs as an Equilibrium Phenomenon," *Journal of Political Economy*, 95 (June 1987), pp. 485–491.

Weber, Thomas E., "Glitches Short-Circuit Miracle of Paying Bills On-Line," *Wall Street Journal*, February 7, 1996, p. B1.

Wenninger, John and David Laster, "The Electronic Purse," *Current Issues in Economics and Finance* (Federal Reserve Bank of New York), 1 (April 1995), pp. 1–5.

White, Lawrence J., "U.S. Public Policy Toward Network Industries." American Enterprise Institute, Washington, D. C., 1999.

White, Lawrence J., "Technological Change, Financial Innovation, and Financial Regulation in the U.S.: The Challenges for Public Policy," Chapter 12 in this volume (2000).

## 12

# Technological Change, Financial Innovation, and Financial Regulation in the U.S.: The Challenges for Public Policy

Lawrence J. White[a]

## 1 Introduction

The financial services sector in the United States is experiencing an era of rapid innovation. These changes are fueled by the rapid improvements in the two technologies – data processing and telecommunications – that are at the heart of financial services. The financial services sector is also one of the most heavily regulated sectors in the U.S. economy – despite two decades of widespread deregulation.

Though technological improvements and innovations are almost always healthy and beneficial for an economy, they can place serious strains on the incumbents in a particular industry or sector on which they are focused, and they may create challenges for public policy, especially in a heavily regulated industry. This has certainly been true for financial services. Further, the heavy overlay of government regulation on the financial services sector has certainly influenced the course of financial innovation and, in turn, been influenced by it.

This chapter will provide an overview of these interactions between financial innovation and financial regulation.[1] Regulation clearly can be a hindrance to innovation; sometimes it may be a spur to innovation. And actual or prospective innovation may, in turn, be an important precursor to subsequent regulation. The social welfare consequences of

[a] Stern School of Business, New York University.

[1] This chapter draws heavily on White (1996a); see also Saunders and White (1986). I have also benefitted greatly from the New York Academy of Sciences' discussion series on "Technology and Finance" held during the spring of 1996. An earlier version of this chapter was prepared for that series.

these complex interactions, and the implications for the development of public policy, are themselves a challenge to disentangle; but an understanding of the processes of innovation and of regulation can clarify the interactions and thus help to structure the public policy debate.

The remainder of this chapter will proceed as follows: The remaining portion of this section will establish an important distinction among types of financial institutions, which will prove useful in the subsequent discussion of financial regulation. Section 2 will provide an overview of financial innovation. Section 3 will describe the broad picture of U.S. financial regulation: its structure, processes, and rationale. Section 4 will then focus on a number of current areas in financial services where issues of innovation and regulation intersect. Section 5 will provide a brief conclusion.[2]

### 1.1 A Classification of Financial Services Providers

At the beginning, an important distinction in function among firms in the financial services sector – between financial intermediaries and financial facilitators – is worthwhile (although, as we discuss below, firms are increasingly offering multiple financial services and thereby encompassing both types of function). *Financial intermediaries* are firms that hold financial assets (e.g., loans, mortgages, bonds, equity securities) and issue liabilities (such as deposits, insurance policies, pension obligations, mutual fund shares, etc.) on themselves, thereby intermediating between their liability holders and the ultimate investments to which their liability holders' funds have been devoted. Familiar types of financial intermediaries include banks and other depository institutions (such as savings banks, savings and loan associations, and credit unions); insurance companies; pension funds; mutual funds; mortgage conduits; finance companies; leasing companies; and venture capital firms. The liabilities of these financial intermediaries constitute important assets for the non-financial business and household sectors of the U.S. economy. In addition, firms that are not usually considered to be part of the financial sector are increasingly acting as financial intermediaries. Every company that extends trade credit to its customers (e.g., allowing payment to be due 30 or 60 days after the delivery of goods or services) is acting as a lender; in some cases, these trade credit arrangements have subsequently led to formal finance company arrangements, such as General Motors'

---

[2] Also, because discussions of technology and of government regulation inevitably involve concepts and organizations that are identified through abbreviations, we also provide an appendix with a glossary of the abbreviations used in this paper.

GMAC affiliate or General Electric's GE Capital. And some companies, such as AT&T, have explicitly plunged into financial services through the issuance of credit cards.

The second category of firms – *financial facilitators* – facilitate the financial transactions between the primary issuers of financial liabilities – e.g., governments, enterprises, and household borrowers – and the investors who purchase these instruments (and in whose hands they are financial assets). In this category are stockbrokers, securities underwriters, market makers, dealers, investment bankers, mortgage bankers, mortgage brokers, financial advisers, rating agencies, accountants, financial analysts, and the financial press. Though firms in some of these categories may hold some financial assets, their holdings are largely incidental to their facilitating roles.

Many firms in the financial services sector straddle the intermediary/ facilitator boundary. For example, many stock brokerage firms also manage and sell mutual funds; and commercial banks are increasingly entering various aspects of the securities industry. Indeed, the continuing evolution of financial innovation and financial deregulation is highly likely to increase the extent to which financial sector firms will encompass services embodying both intermediary and facilitator functions. Still, the distinction between *intermediaries* and *facilitators* will prove useful in understanding the structure and role of financial regulation in the U.S. and in understanding the pressures and strains that some forms of technological innovation (e.g., the expansion of non-traditional lenders, and the processes of securitization) are placing on some financial sector firms (e.g., traditional portfolio lender intermediaries, such as banks).

## 2 Financial Innovation

### 2.1 Some General Concepts

Innovation consists of firms' developing new products (or services) and/or new production processes. Often, but not always, the new products are based on new processes; sometimes also new organizations – organizational innovations – are involved. In essence, innovation involves new ways of doing things.

The conditions that spawn or encourage innovation are multi-faceted (Cohen and Levin, 1989; Scherer and Ross, 1990, ch. 17). Among the important influences are:[3]

---

[3] Of course, in a market-oriented economy the profit-seeking behavior of individuals and enterprises is the underlying basis for innovation.

- the nature of the technology underlying the industry and the rate of change of that technology;
- the structure (e.g., firm size) and competitiveness of the industry;
- the economic environment of the industry; and
- the regulatory environment of the industry.

### 2.2 Applications to the Financial Sector

Innovation – product and process – is not new to the financial services sector. Firms in the various subsectors of finance (e.g., banking, securities, insurance, etc.) have a long history of developing new instruments and services and of developing improved "back office" processes to reduce the costs of existing services and to support the offering of new ones (Van Horne, 1985; Miller, 1986, 1992; Finnerty, 1992; Merton, 1992; Allen and Gale, 1995; Lea, 1996). Further, even the electronics-based technological innovations that have attracted much attention recently are not new to financial services. The development of the telegraph in the 1840s soon led to its use for wire transfers of funds and for the dissemination of price information ("quotes") with respect to gold and securities that were traded on various exchanges, nationally and internationally (Garbade and Silber, 1978). The invention of the telephone in 1876 was followed the next year by the first commercial installation of telephones – by two bankers (Brooks, 1975, p. 3). Large branch-office brokerage firms' extensive use of the telegraph and the telephone soon earned them the descriptive term "wire houses." The electronic funds transfer (EFT) system of the FedWire was developed shortly after the establishment of the Federal Reserve in 1913.

Nevertheless, the pace of innovation clearly has quickened dramatically since the late 1960s; by contrast, the pre-1960s decades seem quite placid and staid. Consistent with the list provided above, there are at least four underlying causes, often with mutually interacting effects on innovation, that can help explain this near-revolution in financial innovation that has occurred.[4] First, the underlying technologies of finance – data

---

[4] In addition to the causes discussed in the text, there appears to be at least one additional motive for financial innovation: reducing the tax burden on financial instruments and transactions. To the extent that some kinds of instruments and transactions are taxed less than others, there is a strong incentive to try to recast or re-engineer those that are in the high-tax categories so that they then qualify for more favorable tax treatment. For example, if capital gains are taxed more lightly than other forms of income (or they are taxed on a realization, rather than accrual, basis), there is an incentive to create instruments that convert dividend or interest payments into capital gains; similarly, if interest payments are a deductible expense to companies but dividend payments are not, innovation will focus on instruments that convert the latter into the former (Campbell, 1988, ch. 16).

processing and telecommunications – have themselves undergone near-revolutions, becoming dramatically more powerful *and* less costly on almost a daily basis. These improved technologies have allowed "financial engineers" better to amass data, assess risks, and thereby design new products and services that can better meet the financial demands of individuals and enterprises. And these products and services can be offered across wide geographic areas. The securitization of many categories of previously illiquid loans – most notably, residential real estate mortgages and credit card receivables – and the offering of credit card services nationally from remote locations (e.g., South Dakota) are good illustrations of these developments.

Second, legal and regulatory changes – generally in the direction of less restrictiveness and less protectionism (i.e., deregulation) – have reinforced these technological improvements, yielding heightened levels of competition throughout the financial services sector. In turn, these greater competitive pressures have forced incumbents to find improved and less costly ways of providing financial services, and deregulation has made it easier for innovators to enter these markets.

Third, the U.S. economic environment changed sharply. After two postwar decades of relatively steady economic growth, low inflation rates, low interest rates, and fixed foreign exchange rates – in short, an economic world of modest fluctuations and apparently low risks – the U.S. economy began traveling over a much rockier road. Inflation rates became higher and more variable in the late 1960s and the following decade and a half, as did interest rates. Foreign exchange rates were unfixed in 1971 and have mostly fluctuated since then. In sum, the world had become a much riskier place by the early 1970s, and the demand for financial instruments to buffer and hedge some of these heightened risks grew commensurately. The development of financial futures and options, most notably by the exchanges located in Chicago, was a direct response to this demand.

Fourth, the dense regulatory structure (to be discussed in Section 3) that envelops much of the financial sector has also been influential in inducing innovation.[5] In the 1970s, especially, some important innovations were inspired by efforts to avoid or circumvent regulatory restrictions. For example, the Banking Act of 1933 required that the Federal

---

[5] Regulation can also inhibit innovation. For example, U.S. securities regulation for many decades prohibited the development of mutual funds that held as assets the shares of other mutual funds; and options on commodities have been prohibited since the 1930s.

Reserve (through its "Regulation Q") restrict the interest that banks could pay on deposits.[6] In the inflationary and higher-interest-rate environment of the 1970s, these constraints became tightly binding, which motivated a number of circumventing innovations. Three notable innovations were the development of the money market mutual fund, the offering of interest-paying checking accounts by credit unions and by savings banks in the Northeast, and the development of the "sweep account" by commercial banks (whereby banks would "sweep," on an overnight basis, idle checking account funds of their customers into interest-bearing securities).[7] Similarly, the Glass-Steagall Act of 1933 has prevented securities firms from owning and operating a commercial bank (and vice versa).[8] This constraint was part of the motivation for Merrill Lynch to develop (and to patent) its "Cash Management Account" (CMA), which allowed customers to buy and sell securities, earn interest on idle funds, write checks, and have a credit card – all linked to a common account. Since the late 1980s, the progressive easing of many regulatory restrictions has in turn encouraged financial innovation; the development of customized swaps, hedges, and other derivative instruments in the late 1980s and early 1990s – by commercial banks as well as by securities firms – is a good illustration of the results of this regulatory loosening.

In sum, financial innovation has been influenced by a number of important environmental factors, including the regulatory framework in which much of finance is embedded. It is to an elucidation of that framework that we now turn.

---

[6] Most of the "Reg Q" restrictions were phased out in the early 1980s; the prohibition on banks' paying interest on the checking accounts of commercial customers still stands, however.

[7] Also, though Regulation Q did not directly cause the development of "repurchase agreements" or "repos" (which are, in essence, short-term loans involving securities as the collateral), it greatly encouraged their use by banks as substitutes for deposits.

[8] In the past two decades, sharp-eyed lawyers, aided and abetted by bank regulators and the courts, have found a number of loopholes in the Glass-Steagall barrier between commercial and investment banking, so that the barrier has become increasingly porous. Nevertheless, as a first approximation, the separation remains a significant phenomenon – as is witnessed by the substantial (but thus far futile) lobbying efforts that the commercial banking industry has devoted (for over 20 years) to erase it legislatively and the equally substantial (and thus far successful) efforts of the securities industry and more recently the insurance agents to maintain it. Similar erosions have occurred in the barrier erected by the Bank Holding Company Acts of 1956 and 1970 between the banking and insurance industries; but, again, as a first approximation, the barrier remains a significant phenomenon.

### 3 Financial Regulation

There is no satisfactory way to provide the full picture of financial regulation, with its excruciating detail and labyrinthine complexities, in any compact form.[9] Nevertheless, in this section we will attempt, with the aid of some clarifying devices, to provide some of the flavor and main features of financial regulation in the U.S.[10] We will first develop some broad principles concerning regulation in general and then turn our focus specifically to financial regulation.

### 3.1 A Clarifying Trichotomy

At first glance, regulation may appear to be an undifferentiated mass of governmental intervention into the operations of private-sector firms and markets. There are, however, enough regularities and patterns in regulation generally that it is useful to classify regulation into three major categories:

1. *Economic regulation*. This encompasses direct controls on prices, profits, entry, and/or exit, including "must serve" requirements. Familiar nonfinancial examples include the states' regulation of electricity prices and profits and localities' regulation of taxicab fares and entry.
2. *Health-safety-environment regulation*. This encompasses restrictions on production processes and product types and qualities. Familiar examples include the U.S. Environmental Protection Agency's restrictions on air pollutant emissions by electric utilities, the Occupational Safety and Health Administration's restraints on workplace hazard exposures, and the Consumer Product Safety Commission's restrictions on unsafe consumer products.
3. *Information regulation*. This involves requirements that specific types of information be attached to products and services. The U.S. Department of Agriculture's food labeling requirements and the Food and Drug Administration's labeling requirements for pharmaceuticals are ready examples.

These three categories are not always airtight or mutually exclusive. Some forms of regulation defy easy categorization or seem to encompass more than one category. Still, as will be seen below, these three categories will help us organize financial regulation into comprehensible bundles and will help link the types of financial firms, the motives for regulation, and the forms of regulation.

---

[9] Indeed, the texts of the complete sets of laws and regulations that apply to the financial sector occupy multiple linear feet on the bookshelves of any legal library.
[10] Further and more detailed descriptions of financial regulation can be found in White (1986, 1994a, 1994b), Campbell (1988, chs. 13–15), Kopke and Randall (1991), Bronfman et al. (1994), and Gramm and Gray (1994).

### 3.2 Motives for Regulation

In an ideal world, governmental regulation would be a "public interest" tool for correcting the shortcomings of private-sector markets. These potential market imperfections include:

- The exercise of market power by sellers (monopoly, oligopoly) or by buyers (monopsony);
- Pervasive economies of scale in production;
- Positive or negative externality (spillover) effects;
- Public goods problems;[11]
- Pervasive uncertainty;
- Asymmetric information on the part of marketplace transactors;
- "Widow and orphan" marketplace transactors who cannot be trusted to make appropriate choices for themselves.

In addition to these deviations from the textbook model of the ideal market, regulation may be motivated by a society's dissatisfaction with the income-distribution outcome of even perfectly efficient market processes and thus by the desire to redistribute income in directions that are deemed socially more desirable.[12]

In this ideal world, regulators would costlessly and perfectly correct the imperfections of markets and improve the distribution of income and thus improve the social efficiency of markets. For example, economic regulation would be used to limit the exercise of market power, health-safety-environment regulation would be used to correct externalities, information regulation would be used to correct information asymmetries, etc.

Unfortunately, in the real world, governmental organizations and their regulatory processes too are possessed of imperfections (Demsetz, 1969; Wolf, 1989; White, 1996b, 1996c). These include:

- Difficulties in formulating clear and implementable goals;
- Difficulties in establishing incentives for efficiency;
- Difficulties in attracting and retaining capable managers; and
- Problems of asymmetric information between regulators and the parties they are supposed to regulate.

Further, because the consequences of regulations are often substantial and the rewards to influencing the regulatory processes in one's

---

[11] "Public goods" are goods or services for which the extra costs of serving an extra user are very low or zero and from which extra users cannot be excluded. Familiar examples are police protection, national defense, an unscrambled broadcast signal, a public health/disease eradication campaign, and the availability of a new idea.

[12] Though taxes and subsidies are the more common tools for effecting income redistribution, some regulatory measures clearly have this goal as well (Posner, 1971).

favor are quite large, the pursuit of that influence and success in achiev-ing it[13] can lead to serious distortions and inefficiencies, as affected parties pursue (and achieve) regulatory restrictions and protections that enrich these successful participants at the expense of others and at the expense of marketplace efficiency (Stigler, 1971; Posner, 1974; Krueger, 1974; Peltzman, 1976; Noll, 1989). The end result could well be inefficiency losses that are at least as substantial as the market imperfections that the regulatory process was nominally supposed to correct. Indeed, the wave of deregulation that swept through the U.S. economy in the late 1970s and early 1980s – which involved the dis-mantling of much *economic* regulation of airlines, railroads, trucking, telecommunications, and banking[14] – represented a political judgment, supported by many economists (Winston, 1993; Joskow and Noll, 1994), that the costs of economic regulation in these areas exceeded their benefits.[15]

With imperfections present in regulatory processes, as well as in market processes, there are no assurances of purity of motives in regu-lation nor of efficiency of outcomes. All judgments about the necessity for and efficacy of regulation must have an empirical basis and cannot be settled solely by *a priori* reasoning about the imperfections of markets or of governments.

### 3.3 The Structure of American Financial Regulation

There is no uniform or neatly delineated way of describing the regula-tory structure that applies to the American financial services sector. American financial regulation is a complex interweaving of multiple federal and state regulatory agencies, often with overlapping juris-dictions and responsibilities among the federal agencies and between the federal and state authorities.[16] Rather than attempt any grand syn-

---

[13] This success is frequently described as the "capture" of a regulatory agency by a specific interest group.

[14] The dismantling in the early 1970s of the system of fixed commissions for securities transactions, which had received regulatory support during the previous 40 years, should also be included in this category.

[15] Unfortunately, in one instance (savings and loan associations), crucial safety regulation was swept aside as well, with disastrous consequences (White, 1991).

[16] For the banking sector alone, efforts to portray regulatory structure and responsibilities yield multi-page charts and/or diagrams that could easily be mistaken for radio wiring diagrams (White, 1991, pp. 190–191).

thesis, we shall proceed case-by-case through the major sub-sectors of finance.[17]

1. *Banking*. Banks and other depositories are regulated by both the federal government and the individual 50 states. At the federal level, there are three agencies (the Federal Reserve, the Federal Deposit Insurance Corporation [FDIC], and the Office of the Comptroller of the Currency [OCC]) with regulatory responsibilities for commercial banks and their holding companies. Another agency (the Office of Thrift Supervision [OTS]) regulates savings institutions (as does the FDIC, because of its deposit insurance responsibilities); and yet another federal agency (the National Credit Union Administration [NCUA]) regulates credit unions.[18] At the state level, each state has a banking regulatory agency, which usually encompasses all depository institutions; a few states have separate agencies for separate types of depositories.

   Over time, the federal government has tended increasingly to centralize bank regulation and to reduce the states' powers. Nevertheless, the tradition of a "dual banking system," with bank charters granted (and regulated) both nationally and by the states, is a strong one (Scott, 1977), and the states still play an important role in bank regulation.

2. *Securities and related instruments*. The federal government and the 50 states share responsibility for regulating this area. At the federal level, the Securities and Exchange Commission (SEC) supervises securities (and mutual fund) issuance and trading and the information disclosure that surrounds these transactions, as well as corporate governance procedures; the Commodity Futures Trading Commission (CFTC) has jurisdiction over commodity and financial futures and options on futures. At the state level, the primary focus is on securities (and mutual fund) sales and corporate governance, the latter through state corporate chartering and corporate law development.

3. *Insurance*. Regulation of the insurance industry is the sole responsibility of the individual 50 states; also, virtually all states operate mutual guarantee funds that honor the obligations of an insurance company that fails.

4. *Pension funds*. The regulation of pension funds is largely a federal

---

[17] In addition to the specific regulatory structures mentioned, the U.S. Department of Justice's (DOJ) Antitrust Division maintains antitrust scrutiny over the financial sector, and the DOJ's Civil Rights Division enforces the anti-discrimination laws that apply to the provision of financial services. Also, virtually all firms in the financial sector are subject to the general reach of the U.S. workplace safety laws, anti-employment discrimination laws, etc.

[18] Also, the Farm Credit Administration (FCA) regulates a panoply of specialized agricultural lending institutions, and the Federal Housing Finance Board (FHFB) regulates the 12 Federal Home Loan Banks (FHLBs), which provide wholesale credit to savings institutions and commercial banks for the purpose of housing finance.

responsibility. The Department of Labor's (DOL) Pension and Welfare Benefits Administration has broad responsibility for all private-sector pensions; the Pension Benefit Guaranty Corporation (PBGC) focuses exclusively on defined-benefit pension plans.

5. *Mortgage conduits.* The Federal National Mortgage Association ("Fannie Mae") and the Federal Home Loan Mortgage Corporation ("Freddie Mac") are Congressionally chartered private corporations[19] that purchase residential mortgages and then package and sell (securitize) most of them and hold the remainder in portfolio.[20] The U.S. Department of Housing and Urban Development's Office of Federal Housing Enterprise Oversight (OFHEO) has regulatory responsibility for these two housing conduits.

6. *Finance companies and leasing companies.* There are no formal regulatory structures that apply to finance companies and leasing companies, though they are affected by some of the regulatory strictures (e.g., some states' usury ceilings on loan interest rates) that apply to other financial sector firms.

### 3.4 The Content of American Financial Regulation

As is true of the structure of financial regulation, the content of financial regulation defies easy or compact description. Again, we shall proceed on a case-by-case basis through the sub-sectors of finance, employing also the trichotomous classification of regulation established above.

1. *Banking.* The burden of *economic regulation* has been growing lighter on banks, in keeping with the general trend of deregulation in the U.S. economy over the past two decades. Nevertheless, the vestiges are significant. Some important examples follow: At the federal level, banks cannot pay interest on the checking accounts of commercial customers. Their activities in the securities and insurance areas are restricted, and both they and their holding companies are restricted to owning enterprises that are closely related to banking.[21] Banks have a regulatory obligation to meet the financial needs of the communities in which their offices are located. At the state level,[22] a number of states have retained limits on intrastate and interstate branching and on the share of the

---

[19] The term "government sponsored enterprise" (GSE) is frequently used to describe these (and similarly structured) companies.

[20] The third major federal mortgage conduit, the Government National Mortgage Association ("Ginnie Mae"), is directly a part of the U.S. Department of Housing and Urban Development (HUD).

[21] Savings institutions ("thrifts") enjoy a loophole in this area. Thrift holding companies that own only one thrift have few restrictions on the types of enterprises that they can own.

[22] Most of the state restrictions apply to banks operating in their states, regardless of whether the bank is state-chartered or nationally chartered.

state's deposits that can be amassed by any individual bank or bank holding company. Some states have usury ceilings on the interest rates that can be charged on certain kinds of loans; and some states place limits on certain kinds of loan fees, such as credit card fees.

*Safety-and-soundness regulation* is a primary concern of the federal bank regulators, with the states playing a supporting role. The primary regulatory instruments employed include minimum capital (net worth) requirements, deposit insurance requirements,[23] activities and portfolio limitations, "good character" requirements for senior bank personnel, business competence requirements, and overall risk limitations. Enforcement occurs through the processes of "examination and supervision."[24]

*Information regulation* is primarily a federal responsibility. Banks are required to inform borrowers and depositors of interest rates and other fees, calculated in a standardized way (so as to ease comparisons among competitive institutions' offerings). A bank must also provide a copy of its most recent financial statement to any customer who asks for it.

2. *Securities and related instruments.* The financial firms that operate in this sub-sector enjoy a relatively light burden of *economic regulation.*[25] Nevertheless, the Glass-Steagall Act, which restricts banks from entering the securities business, equally restricts securities firms from entering banking.[26] The SEC supervises the creation and operation of securities exchanges and the types of instruments that can be traded on them; the CFTC does the same for the exchanges and instruments that are within its domain. Also, the Federal Reserve continues to have the power to set margin requirements – the percentage amount that a securities firm or bank can lend to an investor who puts up his/her securities as collateral for the loan.

The *safety regulation* burden on this sub-sector (and on corporate governance generally) is heavier. An important goal of the SEC, the CFTC, and the states is to protect investors from arbitrary or abusive practices. Thus, corporate governance requirements can be seen as efforts to make corporate managements accountable to the corporations' boards of directors (who are elected by and are supposed to represent the shareholder owners) and ultimately to their shareholders, thereby providing a less arbitrary environment for investors; similarly, regulatory limitations on exchanges, their instruments, and their trading

---

[23] Depositors in banks, thrifts, and credit unions are covered by deposit insurance, up to $100,000 per insured account.

[24] Important changes in safety-and-soundness regulation of the early 1990s are summarized in Benston and Kaufman (1997); some empirical consequences of those changes are explored in Angbazo and Saunders (1999).

[25] It should be noted, however, that prior to the early 1970s the SEC supervised and protected the securities industry's system of minimum fixed commissions on securities transactions (Mann, 1975; Schwert, 1977; Ofer and Melnik, 1978; Roberts et al., 1979; Tinic and West, 1980).

[26] But see the caveats of footnotes 8 and 21 above.

practices and on the practices of the personnel of securities firms and investment advisers are efforts to protect investors from abusive practices by more knowledgeable or manipulative securities (or futures) firms. In addition, the SEC imposes minimum capital requirements on broker-dealers,[27] and it restricts the percentage of low-quality (high-risk) debt securities that money market mutual funds can carry in their portfolios.

Finally, the securities sub-sector (and the larger world of publicly owned companies with traded securities) carries an extremely heavy burden of *information regulation*. When companies issue new securities, they (and their underwriters-distributors) are required to make extensive disclosures. Thereafter, as publicly traded companies, they are required to make extensive financial information available on a quarterly and annual basis and to reveal important new financial developments as they occur. Further, as a means of enhancing disclosure and also enhancing comparability among companies, the SEC enforces the basic accounting system (usually described as "generally accepted accounting principles" [GAAP]).[28] In addition, mutual funds are required to report their net market values on a daily basis and to report other information (such as recent returns) on a standardized basis, so as to enhance comparability.

3. *Insurance.* The state regulatory regimes that apply to the insurance industry roughly parallel the overall regulatory structure that applies to banking (Kopke and Randall, 1991; Randall, 1995; White, 1996d). In the realm of *economic regulation*, many states maintain minimum and/or maximum rate regulation on various lines of insurance and impose "must serve" requirements.[29] Also, the federal Bank Holding Company Acts of 1956 and 1970, which restrict banks from owning insurance companies, similarly limit the ability of insurance companies to own banks. *Safety regulation* largely mimics federal banking regulation, with minimum capital requirements, portfolio and activities limitations, etc. Finally, *information regulation* calls for the disclosure of key features of insurance policies, often in standardized terms so as to facilitate comparisons.

4. *Pension funds.* The federal government's regulatory efforts constitute a mixture of *safety regulation* and *information regulation*. Pension funds are expected to meet "prudent person" standards with respect to invest-

---

[27] Also, investors who trade through and have an account with a securities firm (which often involves leaving securities and/or cash on accounts with the firm) are protected through insurance up to $500,000 provided by the federal Securities Investor Protection Corporation (SIPC).

[28] The initial arbiter of GAAP is the Financial Accounting Standards Board (FASB), an independent non-governmental body; but the SEC can overrule the FASB in the setting of GAAP (and the Congress can ultimately overrule the SEC).

[29] Automobile liability insurance and health insurance are "popular" areas of maximum rate regulation; flood and disaster insurance, homeowner insurance, and auto insurance are areas of "must serve" requirements.

ments and diversification and are required to provide pension plan participants with periodic summaries of their plans. Further, the Pension Benefit Guaranty Corporation (PBGC) enforces adequate funding standards for the defined-benefit plans that it guarantees.

5. *Mortgage conduits.* The OFHEO focuses on *safety regulation* of Fannie Mae and Freddie Mac, primarily through minimum capital requirements.

6. *Finance and leasing companies. Information regulation* is the major form of regulation that affects these companies, through disclosure requirements of lending terms. As noted above, these companies are subject to any state-imposed usury ceilings or credit card fee limitations.

### 3.4 A Summing Up

Though the landscape of financial regulation is exceedingly complex and variegated, there are some patterns – incorporating the intermediary-facilitator dichotomy of financial firms and the economic-safety-information regulatory trichotomy that we have developed – that can be discerned.

First, the widespread nature of financial regulation is not accidental. Finance is a vital input for every business enterprise and governmental entity, and virtually all households are customers of one or more financial services (as depositors, investors, pension beneficiaries, and/or borrowers). The liabilities of major classes of financial intermediaries – i.e., bank deposits, insurance company policies, pension plan benefits, and mutual fund shares – constitute significant fractions of the assets of households and businesses. At the same time, financial markets do seem to be especially susceptible to the types of potential market failures that invite governmental intervention.

Second, of the three categories of regulation, *information regulation* extends most widely across the financial sector. Again, this ubiquity is not accidental. It arises because of the politically expressed belief that finance is complicated and thus that many or most of the customers of financial services are at an informational disadvantage vis-a-vis the purveyors of these services.

Third, *safety regulation* applies most directly and forcefully to the groups of financial intermediaries – depositories, insurance companies, and pension funds – whose liabilities (deposits, policies, and benefits) are widespread and important assets for households.[30] These are also the

---

[30] Mutual funds are the exception here. They are a newer form of intermediary than the ones mentioned in the text, and they are explicitly recognized to be risky. But money market mutual funds – the exception to the exception – are subject to safety regulation.

categories of intermediary that have government-backed insurance or guaranty plans backstopping their liabilities, though in all instances the safety regulation of these institutions (and thus the governmental concern about the safety of their liabilities) has preceded these backstop plans. Political concerns about the inability of these institutions' liability holders to protect themselves against losses, as well as concerns (in the case of depositories) about depositor runs and financial contagion, have clearly been important motivators for this safety regulation and for the governmental backstopping efforts.[31]

The safety regulation that applies to securities firms and other financial facilitators (and, via corporate governance regulation, to the entire corporate sector) is less forceful and less direct. It does not try to provide complete safety of investments to investors but rather to reduce the possibilities of losses due to fraudulent dealings, unsuitable advice, manipulation, or other abusive practices.

Fourth, *economic regulation* applies most extensively to banks and other depositories, and to a lesser extent to the insurance industry. This focus on banks is surely a legacy of 19th century American populism and the perception that banks are large, financially powerful, and somewhat mysterious in structure and operation.[32] The reality that banks are increasingly embedded in competitive markets for financial services and that banks collectively account for a steadily shrinking share of the U.S. economy's financial assets[33] – as of 1997, commercial banks accounted only for about 20% of the assets of all financial institutions in the U.S. (Samuelson, 1998) – has helped underpin the economic deregulation of banking that has occurred since the late 1970s (White, 1986, 1994a). Still, the political perceptions and fears of size,

---

[31] Though the presence of these backstopping plans supports a legitimate interpretation of safety regulation as an effort by government to prevent these financial intermediaries' failures so as to protect *its* obligations, the extensive safety regulation that *preceded* these plans argues strongly that there are deep political concerns about preserving the safety of these liability obligations in the hands of households and nonfinancial businesses, irrespective of the presence or absence of government guarantees.

[32] This last element is again the product of the perception that finance is complex. Also, banks (and insurance companies) are among the few retail operations frequently encountered by households and small businesses that may *decline* to "sell" their products (loans or insurance) to potential customers, thus giving rise to popular perceptions of great and arbitrary power and to political demands to tame that power through economic regulation (White, 1993, 1995; Shull and White, 1998).

[33] This decline has been more or less continuous for well over a century (Litan, 1986; Edwards, 1996; Kroszner, 1996).

power, and mystery persist, as does a substantial amount of economic regulation.[34]

We now turn to some of the interactions between financial innovation and financial regulation.

### 4 Financial Innovation and Financial Regulation: Current Issues

As Section 2 indicated, financial innovation is proceeding rapidly. It has multiple manifestations:

- New instruments, such as financial options and futures and stored-value and "smart" cards;
- Modifications to traditional instruments, such as securitized loans;
- New services, such as PC-based home banking;
- New exchanges for trading securities, such as the Cincinnati Exchange (which is exclusively computerized);
- New opportunities for the users and purveyors of financial services to access each other, over wider geographic areas (including the crossing of national boundaries).[35]

In turn, this innovation has important consequences for financial markets:

- The users of financial services have more choices and opportunities, including the opportunities to make mistakes;
- The incumbent purveyors of financial services face more competition, as do exchanges and even regulators (Coffee, 1995; White, 1996c);
- The possibilities and probabilities of financial failure among the purveyors of financial services may well increase;[36]
- The tasks of financial regulation become more complex.

In this section, we will explore a number of important issues involving the direct and indirect interactions between financial innovation and financial regulation. We will begin with the potential effects of

---

[34] Paradoxically, much of the economic regulation of banks has *inhibited* competition among banks and between banks and other financial services providers, thereby exacerbating market imperfections and inefficiencies rather than ameliorating them (White, 1993, 1995).

[35] The dismantling of geographic and product-line regulatory barriers, nationally and internationally, is clearly aiding this process.

[36] The increased opportunities yielded by financial innovation can have two consequences for financial stability or failure. On the one hand, the new opportunities can be used for diversification and/or hedging, which should provide greater stabilization; on the other hand, the increased opportunities may yield greater opportunities for mistakes in strategies in entering unfamiliar businesses or functions or may be used for deliberate increases in risk-taking, which would increase the likelihood of financial failure.

regulation on innovation; we will then discuss the challenges for regulation (i.e., for public policy) that are posed by the rapid pace of innovation in and around the financial sector.

### 4.1 The Effects of Regulation on Innovation

It is clear that financial regulation may, in some circumstances, encourage innovation; in others, it may inhibit innovation. These circumstances, and their consequences, warrant further discussion.

1. Regulation is intended to prevent enterprises and individuals from pursuing specific courses of action. As the Regulation-Q-induced examples of Section 2 illustrate, the gain-seeking inclinations of enterprises and individuals are likely to induce innovations that allow them to achieve the same or similar ends through alternative means.

   Are such innovations socially beneficial? Or are they anti-social regulatory evasions? The answers to these questions must hinge largely on a "from-the-outside" perspective on the specific regulation itself and a weighing of its social worthiness. If, for example, one believes that the regulation is wrong-headed[37] (as is this author's judgment about Regulation Q, including its current vestiges), then the innovations are a welcome and beneficial relief from the ill-advised regulation – albeit, at some extra costs (of developing the innovation and also of pursuing the desired activities through the indirect innovation-linked route rather than through the original but-for-the-regulation route). If, instead, one believes that the regulation serves a worthy purpose (and the innovation does not avoid or cure the social problem that is the target of the regulation but just permits the privately pursued activity to continue under another guise), then the innovation is simply regulatory evasion and is clearly a poor use of the economy's resources.

   This "outside" perspective and the judgments based on it are thus crucial for any specific judgments about regulation-induced innovations.

2. The Balkanized structure of financial regulation in the U.S. – with multiple federal agencies and 50 states – has the potential for either encouraging or inhibiting innovation (Kane, 1986, 1991; Coffee, 1995; White, 1996c). This structure may encourage innovation by offering multiple alternative forums – multiple federal regulators and/or 50 states – in which an innovator may achieve any needed regulatory approval. A single "no" from a single all-encompassing regulatory agency need not mean the final foreclosure of an innovation. On the other hand, if an innovation requires the scale of a national market and the 50 states have jurisdictional authority, the transactions costs of securing multiple approvals may discourage the innovation in the first place. Further, jurisdictional "turf wars" among regulatory agencies could delay

---

[37] And has arisen and been maintained because of one or more of the governmental imperfections discussed in Section 3.

approvals of innovations and thus discourage their development (Coffee, 1995).

Which of these effects would prevail would be dependent on the particular innovation and jurisdictional arrangement; no sweeping conclusion can be offered. Further, a judgment about the social value of the innovations that arise when innovators can "forum shop" among regulatory agencies again depends on an outside perspective on the social worth of the regulation that prohibits the innovation in some jurisdictions. If one believes that the regulation is worthwhile, then such forum shopping constitutes anti-social regulatory evasion and could lead to a "race to the bottom" by compliant regulators who are reluctant to lose "market share"; alternatively, if one believes that the regulation is wrong-headed, then the forum shopping is beneficial and could lead to a "race to the top."

Again, the outside perspective is crucial for making any judgments.

3. The specialization confinements of financial regulation (e.g., restricting banks or bank holding companies from entering the securities or insurance fields, and vice versa, and restricting banks from entering nonfinancial areas) may again have positive or negative effects on innovation. The nominal confinements may induce "evasive" innovations. Alternatively, these confinements may be inhibiting some innovations that would occur in and take advantage of the multi-product environment of the "financial supermarkets" that could arise in a less constricting regulatory framework.[38]

In sum, it is clear that financial regulation may be having both positive and negative effects on financial innovation and that any judgments as to the merits of these influences hinge crucially on one's views of the merits of the specific regulations themselves.

### 4.2 The Effects of Innovation on Regulation

1. The financial innovations that have geographically widened financial markets have clearly placed pressures on financial regulation to be centralized at the federal level and away from the states. This trend has been most prominent for banking and securities. It is likely to continue.

2. These same innovational forces are causing the markets for some financial products and services to widen beyond national boundaries. Not too surprisingly, there are consequent calls for and efforts at *international* harmonization of financial regulation (Siegel, 1990; England, 1991; Edwards and Patrick, 1992; Stansell, 1993; Barfield, 1996). These efforts have gone the furthest in banking, followed by securities and then insurance.

---

[38] It should be noted, however, that one of the major attempts to construct a "financial supermarket" – consisting of Sears (retailing), Allstate (insurance), Dean Witter (securities), Discover Card (credit cards), and MountainWest Savings and Loan Association (banking) – did not prove successful.

Though there can be potential gains from international harmonization of financial regulation, there are serious dangers as well (White,
1996b, 1996c). The gains can come from the harmonization of information regulation (e.g., in standardizing accounting frameworks and
reporting requirements), so as to reduce the transactions costs of both
the purveyors and users of financial services that cross national boundaries. Also, harmonization that serves as a guise for reducing protectionist barriers or governmental subsidies for financial firms among
countries can be beneficial. But even the harmonization of information
regulation carries the dangers that worthwhile local variations may be
squelched and/or uniformity may be achieved at wholly inappropriate
levels. More important are the dangers that international harmonization efforts could become smoke screens for international regulatory
regimes that are protectionist and anti-competitive; unfortunately, there
are precedents (in airlines, ocean shipping, and telecommunications) for
this type of protectionist international regulatory regime to arise.

In short, there is much to be said for international competition, even
among regulatory regimes,[39] and efforts at international harmonization
should be approached gingerly at best.[40]

For the U.S. securities industry, a crucial issue will be whether international competition will place pressures on the SEC to loosen accounting and reporting standards – because overseas capital markets, with
looser standards (and consequent lower costs), become increasingly
attractive to issuers and to investors (Baumol and Malkiel (1992)[41] – or
whether the higher standards of the U.S. financial markets will prove so
attractive to investors that overseas issuers will be drawn to these
markets.

3. The increased competition created by the rapid pace of financial innovation is generally a beneficial force for the efficiency of financial
markets and for the U.S. economy as a whole. Inevitably, this rapid
change will create strong and uncomfortable pressures on incumbents.
Some incumbents will successfully adapt; others will falter, merge, or
possibly fail. Other firms will rise to take their places.

This pattern is to be expected and encouraged in a system of competitive markets. Nevertheless, the American political system is rarely
comfortable with the prospect of substantial numbers of firms failing.

---

[39] In essence, the case for international competition among regulatory regimes is much
the same case that supports the multiple-regulatory-regime framework in the U.S.
context.

[40] Even the arguments for international harmonization of *safety* regulation that rest on
fears of the consequences of cross-border contagion of financial failures do not withstand close scrutiny: Nationally based safety regulatory regimes, supplemented by informal coordination and communication among national regulators, should be adequate to
deal with potential contagion problems; formal harmonization does not appear to be
necessary (White, 1996b, 1996c).

[41] It seems unlikely that, in the era of the global capital markets of the 1990s, the U.S. government would try to prevent U.S. firms from raising capital in overseas markets or to
try to prevent U.S. investors from purchasing instruments issued overseas.

Incumbents may use this discomfort as the excuse to seek political protection for their incumbency,[42] thereby stymieing or delaying the efficiencies that innovation could otherwise bring.

Further, in the case of the intermediaries that warrant special safety regulation, and especially depositories and insurance companies, the increased competitive pressures do raise a set of legitimate regulatory concerns. In banking, for example, the competitive pressures are coming from a number of directions:

- from other banks, as the combination of improved technologies and reduced regulatory barriers allow banks increasingly to offer their services over wider geographic areas and thereby to invade each others' "turf" more extensively; the low-cost dissemination of financial information through the Internet (e.g., advertising the interest rates on deposits or on loans) will surely quicken this process;
- from other depositories, such as savings institutions, for the same reasons;
- from other intermediaries, such as insurance companies and finance companies, for the same reasons;
- from non-intermediary facilitators, through the process of securitization, which permits the previously illiquid assets (e.g., mortgage loans and credit card receivables) of banks to become securities and thus to be originated, serviced, and sold by financial facilitators (rather than being held in their portfolios only by banks);
- from firms that previously had little to do with finance, such as computer software companies that are likely to become purveyors of home electronic banking programs and services; though these software firms are unlikely to become banks themselves, their brand-name prominence may allow them to insert themselves between banks and their retail customers and to become important "steerers" of those customers; banks will then have to compete to pursue the business (and customers) of these steerers.

Again, these innovations and the competition that they create ought not to be discouraged. But, because banks are special – they do have a special safety regulatory regime, for the reasons discussed in Section 3 – a special regulatory concern should surround this heightened competition.[43] Specifically, the safety-and-soundness scrutiny of bank regulators should be *strengthened* in a period of rapid innovation and heightened competitive pressures, because the owners and managers of faltering banks may be tempted to take "shoot-the-moon" risks at the expense of depositors (or deposit insurers).[44] Primary among the improved safety-and-soundness regulatory instruments should be

---

[42] For example, the insurance agents' lobbyists have been successful in this respect, serving as the current barrier to the Congress's overhaul of the Glass-Steagall Act.

[43] The same special concern should apply to insurance companies and pension funds, for the same reasons.

[44] The incentives for this risk-increasing strategy arise because, in a limited liability legal environment, the owners of the bank receive all of the upside gains from risk-taking but are limited in their liability for losses, which are borne by the liability holders, such as depositors or the deposit insurer who stands in their shoes (White, 1991).

improved capital standards, including better ways of measuring capital (i.e., the employment of a market value accounting framework) and of measuring risks (e.g., financial stress tests).

4. One important aspect of financial innovation has been the development of new financial instruments. Natural questions arise as to how these new instruments should be regulated (e.g., what forms of disclosure are appropriate) and by which regulators.

As the examples below illustrate, there are no automatic answers that can be offered to these questions. Decisions have to be made on a case-by-case basis. But bureaucratic rivalry over regulatory turf (possibly exacerbated by the protectionist fears of incumbents) ought not to be allowed to delay the delivery of the benefits and efficiencies of the new instruments.

5. Some innovative financial products (e.g., financial derivatives) have involved substantially greater levels of complexity than traditional products. As is true for wider opportunities for diversification more generally, when used appropriately these new instruments can be tools for smoothing and hedging and thus reducing risks. But their greater levels of complexity and, often, their greater leveraging possibilities open new opportunities for risk-taking. In turn, these possibilities raise two dangers that are appropriate for regulatory concern. First, the complexity of these products may convert even sophisticated users of financial products into "widows and orphans" who use them inappropriately.[45] Second, the managers of financial intermediaries that pose the greatest safety regulatory concern (i.e., banks and other depositories, insurance companies, and pension funds) may use these instruments carelessly or as part of a deliberate risk-increasing ("shoot the moon") strategy.

Though the regulatory temptations to treat these complex products as the equivalent of nuclear waste and to prohibit their creation and use are great, these temptations should be resisted – because these products' beneficial use as low-cost hedging instruments can also be great. Instead, regulatory remedies should be narrowly crafted to deal with the specific problems. For the "widows and orphans" problems, increased regulatory emphasis on the fiduciary obligations of financial intermediaries and facilitators is appropriate; and for the problems of increased risk-taking by intermediaries, increased regulatory emphases on "know your business and know your risks" and on better capital standards are the appropriate directions for public policy.

6. Stored-value cards and smart cards are electronics-based innovations that represent potential new means of effecting transactions. They are currently offered as telephone cards, transit cards, and university-based

---

[45] Arguably, this was the case for Proctor & Gamble's recent use of derivatives. In some instances, however, derivatives have been improperly blamed for losses that were created by deliberate risk-taking efforts that largely involved "old-fashioned" leverage. This was the case for the highly publicized (but generally misreported) losses of the Orange County, California, investment pool (Figlewski and White, 1995; Jorion, 1995).

transactions cards; and experiments with general-purpose transactions cards are proceeding.

Should these instruments be treated by financial regulators as "money"? To do so would imply that only banks could issue these instruments or that the issuers should maintain adequate capital or otherwise collateralize the outstanding value of cards, thus treating issuers as quasi-banks.

To require this type of regulation at this early stage of development of these instruments seems premature and runs the risk of stunting or distorting their development. Further, the arguments for these strong forms of safety regulation are largely absent. Though most users are unlikely to be in a good position to judge the financial strength of card issuers, users are also unlikely individually to have large sums at risk[46]; and card holder runs seem unlikely and not especially contagious or damaging. Also, as accumulators of stored-value transactions, retail merchants will have stronger incentives (as well as greater capabilities) to monitor the financial strength of card issuers and will decline to accept the cards of weak issuers, thereby sending signals that households can use in their decisions as to whose issuers' cards to buy.

To this author's knowledge, there has not yet been a failure of a major card issuer. When the first failure does occur, there will surely be media attention given to the unfortunate holders of the issuer's cards, and legislators will surely demand to know why financial regulators had not anticipated the failure and taken appropriate preventive actions. Despite these inevitable political pressures, a regulatory stance of "benign neglect" seems most appropriate at this early stage (Horvitz and White, 1999). If these instruments should subsequently assume more of the characteristics of money that call for stronger safety regulation, there will surely be opportunities for the regulatory revisiting of this issue.

7. These new electronics-based instruments may give banks and other issuers substantially enhanced capabilities for capturing quite detailed information about their users' transactions – what, where, when, and how much. This information could be valuable for banks in their "cross-marketing" of various financial services or could be valuable as part of mailing lists sold to other marketers. It is easy to see how users (and their political representatives) could fear the potential abuse of this financial information and would insist on regulatory solutions to prevent such abuse.

In principle, a well-functioning competitive market would solve these potential problems without the need for regulatory intervention. Individual banks would establish and announce their policies with respect to the use of this information. Some banks might proudly announce, "We promise that this information will never be used, even by other

---

[46] The holders of airline tickets on a carrier that fails financially are likely to have larger sums at risk than are the holders of a company's telephone cards.

subsidiaries of the bank!" Others might promise only that the information would never be sold to third parties. Yet others might acknowledge the value of the information and the possibility of its sale but also indicate that the gains would be passed on to customers through lower prices for the bank's services. Or some banks might offer a choice among these options. Bank customers would thus have a set of price-quality alternatives among which they could choose. The absence of any announced policy would likely cause the bank customers to fear the worst and to make their choices accordingly.

Nevertheless, because privacy of financial transactions is an especially sensitive subject for many individuals and because opportunistic (or careless) behavior by some banks might arise, a modest regulatory approach does seem warranted (Horvitz and White, 1999): Banks should be required to establish and announce clearly to their customers a policy with respect to the use of the customers' transactions information. The customers can then choose among banks and policies.

8. The wider use of electronics-based instruments and procedures for the financial system will surely increase the flows of funds through EFT systems. The "wholesale" flows of funds among banks through EFT systems currently amount to hundreds of billions of dollars per day (Humphrey, 1986, 1989). If a major financial institution were to fail and be unable to honor its EFT obligations in the middle of a business day, the damaging ripple effects from such a failure could be substantial.

The Federal Reserve has recently begun to charge modest interest rates for the "daylight overdrafts" (the intraday loans) that give rise to these concerns, hoping to reduce their volume. But there is a more direct way to deal with them, employing a standard tool that is already in the regulators' kit bag: capital-based limitations on the size of loan that a bank can extend to any single borrower (which thereby limits the bank's exposure to loss in the event of the failure of any borrower). These limitations should also apply to banks' exposures to loans to each other through EFT (or any other) systems. A logical extension of this requirement would be the requirement that banks meet their minimum capital requirements on a real-time (i.e., continuous) basis, not just on a periodic (e.g., end-of-quarter) basis, since banks can slip into financial difficulties at any time and not just at the end of calendar quarters.

9. Many of the new electronics-based technologies being developed for banking have "network" attributes (Katz and Shapiro, 1994; Besen and Farrell, 1994; Liebowitz and Margolis, 1994; Economides, 1996; White, 1999), in the sense that the innovations involve combinations of hardware and software and permit bank customers to conduct financial transactions with others, outside of the physical confines of a bank. Accordingly, issues of compatibility among transactors, so as to permit the smooth flow of transactions, and the related issues of technical standards among and between hardware and software components, are important for these innovations. Further, the value of these innovations

to customers increases as the numbers of other actual or potential transactors in a system increase. And economies of scale are often important.

Industry members frequently achieve technical standards among themselves through formal or informal understandings; in essence, markets develop the standards on their own. But regulatory agencies also can be the vehicle for the achievement of technical standards, either by providing a forum and informal encouragement for industry members to reach agreements on standards among themselves or by establishing the technical standards directly through regulatory edict.[47]

Neither unfettered markets nor regulatory processes appear to offer an assured path to efficient and successful technological outcomes (Horvitz and White, 1999). The absence of a critical mass of users may cause promising technologies to languish in competitive markets; alternatively, a firm with a substantial market share and sales momentum may cause a "tipping" process toward an inferior technology. But there are also risks that regulatory processes may force an agreement too soon in the development process and/or the regulatory edict may settle on an inappropriate or inefficient standard.

With many of the new banking technologies in nascent stages and with bank regulators unlikely to be in a better position than industry participants to choose among potential technological candidates, a regulatory stance of benign neglect again seems wisest.

## 5 Conclusion

Rapid technological change and innovation is enveloping the financial sector, with beneficial consequences that are spreading throughout the U.S. economy. Because this sector is heavily regulated, there are important interactions between this rapid innovation and the financial sector's regulation.

As this chapter has argued, there is an important and legitimate logic to much (but not all) financial regulation, which offers a partial explanation of why it has persisted through two decades of widespread deregulation in the U.S. economy. This financial regulation has had and will surely continue to have a role in shaping financial innovation. In turn, innovation will surely continue to pose challenges for regulation.

As the millennium approaches, a major task of public policy will be to ensure that financial regulation does not distort or stifle this rapid and beneficial innovation, while responding appropriately to the challenges that financial innovation will pose.

---

[47] The Federal Communications Commission, for example, which has been in the middle of standard-setting processes for telecommunications, has tried a variety of strategies, from completely hands-off to mandated standards (Besen and Johnson, 1986).

## Appendix: A Glossary of Abbreviations

| | |
|---|---|
| CFTC | Commodity Futures Trading Commission |
| CMA | Cash management account |
| DOJ | Department of Justice |
| DOL | Department of Labor |
| EFT | Electronic funds transfer |
| FASB | Financial Accounting Standards Board |
| FCA | Farm Credit Administration |
| FDIC | Federal Deposit Insurance Corporation |
| FHFB | Federal Housing Finance Board |
| FHLB | Federal Home Loan Bank |
| GAAP | Generally Accepted Accounting Principles |
| GSE | Government-sponsored enterprise |
| HUD | Department of Housing and Urban Development |
| NCUA | National Credit Union Administration |
| OCC | Office of the Comptroller of the Currency |
| OFHEO | Office of Federal Housing Enterprise Oversight |
| OTS | Office of Thrift Supervision |
| PBGC | Pension Benefit Guaranty Corporation |
| SEC | Securities and Exchange Commission |
| SIPC | Securities Investor Protection Corporation |

## References

Allen, Franklin and Douglas Gale, *Financial Innovation and Risk Sharing*. Cambridge, Mass.: MIT Press, 1995.

Barfield, Claude E., *International Financial Markets: Harmonization versus Competition*. Washington, D.C.: American Enterprise Institute, 1996.

Baumol, William J. and Burton G. Malkiel, "Redundant Regulation of Foreign Security Trading and U.S. Competitiveness," in Kenneth Lehn and Robert W. Kamphius, Jr., eds., *Modernizing U.S. Securities Regulation: Economic and Legal Perspectives*. Homewood Ill.: Business One Irwin, 1992, pp. 39–55.

Benston, George J. and George G. Kaufman, "FDICIA after Five Years," *Journal of Economic Perspectives*, 11 (Summer 1997), pp. 139–158.

Besen, Stanley M. and Joseph Farrell, "Choosing How to Compete: Strategies and Tactics in Standardization," *Journal of Economic Perspectives*, 8 (Spring 1994), pp. 117–131.

Besen, Stanley M. and Leland L. Johnson, *Compatibility Standards, Competition, and Innovation in the Broadcasting Industry*. Washington, D.C.: Rand, 1986.

Bronfman, Corinne, Kenneth Lehn, and Robert A. Schwartz, "U.S. Securities Regulation: Regulatory Structure," in Benn Steil, ed., *International Financial Market Regulation*. London: Wiley, 1994, pp. 37–73.

Brooks, John, *Telephone: The First Hundred Years*. New York: Harper & Row, 1975.

Campbell, Tim S., *Money and Capital Markets*. Glenview, Ill.: Scott, Foresman, 1988.

Coffee, John C., Jr., "Competition versus Consolidation: The Significance of Organizational Structure in Financial and Securities Regulation," *Business Lawyer*, 50 (February 1995), pp. 1–50.

Cohen, Wesley M. and Richard C. Levin, "Empirical Studies of Innovation and Market Structure," in Richard Schmalensee and Robert Willig, eds., *Handbook of Industrial Organization*, Vol. 2. Amsterdam: North Holland, 1989, pp. 1059–1107.

Demsetz, Harold, "Information and Efficiency: Another Viewpoint," *Journal of Law & Economics*, 12 (April 1969), pp. 1–22.

Economides, Nicholas, "The Economics of Networks," *International Journal of Industrial Organization*, 14 (October 1996), pp. 673–699.

Edwards, Franklin R., *The New Finance: Regulation and Financial Stability*. Washington, D.C.: American Enterprise Institute, 1996.

Edwards, Franklin R. and Hugh T. Patrick, eds., *Regulating International Financial Markets: Issues and Policies*, Boston: Kluwer, 1992.

England, Catherine, ed. *Governing Banking's Future: Markets vs. Regulation*. Boston: Kluwer, 1991.

Figlewski, Stephen and Lawrence J. White, "Orange County: Don't Blame Derivatives," *SternBusiness*, 1 (Spring 1995), pp. 30–35.

Finnerty, John D., "An Overview of Corporate Securities Innovation," *Journal of Applied Corporate Finance*, 4 (Winter 1992), pp. 23–39.

Garbade, Kenneth G. and William L. Silber, "Technology, Communication, and the Performance of Financial Markets," *Journal of Finance*, 33 (June 1978), pp. 819–832.

Gramm, Wendy L. and Gerald D. Gray, "Scams, Scoundrels, and Scapegoats: A Taxonomy of CEA Regulation over Derivative Instruments, " *Journal of Derivatives*, 1 (Spring 1994), pp. 6–24.

Horvitz, Paul M. and Lawrence J. White, "The Challenges of the New Electronic Technologies in Banking: Private Strategies and Public Policies," Chapter 11 in this volume (2000).

Humphrey, David B., "Payments Finality and Risk of Settlement Failure," in Anthony Saunders and Lawrence J. White, eds., *Technology and the Regulation of Financial Markets: Securities, Futures, and Banking*. Lexington, Mass.: Heath, 1986, pp. 97–120.

Humphrey, David B., "Market Responses to Pricing Fedwire Daylight Overdrafts," *Economic Review* (Federal Reserve Bank of Richmond) 75, (May/June 1989), pp. 23–34.

Jorion, Philippe, *Big Bets Gone Bad: Derivatives and Bankruptcy in Orange County*. San Diego: Academic Press, 1995.

Joskow, Paul L. and Roger G. Noll, "Economic Regulation: Deregulation and Regulatory Reform during the 1980s," in Martin Feldstein, ed., *American Economic Policy in the 1980s*. Chicago: University of Chicago Press, 1994, pp. 367–440.

Kane, Edward J., "Technology and the Regulation of Financial Markets," in Anthony Saunders and Lawrence J. White, eds., *Technology and the Regulation of Financial Markets: Securities, Futures, and Banking*. Lexington, Mass.: Heath, 1986, pp. 187–194.

Kane, Edward J., "Tension between Competition and Coordination in International Financial Regulation," in Catherine England, ed., *Governing Banking's Future: Markets vs. Regulation*. Boston: Kluwer, 1991, pp. 33–48.

Katz, Michael L. and Carl Shapiro, "Systems Competition and Network Effects," *Journal of Economic Perspectives*, 8 (Spring 1994), pp. 93–115.

Kopke, Richard W., "Financial Innovation and Standards for the Capital of Life Insurance Companies," *New England Economic Review* (January/February 1995), pp. 29–57.

Kopke, Richard W. and Richard E. Randall, eds., *The Financial Condition and Regulation of Insurance Companies*. Conference Series No. 35, Federal Reserve Bank of Boston, June 1991.

Kroszner, Randall S., "The Evolution of Universal Banking and Its Regulation in Twentieth Century America," in Anthony Saunders and Ingo Walter, eds., *Universal Banking: Financial System Design Reconsidered*. Chicago: Irwin, 1996, pp. 70–99.

Krueger, Anne O., "The Political Economy of the Rent-Seeking Society," *American Economic Review*, 66 (June 1974), pp. 291–303.

Lea, Michael J., "Innovation and the Cost of Credit: A Historical Perspective," *Housing Policy Debate*, 7, No. 1 (1996), pp. 147–174.

Liebowitz, S.J. and Stephen E. Margolis, "Network Externality: An Uncommon Tragedy," *Journal of Economics Perspectives*, 8 (Spring 1994), pp. 133–150.

Litan, Robert E., *What Should Banks Do?* Washington, D.C.: Brookings Institution, 1987.

Mann, H. Michael, "The New York Stock Exchange: A Cartel at the End of Its Reign," in Almarin Phillips, ed., *Promoting Competition in Regulated Markets*. Washington, D.C.: Brookings, 1975, pp. 301–327.

Merton, Robert C., "Financial Innovation and Economic Performance," *Journal of Applied Corporate Finance*, 4 (Winter 1992), pp. 12–22.

Miller, Merton H., "Financial Innovation: The Last Twenty Years and the Next," *Journal of Financial and Quantitative Analysis*, 21 (December 1986), pp. 459–471.

Miller, Merton H., "Financial Innovation: Achievements and Prospects," *Journal of Applied Corporate Finance*, 4 (Winter 1992), pp. 4–12.

Noll, Roger G., "Economic Perspectives on the Politics of Regulation," in Richard Schmalensee and Robert D. Willig, eds., *Handbook of Industrial Organization*, vol. 2. Amsterdam: North Holland, 1989, pp. 1253–1287.

Ofer, A.R. and Ari Melnik, "Price Deregulation in the Brokerage Industry: An Empirical Analysis," *Bell Journal of Economics and Management Science*, 9 (Autumn 1978), pp. 633–641.

Peltzman, Sam, "Toward a More General Theory of Regulation," *Journal of Law & Economics*, 19 (August 1976), 211–240.

Posner, Richard A., "Taxation by Regulation," *Bell Journal of Economics and Management Science*, 2 (Spring 1971), pp. 22–50.

Posner, Richard A., "Theories of Economic Regulation," *Bell Journal of Economics and Management Science*, 5 (Autumn 1974), pp. 335–358.

Roberts, Dan, Susan M. Phillips, and J. Richard Zecher, "Deregulation of Fixed Commission Rates in the Securities Industry," in Lawrence G. Goldberg and Lawrence J. White, eds., *The Deregulation of the Banking and Securities Industries*. Lexington, Mass.: Heath, 1979, pp. 151–183.

Samuelson, Robert, "Banking Revolution," *Washington Post*, April 29, 1998, p. A21.

Saunders, Anthony and Lawrence J. White, eds., *Technology and the Regulation of Financial Markets: Securities, Futures, and Banking*. Lexington, Mass.: Heath, 1986.

Scherer, F. M. and David Ross, *Industrial Market Structure and Economic Performance*. 3rd ed. Boston: Houghton-Mifflin, 1990.

Schwert, William G., "Public Regulation of National Securities Exchanges: A Test of the Capture Hypothesis," *Bell Journal of Economics and Management Science*, 8 (Spring 1977), pp. 128–150.

Scott, Kenneth E., "The Dual Banking System: A Model of Competition in Regulation," *Stanford Law Review*, 30 (1977), pp. 1–50.

Shull, Bernard and Lawrence J. White, "The Right Corporate Structure for Expanded Bank Activities," *Banking Law Journal*, 115 (May 1998), pp. 446–476.

Siegel, Daniel R., ed., *Innovation and Technology in the Markets: A Reordering of the World's Capital Market System*. Chicago: Probus, 1990.

Stansell, Stanley R., ed., *International Financial Market Integration*. Cambridge, Mass.: Blackwell, 1993.

Stigler, George, J., "The Theory of Regulation," *Bell Journal of Economics and Management Science*, 2 (Spring 1971), pp. 3–21.

Tinic, Seha M. and Richard R. West, "The Securities Industry under Negotiated Broker-age Commissions: Changes in the Structure and Performance of New York Stock Exchange Member Firms," *Bell Journal of Economics and Management Science*, 11 (Spring 1980), pp. 29–41.

Van Horne, James C., "Of Financial Innovations and Excesses," *Journal of Finance*, 40 (July 1985), pp. 621–636.

White, Lawrence J., "The Partial Deregulation of Banks and Other Depository Institu-tions," in Leonard W. Weiss and Michael W. Klass, eds. *Regulatory Reform: What Actu-ally Happened*. Boston: Little, Brown, 1986, pp. 169–204.

White, Lawrence J., *The S&L Debacle: Public Policy Lessons for Bank and Thrift Regula-tion*. New York: Oxford University Press, 1991.

White, Lawrence J., "The Community Reinvestment Act: Good Intentions Headed in the Wrong Direction," *Fordham Urban Law Journal*, 20 (Winter 1993), pp. 281–292.

White, Lawrence J., "U.S. Banking Regulation," in Benn Steil, ed., *International Financial Market Regulation*. London: Wiley, 1994a, pp. 15–35.

White, Lawrence J., "On the Internationalization of Bank Regulation," *Oxford Review of Economic Policy*, 10 (Winter 1994b), pp. 94–105.

White, Lawrence J., "Tying, Banking, and Antitrust: It's Time for a Change," *Contemporary Policy Issues*, 13 (October 1995), pp. 26–35.

White, Lawrence J., "Technological Innovation and the Regulation of the Financial Ser-vices Sector: Tensions and Interactions," prepared for the "Technology and Finance" Discussion Series of the New York Academy of Sciences, March 1996a, mimeo.

White, Lawrence J., "International Regulation of Securities Markets: Competition or Har-monization?" in A. Lo (ed.), *The Industrial Organization and Regulation of Securities Markets*, Chicago, University of Chicago Press, 1996b, pp. 207–235.

White, Lawrence J., "Competition versus Harmonization: An Overview of International Regulation of Financial Services," in Claude Barfield, ed., *International Trade in Finan-cial Services*. Washington: American Enterprise Institute, 1996c, pp. 5–48.

White, Lawrence J., "The NAIC Model Investment Law: A Missed Opportunity," in Edward I. Altman and Irwin T. Vanderhoof, eds., *The Strategic Dynamics of the Insur-ance Industry: Asset/Liability Management Issues*. Burr Ridge, Il.: Irwin, 1996d, pp. 41–49.

White, Lawrence J., "U.S. Public Policy Toward Network Industries." American Enterprise Institute, Washington, D.C., 1999.

Winston, Clifford, "Economic Deregulation: Days of Reckoning for Microeconomists," *Journal of Economic Literature*, 31 (September 1993), pp. 1263–1289.

Wolf, Charles, Jr., *Markets or Governments. Choosing Between Imperfect Alternatives*. Cambridge, Mass.: MIT Press, 1989.

# 13

## The Effects of Entry Restrictions on Bank Performance in the United States[a]

Jith Jayaratne[b], Philip E. Strahan[c]

### 1 Introduction

Banks in the United States have been subject to a wide range of regulations, including those that limit activities, those related to preserving the safety and soundness of banking institutions and the banking system, and those that constrain pricing. Antitrust laws apply to banks as well, so the current consolidation wave may potentially be affected by rules limiting excessive concentration. Banks also must avoid discrimination and are charged with providing credit to low income areas under the Community Reinvestment Act.[1]

We begin this chapter with a brief discussion of the effects of some of these regulations on the efficiency and structure of the banking industry. We then consider in greater depth the effect of restrictions on entry and expansion that prevented banks from branching outside a single county. As we will show, these entry restrictions had a tremendous impact on the industry, and their effects have not been fully appreciated until recently. Although individual banks and other parties may have benefited from these restrictions, both our own work and the work of others reveal that geographic restrictions increased bank instability by preventing adequate diversification, increased market power, and reduced industry efficiency.

[a] The opinions expressed in this paper reflect the authors' views and do not necessarily reflect the views of the Federal Reserve Bank of New York, the Federal Reserve System, or Charles River Associates. Most of the work done on this project occurred while Jayaratne was at the Federal Reserve Bank of New York.
[b] Charles River Associates.
[c] Federal Reserve Bank of New York, e-mail:philip.strahan@ny.frb.org.
[1] For a review of CRA issues, see Thomas (1998).

## 2 Regulation of Bank Activities and Prices

Regulation of banking has a long history. For example, in the first half of the 19th century, banks were granted charters from the states that typically limited them to "traditional" activities such as lending, note issuance, and deposit taking (Shull and White, 1998). The well-known separation of commercial and investment banking goes back to the Banking Act of 1933 (the "Glass-Steagall" Act). The Bank Holding Company (BHC) Act of 1956 further restricted bank powers by preventing holding companies that own at least two banks from engaging in activities that were not "closely related to the business of banking." In 1987, however, the Federal Reserve reversed course by expanding a BHC's ability to underwrite securities through "section 20" affiliates, and both the Fed and the Office of the Comptroller of the Currency have continued to expand banks' ability to underwrite securities and sell insurance.

Regulations designed to protect bank safety also go back well into the 19th century. In recent years, rules on bank capital have become increasingly stringent. In the early 1980s, banks in the U.S. began, for the first time, to face explicit capital adequacy regulations. In the late 1980s, international regulators agreed to a set of rules designed to make bank capital ratios reflect the risks of their asset portfolios, leading to the 1988 Basle Accord. Recently, the focus has shifted away from formulaic capital standards and towards improvements in transparency in the supervision of risk management systems. Bank regulators and supervisors hope to avoid micromanaging the institutions they oversee, and instead mandate that these institutions have in place the systems necessary to monitor and control their own risk-taking. New capital requirements for market risk are based on the output of banks' internal risk measurement models (Hendricks and Hirtle, 1997), and similar approaches to capital requirements for credit risk are currently under consideration (Federal Reserve Board, 1998).

Regulations have also affected pricing of both bank loans and bank deposits. For instance, all but three states limited credit card interest rates as of 1970 (Mandell, 1990). Although rates were typically capped at a relatively high rate of 18 percent a year, the ceiling appears to have been too low for many banks to earn significant profits. Credit card profits nosedived in the late 1970s and early 1980s when inflation drove up the cost of funds, but usury ceilings prevented banks from passing along higher interest costs to borrowers (Canner and Luckett, 1992). Banks challenged these laws in court, and credit card operations relocated in large numbers to states that lifted usury ceilings (such as Delaware and South Dakota).

A series of court decisions and state legislation relaxed regulatory limits on credit card lending by the mid-1980s. By 1988, 18 states had removed all interest ceilings (Mandell, 1990). The card industry grew tremendously in the 1980s. For example, the percentage of banks that issued MasterCard or Visa cards grew from 71 percent in 1979 to 90 percent by 1985 (Mandell, 1990). Although factors other than deregulation contributed to this growth, the relaxation of interest rate ceilings played a significant role in this trend.

Ceilings on bank deposit interest rates (under Regulation Q) also seriously affected the banking system. During those periods when short-term market interest rates rose above the deposit rate ceilings, banks and thrifts lost deposits to alternative investments, forcing them to cut back on lending. Disintermediation was not a serious problem for the first three decades after Congress legislated deposit rate ceilings through the Banking Acts of 1933 and 1935, mainly because the ceilings were higher than market rates. After the mid-1960s, however, open market interest rates rose, leading to periodic flights of deposits from banks and thrifts, thereby producing periodic credit crunches that were particularly noticeable in the mortgage loan markets.

Disintermediation became particularly acute when inflation took off in the late 1970s, and bank deposits fled into money market mutual funds offered by non-bank firms. In response to the plight of banks, Congress gradually lifted deposit rate ceilings starting in 1980 (Gilbert and Lovati, 1979; Gilbert, 1986). Deposit rate ceilings were designed partly to decrease banks' funding costs, thereby inducing banks to invest in less risky assets (Gilbert, 1986). But banks competed for funds nonetheless, by, for example, expanding their branch networks to provide better access for their customers. This non-price competition dissipated much of the increased profits generated by Regulation Q. Spellman (1980) finds, for example, that half of the increase in net revenues generated by Regulation Q was dissipated by banks in non-price competition for deposits.

### 3 A Brief History of Geographic Restrictions on Banking

Restrictions on bank expansion date back to the 19th century, when states imposed limits on branch office locations, allegedly to prevent unscrupulous bankers from "choosing inaccessible office sites to deter customers from redeeming . . . circulating banknotes" (Kane, 1996, p.

#142). Geographic limits were also justified by the political argument that allowing banks to expand their operations freely could lead to an excessive concentration of financial power. Appearing before Congress in 1939, the Secretary of the Independent Bankers Association warned that branch banking would "destroy a banking system that is distinctively American and replace it with a foreign system . . . a system that is monopolistic, undemocratic and with tinges of fascism" (Chapman and Westerfield, 1942, p. #238).

Inefficient banks probably supported these restrictions because they prevented competition from other banks. Economides, Hubbard, and Palia (1995) show that states with many weakly capitalized, small banks supported the 1927 McFadden Act, which gave states the authority to regulate national banks' branching powers. Moreover, many states used control over bank charters and the expansion of branch banking to raise revenues. Massachusetts and Delaware, for instance, received a majority of their state revenues from bank regulation in the early 19th century (Sylla, Legler, and Wallis, 1987).

Geographic restrictions may not have seriously constrained the banking industry before the appearance of large corporations that required large-scale, multistate banking services. Rapid industrialization and the growth of transcontinental railroads after the Civil War, however, created firms whose need for comprehensive corporate financial services could not be met adequately by the existing system of fragmented unit banks. In response, banks formed "chain banks" – an alliance of several banks whose principal ownership rested with the same group of investors – after 1890. (For a review of strategic issues in banking, see Harker and Zenios, 1999). A few years later, "banking groups" – banks owned directly by a holding company – were created in an effort to get around branching restrictions (Calomiris, 1993).

Nevertheless, branching restrictions persisted, and as late as 1975 only 14 states allowed statewide branching. Twelve states prohibited branching altogether, and the remainder imposed restrictions of varying severity. Pennsylvania was representative of a partially restrictive state. Until 1982, Pennsylvania banks were allowed to branch only in the county where their head offices were located and in contiguous counties.

Many states eased the sting of these branching restrictions by allowing banking companies to expand within the state by forming multi-bank holding companies (MBHCs) long before they allowed branch banking. In 1972, 36 states allowed unrestricted MBHC expansion within the state. If the MBHC structure allowed banks to grow optimally without branching, we would expect branching restrictions to have had little impact.

However, MBHCs are more costly to operate than branch banks because they require multiple boards of directors and separate capitalization of each bank subsidiary. The high cost of the MBHC structure is confirmed by the fact that many multibank holding companies converted their bank subsidiaries into branches once branching was allowed (McLaughlin, 1995). Also, branch banking had important effects on the structure of banking markets – significant entry into local markets occurred after intrastate branching restrictions were lifted via de novo branching and small banking companies lost market share after branching reform (Amel and Liang, 1992; Calem, 1994).

In addition to facing restrictions on within-state expansion, banks have traditionally been limited in their ability to cross state lines. The Douglas Amendment to the 1956 Bank Holding Company Act prohibited a BHC from acquiring banks outside the state where it was headquartered unless the target bank's state permitted such acquisitions. Since no state allowed such transactions in 1956, the amendment effectively barred interstate banking organizations. Although states had the option to allow out-of-state BHCs to enter, none exercised that right until 1978, when Maine permitted such transactions. Even then, however, little changed: the Maine statute allowed an out-of-state BHC to buy a Maine bank only if the home state of the acquiring BHC permitted Maine-based BHCs the reciprocal right to buy banks there; since no other state allowed such entry, interstate bank organizations could not be formed. Banks could not in fact cross state borders until 1982, when Alaska, Massachusetts, and New York permitted out-of-state BHCs to enter.

## 4 The Effects of Geographic Restrictions on Bank Stability

Geographic restrictions limit the ability of banks to diversify their loan portfolios and deposit liabilities, thereby producing a more unstable banking system. This conclusion is supported by several features of the banking system, especially during the period before the national deposit insurance fund was established in 1933.

First, branch banks survived bank panics better than unit banks. For example, Calomiris (1993) compares the bank failure rates in several states that were hit hard by the agricultural bust of the 1920s. In three states that allowed some branch banking and which experienced high overall bank failure rates due to the agricultural depression – Arizona, Mississippi, and South Carolina – Calomiris found that branch banks failed at a much lower rate than unit banks. The branch bank failure rate in Arizona, for example, was 1.6 percent, well below the overall failure rate of 4.3 percent in Arizona.

Second, states that allowed branch banks not only weathered economic downturns and bank panics better but also recovered from such episodes faster than unit banking states. Taking another example from the agricultural recession of the 1920s, Calomiris (1992) finds that bank assets in branching states grew substantially faster than in limited-branching states during the period.[2] In fact, the effects of branch regulation were more important than the effects of (state-level) deposit insurance in this example.

Third, markets appear to have recognized the greater stability of branch banks. For instance, during the American Free Banking Era (1838–60), banks issued debt in the form of bank notes that were perpetual, non-interest-bearing, risky debt claims that could be redeemed at par in specie. These notes traded at a discount, with riskier banks' notes being subjected to steeper discounts. Gorton (1996) finds that notes issued by new banks in branch banking states were discounted substantially less than new banks in unit banking states, suggesting that the market perceived branch banking to be safer than unit banking.

Another piece of evidence in this direction is that branch banks held fewer reserves and less capital than unit banks. Calomiris (1993) reports that in 1856 large branch banks in Georgia held half the reserves of the average state bank. Similarly, Canadian and British banks (nearly all were branch banks) held fewer reserves than U.S. banks in the late 19th century and early 20th century (Calomiris, 1993). California banks decreased reserves and capital when branch banking was introduced in 1909.

Comparing the U.S. and Canada during the 1930s provides further evidence that branching enhances bank stability: Canada experienced no bank failures during the 1930s; in 1933, 27 percent of banks operating in the U.S. failed (Saunders and Wilson, 1998).

Of course, branch banks may be safer because they are, on average, bigger than unit banks – not because they have branches. Not all of the above studies control for bank size when investigating the effects of branching on bank stability. However, Laderman et al. (1991) find that branching helps banks diversify their loan portfolios, suggesting that the greater stability of branch banks is at least partly the result of branching over a wider geographic area. Using data from the early 1980s,

---

[2] This analysis is based on 32 states that experienced severe downturns in their agricultural sectors.

Laderman et al. (1991) find that when statewide branching is permitted, rural banks make more non-agricultural loans and urban banks make more agricultural loans. They interpret this to mean that the average bank can lend at a lower cost to borrowers who are near the bank's branches (perhaps because monitoring costs increase with distance to banks' branches). Hence, having a geographically wider spread in branch networks allows banks to diversify their loan portfolios.

Recent history also suggests that geographically diversified banks are more stable. Mishkin (forthcoming) points out that bank failures in Texas and New England could have been substantially reduced if banks had been permitted to operate in both places. Texas experienced a sharp downturn in the middle of the 1980s in response to the collapse of oil prices. As a result, Texas suffered over 100 bank failures both in 1987 and in 1988. During this period, however, the rest of the country was experiencing strong economic growth. What percentage of bank assets in Texas would have been owned by failed banks if there had been no limits on bank expansion across state lines? While we can not answer this question directly, we do note that in 1987, the year Texas first permitted out-of-state bank holding companies to own Texas banks, less than 10 percent of bank assets were owned by non-Texas banks. This percentage rose to more than 50 percent by 1994 (Berger, Kashyap, and Scalise, 1995).

Keeley (1990), however, emphasizes increases in risk taking that followed deregulation-induced declines in franchise value. Keeley argues that banks behaved conservatively during the 1940s, 1950s, and 1960s in order to protect rents generated, at least in part, by prohibitions on branching and interstate banking. He argues that risk-taking increased in the deregulated environment of the 1980s because banks had, in effect, much less to lose than in the past. Demsetz, Saidenberg, and Strahan (1997) also find that franchise value leads banks to take less risk. Thus, it seems likely that, *ceteris paribus*, branching leads to more stable banks. But if competition increases along with the move toward branching, then it becomes much less clear whether or not bank safety has been enhanced by branching deregulation. Note, however, that estimating the net effect of branching deregulation on safety is difficult in practice because safety and soundness regulations were tightened throughout the 1980s and 1990s.

### 5 The Effects of Geographic Restrictions on Bank Efficiency

How did geographic restrictions affect bank efficiency? Jayaratne and Strahan (1998) find that geographic limits reduced the efficiency of the average bank asset and increased intermediation costs, primarily by limiting the ability of better-managed banks to gain market share.

### 5.1 Moves Toward Deregulation

We investigate the efficiency effects of geographic restrictions by examining *changes* in overall bank efficiency once states lifted most geographic restrictions after 1970. The two decades since 1970 witnessed significant deregulation in banking. Only 13 states allowed unrestricted intrastate branching in 1974. During the next two decades, 35 states and Washington, D.C. substantially eliminated restrictions on intrastate branching. By 1992, all but three states allowed some form of statewide branching. As a first step, states allowed banks to branch only by buying other banks' existing branches (M&A branching). Soon thereafter, they often would allow *de novo* branching as well. As for interstate banking, only Maine allowed out-of-state BHCs to buy in-state banks as of 1978. By the end of 1992, the state-level deregulatory process was essentially completed: all states but Arkansas, Iowa, and Minnesota allowed statewide branching, and all states but Hawaii permitted out-of-state BHCs to enter. Finally, 14 states that had previously restricted BHCs' ability to expand within a state lifted such regulations over the two decades after 1970.

Several developments contributed to the removal of geographic barriers limiting bank expansion. In the mid-1980s, the Office of the Comptroller of the Currency took advantage of a clause in the 1864 National Bank Act to allow nationally chartered banks to branch freely in those states where thrifts did not face branching restrictions. The Comptroller's action was instrumental in introducing statewide branching in several southern states. Another impetus behind deregulation may have been the rash of bank and thrift failures in the 1980s, which increased public awareness of the advantages of large, well-diversified banks (Kane, 1996).

Kroszner and Strahan (forthcoming) suggest that the emergence of new technologies in both deposit taking and lending may have encouraged the elimination of geographic barriers by changing the nature of banking markets. For instance, the introduction of the automated teller machine in the late 1970s and the development of money market mutual funds increased competitiveness in deposit markets and reduced the incentive of banks protected from competition to lobby for the preservation of branching and interstate banking restrictions. At the same time, new information technologies diminished the value of the specialized knowledge that long-established local bankers might have had about the risks of borrowers in the community. These changes enhanced the ability of banks to lend in more distant markets. As a result, protected banks' incentive to defend restrictions on branching and interstate banking has diminished over time, while expansion-minded banks' desire to see the restrictions fall has increased.

The initiative to relax restrictions on interstate banking came primarily from larger banking organizations that were well equipped to pursue better lending opportunities and lower funding costs in neighboring states. Their efforts may have succeeded in the 1980s because it became apparent that banks and nonbanks were already practicing interstate banking.

Geographic deregulation significantly altered the banking landscape. Table 13.1 describes some of these changes. In that table, several state-level measures of bank structure (the number of branches, the number of banks, the number of banking companies, the number of branches per bank, and the number of branches per banking company, the state-level deposit Herfindahl-Hirschmann Index (HHI), and the log of the average amount of deposits per banking company) are regressed on four indicators of the severity of the state's restriction on geographic expansion.[3] In order to exploit the fact that states had different degrees of restrictions on bank expansion, and the fact that states deregulated these restrictions at different times, we construct a panel data set with observations for each state during each year from 1975 to 1991. We then estimate regressions of the following form:

$$Y_{t,i} = \alpha_t + \beta_i + \gamma_1 \, Branch_{t,i} + \gamma_2 Bank_{t,i} + \gamma_3 De \, Novo_{t,i} + \gamma_4 MBHC_{t,i} + \in_{t,i}$$

where $Y_{t,i}$ equals one of the measures of structure; $Branch_{t,i}$ is an indicator equal to 1 for states without restrictions on branching via M&A (i.e., states that permit banks to branch across the state by acquiring the branches of existing banks); $Bank_{t,i}$ is an indicator equal to 1 for states that have entered into an interstate banking agreement; $De \, Novo_{t,i}$ is an indicator equal to 1 for states that permit banks to open new branches anywhere in the state; and $MBHC_{t,i}$ is an indicator equal to 1 for states that do not restrict the ability to form multi-bank holding companies within the state. Because of the panel structure, we can also control for aggregate shocks and time trends with time fixed effects ($\alpha_t$), and we can

---

[3] Data on the number of branches, the number of banks, and the number of banking companies (stand-alone banks plus top tier holding companies), as well as on deposits and the deposit-based HHI, are from the FDIC's *Summary of Deposits*.

Table 13.1. *Changes in the structure of the banking industry following deregulation of geographical restrictions on expansion.*

| | Log of # of banks | Log of # of banking companies | Log of number of branches | Branches per bank | Branches per banking company | Log of deposits per banking company | State-level deposit HHI |
|---|---|---|---|---|---|---|---|
| M&A branching indicator | -0.192*** (0.039) | -0.162*** (0.037) | 0.075 (0.101) | 0.930** (0.432) | 1.146** (0.453) | 0.086* (0.051) | 81.15* (41.04) |
| Unrestricted statewide branching indicator | -0.008 (0.040) | 0.086 (0.059) | 0.055 (0.130) | 0.898** (0.422) | -0.043 (0.574) | 0.011 (0.076) | 31.51 (49.11) |
| Interstate banking indicator | -0.064* (0.035) | -0.052 (0.057) | 0.047 (0.063) | 0.414 (0.326) | 1.064** (0.511) | 0.090* (0.053) | -29.09 (57.98) |
| Multi-bank holding company indicator | 0.023 (0.042) | -0.096* (0.052) | -0.001 (0.112) | -0.832* (0.444) | -0.364 (0.529) | -0.038 (0.058) | -48.08 (48.43) |
| Dependent variable mean [median] | 5.002 [5.236] | 4.881 [5.136] | 6.064 [6.254] | 6.293 [4.327] | 6.649 [5.055] | 11.689 [11.668] | 980.9 [760.6] |

*Source:* Kroszner and Strahan (forthcoming).

*Note:* This table contains regressions of state-level measures of the structure of the banking industry. Each dependent variable is regressed on a set of state indicator variables, a set of year indicator variables, and the set of four deregulation indicators; these deregulation indicators are equal to 1 after deregulation and 0 before. If a state was always regulated, the indicator is 0 throughout; if it was always deregulated, the indicator is 1 throughout. Sample period is 1975 to 1991 and Delaware and South Dakota are dropped, so N = 833. The coefficient on the deregulation indicators is reported, with robust standard errors in parentheses. ***, **, * denote statistically significant at the 1, 5, and 10 percent levels.

control for other unexplained differences across states with the state fixed effect $(\beta_i)$.[4]

Table 13.1 shows that geographic deregulation (1) reduced the number of banks and banking companies; (2) increased the size of banks, (i.e., the number of branches at the average bank and banking company increased, and the amount of deposits at the average bank increased); and (3) increased state-level bank concentration (as measured by the state-level deposit HHI – at least after M&A branching was allowed). These effects are economically large. For example, the number of banks decreased by 19 percent and banking companies by 16 percent after M&A branching deregulation. Interestingly, the biggest changes in bank structure are associated with M&A branching deregulation. Consequently, in the rest of the paper we focus on M&A deregulation when examining the effects of geographic deregulation on bank efficiency.[5]

### 5.2  Changes in Bank Efficiency and Prices After Deregulation

Did banks perform better when they were permitted to operate statewide branch networks? We investigate this question by examining how bank costs – measured by loan losses (net loan charge-offs divided by total loans) and noninterest costs (noninterest expenses divided by total assets) – change, on average, after geographic deregulation. We then consider whether banks' customers are better off following deregulation by examining changes in loan prices (interest income on loans and leases divided by total loans and leases). We look at state-level aggregate data for the 1978–92 period to summarize the overall impact of deregulation on the overall performance of the banking system.

To understand our measures of the cost efficiency of the banking system, consider New York in 1978. We construct the charge-offs ratio by dividing the sum of loans charged off by all banks operating in New York in 1978 by the sum of all loans held by New York banks in 1978. We construct similar aggregates for the noninterest expense and loan price variables in each state and year in the sample.[6] The data for these

---

[4] Note that Delaware and South Dakota are dropped from these and subsequent regressions since banks in these states are dominated by credit card banks.

[5] For further discussion of why we emphasize branching deregulation, see Jayaratne and Strahan (1998).

[6] The noninterest expense variable equals total noninterest expenses incurred by all banks in a state divided by total banking assets held by banks in that state. The loan price variable equals interest earned on all loans and leases in a state divided by total loans plus leases held on bank balance sheets in that state.

performance measures are derived from the year-end *Reports of Income and Condition,* filed by all banks with the federal banking agencies.

We estimate the effects of deregulation using regressions with time and state fixed effects and regulation indicator variables similar in structure to those reported in Table 13.1. The regressions allow us to control for other factors that might influence our measures of bank cost and loan prices – most notably the health of the state's economy. Bank costs, particularly those related to loan defaults, generally move with the business cycle: borrowers tend to pay off loans during boom times but are less able to do so during recessions. If states deregulated their branching and interstate banking restrictions during hard times, average measures of costs could improve after deregulation as states' economies recovered from recession. A simple before-and-after comparison of bank performance would show an improvement in bank loan portfolios and profitability after deregulation, but these advances would largely reflect the timing of deregulation. We address this possibility by controlling for the national business cycle in our regressions.[7]

Our analysis suggests that decreases in loan losses, noninterest expenses, and loan rates after statewide branching deregulation are both statistically and economically significant. This is true even after we adjust for the influence of the business cycle on bank performance and for persistent cross-state differences in bank performance. Figure 13.1 illustrates these findings. We report the average levels of the price and cost measures that would have been observed during the sample period under two alternative regulatory regimes: (1) restrictions in place on intrastate branching, (2) branching permitted.[8] The top panel suggests that if no state had allowed statewide branching between 1978 and 1992, the ratio of charge-offs to total loans in the typical state in a typical year would have been 1.2 percent. Had all states allowed statewide branching in our sample period, average charge-offs in the typical state would have fallen by half, to 0.6 percent.[9] The ratio of noninterest expenses to assets would have fallen from 3.5 percent to 3.3 percent if branching had been permitted throughout the period (middle panel). It appears that most of these reduced costs were passed along to bank borrowers in the form of lower loan rates, which in our estimates declined from 11.5 percent to

---

[7] When we control for the *state* business cycle, the estimated effects of statewide branching decrease but are still both statistically significant and economically important.

[8] We also assume in these calculations that interstate banking is not allowed even if statewide branching is permitted.

[9] We find declines in loan loss provisions and nonperforming loans of similar magnitude following branching deregulation. See Jayaratne and Strahan (1998).

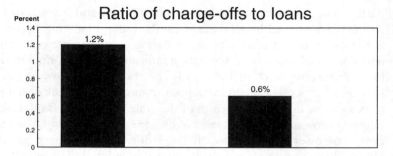

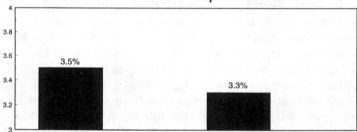

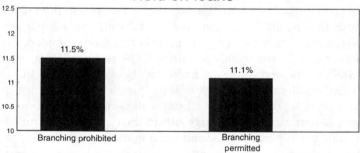

Figure 13.1. Costs and interest rates are lower after deregulation.
Note: This figure shows the average level of price and performance
measures that would have been observed in the 1978–92 period had
all states been subject to the regulatory regimes identified along
the x-axis.

11.1 percent on average.[10] Each of these improvements is statistically significant at the 5 percent level.[11]

### 5.3 Geographic Restrictions and Market Power

Opponents of bank deregulation have argued that deregulation has increased concentration in the banking industry and thereby enhanced market power. While measures of concentration at both the state and national levels have increased in recent years following deregulation, concentration at local levels has remained remarkably constant. For instance, the mean share of deposits held by the top three banking organizations operating in an MSA (Metropolitan Statistical Analysis) went from 66.8 percent in 1980 to 68.3 percent in 1994 (Rhoades, 1996). If enhanced market power were a problem, we would see both increased concentration and higher prices at the local level following deregulation, neither of which has occurred. Similarly, our own estimates of the impact of deregulation on banks' return on equity and return on assets in another study (Jayaratne and Strahan, 1998) showed small increases in profitability that were sometimes statistically significant (at the 10 percent level) and sometimes not. Nevertheless, it appears that most, or perhaps all, of the cost reductions from deregulation are passed along to customers. There is little evidence that deregulation has increased market power.

If anything, geographic restrictions probably *increased* market power by limiting entry. Evanoff and Fortier (1988) find that when local banking markets are more concentrated (measured in terms of the deposit share of the top three banks in a market), bank profitability increases. However, they find this effect only for those states that restrict branching. The potential for entry into local markets by competitors in branching states appears to discipline incumbents in branching states – but not in states that restrict branching. Keeley (1990) finds declines in bank franchise value following deregulation of restrictions on banks' ability to expand, and interprets this as evidence that access to rents declined following deregulation.

---

[10] We find no change in deposit interest rates following deregulation, however. All of the cost declines seem to be passed along to bank borrowers rather than depositors.

[11] The estimates of the effects of deregulation on our performance measures are based on a regression model that assumes that the changes occur immediately following deregulation and are permanent. Because we have only five to ten years of experience after deregulation for most states, we cannot be sure that these effects will continue indefinitely. Nevertheless, we find that the observed improvements in bank performance persist more than five years after branching deregulation.

*5.4 How Deregulation Improves Bank Efficiency*

Limits on bank expansion could have had adverse effects on efficiency in banking for at least three reasons. First, prohibitions on branching and interstate banking may have limited the opportunity for the best-run banks to grow. In unregulated markets, more efficient firms have a natural tendency to gain market share over their less productive competitors, an outcome that will increase average efficiency as the industry evolves over time. By preventing better-run banks from establishing branches, and by preventing BHCs from expanding across state lines, these regulations may have retarded this natural evolution. After the geographical constraints were lifted, the more efficient banks may have expanded, thereby improving the performance of the average banking asset. We call this the *selection hypothesis*.

Second, limited restrictions on geographic expansion may have weakened the market for corporate control, thereby reducing the discipline usually placed on managers of corporations. When interstate banking is prohibited, managers worry less about takeovers. Because their jobs are more secure, they may also be less motivated to increase shareholder value, maximize efficiency, and minimize costs. According to this *disciplining hypothesis*, efficiency in banking improves after deregulation because managers are forced to increase shareholder value in order to preserve their jobs. Note that the disciplining hypothesis predicts that all banks will improve their performance following deregulation, since managers at all banks will come under greater pressure. By contrast, the selection hypothesis predicts only that the more efficient banks will gain market share, not that the efficiency of all individual banks will improve.

A third possible reason why efficiency might improve following deregulation is that barriers to geographic expansion prevent banks from operating at the most efficient size. Most of the studies of scale economies based on data from the 1970s and 1980s suggested that scale economies wane beyond about $500 million in total assets (see Berger, Hunter, and Timme, 1993). According to the *economies of scale* hypothesis, the efficiency of the banking system will improve after branching deregulation as small banks grow and reduce costs. Of course, according to this view, the benefits come from changes occurring at the lower end of the bank size distribution. Since branching deregulation occurred during the 1970s and 1980s, and since banks with assets under $500 million hold a relatively small share of total banking assets, these benefits would likely be quite limited. Recent evidence from the 1990s, however, suggests that scale economies may now extend up to $10 to $25 billion in assets (Deloitte and Touche, 1995; Berger and Mester, 1997; Berger, Demetz, and Strahan, 1999). The effects of improved scale economies may be much larger as a result of the 1994 Interstate Banking and Branching Efficiency Act, which now allows bank holding companies to own banks in all 50 states.

Which of these three explanations best accounts for the performance gains observed following deregulation? We can rule out the economies of scale explanation on two grounds. First, there is scant evidence of scale economies in banking beyond about $500 million in total assets during the 1970s, and 1980s (see Berger, Hunter, and Timme, 1993). The large improvements that we have found in the state-level aggregates cannot plausibly be attributed to the fact that small banks are moving closer to the optimal scale. In 1980, for instance, banks with under $500 million in assets (in 1994 dollars) held less than 30 percent of total assets in the banking system. Second, we have also estimated the change in our performance measures following branching deregulation for small banks (those with assets under $100 million) and large banks separately. We find that the improvements are *greater* for large banks than for small, a finding inconsistent with the economies of scale explanation.[12]

More difficult to evaluate is the hypothesis that management discipline accounts for the beneficial effects of branching deregulation. Because we lack good measures of the degree of managerial effort at banks, we cannot test this hypothesis directly. Nevertheless, we cannot reject the possibility that disciplining played some role in the improved efficiency of banks. Hubbard and Palia (1995) find evidence of greater managerial discipline following interstate banking: the turnover rate for banks' chief executive officers rises and the pay-performance relation tightens once states allow interstate banking. Hubbard and Palia contend that these changes are the effects of a more active market for corporate control after deregulation. Such changes may well have disciplined management to improve bank performance, although neither this article nor the Hubbard and Palia study establishes this point. Shranz (1993) finds that bank profitability is higher in states that allow interstate banking and attributes this effect to a more active takeover market. One problem with this interpretation, however, is that hostile takeovers are quite rare in banking due to regulations limiting the number of potential acquirers to other banking organizations (Prowse, 1997).

The remaining explanation for bank efficiency gains, the selection

[12] These results are available on request.

hypothesis, can readily be tested. To do so, we examine whether better run banking companies grow faster than their less efficient rivals following branching deregulation. First, we classify banks on the basis of their profitability just before deregulation. We then observe the change in the market share after deregulation for the high-profit banking companies. If the selection hypothesis is correct, we should find that profitable banks increase their market share at the expense of unprofitable banks following deregulation.

Specifically, for each state, we first rank banking companies from highest to lowest according to their return on equity at the end of the year prior to the year of deregulation. Next, we go down that ranking until we reach a bank that, together with all previous banks, accounts for 50 percent of the state's bank assets. The banking companies in this group constitute our high-profit firms.[13] We then calculate the group's share of state bank assets five years after branching deregulation. We chose these window lengths because most of the observed changes in bank structure occurred within five years after branching deregulation. For example, nearly two-thirds of the 30 percent increase in the state-level bank asset concentration occurred within five years after branching deregulation. Similar results are reported in Berger, Kashyap, and Scalise (1995), who find that most changes to bank structure occur within five years after geographic deregulation. Some states, however, entered interstate banking agreements during the five-year window. For these states, we use the year just prior to the year in which the state entered the interstate banking agreement as the end of the window. We dropped four states – West Virginia, Tennessee, Oregon, and New Hampshire – that entered interstate banking agreements in the same year or one year after branching was deregulated.

As implied by the selection hypothesis, we find that the high-profit banking companies grow faster after deregulation (Table 13.2): their share of banking assets increases, on average, by 8.5 percentage points (from 51.3 percent to 59.8 percent) after branching deregulation – a statistically significant increase. Of course, we would expect banks enjoying high profits and good loan portfolios to grow relatively faster at all times, even when branching restrictions are in place. In other words, the fact

---

[13] When we substitute loan charge-offs for return on equity as a measure of bank quality, we obtain similar results. To conserve space, however, we do not include these results in this article. In addition, we do not include noninterest expenses in this analysis, because the data are available only beginning in 1984. The lack of earlier data means that we can conduct the exercise in Table 13.2 for only three deregulating states using noninterest expense data.

Table 13.2. *Better banks increase their market share after branching deregulation.*

| Period | Initial market share of high-profit banks – % | Market share of high-profit banks six years later – % | Increase in share (t-statistic) |
|---|---|---|---|
| Prederegulation | 49.9 | 51.7 | 1.8% (0.99) |
| Postderegulation | 51.3 | 59.8 | 8.5% (3.91)* |

*Source*: Authors' calculations, based on data from the *Reports of Income and Condition.*

*Note*: The table reports the change in the share of total assets held by that half of the banking companies with the highest return on equity at the beginning of the specified period. In the prederegulation period, we first rank all banking companies in a given state by their return on equity seven years before the year of deregulation. We define as high-profit banking companies that portion of the ranking whose collective assets represents 50 percent of the state's total bank assets. We then compute the market share of these banking companies in the year before the year of deregulation (six years later). In the postderegulation period, we sort all banking companies in a given state by their return on equity in the year before the year of deregulation. We then compute their market share five years after the year of deregulation (again, six years after the initial ranking). * denotes statistical significance at the 5 percent level.

that banks with good balance sheets grow faster than less profitable banks need not indicate that deregulation caused the weaker banks to lose ground. To isolate the effects of deregulation on selection, we compare the differential growth rates of high- and low-profit banks in a *deregulated* environment with the same differential growth rates in a *regulated* environment.

A striking contrast is evident in the growth rates achieved in regulated and deregulated environments (Table 13.2). High-profit banks increase their market share by only 1.8 percentage points (from 49.9 to 51.7 percent) in the average state over the prederegulation period. This change is so small that we cannot reject the possibility that high-profit banks do not increase their market share at all over the six-year period before deregulation (that is, 1.8 percent is not a statistically significant change). In the postderegulation period, by contrast, the market share of the high-profit banks rises sharply. The evidence in Table 13.2 strongly

Table 13.3. *Changes in the dispersion of bank profitability following deregulation of geographical restrictions on expansion.*

|  | Return on equity | Return on assets |
|---|---|---|
| M&A branching indicator | −0.0262* | −0.0022** |
|  | (0.011) | (0.0007) |
| $R^2$ | 0.358 | 0.368 |
| Dependent variable mean/[median] | 0.086 | 0.0075 |
|  | [0.065] | [0.0060] |
| Dependent variable mean/[median], fully regulated | 0.111 | 0.0090 |
|  | [0.081] | [0.0068] |
| Dependent variable mean/[median], fully deregulated | 0.061 | 0.0059 |
|  | [0.058] | [0.0057] |

*Note*: This table contains regressions of the interquartile range of return on equity (net income/book value of equity) and return on assets (net income/assets) for all banking companies in a given state. The dependent variable is regressed on a set of state indicator variables, a set of year indicator variables, and an indicator equal to 1 after branching deregulation and 0 before. If a state was always regulated, the indicator is 0 throughout; if it was always deregulated, the indicator is 1 throughout. Sample period is 1975 to 1993, and Delaware and South Dakota are dropped, so N = 931. The coefficient on the deregulation indicators is reported, with robust standard errors in parentheses. **, * denote statistically significant at the 1 and 5 percent levels.

supports the hypothesis that branching deregulation forced a process of selection whereby weaker banks lost ground to better-run banks.

Both the selection and disciplining hypotheses imply that the variability of bank performance should decline following deregulation. Banks' performance should converge in unfettered markets. The disciplining conjecture suggests that poorly run banks' managers will improve performance because they face stiffer competition in banking markets, or because they face a greater threat of a takeover if they underperform. The performance of poorly run banks would improve and the variance of bank performance would decrease. The selection conjecture would imply that poorly run banks would exit the industry following deregulation, thereby also reducing the variance of bank performance as the lower end of the performance distribution shrinks.

Table 13.3 indeed shows that the dispersion of bank performance shrinks following branch deregulation. In that table, we measure dispersion as the interquartile range of bank-level return on assets (ROA) and return on equity (ROE). The table shows the results of regressions that have as their dependent variables the interquartile range of ROE and ROA and use the same panel structure used in Table 13.1. Specifically, we regress these two variables on state and year fixed effects and an indicator variable for branching deregulation. We find a significant decrease in ROA and ROE dispersion after branching deregulation. For example, ROE dispersion fell 2.6 percentage points once branching was allowed. We also report the average cross-bank dispersion in ROE and ROA for all states and years when both branching and MBHC formation are restricted (limited branching, MBHC formation restricted both within and across state lines), and when both branching and MBHC formation are unrestricted (statewide branching, no restrictions on MBHC formation either within or across state lines): in regulated environments, the median amount of variability in ROE is 0.081; in unregulated environments, cross-bank variability in ROE falls to 0.058, a decline of about 30 percent.

### 5.5 Geographic Deregulation and Economic Growth

Thus far we have argued that relaxation of geographic restrictions improved the performance of the banking system, enhancing the efficiency of the average bank asset and improving bank lending. How did these changes affect the rest of the economy? Earlier research has shown that countries with better developed banking systems grow faster because savings are channeled into the highest-return investments (King and Levine, 1993). Banks can help to route savings to the most productive uses in two ways. First, they provide information about the profit-potential of different businesses, channeling investment toward good projects and away from bad. Second, banks monitor those firms with which they have lending relationships to ensure that bank funds are put to proper use (Diamond, 1984).[14]

Branching deregulation is likely to enhance the ability of banks to help investors find the best projects and to oversee the successful execution of those projects. As we have seen, banks function better after branching deregulation, and their loan losses decrease sharply. The selection hypothesis suggests that these improvements occur because banks that are better able to screen and monitor loans are able to expand their operations at the expense of less effectively managed banks after

---

[14] For instance, banks write loan covenants that restrict firms' ability to engage in certain activities during periods of financial distress. The writing and exercising of such covenants allow banks to monitor their borrowers effectively (Morgan, 1995).

deregulation. As a result, the economy can grow faster because savings flow more consistently into profitable investment opportunities.

In this section, we investigate whether state-level rates of economic growth did in fact increase following branching deregulation.[15] Specifically, we estimate the change in the average growth rate of two measures of economic activity: real per capita personal income and real per capita gross state product.[16] These two measures differ somewhat in concept: Personal income reflects the income of a state's residents, providing a measure of residents' welfare. Gross state product, by contrast, measures the total incomes of factors of production located within the state, allowing us to assess the economic activity that actually occurs there.[17] As in our estimates of the effects of branching deregulation on bank performance, we control for both business cycle effects and the effects of differences in the long-run growth rate across states.[18] Our tests of the effects of branching deregulation on the state economies show a significant acceleration in growth: annual personal income grows about 0.51 percentage points faster after branching deregulation, and gross state product, about 0.69 percentage points faster (Table 13.4, row 1). This acceleration is not only statistically significant at the 5 percent level but is also economically "large" relative to the 1.6 percent annual average growth rate of real per capita personal income over the sample period.

Of course, there is uncertainty associated with this estimate – with a 5

---

[15] We again focus only on branching deregulation, rather than interstate banking, because we found sharp improvements in bank performance associated with statewide branching but not with interstate banking. Although we looked for evidence of changes in economic growth associated with interstate banking, we found none.

[16] Personal income and gross state product are published annually by the U.S. Department of Commerce. Annual state population figures are from the U.S. Bureau of the Census. We convert nominal personal income to constant dollars using a national price deflator, the consumer price index.

[17] The difference between personal income and gross state product is apparent in how the two measures treat capital income. Capital income is allocated to personal income according to the state of residence of the owner of capital, while for gross state product capital income is allocated according to the physical location of the capital itself. Real per capita personal income grew by 1.6 percent per year during our analysis period (1972–92), while gross state product grew by 1.4 percent per year between 1978 and 1992. (Since the Commerce Department changed the base year for the industry price deflators in 1977, we could not construct a consistent growth series prior to 1978 using gross state product.)

[18] We include a set of time dummy variables that vary across four broad regions to control for regional business cycle effects. For details, see Jayaratne and Strahan (1996), Table 3.2.

Table 13.4. *Economic growth accelerates after branching deregulation.*

|  | Percentage change in personal income growth | Percentage change in gross state product |
|---|---|---|
| (1) Overall increase in growth | 0.51 (2.22)** | 0.69 (2.09)** |
| (2) Increase in growth, years 1–5 | 0.35 (1.75)* | 0.60 (2.07)** |
| (3) Increase in growth, years 5–10 | 0.37 (1.85)* | 0.65 (2.41)** |
| (4) Increase in growth, years 10+ | 0.17 (0.89) | 0.67 (2.48)** |

*Source*: Jayaratne and Strahan (1996), rows 3 and 7 of Tables 2 and 5.
*Note*: T-statistics appear in parentheses below the coefficients.
** Statistically significant at the 5 percent level.
* Statistically significant at the 10 percent level.

percent probability of error, we can only be confident that personal income growth increased somewhere between 0.06 and 0.97 percentage points. Moreover, these figures are estimated under the assumption that the growth pickup persists indefinitely. One possibility is that the economy benefits for a few years as the banking system becomes more efficient, then growth returns to the level that prevailed before the policy change.

We disentangle the short- and long-run effects of deregulation on growth by assessing the average growth rate following deregulation during three distinct time periods (Table 13.4, rows 2–4). We measure the change in the growth rate during the first five years after branching deregulation, the change in growth relative to the years before deregulation during years five to ten, and the change from years eleven and beyond. We find that the beneficial effects of the policy change are greatest during the first ten years. Personal income growth accelerates by 0.35 percentage points in the first five years and by 0.37 percentage points in the next five years. But after ten years, our estimate of the growth effect falls to 0.17 percentage points and is no longer statistically significant. In the gross state product series, however, the increases in growth appear to last beyond ten years.[19]

---

[19] See Jayaratne and Strahan (1996) for details on the growth regressions used to generate these results.

Overall, we lack conclusive evidence on whether the growth effects persist beyond ten years. This limitation is not surprising, however, since we only observe about ten years of growth experience after deregulation for most states. Nevertheless, even if the observed increases in growth do not continue indefinitely, the short-run effects appear to be large.[20]

## 6 Conclusion

Entry and price regulations in banking have proven to be costly. Price controls curtailed the growth of industry segments – such as credit cards – and led to periodic disintermediation of banks. Entry restrictions, in the form of geographic restrictions, increased industry inefficiency (by reducing the ability of better-run banks to grow at the expense of inefficient banks, among other reasons) and increased bank instability (by preventing banks from constructing diversified loan portfolios). Less is known about the effects of price and entry regulation on technological innovation and productivity growth in banking. This is an interesting area of future research since regulation has reduced productivity growth in other industries (Caves et al., 1981).

### References

Amel, Dean. 1993. "State Laws Affecting the Geographic Expansion of Commercial Banks." Unpublished paper, Board of Governors of the Federal Reserve System.

Amel, Dean and Nellie Liang. 1992. "The Relationship between Entry into Banking Markets and Changes in Legal Restrictions on Entry." *The Antitrust Bulletin* 37: 631–649.

Barro, Robert and Xavier Sala-I-Martin. 1992. "Convergence." *Journal of Political Economy* 100: 223–251.

Berger, Allen N. and Robert DeYoung. 1995. "Problem Loans and Cost Efficiency in Commercial Banks." Office of the Comptroller of the Currency, Economic and Policy Analysis Working Paper no. 95–5.

Berger, Allen N., Rebecca, S., Demetz, and Philip, E. Strahan. 1999. "The Consolidation of the Financial Services Industry: Causes, Consequences and Implications for the Future," *Journal of Banking and Finance* 23(2–4), pp. 135–194.

Berger, Allen N., William C. Hunter, and Stephen G. Timme. 1993. "The Efficiency of Financial Institutions: A Review and Preview of Research Past, Present and Future." *Journal of Banking and Finance* 17: 221–249.

Berger, Allen N., Anil K. Kashyap, and Joseph M. Scalise. 1995. "The Transformation of the U.S. Banking Industry: What a Long Strange Trip It's Been." *Brookings Paper on Economic Activity*, 2: 55–218.

Berger, Allen N. and Loretta J. Mester. 1997. "Inside the Black Box: What Explains Differences in the Efficiencies of Financial Institutions?" Chapter 3 of this volume.

[20] Note that there are theoretical reasons to believe that reductions in financial market frictions can increase the steady-state growth rate of the economy. For a survey of the relevant models, see Galetovic (1994) and Pagano (1993).

Calem, Paul. 1994. "The Impact of Geographic Deregulation on Small Banks." Federal Reserve Bank of Philadelphia *Business Review*, December.

Calomiris, Charles. 1992. "Do 'Vulnerable' Economies Need Deposit Insurance?" in Philip Brock, ed., *If Texas Were Chile*. San Francisco: ICS Press, 237–350.

Calomiris, Charles. 1993. "Regulation, Industrial Structure, and Instability in U.S. Banking: A Historical Perspective." In Michael Klausner and Lawrence White, eds., *Structural Change in Banking*, 19–116. New York: New York University.

Canner, Glenn and Charles Luckett. 1992. "Developments in the Pricing of Credit Card Services." *Federal Reserve Bulletin*, September: 652–666.

Caves, Douglas, Laurits Christensen, and Joseph Swanson. 1981. "Economic Performance in Regulated and Unregulated Environments: A Comparison of U.S. and Canadian Railroads." *Quarterly Journal of Economics* 96: 559–581.

Chapman, John and Ray Westerfield. 1942. *Branch Banking*. New York: Harper and Brothers Publishers.

Deloitte and Touche Consulting Group. 1995. *The Future of Retail Banking: A Global Perspective*.

Demsetz, Rebecca S., Marc R. Saidenberg, and Philip E. Strahan. 1997. "Agency Problems and Risk Taking at Banks," Federal Reserve Bank of New York Staff Report, no. 29.

Diamond, Douglas. 1948. "Financial Intermediation and Delegated Monitoring." *Review of Economic Studies* 51: 393–414.

Economides, Nicholas, R. Glenn Hubbard, and Darius Palia. 1995. "The Political Economy of Branching Restrictions and Deposit Insurance: A Model of Monopolistic Competition among Small and Large Banks." NBER Working Paper no. 5210.

Evanoff, Douglas and Diana Fortier. 1988. "Reevaluation of the Structure-Conduct-Performance Paradigm in Banking," *Journal of Financial Research* 1: 277–294.

Federal Deposit Insurance Corporation. 1993. *Historical Statistics on Banking*. Washington, D.C.

Federal Reserve Board. 1998. "Credit Risk Models at Major U.S. Banking Institutions: Current State of the Art and Implications for Assessments of Capital Adequacy." Federal Reserve System Task Force on Internal Credit Risk Models.

Galetovic, Alexander. 1994. "Finance and Growth: A Synthesis and Interpretation of the Evidence." Unpublished paper, Princeton University.

Gilbert, Alton. 1986. "A Requiem for Regulation Q: What It Did and Why It Passed Away." The Federal Reserve Bank of St. Louis *Review* 68: 22–37.

Gilbert, Alton and Jean Lovati. 1979. "Disintermediation: An Old Disorder with a New Remedy." The Federal Reserve Bank of St. Louis *Review* 61: 10–15.

Gorton, Gary. 1996. "Reputation Formation in Early Bank Note Markets." *Journal of Political Economy* 104: 346–397.

Harker, Patrick and Stavros Zenios. 1999. "What Drives the Performance of Financial Institutions?" Chapter 1, this volume.

Hendricks, Darryll and Beverly Hirtle. 1997. "Bank Capital Requirements for Market Risk: The Internal Models Approach." Federal Reserve Bank of New York *Economic Policy Review* 3(4): 1–12.

Hubbard, Glenn and Darius Palia. 1995. "Executive Pay and Performance: Evidence from the U.S. Banking Industry." *Journal of Financial Economics* 39: 105–130.

Jayaratne, Jith and Philip E. Strahan. 1996. "The Finance-Growth Nexus: Evidence from Bank Branch Deregulation." *Quarterly Journal of Economics* 111: 639–670.

Jayaratne, Jith and Philip E. Strahan. 1997. "The Benefits of Branching Deregulation." The Federal Reserve Bank of New York *Economic Policy Review* 3: 13–30.

Jayaratne, Jith and Philip E. Strahan. 1998. "Entry Restrictions, Industry Evolution and

Dynamic Efficiency: Evidence from Commercial Banking." *The Journal of Law and Economics* 41: 239–274.

Kane, Edward. 1996. "De Jure Interstate Banking: Why Only Now?" *Journal of Money, Credit, and Banking* 28 (May): 141–161.

Keeley, Michael. 1990. "Deposit Insurance, Risk and Market Power in Banking." *American Economic Review* 80: 1183–1200.

Kroszner, Randall S. and Philip E. Strahan. Forthcoming. *Quarterly Journal of Economics*.

Laderman, Elizabeth, Ronald Schmidt, and Gary Zimmerman. 1991. "Location, Branching and Bank Portfolio Diversification: The Case of Agricultural Lending." The Federal Reserve Bank of San Francisco *Economic Review*, Winter: 24–38.

Mandell, Lewis. 1990. *The Credit Card Industry: A History*. Boston: Twayne Publishers.

McLaughlin, Susan. 1995. "The Impact of Interstate Banking and Branching Reform: Evidence from the States." Federal Reserve Bank of New York *Current Issues in Economics and Finance* 1, no. 2.

Mishkin, Frederic S. 1999. "Financial Consolidation: Dangers and Opportunities." *Journal of Banking and Finance*, 23(2–4), 675–91.

Morgan, Donald. 1995. "Bank Monitoring Reduces Agency Problems: New Evidence Using the Financial Covenants in Bank Loan Commitments." PaineWebber Working Paper Series no. PW-95-12, Columbia University Business School.

Pagano, Marco. 1993. "Financial Markets and Growth: An Overview." *European Economic Review* 37: 613–622.

Prowse, Steven D. 1997. "Alternative Methods of Corporate Control in Commercial Banks." *Journal of Financial Research* 20(4): 509–527.

Rhoades, Stephen. 1996. "Bank Mergers and Industrywide Structure, 1980–94." Board of Governors of the Federal Reserve System Staff Study no. 169.

Saunders, Anthony and Berry Wilson. 1998. "Bank Capital and Bank Structure: A Comparative Analysis of the U.S., U.K. and Canada," mimeo.

Savage, Donald. 1993. "Interstate Banking: A Status Report." *Federal Reserve Bulletin*, December: 1075–1089.

Schranz, Mary. 1993. "Takeovers Improve Firm Performance: Evidence from the Banking Industry." *Journal of Political Economy* 101: 299–326.

Shull, Bernard and Lawrence J. White. 1998. "Of Firewalls and Subsidiaries: The Right Stuff for Expanded Bank Activities." *Banking Law Journal* 115 (May): 446–476.

Spellman, Lewis. 1980. "Deposit Ceilings and the Efficiency of Financial Intermediation." *The Journal of Finance* 35: 129–136.

Thomas, Kenneth H. 1998. *The CRA Handbook*. New York: McGraw-Hill.

# Part 4

## Performance and Risk Management

# 14

## Risks and Returns in Relationship and Transactional Banks: Evidence from Banks' Returns in Germany, Japan, the U.K., and the U.S.

Kathryn L. Dewenter[a], Alan C. Hess[b]

### Abstract

This chapter examines the effects of banks' organizational structures on their costs of equity capital. We test whether there is a difference in market risk and default risk exposures between transactional banks, found in the U.S. and U.K., and relationship banks, found in Japan and Germany. We find that the market risk of U.S. banks rises during periods of economic contraction, while the market risk of Japanese banks falls during these periods. (The market risk of U.K. and German banks does not change over the business cycle.) We also find that the returns of only the U.S. and U.K. banks show a significant link to default risk. Both of the results support the idea that relationship banks are more effective monitors than transactional banks.

### 1 Introduction

How should we measure the financial performance of financial institutions? Economists use both forward-looking and backward-looking measures. Forward-looking performance measurement assumes the bank is an ongoing concern and uses a bank's value as the performance measure. Value depends on expected future cash flows and the cost of capital used to discount them to their present value. Forward-looking studies often investigate the causes of unusual changes in banks' stock prices such as regulatory changes and mergers.

[a,b] Both authors are at the Department of Finance, Box 353200, University of Washington, Seattle, WA 98195. They can be reached at dewe@u.washington.edu or hess@u.washington.edu.

Backward-looking studies ask why a bank performed the way it did for a specific period of time. Economic profit is a summary measure of past financial performance that combines risk and return. A bank's economic profit is its earnings minus its capital charge. A bank's earnings do not take the risk of the invested capital into account. The capital charge does. It is the product of the bank's invested capital times its cost of capital. The cost of capital is the expected rate of return that an investor foregoes by investing in the bank instead of in another investment of equal risk.

This is a bank cost of capital study. Its results can be used to understand a bank's value and its economic profits. Its key feature is that it uses banking theory to understand cross-country variations in banks' cost of equity. At least since Leland and Pyle (1977), banking theorists argue that banks exist to reduce the adverse selection and moral hazard problems that stem from asymmetric information between borrowers and lenders. Allen and Gale (1995) distinguish transactional and relationship banks as two polar approaches to reducing asymmetric information problems. We ask whether a nation's banking structure, either transactional or relationship, affects the equity risks of its banks. We do this in the context of a multi-factor asset pricing model.

Hess and Laisathit (1996) show that a bank's shareholders demand compensation for the forgone risk-free rate, $r_f$, plus premiums, $\lambda_i$, for the bank's exposures, $\beta_i$, to market risk, default risk, liquidity risk, and yield curve risk. Assuming a linear asset pricing model, the bank's cost of equity capital $k$ is

$$k = r_f + \beta_m\lambda_m + \beta_d\lambda_d + \beta_l\lambda_l + \beta_y\lambda_y \tag{1}$$

The research question is whether the market risk exposure, $\beta_m$, and the default risk exposure, $\beta_d$, differ between relationship and transactional banks. We include liquidity and yield curve risk premiums as control factors.

## 2 Implications of Asymmetric-Information Models for the Coefficients

The risks that a bank's shareholders face start with the exogenous risks of the bank's on- and off-balance-sheet activities. These basic risks are those that all parties would know in an economy with perfect information. Bhattacharya and Thakor (1993) show that these risks are compounded by asymmetric information between the bank and its counterparties. For example, a borrowing firm has superior knowledge of the risks and returns of its projects, the work ethics of key individuals, and the willingness of management to honor their loan commitments. Banks screen potential borrowers to reduce adverse selection, and monitor borrowers to reduce moral hazard. These actions limit the borrower's ability to shirk its labor effort, and to substitute assets that transfer more than the agreed-upon risks to the lender. Through screening and monitoring, a bank can reduce risks due to imperfect information.

Do relationship banks screen and monitor differently from transactional banks? Allen and Gale (1995), Aoki (1994), Aoki, Patrick, and Sheard (1994), Hoshi, Kashyap, and Scharfstein (1990), Prowse (1990, 1996), and Steinherr and Huveneers (1994) report several differences between relationship and transactional banks. Relationship banks, such as the German Hausbanks and the Japanese main banks, provide both debt and equity financing to their clients, have long-lasting ties with them, serve on their boards of directors and in some cases serve as senior managers, and renegotiate debt contracts during periods of financial stress. Transactional banks primarily provide short-term bank loans but not equity financing, monitor loan covenants, have limited interference in corporate management, and are reluctant for legal reasons to renegotiate loans of distressed firms.

Aoki (1994) identifies three monitoring actions that banks take to reduce information asymmetries. Ex ante monitoring consists of credit evaluation and screening to reduce adverse selection and coordination failures across industries with jointly dependent production. Interim monitoring refers to the lender observing and controlling the actions of the borrower after it makes the loan but before the borrower repays it. Ex post monitoring includes verification of the borrower's financial results, punishing poor results, and renegotiating in case of temporary events outside the borrower's control that do not harm its long-run prospects. The Anglo-Saxon, market-oriented, decentralized financial system differs from the Japanese-German, relationship-banking system in who provides each of these three monitoring activities. Separate intermediaries provide specialized monitoring services in the U.K. and the U.S. In contrast, the main banks in Japan and the Hausbanks in Germany do all three types of monitoring.

Banking systems can differ in their monitoring effectiveness because they have different costs of obtaining, analyzing, and acting on information, or because they have different incentives to do so. Relationship banks may have better information about their borrowers and stronger incentives to act at each stage of monitoring than do transactional banks. In the theory of banking, relationship banks may have the same advantages over transactional banks that transactional banks have over public debt. Seward's (1990) model of corporate financing implies that it is optimal for the entrepreneur to be funded with both debt and equity. Equity financing reduces the entrepreneur's incentive to substitute high-risk for low-risk assets, and debt financing reduces the entrepreneur's incentive to lie about the project's payoff. In Aoki's three-part classification of monitoring, relationship banks' equity holdings may improve the effectiveness of their interim monitoring, and their debt holdings may improve the effectiveness of their ex post monitoring.

The literature suggests that relationship banks' have closer ties to their clients than do transactional banks. Relationship banks lend repeatedly to borrowers and maintain their borrowers' daily payment settlements. This provides them with information that reduces noise in credit evaluation. They gain additional information and control by serving on boards of directors and as senior managers. Consistent with this, Lummer and McConnell (1989) find that when a firm announces a renewal of a bank loan agreement, its stock price rises. There is no stock price change when a bank announces a new loan agreement. They view this as saying that banks gain an informational advantage as a result of a continuing relationship with the borrower. If relationship banks have closer ties to their clients, they should have an informational advantage over transactional banks.

The biggest advantage of relationship banks may be in ex post monitoring of firms in financial distress. Borrowers enter financial distress either because the net present value of their projects has turned negative, or because of short-term liquidity problems. It is optimal to discontinue lending to negative value firms, but to keep lending to liquidity-troubled firms with positive values. Chemmanur and Fulgheri (1994) distinguish between the renegotiation decisions of single-period and multiple-period lenders. Renegotiation reputation is important to multi-period but not to single-period lenders. If relationship banks have longer lasting relationships with their borrowers than do transactional banks, they are more likely to renegotiate. This is consistent with Hoshi, Kashyap, and Scharfstein (1990) who show that financially distressed Japanese firms with a main bank are more likely to renegotiate their debt than firms without a main bank. If relationship banks deal better with financial distress, their cash flows and ex post returns will be less affected by contractions than will those of transactional banks.

Sheard (1994) argues that Japanese main banks, a representative form of relationship banks, dominate legal bankruptcy in resolving claims against and opportunities of firms in financial distress. First, main banks have better information than courts and outside claimants about why a firm became distressed, what its prospects are, and how best to resolve the distress. Second, main banks have clearer incentives. By holding numerous types of securities, they avoid many of the conflicts of interest that Seward (1990) found among holders of different classes of securities. They act as delegated monitors for all the claimants. Third, Steinherr and Huveneers (1994) argue that the principle of equitable subordination deters transactional banks from exercising influence over distressed firms for fear of losing their legal status as creditors. As a result, relationship banks participate actively in resolving financial distress whereas transactional banks participate passively.

How do the alleged informational and incentive differences between relationship and transactional banks affect their costs of capital? Relationship banks have lower lending risks than do transactional banks. However, this does not necessarily imply that relationship banks have lower costs of capital. A bank's cost of equity capital depends on the entire composition of its on- and off-balance sheet activities. If relationship banks have lower lending risks, they may hold smaller amounts of securities and be more highly levered. Each of these increases its equity cost of capital. Thus, we are not able to predict which type of bank has a larger beta. However, theory does help us predict changes in betas of relationship banks between economic booms and busts.

- Market-timing hypothesis for relationship banks: $\beta_{m\uparrow Rl} > \beta_{m\downarrow Rl}$.
  If relationship banks are better able to judge borrowers' prospects, they may choose to finance higher-risk loans during economic booms and lower-risk loans during recessions. Let $\beta_{m\uparrow Rl}$ be the market risk exposure during economic booms of relationship banks. The alleged better information of relationship banks leads to a market-timing hypothesis which implies that the banks' market risk exposures are greater in booms than they are in busts.
- Adverse-selection hypothesis for transactional banks: $\beta_{m\uparrow Tr} > \beta_{m\downarrow Tr}$.
  Differences in the effects of monitoring abilities on the costs of capital for relationship versus transactional banks should be greater during an economic downturn when borrowers are more likely to be in financial distress. Effective monitoring matters more when the economy contracts than when it expands. Two opposing forces are at work during downturns: an adverse selection force and a monitoring force. According to Diamond's (1991) adverse-selection model, in normal economic conditions, high-quality borrowers with good credit reputations borrow directly in the credit markets where their cost of capital is lower. Low-quality borrowers without credit histories borrow from banks who are better able than outsiders to screen borrowers. Outside lenders are aware that downturns reduce borrowers' reputational benefits that stem from their consistent repayment of debt. During downturns, the possibility increases that a heretofore high-quality credit will substitute

a high-risk project for the low-risk project that was the basis of external funding. Outside lenders require higher expected returns during downturns to compensate them for this possible asset-substitution. This raises the relative cost of outside financing to high-quality borrowers, and leads them to shift to bank financing.

Ceteris paribus, the costs of capital of transactional banks fall during a downturn.

- Adverse-selection hypothesis for different bank types: $\dfrac{\beta_{m\uparrow Tr}}{\beta_{m\uparrow Rel}} > \dfrac{\beta_{m\downarrow Tr}}{\beta_{m\downarrow Rel}}$.

If borrowers from relationship banks have less access to public markets, as they did in Japan before financial liberalization and as they do in Germany, there is less cyclical movement of borrowers between banks and public financing. Thus, from the adverse selection perspective, the cost of capital at relationship banks should have less cyclical change than at transactional banks. This implies that during economic contractions the market risk of transactional banks falls relative to relationship banks.

- Moral hazard hypothesis: $\dfrac{\beta_{m\uparrow Tr}}{\beta_{m\uparrow Rel}} < \dfrac{\beta_{m\downarrow Tr}}{\beta_{m\downarrow Rel}}$.

However, other things are not equal during a downturn. During downturns, more borrowers enter financial distress. Since a bank's risk is derived from the risk profile of its borrowers, this suggests that a bank's risk profile should rise in a downturn. If relationship banks are more likely to identify distressed firms, help them change their operating decisions, and renegotiate their debt, they should have fewer defaults. On this account, the risks of transactional banks should rise relative to those of relationship banks in downturns. This gives us the moral-hazard hypothesis.

Thus, the existing theories give us two models with opposite predictions. Each can be compared to the null hypothesis of no difference between booms and busts in the ratios of the betas of transactional and relationship banks.

- $H_0: \dfrac{\beta_{m\uparrow Tr}}{\beta_{m\uparrow Rel}} = \dfrac{\beta_{m\downarrow Tr}}{\beta_{m\downarrow Rel}}$.

Which of the two offsetting effects, the adverse selection effect or the moral hazard effect, is larger is an empirical issue to which we now turn.

Different monitoring skills and incentives should also affect banks' exposure to default risk. We would expect to find that the superior monitoring capabilities of relationship banks should be associated with lower exposure to default risks than transactional banks.

### 3 Data and Empirical Tests

We use two different measures of banks' stock returns to estimate their equity costs of capital. In the first, we construct a value-weighted portfolio of monthly returns for the largest, "most representative" banks in that system. For Germany, we use the three major Hausbanks: Deutsche Bank, Dresdner, and Commerzbank. For Japan, we use the six banks that form the center of the six main keiretsu industrial groups: DKB, Fuji, Mitsubishi, Mitsui (Sakura after 4/90), Sanwa, and Sumitomo. For the U.K., we use the Big Four clearing banks: Barclays, National Westminster, Lloyds, and Midland (HSBC after 10/92). For the U.S., we select the 11 banks highlighted as "too big to fail" in the *Wall Street Journal* (9-20-84) and O'Hara and Shaw (1990): Bank of America, Bankers Trust, Citibank, Chase, Chemical, Continental, First Chicago, JP Morgan, Manufacturer's Hanover, Security Pacific, and Wells Fargo. Our second measure of bank returns is Datastream's Retail Bank Industry Index for each country. These indices are value-weighted indices of stock returns for all the commercial or "retail" banks in that country. Table 14.1 describes these and other measures used in the analysis. Dewenter and Hess (1998) extend the data to include two additional relationship bank countries, Switzerland and Netherlands, and two additional transactional bank countries, Australia and Canada. Their results strengthen those we report below.

We also draw our explanatory variables from Datastream. While services such as Datastream have made large amounts of international data available to researchers, we still experience problems finding directly comparable series across all four countries. The primary goal in selecting data series for this study is to get variables that measure similar rates or fundamentals. As we describe each variable below, we highlight some compromises that we made.

The variable for market returns should represent a broad measure of market activity. As a result, we calculate stock market returns from the Commerzbank Index in Germany, the Tokyo NSE Index in Japan, the FT All Share Index in the U.K., and the S&P Composite Index in the U.S.

Our measure of default risk equals a corporate lending rate minus a long-term government rate. For Germany, we take this from the average lending rate for current account credits of DM1–5 million minus the weighted average yield on government and public authority bonds with a life over three years. For Japan, the default risk variable is the end-of-period interest rate on corporate bonds (12 years) minus the end-of-period yield on 8–10 year government benchmark bonds. For the U.K., the default risk variable is the end-of-month London clearing bank base rate minus the long-term government bond yield. For the U.S., the default risk variable is the average prime rate minus the yield on 10-year

Table 14.1. *Description of variables used in the analyses.*

| Variable | Germany | Japan | U.K. | U.S. |
|---|---|---|---|---|
| Banks included in constructed portfolios | Deutsche Bank, Dresdner Bank, Commerzbank | DKB, Fuji, Mitsubishi, Mitsui (Sakura), Sanwa, Sumitomo | Barclays, Lloyds, Midland (HSBC), National Westminster | Bank of America, Bankers Trust, Citibank, Chase, Chemical, Continental, First Chicago, JP Morgan, Manufacturer's. Hanover, Security Pacific, Wells Fargo |
| Market index $(R_m)$ | Commerzbank Index | Tokyo NSE Index | FT All Share Index | S&P Composite Index |
| Default risk measure $(R_d)$ | Corporate lending rate – weighted average yield on government and public authority bonds (>3 years) | Corporate bond rate (12 years) – yield on government benchmark bond (8–10 years) | London clearing bank base rate – long-term government bond yield | Average prime rate – yield on treasury bonds (10 years) |
| Liquidity risk measure $(R_l)$ | Deposit rate (3 months) – annualized discount rate on new issues of treasury bills (3 months) | Deposit rate (3 months) – yield on short-term government securities (60 days) | Deposit rate (3 months) – treasury bill rate (3 months) | CD rate (3 months) – treasury bill rate (3 months) |
| Yield curve measure $(R_y)$ | Yield on second market public bonds (7–15 years) – annualized discount rate on new issues of treasury bills (3 months) | Yield on government benchmark bonds (8–10 years) – yield on short-term government securities (60 days) | Yield on long-term government bonds – treasury bill rate (3 months) | Yield on government bonds (10 years) – treasury bill rate (3 months) |

*Source:* Datastream International is the source for all data, except the U.S. Constructed Portfolio returns (1984–94 only), which are from CRSP. All data series are available from January 1984 through March 1996.

Treasury bonds. The lack of a consistent corporate lending rate and the inability to match perfectly the terms of the corporate and government loans make our default measure an imperfect proxy for the credit risk faced by banks.

We measure the premium that investors receive for bearing liquidity risk as a deposit rate minus a government rate of the same (or close) maturity. For Germany, this equals the average three-month deposit rate minus the annualized discount rate on new issues of three-month Treasury bills. For Japan, we measure liquidity risk as the end-of-period interest rate on three-month time deposits minus the end-of-period yield on 60-day short-term government securities. The U.K. measure of liquidity risk equals the end-of-period interest rate on three-month deposits minus the end-of-period three-month Treasury bill rate. The U.S. liquidity measure equals the monthly average interest rate on three-month CDs minus the end-of-period three-month Treasury bill rate.

We measure term risk with the slope of the yield curve, using a long-term government yield minus a short-term government yield. For Germany, this is the end-of-period yield on 7–15-year secondary market public bonds minus the annualized discount rate on new issues of three-month Treasury bills. For Japan, the yield curve measure equals the end-of-period yield on 8–10–year government benchmark bonds minus the end-of-period yield on 60-day short-term government securities. For the U.K., the slope is the long-term government bond yield minus the end-of-period three-month Treasury bill rate. For the U.S., the yield curve slope is the monthly average yield on 10-year Treasury bonds minus the end-of-period three-month Treasury bill rate. Our inability to match exactly the points on the yield curve from which we select rates across the four countries hurts the effectiveness of this measure.

In order to examine the risk and returns of bank stocks across business cycles, we must identify the growth and contractionary periods in each economy. We do this using leading economic indicators. The indicators are the Manufacturing Trade Production Expectations for Germany, the Composite Leading Index for Japan, the Central Statistical Office's Long Leading Indicator for the U.K., and the Conference Board's Leading Indicator for the U.S. The Japan, U.K., and U.S. measures all represent weighted indices of various economic variables. A comparable indicator for Germany is not available on Datastream. The German measure represents the results of a survey of manufacturing managers. A negative value indicates a majority of respondents were pessimistic about future (three-month) growth prospects.

The business-cycle dating convention in the U.S. is two quarters of consecutive growth (contraction) to signal an expansion (recession). To parallel this convention, we look for six consecutive months of increase (decrease) in the leading indicator to indicate a switch out of a contractionary (expansionary) period. (For the German indicator, we look for six consecutive months of positive or negative values.) We date the beginning of an expansion as the first of the six consecutive months of growth in the indicator. If we stick with the rule of six consecutive months for Japan, there are no contractions in the 1984–96 period. As a result, for Japan, we use a five-month rule. Figure 14.1 depicts the leading indicators for each country, highlighting the periods of expansion and contraction. From the beginning of 1984 through March 1996, we have three contractionary periods in Germany and Japan, four in the U.K., and two in the U.S. We also tried a measure of economic expansion (contraction) which equaled one in any month when the leading indicator increased (decreased) and zero otherwise. This measure yields very similar results to the one above, but with less power.

Our data include monthly observations over January 1984 through March 1996. We begin in January 1984 because the Japanese bank stocks did not actively trade in the early 1980s. Pettway, Tapley, and Yamada (1988) document the inactivity of Japanese bank stocks during that period and their more active trading after early 1984. They argue that the primary force for increased trading activity was financial deregulation that began in the late 1970s and increased throughout the early 1980s.

The research question we address is whether the market risk exposure, $\beta_m$, and the default risk exposure, $\beta_d$, differ between relationship and transactional banks. We are particularly interested in the difference in market risk during periods of economic contraction. We test these relationships across the four countries with a seemingly unrelated (SUR) regression specification which allows for nonconstant disturbances and contemporaneous correlation across countries. Our specification is:

$$r_{nt} = \beta_n + \beta_{m\uparrow}I_{n\uparrow}R_{mnt} + \beta_{m\downarrow}I_{n\downarrow}R_{mnt} + \beta_d R_{dnt} + \beta_l R_{lnt} + \beta_y R_{ynt} + \varepsilon_{nt} \quad (2)$$

where:

> $r_{nt}$ = the monthly market return for our constructed bank portfolio or Datastream's Retail Bank Index for country n
> n = 1, 2, 3, or 4, for Germany, Japan, the U.K., or the U.S. respectively
> t = 1, 2, . . . 147 for monthly observations from January 1984 through March 1996
> $\beta_n$ = the intercept coefficient for the bank portfolio in country n

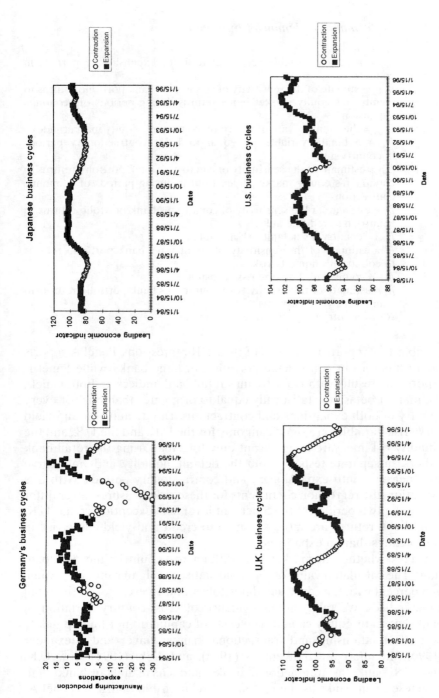

Figure 14.1. Leading economic indicators for Germany, Japan, the U.K., and the U.S.

$I_{n\uparrow}$ = a binary variable set equal to 1 for expansionary periods in country n
$\beta_{m\uparrow}$ = estimate of the sensitivity of country n's bank portfolio returns to country n's equity market index returns during periods of economic expansion
$R_{mnt}$ = the monthly rate of return on country n's equity market index
$I_{n\downarrow}$ = a binary variable set equal to 1 for contractionary periods in country n
$\beta_{m\downarrow}$ = estimate of the sensitivity of country n's bank portfolio returns to country n's equity market index returns during periods of economic contraction
$\beta_d$ = estimate of the sensitivity of country n's bank portfolio returns to country n's credit default risk
$R_{dnt}$ = country n's default risk measure
$\beta_l$ = estimate of the sensitivity of country n's bank portfolio returns to country n's liquidity risk
$R_{lnt}$ = country n's liquidity risk measure
$\beta_y$ = estimate of the sensitivity of country n's bank portfolio returns to country n's yield curve risk
$R_{ynt}$ = country n's yield curve risk measure

Table 14.2 reports the results of the SUR regressions. Panel A reports the results for our constructed portfolios of large banks, while Panel B reports the results with Datastream's retail bank indices. In both panels, the market betas are statistically equal to or greater than one for every country in both expansions and contractions. The default risk and yield curve risk variables are significant only for the U.K. and the U.S., and the liquidity risk measure is significant only for Japan using the retail bank indices. In separate tests, we split the default, liquidity, and yield curve risk measures into expansionary and contractionary periods. With one exception, the regression coefficients for these risk measures never differ across the two periods at the 5 percent level. The exception is that U.K. retail bank returns are more sensitive to credit and yield curve risk in contractions than in expansions.

We test whether the market betas differ across countries during expansions. The calculated value of the Wald statistic is significant at a p-value of 5 percent with the constructed portfolios, and 1 percent with the retail bank indices. We take this as evidence of cross-country variation in banks' costs of equity capital. The costs of capital do not line up neatly between relationship and transactional banks. Mayer and Alexander (1990), Steinherr and Huveneers (1994), and Aoki (1994) view U.K. and U.S. banks as transactional banks, and German Hausbanks and Japanese main banks as the epitome of relationship banks. In Panel A, U.K. banks have the lowest cost of equity capital in expansions, and

Table 14.2. *Seemingly unrelated regression (SUR) results for bank returns against explanatory variables.*

| | $\beta_n$ | $\beta_{m\uparrow}$ | $\beta_{m\downarrow}$ | $\beta_d$ | $\beta_l$ | $\beta_y$ | Adj. $R^2$ |
|---|---|---|---|---|---|---|---|
| *Panel A: Constructed bank portfolios* | | | | | | | |
| Germany | 0.016 | 1.085*** | 1.073*** | -0.004 | -0.002 | -0.005 | 0.762 |
| | (1.400) | (18.191) | (12.751) | (-1.332) | (-0.249) | (-1.370) | |
| Japan | -0.030 | 1.345*** | 0.981*** | 0.005 | -0.009 | 0.012 | 0.605 |
| | (-0.844) | (13.599) | (7.632) | (0.317) | (-1.195) | (1.063) | |
| U.K. | -0.015* | 1.055*** | 1.080*** | 0.028** | 0.011 | 0.030** | 0.682 |
| | (-1.692) | (15.217) | (9.902) | (2.470) | (0.646) | (2.533) | |
| U.S. | -0.041** | 1.253*** | 1.637*** | 0.014* | -0.003 | 0.018** | 0.607 |
| | (-1.970) | (13.296) | (7.773) | (1.862) | (-0.384) | (2.297) | |
| Wald Test | 7.930** | 8.909** | 7.617* | 11.038** | 1.255 | 13.325*** | |
| *Panel B: Retail bank indices* | | | | | | | |
| Germany | 0.013 | 0.943*** | 0.947*** | -0.003 | 0.0001 | -0.005 | 0.809 |
| | (1.541) | (20.803) | (14.804) | (-1.348) | (0.018) | (-1.620) | |
| Japan | -0.032 | 1.306*** | 0.985*** | 0.011 | -0.011* | 0.010 | 0.686 |
| | (-1.086) | (16.082) | (9.337) | (0.736) | (-1.739) | (1.130) | |
| U.K. | -0.016* | 1.056*** | 1.042*** | 0.025** | 0.016 | 0.027** | 0.738 |
| | (-1.942) | (17.348) | (10.800) | (2.443) | (1.029) | (2.443) | |
| U.S. | -0.047*** | 1.086*** | 1.421*** | 0.014*** | -0.003 | 0.019*** | 0.706 |
| | (-3.216) | (16.301) | (9.471) | (2.722) | (-0.462) | (3.471) | |
| Wald Test | 14.125*** | 16.360*** | 8.562** | 14.779*** | 3.259 | 20.331*** | |

*Note:* Model: $r_{nt} = \beta_n + \beta_{m\uparrow} I_{n\uparrow} R_{mnt} + \beta_{m\downarrow} I_{n\downarrow} R_{mnt} + \beta_d R_{dnt} + \beta_l R_{lnt} + \beta_y R_{ynt} + \varepsilon_{nt}$

Table reports results for two seemingly unrelated regressions. Dependent variable equals a value-weighted return of a constructed portfolio of banks (Panel A) and Datastream's value-weighted return for each country's Retail Bank Index (Panel B). Explanatory variables defined in Table 14.1. Data cover monthly observations from January 1984 through March 1996 (N = 147 for each country). T-statistics reported in parentheses. *, **, and *** denote significance at the 10, 5, and 1 percent levels, respectively.

Japanese and U.S. banks have the highest, while in Panel B, German banks have the lowest and Japanese banks the highest cost of equity capital in expansions.

If Sheard is right about relationship banks handling financial distress better than transactional banks, the major difference in costs of capital should occur during economic recessions. We next test whether the market betas differ across countries during contractions. The calculated Wald statistic is significant at 10 percent in Panel A and at 5 percent in Panel B. It appears that banks' equity costs of capital differ across countries during contractions. In both panels, U.S. banks have the highest betas, while Japanese (German) banks have the lowest beta in Panel A (B).

The Japanese market betas for booms and busts are significantly different from each other at the 5 percent level in both panels. The U.S. betas are significantly different from each other at the 10 percent level in Panel A, and at the 5 percent level in Panel B. The decrease in the equity cost of capital for Japanese banks from expansions to contractions is consistent with the market-timing hypothesis for relationship banks, while the increase in U.S. banks' cost of capital is inconsistent with the adverse-selection hypothesis for transactional banks. The market beta estimates for Germany and the U.K. do not change over the business cycle.

A possible explanation for the lack of change in the German estimates over the business cycle is a weak proxy for dating expansions versus contractions. As noted above, dating of the German business cycles is based on the results of a survey of managers, rather than on an index which represents a weighted composite of various economic variables. The Economic Cycle Research Institute (ECRI) provided us a leading economic indicator for Germany, constructed in an analogous manner to the Japan, U.K., and U.S. leading indicators. According to the ECRI measure, Germany had no period over 1984–96 with six (or even five) consecutive months of contraction. This suggests the entire period in our study might constitute an expansion for Germany.

Table 14.3 presents the formal test of our central hypotheses. There we look at changes in the market risk betas of transaction banks relative to relationship banks in expansions versus contractions. The adverse-selection model predicts that the ratio of transaction to relationship bank betas falls from expansion to contraction as the high-quality borrowers return to the transaction banks. The moral-hazard model predicts that the ratio rises from expansion to contraction as the superior monitoring capabilities of relationship banks reduce their overall riskiness during economic downturns. Since we have data on banks from two transaction

Table 14.3. *Hypothesis test of change in relative market betas over the business cycle.*

| | Transaction banks | |
|---|---|---|
| Relationship banks | U.K. | U.S. |

*Constructed portfolios:*
Germany

– Hypothesis $\dfrac{1.055}{1.085} - \dfrac{1.080}{1.073} = -0.0341$ $\qquad$ $\dfrac{1.253}{1.085} - \dfrac{1.637}{1.073} = -0.3707$

– Chi-square statistic $\quad$ 0.048 $\qquad\qquad\qquad\qquad\qquad$ 2.131

– P-value $\qquad\qquad\quad$ (0.824) $\qquad\qquad\qquad\qquad\quad$ (0.144)

Japan

– Hypothesis $\dfrac{1.055}{1.345} - \dfrac{1.080}{0.981} = -0.3166$ $\qquad$ $\dfrac{1.253}{1.345} - \dfrac{1.637}{0.981} = -0.4072$

– Chi-square statistic $\quad$ 2.619 $\qquad\qquad\qquad\qquad\qquad$ 5.355

– P-value $\qquad\qquad\quad$ (0.105) $\qquad\qquad\qquad\qquad\quad$ (0.020)

*Bank indices:*
Germany

– Hypothesis $\dfrac{1.056}{0.943} - \dfrac{1.042}{0.947} = 0.0195$ $\qquad$ $\dfrac{1.086}{0.943} - \dfrac{1.421}{0.947} = -0.3488$

– Chi-square statistic $\quad$ 0.018 $\qquad\qquad\qquad\qquad\qquad$ 2.826

– P-value $\qquad\qquad\quad$ (0.892) $\qquad\qquad\qquad\qquad\quad$ (0.092)

Japan

– Hypothesis $\dfrac{1.056}{1.306} - \dfrac{1.042}{0.985} = -0.2492$ $\qquad$ $\dfrac{1.086}{1.306} - \dfrac{1.421}{0.985} = -0.6110$

– Chi-square statistic $\quad$ 2.319 $\qquad\qquad\qquad\qquad\qquad$ 7.230

– P-value $\qquad\qquad\quad$ (0.127) $\qquad\qquad\qquad\qquad\quad$ (0.007)

*Note*: Model: $r_{nt} = \beta_n + \beta_{m\uparrow} I_{n\uparrow} R_{mnt} + \beta_{m\downarrow} I_{n\downarrow} R_{mnt} + \beta_d R_{dnt} + \beta_l R_{lnt} + \beta_y R_{ynt} + \varepsilon_{nt}$

$H_0$: $\dfrac{\beta_{m\uparrow Tr}}{\beta_{m\uparrow Rl}} - \dfrac{\beta_{m\downarrow Tr}}{\beta_{m\downarrow Rl}} = 0$

Where: $\beta_m$ = the market beta; $\uparrow \downarrow$ represent estimations during expansions and contractions, respectively; and Tr. designates transaction banks and Rl. designates relationship banks. Numbers in the table are based on results reported in Table 14.2. Chi-square test statistic is from a Wald test for non-linear restrictions.

Adverse selection prediction: $\dfrac{\beta_{m\uparrow Tr}}{\beta_{m\uparrow Rl}} - \dfrac{\beta_{m\downarrow Tr}}{\beta_{m\downarrow Rl}} \geq 0$

Moral hazard prediction: $\dfrac{\beta_{m\uparrow Tr}}{\beta_{m\uparrow Rl}} - \dfrac{\beta_{m\downarrow Tr}}{\beta_{m\downarrow Rl}} \leq 0$

and two relationship countries, we have four separate tests for each set of SURs: U.K. versus Germany, U.K. versus Japan, U.S. versus Germany, and U.S. versus Japan. The chi-square test statistic is based on a Wald test for non-linear restrictions. Table 14.3 shows that in seven out of the eight tests, the relative beta ratios rise as the countries move from expansion to contraction. This evidence is consistent with the moral-hazard model. The difference in market betas is significant at the 1 percent level for the U.S. versus Japan (using returns from Datastream's retail bank indices), 5 percent level for the U.S. versus Japan (constructed portfolios), 10 percent level for the U.S. versus Germany (bank indices), and 15 percent level for the U.K. versus Japan (both SURs) and the U.S. versus Germany (constructed portfolios).

The results are consistent with Sheard's contention. However, they are contrary to the prediction of Diamond's one-period loan model that the riskiness of (transactional) banks should fall in economic downturns as the more creditworthy customers shift towards banks. As Diamond suggests, the difference could reflect the increased defaults of outstanding loans overwhelming the lower credit risk of new loans. New loans are a small fraction of the total loans of the bank. Nevertheless, it is interesting that the U.S. bank risk rises during economic contractions, while the Japanese bank risk falls.

The results in Table 14.3 are driven by changes in the U.S. and Japanese market betas over the business cycle. Changes in the composition of banks' balance sheets may explain the changes in their betas. Increases in U.S. banks' market risks could reflect higher leverage or an increase in loans versus less risky securities. Decreases in Japanese bank market risk could be driven by a decrease in leverage or a shift out of loans into securities. To examine this, we collected accounting data from Datastream for German and U.K. banks and from Moody's for the U.S. and Japanese banks. These data cover all the banks included in our constructed portfolios for each year from 1984 through 1995. We classified each fiscal year as contractionary if seven or more months in that year are classified as a contraction based on our method above or if the last six months in the year are classified as a contraction. Table 14.4 reports the results for changes in the mean levels of two accounting ratios, loans/total assets and total assets/equity. For the German and U.K. banks, neither ratio exhibits a significant change between expansionary and contractionary years. The U.S. banks show significant changes in both ratios across the business cycle. The data indicate that U.S. banks shift into loans and increase leverage in the contractionary periods. Both of these changes could contribute to their higher market betas

Table 14.4. *Mean values of accounting ratios for banks in our constructed portfolios.*

|  | Expansion | Contraction | Difference |
|---|---|---|---|
| Loans/Total Assets |  |  |  |
| – Germany | 0.833 | 0.826 | 0.007 |
| – Japan | 0.539 | 0.599 | –0.059*** |
| – U.K. | 0.387 | 0.377 | 0.010 |
| – U.S. | 0.568 | 0.647 | –0.079** |
| Total Assets/Equity |  |  |  |
| – Germany | 29.48 | 28.55 | 0.93 |
| – Japan | 40.94 | 36.83 | 4.10 |
| – U.K. | 22.19 | 22.33 | –0.14 |
| – U.S. | 18.28 | 20.20 | –1.92** |

*Note*: Numbers equal the mean value of accounting ratios across the banks included in our constructed portfolios, identified in Table 14.1. Means calculated for years designated expansion or contraction according to the country's leading indicator. Accounting data are from Datastream (Germany and the U.K.) and Moody's International Manual (Japan and the U.S.). *, **, and *** indicate significant difference based on a T-test for difference in means at the 10, 5, and 1 percent levels, respectively.

during economic downturns. Japanese banks also increase their loan-to-asset ratio in downturns. This shift, however, is inconsistent with both the market-timing hypothesis and with their lower market betas during contractions. Consistent with the lower betas, the Japanese banks do show lower point estimates of leverage during contractions, but the difference is not significant at the 10 percent level. These accounting data, then, provide some alternative evidence for the change in U.S. betas, but little help in understanding the change in Japanese betas over the business cycle.

The asymmetric information models discussed above also provide implications for differences in the sensitivity of relationship versus transactional banks to default risk. The results in Table 14.2 on the default risk variable are consistent with the hypothesis that arms-length or transactional banks show stronger credit risk sensitivity. In Table 14.2, a Wald test rejects equality of the four country default risk betas at the 5 percent level with the constructed portfolios and at the 1 percent level with the retail banks indices. Only the transactional banks in the U.K. and U.S. show significant sensitivity to the default risk measure.

## 4 Conclusion

Short-run measures of a bank's equity cost of capital primarily reflect changes in its stock price. Stock price changes arise from changes in the expected value or risk of the bank's future cash flows. Cash flows change due to changes in market conditions that affect all businesses, and in bank-specific factors, such as default, liquidity, and yield curve risks. Asymmetric information models of banks predict that banks' risk exposures can differ between transactional and relationship banks and between economic booms and busts. Consistent with these predictions, we find that equity costs of capital differ cyclically between U.S. and Japanese banks. During economic downturns, the market risk exposure of equity falls for Japanese main banks and rises for U.S. banks. If the market return falls during downturns, Japanese banks' stock returns fall less than the market falls, and U.S. banks' stock returns fall more than the market falls. The U.S. results are consistent with the decrease in the exogenous risks predicted by Diamond's model being overwhelmed by the concurrent increase in the ex post default risks of existing borrowers. The finding of significant default risk for only the U.S. and U.K. banks supports the notion that transactional banks manage credit risk less effectively than relationship banks. Our results provide evidence consistent with Sheard's contention that relationship banks handle financial distress better than transactional banks.

While we have not studied bank profits directly, our results provide some insights into their likely cyclical behavior. Profits depend on the accounting return on book equity minus the cost of capital. If the return on equity falls during downturns, U.S. banks' profits may fall considerably since their cost of capital is rising while their return on equity is falling. In downturns, investors in U.S. banks require higher returns and get lower returns. Just the opposite happens at Japanese main banks. Investors in Japanese banks require lower returns in downturns, and even if they get lower returns they can still earn zero economic profits. Based on our results, cross-nation comparisons of banks' financial performance must take into account cyclical changes in equity costs of capital.

## References

Allen, Franklin and Gale, Douglas. 1995. "A welfare comparison of intermediaries and financial markets in Germany and the U.S." *European Economic Review* 39: 179–209.

Aoki, Masahiko, 1994. "Monitoring characteristics of the main bank system: An analytical and developmental view." In Masahiko Aoki and Hugh Patrick (eds.), *The Japanese Main Bank System*. New York: The Oxford University Press.

Aoki, Masahiko, Patrick, Hugh, and Sheard, Paul. 1994. "The Japanese main bank system: An introductory overview." In Masahiko Aoki and Hugh Patrick (eds.), *The Japanese Main Bank System*. New York: The Oxford University Press.

Bhattacharya, Sudipto and Thakor, Anjan V. 1993. Contemporary banking theory. *Journal of Financial Intermediation* 3: 2–50.

Chemmanur, Thomas J. and Fulghieri, Paolo. 1994. "Reputation, renegotiation, and the choice between bank loans and publicly traded debt." *Review of Financial Studies* 7: 475–506.

Dewenter, Kathryn L. and Hess, Alan C. 1998. "An international comparison of banks' equity returns." *Journal of Money Credit and Banking* 30, No. 3, Part 2: 472–492.

Diamond, Douglas W. 1991. "Monitoring and reputation: The choice between bank loans and directly placed debt." *Journal of Political Economy* 97: 828–862.

Hess, Alan C. and Laisathit, Kirati. 1996. "A market-based risk classification of financial institutions." *Journal of Financial Services Research*, forthcoming.

Hoshi, Takeo, Kashyap, Anil, and Scharfstein, David. 1990. "The role of banks in reducing the costs of financial distress in Japan." *Journal of Financial Economics* 27: 67–88.

Leland, H. E. and Pyle, D. H. 1977. "Informational asymmetries, financial structure, and financial intermediation." *Journal of Finance* 32-2: 371–387.

Lummer, Scott L. and McConnell, John J. 1989. "Further evidence on the bank lending process and the capital-market response to bank loan agreements." *Journal of Financial Economics* 25: 99–122.

Mayer, Colin and Alexander, Ian. 1990. "Banks and securities markets: Corporate financing in Germany and the United Kingdom." *Journal of the Japanese and International Economies* 4: 450–475.

O'Hara, Maureen and Wayne, Shaw. 1990. "Deposit insurance and wealth effects: The value of being 'Too Big to Fail.' " *The Journal of Finance* XLV: 1587–1600.

Pettway, Richard H., Tapley, T. Craig, and Yamada, Takeshi. 1988. "The impacts of financial deregulation upon trading efficiency and the levels of risk and return of Japanese banks." *The Financial Review* 23: 243–268.

Prowse, Stephen D. 1990. "Institutional investment patterns and corporate financial behavior in the United States and Japan." *Journal of Financial Economics* 27: 43–66.

Prowse, Stephen D. 1996. "Corporate finance in international perspective: Legal and regulatory influences on financial system development." *Economic Review*. Federal Reserve Bank of Dallas Third Quarter: 2–15.

Seward, James K. 1990. "Corporate financial policy and the theory of financial intermediation." *Journal of Finance* 45: 351–377.

Sheard, Paul. "Main banks and the governance of financial distress." In Masahiko Aoki and Hugh Patrick (eds.), *The Japanese Main Bank System*. New York: The Oxford University Press.

Steinherr, A. and Huveneers, Ch. 1994. "On the performance of differently regulated financial institutions: Some empirical evidence." *Journal of Banking and Finance* 18: 271–306.

# 15

## Acceptable Risk: A Study of Global Currency Trading Rooms in the US and Japan

Srilata Zaheer[a]

**Abstract**

In this study, I explore the idea of "acceptable risk" at the organizational level of analysis in a sample of currency-trading rooms embedded in different national cultures. I develop and test a model of how national culture and the organizational context, in particular the control strategies and the norms of acceptable risk within risk-taking units, shape their risk-taking behavior and their performance. The results show that "acceptable risk" as defined within the trading room does influence actual organizational risk-taking, though national culture does not. In addition, market control strategies are related to better risk transformation in these trading rooms.

## 1 Introduction

The influence of context on risk-taking has begun to receive an increasing amount of theoretical and empirical attention in the literature on risk (Tetlock, 1985; March and Shapira, 1987; Schoemaker, 1989; Bromiley and Curley, 1992). Studies of risk preferences expressed by samples of managers exposed to different situational contexts have shown little consistency in individual risk-taking across situations (MacCrimmon and Wehrung, 1986 and 1990). At the same time, theorists in sociology have

[a] Associate Professor, Department of Strategic Management and Organization, Curtis L. Carlson School of Management, University of Minnesota, 321 19th Avenue South, Minneapolis, MN 55455. Phone: (612) 624-5590. Fax: (612) 626-1316. Email: szaheer@csom.umn.edu.

begun to stress the role of social and institutional influences on the norms that define what risks are considered "acceptable" (Douglas and Wildavsky, 1982; Douglas, 1985) or legitimate at the *societal* level of analysis. Yet there has been little systematic work on the norms of "acceptable risk" that might exist *at the organizational level* and how these might influence risk-taking in business organizations. In this study, we explore the idea of acceptable risk at the organizational level of analysis in a sample of real organizations embedded in different national cultures, and develop and test a model of how national culture and the organizational context, in particular the control strategies and the norms of acceptable risk within risk-taking units, shape their actual risk-taking behavior and performance.

I define "acceptable risk" at the organizational level as the *norms* within an organizational unit regarding what risks are legitimate or acceptable for unit members to take. It is reflected in the collective perception by members of the organizational unit as to what the unit's attitude toward risk or tolerance for risk is. In a business organization, acceptable risk would be defined with respect to risks related to business. Actual risk-taking behavior within the organization is likely to be influenced by the norms of acceptable risk, to the extent that behavior is driven by collective attitudes or norms. However, acceptable risk is an institutionalized concept that is likely to be more stable than actual risk-taking behavior.

The global currency-trading industry is particularly well-suited to the development and testing of grounded hypotheses on contextual influences on risk-taking. In particular, risk-taking is a core value-adding activity in this industry, and one of the key sources of competitive advantage of firms in this industry is their risk transformation capability, which is simply the ability of the trading room to take "good risks," to maximize returns at a particular level of risk. The level of speculative activity in this industry has grown rapidly (Ohmae, 1990; Bank for International Settlements, 1993). Further, this industry is one in which two clear organizational forms – the market-control-oriented "investment banking" type of organization and the more traditional "commercial banking" type of organization compete in the same global marketplace, providing different organizational contexts in which to study organizational risk-taking and performance.

This study was conducted in three phases. An exploratory, inductive phase of observation and interviews in nine trading rooms led to the surfacing of the concept of "acceptable risk," and to the development of a model, derived from both theory and field observations, on the influence

of national culture and organizational context on risk-taking and performance. This model was then tested in a sample of 28 currency-trading
rooms of Western and Japanese banks in New York and Tokyo. Finally,
the results were validated through a set of follow-up interviews in a
subset of the trading rooms in the sample.

In the sections that follow, I first briefly discuss the industry context
and then discuss the theoretical background. In the theory section, I
focus in particular on the conceptualization and measurement of actual
risk-taking behavior in organizations, and on acceptable risk. I illustrate
acceptable risk with examples from the qualitative work that led to my
importing this concept from the societal level of analysis to the organizational level of analysis. I then develop the model and hypotheses. This
is followed by sections on the research design and the measures, and by
a section on the analyses and results. I conclude with a discussion of the
implications of the results for theory and practice.

## 2 Currency Trading Rooms as a Research Context

Currency trading, also known as foreign-exchange (FX) trading, is a
setting in which a major part of value-added comes from speculative risk-
taking (Ohmae, 1990). The FX trading room is thus an ideal context in
which to test for the influence of organizational patterns and practices
on risk-taking. The foreign-exchange market originally grew out of a
need to service corporate customers in buying and selling foreign
exchange for their import and export requirements. However, after the
breakdown of the Bretton Woods agreement and fixed exchange rates
in 1973, the door was open to speculation in foreign-exchange, and the
market saw an explosive growth in volume. The volume of currency
trading currently stands at over a trillion dollars *a day*. Only 12% of that
volume appears to be related to genuine trade and investment flows
(Bank for International Settlements, 1993).

In this research context, the decision problem is identical across all
organizations in the sample, i.e., what speculative risk-positions (open,
uncovered positions in different currencies) should the room take at
a point in time. Competitive and technological factors are very similar
across all trading rooms worldwide because technology suppliers in
this industry are global (essentially three major technology supply
firms supplying all rooms worldwide), and many of the customers are
also global. Regulatory influences are minimal. The macro-economic risk
that comes from exchange-rate volatility is identical across all trading
rooms. This setting therefore enables us to concentrate exclusively on

organizational and economic drivers of risk transformation in financial services.

### 3 Theoretical Background

Research on risk-taking behavior has traditionally taken one of three major approaches on how the entity being studied (whether an individual, a firm, or a society) takes risks: the economic, the behavioral, and the sociological. The economic perspective (von Neumann and Morgenstern, 1947; Arrow, 1971) which permeates much of the research in economics, finance, and statistical decision analysis, essentially treats decision-making agents as unitary and free of contextual influences, whether they are individuals, firms, or teams within firms. The role of context in this perspective has been largely restricted to the interaction of individual wealth and risk aversion (Pratt, 1964; Arrow, 1971) and in the finance literature to portfolio effects (Markowitz, 1959; Ball and Brown, 1969).

The second approach is that of the behavioral decision theorists (Slovic, 1972; Payne, 1973; Kahneman and Tversky, 1979; Goldstein and Einhorn, 1987). These researchers tend to describe the actual risk-taking behavior of individuals in relation to their information-processing limitations. In this perspective, context begins to play a role in influencing risk-taking behavior, but it is largely the immediate decision context (for instance, the framing of the problem, the order of presentation, or the salience of the alternatives) rather than the broader organizational or social context in which the decision-maker is embedded. As Tetlock (1985:300) puts it,

> ... the dominant research program on judgment and decision-making has clearly been the cognitive or information-processing approach. ... Thought and action are seen as products of the cognitive operations of the individual thinker, rather than as products of the social, organizational and technological settings in which the individual is embedded.

The third perspective on risk-taking is that of sociology (Douglas and Wildavsky, 1982; Douglas, 1985; Johnson and Covello, 1987), where risk-taking is seen as having little to do with individual preferences. Acceptable risk (Douglas, 1985), which drives actual risk-taking in this perspective, is socially constructed and determined largely by the social and institutional contexts within which choice takes place. In a similar vein, the work of Hofstede (1980) and of Cummings, Harnett, and Stevens (1971) has tended to attribute the different levels of uncertainty avoidance exhibited by individuals to their respective nationalities.

### 3.1 Actual Risk-Taking Behavior in Organizations

The reality of risk-taking behavior in organizations probably lies somewhere along a continuum between the largely unsocialized view of the decision-making entity taken by the economists to the view of risk as a collective construct proposed by sociologists. Other researchers (Tetlock, 1985; March and Shapira, 1987; Schoemaker, 1989; Bromiley and Curley, 1992) express a similar view of the factors influencing risk-taking, as is evident in the following remarks:

> Although they (managers) undoubtedly vary in their individual propensities to take risks, those variations are obscured by processes of selection that reduce the heterogeneity among managers and encourage them to believe in their ability to control the odds, by systems of organizational controls and incentives that dictate risk taking behavior in significant ways, and by variations in the demand for risk taking produced by the context within which choice takes place.
>
> (March and Shapira, 1987:1414.)

As for the specific contextual factors that might influence actual risk-taking behavior in organizations, the influence of structural factors such as incentive and control systems (March and Shapira, 1987) has been mentioned in the strategy and organization literature. Bureaucratic control strategies (Ouchi, 1980), with their association with uncertainty avoidance (Thompson, 1967), can be expected to result in lower risk-taking in organizations. Market control mechanisms, on the other hand, are considered efficient and should result in risk-neutral behavior (Arrow, 1974).[1] Social norms of "acceptable risk" are also likely to influence actual risk-taking, and I will examine the concept of acceptable risk in organizations after discussing how actual risk-taking is defined and measured in this study.

---

[1] The influence of these two types of control strategies is particularly interesting in the financial services industry as both types are clearly identifiable – the bureaucratic control pattern (little discretion to traders, strict limits and controls, low incentive compensation) typically associated with a "traditional commercial banking" type of organization, and the market-control pattern (high authority to traders, no limits, high incentive compensation) with an "investment-banking" type of organization. Both organizational types increasingly compete in some of the same segments (including currency trading) in the global financial services industry.

*3.1.1 Measuring Actual Risk-Taking in Organizations.* Risk has been measured in many ways even within the academic community, most commonly perhaps as the variance of the probability distribution of possible outcomes (Pratt, 1964; Arrow, 1971). Criticisms of variance definitions of risk (Markowitz, 1959) as confusing downside risk with upside opportunity led to models where risk was interpreted as the negative semivariance of a distribution of outcomes (Fishburn, 1977; Coombs, 1983). Researchers on risk in financial markets have chosen instead to estimate risk from the covariance of stock returns with returns on a market portfolio (Jensen, 1972; Blume and Friend, 1975).

Some of this research (Macrimmon and Wehrung, 1990; March and Shapira, 1987) suggests that conceptions of risk and risk-taking *held by managers* differ *substantially* from the views of classical decision theorists. These studies point out that managers do not equate the risk of an alternative with the variance of the probability distribution of possible outcomes. The *magnitude of possible poor outcomes* was far more salient to their decision making than the magnitude weighted by their likelihood.

In the currency trading rooms of major US and Japanese banks where I carried out the initial exploratory research, traders viewed risk in much the same way – as the magnitude of open positions (the speculative holdings) on each currency, particularly the overnight (rather than the intraday) positions, and the magnitude of the possible loss that could arise from carrying such a position. Most of the trading rooms had set limits, valid for six months to a year, on the size of open positions for each currency, or for the room as a whole. Limits were not adjusted during periods of higher or lower volatility in the foreign-exchange markets. The actual exposures to any particular currency that trading rooms carried varied day by day (and minute by minute).

However, on examining the exposures over longer periods, I found a fairly consistent range in "open" (uncovered) positions, and there were major differences between one trading room and another in the size of this range. In the setting in which the model is to be tested where all organizations face the same exogenous volatility in exchange rates, I decided to measure *actual risk-taking* simply by looking at the magnitude of the organization's usual exposure (the size of open positions, in dollars[2]) to a potential loss over a period of time. This is analogous to

---

[2] As dollars tend to be on one side of most currency transactions worldwide, examining open positions in dollar terms eases the task of evaluating risks across different trading rooms, which may trade different mixes of currencies. The qualitative field work in dif-

measuring risk as "bet-size" when the odds are the same (March and Shapira, 1992).

This measure of actual risk-taking has the benefit of being a measure of risk that is understood in the trading rooms. It avoids the problems that arise in attempts to measure subjective probabilities (Wallsten and Budescu, 1983; Budescu and Wallsten, 1985) through question-naires or experimental methods. It is also an ex ante measure of organi-zational risk-taking, while most empirical research on organizational risk-taking has tended to use ex post measures, based, for instance, on the variance of historic accounting returns (Libby and Fishburn, 1977), despite risk being essentially an ex ante concept (Ball and Brown, 1969). Using an ex ante measure seems particularly appropriate in the trading context, as taking risks in trading comes from a conscious deci-sion to maintain an open position, and precedes in time any possibility of return.

### 3.2 Acceptable Risk in Organizations

One of the contextual factors that may influence actual risk-taking behavior in an organization is the norms of "acceptable risk" that prevail in that unit. Douglas and Wildavsky (1982:186) developed the idea of acceptable risk as a collective construct essentially at a societal level of analysis, "to understand the social forces that speak on behalf of envi-ronmental protection in America." The exploratory part of this study, which was based on over 60 hours of observation at nine trading rooms in three countries, and over 50 interviews with traders, managers, and bankers, revealed that the idea of a collectively constructed view of acceptable risk appeared to be equally valid at the organizational level of the currency trading room.

One of the key observations that emerged from the exploratory research was that there were differences between trading rooms in the way acceptable risk (Douglas, 1985) was defined within the room (perhaps what could be called the room's "risk culture"). In interviews with traders within each room, it was clear that they had a shared under-standing of the orientation towards risk that prevailed in their trading rooms, in particular whether aggressive risk-taking was positively regarded or not, and further, that were influenced by it. These values appeared to have developed and been reinforced through the past

ferent countries led me to realize that traders in fact thought of and measured their posi-tions as whether they were "long" or "short" in dollars, whether they traded in Singapore or Tokyo or the US.

history of the trading room, and been disseminated to succeeding generations of traders through the socialization process (Van Maanen and Schein, 1979), and through the controls and sanctions in place in the trading room. The risk cultures of these trading rooms were evident in the stories that were told in these rooms of traders who had "succeeded" or "failed" in the past.

I provide one of these stories as an illustration of how acceptable risk appeared to vary across trading rooms, as manifest in how traders in different rooms provided very different interpretations of the same story. Essentially, these traders had different opinions about the same legendary trader (let us call him Joe) who was said to have made over $300 million in profits in one year for a major bank some years ago. In some rooms, traders were unabashedly admiring of Joe. Joe was said to have been given a more or less free hand by his bank, and was said to have taken enormous (and successful) risks. In other rooms, traders had very negative impressions of Joe ("that couldn't happen here") – I was told Joe took excessive risks and had not really made anywhere near as much money as was claimed. It appeared that Joe's aggressive style of trading was either viewed positively or negatively in different rooms depending on the norms of acceptable risk within that trading room.

Finally, the organizations I study are themselves embedded in national cultures, sometimes in multiple national cultures (if they are located in a country other than their country of origin), which could affect both their norms of acceptable risk and their actual risk-taking behavior.

## 4 A Model of Organizational Risk-Taking[3] and Performance

The hypotheses that are tested in this study are built from theory and from the inductive exploratory phase of this research. The links among the hypotheses and the overall model are given in Figure 15.1. In brief, the room's host-country culture and its parent bank's nationality (home-country) are expected to be associated with its control strategies (market or bureaucratic control), and with its shared norms of acceptable risk. In turn, I expect the trading room's control strategies to be associated with performance, and both control strategies and the norms of acceptable risk to be associated with actual risk-taking, which in turn is positively related to performance (measured as profits per trader). In the model, I control for certain economic explanations for risk-taking and perfor-

---

[3] When I refer to organizational risk-taking, I specifically mean the average actual risk-taking by individuals within the organization.

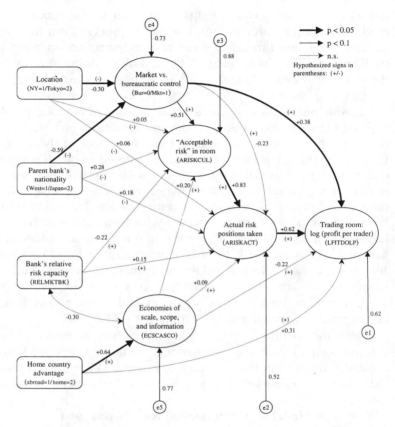

Figure 15.1. Path analysis model for the trading room (Model 1), actual risk-taking (average open positions), and profits per trader.

mance. Some of the behavioral explanations for risk-taking (such as the nature of the decision and exogenous uncertainty) are controlled for by the choice of setting.

I begin a detailed discussion of some of the key hypotheses[4] by drawing on extant research on differences in risk-taking between Japanese and Western organizations. I then go on to discuss the organizational factors that are the specific object of this study, such as the organization's

---

[4] The formal hypotheses as framed are all "alternative hypotheses" that specify that there will be a difference between the factors being compared, and specify the expected direction in which they will differ. The null hypotheses in all these cases are that there will be no difference.

control strategies and its shared values toward risk (acceptable risk). This leads to two sets of hypotheses – the first set links the societal-level effects to the organizational-level factors, and the second set links the organizational context to actual risk-taking and performance.

### 4.1 National Culture[5] and Organizational Risk-Taking

Studies of risk-taking in organizations appear to support the idea of greater risk-aversion among both managers of Japanese ethnicity (Cummings, Harnett, and Stevens, 1971) and in organizations located in Japan (Hofstede, 1980), with researchers essentially reporting a much greater degree of uncertainty avoidance in Japanese managers and organizations than in American managers and organizations. Drawing a parallel from this research to the organizational level of analysis, we come to the first set of hypotheses:

> **H1:** *Trading rooms of Japanese banks will take lower risks than those of Western banks, all else being equal.*

> **H2:** *Trading rooms in Tokyo will take lower risks than trading rooms in New York, all else being equal.*

### 4.2 Organizational Context

*4.2.1 "Acceptable Risk."* As described earlier, one of the critical observations that emerged from the exploratory research was that there were differences between trading rooms in the way acceptable risk (Douglas, 1985) was defined within the room. Interviews with traders suggested that these norms about what levels of risk were acceptable influenced the risks that they actually took. These norms were in many cases "tighter" than the formal limits traders had been assigned – i.e., in

---

[5] A word of explanation is required on the use of the term "national culture" in this paper. The hypotheses developed in this paper on the influence of national culture relate to the effect of the broader social context, which is most readily identifiable with the nation in which the risk-taking units are either located (the host country or location) or from which they originate (the home country or the nationality of the parent bank), on the organizational context, on actual risk-taking, and on performance. One could conceivably argue that the "national cultures" referred to in this paper are really the cultures of two cities, New York and Tokyo, which overwhelmingly dominate the activity we investigate in their two nations. In developing the hypotheses, I draw from the literature that has essentially categorized the business cultures of different nations (Hofstede, 1980; Hofstede et al., 1990). The term "national culture" as it is used in this paper might therefore best be defined as the business culture of the US compared to the business culture of Japan, as manifested in the financial services industry in New York and in Tokyo.

many cases, formal controls were *less* binding than the collectively constructed informal norms of acceptable risk in the room. Actual risk-taking behavior is therefore likely to be associated with these norms of acceptable risk, as well as with the control strategies in place, after controlling for the economic strength of the parent bank.

The primary focus of this study is the direct influence of these internally developed shared norms of acceptable risk and of control strategies on actual risk-taking behavior in the trading rooms.[6] This leads to the following hypothesis linking organizational norms to behavior:

> **H3:** *High levels of acceptable risk will be positively associated with high levels of actual risk-taking behavior.*

*4.2.2 Control Strategies.* The organization's control strategies, whether "bureaucratic" control (Weber, 1946; Crozier, 1964; Thompson, 1967; Ouchi, 1979; Meyer, 1990), or "market" control (Arrow, 1974), should influence the norms of acceptable risk in the room, by providing a formal system of limits and sanctions on acceptable behavior. These control strategies should also influence actual risk-taking and performance in the trading rooms.

As a general rule, control strategies legitimize the level of acceptable risk within the organization. For instance, "bureaucratic" control (Ouchi, 1980), which is high on formalization, centralization, and standardization (Pugh et al., 1969), is a method of uncertainty avoidance and is therefore likely to result in lower risk-taking. "Bureaucratic" control is also likely to lower the levels of acceptable risk within the room by its emphasis on the enforcement of position limits and stop-loss limits in the trading room. "Market" control mechanisms, by contrast, should result in higher levels of acceptable risk and actual risk-taking within the organization.

The "investment banking" type rooms, where market-control practices such as high incentive compensation are most likely to be found, also typically do not have strict limits on overnight and intraday risk positions. These factors should be reflected in greater risk-taking by trading rooms that are "high" on market control (versus bureaucratic control)

---

[6] As mentioned earlier, acceptable risk represents the institutionalized, stable norms within the organization toward risk, while actual risk-taking is a measure of behavior. These two concepts were also shown to be different when the measures used to operationalize them were subjected to a discriminant validity test using structural equations modeling.

compared to rooms that are "low" on market control. By extension, market controls should also go with higher levels of acceptable risk within the trading room. Finally, one could argue that market control, as it usually involves significant incentive-based compensation (Ouchi, 1979), will result in better performance at the organizational level.

These arguments lead us to a set of hypotheses linking control strategies, acceptable risk, organizational risk-taking, and performance:

> **H4:** *High reliance on market (versus bureaucratic) control will be associated with high levels of acceptable risk in the trading room.*

> **H5:** *High reliance on market (versus bureaucratic) control will be associated with high levels of actual risk-taking in the room.*

> **H6:** *High reliance on market (versus bureaucratic) control will be associated with high trading-room performance.*

### 4.3 The Risk-Return Relationship

Researchers in strategic management (Bowman, 1980 and 1982; Bettis, 1983; Baird and Thomas, 1985; Jemison, 1987) have begun to address the relationship between risk and return in firms. Bowman's study showed a negative relationship between firm-level risk and average return in several industries. In the trading room, however, we do expect the traditional positive relationship between actual risk-taking (the size of open positions) and average returns.

Several authors (Bowman, 1982; Bromiley, 1991) have also shown in longitudinal studies that there is a feedback effect (in some cases positive, and in others negative) from performance to risk-taking. However, certain features of the trading-room context render the modeling of a feedback effect difficult, and perhaps unnecessary. First, in a trading room, there can be no return without an antecedent risk position having been consciously taken, i.e., a particular risk position has to precede the return associated with that position. While I have no doubt that how a trader has performed in the last few minutes or hours influences her immediately following risk-taking behavior, in this study, we are interested in the *habitual, institutionalized* element of risk-taking, measured as the "usual positions over the last year" rather than in the immediate cognitively driven variations. At this macro level, we expect that the traditional direction of the risk-return relationship to hold. This leads us to the hypothesis:

> **H7:** *Higher levels of actual risk-taking will be associated with higher levels of performance.*

### 4.4  Control Variables

*4.4.1  Economic Strength.* The economic strength of the bank to which the trading room belongs is expected to affect its actual risk-taking, as the strength of the bank should reflect the banks' economic value and its ability to raise risk capital. Drawing an analogy at the organizational level from the postulates of the top end of the Friedman and Savage (1952) preference curve for individuals (that wealthy decision-makers should be more risk-neutral), rooms of banks that have high economic value should also have the ability to take greater risks. In this sample of 16 banks, all of which are among the largest in the world, we can expect to see the behavior of the top end of the Friedman-Savage curve, and we therefore control for the parent bank's economic strength.

*4.4.2  Economies of Scale, Scope and Information, and the Home-Court Advantage.* That skills influence risk-taking is both logical and established at an individual level. At the organizational level, skills can be taken to refer to the sources of competitive advantage in risk-taking that the organization has, such as its economies of scale, scope, and information, and the home-court advantage of operating in its home country (Hymer, 1976; Kindleberger, 1969). Both of these factors are controlled for in the model (how these factors were measured is described in the section on measures).

### 5  Research Design

The research consisted of three phases. The first phase was an exploratory phase, conducted to understand the setting and build theory; the second was a model-testing phase where traders and trading-room managers in a paired sample of trading rooms in New York and Tokyo were surveyed; in the third phase, a few of the rooms that participated in the study were revisited to validate the findings.

### 5.1  The Exploratory Phase

In this phase, I visited nine trading rooms (three in the US, five in Tokyo, and one in Singapore) belonging to six parent banks (four US, one European, and one Japanese) for observation of trading and interviews. I interviewed all nine heads of trading in these rooms, and typically observed one to two traders as they traded. At three of these banks, I also interviewed managers in charge of accounting for trading operations. My visits to these banks lasted from half a day to two days. A key informant was particularly helpful in initiating me into the language of trading. In addition to visiting these sites, I also interviewed over 20 other traders, trading-room managers, senior bankers, and suppliers to trading rooms.

### 5.2 The Model-Testing Phase: Sample and Data Collection

Initially, I decided to use a paired sample of trading rooms of US and Japanese banks in New York and in Tokyo, in order to focus on the two levels of analysis I was interested in – the national level, and the trading room level, with the trading room as the unit of analysis. A paired design (two trading rooms of the same parent bank in New York and Tokyo) would effectively control for unobserved parent-bank effects (for example, how important trading was in the overall scheme of things for the parent bank) in assessing the role of national culture and the trading-room context on risk-taking and performance. The exploratory phase had revealed that trading rooms of the same parent in different locations differed in their organizational contexts – their control and incentive systems differed as did their shared norms of acceptable risk. They also worked independently in the currency markets, at a different time of day, and as independent profit centers. What interdependencies existed across these pairs of trading rooms appeared to exist at the individual level, whereby a trader in New York might ask his counterpart in Tokyo to wake her up if, for example, Dollar-Mark reached some specified level during Asia-Pacific trading (but even in this, the parent-bank connection was not universal – some of the traders interviewed mentioned calling "friends" in other banks for this purpose).

Using the list of foreign banks in Tokyo published by the Federation of Bankers Associations of Japan (Zenginkyo, 1989) and the Hambros Bank Foreign Exchange and Bullion Dealers Directory (1989) as a guide, nine New York-based US commercial and investment banks were identified as having operations and being "authorized foreign-exchange banks" in Tokyo. Of the nine, six agreed to participate. Of the ten Japanese commercial and wholesale banks identified as having trading operations in New York and Tokyo, eight agreed to participate in the study. All the banks were promised confidentiality and a summary of the results.

As the study proceeded, I discovered that one of the US banks that had agreed to participate had operations but no FX trading in Tokyo. At this point, I decided to include two European banks in the sample, to increase the number of non-Japanese participants. This required the hypotheses to be framed as a contrast between Japanese and Western banks, rather than as a contrast between Japanese and American banks.

I distributed a total of 251 questionnaires to all spot and forward foreign-exchange traders who took overnight positions in these trading rooms. This left out junior traders and traders dealing in the domestic money market and in derivative products whose risk positions are often more difficult to evaluate. The final sample consisted of responses from 198 traders belonging to 28 trading rooms of eight Western and eight Japanese banks, located in New York and Tokyo. The fully "paired" sample consisted of 24 rooms of six Western and six Japanese banks.

The banks in the sample are all prominent players in the global foreign-exchange (FX) market. Ten of these 16 banks feature in a list of the top 50 worldwide FX dealers over the 1979–91 period, six feature in the list of top 15 interbank FX dealers in 1991, seven feature in the list of the top 10 in Tokyo, and four in the list of the top 10 in New York (*Euromoney*, 1991). Together, these 16 banks account for approximately 20% of the total annual worldwide volume in FX.

### 5.2 The Questionnaires

I personally administered the questionnaires to all spot and forward FX traders at each of these trading rooms, and gave a separate questionnaire to each of the heads of trading, who I also interviewed. In the analyses that follow, I used the aggregated responses of all the traders for room-level constructs. This meant that though the sample consisted of only 28 trading rooms, the room-level measures aggregated from the responses of 198 traders were robust and free from position bias (Phillips and Bagozzi, 1982). I used a Japanese version of the traders' questionnaire, which went through translation, back-translation, and pre-testing, in Tokyo. To verify the accuracy of the translation, I separately calculated the reliability of all the constructs for the Japanese and English questionnaires and found them to be stable (Table 15.1). The overall response rate was 79% with a 63% response rate from New York and 92% from Tokyo. This pattern of response rates (higher response rates from Japan) is consistent with previous survey studies conducted in the US and Japan.

### 6 The Measures

This section discusses the structure of the performance measures, followed by a discussion of how the predictor variables were measured and aggregated. Where scales have been used, Table 15.1[7] provides the details of the variables making up the scales and the reliabilities of the scales (Cronbach's Alpha) for the full sample and across the

---

[7] Please contact the author if you would like the complete wording of the questions on the surveys.

Table 15.1. *Reliability of trading-room-level scales.*

| Construct SCALE NAME | Variables in scale These room-level variables are aggregated from all respondents in each trading room | $\alpha$ Full sample n = 28 | $\alpha$ English questionnaire | $\alpha$ Japanese questionnaire |
|---|---|---|---|---|
| **Perceived room performance** ARMPERF | Room has some of the best traders in city Most profits of any room in city Rating of total profit Rating of room's profit/trader | 0.93 | 0.93 | 0.95 |
| **"Acceptable risk"** ARISKCUL | Compared to other bank trading rooms, our trading room is, in terms of risk-taking, one of the most conservative, average, or one of the most aggressive. In this room, aggressive risk-taking is frowned upon R The limits set by the bank are very conservative R | 0.83 | 0.81 | 0.87 |
| **Actual risks taken** ARISKACT | Usual overnight positions of individual traders Usual stop-loss positions of individual traders Usual overnight positions of each group | 0.91 | 0.92 | 0.91 |
| **Market control** AMARKET | Pay traders for performance Hire from the external labor market High turnover of traders | 0.83 | 0.65 | 0.91 |
| **Bureaucratic control: formalization-standardization** AFORMAL | Clear, written policies exist Clear, written job descriptions exist | 0.73 | 0.73 | 0.71 |
| **Bureaucratic control: centralization** ACENTRAL | Decision-making centralized Even minor exceptions need approval Traders have a lot of authority here R Traders can exceed overnight limits R | 0.77 | 0.80 | 0.77 |

Table 15.1.  *(cont.)*

| Construct SCALE NAME | Variables in scale These room-level variables are aggregated from all respondents in each trading room | $\alpha$ Full sample n = 28 | $\alpha$ English questionnaire | $\alpha$ Japanese questionnaire |
|---|---|---|---|---|
| **Bureaucratic control: microcontrols** ALIMPRE | There are: Overnight position limits by currency Intraday position limits by currency Overnight position limits by trader Intraday position limits by trader | 0.92 | 0.95 | 0.76 |
| **Economies of scope** ASCOPE | Large base of customers: Corporates Institutions Individuals | 0.91 | 0.93 | 0.84 |
| **Information economies** AREPUT | Our room would be called first Close to Fed Fed* intervenes through us Big in city FX Big worldwide in FX | 0.80 | 0.77 | 0.84 |
| **Economies of scale, scope, and information** ECSCASCO | Information economies Economies of scope Number of trades per day | 0.85 | 0.92 | 0.84 |

* In Tokyo, "Fed" was replaced by "Ministry of Finance/Bank of Japan".
R = Reverse coded.

sub-samples of traders responding to the English and Japanese versions of the questionnaire.

All the scales discussed below are simple additive scales with equal weight given to each variable. In only one case (economies of scale, scope, and information) were z-scores of the underlying variables used in the construction of the index, as the variable for economies of scale (number of trades per day in the room) was differently scaled than the other measures (which were drawn from seven-point Likert-type scales).

### 6.1 The Performance Measures

All the variables in the model are aggregated (averaged) at the level of the trading room. I used two measures of trading-room performance in the analysis. The first, used in model 1, is "profits from currency trading per trader" (LFITDOLP), obtained as described below from the questionnaire given to the head of the trading room. This measure is a proxy for return on investment, as the fixed investment in a trading room tends to track the number of traders in it.[8] I used a second performance measure in model 2 – "profits normalized by risk" (NORMDOLP). I computed this measure as the profit per trader reported in the FX head's questionnaire divided by the average of the "usual individual overnight positions" reported by the FX traders in that room. This measure is a measure of a room's "risk-transformation" capability, or how well a room does controlling for the level of actual risk-taking. I used logarithmic transformations of the dollar values in the path analysis models.

In addition, I constructed a perceptual measure of room performance (ARMPERF) from the aggregated responses to four perceptual indicators of performance drawn from the FX trader's questionnaire. The reliability of this construct ranged from 0.93 to 0.95 across the sub-samples (see Table 15.1). This construct also showed high correlations with the head's ratings of the rooms total profit ($0.7, p < 0.01$) and with profit per trader ($0.6, p < 0.01$), providing an external check on its validity.

There was a problem of missing data on the basic dependent variable, profits per trader, drawn from the FX head's questionnaire. Only 18 out of the 28 heads of trading rooms reported this figure. This level of missing data is understandable, as this information is not publicly available anywhere, and it is remarkable that this study generated the level of support and confidence it did from the 18 rooms that did report this figure.

The question then arose of whether to test the model using only the perceptual measure of performance. While the perceptual measure is a good measure, I decided that these 18 data points on actual profits per trader were too valuable to ignore. The missing data were therefore estimated from the perceptual data, and I created a derived variable (LFIT-DOLP), which consists of actual profits per trader for the 18 cases, and predicted profits per trader for the other 10 cases. Some of the heads of trading rooms who I was able subsequently to contact on the phone verbally confirmed that the fitted figures were approximately correct. This fitted measure is at least as good as the perceptual measure (as it basically rescales the perceptual data into dollar figures for the missing cases,

---

[8] The exploratory research and a pre-test of the questionnaire revealed that it would be difficult to obtain comparable figures across trading rooms of the actual return on investment because of inherent problems in defining and measuring investment in the trading room.

to make them comparable to the others), and it benefits from having taken into account the available hard data on actual profits per trader. The parameters of the estimation model for fitted dollar profits are $R^2 = 0.29$ (Sig. $F = 0.003$) and Beta $= 0.54$ (Sig. $t = 0.003$).

### 6.2 Actual Risk-Taking

As discussed earlier, in the FX trading room, actual risk taking was operationalized by two elements: the average net open position on a particular day, and the average level at which traders take their losses in each room. This is partly analogous to operationalizing risk as "bet-size" (March and Shapira, 1992) when the odds are the same.

Individual traders have a good sense of what overnight positions each of them individually, and their currency groups as a whole, usually hold. These data were requested (as ranges), and added to an indicator of at what ranges traders usually took their losses, to form an index of actual risk-taking (ARISKACT) in the room. This index has very high reliability (Cronbach's Alpha $= 0.91$ to $0.92$) across the subsamples and is a reasonable proxy for the room's actual risk-taking (Table 15.1). This measure showed a high correlation ($0.63$, $p < 0.01$) with the head's rating of risk-taking by the room, providing an independent check on its validity.

### 6.3 Organizational Context Variables

6.3.1 "Acceptable Risk." These are the shared values towards risk that prevail in the trading room. This construct has been operationalized through a scale (ARISKCUL) composed of three variables that capture the mean perception among traders of the room's orientation towards risk – "Compared to other bank trading rooms, our trading room is, in terms of risk-taking, one of the most conservative, average, aggressive" (seven-point scale with these values anchoring the points); "In this room, aggressive risk-taking is frowned upon" (Strongly Agree to Strongly Disagree); "The limits set by the bank are very conservative" (Strongly Agree to Strongly Disagree). The reliability of this scale ranges from $0.81$ to $0.87$ across the sub-samples, being $0.83$ for the full sample. Acceptable risk and actual risk-taking also factor out as two distinct constructs when subjected to a discriminant validity test.

6.3.2 Control Strategies. I decided to classify the 28 trading rooms into those following market-control strategies or bureaucratic-control strategies (Weber, 1946; Crozier, 1964; Thompson, 1967; Khand-walla, 1976; Ghoshal and Nohria, 1989; Meyer, 1990). This dichotomous classification was both in the interests of parsimony, and because the inductive phase of the study revealed that banks claiming to follow "investment-banking" types of market-based control strategies tended to have a combination of controls and incentives (for instance, large limits, high incentive compensation) that differed markedly from those that could best be described as banks following more bureaucratic "traditional commercial banking" types of strategies. To classify the 28 trading rooms, I clustered them on four control variables. Three of these variables captured aspects of bureaucratic control: formalization, centralization (Pugh et al., 1969), and the use of "micro-controls." This third measure of bureaucratic control was determined by the specific context of trading and reflected detailed limits on intraday and overnight positions by currency and by trader, institutionally dictated stop-loss limits, and strict enforcement. The fourth variable used in clustering was "market control" (Ouchi, 1979), operationalized from three variables capturing pay for performance, hiring from the external labor market, and high turnover.

*6.3.3 Clustering the Trading Rooms by Control Strategy.* The 28 trading rooms were then clustered on these control strategies using Ward's method. The two-cluster solution had high face validity, and a dendrogram revealed a large distance from the three-cluster solution. In the two-cluster solution, cluster 1 consisted of eight trading rooms, all of Western parentage, six located in New York and two in Tokyo. These trading rooms consisted of investment bank trading rooms and of trading rooms of commercial banks in New York that were "trying to look like investment banks" (this characterization of their strategies captures the expressed views of heads of trading in these banks). Cluster 2 consisted of 20 rooms, 13 Japanese banks' trading rooms in New York and Tokyo, six American commercial banks' trading rooms in Tokyo, and a lone American commercial bank in New York which more closely resembled the Japanese banks in its bureaucratic and non-market modes of control.

In the rest of the analysis, I refer to cluster 1 as "market control" trading rooms, and cluster 2 as "bureaucratic control" trading rooms. For the multivariate models, I created a dichotomous variable (MKTCTRL) with "market-control" rooms coded "1" and the "bureaucratic-control" rooms coded "0". Key differences between the "market-control" and "bureaucratic-control" clusters are given in Table 15.2.

Table 15.2. *Characteristics of "market-control" versus "bureaucratic-control" trading rooms.*

| Variable | Bureaucratic control strategy n = 20 | Market control strategy n = 8 | T-test, 2-tail probability |
|---|---|---|---|
| *Clustering variables:* Aggregated from traders' questionnaires | | | |
| **Market control** | 1.49 | 1.89 | |
| AMARKET | (0.55) | (0.45) | 0.08 |
| **Micro-controls** | 3.58 | 2.12 | |
| ALIMPRE | (0.5) | (1.20) | 0.00 |
| **Formalization** | 1.17 | 0.75 | |
| AFORMAL | (0.25) | (0.18) | 0.00 |
| **Centralization** | 2.55 | 1.96 | |
| ACENTRAL | (0.40) | (0.50) | 0.00 |
| *Related variables:* (Head's questionnaire) | | | |
| **Average bonus to salary** | 25.4% | 60.0% | |
| | (33.0) | (26.6) | 0.03 |
| **Highest bonus to salary** | 46.8% | 361.4% | |
| | (90.4) | (548.7) | 0.18 |

*Note*: Standard deviations are in parentheses.

### 6.4 Control Variables

*6.4.1 Economies of Scale, Scope, and Information.* I measured scale (ASCALE) by the number of trades per day in the room. The measure of scope (ASCOPE) was based on three variables: "Our bank has one of the largest client bases of corporate customers in this country," "Our bank has very strong ties with institutional investors (fund managers) in this country," and "Our bank has one of the largest networks of individual customers in this country." Information economies (AREPUT) were operationalized from five variables: "Our bank would be one of the first to be contacted by other banks in this city for FX trading," "Our bank has a close relationship with the Federal Reserve/Ministry of Finance," "The Fed/MOF often intervenes in the FX markets through us," "We are a major force in the FX markets in this city," and "We are a major force in FX markets worldwide."

These three constructs – scale, scope, and information economies – were normalized to equalize the ranges on the scales, and the z-scores were combined into one index (ECSCASCO).

6.4.2 *The "Home-Court Advantage."* This construct was operationalized as a dummy variable (ABROHOME) where Japanese rooms in Tokyo and American rooms in New York were coded "1" and the others "0."

6.4.3 *Economic Strength.* The average market-to-book value over 1989 and 1990 (Morgan Stanley, 1990, 1991) was chosen as a measure that captured the economic value of the parent bank and therefore the capacity of the trading room to take risks. However, market-to-book values in Tokyo were far higher than those in New York because of the very high P/E ratios that prevailed at that time in the Tokyo stock market. While some of these high market-to-book values perhaps reflect the inherent strength of Japanese banks, much of them can be traced to institutional differences between the US and Japan on stockholding patterns, accounting practices, and tax regulations. As I wanted to distinguish between the influence on risk-taking that came from being Japanese and the impact of the parent-banks' economic capacity, the influence of Japan was partialed out of the average market-to-book values (by standardizing the measures within each country), leaving a measure of relative market-to-book values (RELMKTBK) for each group of trading rooms (Japanese and Western). This measure was used as an indicator of the parent bank's economic capacity to take risks.

### 7 Analyses and Results

Two path analysis models (Models 1 and 2) were tested, essentially varying only in that different measures of trading-room performance were used as the criterion variable – profit per trader, which is akin to a "return" measure in Model 1; and profits per trader normalized by risk taken (a measure of risk-transformation capability) in Model 2. The analyses were run on both the strictly "paired" sample and the full sample, and the coefficients were stable in order of magnitude and sign, and so only the results of the full sample of 28 rooms are reported here.

In Model 2, as the outcome variable is average profits per trader normalized for actual risk-taking, "acceptable risk" has been taken out of the model. Further, Model 1 is an overidentified model (relationships not drawn from theory are not included), while Model 2, which has fewer variables, is a "just-identified" model (Pedhazur, 1982), with relationships

Table 15.3. *Model 1: Risks and profits/trader.*

| Dependent variable | Average profit/trader LFITDOLP | Actual risk taking (average open positions) ARISKACT | "Acceptable risk" ARISKCUL | Control strategy Market = 1 Bureaucratic = 0 MKTCTRL | Economies of scale, scope, and information ECSCASCO |
|---|---|---|---|---|---|
| Equation | 1 | 2 | 3 | 4 | 5 |
| $R^2$ | 0.62 | 0.73 | 0.23 | 0.47 | 0.40 |
| Adj. $R^2$ | 0.55 | 0.66 | 0.05 | 0.42 | 0.38 |
| F | 9.20 | 9.60 | 1.31 | 10.93 | 17.65 |
| Sig. F | 0.000 | 0.000 | 0.290 | 0.000 | 0.000 |
| **Independent variables** | $\beta$ (Sig T) | $\beta$ (Sig T) | $\beta$ (Sig T) | $\beta$ (Sig T) | $\beta$ (Sig T) |
| ARISKACT | +0.62 (0.000) | — | — | — | — |
| ARISKCUL | — | +0.83 (0.000) | — | — | — |
| MKTCTRL Market = 1/ Bureaucratic = 0 | +0.38 (0.016) | −0.23 (0.20) | +0.51 (0.07) | — | — |
| ECSCASCO | −0.22 (0.229) | +0.09 (0.47) | +0.20 (0.34) | — | — |
| RELMKTBK Relative Market to Book | — | +0.15 (0.24) | −0.22 (0.29) | — | — |
| ABROHOME Abroad = 1/ Home = 2 | +0.31 (0.108) | — | — | — | +0.64 (0.000) |
| BRANCH NY = 1/ Tokyo = 2 | — | +0.06 (0.63) | +0.05 (0.83) | −0.30 (0.049) | — |
| JPNONJP West = 1/ Japan = 2 | — | +0.18 (0.26) | +0.28 (0.28) | −0.59 (0.000) | — |

between *all* the independent variables and the dependent variable retained in the model, and both models are recursive (no feedback loops). The regression results are given in Table 15.3.

A caveat to bear in mind as one looks at the path analysis models is that the causal structure in these models has been imposed on these variables from theory, and these models therefore *do not* test for causality. The best we can hope to understand from the path analysis models is that the causal structure imposed is *not implausible* and that it explains the total relationship between the dependent and independent variables (as given by the zero order correlations) reasonably well.

### 7.1 Overall Model Fit

*7.1.1 Model 1: Risk and Return.* All the regressions except for the one on acceptable risk had significant overall explanatory power in Model 1 (Table 15.3). While acceptable risk has been modeled as partially endogenous, the main purpose of the model is to explain *actual risk-taking* and *performance*. The model's role in explaining acceptable risk is limited to the investigation of the influence of control strategies, of home and host-country, and of the bank's economic strength on acceptable risk.

The test of a good path analysis model is to what extent the effect coefficients, which explain the total effect of predictor variable on criterion variable (i.e., the total of the direct and indirect effects in the model) approximate the zero-order $\beta$ (the Pearson's correlation coefficient). By this measure, Model 1 (Table 15.4) is reasonably good, as most of the effect coefficients are within 0.1 of the zero-order $\beta$ (Pedhazur, 1982; Cohen and Cohen, 1983).

In addition, we used a formal "goodness-of-fit" test useful with small samples, and an "over-identified" model which has been suggested by Specht (1975). This involves first setting up a "just identified" and fully recursive model (one with every possible relationship defined in the model, even if some of the relationships are implausible) and calculating the generalized squared multiple correlation, $R_m^2$ of the "just identified" model, which is

$$R_m^2 = 1 - (1 - R_1^2)(1 - R_2^2) \ldots (1 - R_p^2)$$

where $R_i^2$ is the squared multiple correlation coefficient ($R^2$) of the ith equation. A similar statistic M is calculated for the overidentified model that is being tested (which has some paths deleted). As some of the $R^2$'s do not exist in the overidentified model, M can take on values between zero and $R_m^2$. If the overidentified model is a perfect fit (i.e., if the correlation matrix is exactly reproduced), $M = R_m^2$. For Model 1, $M = 0.84$, and with a just identified (though not theoretically meaningful) model with all paths included, $R_m^2 = 0.99$. This shows that Model 1 is a reasonably good fit (0.85).

*7.1.2 Model 2: Risk Transformation Capability.* In this model, the dependent variable is the natural logarithm of profits per trader in each room normalized by the average individual overnight positions taken in that room. It can be argued that this is the best measure of a

Table 15.4. *Model 1.*
A: *Total, direct, and indirect effects on profits/trader.*

| Effect on profits/trader (LFITDOLP) | Direct effect | Indirect effect@ | Total effect | Unanalyzed effect | Zero order β |
|---|---|---|---|---|---|
| ARISKACT | +0.62*** | — | **+0.62** | — | +0.58*** |
| ARISKCUL | — | +0.51 | **+0.51** | — | +0.63*** |
| MKTCTRL | +0.38*** | +0.12 | **+0.50** | — | +0.41** |
| ECSCASCO | −0.22 | +0.16 | **−0.06** | +0.06 | +0.15 |
| RELMKTBK | — | −0.02 | **−0.02** | +0.20 | +0.19 |
| ABROHOME | +0.31 | −0.04 | **+0.27** | +0.04 | +0.43** |
| BRANCH | — | −0.08 | **−0.08** | — | +0.13 |
| JPNONJP | — | −0.05 | **−0.05** | — | −0.04 |

B: *Total, direct, and indirect effects on actual risks taken.*

| Effect on actual risk-taking (ARISKACT) | Direct effect | Indirect effect@ | Total effect | Unanalyzed effect | Zero order β |
|---|---|---|---|---|---|
| ARISKCUL | +0.83*** | — | **+0.83** | — | +0.76*** |
| MKTCTRL | −0.23*** | +0.42 | **+0.19** | — | −0.11 |
| ECSCASCO | +0.09 | +0.17 | **+0.26** | +0.01 | +0.33 |
| RELMKTBK | +0.15 | −0.18 | **−0.03** | −0.08 | −0.09 |
| ABROHOME | — | +0.17 | **+0.17** | +0.01 | +0.26 |
| BRANCH | +0.06 | −0.06 | **0.00** | — | +0.13 |
| JPNONJP | +0.18 | +0.12 | **+0.30** | — | +0.33 |

*Note:* $**p < 0.05$, $***p < 0.01$, @ no significance test.

trading room's performance as it captures a trading room's risk-trans-formation capability.

As both actual risks taken (ARISKACT) and the shared values towards risk (ARISKCUL) were removed from this model, there were few predictor variables, and a set of hierarchical reduced-form equations (Cohen and Cohen, 1983) could be used to estimate the path coefficients (Table 15.5). However, this method, while computationally more efficient, cannot be tested for goodness of fit, as it is a "just-identified" model.

Table 15.5. *Model 2: Risk-transformation capability.*

| Dependent variable | Profit per trader normalized for risk taken (NORMDOLP) | | |
|---|---|---|---|
| Equation | 1 | 2 | 3 |
| $R^2$ | 0.29 | 0.43 | 0.47 |
| Adj. $R^2$ | 0.16 | 0.30 | 0.32 |
| F | 2.3 | 3.33 | 3.16 |
| Sig. F | 0.09 | 0.02 | 0.02 |
| **Predictor variables** | β (Sig T) | β (Sig T) | β (Sig T) |
| RELMKTBK Parent bank strength | +0.33 (0.08) | +0.24 (0.16) | +0.14 (0.43) |
| JPNONJP West = 1/Japan = 2 | −0.39 (0.08) | −0.02 (0.92) | −0.06 (0.78) |
| ABROHOME Abroad = 1/Home = 2 | +0.17 (0.34) | −0.03 (0.88) | +0.22 (0.41) |
| BRANCH NY = 1 / Tokyo = 2 | +0.09 (0.62) | +0.26 (0.16) | +0.30 (0.11) |
| MKTCTRL Market = 1 / Bureaucratic = 0 | — | +0.60 (0.03) | +0.52 (0.06) |
| ECSCASCO Economics of scale and scope | — | — | −0.33 (0.20) |

The overall explanatory power of this model was good ($R^2 = 0.47$, Sig. F = 0.02). As additional variables (in particular, market control strategy) were introduced into the model, the economic strength of the bank and the "home-field" effect, which were significant in the earlier stages, lost their explanatory power, and the use of market control strategies emerged as the only significant predictor of profits per trader normalized for risk.

The direct, indirect, and total effects in Model 2 are provided in Table 15.6. As in Model 1, in Model 2, the differences between the total effects predicted by the model and the zero-order correlations were less than 0.1 for each relationship.

### 8 Results of Hypothesis Tests
Having established that the overall models of contextual influences on risk-taking and performance in the trading rooms were reasonably good,

Table 15.6. *Model 2: risk-transformation capability – total, direct, and indirect effects on profits normalized for risk taken.*

| Effect on NORMDOLP | Direct effect | Indirect effect | Total effect | Zero-order $\beta$ |
|---|---|---|---|---|
| MKTCTRL | +0.52 | +0.08 | **+0.60** | +0.57*** |
| ABROHOME | +0.22 | −0.05 | **+0.17** | +0.17 |
| BRANCH | +0.30 | −0.21 | **+0.09** | +0.02 |
| JPNONJP | −0.06 | −0.33 | **−0.39** | −0.39** |
| ECSCASCO | −0.33 | — | **−0.33** | −0.21 |
| RELMKTBK | +0.14 | +0.19 | **+0.33** | +0.36 |

*Note*: *p < 0.05, ***p < 0.01.

I discuss the results in relation to the specific hypotheses proposed in the paper. As Model 1 (Tables 15.3 and 15.4) is the model that includes both acceptable risk and actual risk-taking as predictors, I discuss the results of the tests on hypotheses 1 through 5 and hypothesis 7 from Table 15.3. I discuss the relationship between market control and performance (hypothesis 6) from Model 1 (Table 15.3) and Model 2 (Table 15.5). Results of all hypothesis tests are reported from the multivariate regression models.

To summarize the results of the hypothesis tests:

### National culture and actual risk-taking

*H1:* Trading rooms of Japanese banks will take lower risks than those of Western banks. *Not supported* ($\beta$ = +0.18, not significant – Table 15.3, Model 1, Equation 2).

*H2:* Trading rooms in Tokyo will take lower risks than those in New York. *Not supported* ($\beta$ = +0.06, not significant – Table 15.3, Model 1, Equation 2).

### Organizational context and actual risk-taking

*H3:* High levels of acceptable risk will be positively associated with high levels of actual risk-taking. *Supported* ($\beta$ = +0.83, p < 0.000 – Table 15.3, Model 1, Equation 2).

*H4:* High reliance on market (versus bureaucratic) control will be associated with high levels of acceptable risk. *Marginally supported* ($\beta$ = 0.51, p = 0.07 – Table 15.3, Model 1, Equation 3).

*H5:* High reliance on market (versus bureaucratic) control will be associated with high levels of actual risk-taking. *Not supported* ($\beta$ = −0.23, not significant – Table 15.3, Model 1, Equation 2).

### Organizational context and performance

*H6:* High reliance on market (versus bureaucratic) control will be associated with high trading-room performance.

Performance measured as profits per trader. ***Supported*** (b = 0.38, p < 0.02 – Table 15.3, Model 1, Equation 1)

Performance measured as profits per trader normalized for actual risk-taking. ***Marginally supported*** ($\beta$ = 0.52, p = 0.06 – Table 15.5, Model 2, Equation 3).

### Risk-taking and performance

*H7:* High levels of actual risk-taking will be associated with high trading-room performance. ***Supported*** ($\beta$ = 0.62, p < 0.000 – Table 15.3, Model 1, Equation 1).

## 9 Discussion and Implications

Overall, the influence of acceptable risk (organizational norms regarding what levels of risk-taking are legitimate) on actual risk-taking was borne out in this study. Control strategies (market versus bureaucratic control) tended to influence acceptable risk rather than actual risk-taking behavior. Market control was clearly related to better risk transformation in these trading rooms, and Japanese banks did not take lower risks than Western banks, contrary to expectations.

### 9.1 Acceptable Risk in an Organizational Context

As expected, acceptable risk (the shared norms towards risk) was the best predictor of actual organizational risk-taking in these trading rooms (Model 1, Table 15.3, Equation 2). This result has implications for research and practice. It points to a great need for researchers studying organizational risk-taking and related concepts in a variety of areas (for instance, in innovation or in market entry or in research and development) to develop a better appreciation of an organization's shared values toward risk, and the role that acceptable risk at the organizational level plays in constraining or facilitating organizational decisions involving risk.

### 9.2 "National Culture" Influences on Risk-Taking

One of the results of the organizational level of analysis is that the "Japan" factor (belonging to a Japanese bank or being in Tokyo) did not have the expected negative effect on organizational risk-taking. In fact, contrary to Hofstede's findings which rated Japanese individuals as low risk-takers, Japanese banks appeared to take larger open positions than Western banks (though this relationship was not statistically significant).

One could speculate on possible reasons for the absence of the expected negative "Japan" effect on risk-taking. For one, the high level of global integration in this industry could mean that "home-country" effects are diluted. Second, it might be explained at the organizational level by the "risky shift" phenomenon (Stoner, 1961; Bem, Wallach, and Kogan, 1965; Dion, Baron, and Miller, 1970) where group decision-making (which is higher in this sample of Japanese banks) results in riskier decisions. A third explanation might be found in agency theory (Jensen, 1972; Shavell, 1979; Nalbantian, 1987), whereby the fact that there is little incentive compensation in Japanese banks implies that risk-averse traders do not share in the risk, which therefore results in more risk-neutral decision-making (i.e., traders in Japanese banks can take larger risks because they do not have to worry about their own compensation being significantly affected).

Clearly, further research is required to determine which of these theories best explains the fact that Japanese banks do not take smaller risks than Western banks, though all the research at the individual level suggests that Japanese individuals are more risk-averse than Westerners. Further, this finding perhaps also should serve as a caution to researchers who attempt to take empirical findings at the individual level of analysis and apply them to the organizational level of analysis.

### 9.3 Control Strategies and Risk Transformation

Contrary to conventional wisdom, though limits on risks (net open positions in different currencies) are typically larger or there are no limits in "market control" rooms, traders in "market control" rooms *did not* take larger risks than did traders in "bureaucratic-control" rooms. However, the average profit per trader and the average profit per trader normalized for risk (which is an indicator of the room's risk-transformation capability) were both significantly higher in trading rooms that followed "market control" strategies. Market control strategies therefore do appear to go with better risk-transformation capability in FX trading rooms, though they are not associated with higher risk-taking. This may be due to self-selection, which would provide an economics-based explanation, whereby smarter traders are drawn towards organizations that provide high incentive compensation, or it may be due to traders exerting more effort when their compensation is influenced by the profits they generate.

As predicted, market control strategies had a positive (though only marginally statistically significant) effect on acceptable risk in the trading room. Market control had a small negative "direct effect" on actual risk-taking, but the positive "indirect effect" on risk through the influence of market control on acceptable risk essentially rendered the association insignificant (Table 15.4B). Market control rooms were positively and significantly associated with higher profits per trader. It is interesting to note that, *even when normalized for risks taken, rooms that followed market modes of control did significantly better than rooms that followed bureaucratic modes of control.* What this means is that rooms that follow market control strategies appear to generate higher profits per trader while taking smaller open positions. Jemison's 1987 study in 20 small community banks in Indiana showed a similar result on risk-taking, though not on returns – in his study, decision centralization (bureaucratic control) did not result in lower risk-taking, though it was related to higher returns.

The results of the present study that bureaucratic control is associated with lower risk-transformation capability support the empirical findings of several earlier studies which have shown that bureaucratic organization often produces dysfunctional behavior and inefficiency (Merton, 1940; Gouldner, 1954; Meyer, 1990) rather than the efficiency often ascribed to it. These results are also consonant with some of the newer thinking on appropriate control strategies in organizations which are characterized by distributed knowledge and decision-making at the periphery rather than at the center (Hedlund, 1986 and 1993; Zuboff, 1988).

### 9.4 Caveats

Some words of caution are required before implications can be suggested from this study. For one, the small population of comparable trading rooms in New York and Tokyo and the attendant small numbers in the sample (though a substantial portion of the population of interest was represented in it) do restrict both the kinds of analyses that can be done and the strength and generalizability of any conclusions we can draw from the study. The follow-up visits to a few of the trading rooms to discuss the results were useful in that they acted to further validate the data and results.

From a normative point of view, while market control mechanisms are related to greater normalized profits even within the subgroup of Western trading rooms, the small sample of market control rooms prevented our testing for more complex interaction effects – for instance, with technology or size – which could influence the relationship between market control and performance. For instance, the exploratory work seemed to indicate that market control requires a great deal of attention to be paid to the selection and retention of high-quality "disciplined professionals," because in the atmosphere of relative autonomy that prevails in market control organizations, even small errors can have large impacts. If the room is so large that assuring quality becomes a problem, a market control system may need to be supplemented by other control mechanisms. Some of the "market control" rooms that were observed during this study already do this; they have substituted micro-level individual limits and controls with non-intrusive "global" controls, where netted positions worldwide can be monitored by top management on a real-time basis through technology, giving traders a great deal of freedom and responsibility to take whatever individual risk positions they choose. This form of "virtual" control could perhaps minimize dysfunctional responses to bureaucratic controls at the individual level while simultaneously ensuring that control occurs at the organizational level. Certainly, the literature on control would benefit from research that explores these forms of control and the relationships between the organizational context and behavior.

## Acknowledgements

This study was supported in part by the International Financial Services Research Center at the Sloan School of Management, Massachusetts Institute of Technology, and by the Center for Telecommunications Management at the University of Southern California.

## References

Arrow, K. J. 1971, *Essays in the Theory of Risk-Bearing*, Chicago: Markham.

Arrow, K. J. 1974, *The Limits of Organization*, New York: Norton, 1–29.

Baird, I. S. and Thomas, H. 1985, "Toward a Contingency Model of Strategic Risk Taking." *Academy of Management Review*, 102: 230–243.

Ball, R. and Brown, P. 1969, "Portfolio Theory and Accounting." *Journal of Accounting Research*, Autumn: 300–323.

Bank for International Settlements 1993, *Survey of Foreign Exchange Market Activity*, Basle.

Bem, D. J., Wallach, M. A., and Kogan, N. 1965, "Group decision-making under risk of aversive consequences." *Journal of Personality and Social Psychology*, 1: 453–460.

Bettis, R. A. 1983, "Modern financial theory, corporate strategy and public policy: three conundrums." *Academy of Management Review*, 83: 406–415.

Blume, M. E. and Friend, I. 1975, "The asset structure of individual portfolios and some implications for utility functions." *Journal of Finance*, 30: 585–603.

Bowman, E. 1980, "A Risk/Return Paradox for Strategic Management." *Sloan Management Review*, Spring: 17–31.

Bowman, Edward H. 1982, "Risk Seeking by Troubled Firms." *Sloan Management Review*, Summer: 33–42.

Bromiley, Philip 1991, "Testing a Causal Model of Corporate Risk Taking and Performance." *Academy of Management Journal*, 341: 37–59.

Bromiley, Philip and Curley, Shawn P. 1992, "Individual Differences in Risk Taking." Chapter 5 of J. Frank Yates, ed., *Risk-Taking Behavior*, Chichester, UK: John Wiley & Sons.

Budescu, David V. and Wallsten, Thomas S. 1985, "Consistency in Interpretation of Probabilistic Phrases." *Organizational Behavior and Human Decision Processes*, 36: 391–405.

Cohen, J. and Cohen, P. 1983, *Applied multiple regression/correlation analysis for the behavioral sciences*, Hillsdale, NJ: Erlbaum.

Coombs, C. H. 1983, *Psychology and Mathematics*, Ann Arbor: University of Michigan Press.

Crozier, M. 1964, *The Bureaucratic Phenomenon*, Chicago: University of Chicago Press.

Cummings, L. L., Harnett, D. L., and Stevens, O. J. 1971, "Risk, Fate, Conciliation and Trust: An International Study of Attitudinal Differences Among Executives." *Academy of Management Journal*, 14: 285–304.

Cyert, Richard M. and March, J. G. 1963, *A Behavioral Theory of the Firm*, Englewood Cliffs, NJ: Prentice-Hall.

Dion, K. L., Baron, R. S., and Miller, N. 1970, "Why do groups make riskier decisions than individuals?" *Advances in Experimental Social Psychology*, 5: 306–377.

Douglas, M. and Wildavsky, A. 1984, *Risk and Culture*, Berkeley, CA: California University Press.

Douglas, Mary 1985, *Risk Acceptability According to the Social Sciences*, New York: Russell Sage Foundation.

*Euromoney*, 1988, 1989, 1990, "Survey of Foreign Exchange Markets," May.

Fishburn, Peter C. 1977, "Mean-risk analysis with risk associated with below-target returns." *American Economic Review*, 67: 116–126.

Foreign Exchange Committee, Annual Report, 1989, Federal Reserve Bank of New York.

Friedman, M. and Savage, L. J. 1952, "The expected-utility hypothesis and the measurability of utility." *Journal of Political Economy*, 60: 463–475.

Gersick, Connie 1990, "Revolutionary Change Theories: A Multilevel Exploration of the Punctuated Equilibrium Paradigm." *Academy of Management Review*, 31: 9–41.

Ghoshal, S. 1987, "Global Strategy: An Organizing Framework." *Strategic Management Journal*, 8: 425–440.

Ghoshal, S. and Nohria, N. 1989, "Internal Differentiation within Multinational Corporations." *Strategic Management Journal*, 104: 323–337.

Goldstein, W. M. and Einhorn, H. 1987, "A Theory of Preference Reversals." *Psychological Review*, 942: 236–254.

Gouldner, A. W. 1954, *Patterns of Industrial Bureaucracy*, Glencoe, Ill: Free Press.

Hambros Bank 1989, *Foreign Exchange and Bullion Dealers Directory*, London.

Hedlund, G. 1986, "The Hypermodern MNC – A Heterarchy?" *Human Resource Management*, 25: 9–35.

Hedlund, G. 1993, "Assumptions of Hierarchy and Heterarchy." In S. Ghoshal and D. Eleanor Westney, eds, *Organization Theory and the Multinational Corporation*, London: Macmillan.

Hofstede, G. 1980, *Culture's Consequences: International Differences in Work-Related Values*, Beverly Hills: Sage.

Hofstede, G., Neuijen, B., Ohayv, D. D., and Sanders, G. 1990, "Measuring Organizational Cultures: A Qualitative and Quantitative Study across Twenty Cases." *Administrative Science Quarterly*, 35: 286–316.

Hymer, S. H. 1976, *The International Operations of National Firms: A Study of Direct Investment*, Cambridge, MA: MIT Press. Previously unpublished doctoral dissertation, 1960.

Jemison, David B. 1987, "Risk and the Relationship among Strategy, Organizational Processes and Performance." *Management Science*, 339: 1087–1101.

Jensen, Michael C. 1972, "Capital Markets, Theory and Evidence." *Bell Journal of Economics and Management Science*, 3: 357–398.

Johnson, B. B. and Covello, V. T. 1987, *The Social and Cultural Construction of Risk*, Dordrecht: D. Reidel.

Kahneman, D. and Tversky, A. 1979, "Prospect Theory: An analysis of decision under risk." *Econometrica*, 47: 263–291.

Khandwalla, P. 1976, *The Design of Organizations*, New York: Harcourt Brace Jovanovich.

Kindleberger, C. 1969, *American Business Abroad*, New Haven, CT: Yale University Press.

Kogut, Bruce 1985, "Designing Global Strategies: Comparative and Competitive Value-added Chains." *Sloan Management Review*, Summer, 15–28.

Kogut, Bruce 1993, "Learning, or the Importance of Being Inert: Country Imprinting and International Competition." In S. Ghoshal and D. Eleanor Westney eds., *Organization Theory and the Multinational Corporation*, London: Macmillan.

Libby, R. and Fishburn, P. C. 1977, "Behavioral Models of Risk Taking in Business Decisions: A Survey and Evaluation." *Journal of Accounting Research*, 15: 272–292.

MacCrimmon, K. R. and Wehrung, D. A. 1990, "Characteristics of Risk Taking Executives." *Management Science*, 364: 423–435.

March, J. G. and Shapira, Z. 1987, "Managerial Perspectives on Risk and Risk Taking." *Management Science*, 33 11: 1404–1418.

March, J. G. and Shapira, Z. 1992, "Variable Risk Preferences and the Focus of Attention." *Psychological Review*, 99: 172–183.

Markowitz, Harry 1959, *Portfolio Selection: Efficient Diversification of Investments*, New York: Wiley.

Merton, R. K. 1940, "Bureaucratic Structure and Personality." *Social Forces*, 18: 560–568.

Meyer, Marshall W. 1990, "The growth of public and private bureaucracies." In S. Zukin and P. DiMaggio eds. *Structures of Capital: The social organization of the economy*, Cambridge, UK: Cambridge University Press.

Morgan Stanley 1990, 1991, *Capital International Perspective*, New York.

Nalbantian, H. R. 1987, *Incentives, Cooperation and Risk Sharing*, Totowa, NJ: Rowman & Littlefield.

Ohmae, K. 1990, *The Borderless World*, New York: Harper Business.

Ouchi, W. G. 1979, "A Conceptual Framework for the Design of Organizational Control Mechanisms." *Management Science*, 259: 833–849.

Ouchi, W. G. 1980, "Markets, Bureaucracies and Clans." *Administrative Science Quarterly*, 25: 129–141.

Ouchi, W. G. 1981, *Theory Z*, Massachusetts: Addison-Wesley.

Payne, J. W. 1973, "Alternative Approaches to Decision Making Under Risk: Moments vs. Risk Dimensions." *Psychological Bulletin*, 806: 493–553.

Pedhazur, E. J. 1982, *Multiple Regression in Behavioral Research*, New York: Holt Rinehart Winston.

Phillips, L. W. and Bagozzi, R. P. 1982, "On Measuring Organizational Properties: Methodological Issues in the Use of Key Informants." Working Paper, Stanford University Graduate School of Business.

Pratt, J. W. 1964, "Risk aversion in the small and in the large." *Econometrica*, 32: 122–136.

Pugh, D., Hickson, D. J., and Hinings, C. R. 1969, "The context of organization structures." *Administrative Science Quarterly*, 14: 91–114.

Schoemaker, P. J. H. 1989, "Conceptions of Risk-Taking: Do Intrinsic Risk-Attitudes Matter?" Working Paper, University of Chicago, Graduate School of Business.

Shavell, S. 1979, "Risk Sharing and Incentives in the Principal and Agent Relationship." *Bell Journal of Economics*, 10 (Spring): 55–73.

Slovic, P. 1972, "Information Processing, Situation Specificity, and the Generality of Risk-Taking Behavior." *Journal of Personality and Social Psychology*, 221: 128–134.

Specht, D. A. 1975, "On the evaluation of causal models." *Social Science Research*, 4: 113–133.

Tetlock, P. E. 1985, "Accountability: The Neglected Social Context of Judgement and Choice." *Research in Organizational Behavior*, 7:297–332

Thompson, J. D. 1967, *Organizations in Action*, New York: McGraw-Hill.

Van Maanen, J. and Schein, E. H. 1979, "Toward a Theory of Organizational Socialization." In B. Staw and L. L. Cummings eds., *Research in Organization Behavior*, Vol. 1, Greenwich, CT: JAI Press, 209–269.

Von Neumann, J. and Morgenstern, O. 1947, *Theory of Games and Economic Behavior*, Princeton, NJ: Princeton University Press.

Walter, Ingo 1988, *Global Competition in Financial Services*, Cambridge, MA: Ballinger.

Weber, M. 1946, "Bureaucracy." In H. Gerth and C. Wright Mills eds., from *Max Weber: Essays in Sociology*, New York: Oxford University Press.

Zaheer, A. and Zaheer, S. 1997, "Catching the Wave: Alertness, Responsiveness and Market Influence in Global Electronic Networks," *Management Science*, 43(11):1493–1509.

Zenginkyo Federation of Bankers Associations of Japan 1989, *The Banking System in Japan*.

Zuboff, Shoshana, 1988, *In the Age of the Smart Machine*, New York: Basic Books.

# INDEX